KT-567-467

Twentieth-Century Germany:
From Bismarck to Brandt

WITHDRAWN FROM STOCK

By the same author

THE GERMAN REVOLUTION, 1918–19 (Historical Association pamphlet)

THE GERMAN REVOLUTION OF 1918 (Cambridge University Press)

Twentieth-Century Germany:
From Bismarck to Brandt

A. J. Ryder

Senior Lecturer in History
St David's University College, Lampeter

MACMILLAN

© A. J. Ryder 1973

All rights reserved. No part of this publication
may be reproduced or transmitted, in any form
or by any means, without permission.

First published 1973 by
THE MACMILLAN PRESS LTD
London and Basingstoke
Associated companies in New York Dublin
Melbourne Johannesburg and Madras

SBN 333 01997 0

Printed in Great Britain by
WESTERN PRINTING SERVICES LTD
Bristol

BEXLEY LIBRARY SERVICE

Acc No. J02355 A £10·00 P

10 OCT 1973

Cl No. 943.09 RYD

To my Mother
in gratitude

Contents

List of Plates

Photographs by courtesy of Radio Times Hulton Picture Library
(1–19, 23, 24), the Imperial War Museum (20, 22), Camera Press (25),
Ullstein, Berlin (26), Associated Press (27), United Press International
(28), Landesbildstelle, Berlin (29, 31, 32), and I.N.-Bild, Bad Godesberg (30). Two of the cartoons in the text are reproduced by courtesy
of the Estate of George Grosz, Princeton, N.J.; in the case of the
five reproduced from *Simplicissimus* (Fackelträger-Verlag, 1954) every
effort has been made by the publishers to trace the copyright-holders.
The eagle on the cover is taken from the fountain in the marketplace
at Goslar in the Hartz mountains.

List of Maps

Preface

The eight decades of German history which form the subject of this book have seen more dramatic events, more drastic changes and more destructive violence than any comparable period in the history of another nation. Germany has been a political laboratory, a seed-bed of extremism, a physical and ideological battleground, the most formidable military power and the most heavily defeated nation of modern times. Culture, economics and social life have all been moulded by these pressures. In 1960 an American historian, reviewing German history in the previous half century, identified five images: the prosperous and on the whole admired Empire of William II; the militarist, expansionist Germany of the First World War; the troubled, sympathy-evoking Republic of Weimar; the aggressive, genocidal Nazi Reich; and the post-war democracy of Bonn, whose acknowledged virtues could not quite obliterate the shadows of the recent past. In the 1970s the range of images is further extended. The Federal Republic of Brandt and Heinemann differs in many ways from that of Adenauer and Heuss, while despite its imported Communist trappings the East German Republic or D.D.R. is yet another manifestation of the German *Wesen*. Events since 1969 have placed the story in a new perspective, and provide a vantage point from which to reconsider the whole post-Bismarckian epoch.

A theme which has occupied some historians lately is the continuity of German history, which is often discernible, despite the transformations, within the period 1870–1945, even between 1848 and 1949. More obvious is the parallel between the two world wars, and the unity of that epoch (1914–45) in which the inter-war years were little more than an extended and uneasy truce. It is not hard to see the 'master race' of the Second World War as the successors of the Pan-Germans of the First, while Ludendorff anticipates Hitler, both in his territorial ambitions and in his conception of total war. A 'continuity of errors' has been perceived in German policy running from the imperial government before and during the First World War to the Third Reich. In both wars the Germans overestimated their own strength and under-estimated that of the hostile coalition. In particular, they seriously

underrated the military capability of the United States. The defeat of
1918 was never fully acknowledged. In both wars moral and political
assets were sacrificed for short-term military advantage. German territorial ambitions coincided to some extent in the two struggles, although
Hitler went far beyond the dreams of Bethmann Hollweg. Yet some
errors were not repeated. Hitler managed to avoid the more obvious
mistakes of his predecessors. He deliberately forbore from provoking
England by a world and big navy policy such as had been the Kaiser's
undoing, and, by signing the Nazi-Soviet Pact, he ensured that Germany was not, as in 1914, 'encircled'. What even Hitler could not
eliminate was the challenge to the West implicit in his claim to dominate Eastern as well as Central Europe. Certainly his preoccupation
with continental rather than global aims gave the Second World War
a different emphasis from the First, and for Hitler, whatever his eventual overseas demands might have been, hostilities with the western
powers were an unwanted by-product of his desire for *Lebensraum*.
Yet since Britain was the guarantor of the European balance of power
as well as of the colonial *status quo*, Anglo-German conflict remained
a basic issue in both wars, with the United States playing first a supporting and ultimately a decisive role. Nevertheless the tendency of some
contemporary historians to minimise the difference between the 1914
and 1939 situations obfuscates rather than clarifies. There was no
element of preventive war in 1939 as there had been twenty-five years
earlier. Given the existence of some common ground between Bethmann Hollweg and Hitler, the two men differed fundamentally in
objectives and methods, above all in their mental and moral attitudes.
And although, taking the analogy a stage further, resemblances can be
found between the policy of Stresemann after the First World War
and that of Adenauer after the Second, yet when we consider the post-
1945 period it is the differences between that and its predecessors which
impress. The year 1945 marked a break in German history of a unique
kind. The revolution of 1789 transformed France, but was followed by
the Napoleonic counter-revolution. The Bolshevik seizure of power in
1917 inaugurated a new era in Russian and world history, but did not
divide Russia down the middle. Whatever pattern there was in German
history before 1945 hardly survived the *Götterdämmerung* of the
Third Reich, especially as the break coincided with a basic shift in the
global balance of power which Germany itself had helped to bring
about.

Another way of looking at German history of the last hundred years
is to see it as an unsuccessful attempt to find a synthesis between *Macht*
(power, force) and *Geist* (mind and spirit). In one sense the failure
to reconcile the two had bedevilled German history for centuries, but

since 1871 it has been acute. Bismarck's Reich gave obvious priority to power: the Weimar Republic, culturally so rich, perished from weakness. Hitler's Germany represented the adulation and abuse of power to a monstrous degree. Whether the Federal Republic, despite being a product of defeat and the cold war, will find the elusive balance between the two extremes is something on which only an interim judgement can be offered, but the signs indicate that a compromise is at last being achieved. The keynote of West German politics in the 1970s is a sober realism of a kind rare in the century's earlier decades.

In January 1971 West Germans remembered – rather than celebrated – the centenary of Bismarck's refoundation of the German Empire. The tone was subdued, there was little enthusiasm or self-congratulation. A hundred years after Bismarck's achievement it still looked impressive, but its disastrous consequences inevitably raised the question whether it had not after all been a tragic mistake. Assumptions taken for granted in earlier decades were critically scrutinised. Indeed the whole Bismarckian contribution has been re-examined in the light of bitter experience: the master of *Realpolitik* has himself been reassessed with a new realism, as part of the general demythologisation characteristic of recent German historiography. No doubt the unification of Germany, incomplete though it was in 1871, brought many benefits. It lay in the logic of history and was long overdue. The economic unification under Prussia which preceded it was certainly advantageous. But the methods used to unify Germany, and the form it took, seem as questionable now as they were to a few far-sighted people at the time. A change of some kind was no doubt inevitable in the middle of the nineteenth century. It is hardly conceivable that the Confederation of 1815, in which an ambitious Prussia took second place to a dynastic and ethnically divided Austria, could have lasted indefinitely. But that a less one-sided and more permanent solution than Bismarck's could have been found, such as the federated Central Europe advocated at the time by some, must appear the greatest missed opportunity of modern German history. Even so a doubt remains whether a Germany peacefully united under liberal auspices could have avoided a military collision with the other major countries, given the temper of German nationalism, the skill and resources at its disposal, and the explosive nature of great power rivalry in that epoch. But that is speculation.

Whether the still divided portions of the Bismarckian Reich will ever reunite is also speculative. In some quarters people are already sceptical, viewing the seventy-five years of unity as an 'episode' unlikely to be repeated. A hundred years ago the question of German unity was primarily one for the Germans themselves, even if other interested powers had to be conciliated or 'compensated' in one way or another.

Today the German question cannot be isolated. Both German states are deeply enmeshed in the structures of alliance and the balance of security headed by the two super-powers, who between them divide the German inheritance. Since virtually no one now believes that unification, if it comes, will be attained through strength, power has lost much of its appeal: hence, incidentally, the main reason for the success of liberalism under Bonn compared with its failure under Weimar. For it is in foreign policy that the contrast between Germany at almost any time between 1890 and 1945 and the Germany of today is most marked. Chancellor Bülow was applauded when in 1900 he declared that in the coming century his country would be either the hammer or the anvil of world politics. His later successor, Brandt, had the support of the great majority of his compatriots in his determination that it should be neither. All that can be said at present is that although German nationalism may be a spent force, the energies released by unification are still at work in various fields. The recovery of the German people, moral as well as economic, from a catastrophe which might have been fatal to many nations, deserves more recognition than it often receives. Few who knew Germany in 1945 could have expected that within a quarter of a century its people would have gone so far to redeem themselves from a terrible legacy. Whatever fate has in store for the Federal Republic and the D.D.R., there is reason here for satisfaction, even for pride.

I should like to thank Mr Anthony Nicholls of St Antony's College, Oxford, Dr John Röhl of the University of Sussex, Mr Evan Edwards of University College, Cardiff, and Dr Eleanor Breuning of University College, Swansea, who at one time or another read all or part of the typescript and saved me from numerous errors. I owe much to their helpful advice, as I do to that of the late S. H. Steinberg, who saw and commented on the first chapters. I am grateful to the staffs of the Wiener Library, London and of the library at St David's University College, Lampeter, for helpfulness at all times; to Mrs I. Crowdy, Mrs G. Evans and Mrs R. Shaw for typing the script, often more than once; to the Pantyfedwen Fund Committee, Lampeter, for a grant towards expenses; to the German Embassy, London, for a loan of photographs; and to my publishers for their encouragement, consideration and assistance, including the drawing of maps. I hope that the many others who have kindly aided me in one way or another will accept this general acknowledgement of my appreciation. Last, but most of all, I thank my wife for her patience, advice and invaluable help, especially in reading the proofs and in making the index.

A. J. R.

List of Abbreviations

A.H.R.	*American Historical Review*
H.J.	*Historical Journal*
H.Z.	*Historische Zeitschrift*
J.C.H.	*Journal of Contemporary History*
J.M.H.	*Journal of Modern History*
P. & P.	*Past and Present*
V.J.Z.G.	*Vierteljahrshefte für Zeitgeschichte*
B.D.	*British Documents on the Origins of the War, 1898–1914*
G.P.	*Die Grosse Politik der Europäischen Kabinette, 1871–1914*
D.B.F.P.	*Documents on British Foreign Policy, 1919–1939*
D.G.F.P.	*Documents on German Foreign Policy, 1918–1945*

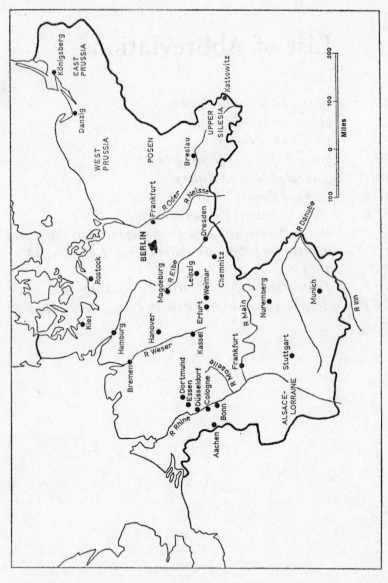

Map 1 Imperial Germany in 1890

CHAPTER I

Introductory: The Age of William II

1890, the year of Bismarck's dismissal as German Chancellor, was a turning point in both European and German history. It marked the arrival of a new era, that of William II. Its immediate consequence, the non-renewal of the Russo-German Reinsurance treaty, was quickly followed by the Franco-Russian pact that restored the balance of power and established the system of rival alliances which lasted until the First World War. In German foreign policy the control and prudence exercised by Bismarck gave way to a less coherent course and later to a policy of expansion that proved ultimately disastrous. It would be wrong to exaggerate the changes caused by the disappearance of one man: the legacy left by Bismarck was less solid than it looked, and his network of treaties had already begun to disintegrate. Bismarck's most recent English biographer speaks of the 'virtual collapse' of his diplomacy, largely by circumstances beyond his control.[1] Russia, on whose friendship Bismarck relied to neutralise French hostility and minimise the chances of an Austro-Russian war, showed in 1887 that she set a diminishing value on the German alliance, and was alienated by Bismarck's transparent displays of displeasure. Although Bismarck's aim, acknowledged by the other powers, was preservation of the *status quo*, his previous record (three wars), occasional sabre-rattling (the war scare of 1875), calculated duplicity and attempts to embroil other nations with each other inevitably left a certain distrust among his neighbours. Still, compared with a revisionist France and an expansionist Russia, and even with an Austria-Hungary seeking a new sphere of influence in the Balkans, Germany represented a force for peace. Even at the end of the century this assessment seemed valid in the eyes of Great Britain, Europe's only major uncommitted power. Inside Germany the consequences of Bismarck's fall were also far-reaching. Although William II came to the throne in 1888, he could not be master in his own house so long as Bismarck stood in his way. As the directing hand of the Iron Chancellor was removed, domestic politics became fluid and unpredictable.[2] The end of the Bismarckian age was symbolic of a more general change in state and society. The complicated system of government created by Bismarck worked less smoothly under his successors, and a period of transition and extended crisis was ended only in 1897 with the establishment by William II of his 'personal rule' exercised through men of his own choice in key ministerial posts. The stage was set for the dynamism which was to characterise the new reign both in its foreign policy and in an ever more impressive rate of economic growth. Tenniel's cartoon in *Punch* showing Bismarck as the dropped pilot was apt: the German Reich was a powerful ship whose new pilot was not quite sure where he intended to go but wanted to get there fast. The new national state, which Bismarck had founded and ruled for nineteen years, was a country of bursting energies, unresolved conflicts and undefined ambitions. The fifty-five years which followed his retirement were to see the consummation and destruction of those forces which, directly or indirectly, he had set in motion, and the ruin of his grandiose political achievement. Even in 1890 there were a few far-sighted prophets of disaster, who had no faith in the brash new Emperor.[3] Yet few people at the time, whatever they thought of Bismarck or William, would have dared to predict so stormy a future for what appeared to be one of the most successful states of Europe, or have imagined that in less than sixty years the very name of Prussia would be erased from the map.

The choice of the name Empire (*Kaiserreich*) evoked memories of the Holy Roman Empire with its legendary rulers and its roots in Germany's romantic past. In structure too the new state was a blend of the old and the new. It represented an uneasy compromise between Prussian particularism and German nationalism, between absolutism and constitutionalism. Formally the Empire consisted of a federation of twenty-five states, ranging in size and importance from Prussia, which contained three-fifths of Germany's area and population, to dwarf principalities like Schaumburg-Lippe, comparable to Rutland, and venerable Hanseatic cities such as Lübeck, proud of their inherited status as 'free cities'. After expelling Austria, Prussia's defeated rival, from Germany, Bismarck was faced with two main problems. The first was how to reconcile the claims of the other twenty-four states with the *de facto* predominance of Prussia. The second was how to satisfy the nationalist and parliamentary aspirations of German liberals while retaining for Prussia her autocratic monarchy and highly conservative social system. The solution was found in an elaborate, hybrid constitution that included a Federal Council or *Bundesrat* as its key body. For although this assembly, on which all the states were represented by ministers, was constitutionally sovereign, in practice Prussia, whose delegation was headed by her Prime Minister (who was also Imperial Chancellor) controlled enough votes to have the decisive say. At the same time an all-German parliament or Reichstag, elected by manhood suffrage, was set up as a second legislative chamber with control over the federal budget. The democratic franchise for the Reichstag was a concession to the liberals, but given by Bismarck with his tongue in his cheek, for he hoped that the middle and lower classes would vote for the 'party of order' as they had done in France in 1848 and under Napoleon III. The Reichstag was not granted power to appoint or dismiss the Chancellor, and its financial control was limited in two ways: all direct taxation was reserved to the governments of the states (which also had their own bi-cameral parliaments), and the army estimates, which made up the greater part of the federal budget, were voted for a term of years. In order for the system to work, the Chancellor needed the support of the parties having a majority in the Reichstag at any given time. The composition of this majority could easily change within the period of office of one Chancellor, depending on the nature of the legislation he introduced. The Chancellor had to come to terms with the party leaders. If they proved obdurate he could always ask the Emperor to dissolve the Reichstag, and use his influence in the ensuing general election to obtain the majority he wanted. On the other hand, dissolution of the Reichstag was not a step to be undertaken lightly, and the Chancellor, especially if he was not a Bismarck, was just as likely to abandon an unpopular bill as to challenge the nation's representatives. The Emperor, on whom alone, according to the constitution, the Chancellor depended, had no wish to see his power diminished by the Reichstag, and Bismarck, as a devoted monarchist, took every opportunity of upholding the powers which the Emperor as King of Prussia inherited from before the revolution of 1848. Thus in practice Bismarck's compromise was tilted, as he intended, in favour of Prussia and authoritarianism. It was not in Bismarck's character to allow the fruits of victory, which had given Prussia the mastery of Germany, to be squandered in peace: hence his hostility to those forces, such as Catholicism and socialism, which challenged the existing order. The German constitution, in a misleadingly liberal phrase, spoke of the Chancellor's 'responsibility', but failed to give this principle any practical application. Max Weber, Germany's leading sociologist, described the Bismarckian system as 'sham constitutionalism'.

The nature of the Prussian government is the key to much in the history of the second German Empire that would otherwise be inexplicable. Autocracy is hardly the right word to describe it, for the sovereign was buttressed by a closely knit, strongly entrenched ruling class which, at least as far as domestic politics was concerned, prescribed the limits within which he could move. This élite held an important if diminishing share of leadership in the civil service and army, and owned the large estates which east of the River Elbe formed the basis of the rural economy and of the social pyramid. Though men of middle-class origin were steadily infiltrating into key posts in the central administration and even into the almost sacrosanct General Staff, in rural Prussia the rule of the landed gentry (Junkers) remained virtually unchallenged.[4] Conservatives also dominated in the Prussian parliament, thanks to the three-class franchise which, by making an elector's voting strength depend on the amount of direct taxes he paid, produced a permanent right-wing majority. The first class might consist of only five or six people, the second of fifty or sixty, the third of five to six hundred: as each class had equal weight, a wealthy man's vote might be worth a hundred times as much as the vote of an ordinary wage-earner. This anachronistic system was combined with a two-tier method of election and open voting, which permitted intimidation. As a reflection of public opinion it was further distorted by a distribution of seats which failed to take into account substantial shifts of population brought about by the growth of towns. The Reichstag, on the other hand, although it too gave inadequate representation to the new urban areas, mirrored the wishes of the electorate with tolerable accuracy. An example will illustrate the difference between it and the Prussian Lower House. In the Prussian elections of 1903 the Conservatives, with less than a fifth of the votes, gained nearly a third of the seats, while the Socialists who, with nearly as many votes as the Conservatives, would on a proportional basis have been entitled to 81 seats, did not obtain even one.[5] The Reichstag elections in the same year gave the Socialists 81 seats out of 397, six more than the Conservatives and free Conservatives combined. The virtual disfranchisement of the propertyless majority in the Prussian *Landtag* was inevitably a standing grievance on the left, and did more than anything else to keep alive the Marxist belief in class war and in the necessity of revolution. Yet without the weighted franchise the Junkers would have lost mastery of the Prussian parliament and the means it gave them of exerting pressure on the Prime Minister-Chancellor. But their use of the conservative *Landtag* to neutralise the relatively left-wing Reichstag put the Chancellor in a position of increasing difficulty. As the agrarian Prussia of the nineteenth century was transformed into the mainly industrial state of the twentieth, the survival of the three-class franchise became more anomalous but to its beneficiaries still more vital if they were not to be submerged in an alien majority. The internal conflict provoked by this constitutional anachronism was to prove a source of weakness to the Empire.

The political parties fell into six main groups. On the far right were the Conservatives, a high Tory party representing the Prussian squire-archy and closely associated with the established Lutheran Church; in foreign policy they upheld the tradition of the Holy Alliance – mon-archical, anti-revolutionary, pro-Russian. Next to them were the Free Conservatives or Reich Party, a Bismarckian offshoot which had broken away from the main stem after the foundation of the Empire. Their interests were industrial as well as agrarian, and they diluted their Prussian particularism with German nationalism. The right centre was formed by the National Liberals, the party of big business which was supported by most of the Protestant bourgeoisie. This was a party in which the adjective, with its emphasis on the Empire rather than on Prussia, was more important than the noun: originally standing for parliamentary control of the executive, most German liberals had come to terms with Bismarck's authoritarian state in return for the blessings of unity, prosperity and greatness. The National Liberals, many of whom belonged to the Pan-German League, were the chief protagonists of imperialism and a big navy. In the middle of the poli-tical spectrum, and after 1890 more often than not holding the balance of power in the Reichstag, was the Centre, the party of the Roman Catholic Church. As a confessional party its main concern was to defend the interests of the Church and of the large Catholic minority against the Protestant Hohenzollerns, but also against liberal anti-clericalism and the atheism of the Social Democrats. Socially the Centre represented a cross-section of the population from the Catholic nobility of South Germany to the peasants of the Rhine and the miners of the Ruhr. Politically far from united, it accepted, on the whole, the Bismarckian constitution, though in the years before the First World War there were signs of a more democratic and less sectarian approach. To the left of the Centre were the radicals, successors of the left-wing revolutionaries of 1848, whose main groups, the *Liberale Vereinigung* and the *Freisinnige* People's party, had come together, though not for very long, to form the *Freisinnige* (Progressive) party. (There was also a sizeable left-wing group in South Germany called the German People's party.) The tendency of these radicals to split and reunite was a symptom of their somewhat uncertain position in German politics. As believers in parliamentary democracy they opposed the Bismarckian system on principle. Yet as time went on they were drawn into support of the government on specific issues, notably in foreign and colonial policy, and in 1907 they were to join the Bülow bloc. The Progressives, in their several groups, drew most of their following from the middle-class (especially Jewish) intelligentsia, from small businessmen and artisans. Still further to the left were the Social Democrats, the party of the rapidly growing industrial working class, whose programme combined the revolutionary ideology of Marx with a demand for comprehensive social reform. So far as they had a foreign policy the socialists favoured a western orientation – closer ties with the liberal states of Europe – and shared Marx's russophobia. They subscribed to the internationalist ideals embodied in the First and Second Internationals, and in the latter, which was founded in 1889, they played the leading part, as befitted the world's largest Socialist party. In the Reichstag their position was one of permanent opposition on principle, though significantly in the parliaments of the South German states they collaborated on certain issues with the Progressives. For the rest, the Reichstag contained representatives of the smaller parties standing for ethnic minorities (Poles, Danes and French) in the border areas of the Reich, while the Hanoverian Guelf party, loyal to the dynasty deposed when Hanover was absorbed by Prussia in 1866, was a picturesque 'Jacobite' survival. On the extreme right a new group made its appearance towards the end of the 1880s: the Anti-Semites. They increased in numbers during the next decade, but later declined and never had more than sixteen deputies in the Reichstag. It was essentially a protest party of a Populist kind, identifying the Jews with materialism and big business.

Although these small parties were normally of only marginal importance, there were times when the difference between government and opposition parties was so narrow that they held the balance. By comparison with Britain, Germany had no Tory Democrats, and her National Liberals had almost nothing in common with the party of Gladstone. Bismarck had described the Centre and the Social Democrats, the two ideological, internationally-minded parties, as 'enemies of the Empire' and had persecuted them both. He felt the same resentment against the left-wing Liberals. His campaign against the Church, the so-called *Kulturkampf*, for which he had National Liberal backing, ended in 1878, when a gradual reconciliation between Chancellor and the Centre began. From 1879 to 1887 Bismarck governed with the help of a new Reichstag bloc that included the Centre, whose support he needed after switching to a tariff policy approved by industrialists and agrarians but unacceptable to a traditionally free trade party. The Centre became, though to a lesser extent than the Conservatives and the National Liberals, a 'state-supporting' or establishment party. The appointment in 1894 of Hohenlohe, a Catholic, as Chancellor was less significant than it appeared because he was an old opponent of the clerical party. During his last three years in power (1887-90) Bismarck again changed his tactics and controlled the Reichstag with the help of a 'cartel' of Conservatives and National Liberals, but this bloc lost its majority in the general election that immediately preceded his fall. Bismarck's reaction was to threaten a *coup d'état*: this was tantamount to an admission that his own constitution involving co-operation between a Chancellor responsible to the Emperor and a Reichstag responsible to the people had proved a failure. His real purpose was probably to stay in power by making himself indispensable. The problem which defeated Bismarck was to be still less amenable under his successors, though some of them showed more adroitness in handling the parties. The number of Socialists in the Reichstag rose from 35 in 1890 to 110 in 1912, when about one elector in three voted for them and the 'national' parties found themselves in a minority. As a professedly republican and revolutionary party the Socialists continued to suffer official ostracism and discrimination, but sheer weight of numbers made it impossible to ignore them.

German socialism had become a political force in the 1860s, when several organised workers' groups came into existence, influenced in varying degrees by the ideas of Lassalle, Marx and the radicals of 1848. In 1875 the two main groups merged to form a united workers' party, later renamed the Social Democratic party of Germany or S.P.D. Although at first progress was slow – there were only two Socialists in the North German Reichstag in 1870 – the party incurred the wrath of Bismarck, who in 1878 took advantage of an attempt on the life of the Emperor to pass a law outlawing all socialist activity except in the Reichstag. This repressive measure, which was regularly renewed as long as Bismarck was in power, failed in its purpose. Although hundreds of leading Socialists had to go into exile with their funds and their press while 1,500 were imprisoned in Germany, support for them continued to rise, and by 1890 they had won more votes than any other party. The growth of industry and big towns favoured the spread of socialism, and when William II began his reign by refusing to renew the Anti-Socialist law and by actually summoning an international labour conference to meet in Germany, new perspectives opened for the S.P.D. In 1891 the party held a conference at Erfurt, the main object of which was to draw up a new programme. This inevitably reflected a 'harder line' provoked by Bismarck's persecution, and the new programme pledged the party to overthrow the autocratic state and the capitalist economic order. Yet it also included a number of reforms, which could be achieved within the existing system and which obviously had more immediate relevance to a period in which a revolution in Germany seemed an unlikely prospect. The struggle between revolutionary and reformist forces within the S.P.D. was to absorb much of the party's energies during the ensuing period. It was significant of the new trend that as early as 1891 the Bavarian Socialist leader, Vollmar, declared that while principles were unalterable, tactics were flexible, and promised goodwill to a government that met them in the same spirit. William II soon showed that he was really no better disposed to the Socialists than Bismarck had been, though he did not act on his threats. The German government made little or no response to the signs of a more conciliatory attitude in a party that in its internationalism as well as in its revolutionary aims was sharply opposed to all that the German Empire stood for.

If Bismarck's attempt to stamp out socialism had been a failure, his campaign against the Liberals had succeeded only too well. Despite its defeat in 1848, Prussian liberalism was a force to be reckoned with, as was shown by the Progressives' challenge to the government over the military budget during the early 1860s. After his wars with Denmark and Austria Bismarck persuaded the majority of Progressives to abandon the fight for parliamentary government and to accept a kind of constitutional authoritarianism: this became the ideology of the National Liberals, while the left-wing minority remained in opposition. Bismarck split the Liberals a second time at the end of the 1870s when the National Liberals disagreed with Bismarck over the tariff and other issues, and a free trade minority seceded which later joined the Progressives. The latter, ground between the authoritarian state on the one side and the rising force of socialism on the other, were soon in decline: the number of their seats in the Reichstag fell from 76 in 1890 to 42 in 1912. During the same period Social Democratic membership of the Reichstag more than trebled. The figures reflect the growing number of working people who moved from the country to the towns and, for the first time, became politically conscious. The weakness of German liberalism left a significant gap in the country's political spectrum. The question which immediately springs to mind is why the German middle classes, in contrast to their counterparts in England and France, were content to remain excluded from political power. Important as was Bismarck's defeat of liberalism (representing broadly middle-class aspirations for a parliamentary regime) there are older and deeper forces to be considered. Germans had a long tradition of indifference to politics, and were inclined to regard themselves as a non-political people. For intellectuals there was the example of Goethe with his olympian detachment. A more general influence was the Lutheran concept of public affairs as by nature sinful. In practice, in a wicked and violent world Christians needed a strong ruler, and the effect of this belief was to forge an alliance between throne and altar, the various Lutheran churches of fragmented Germany leaning heavily on their secular patrons. Unlike more fortunate countries which emerged from the Middle Ages as unified nation-states, the German lands retained an uneasy balance between universalism (embodied in the Holy Roman Empire) and particularism (exemplified in state rights). The number of states, large and small, was over three hundred, and the divisions were widened and deepened by the Reformation and the Thirty Years' War which followed it. While the exact nature and extent of the destruction caused by the war is the subject of dispute among historians – much of it was local in character – there is no doubt that the long and sterile struggle brought appalling loss of life and the ruin of much inherited wealth, and that it had a generally blighting and retarding effect on the progress of civilisation. It also confirmed the tendency to see in absolute government the only alternative to a Hobbesian state of brutalised anarchy. This trend was emphasised by the independence won by the princes at the expense of the much weakened imperial authority. The state which gained most from the Thirty Years' War, Brandenburg-Prussia, was culturally the least developed, so that political leadership parted company with the historic centres of German civilisation in the south and west. Neither the dynastic Habsburg Empire nor the militarised frontier kingdom of Prussia ('Germany's greatest act of colonisation'), nor the innumerable petty states with their autocratic courts and narrow horizons could foster the qualities appropriate to a self-governing nation-state.

There were indeed small states, such as Goethe's Weimar, which were well governed by enlightened rulers, just as there were free cities, like Frankfurt or Hamburg, which had a tradition of self-government that gave the bourgeoisie a status it lacked elsewhere. And it was always possible for those who could afford it to move to another state, if, like Schiller in Württemberg, they fell foul of the local censor. If music and letters flourished in eighteenth-century Germany, as they did, it was largely due to princely patronage. To this day Germany owes its remarkable diversity of provincial culture to the electors and grand dukes who vied with each other in collecting pictures, commissioning music and building a local equivalent of Versailles, benefits paid for by their hard-pressed subjects. The medium-sized states were probably the best to live in: their inhabitants were less likely to get involved in aggressive wars like those of Prussia, while living in less constricting conditions than were found in the dwarf states. But Germany was an irrational patchwork, its Empire little more than a fiction, its *Kleinstaaterei* often stultifying. Germans were safe neither from their own rulers, who could sell them as mercenaries in foreign wars as Hessians were sold to George III for use against the American colonies, nor from outside aggression as when Louis XIV devastated the Palatinate.[6] Apart from Austria, which was really a vast dynastic estate carrying the imperial title, Prussia was the only German state of great-power status, which it owed almost entirely to its military prowess. Nearly all initiative in Prussia came from the king on whom, as in France, the aristocracy depended, and there was little sign of that 'civil society' which elsewhere was the seed-bed of responsible government. It would be wrong to suppose that Prussia, despite its militarism, lacked a liberal tradition: the religious tolerance of Frederick the Great, the reforms of Stein and Hardenberg, the educational work of Wilhelm von Humboldt and the Zollverein are enough to refute such a charge. But liberalism in Prussia owed more to the government than to private citizens: the state shaped society rather than society the state. In his will, Frederick the Great bequeathed his kingdom to his nephew as if it had been his private property.

The Napoleonic conquest and occupation of Germany, though it brought certain benefits such as the Code Napoleon, especially to the western provinces, was on the whole a costly and humiliating experience. Seen in retrospect, it was also part of the price paid for disunity, though at the time particularism was still so strong that few people felt that unification was a necessity. Most Germans were content with the loose Confederation set up by the Congress of Vienna in 1815, which retained the partial consolidation introduced by Napoleon (there were now 39 states instead of over 300), yet still gave free play to inter-state rivalry, notably the long-standing duel between Austria and Prussia. Revulsion against Jacobinism made many people agree with Metternich that order was society's first need, and Metternich was successful in reimposing for a generation his old-fashioned brand of Toryism on a society that was beginning to burgeon with new ideas. Hegel gave Metternich's system powerful intellectual support by idealising the state ('the real is rational') and by providing absolutism with a new metaphysical and moral sanction. The Prussian monarchy was thus, according to Hegel, the realisation of the Divine Idea on earth. The state was by its very nature superior to any political party, a concept which was bound to prejudice the later acceptance of parliamentary government. Partisanship could thus be disguised, if exercised by the state, as superior wisdom. And so after 1815, as before, Germany continued to be a country of subjects, not citizens. Herder had described it as a land of obedience, and Heine mocked the Germans for being content to rule the 'misty realm of dreams', while other, more practical nations governed the land and sea. Yet it should also be recorded that Hegel was not a nationalist, still less a racialist: it was the protagonists of these creeds which were to use Hegel's ideas for purposes which he would not have approved.[7]

The reaction against Metternich's oppressive regime, with its press censorship and gagging of intellectual opinion, took broadly two forms. On the left there was the group known as Young Germany, a literary fraternity to which Heine belonged, and the philosophic radicals who called themselves the Young Hegelians and included the youthful Dr Marx. The Young Hegelians transformed Hegel's theory of history as the unfolding of a divine purpose into a radical ideology that would justify and even require revolution. This revolution, Marx hoped, would do for Germany (whose backwardness he deplored) what the English and French revolutions had done for their respective countries – modernise their institutions and open the way to power for the middle class. But he believed that it would go even further, since the arrival on the scene of a new factor, the proletariat, would enable a socialist revolution to follow the middle class one 'immediately', as the Communist Manifesto claimed with more boldness than insight. This would inaugurate the millennium. Yet socialism in Germany, as the events of 1848 soon showed, had little support. The other rebellion against Metternich came from the radical right, where a *völkisch* or exclusive nationalism grew up that rejected the ideas of the Enlightenment and the French Revolution, which up to 1792 most thinking Germans had been inclined to welcome, and reacted violently against the Napoleonic imperialism to which Jacobinism had given birth. The roots of this new movement lay in romanticism, which became a powerful force in shaping the new German nationalism. Inspiration was found in nature, blood and race rather than in the self-determination and Rights of Man ideals of the French Revolution. The new nationalists like F. L. Jahn rejected, as emphatically as the radical left, the cosmopolitan hierarchical system of Metternich, and were already beginning to exhibit signs of xenophobia, anti-liberalism and Pan-Germanism.

The 1848 revolution – 'the turning-point at which history failed to turn' – gave the German middle classes for the first time the opportunity of seizing power. Then, if ever, Germany could have been united on a basis of consent and achieved the synthesis of force and spirit that has been so rare in German history. For a number of reasons, including the lack of genuine revolutionary zeal among the respectable middle-class leaders, fear of lower-class radicalism, the strength of particularism and the refusal of the King of Prussia to play the part assigned to him, the revolution failed.[8] The honeymoon of liberalism and nationalism was over. The desire for power proved stronger than attachment to freedom; in the words of Dahlmann, one of the leaders of the Frankfurt Parliament: 'The path of power is the only one which will satisfy and satiate the swelling desire for freedom, because it is not merely freedom which the German has in mind. For the most part it is the power which he has hitherto lacked for which he lusts.'[9] Hence German nationalism became dependent on Prussia, the most successful state, the only one with the resources of a great power apart from Austria whose dynastic character and racial heterogeneity disqualified it from national leadership. In the pre-Bismarck era a reformed Prussia, acceptable to liberal opinion, was still a possibility, but it was Prussia, with or without reform, that was important. Bismarck, once in power, made use of Prussia's economic ascendancy, exercised through the Zollverein, and of its military strength. He unified Germany, so far as he wanted, on his own terms. He also used the war of 1870 to change the climate of opinion in South Germany, where traditional dislike of Prussian militarism gave way to admiration. By successfully resisting the middle class demand for self-government, Bismarck deflected its energies into other channels. These were largely economic, for since the middle of the century Germany had begun to experience the industrial revolution. The impact of industrialisation on an authoritarian state was bound to differ from its effect on countries like France and England, where the bourgeoisie was already in power or on the way there. Despite the rapid tempo of economic change in Germany, the country remained substantially unmodified in its institutional and social structure. The 'anarchy' and excessive individualism elsewhere associated with early capitalism were not to be found in Bismarck's Reich where the paternalist tradition, exemplified in protectionism, state welfare and public ownership of sections of the economy, adapted itself to the new conditions by extending its activities. A significant feature, also illustrative of the *dirigiste* nature of the German economy, was the growth of agreements among business firms for the fixing of prices, production and profits. The important part played by these cartels, by vertical and horizontal integration of industry and by the great banks in financing and controlling investment meant that economic power was concentrated in relatively few hands. What was still in a political sense a 'feudal' state acquired the most advanced technology in Europe. Yet while the new industrial middle class might accept its exclusion from power (except for the favoured few who were ennobled), the new proletariat with Marx as its guide presented a new and more dangerous challenge. Just because it combined to an unique degree political backwardness with economic maturity, Germany was seen by socialists as the country most likely to experience the revolution to which they looked forward.

The Reichstag was the forum where the politicians, representing the popular forces, confronted, on very unequal terms, the holders of power. Members of the Reichstag fought elections, made speeches and interpellated ministers, but were rarely given office.[10] If a politician did become a minister, he had to resign his seat, because according to the constitution ministers belonged to the Federal Council for which no member of the Reichstag was eligible. However lively parliamentary

debates might be, they could not acquire the significance they would
have had in a parliamentary regime. Politics was not a career which
appealed to the ambitious. Able young men whose lack of aristocratic
credentials debarred them from the higher ranks of the army, bureaucracy or diplomatic corps (the professions from which the rulers of
Germany were mostly drawn) could make a career in business, where
opportunities multiplied as the economy expanded. But wealth was not
the most coveted reward. As in England, though to a lesser extent,
outstandingly successful businessmen could hope for ennoblement and
admission into the highest society, including that of the Emperor.
Ballin, the director of the Hamburg-Amerika shipping line, and
Rathenau, head of the giant electrical combine A.E.G., became personal friends of William II and were consulted by him on questions
of policy. Both were of middle-class birth and both were Jews.[11] Tirpitz,
the Minister for the Navy, was another man of modest social origin
who made a successful career, while Bethmann Hollweg, the Chancellor from 1909 to 1917, came from a banking family that had been
ennobled. After 1870 the middle classes, who earlier in the century
had been imbued with liberal or radical views, came round to support
of the dynasty and the regime, and eagerly accepted the prevailing
ethos. They did their best to get their sons into fashionable regiments,
and were never so happy as when wearing the uniform of a reserve
officer. They had no desire for the constitutional crisis which a demand
for parliamentary government would have provoked, and were reluctant to do anything to disturb the prosperity from which they benefited.
Caprivi's tariff policy showed that the government was paying more
attention to their interests. Werner Sombart, the economist, accused
the bourgeoisie of completely lacking the will to power; their highest
aim, he declared, was to become Junkers.[12] Like the academic intelligentsia with whom they had close ties, the professional and managerial
élites did not feel deprived: they had as much freedom under law as
they desired. Moreover they feared with some reason that a democratic
system of government would bring the Socialists to power. Max Weber
warned in vain of the danger of allowing political power to remain
the monopoly of an economically declining class, the Junkers, while
the middle and lower classes were still too immature to take their place.
Weber's fears were to be borne out by the experience of the Weimar
Republic, but in Wilhelmine Germany few heeded them. Nor was
much attention paid to Rathenau's criticism of the waste of talent
implied by the exclusion of able men without aristocratic qualifications
from the highest posts.[13] The diffusion of power had not been Bismarck's intention.

The system had other weaknesses. One was that the federal government was inadequately equipped, administratively and financially, to accomplish its tasks, which inevitably became more complex. There was no federal cabinet: policy was made by the Chancellor alone. Only when experience showed the impossibility of one man's directing all aspects of government were new offices created for such functions as railways, justice, finance, the interior, the post office and the navy. And even then the secretaries of state in charge remained formally assistants to the Chancellor. Nor did they have their own civil servants, except in Berlin, but had to use those of the *Länder*. The main financial handicap of the central government was that it drew no revenue from direct taxes, which were levied by the states, so that it depended on their contributions to the federal budget. Even import duties, which were a federal tax, were payable to the states if they exceeded a certain amount. Consequently when in the post-Bismarckian period its expenditure on arms (especially the navy) and on social services rose sharply, the federal government found itself with an unbalanced budget. But the main defect of the system was that it relied for its successful functioning on a single person, the Chancellor, who needed to be exceptionally able. It is not surprising that Bismarck's successors, lacking his unique prestige and special talents, were often unequal to the task. Nor was William II the kind of ruler who would allow his Chancellor to govern without interference as Bismarck had been allowed to do by William I. Yet without a harmonious relationship between Chancellor and Emperor the machine was almost bound to break down. Apart from Bismarck, the German chancellors had too little power for their responsibilities. They did not control the army or even the navy; they were at the mercy of an unpredictable emperor who was often more inclined to listen to courtiers than to his chief minister; and they had to keep federal policy in step with the narrower needs and more rigid not to say archaic structure of Prussia. Authority was no longer concentrated, as in Bismarck's time, in one person; and no one knew exactly where it lay. Lord Haldane, visiting Berlin on his unsuccessful mission in 1912, commented: 'When you mount to the peak of this highly organised people, you will find not only confusion, but chaos.'[14] The Austrian Foreign Minister Berchtold's historic question in July 1914 when he received conflicting advice from Bethmann Hollweg and Moltke, 'Who rules in Berlin?' echoes the same thought. Stampfer, the socialist journalist, described Germany on the eve of the First World War as the best administered but worst governed country in Europe.[15]

Yet to the great majority of Germans the benefits conferred by Bismarck were very real. 'We Germans', the famous historian Meinecke wrote later, 'often felt so free and proud, in contrast to the whole previous German past, in the mightily flourishing Empire of

1871 which gave living space to every one of us.'[16] This was a general view, though it is perhaps curious that Meinecke should have included freedom as well as pride and prosperity among the gains.[17] Meinecke too was optimistic about the new intellectual trends after 1890. But there was a minority which shared Nietzsche's fears. A professor at Jena regretted that the Germans had ceased to be a nation of thinkers, poets and dreamers, and aimed only at the domination and exploitation of nature: 'In the nation as in the individual we see with the increase of wealth the decrease of moral feeling and moral power.'[18] Germany, it seemed, was incapable of finding a middle way between the impractical idealism of the past and the power worship of the present. All agreed that wealth was increasing, and with it a luxury and ostentation quite foreign to the frugal tradition of Old Prussia. Rathenau, returning to Berlin in 1899 after a long absence, was struck by the change:

> We had become both rich and powerful and we wanted to show it to the world. . . . The feverish life of a great city, hungry for realities, intent on technical success and so-called achievement, clamorous for festivals, prodigies, pageants and suchlike futilities . . . all this produces a sort of combination of Rome and Byzantium, Versailles and Potsdam.[19]

The 1890s saw a continuation and in some respects an acceleration of the industrial and commerical growth which had been furthered by unification and the injection of capital provided by the French war indemnity in the early 1870s. The expansion of world trade and the development of new technologies brought a more rapid tempo and a greater concentration of wealth.[20] The survival of what was, by contemporary western standards, an obsolete political and social structure seems to have done little to impede Germany's economic progress; in some ways it may even have furthered it, by enabling captains of industry to exercise an almost military discipline in their factories.[21] But the social discrimination which prevailed in politics and the administration did not apply in trade and industry, where promotion went by merit, not birth. Moreover despite the agrarian bias inherent in the Prussian governmental system, the authorities did much to encourage industrial growth by their tariff policy, by building canals, by providing capital through the Reichsbank, by tax concessions to exports, and in other ways. The government also promoted social welfare in a paternal fashion. Bismarck's sickness, accident and old age insurance policies, while no doubt shrewdly aimed at reducing support for the Socialist party, showed an insight and concern matched by few European statesmen of his day.[22] A falling death-rate (Germany's infant mortality rate was about two-fifths of France's)[23] and diminished emigration were largely responsible for the rise in population from 49 million in 1890 to 67 million by 1914. During the same period the proportion of Germans living in towns went up from under a half to over three-fifths. Whether measured by bigger earnings, consumer spending, increases in savings bank deposits or national income, the standard of living rose. Average wages of coal miners, for example, doubled. Altogether, German economic achievements were impressive in the quarter of a century before 1914. Coal output trebled, steel production increased eightfold, total manufactures and imports more than doubled, exports more than trebled.[24] German travellers, goods and ships were seen in every part of the world, and German banks and investments were active, especially in the Near and Far East and in South America. Engineers like Bosch and Siemens acquired an international reputation. The electric dynamo, the gas engine, the petrol and the diesel engine were German inventions. Although as a trading nation Germany still ranked behind Britain, as an industrial power it was in the first place except for the United States. Britain was falling behind. Ballin, on a visit there in 1910, reported to the Emperor William: 'I confess that as far as England is concerned, I see things pretty pessimistically. The English cannot really compete with us any longer, and if they didn't have the power of capital and a stream of gold didn't pour from the great colonies into the mother country, because of their complacent and conservative habits they would soon be a *quantité negligeable* for us in world markets.'[25] One reason for Germany's success was that her engineers and technicians were better trained, and there were closer links between industry and research. Britain had no real counterpart to the fourteen German Technical High Schools of university standing. The German educational investment as a whole was bigger: with a population less than double that of England and Wales the Reich had more than three times as many university students.[26] Thanks to its new wealth Germany was able to sustain the burden of armaments better than most of its rivals. Though German arms expenditure per head had trebled between 1890 and 1914 (in which year it was almost the same as the British) when war broke out Germany was spending only 2·88 per cent of its national income on defence compared with the British figure of 3·26 per cent.[27] The formidable cost of modern weapons could be borne, but the German economy's growing dependence on overseas trade made it vulnerable to blockade in time of war. Those who in 1914 expected the imperial navy to play a decisive part in the war had overlooked both Germany's unfavourable geographical position in relation to the world's oceans (a permanent disadvantage) and her inability to challenge the British navy while she was still so far short of equality in tonnage. As Rathenau was to point out when war came, the government had relied entirely on its military preparedness and had neglected the economic factor, though in the long run, he argued, armaments alone could not maintain a state above the level determined by the interplay of its industrial, intellectual and moral resources.[28] So far as the General Staff had given thought to this problem, it did not foresee a long war or even believe that a complex industrial society such as Europe had become would be able to support one.

Germany's commercial rivalry with other nations, especially with England, whose industrial leadership had been unchallenged before the 1870s, was matched by a political rivalry that, in the age of imperialism, reached global proportions. The last quarter of the nineteenth century saw the process of empire-building reach its climax with the scramble for Africa as its most spectacular achievement. Before 1875 less than one tenth of the African continent had belonged to the European powers; by 1895 all but a tenth had been annexed. Each power justified its expansion by asserting the superior virtues of its race or civilisation. The combination of nationalism and *Realpolitik* had triumphed in Europe with Cavour and Bismarck; now such policies were carried further afield, and, as befitted a mass age, in a demagogic spirit. The new creeds of imperialism and racialism were buttressed and made intellectually respectable with ideas borrowed from the new sciences of biology and anthropology, psychology and sociology, and became competitors with socialism for popular favour. This was the seed-time of the totalitarian ideologies that came to fruition in the twentieth century. The new technologies established man's mastery over nature as never before. 'Social Darwinism' was invoked to justify the struggle of the strong against the weak, and even Lord Salisbury made a speech about 'dying nations'. Kipling sang the praises of those who bore the white man's burden, usually not without some advantage to themselves. Cecil Rhodes affirmed the superiority of English civilisation. Joseph Chamberlain proclaimed the glories of a British Empire, which, as colonial secretary, he considered it his duty to enlarge whenever the opportunity presented itself. Russia was the headquarters of the Pan-Slav movement which, beginning, like so many nationalist revivals, as a cultural awakening, developed into a political force, especially in the Balkans where it became a threat to the survival of both the Habsburg and Ottoman Empires. France, where the defeat of 1870 left smouldering resentments and sharpened grievances, had its League of Patriots, its Boulanger crisis, its nationalist novelist in Barrès, its anti-semitic publicist in Drumont whose scurrilous campaign bore fruit in the Dreyfus Affair. In Germany unification and the dramatic victory over France had an intoxicating effect: 'The whole nation', Bebel, the Socialist leader, told Valentine Chirol of the *Times*, 'is still drunk with military glory, and there is nothing to be done until some great disaster has sobered it.'[29] Treitschke, the historian, inculcated generations of students with the glorification of Prussia, and the doctrine of the superiority of the Aryan race (of which the Germans were the élite (already familiar through the writings of Gobineau (a French diplomat) and Lagarde (a German orientalist) gained a wider public through the writings of Houston Stewart Chamberlain, the son of a British admiral who became a German citizen. 'Today', Chamberlain assured his admirer William II in 1901, in explaining the Mission of Germandom, 'God uses only Germans.' The internal struggle was against ultramontanism, materialism and the 'caustic poison' of Jewry.[30] The prominence of some Jews, following their emancipation, in banking and other forms of business and also in left-wing politics, made them a special target for criticism: to the right they were objectionable as revolutionaries, to the left as capitalists. Treitschke in his generation had disliked the Jews because they were different: if they wanted to be considered part of the new German nation they must give up their separate practices and beliefs and accept assimilation. But this liberal anti-semitism soon gave way to a racial form, in which it was the assimilated Jew who constituted the real danger, because he was pretending to be something which he could not be. For a time the Conservative party adopted an anti-Jewish programme in order to win popularity, but in this they were outbid by the specifically Anti-Semitic party, which won a number of seats in the Reichstag in the nineties but failed to develop any real momentum.

Although anti-semitism hardly became a serious political force during the Second Empire, the conservatives' discovery that there were votes to be had in attacking the Jews was a significant portent.[31] In a more general sense, the cult of race, with its adulation of the Nordic people above the decadent Latins and uncivilised Slavs, confirmed the misgivings expressed by Nietzsche when he protested against the current belief that the defeat of France proved that German culture was superior to French, and feared 'the expiration of the German spirit in favour of the German Empire'. 'One pays a high price for coming to power; power stupefies. . . . The Germans were called a nation of thinkers; do they think at all today? *Deutschland, Deutschland über Alles*, I fear that was the end of German philosophy.'[32] It was not the end of German philosophy, but the cruder aspects of nationalism, combined with the materialism which was characteristic of the age, were to have more far-reaching consequences than Nietzsche imagined. Nietzsche himself cannot be absolved from all blame, since one effect of his influence was to make intellectually respectable ideas which challenged the assumptions of the liberal civilisation to which despite many reservations Germany belonged. Racial theories also exacerbated foreign relations, so that the German-Austrian alliance against the Franco-Russian combination easily became a test of ethnic superiority.

The new, strident nationalism was preached by professors and politicians, journalists and pressure groups. Among the last named three were of particular importance: the Colonial Society, the Pan-German League and the Navy League, founded in 1882, 1890 and 1898 respectively. The Navy League, which has at one time had a million members, was the most highly organised.[33] Patronised and subsidised by the government, and heavily backed by the steel firm of Krupp, it has been described as the first example of state-directed propaganda; by persuading the people to push it in the direction in which it wanted to go, the government was making sure of support for the expensive big-navy programme. The Pan-German League, which began as the German League and was renamed in 1894, was in some ways more significant because it had a longer life and was concerned with a wider range of policy.[34] By 1914 some 60 members of the Reichstag (mostly National Liberals) belonged to the League. Its aims were to arouse patriotic feeling and to combat unpatriotic trends; to help Germans living beyond the national frontiers, whether in Europe or overseas, and to encourage them to uphold their German character and culture; to promote German interests abroad, and to carry the colonial movement forward to practical results. It was natural that Germany, as a recently united country, should wear its nationalism somewhat self-consciously and aggressively, just as it was inevitable that, as a late-comer to the colonial field, it should join in the scramble for territory with exceptional ardour. The Pan-German League actually originated as a protest movement against the Heligoland-Zanzibar treaty of 1890, and an active part was played in its formation by Karl Peters, the African explorer and governor of German East Africa. Bismarck had acquired for Germany four African territories (East and South West Africa, the Cameroons and Togoland) and some possessions in the Pacific, including part of New Guinea. These gains were small by comparison with those made by Britain and France between 1870 and 1890, especially if the British and French colonial empires acquired earlier are also taken into account. The Pan-German League asserted that Germany was entitled to a share of the world's colonies commensurate with its great power status and growing population. Bismarck's dictum that Germany was a satisfied power was no longer accepted. The difficulty was that by 1890 nearly all the land available for distribution as colonies had already been allocated. Germany, owing to its retarded unification and Bismarck's caution had staked its claim too late. Hence the use by the German government of the 'blackmail'

tactics of which Joseph Chamberlain complained, particularly in relation to England as the chief colonial power.[35] It was probably the only
weapon at Germany's disposal but it caused resentment and distrust
in excess of any benefits. In the long run Germany's economic ascendancy could well have brought political advantages of the sort it coveted
had the First World War not broken out. But Germany was not disposed to wait, though in territorial terms the results of its impatience
were meagre. In contrast to peaceloving *beati-possidentes* such as the
British, Germany, a have-not power, was bound to appear a disturber
of the peace.[36]

Although German colonial demands sprang from a desire for prestige
and general 'greatness' what Bülow called 'a place in the sun' – they
were closely linked in men's minds with the pressure of a growing
population on limited resources in an economy increasingly dependent
on overseas trade. The problem was illustrated by the high rate of
emigration, which was running at an average annual level of well
over 100,000 in the eighties and early nineties. All these emigrants,
most of whom went to the United States, were lost to Germany. It was
strongly felt that there ought to be a place to which Germans could
emigrate without giving up their nationality. Of existing German
colonies only South West Africa had a climate suitable for European
settlement, and it lacked resources. The fertile colonies on the other
hand were unhealthy. This problem was ultimately solved by the economic expansion at home which more than absorbed the entire labour
force and reduced emigration by the turn of the century to negligible
proportions. Another argument in favour of colonies was that by owning the sources of imported raw materials Germany would pay for them
in its own currency and need not depend on imports from other
colonies where trade discrimination was practised. The German objective was not universal free trade but neo-mercantilism, the formation
of a protectionist bloc capable of competing with other blocs; though
the German tariff on manufactured goods was a good deal lower than
that of most European countries.[37] But the notion that Germany with
a colonial empire could become self-sufficient in vital raw materials
was chimerical; even the British Empire was not. Financially Germany's colonies, which absorbed only a fraction of its total foreign
investment, brought loss, not gain.[38] Their main advantage was providing an opportunity for German explorers, administrators, missionaries
and traders to work under their own flag; and the nationalists derived
psychological satisfaction from the colonies as symbols of German
power and prestige. The extent to which, influenced by popular sentiment, the German government pursued colonial objectives with little
regard to their economic importance is exemplified by its insistence on

acquiring from Britain part of the Samoan group of islands, which it henceforth shared with the United States. The launching of the naval programme brought a demand for coaling stations and naval bases, such as the port of Kiao-Chow, leased from the Chinese government for 99 years. It was a general belief at the time – not only in Germany – that a great industrial power must have colonies to keep up its position and to supply its economy with raw materials, expanding markets, and new opportunities for investment.[39] The definitive carve-up of the world appeared to be in progress; few would have predicted that within two generations nearly all the colonies would govern themselves. Finally, behind the general support for 'world policy' which was particularly marked among the academic intelligentsia, lay the idea expressed by Max Weber at his inaugural address to the students of Freiburg University in 1895: that the foundation of the Reich would have been simply a youthful prank if it had not been intended to lay the foundation for further expansion.

Equally significant in view of later events, was the interest of the Pan-German League in the future of the German race in Europe, and particularly in the 13 millions in the Habsburg Monarchy whom Bismarck had excluded from his Empire. In opening branches in Austria and strengthening the ties with Germans across the river Inn (the Bavarian-Austrian frontier) the League was in fact reviving the *grossdeutsch* policy of 1848, which had envisaged the inclusion in a united Germany of those parts of the Habsburg domains (mainly Austria proper and Bohemia) that had belonged to the German Confederation before 1866 and earlier to the Holy Roman Empire. Bismarck's Reich, as one of his critics pointed out as early as January 1871, was a still incomplete nation state, which 'must . . . reserve the right to pull into its framework at the next favourable opportunity those areas of German nationality which still stand outside it'.[40] Such an opportunity appeared likely to occur with a change of monarch in Vienna. There was a general expectation that after the death of the Emperor Francis Joseph, who by 1890 was sixty years old, his Empire would break up, and that the German provinces would then unite with Germany. In the meantime the Pan-German League encouraged the German population in Austria, which though a minority was politically and culturally dominant, to resist the rising tide of Slav nationalism. In particular the League opposed the Habsburg policy of making concessions to the subject peoples in order to keep the Monarchy together. German nationalism in Austria came under the influence of Georg Ritter von Schoenerer, who led a virulent propaganda campaign against both the dynasty and the Catholic Church ('Los von Rom'), and preached anti-semitism despite Jewish support for the Germans against the other nationalities. It was hardly an accident that the man who was to fulfil, though in ways no one could foresee, the dreams of Pan-Germans, Adolf Hitler, was born in a part of Austria where the influence of Schoenerer was strong, and spent part of his early manhood in the racially heterogeneous city of Vienna. So long as Austria-Hungary was allied to Germany, the Austrian Germans were not likely to disrupt the Habsburg Monarchy; but to the racialists blood ties obviously meant more than dynastic and confessional loyalties. This was another difference between the age of Bismarck and that of William II.

Emphasis on the Germanic race had implications in other directions. Early in the nineteenth century Ernst Moritz Arndt had urged the desirability of incorporating in the German Confederation bordering peoples which had formerly belonged to the Empire, such as the Swiss, the Dutch, and the Flemings (as well as those of Alsace and Lorraine). After 1870 such demands had a very different significance, for Germany was now the strongest power in Europe. The Pan-German League took up these claims, though without encouragement from the populations concerned. The League also cultivated closer relations with the Nordic peoples of Scandinavia. The obverse of this notion of extending the Empire to include their racial brethren was the germanisation of foreign nationalities inside it. There were French in Alsace-Lorraine, Danes in Schleswig, and, by far the largest group, three or four million Poles in West Prussia, Posen and Silesia.

These Poles, who had become Prussian subjects through the partition of their country in the eighteenth century, were the object of a germanisation campaign which included the suppression of the Polish language and the buying up of Polish estates for re-sale to German farmers; it was pursued with greater or less severity according to who was Chancellor in Berlin.[41] Caprivi, who succeeded Bismarck, introduced (as elsewhere) a more liberal policy, but a tougher attitude was marked by the foundation in 1894 of an *Ostmarkenverein*, and during the chancellorship of Bülow (1900–1909) anti-Polish measures became more stringent. In the eyes of Pan-Germans, the national minorities represented a 'mortal danger' to the state, and the League encouraged the work of forced assimilation. Germany's 'colonial' relation to her Polish lands, which in some ways resembled that of England to Ireland during the English ascendancy, had strong emotional roots in the centuries-long struggle of the Teutonic Knights against the Slavs. Prussians, themselves a germanised heathen tribe of Baltic origin, did not forget that the whole of their state east of the Elbe was conquered territory, and viewed the Slavs on German soil as a subjugated race. But historical memories could nourish Polish as well as German nationalism, and the Poles, though without a government behind them, resisted germanisation with remarkable success. Well organised, backed by their priests and with a higher birth rate than the rivals, they refused to abandon hope of the eventual restoration of a Polish state. The Poles were neither assimilated nor appeased. The problem remained unsolved until the end of the First World War, when the simultaneous defeat of the Russian and German Empires opened the way for the revival of a fully independent Poland. For Germany the settlement of 1919 was to be simply a source of new grievances, and the German-Polish struggle thereafter became international in character.

No introduction to Wilhelmine Germany, however brief, should fail to mention its remarkable cultural diversity. German artists and intellectuals were, of course, affected by the same influences as the rest of Europe and there was the same mixture and clash of styles in an age which was experiencing an aesthetic revolution. Just as in politics there was a confrontation between the 'national' or establishment parties and the Socialists (whom the Emperor considered a disloyal faction, men without a country), so in literature and the arts there were the officially approved artists in the one camp and the rebels and avant-garde in the other. Official art reflected the taste of the court. William II, modern in his interest in technology and the navy, was a traditionalist when it came to painting, architecture or sculpture. 'An art which transgresses the laws and barriers outlined by Me ceases to be an art' was one of his public pronouncements.[42] The artist's task, he declared, was to preserve the ideals of the past.[43] This in fact meant imitating the past. Every historic style was revived for a purpose: there were Gothic factories, Baroque post offices and Romanesque railway stations.[44] If this was a sign that Germany had not come to terms with her own modernity, it was a trait which was characteristic of the age and far from unique. Despite the lack of a unifying style, German buildings of the period had certain characteristics in common. What struck one contemporary British observer was the cult of force. 'Everywhere one sees the worship of massivity, the striving after crude, imposing effects . . . wherein form is subordinated to size.'[45] The Protestant cathedral in Berlin was one example of this heavy, ornate style, which the same critic described as body without soul – a devastating thing to say about a church. It was as though the rhetorical superlatives of William II's speeches were transposed into stone. Perhaps the most typical manifestation of the official style was the thirty-two white marble statues of Prussian kings and generals in Berlin's central park, the Tiergarten. This was known as Victory Avenue and dubbed 'Dolls' Avenue' by the irreverent. The patriotic theme was in evidence everywhere: each town had its Bismarckstrasse, its streets and squares named after Kaiser Wilhelm, Roon or Moltke. Bismarck memorials, sometimes of formidable size, became a feature of the German landscape, which already had national monuments commemorating the victory over the Romans of Hermann (Arminius) and other heroic exploits.

Yet besides the rather grandiose buildings which seemed the appropriate setting for patriotic rhetoric and imperial swagger, there were interesting experiments by young architects who were feeling their way to a simpler, more radical style that was to become widely popular during the Weimar Republic. One problem was the use of inferior standards when craftsmanship was replaced by mass production. To improve industrial design was the purpose of an association founded in 1907 called the *Werkbund*, which encouraged the output of machine-made articles that were both pleasing and practical. Among the architectural pioneers was Alfred Messel, who designed for Wertheim, a large department store in Berlin, a building in which the space between the supporting columns was filled by expanses of glass. Another innovator was Walter Gropius, the head of the later Bauhaus, who built model factories at Cologne and elsewhere. The emphasis was on functionalism (*Sachlichkeit* was the word used) which made full use of new materials and techniques while rejecting archaic mannerisms and superfluous ornament. By 1914 the twentieth-century style had been achieved in Germany.[46] Nor were the social aspects of architecture neglected: Gropius was interested in the financing and mass production of small houses, and Germany led the way in industrial town planning (Siemenstadt in Berlin and the Krupp estate in Essen). Her manufacturing towns, while often drab, were less mean and squalid than their British counterparts. There was greater emphasis on amenities, and more concern for preservation of the environment.

Despite, perhaps because of, the growth of luxury and security, and the obvious signs of moral as well as material progress, a certain spiritual restlessness was characteristic of the last decades of the century. Orthodoxy was being challenged from all sides. There were radical new creeds and cults: socialism in its various forms, anarchism, the cult of race, and Social Darwinism already referred to, feminism and theosophy, the aesthetic movement. The spread of education helped the proliferation of new ideas, and cheap printing gave them a wide circulation. An enterprising Berlin publisher introduced Tolstoi and Dostoevsky to the German public, and with Ibsen and Strindberg naturalism conquered the German stage. The Berlin theatre entered its golden age, with Otto Brahm founding the *Freie Bühne* in 1889. This was an experimental theatre, free of censorship and non-profit making. A year later a *Freie Volksbühne* designed to produce plays for the working-class audiences came into existence. In 1904 Max Reinhardt succeeded

Brahm as director of the *Freie Bühne*, and soon became Germany's most famous producer, with his own theatre and an international reputation. Berlin, rapidly losing its provincial character, became the metropolis which Germany had lacked. It was a study in contrasts: an industrial giant set among the sandy forests of Brandenburg, the radical capital of a highly conservative state, a centre of avant-garde artists in a metropolis characterised by ostentatious new wealth and the grey proletarian suburbs with their swarming tenements. Some new writers, such as the dramatist Gerhard Hauptmann, were concerned with social problems and roused humanitarian sympathy, though the orthodox were often disgusted. Others, like Frank Wedekind were more interested in adolescence and sexual emancipation. Painting moved from Impressionism (represented, among others, by Corinth and Slevogt) to Post-impressionism and Expressionism, this last being roughly the German equivalent of the French Fauves and Cubists. In the year when William II opened the Victory Avenue in Berlin, the capital saw its first exhibition of Cézanne. The Emperor strongly disapproved, but did not ban it, though in 1908 he forced the director of the National Gallery to resign because it contained too many French impressionists. The man was given a similar post in Munich, which was a more tolerant and also more important artistic metropolis. The first *Sezession* exhibition (of rebel painters) was held there in 1892, followed by many. Munich was also the focal point in Germany of the *Jugendstil*, the Art Nouveau movement named after a periodical called *Die Jugend*. It sprang from the decorative arts, and received a powerful impulse from the Vienna *Sezession* of 1897. The interest in line, characteristic of Art Nouveau, led naturally to an emphasis on pure form, and so to abstract art. One of the pioneers of abstract painting was Kandinsky, a Russian artist who settled in Munich in 1896 and soon began to experiment in colours at about the same time as Picasso was experimenting in forms. Other original talents who worked in Munich shortly before the First World War were Franz Marc, who was killed at Verdun, and Paul Klee, who came from Switzerland. Both, like Kandinsky, belonged to the *Blaue Reiter* group named after one of Kandinsky's pictures. Their aim was to discover the harmonies of nature and to discern what Marc called the 'inner mystical construction of the world'.[47] In Dresden, Germany's greatest Baroque centre, another avant-garde group of painters founded the community known as *Die Brücke*: this included the expressionists Kirchner, Pechstein and Schmidt-Rottluff, and its object was defined as 'to attract all the revolutionary and insurgent elements'.[48] For a time they were joined by Nolde, one of the most intense and individual artists, who was to live to incur Hitler's displeasure. Another expressionist was Käthe

Kollwitz, the wife of a doctor in a poor district of Berlin whose drawings and prints usually took as their theme social protest and suffering. The two most gifted German sculptors of the age were Lehmbrück, another victim of the war, and Ernst Barlach, the North German whose art owed much to medieval wood-carving and the later creator of many war memorials which were destroyed by the Nazis. The founder and president of the Berlin *Sezession* was Max Liebermann, one of the first and most distinguished impressionists, whose life and work formed a kind of bridge between German and French painters. But more typical of the younger generation in Berlin was the movement associated with the periodical *Der Sturm*, which was also the name of a gallery to promote modern art whose influence was felt throughout Germany.

In literature too, expressionism and symbolism (Stefan George) competed with naturalism. Thomas Mann's novels depicted the bourgeoisie in decline: his favourite themes, the clash between the bourgeois and the artistic temperament, and the pathology of artistic inspiration, suited an age that was fascinated by art for art's sake and was beginning to discover Freud. Thomas Mann's brother Heinrich was writing novels which, while less profound, were fiercely critical of the defects of Wilhelmine society, such as the arrogance of the newly enriched middle classes towards their inferiors and their servility towards their betters. Equally pointed satire came from *Simplicissimus*, the left-wing humorous weekly published in Munich, which mocked the foibles of rulers and ruled through the eyes of a particularly brilliant group of artists. Another notable journalistic centre, also started in the early nineties, was *Die Zukunft*, an intellectual review edited by Maximilian Harden, an outsider with a trenchant pen who had begun his career in political journalism as a confidant of Bismarck.[49] *Die Zukunft* was highly critical of the Kaiser and his court, and Harden was twice sent to prison for *lèse-majesté*. Despite censorship the socialist press enjoyed a good deal of free speech, and the fiery Rosa Luxemburg was an instructor in the S.P.D. party school. One of the main targets of the radicals and socialists was the cult of militarism, not only in the sense that the army had too much power over policy, but that the civilians showed excessive deference to uniforms.[50]

To some foreign observers even the Social Democratic party was excessively disciplinarian. Zuckmayer's classic comedy on the theme of uniform-worship, *The Captain of Köpenick*, though written long afterwards, was based on an incident that actually occurred in 1906. The Reichstag debate on the Zabern affair in 1913, when a clash between army and civilians occurred at a small Alsatian town, showed that politicians resented the high-handedness of the military, even if they stopped short of action that would have ended it. Criticism of the army was invariably met with a reference to the danger of rocking the boat at a time when Germany's international position was unfavourable.

Besides the political protest (Social Democracy) and the artists' *Sezession*, there was a third kind of protest which was particularly characteristic of Germany: the youth movement.[51] This started modestly in a Berlin suburb in 1896, and by 1914 had affected the lives and outlook of thousands of young people. The *Wandervögel*, as they were called, were adolescent boys and girls who spent their weekends and holidays in mountains and forests, carrying a rucksack and singing folk songs to the accompaniment of a guitar. A generation reared in the big cities, reacting against the 'asphalt culture' of a mechanised society, rediscovered the beauties of nature, the joys of the simple life. The movement claimed to reject the materialism, artificiality and philistinism of official Germany. Like so much else, it was a product of romanticism, sharing its adulation of the past, the 'dear dead days', its misty nostalgia for a bygone age. Some members of the youth cult, especially those who were not committed to a definite ideology like Roman Catholicism or socialism, were later to be attracted by the cloudy metapolitics of racialism: there is a connection between them and the '*völkisch*' youth groups of the twenties, just as there is between the latter and the Hitler Youth. But in the pre-1914 period the movement kept its pristine idealism; it was patriotic rather than nationalist. The greatest moment in the history of the *Wandervögel* came in October 1913, when they held a huge rally on the Hohe Meissner mountain near Kassel to celebrate the centenary of the battle of Leipzig. This was, significantly, a counter-demonstration to the official celebrations being held at the same time. The young people pledged themselves to such noble principles as self-determination, responsibility, sincerity and 'inner freedom'. Wyneken, one of the leaders, expressed the hope that the day would never come on which they would be forced to carry war into the villages of a foreign people. His words were tragically ironic.[52] A year later many of his audience were dead. In August 1914 they had volunteered enthusiastically for the army, and in October were thrown into the first battle of Ypres where they suffered heavy casualties. Like the English poet Rupert Brooke, who compared volunteers for the war to 'swimmers into cleanness leaping' they did not live long enough to become disillusioned.

The picture presented by the Germany of William II is thus far from homogeneous. Viewed after the lapse of half a century, and one that has included two world wars, Auschwitz and Hiroshima, the pre-1914 world seems one of almost legendary calm and security. That was not how its contemporaries saw it. What struck them was the rapidity and diversity of change, the constant erosion of old values and traditional habits. Technology was transforming the world. Social stability was threatened by war from without and by revolution from within. After 1904 and still more after 1907 Germans felt the pressure of encirclement, while the Socialists' electoral triumph in 1912 showed that the 'internal enemy' had been neither crushed nor conciliated. The antagonisms in German society became more marked. There remained the contrasts inherent in a powerful industrial state encased in medieval trappings, in the largest Socialist party in Europe facing the strongest army. Despite the acknowledged excellence of German scholarship and research in every field and the high general standard of education, the popularity of pseudo-philosophic writings like those of H. S. Chamberlain was a disquieting symptom just as were the signs of a morbid and regressive nationalism. It was during the reign of William II that such slogans as 'blood and soil', 'master race' (used by the Pan-German League) and 'living space' (meaning agricultural land to be acquired for German settlement, if necessary by conquest) began to be heard.[53] To some extent they were an attempt to externalise internal conflicts, to find through foreign conquest solutions unattainable at home. They also testified to Germany's political immaturity: owing to her late development, Germany was still hardly an integrated society like the older nation states, and she was still not sure of her place in the world.[54] The 'adolescent empire' had the faults as well as the enthusiasm of youth.[55] Yet these weaknesses were hidden by the strength and discipline of the state, its outward glitter and prosperity. The structure built by Bismarck was solid enough to survive four years of world war, and collapsed only after defeat brought on by an over-ambitious foreign policy.

CHAPTER II

From the Fall of Bismarck to World Policy (1890-1902)

(i) WILLIAM II AND THE NEW COURSE

Bismarck's dismissal, which was to have so many unforeseen consequences, was the result of a clash of policy and personality between the Iron Chancellor and his new master, William II. William came to the throne at the age of 29 in succession to his father, Frederick, whose reign of 99 days formed a brief, unhappy intermezzo after the long and successful reign of William I. The Emperor Frederick's death from cancer of the throat, after a painful illness embittered by disagreement between his German and British doctors was a political as well as a personal tragedy, for it ended the hopes of a generation that he would inaugurate a fundamental change in German policy. William II was known to be an admirer of Bismarck, and at first it seemed certain that Bismarck would stay in office despite his advanced age. Relations between the two soon reached breaking point however, and in March 1890 Bismarck had to go. William was resolved to be his own Chancellor. But he lacked the application and patience needed for the continuous exercise of power, and his nervous restlessness caused him to spend a great deal of time travelling. He governed sporadically, interfering dramatically from time, especially in foreign affairs, often to the great embarrassment of his Chancellor. A feature of the earlier part of the reign was the role played by courtiers, especially by Count Philipp Eulenburg, the Kaiser's best friend. His 'personal rule' was most evident between 1897 (when Bülow became Foreign Secretary) and the *Daily Telegraph* crisis of 1908, which shattered much of his self-confidence and curbed some of his natural exuberance; not until the First World War did he withdraw almost completely from decision-making.[1]

William had many engaging qualities: an inquiring and versatile mind, energy and enthusiasm, receptiveness to new ideas, good intentions and the desire to be liked. Unfortunately he was also an incurable dilettante. His knowledge, if wide, was superficial, his interests were rarely sustained. With a highly strung temperament he could be easily swayed, and he changed his mind with bewildering rapidity. His impulsiveness made him unpredictable, but he could also be very obstinate. At times he combined the touchiness of a prima donna with the conceit of a spoilt child. Already as a youth William had shown an intractable nature, and some of his subjects viewed his accession with considerable doubt. No one could have been franker than his mother, who told Bülow's mother-in-law in the 1890s: 'Mon fils sera la ruine de l'Allemagne'.[2] The cocksureness which experience might have mellowed was exacerbated by his semi-autocratic position, surrounded by advisers and courtiers who shielded him from unpleasant facts and fed him on a heady diet of flattery. Yet he was capable of humility and even at times of laughing at himself. Theodore Roosevelt perceptively remarked that in his heart of hearts the Kaiser knew that he was not an absolute ruler.[3] But the Kaiser whom the world saw was the man whose brash speeches caused dismay at home and alarm abroad. The bristling moustaches and glittering, frequently changed uniform might strike a highly theatrical note, but behind them was the strongest army and the most highly organised state in Europe. As far as public pronouncements were concerned William was his own worst enemy. In action – especially at a crisis – he revealed a caution that gained him a reputation for timidity. His character was complex and inconsistent. Such different judges as Salisbury, Rathenau and Grey considered him not quite normal, and he was certainly subject to moods of abnormal excitement that help to explain some of his more foolish acts. Despite his insistence on a degree of personal power that was not compatible even with the Prussian constitution, William liked to think of himself as a modern ruler, as much at home on the bridge of a battleship as in the saddle of a Prussian cavalry regiment.[4] He tried at first to follow a 'social' policy, and his friends included industrialists and bankers as well as members of the traditional governing class. He encouraged the teaching of modern subjects in schools, and against opposition ensured that the Technical High Schools should, like the Universities, be represented in the Prussian Upper House. He was aware of the importance of science and technology, and played a leading part in establishing the Kaiser Wilhelm Society for the promotion of the natural sciences. He could also take a long view on many subjects. But in politics he remained an amateur dabbling in matters whose significance he never really understood. Rathenau compared him to a medieval surgeon operating on the body politic with a knowledge of anatomy derived partly from the Bible, partly from a patchwork of the very latest ideas of court professors.[5] Fontane the novelist saw the Kaiser's modernising policy as an unsuccessful attempt to graft new techniques on to archaic structures, like trying to make bulletproof a knight's armour of the year 1400.[6] As Bismarck saw, William lacked a sense of proportion. He believed what he wanted to believe, and his judgement was most erratic. Few careers illustrate so dramatically the catastrophic effects of an inability to come to terms with reality. What the Kaiser represented not only seemed an anachronism to foreigners but embarrassed many of his own subjects. Max Weber, the sociologist, complained that Germans were treated with contempt abroad because they tolerated the regime of William II.[7]

In both its positive and negative aspects William's character bore the marks of his parentage and upbringing. His home life had been strained and unhappy. His father, the well-meaning but somewhat ineffective Frederick, was overshadowed by his able, intelligent and masterful wife, Victoria ('Vicky') Queen Victoria's eldest daughter, whose marriage to the Prussian Crown Prince in 1858 could have been the start of a new, closer relationship between the two countries. In fact things turned out otherwise. Bismarck's wars offended pro-Danish sentiment in Britain and estranged liberal opinion. Whether Vicky with her British background and ideas would ever have felt at home in Prussia-Germany is doubtful. What is certain is that in the Germany created by blood and iron she felt increasingly alienated and unhappy. Like her son, she was opinionated and inclined to lecture others. As a convinced liberal with a strong sense of freedom and justice, she detested Bismarck's regime. She had always found Germany backward and unenlightened, and Bismarck, with his support of autocracy and militarism, was encouraging the worst elements. Political differences were exacerbated by personal dislike and distrust. She and her husband became the focus of opposition to Bismarck, and liberals looked forward to the day when Frederick would succeed his aged father, introduce a parliamentary regime and link Germany firmly to the liberal West instead of to reactionary Russia. William, brought up by a Calvinist tutor to be a Prussian patriot and admirer of Bismarck, resented his mother's attitude, and his experience as a young guards officer strengthened his autocratic tendencies. His love-hate relationship to his parents extended to his mother's home country. William visited England repeatedly from earliest childhood onwards. He was impressed by, and genuinely fond of, his grandmother, the venerable Queen Victoria, and some of his earliest and happiest memories were of Windsor Castle and Buckingham Palace. But there was one Englishman he did not like – his uncle Bertie, the Prince of Wales and later Edward VII. Whereas in early life he associated England with his mother and grandmother, in later life it was Edward who became symbolic of a land for which he felt simultaneously admiration and resentment. The two men were a striking contrast: the nephew tense, ardent, assertive; the uncle relaxed, pleasure-loving, lazy, yet with a shrewd ability to manage men that seemed to bring effortless success.[8] Each, in his way, personified his country. William represented Germany, the parvenu power, striving ceaselessly for status and expansion, but spoiling her chances through clumsiness and miscalculation; Edward stood for the British Empire, mellow, self-assured and complacent. William disapproved of Edward's scandalous private life; Edward's wife, Alexandra of Denmark, could not forgive Prussia for her country's defeat in 1864. Nor could Edward forget William's unfilial treatment of his mother, Edward's sister. William was personally jealous of Edward, while Edward usually found his nephew insufferable.

Despite his earlier enthusiasm for Bismarck, William was not prepared, like his grandfather, to play second fiddle to his distinguished minister, and quite early in the reign a number of issues arose on which the two men disagreed. The most important was the policy to be followed towards the Socialists. In 1890 the Anti-Socialist law was due for renewal. Bismarck insisted that, when the bill was next introduced in the Reichstag, it should contain a clause providing for the expulsion of socialist agitators and should have no time limit. This was too much for the National Liberals, whose support was essential. They and the Free Conservatives drew up an amended version of the bill, making the controversial clause subject to review every three years. The Emperor favoured a settlement on these lines. But Bismarck refused to compromise: he knew that his draft of the bill would never pass the Reichstag, but he calculated that the Socialists, once the law against them had run out, would create disturbances that would give the government an excuse to suppress them by force. This cynical attitude did not suit William, who had no wish to begin his reign with civil war and had already decided to conciliate the workers by summoning an international labour congress in Berlin. He wanted to be known, William told his ministers, as a 'roi des gueux' or poor man's emperor. When, early in 1890. Bismarck outlined his plans for a *coup d'état* and thus for the overthrow of his own constitution, William at first agreed, but on second thoughts rejected them as impractical. When the subject was raised with the ministers they sided with the Emperor, and Bismarck found himself, to his consternation, in a minority of one in a body he had been accustomed to dominate. Bismarck also annoyed William by interviewing Windthorst, the leader of the Centre party which, after the elections of February 1890, held the balance of power in the Reichstag. William suspected that the wily old Chancellor was hatching a plot with the Centre behind his back with the object of forming a Conservative-Centre coalition. At this juncture Bismarck refurbished an old weapon against the Kaiser: he insisted on the observance of a Prussian decree of 1852 which laid down that ministers might advise the King only through the Prime Minister, i.e. through Bismarck himself. Matters came to a head when William demanded the withdrawal of the decree or Bismarck's resignation. At a stormy interview between the two men, in the course of which Bismarck almost threw an inkpot at William's head, the argument spread to foreign affairs, and the Kaiser was provoked to snatch a letter from the German ambassador to England in which the Tsar of Russia was quoted as having described him as 'un garçon mal elevé et de mauvaise foi'.[9] Bismarck now knew that he must quit. In his letter of resignation he gave the impression that the main reason for the break was their disagreement on foreign policy; this was what he wanted the world to believe, but his purpose was not achieved because the Kaiser did not allow the letter to be published. William's reply accepting the resignation, but suggesting that it was mainly for health reasons, was even more misleading; and his assurance that he would seek Bismarck's advice in future proved to be a mere form of words. Yet, as Lord Rosebery said, Bismarck was hoist by his own petard. Having reached the age of 75, he would probably have had to retire before long, and there were already signs of failing powers, but the manner and abruptness of his going left a resentment expressed in the bitterness with which he criticised his successors. Like Wolsey before him, he no doubt reflected on the ingratitude of Kings. To the Kaiser the issue was simple but fundamental; as the Grand Duke of Baden told Hohenlohe, it was whether the House of Hohenzollern or the House of Bismarck was to rule.[10]

Now that Bismarck had gone, how much of his policy would remain? This was the question that everyone inside Germany and abroad was asking. In a telegram to his fellow princes the Kaiser denied any intention to change: 'It has fallen to me to be the officer-of-the-watch on the ship of state. The course remains the same, and now full steam ahead.' In fact, as has already been seen, William's attitude to social problems was very different (at least at the beginning of his reign) from Bismarck's, and he was soon to show a different approach to foreign relations.[11]

The new Chancellor was General Leo von Caprivi, a staff officer who had been in succession head of the navy and a divisional commander in Hanover. He was a man of sense and integrity and a first class administrator, but of limited political experience and without political flair. The new Foreign Secretary, Marschall von Bieberstein, was also a novice in foreign affairs. The end of the Bismarck era therefore meant not only the absence of a single directing hand, but a lack of expertise

at the highest level. William's frequent shifts and his susceptibility to
advice from different quarters made the course of German politics after
1890 anything but consistent. The Chancellor had to manage the
Reichstag as well as please the Emperor, who at times would boast of
his inherited powers, at others would stress the constitutional nature of
the monarchy. Post-Bismarckian Chancellors had to authorise many
moves of which they privately disapproved in order to keep their job
and to prevent worse.[12] It was not easy to occupy Bismarck's chair
without his skill and with an Emperor who took Frederick the Great
as his model.

The vital change that followed Bismarck's fall was the non-renewal
of the secret Reinsurance treaty with Russia, which Bismarck had
considered his diplomatic masterpiece because it simultaneously ensured
peace in Eastern Europe and the continued isolation of France. The
Russian government was anxious to renew the treaty when it expired
in 1890, and William at first gave the Russian ambassador an assurance
to that effect. This decision was, however, soon successfully challenged
by the man who now emerged (behind the scenes) as the 'grey
eminence' of the Foreign Ministry, Baron von Holstein. It was almost
inevitable that the new ministers should lean heavily on a man who
possessed, as Holstein did, an unrivalled grasp of foreign affairs and a
unique knowledge of the foreign service. Although Holstein was not
the highest official (his rank was that of senior counsellor), with his
established reputation as an oracle, his direct access to the Foreign
Minister (their offices were adjoining) and his friendship with the
Kaiser's confidant, Eulenburg, he was by far the most influential. In
view of the power he exercised it is hardly surprising that Holstein
should have been blamed for the mistakes which led to Germany's
diplomatic isolation and ultimate ruin, especially since his name was
connected with several scandals, and as a misanthropic back-room
figure he easily became an object of suspicion. The publication in recent
years of the Holstein Papers shows that Holstein played a less sinister
part than was formerly imagined, and certainly not all the errors of
German foreign policy during the period of his acendancy (1890–1906)
can be laid at his door. He was not responsible for the Kruger telegram
or for the big navy policy. But it was he who insisted on ending the
Russian alliance and on the Morocco policy of 1905-6 which ended so
disastrously for Germany. With all his industry and intelligence Holstein
had a warped judgement. He was a bad psychologist, and was swayed
by personal antipathies. His distrust was pathological, and there was
a malicious streak in his make-up. He was feared and respected rather
than liked, though his courage was undeniable. A German diplomat
who had known Holstein as a young man described him as having 'the

spirit and character of a hunchback'.[13] Yet Holstein was opposed to
the Kaiser's personal rule, which he saw as an anachronism, and
Valentine Chirol, the *Times* editor who knew Holstein well, paid him
this tribute: 'In an atmosphere of gross adulation and servility he
preserved an independence of character and showed a contempt for
stars and ribands and plumed helmets, which were proof against all
blandishments from the highest quarters.'[14]

There were several reasons, Holstein argued, why the Reinsurance
treaty should not be renewed. It was incompatible with Germany's
obligations to her other allies; it violated the spirit of the secret letter of
the Triple Alliance, and if the terms of the secret treaty were divulged
by Bismarck in a spiteful attempt to embarrass the government, Germany would be discredited. Only a man of Bismarck's unique skill and
authority could, it was urged, control the complicated and overlapping
system of alliances he had built up. The Russian alliance was not
popular in Germany, whose Foreign Ministry was suspicious of the
Pan-Slav movement which had a good deal of popular if unofficial
backing in Russia, and had watched with growing alarm other symptoms of anti-German feeling in Russia, including the new *rapprochement* with France. Russia was also believed, wrongly, to be planning
a new stroke in the Balkans, and the German General Staff had been
urging the need of a preventive war. In Russia too expansionist trends
in Germany (symbolised by the formation of the Pan-German League)
caused some fear; the Tsar, Alexander III, distrusted William II as a
person, and even he shared the view that foreign policy now had to
take account of public opinion. Nevertheless, had the German government been willing, the Reinsurance treaty could have been renewed,
with modications to allay German anxieties in the Balkans; but its
complete and brusque rejection (after the Kaiser's initial promise of
renewal) worried the Russians and forced them to seek an ally elsewhere. The result, soon apparent, was the Dual Alliance between
Russia and France.

The alternative for Germany to the Russian alliance was a closer
relationship with England, the country to which, despite his feud with
his mother, William was bound by many emotional ties. Moreover as
a 'modern' Emperor it was natural for William to look to the West.
The moment seemed not unpropitious. In London a Conservative
government was in power under Lord Salisbury, who in 1887 had
concluded the secret Mediterranean Agreements which associated
England with the Triple Alliance in the preservation of peace against
possible encroachments by France and Russia. The British government
was traditionally in favour of a strong Central Europe against the two
expansionist flanking powers, and as long as Bismarck ruled in Berlin

the British knew that Germany was a peaceful state. Friction had arisen between England and Germany over spheres of influence and colonial boundaries in Africa, but it was of a less serious kind than disputes with France over Egypt and the Nile Valley. Salisbury was anxious to clear up outstanding differences with Germany in East Africa, while nearer home the Germans had their eye on Heligoland. This North Sea island, formerly Danish and held by the British since 1815, had strategic importance for the German coast and especially for the Kiel Canal which was about to be built to connect the North Sea with the Baltic. The upshot of negotiations initiated by Salisbury was a treaty, signed in June 1890, whereby Heligoland was ceded to Germany in return for the island of Zanzibar (which became a British protectorate), a strip of the African mainland and the abandonment of German claims in neighbouring territory. The treaty proved very unpopular in nationalist circles in Germany, where the great disparity between the size of the areas exchanged was the subject of bitter comment and the German government was blamed for having made a bad bargain. A new agitation for more German colonies began, marked, as we have already seen, by the foundation of the Pan-German League. In Europe as a whole the agreement was interpreted as indicating a new relationship between England and Germany, and many people expected England to join the Triple Alliance and make it Quadruple. The Emperor, who had visited Cowes Regatta in 1889 and 1890, paid his first official visit to London in 1891. He was given a cordial reception, and in a speech at the Guildhall he toasted the 'historic friendship' between the two countries. The British fleet (of which William was made an Admiral) visited Italy, a reassuring gesture to the Italians who feared an attack by France, and one which helped to preserve the Triple Alliance; while Austria seemed to have good reason to believe that the British policy of containing Russia in the eastern Mediterranean would continue.

The Emperor did not neglect Russia, despite the non-renewal of the Reinsurance treaty, and visited St Petersburg immediately after London in the summer of 1890, taking with him Caprivi, who created a favourable impression, thus making up to some extent for the loss of confidence involved in the departure of Bismarck. Nevertheless, the Russians, who were preparing to expand in the Far East and needed to safeguard their western flank against Germany and Austria, put out feelers to the French which were soon reciprocated. In July 1891 the French fleet paid a successful visit to Kronstadt, the Russian naval base in the Baltic, where the Tsar made the unprecedented gesture of standing to attention while a band played the revolutionary Marseillaise.

Alexander was not keen on an alliance with radical and 'atheistic' France, whose republican regime was badly shaken by a series of scandals that cast doubts on France's military value. Nor were French radicals happy about an attachment to the most reactionary regime in Europe. But each country felt that it needed the other, and self-interest proved stronger than ideology. A Franco-Russian agreement was signed before the end of the year. In 1893, after Germany had strengthened its army through a bill introduced by Caprivi, the Russian navy paid a return visit to Toulon, where an enthusiastic welcome proved the popularity of the new alliance. The result was a military convention which put teeth into the Franco-Russian agreement and made it a military counterpart of the Triple Alliance. Both countries professed purely defensive intentions, but each hoped for the support of the other in its ultimate aims: the extension of Russian power in the Near East on the one hand, the recovery of Alsace-Lorraine on the other. The Franco-Russian financial link was also important: between 1888 and 1896 Russia borrowed five and a half milliards of French francs, much of which was spent on developing Russia's inadequate railway system.

Thus the hegemony established by Bismarck was superseded by a balance of power, and Germany was faced with the certainty that, if a European war broke out, it would be on two fronts. The Germans knew that the Dual Alliance was directed against England as much as against themselves, for France was still, as in previous centuries, Britain's main colonial rival, and Russia her traditional antagonist in the Near East (and more recently, in Central Asia too). It seemed reasonable for Germany to count on a continuation of these rivalries, and on the consequent unlikelihood of any lasting understanding of England with either France or Russia. Therefore, the Germans argued, sooner or later the British would have to seek an alliance with Germany if not with the Triple Alliance. But in the meantime the Liberals had returned to power under Gladstone who, as a convinced Little Englander, shrank from a policy of continental entanglement. In disappointment the Germans turned back to Russia which they still believed was not irretrievably lost to France, and a Russo-German 'most favoured nation' treaty which lowered tariffs between the two countries was intended to gain Russian goodwill. Since the British (who had started to strengthen their navy – a reaction to the Dual Alliance) drew back, the German government must make use of its unattached position between England and Russia and in particular must profit by any embarrassment in which England found herself, to drive home the advantage of belonging to the Triple Alliance. Such a situation appeared in 1893 to have arisen in South East Asia, where the French from Indo-

China were threatening the British-backed buffer state of Siam, and the two powers were on the brink of war. William II happened to be staying at Cowes when the crisis broke, and the British government appealed to him for support. The alarm however soon proved to be false, the crisis passed, and Germany's aid in a hypothetical war with France was not required. Rosebery, who had succeeded Gladstone as Prime Minister, felt relieved; but the Germans were unfavourably impressed by what they considered the pusillanimity of British policy.[15]

There were nevertheless other reasons why England should seek the safety of alliance with the central powers. The Dual Alliance had altered the balance of power in the Mediterranean, for it meant that in case of war the British navy would have to face both a Russian navy at the Dardanelles and a hostile French fleet in its rear. It seemed obvious to Rosebery that England needed the help of the Triple Alliance to keep France in check. The Austrians, fearful of Russian designs on Constantinople and uncertain of the backing of Germany (which was now veering in a pro-Russian direction), appealed to Rosebery for support, informing him that Austria could not maintain her traditional policy of defending the Straits without it. Rosebery, however, replied that Britain could maintain her traditional policy at the Straits only with the co-operation of the Triple Alliance (meaning Germany). The Austrians professed to be satisfied with this answer, but the attempt to get the British to extend their commitments in the eastern Mediterranean (the support promised in 1887 had been purely diplomatic) had not succeeded. The Austrians failed to persuade the Germans to press the British to co-operate; Rosebery, who was annoyed with the Germans for their opposition to the Congo treaty and on other counts, let it be known that if Germany would not undertake to oppose Russia at the Straits he was no longer interested in the Triple Alliance.[16] The Germans feared that Britain would involve them in war with Russia and then expect them to fight it on her behalf. Therefore they insisted on her committing herself before they did. They still wanted the British alliance, but they believed that Britain would abandon isolation only if she were forced to do so by difficulties. By adding to these difficulties Germany would increase England's need of help, and enhance her own value as an ally.[17] This reasoning was to underlie German policy throughout the nineties and beyond.

The new German tactic towards Britain was also shown in the crisis that developed in the same year (1894) over the Congo. The British were anxious to prevent the French from extending their rule eastwards from French Equatorial Africa to the Upper Nile Valley. In 1894 they signed a treaty with Leopold, the King of the Belgians, whereby a block of territory west of the Nile, the Bahr el Ghazal, was to be ceded to the Congo Free State, which belonged to Leopold, in return for the cession to Britain of a corridor between lakes Victoria and Albert Edward, along the frontier between the Congo Free State and German East Africa. The French objected to the treaty as disposing of territory to which the British had no legal right, and were supported by the Germans, who did not wish to have the British on the western flank of their colony, and took the opportunity of embarrassing the British government and improving their relations with France. Yielding to pressure from both France and Germany, King Leopold abandoned the plan of occupying the Bahr el Ghazal, and Britain gave up the proposed corridor. This success for French diplomacy left the way open for the French expedition to the Upper Nile which materialised under Marchand four years later. Anglo-German relations became still cooler.[18] The Germans had calculated on the British coming to terms with Austria-Hungary in order to buy off German opposition in Central Africa; instead, Rosebery threatened to turn away from the Triple Alliance and to improve relations with France and Russia. Although the view in Berlin was that Rosebery was bluffing, suspicion between London and Berlin increased, and it was evident that Germany had made no gains commensurate with the loss of the Russian alliance. Mutual distrust, kept alive by minor colonial disputes, continued to overshadow Anglo-German relations.

At home the New Course had achieved more. The Caprivi government was responsible for a number of reforms, including an advance towards local self-government in the seven eastern provinces of Prussia and the re-organisation of taxation (both of which had to be modified to placate the Conservatives), a law setting up industrial arbitration courts, and a workers' protection law which made Sunday a day of rest, limited the working hours of women and children, and forbade the truck system of wages. Caprivi hoped by such methods to wean the workers away from socialism, the importance of which he did not underestimate. 'The struggle against Social Democracy is the most serious question of our time . . . which could be the dominating one for the end of this century, and perhaps for decades in the next century', he told the Reichstag in 1891.[19] Caprivi also understood the dependence of social policy on a flourishing economy, and he realised that having become a mainly industrial country, Germany needed exports to pay her way in the world and keep her growing population employed. Bismarck, who as a Junker naturally sympathised with the agrarians, had switched to a protectionist policy, especially for agriculture, in 1878, and the tariff on imported corn had actually been raised in 1887. Producers' cartels also helped to keep prices up. The high price of bread bore heavily on the consumer, while exporters were handicapped by the high cost of imported raw materials and by retaliatory tariffs in other countries. Caprivi's solution of the difficulty was to negotiate most-favoured-nation treaties with a number of countries – 38 in all – which led to a lowering of tariffs. He justified his policy in a speech to the Reichstag in which, referring to the high rate of emigration, he declared that Germany must either export human beings or goods, and that the only way to lower the emigration figures was to make the economy expand as fast as the population. It was the first time a German Chancellor had come to grips with this problem and had dared to reduce the economic privileges of the Junkers and thus to weaken their political position. Caprivi became bitterly unpopular among Conservatives, and an Agrarian League, a pressure group which soon had 190,000 members, was formed to fight the new policy which was described as ruinous to agriculture. The agrarians did not, how-ever, deter Caprivi from signing the commercial treaty with Russia which let in more Russian grain and so reduced the price of bread. The querulousness of Conservative opposition annoyed even the Kaiser, who announced that he would not go to war for the sake of a hundred crazy Junkers.[20] The Germans were facing the same problems as England before the repeal of the Corn Laws, but Germany never sacri-ficed agriculture to industry to the same extent, and her percentage of homegrown food remained much higher (roughly four-fifths compared to a half or less). The clash between landowners and industrialists was the economic counterpart to the political clash between Conservatives and Liberals over the question of franchise reform; but on the latter issue a compromise was reached, and when Bülow became Chancellor he tilted the tariff balance back in favour of agriculture. There is little doubt that Caprivi's commercial policy played its part in the rapid expansion of German exports which more than doubled in the next thirteen years, and reduced the rate of emigration from 87,000 in 1893 to an almost negligible 22,000 by 1900.[21] In the last years before 1914 Germany was a net importer of labour. In 1912-13 more than half a million foreigners, mostly Slavs from the east and south east of Europe, were employed in agriculture alone.[22]

It was William II's wish to keep the army strong, and even before the signing of the Franco-Russian alliance in 1891 he demanded a bill to make its size more commensurate with that of its potential enemies. The peace time strength of the German army was only 511,000 com-pared with France's 570,000 and Russia's 843,000. Moreover, with a population of ten million more than France, Germany was training only 191,000 recruits a year compared with France's 220,000. Caprivi accordingly asked the Reichstag to authorise an increase of the army's annual intake by 86,000; but to placate the Liberals, the period of training would be reduced from three years (which was often nominal) to two. The bill, however, was rejected by the Reichstag as falling between two stools; and when it was re-submitted to a new Reichstag after the elections of 1893, it was, ironically, passed only with the help of the Polish deputies, who were grateful to Caprivi for his relatively liberal attitude towards their community. One incidental by-product of the army reform bill was a fresh split among the fissiparous Progressives or *Freisinnige*: one section of them continued to support the government, while another (the left) went into opposition. Caprivi had still more trouble with his Prussian School bill, which was intended to win the goodwill of the Centre party, whose support he needed to secure a Reichstag majority. The bill gave the churches a large say in primary education and made it easy for them to establish their own schools. The Liberals resisted the bill, and Protestant opinion generally was unhappy about it. Miquel, the National Liberal Finance Minister of Prussia, resigned, but was persuaded to stay in office. Caprivi also resigned as Prime Minister of Prussia and was succeeded by Botho von Eulenburg, a man of reactionary views and a cousin of the Kaiser's friend Philipp Eulenburg. This was only the second time during the Second Empire that the posts of Chancellor and Prussian Prime Minister were separated, and the experiment was not a success: it facilitated the tendency of Prussia and the Reich to pull in opposite directions. The School bill was ultimately withdrawn after William II, who had at first welcomed it, threw his weight against it when he realised its unpopularity among large sections of the public. It was Caprivi's biggest setback. 'William II was not a ruler; he was a medium. He reflected the political mind of Germany and expressed it with genius.'[23]

The Emperor's volatile temperament combined with the enmity of the Junkers proved Caprivi's undoing. 1894 was a year of anarchist violence (the French President Carnot was assassinated, and an attempt made on the life of the Italian Prime Minister Crispi) and of strikes inside Germany. William, who now equated socialism with anarchism, abandoned his earlier role of the poor man's friend and led a demand for stricter measures against the forces of revolution. In a speech at Königsberg in September he declared war on these forces in the name of religion, morality and order. Caprivi, who had not been consulted about the speech, was told to introduce a bill against sedition. This amounted to a revival of the anti-socialist policy of Bismarck. Caprivi was willing to consider a moderate extension of the law, but doubted whether an extreme measure would have the desired effect – Bismarck, after all, had failed – or whether the Reichstag would pass it. He proved right about the Reichstag, whereupon the Emperor, who had now been formally reconciled with Bismarck, toyed with the idea of a *coup d'état* and abolishing manhood suffrage, a course favoured by the new right-wing Prime Minister of Prussia. In these circumstances Caprivi's resignation, which had been offered and rejected several times before, became inevitable. Caprivi was personally respected but he lacked the politician's ability to make himself popular, and in one way or another he had offended most of the parties and pressure groups. Nor had his foreign policy improved Germany's position. It was the end of the New Course. Both domestic and foreign policy had returned to the Bismarckian path: repression of subversion at home, the search for an accord with Russia abroad. The Emperor threatened the kind of unconstitutional action he had criticised Bismarck for proposing. Caprivi, who had taken office from a sense of duty and preferred principles to expediency, left it without regret. He was on the whole an honourable failure except for his economic policy, which must be accounted a success.

(ii) HOHENLOHE, SOCIAL DEMOCRACY AND THE ARMY

Caprivi's successor as Chancellor was Chlodwig, Prince of Hohenlohe-Schillingsfürst, whose name was suggested to the Kaiser by his confidant Philipp Eulenburg. Apart from his age (75) Hohenlohe seemed in many ways a suitable choice. Unlike Caprivi, he brought to the post considerable political experience, having been in succession foreign minister of independent Bavaria, a member of the Reichstag, German ambassador in Paris and governor of Alsace-Lorraine. As a Bavarian, a liberal and a tolerant Catholic, Hohenlohe would help to cement relations between the constitutionalist South German states and conservative, Protestant Prussia. As an elder statesman and *grand seigneur* Hohenlohe soon established an avuncular relationship with the Emperor, to whose wife he was distantly related. Hohenlohe was also a kinsman of the royal family of Russia, where his wife had large estates. Another advantage hoped for from his appointment was an improvement of German-Russian relations; German foreign policy, having failed to draw Britain into the Triple Alliance, now sought, unsuccessfully, to restore the alliance with Russia abandoned four years before. The death of the slavophile Tsar Alexander III and the succession of the more pliant Nicholas II seemed a good augury for a return to the old dynastic cordiality between the Prussian and Russian courts. On the other hand, Hohenlohe's bad memory, lack of speaking ability, indifferent health and lack of energy – hardly surprising in a man of his years – were serious handicaps.[24] He had little stomach for wrangling with the Reichstag or for those foreign adventures so dear to William's heart. Hohenlohe in turn became disillusioned with the Kaiser, who tended to lean on his other advisers, especially after 1897 when the ambitious Bülow was made Foreign Secretary. Hohenlohe never became a mere tool in the hands of his impulsive and unpredictable sovereign, but he was ineffective in a situation that called for a strong hand. Hohenlohe reacted to events; he did not shape them.

The new Chancellor's first hurdle was the Emperor's insistence on repressing the Socialists, the policy which had been Caprivi's undoing. Early in 1895 the Kaiser wrote to his cousin, the Tsar of Russia in his own idiomatic brand of English: 'My Reichstag behaves as badly as it can, swinging backwards and forwards between the Socialists egged on by the Jews and the ultramontane Catholiks (sic); both parties being soon fit to be hung all of them as far as I can see.'[25] Hohenlohe presented to the Reichstag a sedition bill containing severer penalties for breaches of the criminal code, military and press laws. At the same time he warned the Emperor that he too would resign rather than sponsor a measure so illiberal that it would lead to conflict with the Reichstag, make a coup d'état inevitable, and in the end only strengthen the opposition as Bismarck's Anti-Socialist laws had done. Even the modified sedition bill was in fact rejected by the Reichstag, after debate in committee. Each party, while prepared to curb its opponents, was jealous of its own freedom, with the result that no general agreement could be reached and in the end the measure was found impracticable. When the Kaiser heard the Reichstag's decision he took it calmly, but in a telegram to Hohenlohe characteristically added: 'We are left with fire-hoses for everyday use and cartridges as a last resort.'

Hohenlohe was no doubt relieved to see the end of the sedition bill, but William II came increasingly under the influence of men who urged the need to act more forcefully against the Socialists and their allies the trade unions.[26] Among these advisers was a recently ennobled industrialist from the Saar and member of the Reichstag, Karl Ferdinand Freiherr von Stumm-Halberg, who was well known for his belief in the application of army discipline to industry. 'If a factory is to flourish, it must be organised on military, not parliamentary lines' was his dictum, and the Emperor was disposed to agree.[27] Was not industrial autocracy the logical counterpart of the political autocracy for which the Hohenzollerns stood? In September 1898 William made a speech at Bad Oeynhausen in which he declared that anyone inciting to strike, or picketing, should be sent to gaol. The Minister of the Interior, Count Posadowsky, was surprised and dismayed by this announcement, as was Hohenlohe, but to please the Emperor they had to draw up an anti-strike bill and introduce it into a largely hostile Reichstag.[28] During the ensuing debate the Emperor was criticised, and the prestige of the monarchy as well as of the government suffered

King and People

(H. Schlittgen, 1896)

Bodyguard (sent by the king to inquire about the demonstrators) reports:
'Socialists, Your Majesty.' King: 'Give the people my compliments, and
tell them that nothing will come of that – nothing at all.'

(*Simplicissimus*, 1896)

when the 'prison bill' as it was dubbed by the left-wing parties was unceremoniously rejected after criticism by Liberals and Catholics as well as by Socialists. This episode, like the earlier rejection of the sedition bill, showed the value of the Reichstag as a guardian of popular liberties, and proved that, faced with resolute opposition, William would give way. With the collapse of the anti-strike bill the 'Stumm era' ended: Bülow, the next Chancellor, was to use more subtle methods of defeating the internal enemy. Other manifestations of the Reichstag's concern for freedom in this period were its amendment of an earlier law banning political associations, and its refusal to pass a bill against public immorality (the so-called Lex Heinze) after hearing the determined objections of a Liberal and Socialist minority.[29]

While the Emperor, encouraged by Stumm, was contemplating ways of combating Social Democracy, more far-sighted people were trying to solve the same problem by a policy of reconciling the Socialists to the Empire. A leading exponent of this approach was a Lutheran pastor who went into politics, Friedrich Naumann.[30] Like the Emperor, Naumann knew that, as a revolutionary party, the Socialists were, at least in theory, committed to the destruction of the existing order; but he also realised that the workers had genuine grievances and that until these were redressed the gulf between them and the rest of society could not be bridged. Initially Naumann was an adherent of Adolf Stöcker, the court chaplain who became leader of the Christian-Social Union, a movement which tried to enlist working-class support by appealing to anti-semitic sentiment in Berlin and other big cities. While Stöcker was theologically orthodox and politically conservative, Naumann was theologically liberal and politically inclined to socialism. In 1896 he became founder-president of the National Social Union which like Stöcker's Union sought to appeal to the masses but rejected anti-semitism. It put up candidates for the Reichstag in the general elections of 1898 and 1903 but without success. Naumann, who had been much impressed by Max Weber's emphasis on nationalism and the importance of power in politics, summarised his beliefs in a book published in 1900 under the title of *Demokratie und Kaisertum*. A Germany in which the Emperor and the workers had become allies would, he announced, be invincible. He tried to persuade the government to adopt a popular social policy, while he told the Socialists that if they wanted to govern Germany they must come to terms with the monarchy and the army. His object was to reconcile the state and its nationalist supporters with the internationally-minded working class, in order to win over the latter for a policy of 'democratic imperialism'. The three-class franchise, symbol of privilege and mistrust, must go, and the workers must receive a large share of the wealth they created.

The steady rise of the Socialist vote, despite half-hearted repression and paternalistic welfare, was a continual reminder of a challenge that could not be ignored. Naumann would have endorsed what a German diplomat was to write in 1906:

> In the long run a country cannot be ruled without the working man or against them, for, whether we like it or not, Germany has already become an industrial state. The principles of the old Prussian class state are no longer applicable, particularly when the ruling classes show so little political judgement.[31]

Meinecke, the historian, saw Naumann as standing for the new German industrial state against a Prussian particularism which the powerful Reich no longer needed.[32] Naumann was thus in many ways the most significant political figure of his age, though this was hardly apparent to the Emperor and his advisers. It was, indeed, never a practical possibility that William II would sacrifice the privileges of the Prussian ruling class, in which his own power as Prussian king was rooted, for the sake of greater social cohesion in Germany. For similar reasons he could not take advantage of another opportunity – the crisis through which German Social Democracy was passing at the turn of the century. Numerous influences combined to wean the S.P.D. away from its revolutionary fundamentalism and to turn it on an evolutionary course. The reformist trend which had emerged under the lead of such men as Vollmar, the ex-officer who headed the Socialist party in Bavaria, and David, the party's agrarian expert, was reinforced at the end of the 1890s by the 'revisionism' of Eduard Bernstein, whose *Voraussetzungen des Sozialismus und die Aufgaben der Socialdemokratie* (translated into English as *Evolutionary Socialism*) refuted many of the assumptions on which the S.P.D's Marxist orthodoxy was based. The general effect of this re-thinking among Socialists was to strengthen the libertarian and democratic wing of the party at the expense of those who continued to preach the need for a revolution, and who believed that socialism must precede not follow the introduction of democracy. It was far from easy for even non-violent Socialists to abandon their revolutionary beliefs while Germany was ruled on authoritarian lines and they themselves were treated as second-class citizens.[33] Kautsky, as an orthodox Marxist, was committed to belief in the revolution, but he tempered this with the suggestion that it might after all be bloodless, thus keeping his options open and satisfying his party's pacifist sympathies. The need to reform the Prussian franchise was recognised by liberals, but attempts to do so by the government, before and even during the First World War, were defeated by the forces of conservatism. For a Prussian parliament to accept so basic a change as liberalisation of the franchise it would have had to undermine the very status of Prussia. As for the other institutions to which Social Democracy objected – the monarchy and the army – some Socialists were to show a willingness to compromise, despite their lip-service to Marx. What would have happened had the Emperor and the Socialists become reconciled, as Naumann wanted, can only be surmised, though it is an interesting speculation. In the event, Naumann was pilloried by the Conservatives for his radicalism, while the Socialists denounced him as an apostle of imperialism. William II had no understanding for Naumann's ideas, as Naumann reluctantly recognised, and his influence on German politics was slight. Having failed to get elected to the Reichstag as a National Social candidate, Naumann succeeded when he stood at the general election of 1907 as a Progressive. Among his followers two were to be outstanding: Theodor Heuss, the future West German President, and Hjamar Schacht the banker, who was to end his political career in the dock at Nuremberg.

During the chancellorship of Hohenlohe another dispute occurred which illustrated the uneasy relationship between civilian and military authority in the Second German Empire. During the three wars of unification Bismarck had successfully upheld the principle that the civilian power (himself) had precedence over the army chiefs. Yet the Elder Moltke, who was head of the General Staff from 1857 to 1888 and shared the laurels of Bismarck's victories, yielded to the latter with great unwillingness and remained convinced that, at least in wartime, the military will should prevail.[34] *De facto* if not constitutionally the head of the General Staff ranked equally with the Chancellor as adviser to the Emperor, who was of course the final authority for both. The situation was complicated by the fact that power within the army was divided between the General Staff and the Emperor's Military Cabinet. Like its civilian counterpart, the Military Cabinet had been growing in importance, and was much more than a secretariat.[35] It was an instrument for the exercise of the royal prerogative in a sphere which the King of Prussia regarded as specifically his own. Both General Staff and Military Cabinet were jealous of the Ministry of War, whose head, usually a Prussian general, was the spokesman of the army in the Reichstag and was responsible for seeing that supplies were voted. The Minister of War, Kameke, was criticised by the General Staff and Military Cabinet for being too conciliatory to the army's Reichstag critics. In 1883 Bismarck showed his displeasure at the tendency to allow civilians a say in military affairs by forcing Kameke to resign. 'A parliamentary general on active service,' declared Bismarck, 'is always an un-Prussian phenomenon, and as Minister of War a dangerous one. It would pave the way for a future in which the monarchist tradition of our army would slowly but surely decline.'[36] This sounded like an echo of the 'time of conflict' of the 1860s, when Bismarck had uncompromisingly rejected demands for parliamentary control of the Prussian army. Now as then, Bismarck's main concern was to shield the army from civilian interference (especially if such interference had a democratic character) for the sake of the monarchy. The new Minister of War, Bronsart von Schellendorf, was obliged to acknowledge the right of both General Staff and Military Cabinet to have direct access to the Emperor, and thus to be independent of himself.

William II, as was to be expected, lost little time after his accession in asserting and extending his rights over the armed forces. One of his first acts was to create for the navy a tripartite division similar to that which existed in the army. The Naval High Command was detached from the Imperial Admiralty to which it had hitherto belonged and placed directly under the Emperor, while a separate Naval Cabinet was also constituted. Bismarck justified this change in the Reichstag as necessary to prevent the Chancellor – and through him the Reichstag – from interfering in matters of naval and military command.[37] By thus supporting William's desire to bring the services more under his personal control Bismarck bears no little responsibility for the embarrassing independence which, later in the reign, the service chiefs were to exercise *vis-à-vis* the Chancellor and which Bismarck himself would not have tolerated. The chief beneficiary of the naval reorganisation was Tirpitz, who at the time was Chief of Staff to the Naval High Command and was soon to be Minister of Marine. Like many other royal advisers, Tirpitz played on his master's vanity. 'Your Majesty', he assured the Emperor in 1899, 'can now be your own admiral.'[38] William was genuinely fond of and interested in naval matters, but he lacked the professional training that would have enabled him to be more than a titular head of the fleet. His policy of reducing the civilian share of control over the forces, like his preference for military rather than civilian advisers, widened the breach between the army and large sections of the nation and increased the temptation to solve intractable domestic problems by a military *coup d'état*.[39]

Civilians and soldiers clashed again in 1894, when Bronsart decided that the Prussian code of military justice which had been drawn up in 1845 was out of date, and in particular that the practice of holding courts martial *in camera* must be changed. The Reichstag agreed that reform was overdue, but the Emperor sided with the army chiefs when they contended that this amounted to unwarranted interference by civilians in military affairs. General von Hahnke, the Chief of the Military Cabinet, issued a memorandum stating frankly that the army must remain an insulated (*abgesonderte*) body into which no one might peer with critical eyes.[40] This amounted to a claim that the army was a state within a state. The crisis caused by this clash between army and Reichstag was sharpened when a minister of the Prussian government, Köller, was found to have leaked confidential information to the Emperor, and was dismissed, to William's annoyance, by the Chancellor. At this juncture the army needed the Reichstag to vote supplies; the Reichstag decided to grant them provided the army accepted the abolition of private courts martial, and Hohenlohe promised that a bill to this effect would be introduced. The Emperor, who was annoyed because the Reichstag had recently reduced the naval estimates, described the opposition in a telegram to his brother as unpatriotic scoundrels, and spoke wildly of staging a *coup d'état*.[41] Hohenlohe patiently insisted on the need for reform of court martial procedure, and in the end (as usual) it was William who yielded, though with bad grace.

Serious as was the continued division of authority within the army from a military point of view, a graver problem politically was the army's pursuit of independence in matters of high policy that far exceeded military technicalities. It was in the years after 1891, when Schlieffen became Chief of the General Staff, that the Plan which bears his name was adopted. Up to then German plans for a two-front war, worked out while the elder Moltke was Chief of the General Staff, assigned the bulk of the army to the Russian front, where the offensive was to be launched, with a defensive action against France. Schlieffen made the momentous decision to reverse these roles and to concentrate the main strength against the West. There were several reasons for the change. The main one was that Germany, facing a superior coalition, could win only if victory was gained in the first few weeks, and that this was possible only in France. Russia, because of its size and poor communications, would take too long to conquer, but once France was defeated, the whole German army would be available to deal with Russia at its leisure. Given the strength of French defences and the protective nature of the frontier region, the only way of knocking France out of the war quickly appeared to lie in outflanking the French army from the north. The use of a powerful right wing involved marching through Belgium and Luxembourg, two countries whose neutrality was guaranteed by the powers, including Germany. By 1897 the Schlieffen Plan had been amended to take in these two countries. This was made known to Hohenlohe at an unspecified date during his chancellorship, and to Holstein. Neither made any objection, nor did Bülow, who also knew of it.[42] Holstein's comments on the Plan are worth quoting:

If the head of the great General Staff, and especially a strategic
authority like Schlieffen, considers such a measure [the violation
of Belgium and Luxembourg] essential, then it is the duty of diplomacy to adjust itself accordingly and to prepare for it in all possible
ways.[43]

As a recent German historian has written: 'To raise political objections to a strategic plan worked out by the General Staff would have
appeared, in the Germany of William II, unwarranted interference in
a foreign sphere.'[44] This was to be Bethmann Hollweg's defence at the
outbreak of war in 1914 and after – that it was not the business of the
politician to stand in the way of military necessity. This was hardly
consistent with the view of Clausewitz that war is the extension of politics, not the other way round. The inability of civilians to control
soldiers has seldom had more disastrous consequences than in August
1914. Another example of army interference in politics occurred during
the Balkan crisis of 1908-9, when Austria, against Serb opposition,
annexed the provinces of Bosnia and Herzegovina, and Russia abandoned her protégé Serbia under German threats. It was clear this time
that the Austro-Serb quarrel could easily trigger off a European war.
In this dangerous situation much depended on the extent to which
Germany would restrain her Austrian ally. When the Austrian Chief
of Staff, Conrad von Hoetzendorff, wrote to his opposite number in
Germany, Moltke, asking for an assurance of German backing in case
of war with Serbia, Moltke's reply 'amounted to an admission that
Austria had a right to expect German support even if a war caused by
her own provocation', thus giving the Dual Alliance a sense never
intended by Bismarck.[45] The service chiefs also tried to influence
German diplomacy through the activities of the military and naval
attachés, who were encouraged to pursue their own policies, which –
especially the latter – frequently clashed with those of the Foreign
Ministry. When Chancellor Bethmann Hollweg complained that his
efforts to reach a naval agreement with Britain were being foiled by
the German naval attaché in London, the Emperor refused Bethmann's
request to discipline the attaché and summed up his views in a marginal comment that as the attaché was an officer he could not be removed by a civilian superior.[46]

Hohenlohe had not long been in office when Germany began to
develop an overseas or world policy. Bismarck had acquired colonies
for Germany in Africa and the Pacific, but his colonial policy was
always subordinate to his main purpose, the maintenance of Germany's
de facto hegemony in Europe. His successors sought a wider field of influence, but at a time when, as a result of the Franco-Russian alliance,

Germany's continental position was much less favourable. Already Caprivi had declared that a nation which did not play a part in world affairs might cease to count as a great power.[47] Imperialism was seen as a logical corollary of unification. William II told his subjects in January 1896: 'The German Empire has become a world Empire.' The implications of this statement – an aspiration rather than a fact – were soon apparent: Germany was about to embark on a substantial naval building programme and to stake a claim for a larger colonial empire, commensurate with her growing population, economic needs and great power status. The continental policy that had satisfied Bismarck was no longer adequate. There was nothing unique to Germany in this urge for overseas possessions; but Germany started late, and with the peculiar geographical handicap of being surrounded by great powers, two of which were in a military alliance against her. This was a mortgage on German diplomacy of which too little account was taken.

In 1894 the Far East became for the first time the focal point of European diplomacy when war broke out between the giant but declining empire of China and the new ambitious power of Japan. To the general surprise the Japanese were victorious, thanks to their mastery of western techniques, and China was faced with terms of peace that included the surrender not only of Korea (the future of which had been the immediate cause of the war), Formosa and some fishing islands but also of the Liaotung peninsula that contained the warm-water harbour of Port Arthur. This sudden shift in the balance of power alarmed the Russians, who had designs on North China and had begun to build the Trans-Siberian railway in 1892. In particular the Russians hoped to acquire Port Arthur as an alternative railway terminus to Vladivostok, which was ice-bound several months of the year. Russia accordingly came forward as self-appointed protector of China against Japan, being supported by France, anxious not to lose the goodwill of her ally and, less predictably, by Germany, hoping to win Russian favour and to acquire for herself some of the territory claimed by Japan. The Japanese reluctantly yielded to this *démarche* by three European powers, and Port Arthur kept (until its seizure by Russia a few years later) a precarious independence. Japan bore a grudge against Russia for depriving her of the fruits of victory, but also against Germany, whose protest against the original peace terms had been unnecessarily offensive. Nor had Germany won Russian friendship for her pains: when the Russians had to lend money to China to enable the Chinese government to pay the larger indemnity that offset the smaller territorial loss, they had no difficulty in borrowing it from the French. Besides the reasons for backing Russia already mentioned,

William genuinely believed that it was the duty of the white nations to defend themselves against the 'yellow peril', and Christianity against the heathen. Less altruistically, he also calculated that the more Russia became involved in China, the less likely she was to cause trouble in the Balkans.[48]

Yet in the Near East, too, continued unrest gave rise to fresh speculation about the future of the Ottoman Empire. When Salisbury came back as British Prime Minister in June 1895 he was under considerable pressure to do something to help the Sultan's Armenian subjects, thousands of whom had been massacred. The British public were roused by these atrocities in much the same way as they had been roused by the Bulgarian atrocities in 1876. Salisbury had long been sceptical of the Sultan's repeated promises of reform, and had come to believe that this empire was bound to disintegrate. In the summer of 1895 conversations on the future of the Ottoman territories took place between Salisbury and Hatzfeldt, the German ambassador in London, in which, according to Hatzfeldt, Salisbury put forward the idea of partition. There is evidence that Hatzfeldt, for reasons of his own, misrepresented Salisbury's views so that they appeared more solid and less tentative than they were in fact.[49] In Berlin the immediate reaction to what seemed a complete reversal of the traditional British policy of shoring up Turkey against her predatory neighbour, Russia, was unfavourable. Holstein, suspicious as ever, feared that England was trying to embroil the other powers for her own advantage, and more particularly that Salisbury aimed at making Germany quarrel with Russia over the share each would receive in partition, and at breaking up the Triple Alliance by encouraging Italy to take Albania and so falling foul of Austria-Hungary. Later, in the light of Hatzfeldt's explanations of British policy, the German Foreign Ministry took a less jaundiced view of Salisbury's intentions, seeing in the satisfaction of Russian claims to Constantinople a possible means of inducing Russia to abandon her French alliance. The Turkish question was broached in a conversation between Salisbury and the German Emperor during the latter's visit to Cowes in August. Salisbury was left with the erroneous impression that the Germans would not support him in efforts to bring pressure to bear on the Sultan to stop ill-treatment of the Armenians. In fact, as the Emperor made clear to the British military attaché in Berlin soon afterwards, he had no objection to a partition of Turkey that provided for adequate indemnification to Austria-Hungary and Italy. This went too far for Salisbury, who now drew back, leaving William to complain of British perfidy.[50] Relations between the two had not been improved by a misunderstanding that occurred at Cowes during the Emperor's visit, when Salisbury unexpectedly failed to appear at a second interview arranged between them. Salisbury's soundings confirmed Holstein in his belief that Britain was interested in stirring up trouble rather than at a genuine settlement. What in fact inhibited Salisbury, who was disturbed by further massacres of Armenians, was the unwillingness of the other powers, especially Russia, to support British attempts to exert pressure on the Sultan, so that Salisbury was left with the alternative of single-handed action or none. A seizure of Constantinople by the British navy would have involved the risk of an Anglo-Russian war, for which the cabinet was unprepared. It decided that a continued attempt by Britain to hold the Straits was no longer either feasible in view of the Franco-Russian alliance, or necessary for strategic purposes, since British mastery of the Eastern Mediterranean was assured by the occupation of Cyprus and Egypt. The Royal Navy was withdrawn from the Aegean, and Salisbury refused an Austrian request to guarantee Constantinople against Russia. Thereupon the Austrians decided not to renew the Mediterranean agreements, and a historic link between England and the Triple Alliance was severed.[51] The burden of upholding the Ottoman Empire, the survival of which was judged in Vienna to be essential to the survival of the Habsburg Empire, now fell on Germany. But the Germans did not share the Austrian view that any expansion by Russia was to be opposed. They never – especially the Emperor – abandoned the hope of detaching Russia from France (for which a price would have to be paid in the Balkans), and William used his influence on his cousin, the young and impressionable Nicholas II, to discredit France and sow mistrust of England. William liked to speak of reviving the Holy Alliance and stressed the need for monarchical solidarity against the forces of democracy and revolution. More concretely, William had in the previous year (1894) offered to let the Russians take Constantinople.[52] This policy was crossed, not only by discussions on the partition of Turkey with Britain, but also by the extension of German influence in Turkey through the Baghdad Railway. Fortunately for Germany, Russia was now preoccupied by the Far East and willing to preserve the *status quo* in the Balkans, as was shown by the Austro-Russian agreement of 1897. For the next ten years, despite occasional rumblings, the Balkans were quiet, and the basic Austro-Russian conflict that contained the seeds of a general war remained dormant.

German-Turkish relations became closer after 1898, when the Kaiser, at the invitation of the Sultan visited Constantinople, Damascus and Jerusalem. A speech in which he declared that the 300 million Moslems would always find a friend in the German Emperor caused a raising of eyebrows in Britain and France, both of which had millions of Moslem subjects in their empires. A practical outcome of the journey was the advancement of German plans for the proposed railway from Constantinople to Baghdad, for the first length of which a concession had been granted to Georg Siemens, a director of the *Deutsche Bank* and of the well-known electrical engineering firm started by his family. Unlike Bismarck who, in deference to Russian suspicions, was not keen on German commitments in Turkey, William gave his support to Siemens' project, which was extended to include a branch line to Basra on the Persian Gulf. Originally conceived as a purely commercial enterprise, the Baghdad Railway soon acquired political significance, despite Bülow's assurances that Germany had only business interests in Turkey. The Russians became worried when the Kaiser's visit to Turkey was followed by a number of other concessions to Germans, including permission to build a harbour at Haidar Pasha on the Asiatic side of the Bosphorus. Russia had long regarded herself as the paramount European power in Turkey and as the principal prospective beneficiary when, sooner or later, the Ottoman Empire would fall to pieces. That the Germans should now oust Russian influence, dominate the Straits through which passed most of Russia's trade, and strengthen the Turkish economy by building railways and ports, was highly obnoxious to the Russians, who successfully insisted that any railways to be built in Northern Anatolia must be built by them.[53] Marschall von Bieberstein, the German Foreign Minister who became ambassador to Turkey in 1897, drew conclusions from the new policy:

> One can look forward to the time when [Bismarck's] famous saying that the whole East is not worth the bones of a Pomeranian grenadier will be an interesting historical reminiscence, but no longer actually true.[54]

The Baghdad Railway had an adverse impact on Anglo-German relations. Initially the British government looked benevolently on the project, though there was some nervousness about the effect of the railway on the safety of the route to India and the Persian Gulf. But the railway could not be insulated from other aspects of German policy, and the sinister significance it had acquired in the eyes of the general public was shown in 1903 when the German consortium financing the Baghdad railway ran short of capital and appealed for financial co-operation from Britain, France and other countries. The British government was in favour of participation, for in that way the project would have acquired an international character, but in the end it yielded to the public outcry and the German offer was turned down. In Russian eyes Germany had displaced England as the stumbling block to Russian expansion in Turkey and Persia; in British eyes Germany as well as Russia now seemed to threaten the western approaches to

India.[55] The Anglo-Russian agreement of 1907, which was mainly concerned with Persia, marked a common determination by both powers to set a limit to intrusion by a third. Yet once again the pattern changed: Anglo-German differences over the Baghdad Railway were to be overcome on the eve of the First World War.

Meanwhile the Kaiser had turned his attention to Southern Africa, where the growing antagonism between British and Boers foreshadowed the approaching war. To escape British rule, an earlier generation of Boers had established themselves in the two inland republics of Transvaal and Orange Free State. Thanks to the propaganda of the Pan-German League and other nationalist bodies, German interest in Africa had increased since Bismarck's day, and the Kaiser, not without encouragement from the Boers, decided to support them in their struggle for independence. Most European nations felt a natural sympathy for the Boers as a small peasant people bullied by predatory imperialists; and the Germans had a strong fellow-feeling for them as kinsmen. There were considerable German investments in the Transvaal where 15,000 Germans were living, and the railway from Johannesburg to Delagoa Bay, the republics' only independent link with the outside world, was German-built. The British on the other hand resented German interference in a part of the globe where they had hitherto been unchallenged from outside and in what was to them a domestic quarrel. The London Convention of 1884 had specifically stated that in matters of foreign relations the Boers must act in consultation with Britain. In offering their alliance to the discontented Boers, the Germans were encouraging the latter to breach the treaty and to resist British claims, such as the demand for political rights for foreigners in the Boer republics. At the end of December 1895 the ill-starred Jameson raid prompted the Kaiser to send a telegram a few days later congratulating the Boer president, Kruger, on having preserved the independence of his country 'without appealing to the help of friendly powers'. William was in one of his moods of abnormal excitement, and the raid was an act of aggression; but the telegram, suggested by Marschall to avert worse action by William II, was a major political blunder. Germany was unable to give Kruger any effective help, despite the Kaiser's brash talk about sending troops to the Transvaal, because of the British navy's command of the sea. In England the telegram raised a storm of protest out of proportion to its intrinsic importance, though not out of keeping with an age in which wars could be provoked by trivial acts and national pride took offence at the slightest pretext. William II, who had hitherto been regarded as a friend of Britain, was blackballed as a traitor; and the popular wrath erupted in a press campaign, anti-German riots and a trade boycott. Hatzfeldt, the German ambassador in London, reported to his government on 21 January 1896: 'I cannot doubt that the general atmosphere was such that had the government too lost its head or for any reason wanted war, it would have had the whole of public opinion behind it.'[56] Much of the indignation displayed had deeper origins, such as a long-smouldering resentment at German commercial rivalry. Germany earned an unpopularity for which she could show no gains; when the long threatened Anglo-Boer war broke out the German government was ostentatiously neutral. William sternly forbade his officers to be given leave of absence to South Africa. 'I am not in a position', he wrote to Bülow, 'to go beyond the strictest neutrality, and I must first get myself a fleet. In twenty years' time, when the fleet is ready, I may use another language.'[57] Fortunately for William, his subjects did not know the terms of a fulsome but patently insincere letter of apology for the Kruger telegram which he wrote to his grandmother, Queen Victoria. Nor did the British public, in its sense of outrage, at first realise, as Salisbury did, that the ultimate object of German diplomacy, despite its short-term aim of uniting Europe against England, was to force the British to join the Triple Alliance; and when the *Times* correspondent pointed this out the idea was received with bitter cynicism. 'Kicking a Briton into submission', wrote the *Spectator*, 'is a possible expenditure of energy; but even a man like the German Emperor, who seldom judges men right, would hardly dream of kicking him into friendship.'[58]

(iii) BÜLOW, TIRPITZ AND THE KAISER'S 'FREE HAND'

The emphasis on world policy became more marked in 1897 with the appointment as Foreign Secretary of Bernhard von Bülow, another friend of Philipp Eulenburg, who had already been noticed by the Emperor as a likely future Chancellor.[59] Bülow, a member of an old noble family in Mecklenburg, was a career diplomat who had been in succession German ambassador in Bucharest and Rome. He had an Italian wife, and in character could perhaps not unfairly be described as a *tedesco italianato*. Witty, urbane, eloquent and resourceful, Bülow pleased William by his expansive tastes in foreign policy and his skill in managing the Reichstag. Bülow was a man of facile optimism, glib and not very scrupulous, and his flattery of William encouraged the latter's worst qualities. He had too much of the courtier in him to be a statesman. Behind the scenes Holstein continued to be a major influence on foreign policy, though he was less dominant than before the ascendancy of Bülow and Tirpitz.[60]

One of Bülow's first achievements was the annexation of the Chinese port of Kiao-Chow, which occurred after the Kaiser, on a visit to St Petersburg, had persuaded a reluctant Tsar to agree to the German navy's sharing that port jointly with the Russian navy. The murder of two German Catholic missionaries in Shantung province soon, however, provided an excuse for Germany to demand and receive from China a lease assigning Kiao-Chow to Germany for 99 years. The Russians compensated themselves by seizing Port Arthur; the British and French, not to be outdone, helped themselves to Wei-hai-wei and Kuangchowwan respectively. The partition of China, under the guise of protecting her, seemed to have begun. The despatch of a German naval squadron to Kiao-Chow under Prince Henry, the Emperor's brother, gave William the opportunity to make one of his most notorious speeches in which he proclaimed the policy of the mailed fist, and Prince Henry replied in kind: 'My sole wish is to preach Your Majesty's gospel to everyone abroad, no matter whether they want to hear it or not.'[61] The occupation of Kiao-Chow fitted in well with German plans for a larger navy, indicated by the appointment of Tirpitz as Minister of Marine at about the same time as Bülow became Foreign Minister. Alfred von Tirpitz was an ambitious, energetic naval officer with a talent for organisation and a flair for publicity.[62] William had been much impressed by Mahan's books on the influence of seapower in history, and recent events, such as the Spanish-American war of 1898 and the German-American naval confrontation at Manila in the same year, seemed to confirm Mahan's thesis. Britain, above all, owed her world position to her navy. Germany needed a powerful fleet to protect her overseas possessions, her growing merchant marine and world trade; also for 'general purposes of greatness'. Just as continental policy presupposed the existence of a strong army, so world policy could be pursued only by a country with an effective navy. And just as her army had made Prussia a great power, so her navy would make Prussia-Germany a world power. In Tirpitz William believed he had the man who would realise his dreams. Largely owing to the propaganda launched by the Navy League in which he played a leading part, Tirpitz persuaded the Reichstag to pass a bill providing for the construction, over a period of six years, of 19 battleships, 12 large and 30 small cruisers and 8 armoured ships for coast defence. The official intention was to make the new fleet half as strong as the combined fleets of France and Russia. Tirpitz's real purpose – not for public consumption – was to create a navy able to defeat the British.[63] This was a triumph for him, since he had succeeded with the Reichstag where his predecessor in office, Hollmann, had failed. With Tirpitz and Bülow as his enthusiastic assistants the Emperor could pursue world policy unhampered.

The creation of a powerful navy was one of the most significant events in the Second German Empire. Externally it worsened Anglo-German relations at a time when, for several reasons, Britain was becoming alarmed at Germany's preponderance in Europe, and the ensuing naval rivalry of the two countries was to make impossible the political understanding between them which was desired (especially after 1908) by the German government and by much public opinion in Britain. Internally the German navy became a rival to the army in its claims on national resources. Tirpitz's skill in mobilising parliamentary votes and public support for the navy assured it of the funds needed for rapid growth. Tirpitz established himself as a formidable political figure who, thanks to the backing of the Kaiser, exercised a fatal influence on German foreign policy. The navy had a strong emotional appeal. It was a symbol of pride and ambition. It was a middle-class creation, free from the caste spirit of the army and, being a product of unification, acted as a binding force, again unlike the army in which state differences remained. The navy had close links, which the Navy League fostered, with the business and scientific worlds. To industrialists naval building meant contracts, to the workers jobs; to merchants its was recommended as an insurance against foreign interference with German overseas trade. It had the glamour of world policy. Few realised (or, if they realised, dared say) how useless the Imperial Navy would be when war came.[64]

The year of Tirpitz's first naval law (1898) was also that of Fashoda, the Sudanese town where Britain successfully opposed a French attempt to occupy the Upper Nile Valley. France yielded to superior seapower, a lesson not lost on the Germans. The Boer War, which began in October 1899, was another example of the value of a navy: despite the disapproval of Europe and her preoccupations in the Far East, England was able to ensure the defeat of the Boers by denying them outside help. Germany's only advantage from the war, an indirect one, was the acquisition of part of the Samoan group of islands which hitherto had been jointly administered by Britain and America. However a new source of friction arose when the British stopped and searched for contraband several German mailboats bound for South Africa. An angry exchange of notes between the two governments followed, and public opinion was roused on both sides. The British had acted on inadequate evidence, and compensation was paid to the Germans. The only beneficiaries were the advocates of a greater German navy: when Tirpitz heard of the incident he is said to have exclaimed: 'Now we have the wind we need to bring our ship into the harbour; the new naval bill will pass.'[65] This bill, which was presented to the Reichstag in 1900, doubled the strength of the German fleet. The new ships were to be built at the rate of three a year over a period of 16 years. The programme could be completed only if the yards were fully equipped and assured of a regular flow of orders, so that a certain inflexibility was inevitable.[66] While at the time of his first naval bill Tirpitz had declared that the German navy was not being built against England, in introducing his second bill he admitted that the German navy must be equal to its most difficult task, a 'naval battle in the North Sea against England'.[67] The British were not perturbed; they had a long lead over all other countries in battleships, and Germany still had fewer completed battleships than France. During the Boer War the Emperor had risked his popularity at home by twice visiting England: on the first occasion he took Bülow with him and the question of an Anglo-German understanding was discussed between Bülow and Chamberlain. The second visit was to Queen Victoria before her death. His obvious affection for his grandmother, and attendance at her funeral, did much to restore William's tarnished reputation among the British people. William emphasised his neutrality during the Boer War by refusing to receive President Kruger when the latter was in Germany in December 1900. By contrast, the German press in the latter stages of the war was full of reports of British inhumanity, and great indignation was roused over the concentration camps in which large numbers of Boer women and children died. Anglophobia was rife.

In a memorandum supporting his policy Tirpitz explained his object: the German navy must be so strengthened that even the most powerful naval power could not attack it without losing enough ships to jeopardise its own position.[68] This was the famous risk theory on which Tirpitz set great store. What did it imply in practice? The chief naval power was Great Britain, whose fleet was dispersed in different parts of the world, and could not be at full strength in the North Sea. Germany must have a battle fleet capable of inflicting on the British navy damage sufficient to bring it below the two-power standard which Britain sought to maintain (the Royal Navy had to be equal to the two next strongest fleets taken together). The possession of such a fleet would enable Germany to neutralise Great Britain. So long as the latter was isolated and on bad terms with France and Russia the risk theory made sense; once she had an *entente* with one of them, it did not. German naval thinking, like German diplomacy, assumed a permanent antagonism between England and Russia; and took it for granted that France could not come to an understanding with England without giving up her alliance with Russia. There remained one danger: that the new German navy would be 'copenhagened' by the British on the precedent of Britain's destruction of the Danish fleet in 1807. Tirpitz rightly judged that, while some Englishmen might favour a preventive blow of that kind, public opinion would not allow it –

certainly not in the early stages when the German navy would be too weak to defend itself. Some Germans thought that Britain might go to war to destroy Germany as a trade rival, but this irritant in Anglo-German relations became less important after 1900. Between then and 1914 British exports grew only slightly less rapidly than Germany's, a sign that there was room for both. They were also important to each other's trade: England was Germany's best customer, Germany England's best in Europe. It was not British manufacturers and businessmen who urged a preventive war. The first British reaction to the German naval programme was on the whole slow and sober; but in March 1903 the Admiralty announced that a new naval base would be built at Rosyth on the Firth of Forth. This indicated a concentration of the British fleet on the North Sea, a move prompted by German naval policy. The *rapprochement* between England and France about that time made Tirpitz's risk theory out of date. The *Times* referred approvingly to the improvement in Anglo-French relations and stressed the need to adopt a 'more scientific and elastic formula' than the two-power standard (25 November).[69] But the Germans continued to build, while the introduction of a new and more powerful battleship, the *Dreadnought*, was shortly to alter the whole picture of naval rivalry. Tirpitz did not abandon his privately admitted intention to outbuild the British fleet.[70] His calculation that a strong German fleet would raise Germany's value as any ally proved, as far as Britain was concerned, a disastrous illusion.

Ironically, the years of Tirpitz's first two naval laws were the time when the British government was most anxious to reach a general agreement with Germany. In the British cabinet Chamberlain, the Colonial Secretary, had begun to question the wisdom of isolation. Even for England, world policy imposed a strain on limited resources, as the Boer War was soon to show, and there were risks in having no friends. A way had to be found of containing Russia in the Far East. France, unreconciled to the British occupation of Egypt, was Russia's ally. If a partner had to be found it could only be Germany, the one power capable of exerting simultaneous pressure on both Russia and France. Chamberlain liked the idea of an agreement between the three strongest powers, Britain, Germany and the United States, to keep world peace, and the Germans' common ancestry with the Anglo-Saxons was an additional rcommendation. In March 1898, shortly after the Russian seizure of Port Arthur, Chamberlain had the first of a number of talks with the German ambassador, Hatzfeldt. Chamberlain offered an alliance. The German reaction was negative, mainly for two reasons. Firstly, the Germans had no vital interests in China, certainly nothing that could justify a war with Russia of which they, not

England, would have to bear the brunt. Secondly, it was assumed in Berlin that Britain's need of an ally would increase until she would eventually have to accept Germany's terms and join the Triple Alliance. Holstein in particular was convinced that time was on Germany's side and that she must keep her free hand as long as possible and on no account pull England's chestnuts out of the fire.[71] The German confidence in the soundness of their analysis made them ignore as bluff Chamberlain's warning that if he could not reach agreement with them he would turn to France and Russia.

His policy of keeping in with the Russians as far as possible led William to try to turn Chamberlain's proposal to advantage by telling his cousin the Tsar about it and asking bluntly what the Tsar would give him if he rejected the British offer. This was a move towards a continental bloc directed against England. Nicholas, in his reply, ignored that question but said that he too had been approached by the British government, thus increasing William's suspicions. Nor did the Emperor's manoeuvre prevent France and Russia tightening the terms of their alliance in 1899 by agreeing that it was intended to preserve the balance of power in Europe as well as to maintain peace. Late that year the second round of Anglo-German talks began between Chamberlain and Bülow, who had accompanied the Emperor to England after the end of the Samoa negotiations. Chamberlain, whose approach to politics was that of an ambitious industrialist rather than of a cautious diplomat, was encouraged to make a speech at Leicester in which he publicly advocated an Anglo-German-American alliance as the most natural. Bülow's reply was cool. German distrust of England had understandably been revived when the British, after signing a treaty with Germany providing for the partition of the Portuguese African colonies between them in the case of Portugal having to give them up, in the following year made another treaty with Portugal guaranteeing the colonies, the object being to buy off any possible Portuguese help to the Boers in the Boer War.[72] The Germans noted too that the war began with a series of British disasters; and many expected a British defeat.

Yet while events in South Africa drove England and Germany apart, events in the Far East drew them – for a time – together. The Boxer Rising of 1900, the first large-scale manifestation of Chinese resentment against foreign imperialism, forced the European powers to co-operate in common defence. The Emperor was delighted when it was decided that the international force to be sent to China should be commanded by Waldersee, the former Chief of the German General Staff. Before Waldersee set off, he and his troops were addressed by William in a speech that, in years to come, was to do Germany untold harm: the soldiers were urged to behave like Huns, to take no prisoners and show no mercy. Bülow did his best to censor the text before it was given to the press, but a local journalist took the speech down in shorthand, and the damage was done. In any case, the Emperor's advice was hardly needed, for before Waldersee could reach China the Boxers had been defeated and the Europeans in Peking liberated. Britain, however, appeared undismayed by the Emperor's outburst; she still hoped for German backing against Russia. In October 1900 the two countries signed the Yangtse agreement, pledging themselves in general terms to uphold the territorial integrity of China. But the divergence of interests between the two signatories was soon apparent. The British contended that the treaty applied to Manchuria as to the rest of China; the Germans, unwilling to offend the Russians who intended to annexe Manchuria, denied it. The British realised, rather late in the day, that they could not rely on the Germans in the Far East and that they must look elsewhere for an ally. They soon found one in Japan.

By this time Hohenlohe had resigned. The weakest of post-Bismarckian Chancellors, he had long been embarrassed by what Hatzfeldt once described as the Emperor's 'incessant vacillations' in foreign affairs, and had been overshadowed by the more energetic Bülow, who succeeded him. Disillusioned by the German's negative attitude in China, Chamberlain had now given up hope of an Anglo-German agreement, but other members of the cabinet, especially the new Foreign Secretary, Lord Lansdowne, still thought the idea worth pursuing. Salisbury's retirement from the Foreign Office (though he remained Prime Minister) made this a suitable moment for trying again. Salisbury had been the most isolationist minister in the government; he disliked the Emperor and in Germany had been the object of distrust ever since the discussions on the partition of the Turkish Empire in 1895. Lansdowne, less sceptical and anxious to score a success, foresaw a further reason to seek Germany's friendship: in the approaching war between Russia and Japan, German pressure would be needed to prevent France from siding with Russia. During the early and middle months of 1901 the project of an Anglo-German alliance was again mooted with the German embassy. As Hatzfeldt was ill for much of the time, the German spokesman was Eckardstein, the first secretary, who had married an English heiress and was a familiar figure in English social circles. Unfortunately Eckardstein, in his eagerness to pull off a diplomatic coup and to win personal credit, exaggerated to the German Foreign Ministry the British desire for a settlement in order not to let Holstein think that he had taken the initiative.[73] It is, however, doubtful whether the result would have been different had Eckardstein not misrepresented the British attitude. When Landsdowne proposed a defensive alliance between Britain and Germany, and had a draft treaty prepared, the Germans replied that the treaty must be with the whole Triple Alliance.[74] This, so far as it was a genuine condition, made it harder for the British to agree, since there was little disposition in London to underwrite the 'moribund' Habsburg Monarchy.[75] Berlin's insistence on the participation of its allies came oddly at a time when the Italians, through a separate treaty with the French over Morocco and Tripoli, had just made a significant move towards detaching themselves from their partners. The Germans' failure to put forward any counter-proposals, and Salisbury's continued advocacy of isolation in a cogently argued memorandum, made Lansdowne abandon the plan of a general agreement.[76] There remained the possibility of a local agreement, like those over Samoa and the Yangtse. Lansdowne suggested Morocco, where the breakdown of the Sultan's authority and French encroachments created a dangerous situation: Germany could have the Atlantic coast of Morocco in return for co-operation against France. The offer had been made before notably by Chamberlain in November 1899; as before, it was turned down. Germany's refusal to quarrel with Russia over China had been sensible; but to argue, as Holstein did, that Germany could not risk becoming involved in war with France over Morocco, was to overlook a vital difference between the two cases. Russia could hardly have supported France in such a war (as she did not support her over Fashoda), and with England as her ally Germany would have had nothing to fear from France. Finally, Lansdowne proposed an agreement with Germany for maintenance of the *status quo* over a wide area of territory – the Mediterranean, the Adriatic, the Black Sea and the Persian Gulf. Metternich, the new German ambassador, replied that nothing short of a defensive pact with the Triple Alliance would meet the case.[77] It was not, in any case, obvious what advantages such a package deal would have for Germany. Another consideration in Berlin was that so long as the German navy was in its infancy, a British alliance was to be avoided, for it would have weakened the case for a strong fleet. Thus negotiations for an Anglo-German understanding petered out. There was no formal breach, but German reluctance to make a binding commitment was sufficiently evident to discourage further British overtures. Public opinion, especially in Germany, had been unfavourable. The press campaign against England during the latter stages of the Boer War continued unabated; even Bülow was embarrassed by it, but he would not court unpopularity by ignoring it.[78] Stung by German accusations of 'methods of barbarism' in South Africa, Chamberlain made a speech at Edinburgh in which he criticised German troops for their behaviour in the Franco-Prussian War. This roused the nationalists to fury; bitter remarks were passed in the Reichstag, and Bülow replied in a tone of cold contempt. Metternich wrote to Bülow on 21st February 1902: 'For the moment I would summarise the situation by saying: "I wouldn't give twopence for Anglo-German relations".'[79]

The Germans continued to believe that if they showed patience and adroitness England would ultimately have to accept their terms. The balance of power in Europe, William told Lansdowne, was himself with his twenty-two army corps: he was *arbiter mundi*.[80] In reality, as Francis Bertie, of the British Foreign Office, pointed out at the time in a memorandum, it was Germany's position which was deteriorating.[81] She was surrounded by countries which feared and distrusted her, and her only reliable ally, Austria-Hungary, was an uncertain quantity. In the British press germanophobia was beginning to answer the anglo-phobia across the North Sea. Current dislike of Germany was graphically illustrated by two contemporary events: the public outcry in England at German attempts to embroil England with America during a punitive expedition to collect debts in Venezuela by British and German warships;[82] and the refusal of the British public – not the government – to respond when the German sponsors of the Baghdad railway sought to raise a loan in London. The *Frankfurter Zeitung*, one of Germany's leading liberal newspapers, wrote in January 1903:

> Thirty years after Sedan we are still looked upon as a parvenu with the characteristics of an intruder. Wherever anything is going on in the world, we want to be 'in it'. If two millstones are grinding against each other, we should like to have our fingers between them. Whenever a sunbeam falls, we want to be there in order to warm ourselves.[83]

CHAPTER III

The Years of Crisis:
Germany's 'Encirclement'
and the Arms Race

(i) MOROCCO AND ALGEÇIRAS

In February 1902 Eckardstein reported from the German embassy in
London to his Foreign Ministry that at a reception at Marlborough
House he had seen Joseph Chamberlain and the French ambassador,
Paul Cambon, talk to each other for nearly half an hour with great
animation, but that the only words he had been able to catch were
'Morocco' and 'Egypt'. This was only one of several warnings that
reached the German government of what was soon to blossom into the
Entente Cordiale. In the summer of 1902 Chamberlain, on his way to
sign the peace treaty that ended the South African war, stopped in
Cairo, where he told the French representative that he would like an
understanding with France. Edward VII, whose francophile sympathies were well known, gave full backing to these feelers; and his
state visit to Paris in May 1903 did much to break down the hostility
engendered by Fashoda and the long feud over Egypt. Two months
later President Loubet paid a return visit to London, and a favourable
atmosphere had been created for serious Anglo-French negotiations.
Loubet was accompanied by Delcassé, the Foreign Minister, who had
long aimed at an understanding with Britain. Delcassé had conversations with Lord Lansdowne, the British Foreign Secretary, about
matters of mutual concern, including two countries where they had
conflicting interests – Morocco and Egypt. The French had never been
reconciled to Britain's sole occupation of Egypt which they had regarded as their protégé, while Morocco, on which the French had
their eye, was close to Gibraltar, one of the British Empire's most
sensitive spots. The approach of the Russo-Japanese war, which he
had foreseen, made Delcassé treat the Anglo-French talks as a matter
of urgency. There was a danger that France, the ally of Russia, might
become involved in hostility with Japan, since January 1902 the ally

of Britain. The British were not at this time thinking in terms of a general alliance with France, but they saw the advantage of settling disputes that had long been an irritant to both countries. The Entente Cordiale, which was finally signed in April 1904, covered a wide range of territories including the Newfoundland Fisheries, West Africa, Siam and the New Hebrides as well as the more controversial Egypt and Morocco. The French recognised the *status quo* in Egypt; the British promised non-interference in case the French acted to change the *status quo* in Morocco. This was a diplomatic way of allowing Morocco, nominally an independent Moslem state but in fact on the brink of chaos and largely surrounded by the French colony of Algeria, to be added to the French Empire at a time convenient to France. It was also agreed that Tangier, the harbour opposite Gibraltar, and its immediate neighbourhood should be ceded to Spain.[1] Thus Spanish opposition was bought off, and British doubts for the safety of Gibraltar set at rest. By a secret treaty between France and Italy signed in 1900, Italy was (at a later date) to be allowed to seize Tripoli from Turkey in return for acquiescence in France's Morocco policy.

The German government heard of the Entente with some surprise. The Germans believed that the British would never let the French have Morocco, and they assumed that France could reach an understanding with Britain only at the cost of the alliance with Russia, which was for the French, in a military sense, much more important. Hence Eckardstein's warnings that a new Anglo-French-Russian understanding was in process of formation were not taken seriously in Berlin. Bülow assured the Emperor in May 1903 that the chances even of an Anglo-French agreement were not at all promising.[2] He calculated that Germany's position could only improve as Russia, moving closer to war with Japan, would be forced to make concessions to Germany in order to induce her to keep Austria-Hungary and the Balkans quiet while Russia was preoccupied. William II saw in Russia's difficulties a welcome opportunity to press for the Russo-German agreement that remained one of his most cherished hopes. Indeed the outbreak of war between Russia and Japan in February 1904 was for Germany the one advantageous event to offset the Anglo-French *rapprochement*. Privately the German authorities did not disguise their fear that the Entente would reduce Germany's importance in Europe and tend to attract Italy, whose loyalty to the Triple Alliance was now more than questionable, fully into the Anglo-French orbit. Somehow Germany had to assert herself, and to prevent England or France from reaping the benefit of the Entente. 'Not only for material reasons but even more to preserve her prestige Germany must oppose the annexation of Morocco by France' wrote Holstein in a memorandum of 3 June 1904.[3]

The Germans still hoped that the war in the Far East would lead to an open breach between England and Russia and that France would be torn between them. An incident nearly proved them right. In October 1904 some Russian warships on the way from the Baltic to the Far East mistook a group of British fishing vessels on the Dogger Bank for Japanese torpedo boats and sank them. The British, who had no desire to become embroiled in war with Russia, accepted compensation from an embarrassed Russian government, and the danger point was safely passed. The Germans were supplying the Russian navy with coal. They told the Russians that if they were to share the risks of war they must receive adequate guarantees. William proposed to the Tsar a defensive alliance between their two countries, which France would have to accept whether she liked it or not, though under no circumstances must it be allowed to draw Germany into war with Britain.[4] A draft treaty was prepared which the Russians, after some delay, insisted must be shown to the French. The Germans, unwilling to expose themselves to possible retaliation by the British fleet, let the project lapse for the time being.

There was, however, another way whereby Germany could profit by Russia's difficulties, which now included revolution at home as well as defeat in the Far East. She could apply pressure to a temporarily isolated France. In January 1905 a French mission arrived at Fez, the Moroccan capital. This was seen as the first stage of a French take-over of Morocco, whose government was on the verge of collapse. It was quite in accord with the Entente Cordiale. But the German government decided to protest. To show that it meant business the Emperor himself would go to Morocco. 'Your Majesty's visit to Tangier', Bülow told William, 'will embarrass M. Delcassé, frustrate his plans, and benefit our economic interests in Morocco.' William's comment was: 'So much the better.'[5] It was, nevertheless, with considerable reluctance that the Emperor actually set foot in Tangier, where his arrival triggered off an international crisis. The French, unprepared, faced the Germans alone. What did the Germans want? This was far from clear at the time, and has been much debated since. Not, the Emperor declared, the annexation of Morocco by Germany. Legally, as a signatory to the Madrid Convention of 1880 concerning Morocco, Germany had the right to be consulted on any change in its status. In real terms Germany was interested in trade with Morocco, the economic importance of which was much exaggerated, and in its iron ore, though as yet, owing to French opposition, no German mining firms had been able to establish themselves there. Such hopes would be frustrated if Morocco was incorporated in the French customs union. There was also the prestige aspect to which Holstein had drawn attention in his memorandum of June 1904. The Germans thus believed, not without reason, that in protesting against the French move they had a good case. They appeared as guarantors of the *status quo* against a French encroachment, and as upholders of the Open Door (the principle recently invoked by the Anglo-Saxon powers in China) against French protectionism. But the real significance of the crisis was political. The basic German motive was to prove to the French that they could get nowhere without German goodwill, and that this goodwill must be paid for.[6] It was a rough method, similiar to the tactics used by Berlin to dragoon the British into alliance. Holstein saw it as the counterpart of British policy towards France at the time of Fashoda, when by standing firm the British had forced the French to accept friendship on their terms.[7] What Holstein forgot was that, despite Gallic anglophobia, for France there was a fundamental difference between Britain and Germany, and that, in the existing balance of power, a France allied to Germany would have been so much a junior partner that the Germans would have had the mastery of Europe. The German government backed its demands with threats. Delcassé believed that the threats were bluff, but his colleagues were not so sure, and they knew that France could not fight Germany single-handed. Delcassé thereupon resigned, and Rouvier, the new Premier, who was known to be more cautious, took over the Foreign Ministry. This was seen as a great victory for Bülow, whose jubilant Emperor made him a prince.

The French hope that Rouvier would be treated more leniently than Delcassé proved illusory; the Germans dismayed their friends in Paris by rejecting a settlement and demanding an international conference to decide the Moroccan question. This proved a tactical mistake, for when the conference met at Algeçiras in January 1906 all the participants, including Italy and the neutral United States, took the French side. By gaining the approval of the conference for control of Morocco to be in French hands, France had won her point, and emerged from the conference as the victor. The Germans had spoiled a good case by pressing it too hard, by miscalculation and by their own disunity; the Emperor, Bülow and Holstein were pursuing different policies.[8] Though some highly placed people in Berlin favoured a preventive war against France, Bülow realised that the nation as a whole would not understand or approve of a war for Morocco.[9] The German object was, in any case, to lever France into alliance, not to defeat her. The most serious aspect of the crisis from the German point of view was that it brought France and England closer together, instead of driving them apart as had been intended. Grey, the new British Foreign Secretary, warned Metternich, the German ambassador in London, that 'in the event of an attack upon France by Germany, arising out of our Morocco Agreement, public feeling in England would be so strong that no British government would remain neutral'.[10] Grey believed that if Britain left France to fight Germany alone France would never forgive the desertion, and Britain would be left without a friend. Grey could not promise the French military help, but he allowed the informal conversations between the French and British military staffs, which had begun under his predecessor, to continue. These were non-commital, but in time established, at least in French eyes, a moral obligation, and their scope was to increase as time went on. The Germans knew of the talks and saw that they were faced with a combination of three powers. Their Morocco policy, which had begun as an exercise in brinkmanship, had ended in their isolation.

Meanwhile Germany's wooing of Russia, which contrasted markedly with her attempt to browbeat France, had suffered a further rebuff. In the summer of 1905 William II, elated by the fall of Delcassé, and determined to take advantage of Russia's plight, met the Tsar on the Finnish island of Björkö in the Baltic and persuaded him to sign a Russo-German defensive alliance against attack by a third power. The Tsar's ministers soon rejected, however, this essay in personal diplomacy as incompatible with Russia's obligations to France, and nothing came of it. The Tsarist regime survived defeat and revolution, and Russia's military recovery was a matter of time. French morale had revived, and the Franco-British Entente had been strengthened and extended. England had in effect notified Germany that she would not allow the destruction of France as a great power. The Germans were soon to realise that so favourable a constellation of circumstances as those of 1905 would not recur. On the contrary: all Germany's future moves were liable to be interpreted as a bid for continental hegemony; even her bids for friendship were suspect. Nor would it be easy for Germany to profit, as in the past, from Anglo-Russian quarrels. In 1907 Britain and Russia signed an agreement over areas in Central Asia – Persia, Afghanistan and Tibet – where their interests had clashed. Anglo-Russian relations were strengthened and German fears of encirclement heightened, by a state visit of Edward VII to Nicholas II at Reval (Tallinn) in the Baltic in June 1908.

(ii) ANGLO-GERMAN NAVAL RIVALRY

The tendency in Whithall to watch every German move with wariness, if not suspicion, was marked by a memorandum on British Relations with France and Germany circulated to his colleagues by Eyre Crowe, Senior Clerk in the Foreign Office, on 1 January 1907.[11] Crowe suggested that Germany was aiming at general political hegemony and maritime ascendancy, and that she sought to achieve it by fostering mutual antagonism among the other powers, as when she had tried to divide France from England over Morocco. The spirit of aggrandisement 'achieved mainly at the point of the sword' characteristic of Prussia had been inherited by united Germany, whose desire to become a world power inevitably brought her into opposition to England. England, Crowe wrote, should not discourage Germany's 'legitimate claims' to colonial expansion or naval power, but she must resist the kind of indiscriminating appeasement that would only whet the German appetite. 'Legitimate claims' was a question-begging phrase. No doubt Crowe used it to distinguish between Germany's desire for, say, Morocco as a colony and her wish to use it as a lever to bring France into dependence. But clearly the Germans would not allow the British to judge what was legitimate for them. They were convinced that their newly united country had an unquestionable moral right to a larger share of the world and say in world affairs commensurate with its population, needs and importance. And whereas Germany was increasingly feared by her neighbours as a dangerous concentration of power, the German people saw themselves threatened by two unfriendly neighbours (a vengeful France and an expansionist Russia) and wilfully obstructed in their justified naval and colonial aspirations by a jealous and selfish Britain. Even Crowe admitted in his memorandum that German 'aggressiveness' might be less the result of a great design than 'the expression of a vague, confused and unpractical statesmanship, not fully realising its own drift'.

If to the British Foreign Office the German challenge presented itself primarily as a threat to the time-honoured balance of power, the average Englishman saw it in more concrete terms – the efficient and rapidly growing German navy. In 1904 began the most crucial period in the two countries' naval rivalry. Although the second German navy law, passed in 1900, led to no immediate counteraction in Britain, its significance did not go unobserved. The First Lord of the Admiralty, Lord Selborne, told the cabinet in September 1902 after a visit to German naval establishments by his Parliamentary Secretary, H. O. Arnold-Forster, that the German fleet could be designed only for possible war with England: it could not be used against France and Russia.[12] In his memorandum Selborne referred to the 'malignant hatred' of the German people for Britain. This was symptomatic of a widespread view. The British public had become aware, through the reports of journalists, Reichstag speeches and the German press, of the anglophobia which had been virulent in Germany during the Boer War. Now this was matched by a germanophobia in Britain that

showed comparable hostility and suspicion.[13] Behind the hostility on
both sides was fear. The British realised that the greatest military power
was setting out to dispute with them the mastery of the seas: what could
this mean but a bid to dominate the world? The German fear, more
immediate, was that the British would destroy their small fleet before
it was capable of self-defence. Such apprehensions, though greatly
exaggerated, were not entirely unjustified. Sir John Fisher, who became
First Sea Lord in October 1904, actually proposed to 'copenhagen' the
German fleet, an idea promptly rejected by Edward VII.[14] The
Germans did not hear of this incident, but they reacted to Fisher's
irresponsible impulsiveness much as the British to William II's sabre-
rattling. They read about a speech by Arthur Lee, the Civil Lord of the
Admiralty, who in February 1905 declared that in case of war 'the
Royal Navy would get its blow in first before the other side had time
even to read in the papers that war had been declared'[15] – presumably
on the analogy of the Japanese, who in the current war destroyed
Russian ships in Port Arthur without warning, with the cynical
approval of some British newspapers. Lee's speech understandably
evoked a sharp reaction in Berlin, where the threat of a British preventive war at sea had long been taken seriously, and added to the nervousness already caused by the danger Germany incurred through her
support of Russia against Japan. There was panic at Kiel and other
places in Schleswig Holstein where the British were expected to land.[16]
The main result of all this was a worsening of Anglo-German relations,
further support for the Navy League, and greater readiness on the
part of the Reichstag parties to vote larger naval estimates. In November 1905 a supplemental naval law was passed which provided for the
construction of six big cruisers and 48 destroyers over and above those
already approved: at the same time the size and armaments of battleships already laid down were increased. Almost immediately the British
Admiralty issued a statement which made it clear that the pace of
British naval building would depend on that of Germany. This was a
warning to the Germans of Britain's determination to keep her lead
at all costs, and a refutation of Tirpitz's thesis that the British were
a *Krämervolk* (nation of shopkeepers), unwilling to make sacrifices for
patriotic ends.[17]

Tirpitz's hopes that the British would weary of the naval competition were raised when the Liberals came to power at the beginning of
1906. The new government was pledged to retrenchment, and was also
under strong pressure from its supporters and even from some of its
members to reduce expenditure on the navy in order to finance the new
social services which they intended to introduce. There seemed at first
a slight prospect that the Second Peace Conference, due to meet at

The Hague in 1907, would do something to slow down the arms race. The conference coincided however with a sharpening of Anglo-German naval rivalry. The German government had in any case decided to oppose any proposals for disarmament; and though most of the continental states agreed with her, it was Germany who had the odium, in the eyes of peace-lovers, of leading the campaign against any serious progress on compulsory arbitration as well as on armaments limitation. The Germans accused the British of trying to freeze naval strength at a level favourable to themselves, while the British blamed the Germans for barring the way to any arms agreement.

Meanwhile, in February 1906, the British government had launched the first dreadnought, the new type of fast, heavily armed battleship which would make all other types obsolete. In November 1907 the Germans announced that they would also build dreadnoughts, initially at the rate of three a year compared with the British rate of four. The British did not regard this ratio as compatible with their own safety.[18] German naval ambitions were now causing real alarm across the North Sea, as Metternich, the German ambassador, repeatedly told his government. An attempt by the Emperor to allay this anxiety by writing privately to Lord Tweedmouth, the First Lord of the Admiralty, to assure him that the German fleet was not meant to challenge the British and suggesting that the British slow down their rate of building, did more harm than good in London, where it was resented as an unwarrantable attempt by a foreign head of state to influence a British minister. In July 1908 Grey, the Foreign Secretary, and Lloyd George, the Chancellor of the Exchequer, warned Metternich that good relations between England and Germany were impossible so long as the naval building race continued. The British fleet, they pointed out, could not invade Germany, whereas England's existence as a great power rested on her navy. Lloyd George asked for a reduction in the tempo of German building, and suggested a ratio of 3 to 2 between the two fleets. The Emperor minuted on Metternich's report:

> It must be pointed out to him [Metternich] that I have no desire for a good relationship with England at the sacrifice of the increase in Germany's navy. The [navy] law is to be put into effect to the last detail; whether that suits the British or not is no matter. If they want war, they can begin, we do not fear it.[19]

Metternich, frustrated because his advice was consistently ignored, after a further conversation with Lloyd George wrote of the spectre of war looming up on the horizon as a result of the 'poisoning of public opinion'.[20]

In August 1908 Edward VII, who had been watching the postures of his nephew, the Kaiser, with growing concern, paid him a visit at Friedrichshof Castle at Kronberg in the Taunus mountains. He was accompanied by Sir Charles Hardinge, Permanent Under-Secretary at the Foreign Office, and carried a memorandum in which Grey had written:

> The British government would not think of questioning the right of Germany to build as large a navy as she thinks necessary for her own purposes, nor would they complain of it. But they have to face the fact that at the present rate of construction the German naval programme will in a very few years place the German navy in a position of superiority to the British as regards the most powerful type of battleship [the dreadnought].[21]

Hardinge had a highly embarrassing interview with the Emperor in which he said with a bluntness to which the All-Highest was not accustomed: 'You must stop or build slower', to which William replied: 'We shall fight then, for it is a question of national honour and dignity.'[22] Yet there was an alternative. The Germans soon showed that they would be willing to slow down their naval building in return for concessions in other fields – if, for example, England would promise to be neutral in a war between Germany and France. This was something which Grey could obviously not undertake without imperilling relations with France and Russia, and allowing Germany to become master of the Continent. The British government was in any case unwilling to buy German recognition of a naval superiority which it was determined to uphold, whatever the cost.

During the winter of 1908–9 British fears were increased by the belief that in Germany some advance ship-building was going on which was not shown in the published figures.[23] This, of course, had been denied by Metternich in his talks with Grey, who in November 1908 declared that there was no half-way house between complete safety and absolute ruin.[24] The new First Lord of the Admiralty, McKenna, overestimated the German rate of building, and there was almost a panic. Lord Roberts warned the House of Lords of the danger of German spies. The popular outcry led by the Conservative opposition was 'We want eight and we won't wait', meaning that Britain would build eight dreadnoughts – four at once, and a further four if Germany did not reduced her tempo. The marked jump in British expenditure had to be justified by reference to the German example, which caused fresh criticism in the German press. When Metternich urged the German Chancellor to pay more attention to British public opinion, Tirpitz as the Navy Minister warned Bülow that any reduction of the building programme would be an 'intolerable humiliation' for Germany and would lead to his resignation. Bülow was not the sort of man who would resign rather than give way; and in any case, after October 1908 his days were numbered. His attempt to come to terms with England failed on the one hand because of the intransigence of Tirpitz (backed by the Emperor) on the other because Britain could not promise the neutrality for which Germany asked. Grey wrote in October 1909:

> An entente with Germany such as M. Kiderlen-Waechter [the Chancellor's envoy at the time, and later Foreign Secretary] sketches would serve to establish German hegemony in Europe and would not last long after it had served that purpose. It is in fact an invitation to help Germany to make a European combination which could be directed against us when it suited her so to use it.[25]

In another minute Grey put the same point more bluntly: 'If we sacrifice the other powers to Germany we shall eventually be attacked.'[26] Sir Ernest Cassel, Edward VII's banker friend who had close ties with Ballin, the Hamburg shipowner, wrote that Germany's naval programme was the alpha and omega of all English mistrust, as of all English machinations. Naval rivalry was the most sensitive area of Anglo-German relations, but it was also the symbol of a more general uneasiness and irritation that sprang from several sources, as Rathenau had pointed out in a report to Ballin which the latter sent on to Bülow:

> Germany is a competitor and a rival. This feeling has been apparent in all my conversations with cultured Englishmen. Sometimes it takes the form of a compliment, sometimes it is said ironically, sometimes it becomes a direct reproach. . . . Outsiders who cast their eyes over Europe see a seething mass, a people of restless activity, and enormous spiritual and mental vitality, hemmed in by older, more stagnant nations. Eight hundred thousand fresh Germans a year! Every five years an additional population nearly equal to that of Scandinavia or Switzerland! And one asks how long declining France can withstand the atmospheric pressure of such a neighbour. So that every English discontent is beginning to be crystallised and summed up in this very concept – Germany. What, in the educated classes, has become a reasoned conviction, comes out in the rank and file, in provincials and in young people, in the form of prejudice, hate, fantastic misconception, to an extent far surpassing our best journalistic efforts. . . . Only the ensemble of our policy is capable of at last giving England the impression that, on Germany's side, there is no irritation, no fear, no pressing need to expand and take an offensive attitude. . . .[27]

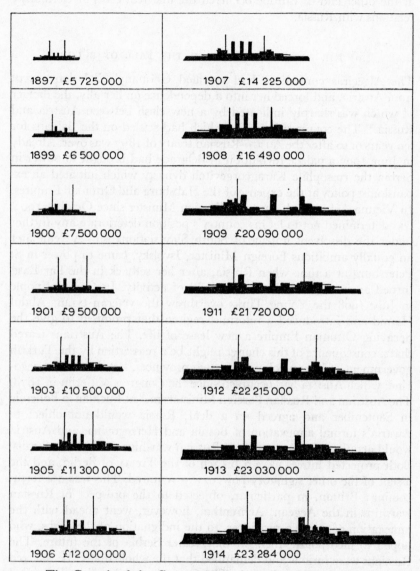

1897 £5 725 000	1907 £14 225 000
1899 £6 500 000	1908 £16 490 000
1900 £7 500 000	1909 £20 090 000
1901 £9 500 000	1911 £21 720 000
1903 £10 500 000	1912 £22 215 000
1905 £11 300 000	1913 £23 030 000
1906 £12 000 000	1914 £23 284 000

The Growth of the German Navy in terms of Expenditure
(Radio Times Hulton Picture Library)

Rathenau's advice was, unfortunately, little heeded in Germany. Anglo-German naval rivalry created an unbridgeable gulf. Meanwhile at the other end of Europe occurred the first real crisis in Germany's relations with Russia.

(iii) THE BOSNIAN CRISIS AND THE FALL OF BÜLOW

The Algeçiras conference had revealed Germany's isolation except from Austria, and forced her into a dependence on her ally, the danger of which was sharply indicated by a new clash between Austria and Russia.[28] The comparative quiet which had settled on the Balkans for ten years or so after the Austro-Russian treaty of 1897 was over. Already in June 1903 a palace revolution in Belgrade had brought to power in Serbia the russophile Karageorgevitch dynasty which initiated an expansionist policy at the expense of the Habsburg and Ottoman Empires. In Vienna Aehrenthal, Austrian Foreign Minister since October 1905, was determined not to let his country's position deteriorate any further under the dissolvent impact of South Slav nationalism. A year later an equally ambitious Foreign Minister, Isvolsky, came to power in St Petersburg at a time when Russia, after her setback in the Far East, turned again to the Balkans as a field of activity. In Constantinople in July 1908 the Young Turks overthrew the veteran tyrant Abdul Hamid and introduced a reformist regime that promised to give the decaying Ottoman Empire a new lease of life. The Austrians feared that a consequence of this change might be a reassertion by the Turkish government of its control over the two provinces, Bosnia and Herzegovina, which Austria had occupied since the Congress of Berlin in 1878. The Austrian and Russian Foreign Ministers met at Buchlau in Bohemia in September and agreed on a deal: Russia would not object to Austria's formal annexation of Bosnia and Herzegovina, and Austria would acquiesce in the passage of Russian warships through the Straits. Both projected moves were a breach of the Treaty of Berlin, and the assent of the other signatory powers was required. This was not forthcoming: Britain, in particular, objected to the prospect of Russian warships in the Aegean. Aehrenthal, however, went ahead with the annexation of the two provinces, to the indignation of the Serbs, who hoped to incorporate them in the greater Serbia of the future. The Russians were furious and demanded that the whole matter be referred to an international conference. The Germans, while privately critical of Austria for having acted in such a way as to upset the Turks, would have nothing to do with the conference, which they feared might prove a second Algeçiras. Publicly Berlin gave Vienna full support, and the Emperor in a much publicised speech promised to defend his ally 'in shining armour'. Bülow needed a diplomatic victory to offset the loss of prestige caused by the Emperor's *Daily Telegraph* interview (see below). The Russians had not recovered sufficiently from the defeat of 1905 to take up Germany's challenge. Aehrenthal contemplated invading Serbia to destroy South Slav nationalism at its source, but then drew back, unwilling to add millions of Slavs to the population of the Empire through partitioning Serbia. Thus the Austrians rejected the opportunity of a localised preventive war. The French were relieved not to have to back Russia in a Balkan quarrel in which their interests were not directly involved. At the same time the French government took advantage of Germany's preoccupation to obtain her assent to their freedom of action in Morocco in return for the safeguarding of German economic interests there. Russia's grudging acquiescence in the new *status quo* of Bosnia and Herzegovina was the last success of Austro-German diplomacy before the outbreak of the First World War. It was dearly bought. Serbia nursed a grievance and waited for an opportunity of revenge; Russia resented her humiliation and would not give way again. France, despite misgivings, held fast to the Russian alliance. England was confirmed in her determination not to abandon her friends in Europe. Just as German threats over Morocco quickened into life the Anglo-French Entente, so did those over Bosnia help to transform the Anglo-Russian agreement, which applied only to Asia, into a more general understanding about Europe.[29] The hands of those in Austria who urged the necessity of a preventive war against Serbia were strengthened by the knowledge that they could count on German support. It was only too plain that the next Balkan crisis could precipitate a general war. Privately Bülow sensed the danger: his parting advice to the Emperor is said to have been: 'Do not repeat the Bosnian affair.'[30] Yet it was also evident that time was not on Germany's side: every year saw Austria further in decline, while Russia, helped by French loans, was recuperating. The temptation to those in power in Vienna to destroy Serbia before Russia was ready was growing stronger.

Bülow did not long survive his hollow triumph. By the time the Bosnian affair reached its climax, he had fallen out of favour with the capricious Emperor over the most celebrated if not the most fateful of imperial howlers. The *Daily Telegraph* of 28 October 1908 published the account of an interview which William II had given to a British friend, Colonel Stuart-Wortley, with whom he had stayed at a country house near Bournemouth. In the article William sought to allay the fears of the British public about himself by declaring that, as an anglophile, he had actually advised the British government on how to defeat the Boers during the South African war. The British were amused rather than impressed by this clumsy but well-meaning essay in public relations. The Germans were horrified. There was a public outcry, and a stormy debate in the Reichstag in which the Emperor came under heavy fire from the conservatives as well as from the radicals. Technically Bülow was to blame, for the offending article had passed through his hands on its way to the Foreign Ministry, where only minor changes were made. Instead of defending his master in the Reichstag, as the Kaiser expected. Bülow virtually apologised for him and exculpated himself. William turned bitterly against his former favourite. Even the future of the Emperor's 'personal rule' seemed to be in doubt. The *Berliner Tageblatt* wrote that it was intolerable for a nation of sixty millions which had risen by its own efforts and was of the highest intelligence to be dependent on the whim of one man.[31] William suffered a nervous breakdown. He issued a statement promising that in future he would pay due regard to his constitutional responsibilities. Thereafter he made fewer brash speeches, though from time to time he continued to invoke Divine Right and to treat his ministers like subordinates.[32] The *Daily Telegraph* incident caused the only major constitutional crisis of the pre-war period, and had temporarily created a mood favourable to the introduction of a parliamentary regime, for which the radicals had long pressed. But Bülow did not intend so revolutionary a step, and the Bosnian crisis which occurred just afterwards was hardly a propitious background for experiment. So the chance was allowed to slip.[33] Bülow himself remained in office, but few doubted that, having lost the Emperor's goodwill, he would not be there much longer.

A party clash over finance was the immediate cause of Bülow's fall. Bülow had shown more skill in managing the Reichstag parties than any Chancellor since Bismarck, and his home policy was initially successful. Until the end of 1905 he kept the support of both Conservatives and the Centre, thus assuring himself of a majority. The Centre was rewarded by the abolition of the anti-Jesuit law, a last vestige of the *Kulturkampf*. The *quid quo pro* to the Conservatives was material, an increase in the tariff of imported grain. The duty on wheat rose from £2.10.0 to £3 a ton, on barley from £2.10.0 to £4, on oats and rye from £2.10.0 to £3.10.0.[34] Under Caprivi tariff policy had been equally balanced between agriculture and industry. Bülow, who liked to be considered an agrarian Chancellor, re-established the priority of agriculture. Still the landowners were not satisfied, and fought hard in the Reichstag for a higher tariff. They also resisted a government plan to construct an inland waterway between East and West Germany because they feared that easier communications would lower the price of grain. Although parts of the projected network were completed, the central section from Hanover to the Elbe remained unbuilt. As for industrial tariffs, Bülow renewed the commercial treaties with foreign countries as they fell due on much the same lines as before, with a moderate duty on manufactured goods and little or none on raw materials. The higher cost of living caused by the new taxes on food was one reason for the marked increase in the number of votes for the Social Democrats in the Reichstag election of 1903.[35] This was a setback to Bülow who, however, retained his Reichstag majority. The next general election was fought in the shadow of a colonial war. In South West Africa a native tribe, the Hereros, had risen against German rule and been suppressed with considerable cruelty. Certain scandals over military contracts involving ministers also came to light. The government was heavily criticised by the Socialists, but also by the Centre, whose attitude to the Hereros was influenced by the reports of Catholic missionaries. Bülow rallied the Conservatives and Liberals under the banner of world policy or imperialism, and in the ensuing general election the number of Socialist deputies fell from 79 to 43. It was the first reverse the party had suffered, and Bülow was jubilant. Yet the total Socialist vote had risen, not fallen, and the Centre held its position as the strongest party with 104 seats. Henceforth Bülow governed with the backing of a new bloc, named after himself, consisting of the Conservatives, National Liberals and Progressives, with the Centre, like the S.P.D., in opposition. To satisfy the Progressives Bülow included in the speech from the throne in October 1908 the promise of an 'organic evolution' of the Prussian franchise, a euphemism for reform. Demonstrations and street marches in favour of a change in the franchise were held by Progressives as well as by Social Democrats. But even the modest measure Bülow introduced into the Prussian *Landtag* failed to overcome conservative opposition – the first of several unsuccessful attempts of the kind between 1908 and 1918. Bülow also pleased liberal opinion by getting the Reichstag to pass a bill giving more freedom to political meetings, in which henceforth women and young people were allowed to take part.

Another consequence of Bülow's quarrel with the Centre was the dropping from the government of Posadowsky, who had close ties with that party. Count Posadowsky-Wehner, known as the 'Red Count', had been Secretary of State for the Interior since 1897, and had successfully piloted through the Reichstag a series of social reforms. He had extended and improved invalid, sickness, old age and accident insurance, reduced child labour and 'sweating' and restricted hours of work in shops and offices. Inspectors of factories were appointed. Industrial courts were set up to deal with disputes between employers and workers, and funds were allocated for workers' housing. A liberal administrator and able parliamentary speaker, Posadowsky did much to repair the damage caused by the repressive policy of the nineties exemplified by the Sedition bill. His approach to social problems was positive; he recognised the Social Democrats as legitimate spokesmen of the working classes, and his insurance legislation received their support. None of the Prussian governing class did more, and few did as much, to reconcile the workers to the regime by improving their lot. His successor as Minister of the Interior, Bethmann Hollweg, continued Posadowsky's work, and in 1911 (by which time Bethmann had become Chancellor) the Reichstag approved an improved comprehensive Insurance Bill covering seven million people. This was followed by a similar insurance scheme for white-collar workers. Bethmann even tried, unsuccessfully, to establish works councils (*Arbeitskammern*) in which employers and workers would collaborate to regulate industrial questions.

These social services cost money. Expenditure on the armed forces, especially the navy, was also rising. One of Bülow's urgent problems was how to raise new revenue to cover a budget deficit of RM.500 million. The economy continued to prosper, and national income per head rose by 45 per cent between 1890 and 1914.[36] But the proportion of national wealth that went to the federal government was wholly inadequate to its needs. This was mainly because all direct taxation was levied by the state governments, so that apart from state contributions to the central budget (the so-called matricular contributions) the federal government had to depend on revenue from customs, excise and stamp duties and on profits from nationalised enterprises such as the railways. As these sources of income were insufficient, it was forced to borrow, and the national debt trebled between 1890 and 1904.[37] Bülow had raised the duty on beer and tobacco in 1902, and was to do so again on these and other articles of consumption. But there was a limit to the amount of indirect taxation that was socially acceptable if not to what was fiscally practicable. The left-wing parties demanded that the direct taxpayer should share the burden. Bülow proposed an inheritance tax, an equivalent to the British death duties. The Conservatives were bitterly opposed, arguing that such a tax would ruin their estates.[38] In June 1909 the Inheritance Tax bill was lost by a small majority, most of the Conservatives having turned against the government. Yet the measure would have passed had not the Centre and the Poles voted against it for reasons of their own – the Centre still bore a grudge from the government's hostility during the 1907 elections, the Poles resented Bülow's germanisation policy in the eastern provinces. The result was fatal to Bülow. His bloc had fallen to pieces, and having lost the confidence of the Reichstag, his usefulness to the Emperor was exhausted. Despite a formal reconciliation between the two men,

William had not forgotten what he saw as his minister's perfidy the year before, and Bülow's resignation was now accepted. Bülow was not unwilling for his departure to be interpreted as a victory for the Reichstag over the executive – a vindication of the liberal principles in which he half believed – and he blamed the Conservatives, with some justice, for their 'frivolous' opposition.[39] No doubt he could have stayed had William wished to keep him, though it is not easy to see how he could have forced the inheritance tax through the Reichstag, which failed to take advantage of the opportunity somewhat unexpectedly presented by the Emperor's loss of prestige and Bülow's defeat.

So Bülow left the scene, after being Chancellor for nine years and having guided German foreign policy for twelve. When he came to power Germany still had considerable freedom of action. Britain saw her as a potential ally, and her neighbours' embarrassments were her opportunities. When he resigned, the nightmare of coalitions so dreaded by Bismarck was a reality, and the friendship of her remaining ally, Austria-Hungary, more a liability than an asset. Some of Germany's difficulties were inherent in the situation which Bülow inherited – the enmity of France caused by the amputation of Alsace-Lorraine, the irreconcilability of Russian and Austrian interests in the Balkans. Others sprang from miscalculation and ineptitude. The assumption that time was on Germany's side in her negotiations with England, reiterated by Holstein as late as November 1901,[40] was disproved by the British decision to act as a counterweight to Germany's super-power, and more specifically, by the predictable British reaction to Tirpitz's naval programme. Could the anti-German turn in British policy have been foreseen? Caprivi had warned Tirpitz as early as 1893 not to start a big navy until Germany had settled with France and Russia.[41] Yet such a settlement was, in the circumstances, almost impossible; no German government could have paid the price – renunciation of Alsace-Lorraine, abandonment of the Habsburg Monarchy. The British government had hinted more than once during Anglo-German negotiations at an agreement with France or Russia as an alternative to one with Germany, yet such warnings were treated in Berlin as bluff. Other developments could hardly be anticipated by the Germans, such as Japan's victory over Russia (which relieved Britain of the need to pursue an anti-Russian policy in the Far East), or the extent to which colonial disputes which had divided Britain from France and Russia (Egypt and Morocco, Persia and Afghanistan) could provide the means of their reconciliation. Germany had less comparable territory with which to bargain, though the Baghdad Railway was to be a case in point, nor would France have accepted any colonial territory as a *quid pro quo* for Alsace-Lorraine. Holstein drew the right conclusion after the conference of Algeçiras, so disastrous to German prestige, when he advocated that Germany should draw in her horns as Russia had done after the Crimean War.[42] But such advice was unpalatable to the Emperor, who could not stand pessimists, and he and Tirpitz continued on their collision course.[43] Although Russia's defeat by Japan favoured Germany in its immediate consequences, in the long run, by eliminating the main obstacle to an understanding between Britain and Russia, it facilitated the formation of the Triple Entente, which after 1907 deprived Germany of much of the self-confidence with which she had begun the century.

(iv) THE AGADIR CLASH AND THE HALDANE MISSION

Bülow's successor as Chancellor was Theobald von Bethmann Hollweg. Bethmann Hollweg, son of a well-known Frankfurt banking family with liberal associations, was a distinguished jurist and official who had been in succession Prussian Minister of the Interior and federal Secretary of State for home affairs. He had the virtues of a senior civil servant: caution, seriousness, a capacity for hard work and a highly developed sense of responsibility. There was also much of the pedant in his character. Unlike the brilliant but slippery Bülow, Bethmann seemed a man to be trusted. Edward Goschen, the new British ambassador in Berlin, described him as honest and straightforward,[44] and there were hopes that with Bethmann at the Chancellery the peace of Europe would be in safer hands. Unfortunately however the Emperor continued to treat foreign affairs (of which Bethmann confessed he knew very little: unlike his well-travelled predecessor he had hardly been outside Germany) as his own preserve. Despite the *Daily Telegraph* affair, William went on exercising his 'personal rule' in sporadic fashion, through the military, naval and civilian cabinets. Moreover Bethmann was under constant pressure from the Pan-Germans not to 'truckle slavishly' to foreign powers. He did his best to neutralise their influence and that of Tirpitz so far as they obstructed his own plans, but with little success. On the home front Bethmann's conciliatory attitude to the parties helped him to manage the Reichstag, and his liberal record in office made him acceptable to the left. As a Chancellor he took it for granted, in the Bismarckian tradition, that his office was above parties, as an administrator he found partisanship uncongenial, and as a patriot he believed that heated internal conflict would be interpreted abroad as a sign of German weakness and would harm Germany's prestige.[45] For these reasons Bethmann shrank from pursuing his policies, so far as they involved reform, to a point of crisis. He knew the limits of his power: he was the Emperor's nominee, and like the unhappy Bülow he needed the confidence of the Emperor as well as the co-operation of the Reichstag. He was not without courage but lacked resolution.

Bethmann Hollweg saw that improved relations with Britain were the key to any improvement in Germany's international position, and he lost no time in telling the British government of his desire to reach a settlement on the vexed question of naval building. He offered to reduce by three the number of capital ships due for completion by 1914 in return for a general political assurance on the part of Great Britain. Grey was chary: 'I want a good understanding with Germany, but it must be one which will not imperil those we have with France and Russia.'[46] Both Paris and St Petersburg – especially Paris – were suspicious of any move suggestive of an Anglo-German *rapprochement*. Grey, briefed by his Foreign Office advisers, showed sensitivity to French susceptibilities by refusing a German proposal to sign a declaration guaranteeing the territorial *status quo*, on the lines of a declaration on the Baltic recently signed by Germany, Russia and Sweden. The official British view was that any formal recognition by the British of the German possession of Alsace-Lorraine would have destroyed French confidence and put an end to the Entente Cordiale. British policy had to take account of those in France who feared being drawn into an Anglo-German confrontation and saw advantages in better relations with Germany. As in 1905, both Britain and Germany were competing for French favour, the one to keep, the other to gain it. In February 1909 France and Germany signed an agreement on Morocco by which the latter accepted a greater measure of French political control of that country in return for recognition of Germany's equality as a trading partner. When Grey, anxious not to give any offence, suggested that France and Russia be invited to share in the proposed declaration, nothing came of it. The French would not have given way on Alsace-Lorraine, and the Germans would not have been nearer their objective, which was British neutrality in the event of a war between themselves and the Dual Alliance. The British calculation was that France and Russia together would not be equal to the German challenge: 'The one obstacle to German hegemony in Europe has been the strength and independence of the British navy', as Eyre Crowe put it in a minute approved by Grey.[47] The furthest Grey would go in meeting German wishes was to offer a statement that Britain had no hostile intentions against Germany and no understanding with other powers directed against her. This was not good enough for the German government, which insisted that if England genuinely wanted a reduction of Germany's naval programme she would have to pay a political price for it. British reluctance to pay this price was reinforced by doubts whether Tirpitz would allow Bethmann Hollweg to make any significant modifications in the naval building timetable.[48] No agreement proved possible. Nor was any progress made when Anglo-German talks were resumed in 1910. While the Germans were suspicious of the Anglo-Russian understanding, Grey knew how precarious it was. Russia's fickleness seemed to be confirmed by a Russo-German *rapprochement* towards the end of 1910 when the Tsar, accompanied by his new Foreign Minister Sazonov, visited William II at Potsdam and took part in talks with Bethmann Hollweg and his new Secretary of State for foreign affairs, Kiderlen-Waechter. Kiderlen promised Sazonov that Germany would not support Austria if Austria followed an expansionist policy in the Balkans, and Sazonov promised Kiderlen that Russia would not join England in a coalition directed against Germany. This understanding paved the way for another signed in the following year which eliminated Russo-German differences in the Near and Middle East. The Germans recognised Russian predominance in North Persia; the Russians withdrew their objections to Germany's plans for the Baghdad Railway. There was even to be an eventual extension linking the Baghdad line with Teheran, the Persian capital – a project never brought to fruition. The British rightly suspected that in the Potsdam talks the Germans' main object was to compromise the Russian leaders in British eyes.[49] The Russians refused to give the written pledge for which the Germans asked, but Grey was left uneasy. Anglo-Russian relations in Persia, despite the agreement, were anything but smooth. A new diplomatic blunder by Germany, however, soon revived the Triple Entente that had been showing signs of dissolution.

In the spring of 1911 fresh disturbances occurred in Morocco. The Sultan, as on previous occasions, was unable to protect the lives of Europeans, and the French, who had been waiting for this opportunity, marched in and occupied Fez. The Germans objected that this was a breach of the treaty of Algeçiras and of the 1909 agreement. They were convinced that the disorders had been instigated by France, and they demanded that since the *status quo* was being altered to French advantage, they should receive compensation. Germany had promised political disinterestedness in Morocco, but this did not mean that she had to acquiesce in its transformation into a French protectorate. Kiderlen-Waechter, the new 'strong man' of the German Foreign Office, was supposed to represent the Bismarckian tradition, but he behaved more like a second Bülow. At the beginning of July the world was startled by news that a German warship, the *Panther*, had arrived at Agadir, a port on Morocco's Atlantic coast. Kiderlen's object was not to establish a German colony in South Morocco, much as that would have pleased the Pan-Germans and the German mining interests in Morocco, but to use Agadir as a bargaining counter with which to obtain a territory in Central Africa.[50] The 'compensation' demanded was the French Congo. This was more than France was willing to yield. While the French and Germans were still deadlocked over this question, the British Chancellor of the Exchequer, Lloyd George, made the famous Mansion House speech in which he announced, without naming any country, that England would fight rather than let France surrender to German claims. The speech had a dramatic effect, though tension was lowered by a conciliatory speech by the British Prime Minister Asquith shortly afterwards. War between England and Germany was seen to be a real possibility by the people of both countries for the first time. The British fleet was put on the alert. The French continued their negotiations with the Germans on more equal terms, and the result was the signature of a treaty whereby, in return for the recognition that Morocco was French, Germany was to receive a portion of the French Congo connecting the German Cameroons with the Congo river. The newly acquired territory was poor in resources, but Kiderlen hoped that it would be the beginning of a German *Mittelafrika*. Still, it was an ungratifying return for a diplomatic stroke that had sounded the alarm bells ringing and given a new lease of life to the Franco-British entente.

Agadir had grave consequences. In Germany there was baffled rage among the nationalists. In the Reichstag the Conservative leader von Heydebrand denounced the government for having sacrificed German honour, and charged England with having tried to provoke a Franco-German war. He appealed to the Chancellor to use the 'good German sword' at the right time – a warning that a further humiliation like Agadir would not be tolerated.[51] Bethmann Hollweg, to his credit, replied that 'strength does not need to brandish the sword'. Tirpitz called for a new navy law. These developments did not go unheeded in England, where fear based on naval rivalry was not easily allayed by an easing of tension in other fields. It was in this atmosphere of exasperation and frustration that the German government passed a bill creating two new army corps, to be followed in the following year (1913) under the impact of the Balkan wars by an increase in the peacetime strength of the army of 136,000.[52] It was also symptomatic that a book by a former member of the General Staff, General von Bernhardi, *Germany and the next War*, which propounded the thesis that Germany was faced with a choice between world power and downfall,[53] rapidly went through six editions. In France too a patriotic revival was under way. The Caillaux government, which had been engaged in surreptitious negotiations with Germany before Lloyd George's Mansion House speech, was succeeded by that of Poincaré. Poincaré, an incisive nationalist lawyer from the frontier province of Lorraine, soon showed that France would follow a less conciliatory policy, and made himself the spokesman of those who would fight rather than yield to German demands. The symbol of the new French mood was the decision to extend the period of French military service from two years to three, thus making up for France's inferiority in manpower. Meanwhile Italy had seized the opportunity to attack Tripoli, the Turkish province in North Africa which she had long coveted. Though the other powers were embarrassed by this act of aggression, they all, for various reasons, acquiesced in it. But the weakening of Turkey encouraged the irredentist Balkan states to combine for the further liberation of Turkish territory in Europe, and so led directly to the Balkan wars.

The nearness of a European war at the time of Agadir caused alarm to thoughful people in both England and Germany. Among the latter was Albert Ballin, the head of the largest German shipping company, the Hamburg-Amerika Line. Ballin who was often consulted by the Emperor was one of the most influential individuals in the Reich. He was also friendly with Sir Ernest Cassel, the German-born financier who had become a confidant of Edward VII. Ballin suggested to Cassel that a member of the British government should visit Germany in order to make a fresh attempt to put an end to the dangerous and financially disastrous naval rivalry. Grey, under considerable pressure from the radicals to reduce expenditure on the navy, was inclined to take up the suggestion. There was also, Metternich reported from London in December 1911, a growing desire in England to improve relations with Germany. The upshot was the decision to send to Berlin Lord Haldane, the Minister of War. Haldane was chosen because he was known to be an admirer of German culture and had received part of his education at German universities. Accompanied by Cassel, he spent several days in February 1912 talking to William II, Bethmann Hollweg and Tirpitz. Haldane's object was to persuade the Germans to slow down their fleet-building programme in return for a political declaration by the British and concessions in the colonial field.[54] In Berlin Haldane learnt of the new Navy bill, the *Novelle* of 1912, which obviously made agreement harder to reach. Neither country had moved from the positions previously taken up, except that Britain was now prepared to offer Germany territory in Africa: the British would not commit themselves to a declaration that would upset their partners in the Triple Entente; the Germans insisted on British neutrality in case of war between themselves and the Dual Alliance. Haldane found Tirpitz much less willing to come to terms than Bethmann Hollweg, and Tirpitz's intransigence confirmed the scepticism of those in London who doubted whether any German professions of readiness to reduce the naval programme could be taken seriously.[55] Grey finally agreed to a political declaration which ran: 'England will make no unprovoked attack upon Germany and pursue no aggressive policy towards her. Aggression upon Germany is not the object and forms no part of any Treaty, understanding or combination to which England is a party, nor will she become a party to anything with such an object.'[56] The Germans were not impressed. They still wanted nothing less than neutrality, a word which Grey knew would undermine French and Russian confidence in Britain.[57] The British government was already planning to bring its Mediterranean fleet to the North Sea for concentration in home waters. The French would group their navy in the Mediterranean, for the defence of which they would become responsible, while the British would be expected to guard the North French coast. Such an arrangement would be upset by any estrangement between France and Britain. The practical implications of the Entente were beginning to show themselves, and the likelihood of British non-involvement in a Franco-German war was reduced. The failure of the Haldane Mission left Anglo-German relations much as before. In May 1912 the Reichstag passed Tirpitz's *Novelle*, thus adding one capital ship to the annual building total, and in July the British announced that during the next five years twenty-one instead of seventeen ships would be laid down.[58] The construction of light cruisers was also to be accelerated. The slogan of the day in Britain was 'Two keels to one', meaning that each additional German ship would be matched by two British. In Germany Tirpitz had won the day against Bethmann Hollweg, a change symbolised by the recall of the German ambassador in London, Metternich, whom the Emperor considered too conciliatory to the British. He was replaced by Baron Marschall von Bieberstein, who, however, died shortly after being appointed. Marschall's successor was Prince Lichnowsky, a liberal-minded nobleman who, though relatively inexperienced as a diplomat, soon became very popular in English society and to the Kaiser's dismay turned out to be even more anglophile than Metternich. William preferred the advice of his naval attaché in London, Captain Widenmann, who had consistently worked against Metternich and influenced the Kaiser against him.

(v) BETHMANN HOLLWEG'S DOMESTIC DILEMMA: CONSERVATIVE OBDURACY AND THE SWING TO THE LEFT

In home no less than in foreign affairs Bethmann Hollweg inherited a difficult situation. The problems which had defeated Bülow – Prussian franchise reform, the use of direct federal taxation to balance the budget – remained, and even became more urgent with the leftward trend in the politics and the rising cost of the arms race. Now that the Bülow bloc of Conservatives, National Liberals and Progressives had collapsed, the new Chancellor had to find a fresh basis of support in the Reichstag. It was, indeed, possible for him to legislate with the backing of National Liberals, Progressives and Centre, who together commanded a parliamentary majority until 1912.[59] But Bethmann's aim was to win the co-operation of all the major parties (except the Social Democrats, whose opposition was taken for granted) including the Conservatives. Bethmann recognised the significance of the rise of socialism, and was less hostile to it than most of his predecessors. But he did not want to become dependent on the Socialists in the Reichstag because he shared the general view of 'bourgeois' politicians that in matters of fundamental national importance like defence the Socialists were not to be relied on.[60] Bethmann's conciliatory policy was intended to heal the wounds caused by the bitter dissension over Bülow's proposed inheritance tax. In this aim he was only partially successful. He gained the support of the Centre which Bülow had lost, but the Conservatives were no more inclined to compromise with the new Chancellor than with the old. The difficulties confronting Bethmann were evident in the three major tasks he undertook: liberalisation of the Prussian franchise; a new constitution for Alsace-Lorraine; and reform of the federal budget. Conservative opposition in the Prussian *Landtag* defeated a modest attempt to reform the franchise proposed by Bethmann in his capacity as Prussian Prime Minister. He was more successful over Alsace-Lorraine, for which he had Reichstag backing. Against right-wing opposition he introduced a constitution for the province which made it an autonomous federal state with its own parliament based on a democratic franchise. Yet the inhabitants of Alsace-Lorraine remained unreconciled to German rule, the militarist nature of which was displayed by an incident at the small garrison town of Zabern, where a few young officers behaved arrogantly towards a crowd of civilians.

It was the financial problem that caused most controversy, and exemplified the strains to which a Chancellor was subject who was trying to please the democratic forces in the Reichstag while responding to the built-in conservative bias of Germany's hybrid constitution. By 1912 the decision to create two new army corps and enlarge the navy through the Tirpitz *Novelle* made it essential to raise fresh revenue. An increase of taxes on consumption, such as had been resorted to in 1909, was no longer appropriate. The obvious solution was to impose a federal property tax in the form of a death duty, as Bülow had tried to do and failed. The Reichstag presented little difficulty. The general election of January 1912 had resulted in a massive loss of seats by all parties except the Socialists, who more than doubled their representation and emerged as the largest party with 110 seats. For the first time the Centre was displaced from its leading position. The success of the S.P.D. was even greater than it appeared, for had there been proportional representation its total would have been 139 seats, and with the Progressives it would almost have formed a majority in the Reichstag. The left wing and liberal parties were in favour of a federal property tax as the alternative to a further rise in indirect taxes which would have borne heavily on the poor. Bethmann revived the project of an inheritance tax. There were two difficulties. The first was the uncompromising opposition of the Conservatives, who were unwilling to pay for the armaments they supported. The second was the objections of the states, which were jealous of their virtual monopoly of direct taxation.[61] The Federal Council, in which Prussia as the largest state had a power of veto, used its position as the guardian of state rights, and without the Council's approval no bill could become law. After prolonged wrangling Bethmann settled for a tax on the increment in the value of real property. This was a compromise between what the left-wing majority in the Reichstag wanted and what the Federal Council would accept. The Conservatives remained obdurate. Still further revenue was needed to cover the cost of the higher military estimates in 1913, which raised the peace-time strength of the army by approximately twenty per cent. This time it was decided to impose a special levy on all estates worth £2,500 and over, and on all incomes of £500 upwards. This was a non-recurring tax to meet a special situation.

Among those who voted for the defence levy or *Wehrbeitrag* were the Socialists, whose decision was something of a landmark in the party's history. Normally the S.P.D. opposed the budget, but on this occasion it felt able to approve the *Wehrbeitrag*, despite its military character, on the grounds that it fell only on the wealthy. There was, however, a group of Socialist deputies who in the party's internal debate showed that they preferred to stand by traditional anti-militarism even though the new armaments were to be paid for by a progressive tax.[62] This was a sign of a growing split in a party that for some years had been *de facto* divided into reformists or 'revisionists' on the right, neo-revolutionaries on the left and a 'Marxist centre' balancing uneasily between them. Though revisionism had been officially rejected by the S.P.D. at its conference in 1903, since 1906 revisionist practice if not theory permeated it at all levels, and reformist socialists such as Ebert the new general secretary and the future president of the German

republic were now predominant at party headquarters. As the party
became more bureaucratic it became more cautious. The electoral
success of 1912 seemed to bring the S.P.D. one stage nearer its goal in
the long struggle for power, and to vindicate the reformists' preference
for constitutional methods in opposition to the political strike and mass
agitation favoured by the left-wing militants. Indeed, to a party already supported by over one-third of the electorate, the capture of an
actual majority of votes for the Reichstag appeared a far from unattainable objective in a country in which the working-class proportion
of the population was over half and steadily increasing.[63] The party
had rejected the mass strike, and in some of the South German states
reformist socialists had already shown that successful co-operation
with 'bourgeois' parties was possible, despite the official condemnation
of it as 'a sell-out'.[64] The question was whether similar tactics could be
used at federal level in pursuit of aims for which Progressive and perhaps National Liberal support might be forthcoming, such as Prussian
franchise reform, the redistribution of Reichstag seats on a population
basis, and even the introduction of ministerial responsibility into the
system. Such plans went far beyond anything Bethmann Hollweg
was prepared to contemplate, and indeed any attempt to implement
them would have added to his difficulties, already formidable, with the
Federal Council and the Prussian *Landtag*.

Thus in Germany, as in France, the last general election before the
First World War resulted in a victory for the left. The two Conservative
parties, whose total of Reichstag deputies had fallen from 84 to 57,
were increasingly isolated. The pressures behind the reform movement – industrialisation, socialism, the democratic climate of the age –
were growing stronger, while the Junkers and their friends, defiantly
entrenched behind their constitutional privileges, were in no mood to
give way. Bethmann was caught between an irresistible force and an
immovable object. Just as in England the rising cost of armaments
and pressure for social reform, reflected in Lloyd George's 1909
budget, precipitated the constitutional crisis of 1910 and the Parliament Act, so in Germany the demand for Prussian franchise reform
and a federal property tax seemed to be moving towards a showdown
that would alter decisively the balance of power. But whereas in
England the radicals triumphed, in Germany they failed. As we have
seen, the Chancellor was unwilling to provoke a clash, and the day of
reckoning was postponed. It was to come in November 1918; when
the German revolution with its mixture of democratic and socialist
objectives was, in part at least, the deferred crisis of the Wilhelmine
regime.

Some of the anxieties caused by the pre-war tensions in German society found expression in a pamphlet written by the chairman of the Pan-German League, Heinrich Class, under the pseudonym of Daniel Frymann and entitled 'If I were the Kaiser'.[65] The immediate background to it was the election of 1912, which alarmed the Pan-Germans by raising the spectre of a left-wing government granting equal franchise in Prussia and a parliamentary regime in the Reich, and of a Germany permanently dominated by the 'anti-national' parties. The atmosphere engendered by the Agadir war-scare also contributed to the sense of crisis. In this pamphlet, which was described by the League press as the 'quintessence of national anxieties and wishes', a political programme for decades, Class outlined the totalitarian state of the twentieth century. How in such circumstances was Germany to face the prospect of war – for only war could give her the extra territory she needed? If the war proved victorious, the nationalists would hold power indefinitely; but if it ended in defeat, they would have to stage a *coup d'état* and set up a dictator who would crush the Socialists completely (thus going further than Bismarck, who had allowed them to sit in the Reichstag). The Jews, who were branded as the chief instigators of revolutionary Marxism, would be subjected to far-reaching restrictions. They would not be allowed to hold public office, join the army or navy, vote, become lawyers or teachers, manage banks or theatres or work for non-Jewish newspapers. No Jewish immigrants would be allowed. As for other immigrants into Germany, those of Germanic stock would be admitted, but not people from Eastern or Southern Europe. 'Harmful elements' in the nation must be rooted out. The pamphlet foreshadowed the Nazi racial policy, from laws against Jews to those governing marriage and the inheritance of land. As the most recent historian of the Pan-German League has written, from Class's advocacy of a *coup d'état*, racial doctrine, anti-semitic legislation and an aggressive domestic policy to Hitler's Gestapo, concentration camps and one party state was only a short step. These views were expounded by a Rhineland lawyer at a time when Germany was living in peace and prosperity. They were a product of fear, just as the similar views of Hitler himself were based on the apprehensions of the dominant German minority in a declining Habsburg Empire threatened by the rising tide of Slav and other ethnic groups. Such 'politics of cultural despair' were obviously to become of much greater significance at a time of defeat and economic depression after the First World War.

It is a common temptation to a historian to interpret the past in terms of the future, and nowhere is the temptation greater than in the case of Germany. Yet in the light of future events the activities of the Pan-Germans, minority though they were, can hardly be dismissed as insignificant. Some contemporaries were aware of the danger. In an article published in 1911 Walther Rathenau confessed his forebodings:

> I am fighting against the wrong being done in Germany, for I see shadows rising wherever I turn. I see them when I walk through the shrill streets of Berlin in the evening; when I catch sight of the insolence of our wealth gone crazy; when I hear the futility of boastful words or hear reports of pseudo-Germanic exclusiveness, which winces at newspaper articles or the remarks of ladies in waiting. An age is not carefree just because the lieutenant beams and the attaché is full of hope.[66]

On another occasion Rathenau called to mind Belshazzar's Feast, echoing Kipling's earlier warning to his fellow-countrymen in *Recessional*. Since the Boer War the British Empire had passed its noon; with Edward VII began the long imperial sunset. Germany on the other hand felt herself, as Treitschke had said, the youngest of the great nations of Western Europe, with her zenith still to come. Few people shared the presentiments of Rathenau who, besides being a sensitive Jew and a highly successful industrialist, had the vision of an artist. The prevailing mood was a blend of *hubris*, fear and frustration. Germany was powerful, but she was faced by a larger, hostile coalition, and her prospects were visibly diminishing. Some foreigners were alarmed at the streak of morbidity and violence they detected in the spirit of Germany – in the philosophy of Nietzsche and the music of Richard Strauss as well as in the megalomania of William II. Romain Rolland had written in 1899: 'Germany as the All-Powerful will not keep her balance for long. . . . Giddiness blows through her brain. Neroism is in the air.'[67] Despite the untold prosperity and solid achievements of Wilhelmine Germany, the celebrations held in 1913 to mark the Emperor's silver jubilee and the centenary of the battle of Leipzig could not dispel a feeling of disquiet. Bethmann Hollweg sensed a 'strange oppression' burdening the country's political life, a mood of dissatisfaction.[68] People lacked ideals: politics – it was an old and familiar complaint – had become a matter of material self-interest according to Werner Sombart, the economist, in a book published in 1912.

The malaise was not confined to Germany. The sense of satiety, and often of guilt, at the increasing wealth and luxury, the giddy sense of power, an awareness of spiritual decay and a feeling of pessimism about the future are themes to be found in a number of poets of the early twentieth century. Valery Bryusov of Russia in a poem entitled *The Coming Huns* called for a huge catastrophe to cleanse and change the world, while Cavafy, the Alexandrian Greek, in his *Waiting for*

the Barbarians depicted the prevalent desire for a barbarian invasion
to solve current ills as symptomatic of a society that had lost its vitality
and become cynical. Sir Maurice Bowra, whose acquaintance with
European poetry was almost unrivalled in his generation, even suggests
that 'what ultimately brought the war was not the uncertain rivalries
of European powers, nor even the ambitions and fears of Germany,
but the death-wish in the peoples of Europe, a half-conscious desire to
break away from their humdrum or horrifying circumstances to something more exciting or more exalted'.[69] The longing for excitement
was certainly present in Marinetti, the Italian Futurist poet and apostle
of violence, whose movement was one of the spiritual forces behind
Fascism. While the intellectuals spoke in apocalyptic language of war
and 'living dangerously', the Balkan peoples, incited by tribal feuds
and national jealousies, erupted into a new conflagration.

(vi) THE BALKAN WARS AND THE ANGLO-GERMAN DÉTENTE

Foreign policy, it has been observed, seldom follows a straight line;
and it rarely consists of a single thread. During the two years that preceded the outbreak of the First World War the diplomatic pattern,
already intricate, was made more complex by the strains and realign-
ments caused by the Balkan upheaval. The second Morocco crisis
(Agadir) had conformed broadly to the same pattern as the first (Tangier). Germany had put on a show of force to make demands which,
if accepted, would have permanently damaged France's standing as
a great power; England stepped in to support the French and redress
the balance. On both occasions Germany's relations with Russia were
little affected, despite the Franco-Russian alliance; it was Germany's
relations with the West which deteriorated. But the growing danger
of a war arising from the Balkans threw England and Germany together. There was an Anglo-German détente between 1912 and 1914,
and even signs of a relaxation of tension between Germany and France
in the latter year. The First World War was a result of four converging
crises: Germany's world policy, affecting mainly the British Empire;
her bid for continental hegemony, directed against France and Russia;
her commitment to uphold, by war if necessary, the threatened Habsburg Monarchy; and her stake in the Ottoman Empire with its
challenge to Russia. The Moroccan clashes concerned the first two
problems – Germany's relations with Britain and France; those in the
Balkans concerned the last two – Serbia and Russia. Germany was
involved in the Balkans as the ally of Austria, France as the ally of
Russia. Because Germany would not abandon Austria, France would
not abandon Russia and England clung to the Entente Cordiale, the

two western powers and Germany were sucked into the fatal Balkan maelstrom. This was not an accident. It was predictable and almost inevitable that resurgent Balkan nationalism, irredentist and trigger-happy, should challenge the 'honour' or vital interests of the one great power that stood in the way of its ambitions – Austria-Hungary.[70] It was equally predictable and almost inevitable that Austria-Hungary should try to preserve its great power status rather than admit defeat as the difficulties mounted. Both the defenders of the *status quo* and the advocates of radical change could find ample justification for their attitude. Both, on their different assumptions, were right. The small states were neither wholly independent of, nor effectively controlled by, the great powers – a situation clearly fraught with risks. Yet that a general war was, in the short run, preventable, is shown by the experience of the Balkan wars, when British and German diplomacy co-operated to localise the conflict. This was to prove impossible in July 1914.

Italy's brazen seizure of Tripoli in 1911 was an encouragement to the Balkan states to attack Turkey and liberate further territory. The Young Turk regime with its attempts to 'ottomanise' subject peoples acted as an additional irritant. In March 1912 Serbia and Bulgaria formed the alliance against Turkey known as the Balkan League, and were soon joined by Greece. Russia gave general approval to the League, which she dared not oppose, though its aggressive character (against Turkey if not also against Austria-Hungary) was not in doubt. The right of veto possessed by Russia on any war to be declared under the League was a safeguard of little value.[71] Russia even joined Austria in urging the Balkan states not to break the peace, but the warning was unheeded. Early in October 1912 fighting broke out between Turkish garrisons and their subjects in Albania and Montenegro. It soon spread to Thrace, Macedonia and Epirus. Defeated by the armies of Bulgaria, Serbia and Greece, the Turks were forced to abandon almost all of Turkey in Europe, and the Bulgarians had penetrated nearly as far as Constantinople. After about eight weeks of fighting Bulgaria, Serbia and Montenegro (but not Greece) signed an armistice with the Turks, who had appealed to the powers to intervene on their behalf. Soon afterwards a peace conference opened in London under the chairmanship of Sir Edward Grey. Serbia received the lion's share of Macedonia, the ethnically mixed province which had been assigned to Bulgaria at the shortlived treaty of San Stefano in 1878. Bulgaria and Greece also made substantial gains.

These changes profoundly affected the standing and security of the Austro-Hungarian Monarchy, whose seven million Serb, Croatian and Slovene subjects the Pan-Serbs hoped to include the future South Slav state. The Austrians had no clearcut policy towards the South Slav problem – itself a reflection of the basic divisions within the heterogeneous Empire. Some of the political and military leaders advocated a punitive expedition against Serbia in order to absorb or partition her; others thought in terms of a reconstruction of the Monarchy on a tripartite basis, with the Southern Slavs being given equality of status with the Germans and Magyars. Some Austrians would have liked an economic union with Serbia whereby she would be drawn into the orbit of the Monarchy.[72] These conflicting views prevented the emergence of an unambiguous programme. Russia's support of the Serbs was a factor to be taken into account, and a disincentive to the gamble of preventive war. Austria's immediate concern after the first Balkan war was that Serbia should not become too large and powerful. She accordingly held out against Serbia's acquisition of a port on the Adriatic, as the Serb government wanted. Austria was successful in pressing her point of view largely because Russia, fearful lest Bulgaria take Constantinople, did not give full support to Serb aspirations. Within a few weeks of the signing of the treaty ending the first Balkan war, the second one began.[73] It started with an attempt by Bulgaria to seize a larger share of the spoil, and developed into an attack on Bulgaria by Serbia and Greece, with Roumania joining them. The treaty of Bucharest, which concluded the war, was made by the Balkan states themselves, unlike the treaty of London which was the work of the great powers. Now Greece as well as Serbia gained at the expense of Bulgaria, which also lost Dobrudja to Roumania. Enlarged Roumania, though remaining a nominal ally of the Triple Alliance, was showing signs of going over to the Franco-Russian side.[74] Roumania displayed an irredentist interest in Transylvania, where two million people of Roumanian stock lived under the intolerant rule of the Magyars; she also calculated that the balance of military power had passed to the Triple Entente. Austria's only Balkan friend (apart from diminutive Albania) was defeated Bulgaria. During the wars Austria had shown forbearance. She had let pass the opportunity of reoccupying the Sanjak of Novi Bazar, which would have given her a commanding position in the western Balkans, during the first Balkan war, and had abstained from allying with Bulgaria to attack Serbia during the second. Yet at the end of the wars her situation was significantly worse.[75] On the south and east she was almost surrounded by enemies, and the defeat of Turkey was virtually a defeat for herself.

Austria's precarious position inevitably affected Germany, her only certain ally. In Bismarck's time Germany supported Austria only so far as the latter followed a defensive policy; but Bülow at the time of the Bosnian crisis had given Austria a blank cheque, and the annexation of Bosnia and Herzegovina, which Germany approved, was not a defensive move. In November 1912, Kiderlen-Waechter, the German Foreign Secretary, told the Foreign Affairs committee of the *Bundesrat* that if Austria in defence of her vital interests against Slav encroachments was attacked by Russia, Germany would throw her whole weight behind Austria: 'If Austria must fight . . . we must go to her aid lest we have later to fight alone beside a weakened Austria.'[76] In Austria's situation the distinction between defence and attack was anything but clear. Given Serbia's subversive aims against the Dual Monarchy, was a preventive war against Serbia justified? On this point opinion in Berlin, as in Vienna, was divided. The prevailing view was in favour of restraint, which coincided with the policy of Berchtold, the Austrian Foreign Minister. Germany could afford to take a more detached and less partial attitude to Balkan problems than Austria: the Emperor William, in particular, expressed absurdly unrealistic hopes about Serbia and Roumania. He was also optimistic that Greece, under her new king, Constantine, who was married to William's sister, would become an ally of the Triple Alliance.[77] Germany had another reason for not becoming too deeply involved in Austria's quarrels – her wish to keep on good terms with Russia, with whose Tsar William II had a 'most cordial' meeting in the Baltic in July 1912. Finally, the German government was anxious not to put at risk the détente with England which was a by-product of the diplomacy of the Balkan wars, and which was some compensation for the later deterioration in German-Russian relations.

The Balkan wars also reacted adversely on Germany's position in Turkey, whose German-trained army, administration and finances were in disarray. Something had to be done to bolster that country, exhausted as it was by war and defeat, and to prevent it from sliding into the western camp, as other Balkan states showed signs of doing through their need of investment capital, which France, but not Germany, was able to supply. Germany also had to safeguard her interests in the Ottoman Empire, notably the Baghdad Railway. Now that most of Turkey in Europe was lost, how much of Turkey in Asia would remain? When the Turks asked Germany to send another general to reorganise their land forces, the Germans could hardly refuse. The result was the arrival at Constantinople of General Liman von Sanders, who was appointed commander of the first Turkish army corps. This move was watched with suspicion by the other powers, especially Russia. Russia was seriously worried by the German hold on the Straits, through which passed 90 per cent of Russian wheat exports. Growing tension between Germany and Russia followed, which was alleviated when the Germans agreed that Liman should become Inspector-General of the Turkish army without command over troops. But the Russians' misgivings remained, and they speeded up their military preparations. The Kaiser minuted on a report: 'As a soldier ... I haven't the slightest doubt that Russia is systematically preparing war against us; and I shall act accordingly.'[78] He had recently written: 'Russo-Prussian relations are dead for all time. We've become enemies.' There was no universally acceptable solution to the problem of Turkey. Not until after the First World War was a revival of Turkish nationalism in the heartland of Anatolia to fill the vacuum left by the long imperial decline. In the period immediately preceding the outbreak of war Russo-German enmity over the Ottoman Empire added considerably to the atmosphere of belligerence.

The improvement in Anglo-German relations brought about by a common approach to Balkan problems led to a more sympathetic British attitude to German colonial aspirations. It also coincided with a general desire in Britain after Agadir for a friendlier approach to Germany.[79] Radicals were anxious to end the arms race. There was mounting distrust of Russian policy in Persia, and British connivance at Russian sabotage of the efforts of the American financial adviser, Morgan Shuster, to set Persia's finances in order caused criticism and embarrassment.[80] Haldane during his visit to Berlin in February 1912 had tentatively suggested a deal on colonial territories in Africa, a theme which was taken up by Grey later in the year. It was decided to revive, with modifications in favour of Germany, the plan drawn up in 1898 for dividing the Portuguese colonies of Angola and Mozambique in case Portugal herself abandoned them. There was a hitch: Grey with his liberal conscience insisted that the Anglo-Portuguese treaty of 1899 guaranteeing Portugal her possessions be published as well, while the Germans not unnaturally demurred. Although final agreement had not been reached by the time war broke out, the fact that the negotiations reached such an advanced stage suggests a successful outcome. Both sides were counting chickens before they were hatched, and the negotiators might have been surprised to hear that Portugal's African empire would survive their own. But the Germans had, or thought they had, something to look forward to, and England had bought goodwill in someone else's currency. Even the more controversial Baghdad Railway question now proved capable of solution. England withdrew her opposition to Germany's plans in Turkey in return for a pledge that any extension of the line from Basra to the Persian Gulf would be under British control. Two British members were to be appointed to the Baghdad Railways Board. These negotiations were carried on 'in the friendliest spirit', and agreement was reached on the eve of the world war.[81] The chief barrier to good Anglo-German relations remained the naval rivalry, but even here there was some slackening of tension. The First Lord of the Admiralty, Winston Churchill, appealed in 1912 and again in 1913 for a 'naval holiday', meaning a year's cessation of building. The Germans declared this to be impracticable. But the British were less worried than before: their lead over Germany increased after 1911. In 1913 even Tirpitz argued, rather late in the day, that a further rise in the naval building programme could not be justified financially, and agreed to postpone construction of the third capital ship approved by the 1912 *Novelle*.[82] He was now prepared to settle for a building ratio of 10 to 16 which was also acceptable to the British. Germany's decision at this time to increase the size of her army reduced the resources available for the navy. A more general difficulty about Anglo-German relations was that the British did not know exactly what Germany wanted. The Germans themselves did not always know, as von Jagow, the newly appointed Secretary of State for foreign affairs, admitted to a British diplomat in January 1913. More often than not, the general desire for expansion did not take a concrete shape.[83] The large measure of agreement reached between the British and German governments over the Portuguese colonies and the Baghdad Railway was a success for those moderate imperialists in Germany such as Solf, the anglophile Colonial Minister, and Kühlmann, the later Foreign Minister who was on the staff of the German Embassy in London during the period of the Anglo-German détente. Both these men believed that Germany's best chance of enlarging her colonial empire lay not in rivalry with Great Britain but as a kind of junior partner. Such a policy was also advocated in a book by a German journalist published in 1913 and entitled *German World Policy and No War*.[84] Had the German government not provoked the British by their naval policy the latter would have been less inclined to support France and Russia in maintaining the balance of power. The influence of Tirpitz however prevailed in Berlin, thanks largely to the support he received from the Kaiser.

Germany's relations with France in the two years before the great war followed a somewhat different course. The main significance of the rise of Poincaré, who became Prime Minister in January 1912 and President a year later, lay in the strengthening of the Dual Alliance. France told Russia that she would support her in a war arising from an Austro-Serb quarrel provided that Germany intervened on Austria's side. This meant in fact that France would take part in a war provoked by the Balkan League if Germany did so.[85] In the past the French had tried to restrain the Russians from involving them in a

Balkan conflict in which France's vital interests were not at stake. Now they would go along with Russia in all circumstances. They feared, as before, that otherwise Russia might elude them and come to terms with Germany. Such fears were not wholly unfounded. In November 1910 the Tsar visited his cousin the Kaiser at Potsdam and signed an agreement concerning Persia and the Baghdad Railway. In the following year Russia noticeably failed to support her French ally during the Agadir crisis. Such gestures, like the Franco-German treaty of 1909, were examples of the 'inter-penetration of alliances' that showed how far from rigid the alignments were. But after 1912 the French also felt more confident of their own chances in a general war.[86] The three years service law put the French army on a more equal footing with Germany, and the balance of power in south-east Europe had clearly swung against the Triple Alliance. But in France, as in Britain, there were many, especially among the radicals and socialists, but also including bankers and industrialists, who would have preferred an understanding with Germany, just as the German radicals and many businessmen were orientated towards the West. The elections in April and May of 1914 brought a victory for the left (as those of 1912 had in Germany), and Poincaré, much against his will, was forced to appoint Viviani, a Socialist, Prime Minister. Jaurès, the French Socialist leader, was an ardent advocate of reconciliation with Germany, and had close and cordial ties with the German Social Democratic party. Germany had thus much to hope for from a détente with the West, the fruits of which could only be gathered by the exercise of restraint and patience. Meanwhile, however, in Eastern Europe time was not on Germany's side as Russia, helped by French loans, increased her military preparations. It was too late for Austria to fight a localised, preventive war against Serbia, but the longer the Central Powers had to wait for the 'inevitable' general war, the less chance they had of winning it.

Despite the flexibility in the alliance system shown during the Balkan wars, its basic character remained. The British, while willing to make colonial deals with Germany, still believed that she aimed at the hegemony of Europe, and that France must be supported. Even a German move towards France was suspect as an attempt to break the Entente,[87] just as a German move towards Russia was seen as having the same purpose. Not even Russia's breaches of the 1907 agreement in Persia, where she appeared to be aiming at the annexation of the North, were a good enough reason for quarrelling with Russia. Indeed, Sir Arthur Nicolson, Permanent Under-Secretary of the Foreign Office after 1910 and former ambassador at St Petersburg, argued that England had to be on friendly terms with France and Russia because they had more power to harm her than Germany had.[88] This was curiously reminiscent in different circumstances of the earlier reasoning of Holstein, that Germany could force the British into alliance by making them uncomfortable. In fact the British as a whole never feared France or Russia as they feared Germany because neither was a naval power of the same order. Russia's expansion in Asia, while resented as a threat to India, could hardly cause the same concern as a concentration of naval and military power in North West Europe. Nor was there in Anglo-Russian relations the same acrimony at the popular level, including the press, as there had been between England and Germany. On the other hand Russia, unlike Germany, was practically invulnerable to the British.

The number of points of conflict in Europe, the passions roused by them and the feverish intensity of the arms race all pointed to war. Maximilian Harden, editor of the radical periodical *Die Zukunft*, wrote in May 1914: 'This summer will see our fate decided.' In Central Europe few people doubted that war would be the outcome of a situation which seemed to admit no other solution. Statesmen approached the catastrophe with something like fatalism, especially in Austria, where the only choice seemed to lie between an act of desperation (like the ultimatum to Serbia of July 1914) and continued decline under the impact of disruptive forces without and within. Germany's future was bound up with Austria's. Bismarck's decision to opt for Austria in preference to Russia when forced to choose, itself hardly escapable at the time, set Germany on an irrevocable course. Now she had either to shore up Austria as a great power or wait for the time – perhaps on the death of the aged Emperor Francis Joseph – when the Monarchy would disintegrate altogether or be reconstructed as a predominantly Slav State.[89] Although Vienna received conflicting and often uninformed advice from Berlin about Balkan problems, there was no real doubt that in any showdown involving the future of Austria-Hungary, Germany would stand by her. Several times between 1908 and 1914 a European war could have broken out had Austria decided on a preventive war against Serbia. Each time Austria had drawn back. The Germans began to wonder whether there was any point at which the Monarchy would stand and fight rather than lose further prestige and power. There was also a question mark about the whole future of Turkey, the other declining Empire with which the fortunes of Germany were linked. Each crisis that passed made the situation slightly worse since it left behind increasing exasperation and impatience. William II saw it as a struggle between Germans and racially inferior Slavs, with 'decadent Gauls' and perfidious British helping the Slavs.[90] None of the national leaders viewed the impending war as a European civil war, in which all would be losers. No one had the strength to master events, and few had the imaginative grasp to understand them. Colonel House, President Wilson's special envoy who visited the European capitals in the summer of 1914, found militarism run mad, and a preoccupation with immediate gains to the exclusion of long-term goals: 'There's no future in Europe's vision . . . no long look ahead . . . The European powers are mere threats to one another, content to check, the one the other . . .'[91] There was no supranational vision; each country had its own, which clashed with that of its neighbours. There was also a feeling of resignation. It was an age in which war was still an admissible instrument of national policy, in which losses were expected to be justified by gains. The dangerous feature of the situation was that the balance of power was constantly shifting, with the result that whichever side felt threatened soon reached a point at which the temptation to go to war rather than yield territory or prestige became irresistible. This was the position in which the Central Powers found themselves in the summer of 1914.

CHAPTER IV

The First World War:
From the Outbreak to the
Entry of America

(i) BETHMANN HOLLWEG'S BRINKMANSHIP

The outbreak of the long foreseen and almost fatalistically accepted
European war followed from Germany's decision to give her ally Austria
unlimited support in the crisis caused by the assassination at Sarajevo
of the heir apparent to the Habsburg throne, the Archduke Franz
Ferdinand. The crime was carried out by South Slav nationalists and
organised by a secret society known as the Black Hand. Pasich, the
Serbian Prime Minister, knew of the plot and even sent a vague warning to the Austrian government. Sarajevo was the capital of Bosnia,
one of the two provinces (the other being Herzegovina) annexed by
Austria in 1908. On that occasion the direct challenge to South Slav
sentiment led to a confrontation between Germany, as Austria's ally,
and Russia, as Serbia's protector. And although Russia gave way, such
a humiliation was not to be borne a second time, as Bülow, the uneasy
victor, realised. Serbia's victory in the two Balkan wars gave her
new prestige and considerable accretions of territory. Austria felt
threatened, and in October 1913, with German approval, sent an ultimatum to Belgrade requiring the Serbs to evacuate Albania, which
they had occupied. Russia advised her protégé to be patient, but reassured her that the future belonged to Serbia: 'the time would come
to lance the Austro-Hungarian abscess'.[1] Austria as well as Serbia
mobilised during the Balkan wars and the two were on the brink of
hostilities before Serbia climbed down. What distinguished the crisis
of July 1914 from previous Balkan crises was that Russia had so far
recovered from defeat and revolution as to take up the German challenge and stand by Serbia at all costs, while she could count on a support from France which had not been forthcoming in the past. There
was thus dangerous rigidity on both sides. The 'Now or never' with
which William II had accompanied Austria's démarche in October

1913 was repeated in more risky circumstances.[2] On 5 July the Austrian ambassador had a meeting with the German Emperor and his advisers at Potsdam, at which Germany not only gave her ally a blank cheque but suggested the terms in which it should be written. With this assurance, the Vienna government proceeded to take a tough line with Belgrade. The Austrians had been much provoked, and they had good reason to believe that any further concessions to Serb nationalism would be disastrous for the Dual Monarchy. Little value was attached to Serb promises of good behaviour in future. The government in Vienna accordingly presented Serbia with an ultimatum containing a number of demands incompatible with its dignity and independence. The Austrians thereby revealed their intention to solve the problem by war, which was to be followed by the partition of Serbia between Austria, Bulgaria and Albania, though they had discarded this solution not long before. This objective was made even plainer when the Serb reply to the ultimatum was rejected, despite its conciliatory character at least on the surface. The Dual Monarchy declared war on Serbia on 28 July, knowing that the war could not be localised but trusting in Germany to hold Russia and France in check.

The uncertain factor in the calculations of the statesmen in July 1914 was the attitude of Great Britain. This was important for Germany, not because of England's military strength – her regular army of 150,000 was too small a factor to carry much weight in the balance – but because it was reckoned in Berlin that without British active support Russia and France might not be willing to risk a war.[3] Hopes that England might after all stay neutral in a continental war had been revived by the improvement in Anglo-German relations since Agadir, despite certain signs to the contrary, such as secret Anglo-Russian naval negotiations in the early summer of 1914. Bethmann Hollweg believed that the British were unlikely to take sides in a dispute arising in the Balkans. The threat of civil war in Ireland was for Germany another favourable circumstance. On the other hand, clear warnings had been given, by both Grey and George V, that if war broke out between Germany and France, England would come to the help of France. Once Russia was involved, France could not stay out, so that the issue for the British would be the balance of power, not the future of Serbia. Nevertheless the prospect of British neutrality would be strengthened if Russia appeared as the aggressor. For Bethmann Hollweg another consideration was at stake. The Social Democrats, whose support was essential in the interests of national unity, would never fight in a quarrel provoked by Austrian aggression, as they declared in a series of demonstrations all over Germany towards the end of July. But a war of defence against Tsarist Russia was a very different matter. It thus suited Bethmann to allow the Russians, whose decision to back Serbia had been known for some time, to declare general mobilisation some twelve hours before Germany did so. In the case of the Socialists, Bethmann's tactics worked; fear of Russia – 'the Cossacks' – was an easily aroused emotion, especially on the left. In the case of Britain it did not, for Russian mobilisation was seen as provoked by German action. Grey however at first believed in German goodwill, and sought to use Berlin to put a brake on Vienna, as he had successfully done during the Balkan wars. On 27 July Grey sent a message to Bethmann Hollweg asking him to restrain Austria, but this time Bethmann forwarded it with the recommendation that it be rejected.[4] Bethmann's duplicity, of which this is only one example, deceived not only the British government but his own Emperor, whose failure of nerve he no doubt foresaw. The German Chancellor's calculation appears to have been that either the determination to stand by Austria would find Russia irresolute and thus lead to a break-up of the Dual Alliance or that, if it came to a general war, Germany and Austria had a reasonable chance of winning it. Like other Germans, he was haunted by the realisation that time was not on their side. In Western Europe Germany had suffered a humiliation at Agadir which must not be repeated. In the Balkans the balance of power had shifted in favour of the Serbs and Russians; even Roumania, nominally linked to the Triple Alliance, was now in the opposite camp. There was talk in Berlin and Vienna of a preventive war, a strike before Russia was prepared, which was assumed to be about the year 1917. 'We are ready, and the sooner it comes the better for us' was the opinion of Moltke, Chief of the German General Staff, on 1 June 1914.[5] Tirpitz, however, was fully conscious that the German navy was not ready for war, despite the completion of the Kiel Canal that summer.[6] Germany's pledge to Austria was defensive in the sense of preserving the *status quo* in the Balkans. But it was characteristic of the confused situation in that part of Europe that on both sides the difference between the offensive and defensive attitudes was blurred. Though Serbia had an obvious interest in altering the *status quo*, Austria's ultimatum to Belgrade gave its policy an offensive character. From London Germany was increasingly seen as using the Serb crisis as the pretext for unleashing a general war.

On 29 July Grey at last came off the fence of neutrality and warned the German Chancellor that, if France became involved in war, Britain would support her. Although the warning was not new, it came as a shock to Bethmann Hollweg, especially as it coincided with news of mobilisation of the British navy. The Kaiser was filled with gloom and denounced British perfidy. Faced with the virtual certainty of British intervention, Bethmann, even at this late stage, could have halted the escalation to war by persuading the Austrian government (which perhaps was not unwilling to be overruled) to stay its hand against Serbia so as to give time for the attempt at mediation to bear fruit. Instead, Bethmann's support of Grey's efforts was still ambiguous and half-hearted; he failed to respond to a personal appeal for restraint from George V. Then came news of Russia's mobilisation, which left Bethmann, as Tirpitz described him, like a drowning man.[7] He admitted to the Prussian cabinet on 30 July that the situation was out of hand, and his own nerve was evidently failing. It was his tragedy, and the world's, that he rejected British overtures which might have provided Austria with an honourable compromise, and perhaps even left Germany in a stronger position by dividing England from France and Russia.[8] But the German view was that no compromise with Serbia was possible, just as Grey, speaking of the German navy felt that there was no halfway house for Britain between safety and ruin. Bethmann's excuse was that once Russia mobilised, Germany was bound to follow suit. But German mobilisation was not just the spontaneous reaction to a Russian threat which Bethmann wished it to appear. He knew that if Austria went to war with Serbia Russia would come to the help of Serbia. On 26 July Moltke was asked to draft an ultimatum to Belgium demanding the right of entry for German troops, and on the following day Admiral von Müller, the head of the Kaiser's Naval Cabinet, wrote in his diary: 'Tendency of our policy: to keep quiet, letting Russia put herself in the wrong, but then not to shrink from war.'[9] Indeed Bethmann himself said on 28 July, according to Riezler, that Russia must be put in the wrong in all circumstances. Historians seem bound to take the view that Bethmann Hollweg's main concern was not to stop the war but to make sure that the blame for it was fixed on Russia. From then on it was the generals who made the running. A special reason for urgency was that Austria adopted a mobilisation plan that gave priority to the Serbian front and thus put a greater military burden on Germany to keep the Russians out of Central Europe.[10] Under irresistible pressure from the General Staff, the German government declared a 'state of war emergency' on 31 July – the recognised prelude to mobilisation – and sent a message to St Petersburg demanding that Russia's mobilisation be revoked. When no satisfactory reply was received, Germany declared war on Russia. It was 5 p.m. on 1 August. About the same time the Kaiser signed the order for German mobilisation. An ultimatum was also despatched to France, where mobilisation had also begun, requiring her to remain neutral and, as a pledge, to hand over to Germany the fortresses of Toul and Verdun for the duration of the war. The

condition was naturally rejected, and two days later a German declaration of war followed. What Gerhard Ritter has described as the
'unbelievable haste' of Germany's final moves was dictated by the requirements of her only plan of campaign for a two-front war, the
blueprint drawn up by Schlieffen and modified by his successor
Moltke.

It was just after the signing of the German mobilisation order that
there occurred the most bizarre episode in the whole sequence of
dramatic events. News reached Berlin from Lichnowsky, the German
ambassador in London, that Britain might after all remain neutral if
France were not attacked. This was followed by a second telegram
from Lichnowsky suggesting that British neutrality might be possible
even if France as well as Russia were involved in war with Germany.
The Kaiser was overjoyed, and called for champagne. But when he
told Moltke, hastily recalled to the Palace, that Germany would have to
scrap the Schlieffen Plan, remain on the defence in the west and
attack in the east, Moltke was flabbergasted. Only a dilettante like
William II could disregard a quarter of a century of military planning
with such levity. With obvious reluctance Moltke agreed that the bulk
of his army might be deployed against Russia, but he insisted that it
must first assemble in the west if chaos was to be avoided. An army
improvised to invade Russia, he told the Kaiser, would be a mob without proper supplies, not a force ready for battle.[11] In view of the political advantages which Germany stood to gain by not attacking in the
west, including, at least initially, British neutrality, the question whether
Moltke was right has been much debated. Was a last minute switch
of one and a half million men and their equipment from west to
east a practical proposition? Groener, who as Director of Railways in
the General Staff was in the best position to judge, subsequently gave
it his opinion that the change could have been made, though he would
not have favoured it because only in the west could the war be decisively won.[12] Both the Kaiser's hopes and Moltke's misgivings were
however soon dissipated by a further message from Lichnowsky
explaining that he had misunderstood Grey earlier in the day and that
British neutrality was unlikely in any circumstances. By this time William had retired for the night, and Moltke was summoned to the
Imperial bedchamber to receive the news. He now knew that he could
go ahead with the plan for the invasion of Luxembourg, already overdue under the Schlieffen Plan. Two other formalities were needed before the rest of the Plan, including the vital right-wing thrust, could
be put into effect: the ultimatum to Belgium, and the declaration of
war on France to make sense of the march through Belgium. Both
were despatched on 3 August. The following day the Chancellor

announced the breach of Belgian and Luxembourg neutrality to an
expectant Reichstag. The last British doubts about joining in the war
quickly vanished. By midnight on 4 August Germany was at war with
the British Empire. The Schlieffen Plan, her only strategic hope, was
her political nemesis: the earlier failure of the civilian authorities to
control the military now exacted its price. On the purely military
plane British intervention caused no immediate worry: Moltke seems
to have given no thought to it, and he did not even consult Tirpitz
about joint military-naval action against England.[13]

The course pursued by the German government between the Sarajevo assassination and the outbreak of general war amounted to an
enormous gamble: in the idiom of a later day, it was an exercise in
brinkmanship. The two main speculations, that Russia (whose stake in
the Balkans, unlike Austria's, was a matter of prestige, not survival)
would recoil rather than fight when it came to the point, and that
England would prefer neutrality to involvement in a continental war,
proved mistaken. Even when all this was clear Bethmann Hollweg,
instead of cutting his losses and making a face-saving retreat, turned
from the diplomatic to the military gamble, the attempt to knock out
France before dealing with an isolated Russia. Germany's adherence
to this policy even when the chances of success were patently diminishing derived from the fear of waiting too long as well as from the self-
confidence and desire to fulfil its 'destiny' of a nation conscious of its
strength. The mercurial Emperor alternated between ill-founded optimism and black despair. The key figure was Bethmann Hollweg,
whose conduct suggests that he was acting out of character. During
his five years as Chancellor Bethmann had gained a reputation for
sobriety and moderation. With his high sense of responsibility he was
anything but a gambler. He had incurred much criticism on the right
for his conciliatory attitude both at home and abroad, his opposition
to Tirpitz and the Navy League and his alleged anglophilia. During
the war he was to be attacked by the same people for his lukewarmness
over annexations and his refusal to allow unrestricted submarine warfare. That such a man, cautious to the point of pedantry, reflective
and scrupulous like the lawyer and official that he was, should have
unleashed a European war, and have used duplicity in doing so, presents a psychological puzzle. Cases occur in history of statesmen who
are normally prudent and restrained being provoked into folly. Part of
the explanation in Bethmann's case may be that his behaviour in July
1914 was shaped by his reaction to previous Balkan crises rather than
by the particular circumstances of that month.[14] Moreover, while conciliatory to England, he was inclined to take a hard line with Russia,
and it was Russia which stood behind Serbia. Kiderlen-Wächter, the

German Foreign Secretary at the time of Agadir, had said in November 1912: 'If ever Austria must fight for her position as a great power, we must stand at her side in order not to have to fight alone afterwards.'[15] This seems to have been Bethmann's view: he had decided to stand firm, and Sarajevo happened to be the crisis where this decision was tested. There was a sense of inevitability in this attitude, as in that of most of Bethmann's opposite numbers in the other capitals of Europe.

Whatever illusions Bethmann may have had about such use of bluff at that time, it was obvious by 29 July that blood was going to be shed since Russian mobilisation virtually made war inevitable. It was then that, as Albertini indicates, Bethmann lacked the audacity to reverse his policy and call the gamble off. By that date the influence of the military was probably too strong. But also a situation had been reached which Riezler, Bethmann's confidential adviser, described as the most dangerous, when a weak government could not resist nationalist pressure because it could not afford loss of face. Bethmann in effect confessed on 30 July that he was being borne along by forces he was unable to control: the calculated risk on which, according to Riezler, he had decided to embark, had become an unmanageable catastrophe.[16] The lack of consistency discernible in Bethmann's moves during this feverish period suggests a certain confusion of purpose. Later in the war, he was to admit that the war was in a sense preventive for Germany. Despite the frequent mention of preventive war, the German government had made none of the preparations in the fields of diplomacy, public relations and economics which a government deliberately planning a war would have undertaken. The declarations of war on Russia and France, which made Germany technically the aggressor, showed clumsiness and lack of forethought. Most of the German leaders, especially the generals, thought them quite unnecessary, a concession to Bethmann's sense of rectitude and the legal pedantry of the Foreign Ministry, which could not imagine invading a country without first being at war with it. The declarations made it easy for Germany's nominal allies, Italy and Roumania, to escape legally from their treaty obligations. As the Kaiser complained, his allies fell away like rotten apples. Italy's declaration of neutrality, which a less offhand treatment by the German and Austrian governments might have prevented, enabled France to use at the Marne 35,000 troops withdrawn from the Italian frontier, while Roumania's neutrality came as a similar relief to Russia.[17] No attempt was made by Bethmann Hollweg to prepare world opinion for the breach of Belgian neutrality, reaction to which in other countries can hardly have come as a complete surprise. According to Erzberger, one of the leaders of the Centre party who was afterwards active in official propaganda, there was no expectation of war in the Foreign Ministry at the end of July, when leading members of the government were still away on holiday.[18] Though it could be argued that the general holiday atmosphere might have been intended to allay suspicion, such an explanation would hardly apply at the end of the month, when war between Austria and Serbia was already a fact. Nor were any economic measures taken against the outbreak of war. Supplies of grain were allowed to be sent to France during July, and when at the end of the month a large business firm asked the Navy Office if several ships carrying fuel oil and destined for England should not be diverted to Germany the reply was that there was no need. There were no stockpiles of saltpetre, copper, nickel and other essential raw materials.[19] Only in the narrowest military sense was Germany ready for war in August 1914, and then only for a short, continental war of the 1870 type. Yet this was the very kind of war which the German government had made impossible by its own strategy. The generals complained that the diplomats, by giving them one unreliable ally against three great powers plus Belgium and Serbia, had set them an impossible task, but the civilians could reply that it was the Schlieffen Plan which had created so unfavourable a balance. How seriously Bethmann Hollweg miscalculated can be shown by one example. During August 1914 he told Tirpitz that the war with England was a thunderstorm which would pass quickly.[20] He could hardly have been more mistaken, as the precedent of Napoleon might have warned him.

(ii) THE SOCIALISTS AND THE PARTY TRUCE

Disastrous as Bethmann Hollweg's diplomacy had been in the last weeks before the outbreak of war, at home he had managed to unite the whole nation behind the government. Von Müller, the head of the Kaiser's Naval Cabinet, wrote on 1 August: 'The mood is brilliant. The government has succeeded very well in making us appear as the attacked.'[21] At first no one was quite sure how the Social Democrats would react. The S.P.D. had repeatedly pledged themselves at meetings of the Second International to oppose war, not only by using the power of the proletariat to prevent its breaking out, but to end it once it had begun. Exactly what this meant was not spelt out, but it was generally understood to imply some kind of strike action or even refusal of military service. During the crisis of July 1914 the German Socialists gave every indication of sticking to their principles. Articles in the party press, speeches, and demonstrations in many parts of the country warned the government in strong language not to support Austrian aggression against Serbia. This was the S.P.D. line as late as

30 July. On 29 July Hugo Haase, co-chairman of the S.P.D. and chairman of its parliamentary party, told a special conference of the Secretariat of the International at Brussels that the German workers would not allow Germany to go to war for the sake of Austria even if Russia intervened. 'Secret treaties', declared Haase confidently, 'do not bind the proletariat.'[22] But when Haase returned to Germany he found the atmosphere transformed by news of Russian mobilisation. Socialists remembered an article by Engels in 1892 prophesying a war between Germany and Austria on the one hand and France and Russia on the other, and pointing out that since compared with Tsarism even Hohenzollern Germany represented enlightenment and progress, it would be the duty of German Socialists to support their country.[23] There was a general understanding in the S.P.D. that a war against Russia was the one war that could be justified. Bethmann Hollweg knew that if Russia could be made to appear the aggressor – which meant if she mobilised before Germany – the Socialists would be unlikely to give any trouble, and he received assurances to this effect from, among others, a member of the S.P.D. executive (Südekum). By 31 July the S.P.D. press was writing resignedly that if after all war came the Socialists would do their duty like other Germans. But up to the last moment the party was uncertain of the government's attitude. On 30 July the party executive met and decided to send two of its members, Ebert (the other co-chairman) and Braun (the treasurer) to Switzerland with the party funds – an admission that they expected to be declared illegal in case of war and were preparing for the kind of persecution experienced under Bismarck. At the same time another member of the executive, Hermann Müller, was despatched to Paris to try and reach agreement with the French Socialist party on a common line of action should war prove inevitable. The whole future of the party now seemed to depend on whether or not it supported the war credits bill for 5 billion marks to be presented to the Reichstag on 4 August.

It was the greatest crisis in the party's history, and an agonising dilemma. It the S.P.D. opposed the credits they would be condemned for disloyalty and for exposing Germany to a Russian invasion, and would become violently unpopular throughout the country. It they voted for the credits they would be going against their most cherished convictions and breaking solemn pledges. Whichever course they took the party would probably split. Yet a decision could not be delayed. On 3 August the parliamentary party or *Fraktion* met to discuss the issue.[24] Most were by now in favour of supporting credits; under the pressure of events and mounting war fever, opinion had hardened behind the right-wing views. A minority still opposed. A third alternative, abstention, was proposed by Kautsky, the party's intellectual mentor, who

was present by invitation. But Kautsky received no backing: the precedent of 1870, when the two Social Democrats in the North German
Reichstag, Bebel and Wilhelm Liebknecht, had abstained from voting
credits for the war against France on the grounds that it was aggressive, had little weight for a party which represented almost a third of
the electorate. The report of Müller, just back from Paris, that the
French Socialists did not intend to oppose credits in their Chamber if
France were attacked showed the collapse of socialist internationalism
and could only discourage the German anti-war group. In the end a
hard core of fourteen left-wingers clung to their conviction that the
party must oppose an imperialist war; but in order to preserve the
appearance of unity before the outside world the dissentients agreed to
vote with the majority in the Reichstag on the following day. This
was on the understanding that their views would be taken into account
in the drafting of a declaration which Haase, as chairman, was to read
aloud at the time of the vote. The declaration was shown beforehand
to the Chancellor, who persuaded the party to omit the final sentence
containing an assurance that if the war became one of conquest for
Germany the Socialists would oppose it. Even the hint of conquests,
Bethmann explained, would upset the British, whose neutrality was
still hoped for; he knew too, that the Conservatives would object to so
explicit a pledge.[25] National solidarity was the demand of the hour. In
his speech from the throne the Kaiser, resplendent in uniform complete with helmet and sword, told the Reichstag assembled for the
occasion in the White Room of the Royal Palace: 'We are not impelled
by any lust of conquest.' In the same address William II roused his
audience to a pitch of excitement and patriotic fervour by declaring
that henceforth he knew of no parties any more, only Germans. It was
an inspired response to the national mood. Perhaps never before, certainly never afterwards, was William to be so genuinely popular. The
government had announced a *Burgfrieden* or party truce. For the first
time the Social Democrats, no longer social pariahs and unpatriotic
scoundrels, could join wholeheartedly with the rest of the nation. They
had done their duty as citizens in supporting a war of defence. The significance of the vote of 4 August was well understood, though in very
different ways. For the left wing it was soon to be denounced as a shameful betrayal of socialist principles. For the reformist right – men such as
Eduard David – it pointed the way to the reconciliation of the party with
the Hohenzollern monarchy which they had long seen as desirable.
Bethmann Hollweg had the satisfaction of gaining Socialist and trade
union backing for a war which he knew could not be won without it.

Yet already there were grounds for doubts about the government's
good faith. It was on the same afternoon that Bethmann Hollweg, also

in uniform, told the Reichstag of the breach of Belgian neutrality, which had occurred some hours before. He candidly admitted the wrong, which he said would be made good when Germany's military goal was reached, and pleaded that no other course of action was possible, quoting the proverb that necessity knows no law. There were no comments or protests, even from the Socialists. Yet only a year before the Secretary of State for foreign affairs, Jagow, had assured party leaders in the Reichstag budget committee that Germany would respect Belgian neutrality in case of war as long as her neighbours did.[26] Now the government asserted that the French had been the first to infringe Belgian neutrality: later it was to claim that captured Belgian documents proved the Belgian government had in fact abandoned neutrality.[27] As far as the Socialists were concerned, there were some twinges of conscience; but most saw the Belgian issue as subordinate to the larger question of war or peace. To Marxists the question of national sovereignty was of little importance by comparison with the clash of rival imperialisms. Since 31 July martial law and military censorship had been in force. German politicians, like the rest of the public, were dependent on government-controlled news and could have little idea of the situation as seen by other countries. The wildest rumours, invented or endorsed by the authorities, of French and Russian attacks on Germany were in circulation, and in the prevailing hysterical mood were eagerly believed. The fear of Russia was real, as well it might be in view of Germany's thin defence force in the east. It was with Russia in mind that Victor Adler, the Austrian Socialist leader declared: 'If I feel the knife at my throat, I must first push away the knife, rather than argue about responsibility.'[28]

The party truce was the German equivalent of the *union sacrée* proclaimed in France at the beginning of the war, and to the sinking of party differences in Britain which led later to the coalition government that eventually included the Labour party. In Germany the Social Democrats ceased to be second-class citizens: they were no longer debarred from civil service and university posts and commissions in the army; the National Association for the Combating of Social Democracy suspended its activity, and socialist newspapers were allowed to circulate in the forces. The trade unions, too, which before the Reichstag vote of 4 August had already decided to support the government, were acclaimed as patriots. 'The workers', declared one of the union leaders on 4 August, 'have more to lose than their chains – their organisation.'[29] The government was aware of the need for trade union co-operation in planning the war economy and expanding production. It was essential to reduce labour disputes to a minimum; strikes had already been made illegal for the duration. Bethmann

Hollweg won the confidence of the trade unions as he had to a large extent won that of the S.P.D. Socialist members of the Reichstag were invited to visit the front and to go on propaganda tours of neutral countries, and party leaders were consulted by the government. There remained two major obstacles to full co-operation between the party and the government: the three-class franchise in Prussia, and the absence of parliamentary government. Bethmann Hollweg had shown before the war his support for franchise reform. In November 1914 his deputy, Secretary of State Clemens von Delbrück, made a speech promising 'reorientation' after the war – a vague phrase, taken to mean liberalisation of the franchise, if not also parliamentary control of the executive. But Bethmann knew that Conservative hostility to constitutional change remained adamant, and he was loth to do anything that would destroy the new and precarious national unity. This policy made sense on the assumption – reasonable on 4 August 1914, less so in November – that the war would be short, the 'thunderstorm' of which the Chancellor had spoken. The question from that autumn onwards was whether the party truce would last indefinitely, in other words, how long the Socialists would support the government if they did not get any of the constitutional concessions to which they believed themselves entitled. Yet important as the franchise issue was for the party, the question of annexations became even more so as the government abandoned its purely defensive position of August 1914. While the S.P.D. officially condemned annexations, the right-wing parties demanded them. These conflicting pressures killed the *Burgfrieden*. Within the S.P.D. the strains between right and left, only temporarily stilled by the euphoria of 4 August, soon reopened with fresh intensity.

(iii) THE DRAMA OF THE MARNE

The German army that took the field in August 1914 has been described as the most brilliant that the world had seen.[30] Its superiority lay not in numbers – the French mobilised nearly as many men as Germany deployed in the West, not to mention the six Belgian and seven British divisions – but in planning, organisation and training. Mobilisation was carried out with clockwork precision. Of the seven armies grouped along Germany's western border, five were to take part in the massive sweep that was to overrun Belgium and invade France from the north, with the object of enveloping the French armies from the rear. The two other German armies were to defend South Germany against the expected French offensive into Alsace-Lorraine. The conquest of Belgium presented few difficulties, once the initial obstacle, the city of Liège with its twelve forts, had been overcome. This was a feat accomplished almost single-handed by Major-General Ludendorff, the former Chief of the Operations Section of the General Staff who, temporarily attached to Bülow's Second Army, displayed the ruthless energy that was soon to make his name a household word. Yet the march through Belgium was far from the walkover that some had imagined. The Belgian army, before being pressed back into the fortress of Antwerp, fought hard, and the invaders also suffered casualties from *franc-tireurs*. For the Germans losses were less important than speed. Brussels was reached by 20 August. From there von Kluck's First Army wheeled south-west on a course originally destined to take it west of Paris before turning east to surround the French forces. The French, who set their hopes on an offensive in Alsace-Lorraine, were almost wholly unprepared for the Schlieffen strategy, although the plan had been betrayed by a German officer some time before.[31] But the French General Staff did not believe that the Germans would be capable of reinforcing their right wing in such strength, and had to adjust themselves as best they could to the onslaught from the north. According to Schlieffen the German First Army should have been in or level with Paris by the fortieth day after mobilisation. By the thirty-second day (2 September) it was in Senlis, twenty-five miles north-east of Paris, which had been evacuated by the French government and by a large proportion of its inhabitants.

At this moment Moltke made two vital decisions. He issued a general directive ordering an offensive on the entire front, the object being to take advantage of the retreating and, as he believed, disorganised French by bringing the German left wing into play in a pincer movement designed to reproduce a second Sedan. This was a modification of the Schlieffen Plan, which had presupposed a mainly passive left wing acting as a pivot against which the right would execute its gigantic wheel. Moltke's second decision, which was really wished on him by the eager and impetuous Kluck, was that instead of including Paris in the German sweep, with Kluck's army passing west of the city, the German right would swerve south-east and pass east of Paris to link up with the other armies driving south-east across the French lines. This further change of the Schlieffen strategy was dictated by fear lest, as the German armies fanned out on their march deeper into France, the gaps between them would become too wide. But although this risk was averted by a reduction of the area to be enveloped, another danger was created, for Kluck now had on his right flank the armed fortress of Paris and north of Paris a new French army under Maunoury. To meet this threat Moltke ordered his entire army to halt, and the First and Second Armies (Kluck and Bülow) to stand guard against Maunoury. Thus for the first time the Germans lost the initiative. Kluck, who had raced ahead of Bülow and was due east of Paris across the Marne, had to withdraw quickly and engage with Maunoury on his right. But in doing so he failed to close the gap between himself and Bülow into which the small but efficient British Expeditionary Force thrust itself – the first advance after the long retreat. At the same time Joffre, judging that his moment had come, ordered a general offensive against the German armies strung out like a drooping sack between the two French-held strong points of Verdun and Paris. This was the battle of the Marne, which, as Liddell Hart wrote, was a psychological more than a physical victory. Though it would be wrong to deny Joffre the credit for the reward for his cool nerves and strategic skill, the fact remains that the Marne was lost by the Germans rather than won by the French. Small as was the fighting involved, the Marne was the decisive event of the war. Its loss by Germany meant the failure of the Schlieffen Plan, the end of any prospect of a short war (the only kind Germany was equipped to win) and the beginning of attrition and siege warfare. After the Marne came the attempt by each side to outflank the other, the halt of the German drive to the Channel ports, and the hardening of the front into two parallel and continuous lines of trenches, between 30 and 800 yards apart, from the North Sea to Switzerland. Yet even if the battle of the Marne had gone the other way, it is not certain that Germany would have won the campaign, if only because of shortage of supplies. Moreover French morale was far from crumbling. If she had managed to defeat the French Germany would still have been unable to subjugate England. Without air strength and faced by a still potentially formidable Russia, William II would have been in a less favourable position than Hitler in 1940, or even than Napoleon in 1805.

The reasons for the German failure on the Marne have been much discussed.[32] Moltke, who was on the verge of collapse during the whole campaign, was an obvious scapegoat. As Schlieffen's successor as Chief of the General Staff he had modified the original plan by reducing the proportion of troops on the right wing. This, in retrospect, was the fatal change, though one for which justification could be found in the increased strength of the French and Russian armies since Schlieffen's day. His decision at the end of August to order a general offensive instead of concentrating his effort on the right wing, and his withdrawal from that vital wing of two army corps to reinforce the slender defences of East Prussia (they arrived too late to be used at Tannenberg) were errors of judgement. Other opportunities of striking a decisive blow were missed. It was not Moltke's fault that the French were able to dispose of troops which would have stayed to defend the Italian border had Italy not declared her neutrality. But there is no doubt that Moltke was badly out of touch. His headquarters, first at Coblenz, then at Luxemburg, was too far from the scene of battle to enable him to grasp what was going on or keep a firm grip on his commanders. His orders tended to be irresolute and out of date. Kluck was too impetuous, Bülow too sluggish. The growing distances between the advancing German armies made communications more difficult, both between themselves and with the High Command. The sending of messages by wireless did not function well, and the field telephone system was useless over long distances.[33] The sheer exhaustion of the German troops, especially of the footsore right wing which had been marching for weeks in sweltering heat and, in the absence of functioning railways, had outrun their supplies, was a major factor. 'The men stagger forward', wrote one of Kluck's officers on 2 September, 'their faces coated with dust, their uniforms in rags, looking like living scarecrows. They march with their eyes closed, singing in chorus so that they shall not fall asleep . . . It is only the delirium of victory which sustains our men, and, in order that their bodies may be as intoxicated as their souls, they drink to excess, but this drunkenness keeps them going.'[34] The French, despite their long retreat, showed a resilience and offensive spirit which took the Germans by surprise, and Joffre was helped by good communications and railways. But the crucial factor was neither the shortcomings of Moltke nor the errors of individual commanders, but the insufficiency of German numbers for so ambitious a strategy. Schlieffen himself once admitted that the Plan needed eight additional army corps. The heavier than expected casualties in Belgium and the need to guard supply routes and contain the Belgian army in Antwerp reduced the total of men at the Marne, and in any case the Aachen-Liège bottleneck into Belgium was too narrow a base for deployment on such a scale. No doubt if Moltke had been more confident, less highly strung and in better health, the outcome might have been different. Moltke lost his nerve: Joffre did not. The French often spoke of the miracle of the Marne. It would have been a greater miracle if the Schlieffen Plan had come off. It was a gamble whose chances of success were never high. As Groener wrote to his wife in January 1915, on the Marne the German army had run out of breath.

(iv) FALKENHAYN: EAST FRONT OR WEST FRONT

The first consequence of the Marne defeat was a change in the German High Command. Moltke, who had suffered a nervous breakdown – he had never recovered from the shock of the Kaiser's sudden change of plans on the evening of 1 August – was quickly replaced as Chief of Staff by Erich von Falkenhayn, the Prussian general who

since 1913 had been Minister of War. Considerably younger than
Moltke, fitter and less temperamental, Falkenhayn with his alert good
looks and reputation for efficiency at first revived faltering confidence
in G.H.Q. Falkenhayn was one of the few senior staff officers who
knew the outside world – he had spent seven years as a military instructor and staff officer in China. While far from sharing the pessimism of
Moltke, he was sober and realistic in his assessment of Germany's
chances, and did not believe she could win a war of attrition, though
she might avoid defeat. According to Erzberger, he declared on taking
over his new post that the war was lost, but Groener, speaking to
Falkenhayn in the middle of December after the disappointments of
the autumn campaign, found him still hopeful.[35] Privately many leading Germans were doubtful whether Germany, with so vulnerable an
ally as Austria, was capable of defeating two continental great powers
and a maritime world power, but such misgivings could not be
expressed in public. The German people had not been told the truth
about the Marne, and were still intoxicated by the successes reported
during the first weeks of the war.[36] While the battle of the Marne still
hung in the balance the Chancellor had turned down a tentative offer
from the United States government to mediate a peace with France
that would have left the pre-war frontier unchanged but allowed
Germany to claim a war indemnity and any French colonies she
pleased.[37] To a country in occupation of nearly the whole of Belgium
and almost a tenth of France, including the richest industrial areas,
this did not seem an attractive proposition. Elated by the victory of
Tannenberg in East Prussia, still confident of being able to break
through in the west, and pressed by patriotic societies, industrialists
and intellectuals to whom any return to the *status quo ante bellum* was
unthinkable, the German government abandoned the purely defensive
aims professed in its Reichstag statement of 4 August and privately,
though not yet publicly, came down in favour of territorial annexations, many of which were described as guarantees against future
attack.

When Falkenhayn took over his new command on 14 September,
the situation in the west was not, perhaps, irretrievable.[38] Had he followed the advice of Groener, his Director of Railways, he would have
pulled back his entire army for regrouping, and built up a stronger
right wing with which to renew the Schlieffen strategy of envelopment.
The operation would have taken a fortnight, but, in Groener's view,
would have enabled him to advance as far as the mouth of the Somme.
Falkenhayn, however, refused to retreat further, believing that it
would be misunderstood, and was thus unable to reinforce his right
wing in sufficient strength. His attack, when it came, was spread over

three sections of the front and therefore ineffective. The German right wing, exhausted by a gruelling campaign, weakened by losses and short of ammunition, was no longer capable of the same effort as at the outbreak of the war. Falkenhayn too had other things on his mind. The Austrians, who had been promised the transfer to the east of the bulk of the German army by mid-September – six weeks after the beginning of hostilities – were crying out for help. The crucial decision facing Falkenhayn was whether to continue the main effort in the west, or, as many advocated, to transfer troops to the eastern front, where – judging by Tannenberg – prospects of success were brighter. As a convinced 'westerner' Falkenhayn believed that it would be wrong to strive for cheap victories in the east at the expense of the west, the only decisive sector. France, backed by England, would stay in the war even if Russia was beaten. In a desperate effort to break through in the west, Falkenhayn turned a deaf ear to appeals from the east and used his reserves in an attack along the river Yser and against the Ypres salient, with the intention of capturing the ports of Calais, Boulogne and Dunkirk. These ports could easily have been captured in August had the Germans so decided, for the British had evacuated the whole coast as far as Le Havre, and German Uhlans had roamed at will over the north-west of France.[39] The first battle of Ypres (October–November 1914) as this engagement is usually known, was a costly failure, symbolic of the deadlock in the west and the forerunner of other futile, and still bigger blood baths in the Flanders mud. The German army was already handicapped by the loss of many of its best men, and Falkenhayn had to send into the holocaust thousands of half-trained volunteers straight from school or university, commanded by elderly officers. Enthusiastically singing *Deutschland, Deutschland über Alles*, the youngsters were mown down in swathes by the expert marksmen of the B.E.F. 'It was madness', in the words of one British historian, 'to send these lads into action.'[40] Falkenhayn's reputation never recovered from this *Kindermord* or massacre of the innocents. He was also blamed for wasting troops in Flanders who were needed in the east. Falkenhayn can hardly be faulted with having tried to reach a decision in the west before the Allies were reinforced by Kitchener's new levies: it was unfortunate – a measure of the lack of co-ordination between east and west – that Hindenburg simultaneously started an offensive in Poland for which the necessary reserves were lacking. On the day (18 November) that Falkenhayn called off the Ypres battle he admitted to Bethmann Hollweg that victory on both main fronts was no longer within Germany's capacity, and was ready to draw the depressing conclusion that she must be satisfied with a modest peace.[41] He wanted Germany to put out peace feelers. Bethmann Hollweg too could see no end of the war except the exhaustion of both sides and a stalemate. (This did not prevent him from advocating annexations in an open or veiled form). Such views were defeatist, in fact treason, to the new commanders in the east, Hindenburg and Ludendorff.

It was his relations with these two men that constituted Falkenhayn's second main problem. At the beginning of the war the Russian 'steamroller', in which the Allies had great faith, was to roll into Germany to relieve the pressure on France. (Steamroller, though hardly an apt metaphor for an army of peasants notoriously short of mechanised equipment, suggested a sheer weight of manpower, which the Russians certainly had.) The Germans had calculated that the Russian army would take two months to mobilise, by which time France would have been defeated and Germany would be ready for it. In fact Russian mobilisation proved speedier, and by the middle of August, despite material shortages – the army had fewer than 700 motor vehicles of all kinds[42] – it was able to take the offensive both in Galicia, where the Austrians had been badly defeated, and in East Prussia. Heavily outnumbered, the German Eighth Army on the eastern border of East Prussia fell back against the Russian First Army under Rennenkampf, and to avoid being cut off by another Russian army advancing from the south (Samsonov) contemplated withdrawal from the whole province. Moltke now intervened, deposed the army commander, Prittwitz, and appointed in his place Hindenburg, who at the age of 67 was called out of retirement to rescue the fatherland – appropriately he was himself an East Prussian – with the help of Ludendorff, the hero of Liège, who became his Chief of Staff with the title of Quartermaster-General. Working largely with plans drawn up by Colonel Hoffmann, the Chief of Operations Staff of the Eighth Army, the new duumvirate defeated the army of Samsonov at the battle known as Tannenberg in belated revenge for the victory of the Poles and Lithuanians over the Teutonic Knights 500 years before.[43] Tannenberg was a crushing success, in which over 90,000 prisoners were taken. A few days later Rennenkampf's army was routed in the battle of the Masurian Lakes and East Prussia was temporarily freed. Enthusiasm for the victorious generals knew no bounds, and the legend of their invincibility was born. The two were a striking contrast in style and character. Hindenburg was solid, imperturbable, patrician. A veteran of the war of 1866 and 1870, with his square skull, massive neck and handle-bar moustache, he was a decent incarnation of the Prussian military tradition, a father figure whose effigy in wood was displayed in public squares to have nails driven into it by donors to war charities. Hindenburg was to remain a national monument to the end of his life. The much younger Ludendorff was restless, excitable, a man of inexhaustible energy and consuming ambition. His brash manner, often accompanied by a scowl in the pudgy face, suggested a resentful temperament, connected perhaps with the fact that his family had come down in the world through impoverishment. Ludendorff lacked a sense of proportion, and his nationalism was of the neurotic kind that foreshadowed the racial extravagances of the Third Reich. In later years Ludendorff under the influence of his second wife was to belong to the lunatic fringe of German politics. Before the war he had tried unsuccessfully to persuade the General Staff, to which he belonged, to raise the strength of the army by five army corps instead of the two sanctioned by the act of 1913. This was a decision which the military authorities had cause to regret at the battle of the Marne; the reason for it was also significant – reluctance to dilute the aristocratic Officers' Corps with middle-class recruits.[44] In his indifference to the aristocratic ideal Ludendorff also anticipated the future, just as Hindenburg represented the past. Both men had qualities the other lacked, and though Hindenburg, who had greatness thrust upon him, shone only in conjunction with his dynamic colleague, his strong nerves and unruffled manner were a necessary antidote to Ludendorff's excitability. Both became folk heroes, with a prestige far exceeding that of any other German general. Falkenhayn would have been less than human if he had not been envious of them, and the inconclusive argument between easterners and westerners acquired the character of a bitter personal rivalry. The spirit of the blessed Schlieffen, wrote Groener, which had obviously eluded the western commanders, and most of all the High Command, was with Hindenburg and Ludendorff.[45] The difference in success between the fronts owed more to the Russians' technological backwardness: the Germans were able to read the Russians' wireless messages, which were sent uncoded, and so to anticipate their movements; the Germans too had reconnaissance aircraft, a new weapon whose importance was to grow rapidly. The Russian army reflected a more primitive economy and a less organised society.

Between East Prussia in the north and Galicia in the south lay Russian Poland, a large salient thrust into the curve of Germany's eastern border. There a Russian army threatened the industrial province of Upper Silesia. Hindenburg's Ninth Army had intrepidly advanced towards Warsaw in the early autumn, but fell back quickly before superior numbers, destroying the railway line as it did so. To forestall a Russian attack Hindenburg went forward again early in November, though the reinforcements for which he had asked Falkenhayn did not arrive in time to influence the battle. Falkenhayn's critics claimed that had the four army corps in question been at Hindenburg's disposal earlier they would have enabled him to end the campaign and remove the Russian threat to Germany altogether.[46] Even so, the Russians were defeated and forced back to a line east of Lodz. The wrangle between easterners and westerners did not augur well for the future of the German army, and was embarrassing to the Chancellor. The easterners had cogent arguments. The most important was the need to rescue Austria, whose army had lost 1·6 million men by February 1915. The Austrians felt let down because, contrary to promise, the bulk of the German army had not been thrown against Russia two months after the outbreak of war. The multi-national state already showed signs of disintegration: thousands of Czechs and Roumanians in the Habsburg army had already gone over to the Russians. The loss of Galicia exposed the heart of the Empire to Russian attack, plans were made for the royal family to leave Vienna for Salzburg, and there was even talk of the Austrians having to make a separate peace. They had twice failed even to conquer Serbia, for the sake of which they had gone to war, and the Germans saw the necessity of sending troops to occupy at least the strip of Serb territory that lay between Austria-Hungary and Bulgaria so as to open the road to Turkey. Turkey, Germany's new ally, was desperately short of munitions, and these could be supplied only through friendly territory. German success in Europe might encourage Bulgaria to join her (as was to happen in September 1915), and to discourage other neutrals (Italy, Roumania – a vain hope) from siding with the Allies. Finally it was argued that Germany could be strong enough to break through in the west only if she was first victorious in the east.

During the winter of 1914–15, by which time both armies in the east were digging in – though the armies in the east never became so trench-bound as those in the west – the hostility between Hindenburg–Ludendorff and Falkenhayn came to a head. The two eastern commanders ('*Oberost*') who thought little of Falkenhayn's strategic talents suspected him of disbelief in total victory (which was true) and of wanting to 'spare' the Russian army (which was not). Hoffmann, the Chief of Staff of the *Oberost* team, wrote in his diary in December 1914: 'The method of conducting the war in the west terrifies me. Falkenhayn is the evil angel of our fatherland, and, unfortunately, he has His Majesty in his pocket.'[47] Without consulting Falkenhayn, Hindenburg, now in control of the whole German eastern front, promised the Austrian Commander-in-Chief, Conrad von Hoetzendorff, to send several German divisions to the Carpathian front, where they would form a new Austro-German 'southern army'. Falkenhayn thereupon made Ludendorff the new army's Chief of Staff to the commander, General von Linsingen. Hindenburg, who relied heavily on Ludendorff, protested angrily, threatened to resign, and demanded Falkenhayn's dismissal – an odd act of insubordination from so traditional a Prussian officer.[48] Hindenburg was quite willing to become Chief of the General Staff himself if he could take Ludendorff with him. This dispute was referred to the Kaiser, who liked Falkenhayn but detested the arrogant Ludendorff. In the end a compromise was reached: Falkenhayn stayed as Chief of Staff but gave up the Ministry of War, Ludendorff remained with the Ninth Army under Hindenburg, and more reinforcements were sent to the east. Bethmann Hollweg wrote in 1916: 'We risk losing the war strategically with Falkenhayn, politically with Ludendorff.'[49] In was unfortunate for Germany that Ludendorff was not Chief of the General Staff early in the war, when there was a chance of victory, instead of towards the end, when it was almost unattainable. Falkenhayn, a less gifted soldier, had sounder political judgement, and might have accepted a negotiated peace in 1917, to which Ludendorff was totally opposed.

(v) THE WAR AT SEA: THE U-BOAT QUESTION

Nowhere did Germany's performance fall short of her hopes more than in the war at sea, to which the prospect of a long and exhausting struggle gave added significance. Here too the demands of the technical experts (real and imagined) were to override the politicians' scruples with fatal results. Germany had expected a British blockade, but one that would be enforced near her coast, so that the new and still untried German fleet, anxious to show its capabilities but still somewhat in awe of the legendary and much larger British navy, would be able to challenge the latter under relatively favourable conditions.[50] Instead, the British blockade operated at a distance: the exits from the North Sea were controlled and mined, with special submarine traps in the English Channel. To escape possible danger from German mines and submarines the British Grand Fleet was prudently withdrawn to Scapa Flow, its base in the Orkneys (and even, for a time, to the still more remote Galway in Ireland). From harbours along the east and south coasts, British cruisers, torpedo boats and minesweepers kept a constant watch for any sign of German activity. They watched, on the whole, in vain. A few German cruisers at sea when war was declared created a stir by destroying a good deal of Allied shipping in different parts of the world before they themselves were rounded up and sunk. Apart from a few isolated forays by German submarines, British shipping was hardly interfered with, nor was any attempt made to disrupt the flow of men and materials across the

Channel. The High Seas Fleet stayed in port. The war had disproved the two assumptions of Tirpitz's naval policy: the German navy had not deterred England from going to war, and the battleships, into which so much of Germany's effort and expenditure had gone, were of no practical use. With 24 dreadnoughts in the North Sea against 16 German, and twice as many cruisers and torpedo boats, Britain's margin of strength was decisive. The Kaiser and his naval advisers (except Tirpitz, whose advice was ignored) could hardly risk a major battle; they were anxious to preserve the German fleet, if only to strengthen their diplomacy when the time came for peace negotiations. Even during the war their navy was not entirely idle: it protected the German coast, patrolled the Baltic, prevented Russia from receiving supplies from her allies, and safeguarded the iron ore which Germany imported from Sweden. But these objectives could have been attained with a smaller force. The failure of the High Seas Fleet to play a more adventurous role was a bitter disappointment to Tirpitz, who was now an angry and frustrated old man. As Minister of Marine he was present at G.H.Q., but his views were discredited and he was not made chief of the naval staff as he had hoped.[51] He felt that his life's work had been wasted. In vain did Tirpitz blame Bethmann Hollweg for alleged anglophilia and Admiral von Pohl, the Chief of the Naval Staff and later Commander-in-Chief of the navy, for timidity. A cruiser battle with the British off Heligoland at the end of August in which the Germans lost three ships did not encourage the taking of risks. Not until January 1916 was Tirpitz's offensive spirit reflected in the naval command, when Scheer, a man of bolder ideas, replaced Pohl as Commander-in-Chief. Scheer's policy was to send his cruisers out into the North Sea with the object of provoking the British to fight. He also extended the raids made by German cruisers on the British East coast in the course of which civilians were killed; like the Zeppelin raids, such attacks did negligible damage to the war effort but roused popular indignation against the 'shameless Hun'. It was after one of these naval raids that the two main fleets clashed off the west coast of Denmark in what became known as the battle of Jutland or Skagerrak. Despite superior numbers, the British suffered about twice as much in casualties and ships as their opponents. The Germans proved to have better gunnery, stronger armour and in some respects greater tactical skill. The Nelson tradition was tarnished, and Jellicoe, Commander of the Grand Fleet, was criticised for excessive caution. But strategically the battle made no difference. The High Seas Fleet went back to port and stayed there: the British kept their stranglehold.

For some time German naval thinking had been turning to the submarine as the only means of retaliation. As early as November

1914 Tirpitz in an interview with an American journalist had hinted at a submarine campaign to starve out Britain.[52] In February 1915 the German government declared the waters round the British Isles a war zone, in which it would sink without warning neutral as well as Allied passenger and merchant ships. Like the British blockade, which involved stopping and searching neutral vessels and removing contraband of war (of which there was an agreed definition in international law), this move caused great annoyance to neutral countries including the United States. The British reaction was to tighten the blockade by reducing or abolishing the existing distinction between contraband and other types of goods destined for the enemy. Finally Germany ceased to receive extra supplies of goods via neutral ports. In July 1916 England and France formally abrogated their adherence to the Declaration on War at Sea signed in London in 1909. Both the Allies and Germany were in breach of international law, but the German embargo hit America harder in two ways: it affected a much higher proportion of her traffic because she did much more trade with the Allies than with Germany, and it involved the loss of lives as well as property at sea. The Germans' threat was, in any case, premature because at the time they had only twenty-one submarines, most of very limited range, and of these only a third could be in operation at any one time.[53] (Not one of the submarines was capable of making the voyage round the British Isles.) These facts were not, however, made known to the Chancellor, nor was he told that it took two years to build a submarine and another three months to test it.[54] Public opinion in Germany had already begun to see the risks of American hostility. The most famous victim of the new policy was the Cunard liner, the *Lusitania*, which was torpedoed off the Irish coast in May 1915 with the loss of nearly 1,200 lives including 128 American men, women and children. The American public was furious, and President Wilson curtly informed the German government that he would hold them strictly responsible for any further loss of American life and property. The German government (which had actually struck a medal to commemorate the sinking) alleged that the *Lusitania* had been armed as a cruiser and was carrying munitions (which was true); also a warning had been given before she left New York. In German eyes the United States had already compromised its neutrality by supplying the Allies with loans, arms and supplies on a massive scale. Nevertheless Germany could not afford to lose American goodwill at a time when several neutrals, including Italy, looked like joining her enemies. U-boat commanders received instructions to sink ships only when they could be identified as hostile, and not to attack passenger or American ships. Bethmann Hollweg was between two fires. If he did not go some way to meet Wilson he ran the risk of American intervention; if he went too far, he would nullify the effect of the whole submarine campaign, which would become a farce. Tirpitz continued to urge maximum use of the U-boat, which he alleged would terrify neutrals and force England to submit in six weeks. It was in vain that Ballin, who probably knew more about British shipping than anyone else in Germany, warned the Kaiser: 'At least 200 overseas ships enter English ports a day and as many leave them. We can annoy England but we certainly cannot force her to make peace by sinking 30 or 40 ships a day.'[55] The Kaiser too knew that England would fight to the last breath rather than capitulate. But Germany's failure to win the war on land reinforced the arguments for an all-out effort by sea. This was also the opinion of the naval chiefs. After Jutland Scheer was to report to the Kaiser:

> There can be no doubt that even the most successful result of a high seas battle will not compel England to seek peace. The disadvantages of our military-geographical position compared with that of the island kingdom cannot be offset by our fleet to the extent that we can master the blockade or the island itself . . . A victorious end of the war in the foreseeable future can be attained only by the destruction of British economic life, that is through the use of the submarine against English commerce.[56]

Britain's immense geographical advantage was a factor of which Tirpitz had taken too little account. She was able to dominate, at least on the surface, both exits from the North Sea, the twenty odd miles across the Channel and the three hundred miles between Scotland and Norway.

While England steadily tightened the blockade, pressure for unrestricted submarine warfare (meaning the torpedoing of ships without warning) grew stronger in Germany where it was supported by Holtzendorff, the new Chief of the Naval Staff, and by public opinion including the Reichstag majority. At the end of 1915 Falkenhayn, who had hitherto sided with Bethmann Hollweg in opposing it, changed his mind. It was, he now believed, the only way in which England, Germany's strongest and most elusive enemy, could be defeated; but he also intended to use U-boats to provoke a British attack in Flanders to coincide with his planned assault on Verdun. He believed that he would be able to break through the new British levies and thus turn the war again into one of movement. It was doubtful how long the Kaiser would be able to resist the demand for an all-out U-boat campaign, backed as it was by the so-called experts as well as by most of the parties and right-wing pressure groups. Bethmann himself remained sceptical of the admirals' assurance that Germany had enough submarines to force a British surrender within a few months, just as he could not share their under-estimate of the United States. Another reason for not wanting to worsen relations with the latter was the possibility that Wilson might act as a mediator in peace talks. In vain Bethmann warned party leaders in the Reichstag that war with the U.S.A. and the neutral world would be Germany's ruin: 'They'll destroy us like a mad dog.'[57] With some difficulty he settled for a compromise: only armed enemy ships would be sunk anywhere without warning, and in British waters only enemy merchant ships, not passenger ones. This formula did not satisfy the U-boat extremists, including Tirpitz, who resigned (March 1916). In the same month the inadvertent sinking by a German submarine of a French Channel steamer, the *Sussex*, with the loss of American lives caused a new crisis in German-American relations. A note from Washington threatened to break off relations unless German policy changed. It took all Bethmann's political skill to pacify Washington while resisting mounting pressure at home; he had to promise Wilson that in future no merchant ships at all would be sunk without giving a warning and a chance for the passengers and crew to escape.[58] At the same time he vainly urged Wilson to press the British to relax their blockade of Germany, failing which he reserved freedom of action.

The last chance – always slight – that the U-boat question would be settled in a way that would achieve results without provoking America to war virtually disappeared when, at the end of August 1916, Falkenhayn was replaced as Chief of the General Staff by Hindenburg, with Ludendorff as the real boss. Once the over-mighty generals were in control, it was only a matter of time before they would force Bethmann Hollweg to abandon his objections to unrestricted submarine warfare.

(vi) FALKENHAYN: BETWEEN VICTORY AND STALEMATE

In the spring of 1915 Germany's prospects seemed gloomy. The Russian army, in possession of Galicia, presented a standing threat to the heart of the Habsburg Monarchy, whose weakness as an ally had been exposed by defeat in the first weeks of the war. Italy, where public opinion clamoured for intervention on the side of the Allies, was still hesitating. But although the Austrians, under German pressure, promised her territory in return for continued neutrality, the Entente was able to offer her a much bigger bribe, and by April it was fairly clear to the Central Powers that Italy would join their enemies. In the same month the British landed in Gallipoli, where they all but managed to eject the Turks and capture the Straits; if they had been successful they would have knocked Turkey out of the war and have been able to send supplies to Russia. Falkenhayn remained convinced that the western theatre of war was the only decisive one, but he saw that in the coming months Germany's major effort would have to be made in the east. Only in this way could Austrian morale and security be restored, Turkey heartened, and the wavering Balkan neutrals, especially Roumania, dissuaded from joining the Entente. Plans were drawn up for a joint Austro-German offensive against Russia, with Austrian troops for the first time under German command (General von Mackensen). It was a bold project, for it involved stripping the western front (where the Germans were now outnumbered by half a million men) of all but the minimum needed to hold it against expected French and British attacks. It also ignored the possibility of an attack on Austria in case Italy declared war, as she did on 24 May. Mackensen's offensive began at Gorlice between the Carpathians and the Vistula at the beginning of May and was an immediate success. The Russians were thrown back in depth, and their front further north in central Poland became a salient. The Germans now attacked this salient from north and south in a pincer movement which forced its occupants to a headlong retreat which, with its scorched earth policy, was reminiscent of 1812. Warsaw fell on 4 August, and beyond that the Germans pushed on to the railway junction of Brest Litovsk 125 miles further east. Opposite East Prussia the Germans also gained territory and captured the town of Vilna on the main railway line between Warsaw and St Petersburg. The Russians' new front in September 1915, when their retreat had ended, ran south-east from Riga (still in Russian hands) to Dvinsk, and thence almost due south to Czernowitz on the Roumanian border. At some points the line lay 300 miles east of where it had been before the offensive; and Courland, central Poland and Galicia were now under German control. It was a notable victory and Falkenhayn's greatest achievement, but his critics, including the commanders on the eastern front, were convinced that it could have been more complete and indeed decisive for the East had they been given the reinforcements to capture Vilna earlier in the summer and cut off the Russian army's retreat. Falkenhayn had his reasons for not wanting to commit too many troops to the Vilna attack: he had to keep reserves to plug any gaps on the western front, where a French offensive in Champagne was to cause moments of great anxiety, and he had to be ready to aid Austria on her new Italian front. He was also chary of becoming too involved in so vast and inhospitable a country as Russia: the precedents of Charles XII and Napoleon were hardly encouraging.

The victory in the East revived the prestige of the Central Powers in the Balkans, where Roumania did not dare declare war on Austria despite her obvious desire for Transylvania, and Bulgaria moved closer to Germany. In return for a promise of Macedonia (which Bulgaria had gained in the first and lost in the second Balkan war), and other Serb territory, with a prospect of more to come if Roumania or Greece attacked her, Bulgaria agreed to join the German alliance, making it quadruple. Her army was needed to take part in the conquest of Serbia which was the next item on Falkenhayn's agenda, for only through Serb territory could munitions be sent to Turkey. Two attempts by Austria alone earlier in the war to subjugate Serbia had humiliatingly failed. In the autumn of 1915 Serbia finally fell to an attack from three sides in which a quarter of a million troops took part. The Allies were doing everything to 'persuade' Greece, the ally of Serbia, to enter the war, and landed troops in Salonika near the Bulgarian frontier. The result was the opening of the Salonika front, an operation which brought no military advantage to the Entente, since the Bulgarian troops tied down there would not have fought elsewhere, unlike the Allied troops facing them.

Falkenhayn could look back on the year 1915 with some satisfaction. The Russian armies had been greatly weakened and pushed back so that they no longer constituted a threat to Germany; the Serb army had been eliminated, and German domination established everywhere in the Balkan countries except Greece; and all Allied attacks on the western front had been repulsed. In Gallipoli the Turks with German help had defeated the Allied invaders, and the threat to the Straits had disappeared. Germany was able to send supplies to Turkey through Bulgaria, and a Turkish force actually went north to fight on the eastern front against Russia. The Italians had made no progress against the Austrians, who had their backs to the Alps. Yet none of these successes could be turned to political advantage. Falkenhayn hoped for separate peace with Russia for which he was willing to forego territorial gains. The German government had put out peace feelers to Russia in the summer through the King of Denmark, but the Tsar did not respond.[59] He stood by his promise to the Allies in September 1914 not to make a separate peace, in return for which Russia would receive Constantinople and the Straits when the war was won. The loss of territories mainly non-Russian in population was not decisive. So it seemed to Falkenhayn that he must turn once again to the west if the war was to be ended. An all-out attack must be launched on France, England's 'continental sword', whose collapse, combined with a U-boat campaign against Britain, might make both countries ready for peace. The Germans believed that France, after her severe losses, was near the end of her reserves – a calculation which overlooked the half a million or so of French colonial troops. The object of German strategy was to force the French to use up the last of their manpower, and the place chosen, the fortress of Verdun, was one where they would fight and die rather than retreat.

The battle of Verdun, which was for many Frenchmen and Germans the most traumatic experience of the war, began on 21 February 1916, and went on, with varying degrees of intensity, until the end of the year. For the defenders Verdun became a symbol of the will to resist, a touchstone of French morale. French losses were enormous, as Falkenhayn had calculated, but German losses too mounted horribly; and his claim that for five French casualities there were only two German is not borne out by statistics. The long-term effects of this blood-letting on the French army were admittedly serious, and included the mutinies in the spring of 1917; but the German army was too weakened to take advantage of them. Morally the French were victorious since Verdun was held. The costly and inconclusive battle was fatal to Falkenhayn's prestige and also involved him in another dispute with the Chancellor. Bethmann was annoyed to be told by Falkenhayn that Verdun failed because it was not accompanied, as Falkenhayn had assumed, by unrestricted submarine warfare against England. Falkenhayn went so far as to offer the Kaiser his resignation, which was refused. He did not believe that Germany's allies were capable of carrying on beyond the autumn of 1916 – this was some justification for desperate measures such as submarine ruthlessness. Bethmann Hollweg was more concerned not to provoke American intervention. Verdun had a sobering effect on the Kaiser, who told von Müller, the Chief of his Naval Cabinet: 'One must never utter it, nor shall I admit it to Falkenhayn, but this war will not end with a great victory.'⁶⁰ Soundings were taken in Switzerland to find out if the French were ready to make peace, and the German government hinted at relatively minor frontier adjustments such as the exchange of Briey for a part of German Lorraine. The French were not interested. It thus appeared that neither Russia nor France wanted peace on a *status quo ante bellum* basis, apart from what might happen to Belgium which was a problem in itself, the territorial issue of greatest concern to England.

With the object of relieving the hard-pressed French, the Allies unleashed two offensives in the summer of 1916: Brussilov, the ablest Russian general, attacked the Austrians in Galicia and Volhynia early in June, and the new British 'Kitchener army' with some French support went into action on the Somme in July. The Somme was the greatest demonstation yet seen of artillery power and 'frightfulness'.

For every square yard a million tons of steel was blown into the air; yet the defence was far from obliterated, and the territorial gains were trivial compared with the heavy cost in life. Both sides lost over 600,000 casualties, so that the total of killed and wounded at Verdun and the Somme came to over two million. The moral effect was shattering. Brussilov, whose success was more obvious and less expected, kept up his attacks until September. Under good generalship Russian soldiers were still capable of winning. The Germans had to rush reinforcements to the scene, and Falkenhayn withdrew fifteen divisions from the western front, where they could ill be spared. Brussilov's break-through was not matched by his colleagues further north, who showed a reluctance to attack, and full advantage was not taken of his advance. By the end of September the Austrian front had been stabilised, though with much of Volhynia and Bukovina again in Russian hands. Brussilov had inflicted 450,000 casualties on the Austrians, two-thirds of whom were prisoners. This was a further, perhaps fatal blow at the tottering Habsburg Empire, which once again had been rescued by its German ally, as Brussilov had rescued his allies. Germany now demanded unity of command along the eastern front, and the Austrians, swallowing their pride, agreed that Hindenburg should be commander-in-chief from the Baltic to Tarnopol; the small southern section, nominally commanded by the Austrian Archduke Charles, would have the German General von Seeckt as its Chief of Staff and thus virtually also be under Hindenburg. The Russians too paid a heavy price for their victory with something like a million casualties. By the winter of 1916–17 there were reckoned to be over a million deserters from the Russian army. Thus the two anachronistic empires, like a pair of belligerent dinosaurs, ponderously exhausted each other before revolution destroyed the one, nationalism the other.

At the end of August Roumania, encouraged by Brussilov's advance and enticed by lavish Entente promises of Austro-Hungarian territory (including the largely Roumanian Transylvania) now took the plunge and declared war on Austria. Had this move been made two months earlier, it could have been fatal to the Central Powers. Now the Germans were prepared, though they were heavily outnumbered, and much of the 300 mile long frontier with Roumania was thinly manned. But Mackensen, the victor of Serbia, with a largely Bulgarian army invaded Roumania from the south-east, while Falkenhayn, now commanding an army, fought his way in from Transylvania. Bucharest fell early in December, and by the beginning of the New Year the Roumanian army had been driven back to a line not far from the Russian border. The Germans managed to extract some food and oil from defeated Roumania though not as much as they needed because most of the oil installations had been wrecked by a British M.P., Colonel Norton Griffiths. The rump Roumanian army was reinforced in its new position by the Russians, who feared for the safety of Odessa. Thus the eastern front now ran the whole way from the Baltic to the Black Sea.

Roumania's entry into the war had been the signal for the dismissal of Falkenhayn. Opposition to him had been growing for some time, and the eastern commanders had constantly and at times unfairly criticised him. The fundamental reason for a change in the High Command was the desire to give Hindenburg and Ludendorff, to whom almost legendary powers were ascribed, a chance to win the war. The more hopeless Germany's prospects became, the more the public put its faith in a superman and a super-weapon (the submarine). Both the Kaiser and the Chancellor wanted to satisfy the national mood; and they knew that if they had to make a disappointing peace they could afford to do so only with Hindenburg there to shield them from unpopularity.[61] Thus there were political as well as military reasons for the move. Falkenhayn, despite his success on all fronts in 1915, had never been glamorous like Hindenburg and Ludendorff, and his failure at Verdun, like his earlier disaster at Ypres, dimmed the lustre of his other achievements. Burian, the new Austro-Hungarian Foreign Minister, was anxious to see Hindenburg in charge, as were several of the German state governments. Bethmann Hollweg had long been critical of Falkenhayn, and as early as January 1915 he had tried to remove him from the High Command. Their disagreement over the U-boat question added to Bethmann's mistrust. The Kaiser, who had continued to support his Chief of Staff, was now persuaded by his military advisers to drop him. Falkenhayn, depressed and disheartened, bore his dismissal with dignity, and refused the offer of an ambassadorship in Turkey. Instead, as we have seen, he took charge of an army which played a leading part in the defeat of Roumania.

The elevation of Hindenburg and Ludendorff to the High Command marks the beginning of a new phase in the war. Whatever Falkenhayn's private doubts about Germany's ability to win, in public he maintained that she could indefinitely withstand her enemies' attacks by husbanding her resources: his slogan was 'Hold out'. In practice he tried to force a decision at Verdun but even this was not pressed to the furthest extent because of Falkenhayn's habitual caution. Given that, as Falkenhayn knew, Germany could not win a war of attrition, and that overwhelming superiority on one section of a front offered the only chance of success, Falkenhayn's refusal to commit his reserves at critical moments both on the eastern front and Verdun may have deprived her of victory. Falkenhayn would not have objected to a moderate peace; he also accepted the authority of the Chancellor despite their disagreements.[62] The temperamental Ludendorff believed only in victory or defeat, and wished to dominate the government. Ludendorff was a political liability, yet the uneasy balance between civilian and military authority had now swung in favour of the military. Colonel von Marschall, a member of the Kaiser's military cabinet, told Groener that he feared Ludendorff with his unlimited ambition and pride would carry on the war until the German people were completely exhausted and that in the end the monarchy would have to bear the damage.[63] The forecast was exact. Ironically Bethmann Hollweg too found himself in a weaker position. While it was theoretically true that he could more easily have faced an unpopular peace, Hindenburg and Ludendorff in fact had no intention of allowing such a peace to be made. The date of the new appointment, 29 August 1916, was really the beginning of military dictatorship, which in the end proved fatal to Bethmann Hollweg. The Reichstag too was a victim, but a willing one. Capelle, the new Secretary of the Navy, complacently assured the leaders of the Reichstag parties that if the United States entered the war against Germany the effect would be nugatory. On 7 October 1916 the parties commanding a majority passed a resolution that the question whether or not to declare unrestricted submarine warfare was one for the High Command (not the Chancellor). Thus a crucial political decision was put in the hands of the military; and the Kaiser's authority had shrunk as the two generals had only to threaten resignation to get their way on any major issue.

(vii) THE DEBATE ON WAR AIMS

In Germany, as in other belligerent countries, the war gave rise to a widespread feeling that the eventual peace settlement must bring gains at least commensurate with the sacrifices made – gains to be measured both territorially and in terms of prestige and power. Most people would have agreed with the Pan-German League's assessment that the war was being fought for the Greater Germany of the future, though they saw it as a struggle forced upon her by her enemies. At the beginning of the war, when the German army seemed within a hair's breadth of victory, belief in a victorious peace ran high, and continued so in the months and years that followed, however little it was justified by the military situation. The Chancellor was aware of the national expectations, which at first he shared. He knew that public opinion would not allow him to make a peace that would leave Germany empty-handed; yet he was realist enough to understand that she could impose a 'German peace' only after completely defeating both France and Russia – a feat which Falkenhayn told him was impossible. If the best that could be hoped for was successful defence in a war of attrition, with the Allies unable to break German resistance, then a compromise peace would have to be accepted. There were many who, with Max Weber, argued that, if the Reich, like Prussia in the Seven Years' war, could emerge undefeated from a war with three great powers this in itself would amount to a moral victory; and Bethmann himself agreed with them.[64] But few people were willing to speak out in favour of a 'renunciatory' peace, especially as Germany was in possession of large areas of hostile territory which she intended to exploit or to use as bargaining counters for concessions elsewhere. The campaign for annexations began as soon as news of the first victories in the west gave rise to a fresh wave of patriotic fervour, with the towns beflagged and the church bells ringing. A letter from Ballin to Tirpitz on 1 October 1914 conveys the mood:

> I was in Berlin this week and was horrified at the wild schemes entertained not only by Berliners, but by important people from the Rhineland and Westphalia. They view a landing of our army in England as a matter of course. Seizing their best colonies is no longer a matter for dispute. That we keep Calais, Boulogne, Ostend and Antwerp is a foregone conclusion. The British navy has to adjust itself to our expansion, and the war indemnity varies between 30 and 40 milliards. That the British fleet has long since withdrawn from the Channel and is hiding behind the Orkneys is as certain as that Egypt is among the colonies we intend to have served up to us as dessert.[65]

The government's readiness to abandon its purely defensive posture of 4 August is evident from a memorandum drawn up early in September which was intended to serve as the basis of an armistice with France, whose collapse – this was just before the turning-point of the Marne – seemed imminent. This document, which presented the views of Bethmann Hollweg, demanded that France be so weakened as to make impossible for all time her revival as a great power, and that Russia be thrust back from the German border and forced to abandon her rule over non-Russian peoples. France was to cede territory (the fortress of Belfort, the iron-ore towns of Briey and Longwy and a strip along the Channel as far as Boulogne), to pay an indemnity, and to become economically dependent on Germany. Belgium was to become a vassal state with some loss of territory to Germany, Luxembourg was to join the German Empire, Germany's African colonies were to be expanded, and a number of European countries, including several neutrals, were to form an economic association in a German-domin-ated *Mitteleuropa*.[66] The combination of economic with strategic aims showed the lines on which the German government was thinking – lines laid down before the war in schemes discussed between the Chancellor and his political and economic advisers, which the war appeared to give Germany the opportunity of realising. In public however Bethmann Hollweg was cautious. On the one hand, he did not wish to provoke the Pan-Germans, who were always inclined to attack him for pusillanimity in pursuing national ends, especially in relation to England; on the other he had to be careful not to alarm neutral opinion, already upset by the violation of Belgium, or to alienate the Social Democrats who officially supported the war only as long as it was one of defence. For these reasons, and in order not to damage the party truce established on 4 August, Bethmann Hollweg sought to avoid public discussion of German war aims, which he knew were an explosive subject. Yet it was difficult to escape the topic when, every few months, the Reichstag had to be asked to vote supplies for the war. In March 1915 thirty Socialists, including Karl Liebknecht, voted against the third war credits bill, thus showing that the party truce was breaking down on the left. Karl, son of Wilhelm Liebknecht, who had been one of the founder members of the S.P.D., was now de-nouncing the war as imperialist and advocating a return to class war as the only policy compatible with socialist principles. There were few voices at the time which agreed with Liebknecht; Lenin's did, but from neutral Switzerland, where he was living, the impression was less striking than when it came, like Liebknecht's, from the heart of Imperial Germany.

In the course of 1915 annexationist fervour increased. On 20 May the Chancellor was presented with a memorandum from six economic organisations representing German industry and agriculture demand-ing substantial gains of territory at the expense of France, the subjec-tion of Belgium to German control, the attachment to Germany of provinces south of and along the Baltic and an 'adequate' colonial empire. Altogether in the west alone the claim was for 50,000 square miles containing about eleven million inhabitants. This was followed a few weeks later by a similar petition signed by 1,347 professors, artists, writers, journalists, clergymen, teachers, businessmen, lawyers, civil servants, farmers, politicians and retired generals and admirals. The demands were much the same as in the first memorandum, but there was a stronger emphasis on measures against England. The petition declared: 'We must never forget that this war, in the last analysis, is a war of England against Germany's world economy and overseas prestige.'[67] England must be forced to restore the freedom of the seas and to give up Egypt. Germany must acquire a chain of overseas bases to enable her to put an end to British naval predominance.

Behind both petitions lay the propagandist activity of the Pan-German League, which put forward even more extreme demands and was widely influential through the large number of industrialists and intellectuals who belonged to it. The League wanted Germany to annex the French coast as far as the mouth of the Somme, Verdun and Toulon (!), the Polish frontier districts, Lithuania and other Baltic lands. An ominous feature of the League programme was that the territories to be acquired by Germany must be clear of all inhabitants.[68] In this way the problem of enlarging Germany's area without adding to her national minorities would be solved. Another significant aspect of the Pan-Germans' attitude was the anxiety of their leader, Heinrich Class, lest failure to make substantial gains from the war would discredit the government and bring the left-wing parties to power. For Class even the Conservatives were too democratic. He evidently did not believe that the masses could be won for a policy of imperialism, and the party truce of 4 August 1914 with its hint of eventual social reform alarmed him: 'We have lost the war on the home front' was his reaction when he heard the news.[69] For him, maintenance of the political *status quo* was as much a war aim as expansion: thus annexationism abroad and rigid conservatism at home were closely linked. The Conservatives, wrote General Hoffmann, were less afraid of what might happen to their country than of the loss of their political predominance.[70] Bethmann Hollweg's attempt to manoeuvre between the Scylla of his Pan-German censors and the Charybdis of his Socialist critics, was necessarily a tortuous one, leading him into duplicity and double talk which ultimately made him mistrusted by both sides. Nevertheless, thanks to the support of the Kaiser, Bethmann survived for three years. He tried to reconcile his own desire for annexations – though on a less ambitious scale than the extreme nationalists' – with previous disclaimers of aggression demanding 'guarantees and securities', words that made territorial and other claims sound deceptively innocuous. This notion that Germany might extend her power and influence without actually annexing the territory she had occupied appealed to moderate opinion, which also tried to steer a middle course between the territorial acquisitiveness of the Pan-Germans and the renunciation of what had been won implied by a posture of pure defence. Typical of this attitude was a memorandum for the Chancellor drawn up by Theodor Wolff, editor of the liberal *Berliner Tageblatt* and supported by leading public men and intellectuals, including Metternich, the former ambassador to Britain, Hans Delbrück the historian, Dernburg, the former colonial minister, and such academic luminaries as Einstein, Troeltsch, Harnack, Schmoller and Max Weber. The social and professional background of these signatories was much the same as that of those who signed the petition of the 1,347 except that the moderate group included few historians or representatives of heavy industry. The latter had, of course, an obvious vested interest in the acquisition of Briey-Longwy and other areas rich in minerals.

By May 1915 the Conservatives, Free Conservatives, National Liberals and Centre formed, with the Anti-Semites and, at times, the Progressives, an annexationist majority in the Reichstag. These parties formally recorded their views in a resolution passed on 9 December 1915, during a debate on the fifth war credits bill, which ran:

> In complete unity and quiet determination we await the hour which shall make possible peace negotiations in which Germany's military, economic, financial and political interests must be permanently guaranteed to their full extent and by all means, including the necessary territorial acquisitions.[71]

Bethmann Hollweg was content to let the party leaders say what it would have been imprudent for him to admit, if only because of the official attitude of the S.P.D. During the same debate the Social Democrats interpellated the Chancellor on this issue, after a meeting to discuss it between him and Scheidemann. Scheidemann was in as delicate a position in relation to his party as Bethmann was in relation to the Reichstag. During the preceding months arguments about the German war aims and the future of Belgium had led to further dissension within the S.P.D. The left-wing members of the parliamentary party were now thoroughly distrustful of Bethmann's ambiguity and accused the party leaders of being prisoners of the government or 'Kaiser socialists'. In the vote on war credits of December 1915 some twenty voted against them, and another twenty abstained: thus about two-fifths of the socialist *Fraktion* were in rebellion against the party whip. The break-up of the S.P.D. appeared inevitable, especially as on the extreme right of the party were those who, in such periodicals as the *Sozialistische Monatshefte* and the government-subsidised *Glocke*, gave open support to the annexationist camp. The party split was thus threefold, though numerically the deviation on the left was more significant than that on the right. In March 1916 there was a violent scene in the Reichstag when Haase, the former chairman of the S.P.D. and now leader of the parliamentary opposition, refused to follow the party majority in voting for the sixth war credits bill. Haase and his supporters became known as the Social Democratic *Arbeitsgemeinschaft* or Working Group, the nucleus of the Independent Social

Democratic party that was formally constituted a year later. The Working Group not only refused to finance the war, but disagreed with the government (and with the Majority Socialists as the S.P.D. was henceforth known) over a wide range of subjects including almost all aspects of the war. The question was whether, as the war became more unpopular and the government's unwillingness or inability to stand up to annexationist pressure became more apparent, still more of the S.P.D. parliamentary party would cross over to the Working Group, which would then become the majority. This did not in fact happen, though there remained with the S.P.D. a small number who believed that war credits should be voted only in return for concessions, in contrast to the majority view that the credits were for the nation, not the government, and should not be the subject of bargaining. Further to the left of the Working Group was the International Group better known as Spartacists, whose opposition to the war was absolute and not dependent on whether the government intended to make conquests or not. Their two leaders were Karl Liebknecht, who before the war had headed the anti-militarist movement in the S.P.D., and Rosa Luxemburg the Polish-born Marxist, who had been the brain and inspiration of the militant left. Liebknecht, after denouncing the war in the Prussian *Landtag* (where, as well as in the Reichstag, he had a seat) addressed an anti-war demonstration on 1 May 1916 on the Potsdamer Platz in the centre of Berlin and was arrested on the spot. His trial on a charge of 'aiding a hostile power' at the end of June was the signal for the first large-scale strike of the war, a tribute to Liebknecht's sincerity and courage rather than a measure of support for his opinions. Rosa Luxemburg who had already spent some months in prison in 1915 on a revived pre-war charge, was re-arrested in July 1916 and remained till the armistice in 'preventive custody'. The government regarded her, not without reason, as dangerously subversive. What had once been the united Social Democratic party of Germany now stretched from the revolutionary defiance of Liebknecht to the imperialist apologetics of such nationalist socialists as Lensch, Hänisch and Winnig.[72] The rank and file of party supporters tended to move to the left in sympathy with the Working Group, less for ideological reasons than from exasperation at the unending war. In July 1916 the *Büro für Sozialpolitik* reported:

The temper of the masses is at present so bad in many places, that every mention of a war aim beyond the *status quo* . . . would result in numerous voters going over to the [Socialist] minority.[73]

Yet while awareness of the growing desire for peace should have moved the Chancellor to less ambitious war aims, other developments impelled him in the opposite direction. The greater bitterness and savagery of the fighting, the popular desire to take revenge on the enemy and make him 'pay for the war', the extension of German rule in eastern Europe as the Russians were pushed back, the influence of German military governments in these areas and in Belgium, and the knowledge that the Entente's war aims included depriving Germany and her allies of substantial territories, all contributed to harden public opinion against a soft peace. The constant pressure of the Pan-Germans, who received support from the Crown Prince, was another factor. Among Bethmann Hollweg's most virulent right-wing critics was Wolfgang Kapp, the senior administrative official from East Prussia who in 1920 was to lead the Putsch against the Weimar Republic. In view of Bethmann's private commitment to annexations, as shown in his memorandum of 9 September 1914 and elsewhere, it is not at first easy to understand why Kapp and the other Pan-Germans were so hostile. The reasons lie partly in Bethmann Hollweg's pre-war policy, which was allegedly weak and anglophile, partly in his refusal during the war to pursue all-out submarine warfare regardless of the consequences, and partly in Kapp's fear that Bethmann, in his so-called 'diagonal' policy, would reform the Prussian franchise to appease the Socialists and so open the way to a left-wing government.[74]

On 5 April 1916 Bethmann Hollweg pleased the annexationists by telling the Reichstag that there could be no return to the *status quo ante bellum* as far as Belgium was concerned, and he hinted that Germany intended to divide Belgium by playing off the Germanic Flemings against the culturally dominant French-speaking Walloons. In the same debate Scheidemann indicated that his party was thinking on similar lines by declaring that only a simpleton would imagine that a whole continent could go up in flames, with millions destroyed and killed, without a single boundary stone being moved. In an earlier speech (9 December 1915) Bethmann Hollweg had referred to the two 'gates of invasion', Belgium and Poland, which would have to be firmly closed in future. The problems presented by these two conquered countries illustrate the difficulties Germany faced in trying to expand in Europe and to impose a 'German peace'.

The German stake in Belgium – a legacy, like so much else, of the Schlieffen Plan – was basically to ensure that it remained under German control both militarily and economically. Otherwise, it was alleged, Belgium would become a British springboard against Germany. Bethmann Hollweg's pledge of 4 August 1914 to make good the wrong done to Belgium was forgotten, and documents were produced purporting to show that before the war the Belgian government had planned common action with Britain in case of war with Germany, thereby abandoning its supposed neutrality.[75] Occupied Belgium was also to be used as a bargaining counter at peace negotiations to secure the return of Germany's colonies, all of which, except East Africa, had fallen into Allied hands. Falkenhayn expressed a widely-held view when he said that the unconditional military domination of Belgium by Germany was a necessity, without which she would lose the war in the west. Belgium was subjected to German economic penetration and exploitation, and the area east of the river Meuse was to be annexed to the Reich. The long-standing feud between Fleming and Walloon gave the occupying power a chance to divide and rule. Berlin's policy was to win Flemish support by taking up Flemish linguistic and other grievances and by stressing the racial link between Flemings and Germans. On the whole however, common resistance to German domination brought the two Belgian peoples together, though there were collaborators among the Flemings. For Britain the unconditional restoration of Belgium to full sovereignty with restitution for damage was an essential of any peace settlement and an issue of principle, as it was for neutral, especially American opinion. Thus German plans for the permanent reduction of Belgium to vassal status ruled out any real possibility of peace with England, as the abortive peace talks of 1917 were to show. Belgium was in many senses Germany's Achilles heel; and the deportation of thousands of Belgian workmen to war work in Germany in 1916 understandably drew much hostile criticism from abroad as well as from Independent Socialists at home.

The case of Poland was in many ways similar, but more complex because more interests were involved. Russian oppression of the Poles and other subject peoples enabled Germany to play the part of a liberator when she defeated the Russian army in the course of 1915, despite Germany's far from liberal record towards her own Polish population in Posen, West Prussia and Upper Silesia. Even before the war actually broke out the German government had been planning to rouse the Poles in Russia with a promise of independence if Germany won.[76] This was part of a general design to stir up revolution in the Tsarist Empire. Not to be outdone, the Russian government promised the Poles that in case of a Russian victory all the Polish provinces, including the Prussian and Austrian ones as well as the hard core or 'Congress Poland' assigned to Russia in 1815, would be re-united and given autonomy. The Poles themselves were little impressed by these attempts to win their support by promises which, judging from past experience, were unlikely to be honoured. Of the three occupying powers of pre-partition Poland, Austria was the least unpopular because Poles in the Habsburg Monarchy (Cracow and Galicia) enjoyed a good deal of self-government and were treated as a privileged group compared with the non-historic peoples. Pilsudski, the Polish socialist and patriotic leader, organised a Polish Legion largely recruited from Galicia, which fought as a part of the Austrian army. When, after the summer of 1915, the Polish question demanded a solution with the country divided between German and Austrian occupation, the Austrians called for a settlement which would include Congress Poland within the Habsburg Monarchy. Any other solution, it was feared in Vienna, would disrupt Austria, because the Galician Poles would be attracted to a reconstructed rump Poland based on Warsaw, and no Poland would be complete without Cracow, the former capital. Poland would also be a desirable acquisition for the Monarchy, though the Hungarians were bitterly opposed to the inclusion of any more Slavs. The Germans, however, had their own plans: Congress Poland, shorn of a substantial 'frontier strip' to be ceded to Germany, was to become their vassal state, a defensive glacis and part of the new economic order they hoped to establish as *Mitteleuropa*. The Germans were, in any case, for a long time unwilling to commit themselves to a policy in Poland that would nullify their efforts to make a separate peace with Russia. Another reason which made the Germans reluctant to appeal to Polish nationalism was that it would act as a magnet to Germany's own Polish subjects.

Differences between Germany and Austria over the future of Poland might have postponed any solution indefinitely had not the impetuous Ludendorff, when he came to the High Command, insisted on a decision. His main objective was to draw on Polish manpower to make good losses in the Austrian army, and he knew that the Poles would not volunteer unless they had some assurance of independence. By October 1916 Bethmann Hollweg could no longer resist the pressure; his efforts at a separate peace with Russia had all been rejected, and he believed that the Russians were too exhausted to take effective counter-action. So on 5 November an independent Polish kingdom was formally proclaimed. It was to be attached to Germany and Austria-Hungary jointly, though in practice German influence proved predominant. The boundaries of the new state were not defined, and no executive was actually set up. The project remained on paper, and Ludendorff's hopes of Polish recruits remained unfulfilled. By April 1917 only 4,700 recruits had presented themselves instead of the 350,000 (or 800,000 according to the German governor general) expected. The mordant comment of a Polish leader on such speculations was: 'We haven't got so many suicides.'[77] This result was hardly surprising in view of Germany's intention to annex the economically valuable 'frontier strip', her determination to hold on to her existing Polish provinces, and her refusal to treat the Poles as equals. Polish nationalists looked increasingly to the Allies and America; and President Wilson's speech of 22 January 1917 calling for an independent Poland, a demand that was to be included in the Fourteen Points a year later, contrasted with Germany's failure to make any headway with Polish opinion. Pilsudski, after briefly co-operating with the German-sponsored 'state council', broke with the Germans and in July 1917 was arrested and sent to prison on a charge of sabotaging recruitment to the German army. Inside Poland the Germans and Austrians continued their fruitless rivalry, and right up to the end of the war were still arguing about who was to wear the Polish crown.

(viii) THE GERMAN PEACE NOTE AND THE BREACH WITH AMERICA

The desirability of ending the war by a general negotiated settlement was never absent from the mind of Bethmann Hollweg, especially when Germany's military situation worsened, though he would have preferred a separate peace with each of the enemy states as more likely to be favourable. President Wilson wanted not only to end a war which, through the blockade, was causing considerable embarrassment to the United States, but to set up a new world order based on disarmament, security, freedom of the seas and an agreement on colonies, ideals which he later embodied in the League of Nations. America's moral and material support of the Allies showed that Wilson himself and still more his advisers, Colonel House and the new head of the State Department, Lansing, were far from neutral. German distrust of mediation by America was thus inevitable. Nevertheless, the moment might still come when Germany might be glad of a mediator and the United States was the only power capable of playing this part. Moreover, the submarine campaign, with its threat to American lives and property, had already brought Germany and the United States to the brink of war. It was expedient for Bethmann Hollweg not to pour too much cold water on Wilson's peace efforts, if only to prevent American armed intervention, which Bethmann, unlike most of the politicians and service chiefs, believed would be a calamity. When House toured Europe early in 1916 to take soundings for the President on the kind of peace likely to be acceptable, he visited Berlin as well as London and Paris. It was clear that the Entente's terms were a long way from anything Germany would accept: France wanted more than the restoration of Alsace-Lorraine. Bethmann's speech in the Reichstag on 5 April 1916, in which he specifically mentioned annexations, seemed to widen the gap. On 28 May Count Bernstorff, the German ambassador in Washington, reported to his government that Wilson was thinking of calling a general peace conference at The Hague to which neutral countries would be invited. Bernstorff (who worked hard with little support from Berlin to prevent further deterioration of German-American relations) was told to do what he could to kill the project. The Germans were not prepared to return to the *status quo ante bellum* which the President was expected to propose, nor were they interested in his more general utopian ideas. Apart from the reservations about Wilson, they were doubtful about submitting their case to a conference in which they would be heavily outnumbered. On the debit side, in the summer of 1916 the deterioration in Germany's military position marked by the failure at Verdun, the great Allied material superiority manifested at the Somme, the Austrian collapse, the Italian offensive and the imminent entry of Roumania into the war on the side of the Allies, induced a certain caution. Moreover the replacement of Falkenhayn by Hindenburg and Ludendorff increased the pressure on the Chancellor in favour of unrestricted submarine warfare. Before taking such a fateful step, Bethmann Hollweg wanted at least to explore the possibility of American mediation. The moment was favourable: American opinion had moved away from intervention, and with the approach of a presidential election the government was concerned to emphasise its neutrality. At a meeting of government and army chiefs at Pless at the end of August the Chancellor took an 'extremely serious' view of the situation, saying according to Helfferich, the Finance Minister who was present: 'We had to do everything possible to gain peace. The only way out . . . led through Wilson, and this way had to be taken, even though the prospects were uncertain . . .'[78] On 2 September Bernstorff was instructed to find out whether mediation by Wilson had any chance of success if Germany agreed to a conditional restoration of Belgium. But by this time Wilson and his colleagues were immersed in preparations for the presidential election early in November, and nothing more could be done from the American side before that date. At the same time the American government was bluntly told that should mediation be tried and fail Germany would declare unrestricted submarine warfare.[79]

During October Bethmann Hollweg was asked by a Progressive member of the Reichstag, Haussmann, to take the initiative himself in proposing peace, a suggestion which had already been made with some force by the Austrian Foreign Minister Burian. The Habsburg Monarchy, faced with the new threat from Roumania and a third war winter, was not far from breaking point. In the following month the aged Emperor Francis Joseph died, and his successor Charles had a more flexible attitude to the question of peace. All these considerations, and not least Germany's own plight as she entered the bleak 'turnip winter', made Bethmann Hollweg decide to act. It was characteristic of the new power of the military chiefs that Bethmann had to clear his plans with them before proceeding. He also had to come to an agreement with the Austrians, whose war aims, focused on the Balkans, were quite different from Germany's, and who were indifferent to the fate of Belgium and Alsace-Lorraine. Bethmann also wished to anticipate another move by Wilson after his re-election on 7 November on a pledge to keep America out of the war. On 6 December German troops occupied Bucharest, and this fresh triumph of German arms was judged to be the right moment for the Chancellor to produce his Peace Note, which was issued six days later. The terms of peace were unspecified – Bethmann did not believe in prematurely disclosing his hand – but the tone was one of confidence and defiance. Germany and her allies were ready to enter into peace negotiations, but the peace must ensure the 'existence, honour and free development of the peoples' – a vague formula that could mean much or little.

On 18 December Wilson replied to the Peace Note with a proposal that all the belligerent powers should make public the conditions on which they were willing to make peace. Wilson himself, under the impact of recent events such as the crushing of the Irish Easter Rising, the black-listing of American firms by the British under the blockade and the intransigence shown by the new British Prime Minister, Lloyd George, was now more genuinely neutral in sentiment than in previous months, as his speech of 22 January 1917 was to show, with its demand for peace without victors or vanquished and its faint anticipation of the Fourteen Points of a year later. But the German government failed to profit by this shift in American policy, for on 26 December Wilson's offer was formally rejected. On 20 December the German Peace Note was firmly and predictably turned down by the Entente governments, which wrongly believed it to be nothing more than a propaganda move intended to influence German and foreign opinion. They declared that the attempt to impose a 'German peace' was empty and insincere, and the French described it as designed to split the Allies. As for Wilson's proposals, the Allies self-righteously refused to be put on terms of moral equality with the Central Powers; at the same time they made known their conditions of peace.[80] These involved not only evacuation by the Central Powers of all occupied territory but the liberation of the subject peoples of the Habsburg and Ottoman Empires, with hints of the transfer of Alsace-Lorraine to France and a possible threat to Germany's Polish provinces. Thus the main lines of the future Versailles settlement were sketched. Such aims went too far for Wilson, who was annoyed by the Allied attitude and on 26 January asked the German government to let him know confidentially what its peace terms would be. The reply indicated some

frontier changes in Germany's favour in east and west, with the conditional restoration of Belgium, but such value as this disclosure had
was reduced by the proviso that the offer was conditional on acceptance by the Allies of the German Peace Note. By this time the
exchange of views with the United States government was mere
shadow boxing, for on 9 January the German government had taken
its gravest decision since 1 August 1914 – to wage unrestricted submarine warfare from 1 February. This, wrote Ludendorff afterwards,
was seen as the only way of winning the war within a reasonable
period of time.[81] With a heavy heart – he was 'agitated and depressed' according to Admiral von Müller – Bethmann had given way
to the generals and admirals (with whom the Kaiser now agreed) in
taking a step which he had long resisted and still saw as one of desperation.[82] He tried at the last moment to persuade the High Command to postpone the beginning of the U-boat campaign, but they
refused on 'technical grounds'; their real reason was their desire to
strike at a time when England was more than ever dependent on
imports. On 31 January Bernstorff had the embarrassing task of handing over the German reply to Wilson and at the same time announcing
that U-boat ruthlessness was to start the following day, carrying 'in
one hand a palm of peace, in the other a torpedo'.[83] He had been
obliged to keep up the pretence of good faith in the talks with the
American government while knowing that the decision about submarines had already been taken and the last chance of preserving
American neutrality destroyed. The President, who, despite his anglophile sentiments, genuinely wanted to keep his country out of war, was
driven inexorably towards intervention. Diplomatic relations with
Germany were broken off early in February. Yet it was another two
months before Wilson declared war. If the Germans in fact abstained
from destroying American ships and lives, he told Congress, he would
take no action; and even if they made such attacks, he would reply
with armed neutrality.[84] Congress was in a far from bellicose mood.
Yet public opinion was changed by the final German blunder – a
telegram sent by the Foreign Secretary, Zimmermann, to the Mexican
government promising that if Mexico helped Germany in war against
the United States Germany would ensure that the states of New
Mexico, Arizona and Texas, which had been ceded by Mexico in
1845, would be restored. The message was intercepted and de-coded
by the British, who passed it on to Washington, where it created a
sensation. By 6 April 1917 Germany and the United States were at
war. The breach with America had been a blow to Bethmann Hollweg,
who thought of resigning. His reputation would have gained had he
done so. He persuaded himself that it was his duty to stay in office in

order not to make the situation appear worse than it was in the eyes of neutrals, and to save what was left of the party truce at home. Yet effective power had passed to Ludendorff, who was already toying with the idea of finding a new Chancellor.[85] Bethmann remained on sufferance.

There is little to suggest that the peace feelers which followed the German Peace Note had any chance of success. In Germany distrust of Wilson, scepticism about a negotiated peace, belief in the war-winning capabilities of the U-boat and determination not to accept a return to pre-war frontiers raised formidable obstacles. Among the Allies opinion had hardened: the Peace Note was unfortunate in its timing. In Russia and France new governments had recently come to power, pledged to a tougher policy, while in Britain Lloyd George, protagonist of a fight to a finish, had replaced the less militant Asquith. The Allies would certainly not have accepted a return to the pre-war *status quo*, which was in any case ruled out by secret treaties between themselves. Nor was peace-making only a question of territory. The passions of a people's war would not be satisfied by the kind of compromise that could have ended a cabinet war. As Count Lerchenfeld, the Bavarian envoy in Berlin, remarked: 'Peace is not a matter of conditions. We could offer the return of Poland, Belgium and the North of France, it would be of no use. Germany must be defeated, that is what our enemies demand.'[86] The Allies felt that if Prussian militarism was not conquered, the peace would be only a truce. In these circumstances it is hard to see how a negotiated peace could have come about at the end of 1916, even if the German government had been prepared, as it was not, to take advantage of the positively neutral elements in Wilson's policy, and even if its 'experts' had not grossly underestimated America's war capacity. Short of defeat, Germany would not give up Alsace-Lorraine. Nor could she barter away the territory of her allies.

Nevertheless, in the light of subsequent events, the decision for un-restricted U-boat warfare was a fatal mistake. In the short run the calculation that it would enable sinkings of Allied ships to increase from 400,000 a month to 600,000 was correct: indeed in April over 800,000 tons of Allied shipping were destroyed. But thereafter losses fell away, thanks to the convoy system introduced on Lloyd George's insistence in the summer of 1917, which in turn was facilitated by American destroyers. Moreover, once America was in the war, her shipyards would replace British shipping losses. Nor did Germany have enough submarines for the task, in view of the length of the United Kingdom coast to be blockaded and the formidable nature of British sea defences. At the beginning of 1917 the number of German submarines was 134, of which 95 were in the North Sea and Flanders ports, the remainder being distributed between the Mediterranean and the Baltic.[87] In practice the enforcement of the embargo against the British Isles depended on the operation of about 30 U-boats, a small enough total by comparison with the 170 ships or so which then arrived at or left British ports every day. On a more general view, the virtual defection of Russia after the revolution of March 1917 might have forced the Allies to consider a compromise peace had they not been joined by the United States, already an economic super-power. It is arguable that any peace signed in the spring of 1917 would have been favourable to Germany, if only because she was in occupation of so much foreign territory. By provoking America to war, the Germans lost this opportunity, and threw away the possibility of American mediation, which represented another chance of ending the war on equal terms. As in the case of Belgium, Germany sacrificed long-term advantages for a short-term gain based, as it happened, on a miscalculation, and ignored the wider moral and political implications of the gamble. There was some force in the argument used in Berlin that the Americans' commitment to the Allies in the form of loans and supplies of all kinds was already so great that an American declaration of war would make little practical difference; but the assumption, all too readily made by the generals and admirals, either that America would be of no value as a military power or that U-boats would prevent any American troops from landing in France, proved totally unfounded.

CHAPTER V

The First World War:
From the Russian Revolution
to the Armistice

News of the declaration of war was received in Germany with enthusiasm and demonstrations of national solidarity. The Kaiser's speech
of 4 August proclaiming a party truce helped the closing of ranks. In
Berlin throngs of smiling youths cheered the mobilisation order and
flocked to the colours. Girls threw flowers at marching soldiers on their
way to the front. Troop trains, decked with foliage and inscribed with
slogans (*Straight to Paris! The Tsar to the Gallows!*) chalked on the
carriages were hailed by farmers in the fields as they trundled through
a countryside where harvest was in full swing. Crowds in the cities
sang *Deutschland über Alles* and the *Wacht am Rhein*. Such scenes
had their counterpart in other countries, though the jubilation was
probably less. Everywhere men embarked light-heartedly on a war
which they expected to be costly but short. Germans knew that they
faced a more formidable struggle than that of 1870, which the older
ones could remember: this time they were pitted against three great
powers with only one ally (and of uncertain strength). Yet confidence
in Germany's military superiority ran high, and few spared a thought
for the economic consequences of the blockade or the moral implications of the invasion of Belgium. Nationalists were delighted that Germany was at last striking against the hostile coalition that blocked her
justified expansion: the war would cut insoluble problems with the
sword. To idealists and romantics the war was an escape from the
sordid everyday world to a higher realm of courage and selfless
patriotism. Like Rupert Brooke in England many young Germans
hailed it as an ennobling experience, a cure for peacetime decadence.
It was the German people's hour of destiny, wrote the critic Julius Bab
in the foreword to a new magazine entitled 'The German War and
German Poetry', which included from Richard Dehmel, a poet of

some repute, verses ending with the lines: 'As all are safely in God's hand, we'll gladly bleed for the fatherland.'[1] What the patriotic muse lacked in inspiration, it made up in enthusiasm. Even the 'non-political' Thomas Mann described the war as 'purification, libera-tion . . . an immense hope';[2] the perspicacious Max Weber wrote of it as 'great and wonderful'. The war would heal the divisions of German society and give it new meaning and purpose. The historian Meinecke, looking back nostalgically after more than thirty years, recalled the August days of 1914 as one of his most precious and unforgettable memories, and saw in the exaltation a longing for 'spiritual renewal'.[3] Hähnisch, the editor of the left-wing socialist *Leipziger Volkszeitung*, recorded the immense relief he felt at being able at last to join in the general enthusiasm: the theoretical internationalism of Marxist dogma now seemed to belong to a bygone age. The euphoria of the outbreak of war was sustained by news of the first victories. A whole generation of Europeans had been psychologically prepared for this moment, alternately alarmed by the successive crises that had brought their countries to the brink of war, and roused to patriotic fervour by xenophobic propaganda as Bethmann Hollweg once bitterly com-plained about his own nation. There were, even in Germany, a few warning voices. Ballin bewailed the tragedy of an Anglo-German war caused by an irrelevant quarrel in the Balkans. Rathenau wrote in December 1914: 'There is a false note about this war . . . What must the price of victory be to justify so much blood and tears?'[4] But then Rathenau had also told a friend, in words which his nationalist critics were never to forgive, that if the German Kaiser returned victorious through the Brandenburg Gate history would have lost its meaning.[5] In contrast to the many people who saw the war as the start of a new era, Rathenau was pessimistic: 'This war is not a beginning but an end; what it will leave behind is ruins.'[6] The Germans were deter-mined that the ruins would not be on their soil.

For the moment, the sense of revival and unity was uppermost. One manifestation of this was the 1914 Society, founded by Moltke, the Chief of Staff who lost his post after the battle of the Marne, and Solf, the Colonial Secretary. Its object was 'to offer German men of all pro-fessions and classes and regardless of party affiliations the possibility of unprejudiced and informal social intercourse'.[7] Among its members were princes, generals, admirals, industrialists, bankers, members of the Reichstag, artists, professors and publishers. It included all shades of political thought from conservatives to right-wing Social Democrats, extreme annexationists and moderates. Designed as the counterpart of a British club, the society broke new ground in a country where men of different political allegiances and social backgrounds rarely met:

here for the first time socialists could rub shoulders with ministers, generals with intellectuals, businessmen with artists. Politics could be discussed confidentially and in a relaxed atmosphere. A similar but smaller club was the Wednesday Society started by the National Liberal leader Bassermann, which also brought together leading men of different parties and professions. This too was a forum for discussing what became known as the ideas of 1914.

What were the ideas of 1914?[8] The phrase was coined by a Hegelian sociologist at Münster University, who drew a contrast between conservative Germany and revolutionary France ('the ideas of 1789'). The Allies sought from the beginning to give the war an ideological character: it was to save small nations (Belgium, Serbia) from Prussian militarism, more generally to propagate democracy and self-determination, ultimately to be, in the words of H. G. Wells, the 'war to end war'. What had Germany to set against these ideals? For it was not enough to ridicule them or to protest against English hypocrisy. Germany claimed to be protecting Europe from Tsarist tyranny, an argument which carried some weight not only on the German left but in neutral countries such as America. (A deep-set fear of Russia can be traced from Max Weber's warning in 1895 'The Cossacks are coming' to Bethmann Hollweg's remark shortly before the war that there was no point in planting trees in the park of his country house as the Russians would be there in a few years.)[9] Even after the Russian threat was lifted in 1915, Germany could represent herself as the liberator of subject peoples of the Russian Empire such as the Finns, though the Reich's illiberal record towards its own Polish and Danish minorities made such a claim unconvincing. Nor was maintenance of the Habsburg Empire compatible with the aspirations of the Serbs, Roumanians and other ethnic minorities. It was in any case soon clear that the basic struggle inside the war was between Germany and England, not Germany and Russia. What was at stake, wrote Bethmann Hollweg in November 1914 'was the destruction of England's world supremacy'.[10] From the beginning popular fury had been strongest against perfidious Albion, which, ignoring ties of blood, had treacherously sided with Germany's enemies in a life and death struggle. Lissauer's 'Hymn of Hate' showed how war could appeal to the basest as well as the noblest emotions. The Anglo-German duel had to be dressed up in ideological terms. England embodied the cant, mercenariness and selfish individualism of Anglo-Saxondom. Germany, on the other hand, was heroic, idealistic and socially organic. Werner Sombart, the economist, made the point succinctly and without subtlety in the title of a book developing this theme, *Helden und Händler* (Heroes and Dealers). The Kaiser in one of his angriest marginal comments had raged against 'this hateful lying unprincipled nation of shopkeepers'.[11] In reply to the British indictment of militarism German publicists denounced British 'navalism' as a menace to small nations, he praised the German navy as destined to redress the global balance of power, so long weighted in favour of the British Empire. Allied moves to turn the war into one of emancipation for oppressed peoples (with its destructive implications for the Habsburg and Ottoman Empires) were refuted by references to British imperialism in Ireland, Egypt, India and elsewhere. The most bizarre rationalisation of German war aims came from a group of left-wing Socialists such as Hähnisch who, after August 1914, abjured their former internationalism and supported the territorial ambitions of the Pan-Germans with pseudo-Marxist arguments.[12] Germany, they declared, was the leader of the world revolution against the plutocratic West. Such interpretations carried no conviction among the other parties in the Socialist International, whose leaders (both the chairman and secretary at the time were Belgians) leaned heavily towards the Allies. As for Germany's other international link, the Roman Catholic leader Erzberger used his influence in Catholic organisations to present the German case and refute Allied slanders, but with limited success. Though the Vatican was not unsympathetic, neutral as well as Entente opinion was roused against Germany by the sack of Louvain and the sufferings of Catholic Belgium. German publicists included no such masters of propaganda as C. F. G. Masterman of the British Cabinet, Wickham Steed of the *Times* and Lord Northcliffe its proprietor, nor had they such promising material to work with. The ferocity and unscrupulousness of the British press campaign against the 'Huns' made an impact which long outlasted the war.[13] In the United States the Germans could make little impression: common traditions, sentiment and self-interest worked in favour of the Allies, and Germany (who lost her direct cable to America) spoilt her case by blunders, of which the sinking of the *Lusitania* was the most notorious. Lacking a universal idea, Germany was forced on the 'spiritual defensive', and even her claim to be defending Europe from Russia had little credibility after 1915. Her endeavours to break the British blockade threatened neutral lives as well as property.

The most notable, certainly the most profound and thoughtful attempt to establish a rational case for Germany was made by Thomas Mann. If German writers of that generation can be divided into two groups – the politically committed and the uncommitted – Thomas Mann belonged to the latter. He thus differed sharply from his radical brother Heinrich, whose satirical novels such as *Der Untertan* (translated into English as *The Underdog*) and *Professor Unrat* (later made into the film *The Blue Angel*) marked him as an unsparing critic of Wilhelmine state and society. Thomas Mann's interests were philosophic, psychological and musical: the main influences behind his work were Schopenhauer and Nietzsche, and his themes were suggested by the *fin de siècle* movement – the relation of the artist to bourgeois society, genius and sickness, decadence and morality. Mann's writing was marked by a delicate and compassionate irony, and he strongly disapproved of his brother's use of his art to inculcate a political message. It was something of a transformation when very early in the war Thomas wrote to Heinrich: 'Must we not be grateful for this wholly unexpected opportunity of living through such great events?', and a little later referred to 'this great, fundamentally decent and awe-inspiring people's war'.[14] Heinrich, with his democratic sympathies, was guilty, in his brother's view, of siding with Germany's enemies. Even the violation of Belgian neutrality was defended in an essay by Thomas Mann citing Frederick the Great's seizure of Silesia as a precedent. Finally he produced a full-scale study of the issues raised by the war in his *Reflections of a Non-Political Man* which appeared in 1918. The title was misleading: it was political in an intellectual sense, and taken in conjunction with Mann's other writing established him as an apologist of the Hohenzollern Empire. He saw the West, not Russia, as the main enemy and rival. The *Reflections* drew a contrast between civilisation, which is western, and *Kultur*, which is German. Civilisation means democracy, party politics, material comfort and mob radicalism; it is shallow and ephemeral. *Kultur* is aristocratic, reflective, profound and musical; it is not taken in by facile optimism. Western freedom, so vaunted by French and English liberals, is an external freedom; German freedom is that of the spirit. Mann was understandably resentful at the sweeping Allied condemnation of German *Kultur* and the crude lumping together of Nietzsche the European with apologists of Pan-Germanism like Gerhardi. He rejected the charge of barbarism and declared that Germany's 'social empire' was preferable to the 'dirty plutocratic bourgeois republic' across the Rhine.[15] The contrast between civilisation and *Kultur* was not new in German thinking, but it was sharpened by wartime polemics. In more general and less propagandist terms it reappeared in Mann's great post-war novel *The Magic Mountain* with its brilliant intellectual swordplay between Settembrini, the Italian *Zivilisationsliterat* (his brother Heinrich), who is rational, democratic and a believer in progress – in short an old-fashioned liberal – and Naphta, the subtle, pessimistic and mystical Jesuit, a 'revolutionary conservative', who believes in violence, and, for good measure, turns out to be a converted Jew. Mann himself was closer to the position of Germany's conservatives than he was ever to be again and his later political writing in defence of the much abused Weimar Republic and afterwards in defiance of the Nazis involved a reversal of earlier attitudes. In the world of Lenin and Hitler the ideas of 1914 were as out of date as the plumes and lances of the Uhlan cavalry.

Among the most promising and concrete ideas of 1914 was that of *Mitteleuropa*. The notion of a customs union to include Germany and the Habsburg Empire was far from new; it had been suggested by the Austrian Chancellor Schwarzenberg in the aftermath of the 1848 revolution but had been rejected by Bismarck. In the years before 1914 many industrialists came to see the value of forming a large economic bloc with Germany as its centre flanked by her allies and neighbours. In July 1912 Rathenau proposed to Bethmann Hollweg the setting up of a customs union to consist of Germany, Austria-Hungary, Switzerland, Italy, Belgium and Holland. The purpose was to build up a market large enough to hold its own in the world that appeared to be increasingly dominated by big economic groups such as the United States, Russia and the British Empire (which, however, owing to free trade, was anything but a closed system). Such a bloc, of course under German hegemony, would also be a means of preserving the Habsburg Empire from disintegration. When war broke out in 1914 the idea of *Mitteleuropa* was enthusiastically taken up by the German government and by the various groups of annexationists. German conquests indicated the shape such a *Mitteleuropa* might take. As moreover the Reich was cut off from her colonies and her world trade, it was all the more important for her to extend economically into the contiguous areas of Europe and the Balkans. 'All south-eastern Europe' stated a memorandum drawn up in the Chancellor's office in May 1915 'is a cultural colony on our doorstep'.[16] There was a broad similarity between the government's aims and those of Friedrich Naumann, whose much publicised book *Mitteleuropa* came out in October 1915. Naumann stressed the economic rather than the political aspects, and expected the adhesion of the small states to be voluntary. Yet practical difficulties remained. One of the most intractable was the future of Poland, on which the German and Austrian governments could never agree. In south-east Europe and the Ottoman Empire efforts to secure German economic preponderance met the resistance of traditional Austro-Hungarian interests and of Turkish nationalism. *Mitteleuropa* was still an unrealised dream when the war ended, and the break-up of the Habsburg Empire created entirely new circumstances in the Danube valley. The project of a self-contained European bloc under German control was to be revived, in a cruder and more brutal form, by Hitler during the Second World War.

(ii) THE HOME FRONT: THE WAR AND THE ECONOMY

Modern war is the severest test of a nation's economic efficiency and social stability as well as of its political maturity and military strength. How did Hohenzollern Germany, dependent as it had been on international trade and internally divided by caste and other barriers, stand up to the ordeal? How far was its cumbersome and anomalous political structure equal to a struggle that was itself a revolutionary force?

Although it was not until 1916 that the silent but deadly pressure of the British blockade caused real hardship to the civilian population, the problem of organising a war economy under siege conditions had been with the German government since the day hostilities began. Germany in 1914 was completely unprepared for a long war: the only kind of war envisaged by her efficient but not particularly imaginative General Staff was a short, victorious one. She had no stocks of raw materials, and even her supplies of ammunition were soon proved inadequate. As in peacetime, the federal government was handicapped by not possessing its own civil service, and by having to act through the states which watched jealously over their own interests. The first effect of the blockade was to cut Germany off from her overseas markets and supplies, including tropical and colonial produce. Imports accounted for about a third of the food and animal fodder consumed, and included many essential raw materials used for making munitions, such as copper and nickel. Thanks to the foresight of two private industrialists (Rathenau and Moellendorff of the General Electric Company) the Minister of War was persuaded within a few days of the outbreak of war to set up within his Ministry a War Raw Materials Department with Rathenau as its head. The new department proceeded to collect and conserve supplies of iron and steel, metals, chemicals, cotton, leather, rubber and other materials, and to allocate them to firms producing for the war effort. Rathenau brought to the task the vision and drive which had made his own firm so successful, though as a civilian and a Jew he hardly felt at home in the military bureaucracy. It was Rathenau's idea to set up a number of non-profit-making companies which worked under close government supervision, the so-called war companies, representing a half-way house between private enterprise and nationalisation. The War Raw Materials Department did its job well, but Germany could not have stayed long in the war had it not been for the skill of her scientists in finding substitutes for materials that had become unobtainable. The outstanding feat was that of Fritz Haber, a professor of chemistry, who invented the process of synthesising ammonia from nitrogen and hydrogen, so making possible the production of munitions and fertilisers without imported saltpetre. Other discoveries were oil from coal, and synthetic rubber. Great ingenuity was shown in inventing substitutes, especially in food. On the initiative of Ballin a private corporation was formed to buy wheat abroad. Extra foodstuffs were imported from Holland and Scandinavia until gradually this source too was cut off by the blockade. Lack of fodder forced the farmers to slaughter several million pigs prematurely, thus reducing the future supply of meat and depriving the farms of breeding stock and manure. Shortage of fertilisers drastically reduced crop yields, and the land also suffered from the call-up of men and horses, despite the employment of prisoners of war. The result was a fall in agricultural productivity and a lower standard of living for the farmer, who – unlike most of the townspeople in the latter half of the war – had enough to eat, but had to pay more for everything he bought. Bread rationing was introduced early in 1915, and was followed by the rationing (with price controls) of meat, potatoes, milk, sugar, fats, butter and clothing. But the rations were often not met, especially in towns. Potatoes replaced grain as the staple food, to be succeeded in turn by turnips after the disastrous potato harvest of 1916. By the summer of 1917 the average daily consumption of calories, which had been 2,280 before the war, had shrunk to about 1,000 and the proportion of protein foods had fallen very much more.[17] Consumption of fats was a sixth of pre-war, consumption of meat a ninth. What was obtainable was monotonous and of poor quality; cooking was difficult and malnutrition widespread. Acorns, chestnut flour, clover meal, pine cones, green leaves and stinging nettles were added to the diet. The winter of 1916–17, when shortage of coal added to the misery, was probably the worst period of the war for civilians.[18] Thereafter, thanks to increased imports from defeated Roumania, food supplies improved slightly, though clothing became scarcer. In 1918 Germany expected to collect a good deal of grain from the Ukraine with which they signed a special 'bread peace', but the 4,000 tons actually secured was disappointingly small. The civilian death rate in Germany rose significantly in the last two years of the war, and the 'flu epidemic of 1918 wrought havoc among a weakened population. It is estimated that about 763,000 deaths were due to the blockade, apart from indirect consequences such as an increase of deaths from tuberculosis and more miscarriages.[19]

In the summer of 1916, when food riots showed a new unrest among the population, the government recognised the urgency of the problem by setting up a War Food Office to control civilian food supplies. This was a federal body under the Chancellor, headed by a senior Prussian official who was advised by General Groener of the General Staff. Groener represented the army on its central committee, which also included a Social Democrat (August Müller) and a trade union leader (Stegerwald). The presence of these spokesmen of the left, suggested by Groener, was an implicit acknowledgement by the government that working-class participation was indispensable. One of the innovations made by the War Food Office was different rations for 'hard' and 'hardest' working labourers. As in other belligerent countries, the war was imposing a new egalitarianism.

One of the thorniest problems was the chronic shortage of labour. Industry and the armed forces both competed for manpower. Initially, in the effort to build up the strength of the army, industry's need for skilled men was almost totally disregarded. But the shortage of munitions in the autumn of 1914 led to a different attitude. In a war much more mechanised, much more dependent on civilian effort than any previous war, the man in the factory was just as important as the man in the trenches. Skilled workers required for essential war industry were exempted from military service, while less specialised jobs were taken over by youths, women and prisoners of war. The deportation of Belgian workmen to Germany already referred to also made a contribution: this anticipated on a small scale the huge migration of forced labour during the Second World War. Then the realisation came that by using more machines the army would be able to manage with fewer men.[20] When in the late summer of 1916 Hindenburg and Ludendorff were appointed to the Supreme Command they decided to increase production of arms and munitions in a new, grandiose programme named after Hindenburg himself. The generals were impressed by the success of Lloyd George's munitions campaign in England, with results shown in the battle of the Somme, and by the British use of manpower. In an effort to emulate this example the new command set up an organisation known as the War Office. Groener, transferred from the War Food Office, was put in charge, and certain functions hitherto exercised by the Prussian Ministry of War were handed over to the new body, which thus became responsible for labour, weapons and munitions, raw materials, clothing supplies, imports, exports, and food supplies for the army and war industry. Yet the new organisation's performance fell short of its promise. Ludendorff believed that more must be done to comb out men for the war effort. The result was the passing in November 1916 of the Auxiliary Service law which obliged all men not in uniform to work in designated occupations. Though the act did not apply to women, they had already come forward in large numbers, and by the beginning of 1917 some four and a third million working women were employed in insured work, only half a million fewer than the number of insured working men.

While the war abolished some of the barriers in German society, it created others. The soldier in the trenches, risking his life for a meagre wage, the poorly paid civilian clerk and the inadequately pensioned war widow resented the profits made by war-contractors. Such gains were taxed, but there were many who considered that they should not be allowed in the first place. One of the reasons for Groener's dismissal as head of the War Office in August 1917 was his criticism of war profits, which had drawn the anger of the big industrialists who were influential with Ludendorff. Agricultural states like Bavaria disliked having to give up food to feed the Prussians. Higher prices too caused unequal degrees of hardship. Some inflation was inevitable in wartime, but it was made worse by the government's recourse to loans and short-term credits in preference to taxation as a means of paying for the war: the expectation was that, once the war was won, the vanquished would pay a huge indemnity. The extra currency put into circulation combined with Germany's unfavourable trade balance to weaken the mark, which by the end of the war had lost about four-fifths of its 1914 value. The lack of financial discipline was a foretaste of the much wilder inflation of the post-war period.

The main consequences of the war for Germany's social economy were three. Firstly, as in all belligerent countries, there was a marked increase of centralisation and government control. Free market forces had to be subordinated to national needs. The War Food Office, the War Office, and the Auxiliary Service law all exemplified this trend, which anticipated the greater, if chaotic, use of controls during the Third Reich. Secondly the army, through the Prussian Ministry of War in the first half of the war, and through the Supreme Command in the second half, played a major part in determining and enforcing economic policy. The changes were less striking in Germany, with its tradition of public ownership and industrial cartels, than in a country with a *laissez-faire* tradition such as England. War socialism, the name often given to the combination of rationing, controls and conscription, was only accelerating what many people felt was an inevitable process in an age of large-scale technology and mass consumption. This was certainly the view of Rathenau, who added a prophet's imagination to his experience as a major industrialist. In his book *Of Things to Come*, published in 1917, Rathenau predicted that, even after the war, the state would continue to play a leading part in economic life, which would be organised on more collective and egalitarian lines than hitherto.

An improvement in the political and – to some extent – material

status of the working classes, and of the trade unions as their representatives, was the third consequence of the war. This arose partly
from the greater bargaining strength of the workers, especially in war
industry, partly from the recognition by the government and the army
of the need to conciliate them. The insatiable demand for skilled men
in the factories producing for the army forced wages up, in some cases
by more than the rise of the cost of living. And though many working
people suffered from price increases and were unable to afford to buy
on the black market, they gained by comparison with the white collar
employees and people living on fixed incomes. As for the government,
a Chancellery memorandum dated 27 October 1914 suggested the
development of a less divided society:

> There is no doubt that the common danger has won the German
> workers for the nation. It offers perhaps the last opportunity to
> win them not only for the nation but also for the state . . . The
> state must seek to avoid treating the labour movement as an
> enemy.[21]

The authorities' refusal to enact franchise reform during the war,
despite the significance of this for the S.P.D., contrasts with their
willingness to meet the demands of the trade unions, and reflects the
difference in outlook between the conservative civilians and the more
pragmatic generals. The unions obtained what amounted to a new
deal. They achieved *de facto* recognition as the workers' spokesmen
and a pre-war ruling that they were political associations was revoked.
The unions, as we have seen, were represented in the War Food Office
and the War Office. They were successful in getting a number of safeguards written into the Auxiliary Service act. The act's essential feature
was that it limited the individual's right to work where he chose. In
return for this, it was agreed that where a difference of opinion arose
over an employee leaving one job for another, the dispute would be
referred to an arbitration committee on which the workers would
have equal representation with the employers. Another provision of
the act was that workers' committees were to be set up in every factory
employing more than fifty persons. Later in the war the government
re-introduced a bill for the establishment of management–labour committees which it had tried unsuccessfully to pass in 1910. During his
period at the War Food Office and the War Office Groener tried his
best to develop good relations between the civil and military authorities
on the one hand and the trade unions on the other. Long before the end
of the war leading industrialists sought union co-operation in plans for
post-war demobilisation. All this paved the way for an agreement between the industrial employers and the union leaders which was

concluded in the last days of the war and formed an economic counterpart to the Groener-Ebert pact of November 1918.

It is not easy to estimate the success of Germany's war economy.[22]
It fell far short of complete efficiency in the use of both manpower and
materials, just as it failed to secure an equitable distribution of burdens. Too little was done to help agriculture overcome the effects of
the blockade. Raw materials were wasted; selfish interests at times
prevailed over public need. There was too much bureaucracy; yet
despite controls a black market flourished and profiteering was a scandal. Nevertheless, Germany managed for over four years under siege
conditions to sustain the war effort against a vastly superior coalition
and to maintain – though in the last two years in a state of semi-
starvation – the working population. Technically some brilliant results
were achieved, especially in chemistry, a field in which Germans had
long excelled, and great inventiveness and organising skill were shown
in the stretching of limited resources.

(iii) THE CRISIS OF SUMMER 1917 AND THE FALL OF BETHMANN HOLLWEG

As the pinched and dreary winter of 1916–17 drew to an end the
German Chancellor sensed that something must be done to raise the
morale of a country increasingly depressed by the sacrifices of an
apparently interminable war. A conference of opposition Socialists in
January 1917 marked the growth of militance on the extreme left, and
emphasised the danger that the moderate Social Democratic leaders
might lose control of their followers. The main internal grievance remained the degrading three-class Prussian franchise. As early as
November 1914 Clemens von Delbrück, the Secretary of the Interior,
had vaguely promised party leaders in the Reichstag a 're-orientation'
of home policy, which was generally understood to mean franchise
reform. Though Bethmann Hollweg had long been in favour of this
as his unsuccessful franchise bill of 1910 showed, he dreaded the
showdown with the Conservatives which changing the internal power
structure would involve, and hoped to delay action until after the war.
But as the war lengthened, and the government made ever greater
demands on its subjects, the case for a political concession became
more pressing. The Kaiser's speech from the throne at the beginning
of 1916 contained a reference to reform, but no action followed. Then
on 27 February 1917 Bethmann returned to the theme. Striking an
emotional note, he praised the new social unity brought about by the
war, and quoted some lines by a worker-poet which declared that
Germany's poorest son had proved her most loyal. The implication

that class franchise must be abolished was obvious. On 14 March Bethmann addressed the Prussian *Landtag* in similar terms: 'Woe to the statesman who does not recognise the signs of the times.' He spoke more truthfully than he knew, for in Russia revolution had already broken out, and the Tsar, who patently did not discern the signs of the times, had just lost his throne. The same radical pressures were at work in both countries, and Scheidemann issued a warning in the socialist daily *Vorwaerts* on 19 March that Germany too might experience revolution if overdue reforms were not carried out. Many people, not only on the right, were alarmed. On 31 March a conference was held at the Chancellery to discuss the effects of the Russian Revolution. 'Bethmann', wrote the South German Progressive leader Haussmann, 'has openly joined the left, and the struggle for power is beginning in the middle of war under the leadership of the Chancellor.'[23] Bethmann's position in the Reichstag seemed safe enough, for only the Conservatives opposed him. The result of a lively parliamentary debate was the setting up of a constitutional committee of the Reichstag which would enable its members to exercise some influence on the government and would deal with the whole question of internal reform. Germany appeared to be moving slowly towards a parliamentary regime. It was not foreseen that government ministers would in fact boycott the committee, which remained virtually powerless.

On 7 April, Easter Day, the Kaiser issued a Message announcing that the three-class franchise in Prussia was to be abolished and the Prussian Upper House reformed after the war. This had been urged on him by Bethmann, who hoped thereby, temporarily at least, to appease his left-wing critics and reassure his supporters in the S.P.D. Almost at the same moment President Wilson, having at last with the approval of Congress declared war on Germany, made a speech explaining that America's object was to make the world safe for democracy. This declaration, coming on the heels of Russia's liberal revolution, emphasised Germany's ideological isolation. 'The democratic ring', wrote Prince Max of Baden, 'seems to be closing tighter and tighter round reactionary Germany.'[24] Although Socialist opinion was far from satisfied with the Easter Message, since it wanted equal suffrage, not the plural suffrage offered, and was unwilling to wait until the end of the war, the gesture was not without effect on the S.P.D. It made no impact on the Socialist opposition, who at that very moment were setting up the Independent Social Democratic party as a semi-revolutionary rival to the 'pro-war' majority (see below). Nor did the Easter Message avert a wave of strikes in Berlin and other big cities that followed a cut in the bread ration. For the first time the strikers made political demands (one of them being equal franchise) and at

Leipzig the strike was organised by a workers' council, an ominous sign in view of the role of workers' councils in revolutionary Russia. On 19 April the S.P.D., worried at the loss of many supporters to the Independents, issued a manifesto calling for equal civil rights, progress towards parliamentary government and – using a slogan recently made popular by the Petrograd Soviet – peace without annexations and indemnities. The moderate 'bourgeois' parties in the Reichstag, especially the National Liberals, shared the Socialist desire for internal reform but adhered to their previous aim of an annexationist peace. A shift of attitude by the Centre, however, was brought about by Erzberger, the leader of its left wing, whose efforts were to culminate in the Peace Resolution of July. Erzberger was one of the few members of the Reichstag who had read the secret memorandum of 12 April drawn up for the Austrian Emperor by Count Czernin, the Dual Monarchy's new Foreign Minister. This stated bluntly that Austria-Hungary had reached the limit of her endurance and that if the governments of the Central Powers did not make peace within the next few months, their exhausted and disillusioned peoples would do so for them. The memorandum repeated, though from the opposite point of view, the warning of the Zimmerwald Socialist parties that Europe must make peace or be engulfed by revolution. Austria had in fact, thanks to German help, achieved its war aims: Serbia and Roumania were occupied and Russia was defeated. Only Italy remained, and she was hardly formidable. German ambitions were the main bar to peace. The Emperor Charles had already, without informing his ally Germany, begun secret talks with France through his brother-in-law Prince Sixtus of Bourbon Parma, who was an officer in the Belgian army. The Germans were furious when they heard later that the Austrians were willing to let France have Alsace-Lorraine as an inducement to peace; such a gesture of disloyalty could only widen the gulf between two allies who had never really trusted or liked one another.

While Bethmann Hollweg was being urged by the Socialists and by the Austrians to end the war on terms amounting to something like the *status quo ante bellum* (a 'Scheidemann peace') he was under equal pressure from the Supreme Command to insist on the fruits of victory (a 'Hindenburg peace'). The generals watched every move in favour of a renunciatory peace with unconcealed disapproval. Optimism at G.H.Q. was sustained by the failure of Allied attempts to break through on the western front in April 1917, by the apparent success of the submarine war against England (sinkings in that month reached their highest level) and by the virtual collapse of Russia as a military power in the wake of revolution. On 23 April the Supreme

Command drew up a memorandum embodying war aims more far-reaching than those agreed during the previous winter as the basis of the German Peace Note. Bethmann Hollweg dared not reject the generals' demands but accepted them with mental reservations.[25] On 15 May in what was to be his last major speech in the Reichstag he used, as before, language which meant different things to different people. As the gaps between the parties had widened, such a performance required even greater tactical skill; but many were now tired of the Chancellor's equivocations, of what he himself called a 'policy of diagonals'. The Supreme Command was unhappy at the prospect of franchise reform, which would give the left-wing parties more influence and herald the breakdown of Prussia's social structure. Ludendorff described the Easter Message as a 'kowtow to the Russian Revolution'. He had one more reason to be rid of the Chancellor.

By the end of June Germany's position had again changed for the worse. In the west Allied superiority in munitions was now, Ludendorff's spokesman Colonel Bauer told Reichstag leaders, four to one, and would rise to six to one – a bleak prospect for the future. Submarine sinkings of British ships, though still serious, were beginning to taper off as the convoy system introduced by Lloyd George proved effective. Russia was still in the war, and with Brussilov launching what was to be his last offensive there was no immediate prospect of a separate peace with Russia. The western powers still showed no inclination to take part in a general peace settlement. A fourth winter campaign was now inevitable. At home, as the S.P.D. leaders reminded the Chancellor in a memorandum that was almost an ultimatum, discontent and suffering had reached new depths. Scheidemann afterwards described conditions at this time:

> Workmen were collapsing by the hundred from starvation every day in the factories; postwomen were fainting on the doorsteps. Hunger, deprivation and sorrowing for the dead; indignation aroused by Pan-German war proposals; no prospect of an end, and, last but not least, despair verging on revolution.[26]

Riots and disorders in various parts of Germany indicated a serious breakdown in morale and discipline. Bethmann could not ignore the danger signals. The Easter Message did not go far enough, he told the Kaiser. On 12 July Bethmann was authorised to issue a promise that Prussia would receive, before the end of the war, the same franchise (one man one vote) as the Reichstag, and that a bill to that effect would be introduced into the Prussian Landtag. Bethmann, having won the battle for reform, no doubt reckoned on the continued support of the left-wing parties. He was cruelly disillusioned immediately.

For it was at this point that Erzberger's plans, temporarily coinciding with Ludendorff's, brought about Bethmann's dismissal.[27] Erzberger, who had been an ardent annexationist at an earlier stage of the war, was now convinced that Germany must return to the policy of defence with which she had officially entered the war. Austria's desperate situation was one reason for Erzberger's pessimism. Another was the false optimism generated by promises of a British collapse as a result of U-boat sinkings. Having made his own assessment, Erzberger had little difficulty in proving to the Reichstag main committee that the German Admiralty had grossly miscalculated, particularly in ignoring the extent to which the British could call upon other countries, including their new ally America, to replace shipping losses. Erzberger's disclosures created a sensation. He also feared that the Majority socialists would not vote for the next war credits bill, which was imminent. Having inscribed the formula of no annexations on its banner, the S.P.D. could hardly go on supporting a Chancellor who, as Bethmann had told the Reichstag, was in full agreement with the Supreme Command on war aims. And at a time when thousands of Majority socialists were going over to the Independent socialist party the S.P.D. leaders were almost obliged to take a more radical line. Yet if the S.P.D. went into opposition the unity of the German people, demonstrated by the Reichstag majority, would be shattered. Erzberger believed that a peace gesture by the Reichstag would restore internal harmony, reassure the war-weary Austrians, and favourably influence neutral and even hostile opinion. Convinced by Erzberger's arguments, the Reichstag parties formed a new, inter-party committee, from which only the Conservatives and the Independent socialists were absent, to draw up a peace resolution. The draft was shown to Bethmann Hollweg, who considered it a tactical mistake, though he could hardly disapprove the contents. Indeed, in combining assertion of purely defensive intentions with a clause that did not exclude territorial gains in certain circumstances, the resolution was very much in line with Bethmann's own pronouncements. It was this which alarmed Hindenburg and Ludendorff. They had no wish to see a peace resolution passed, especially while the pessimistic and 'flabby' Bethmann was in charge, and they hastened to Berlin to raise opposition to the Chancellor among the politicians. Bethmann, aware of the danger, persuaded the Kaiser to order the generals back to headquarters, where they doubtless had 'more important business'. Instead of putting Erzberger and his friends on their guard, the incident strengthened their determination to get rid of Bethmann. With doubtful constitutional propriety, Ludendorff now brought the Crown Prince into play. The latter, a political lightweight but known to be a supporter of the Pan-Germans and an extreme right-winger, invited the various party leaders to give him their views on the Chancellor. Apart from the Progressives, no party now supported Bethmann; even some of the Social Democrats desired his fall. Since he no longer commanded a majority, Bethmann's usefulness to the Kaiser was at an end. But William did not take the final step of dismissing his Chancellor until Ludendorff threatened that otherwise he and Hindenburg would resign. Bethmann went quietly, making no attempt to rally his friends or seek the support of the Reichstag against a flagrant interference by the Supreme Command in domestic politics.

The dismissal of Bethmann Hollweg could be construed, as it was by some of the more gullible, as a victory for the Reichstag over the executive. In reality it was a victory for Ludendorff, for Bethmann's successor was virtually the general's nominee. Ludendorff had no intention of allowing the Reichstag to thwart his war aims or put a Scheidemann-type government in power. He insisted on influencing the wording of the peace resolution, the significance of which was largely lost when the new Chancellor, Michaelis, declared that he accepted it only as he understood it. Erzberger had given as one of his reasons for opposing Bethmann that the latter had 'soiled his waistcoat' by the violation of Belgium and unrestricted submarine warfare. Yet Erzberger himself and all the Reichstag parties except the Socialists had gone along with these policies and were later to vote for the annexationist treaty of Brest Litovsk. If the new Reichstag majority coalition of Centre, Progressives and S.P.D. had really wished to introduce a parliamentary regime and negotiate a moderate peace they should have made Ludendorff their target, not Bethmann Hollweg. Erzberger had made the worst mistake of his political career by ousting Bethmann without making sure that his successor would be more acceptable; he had let himself be used by people (not only Ludendorff, but National Liberals like Stresemann) whose objects were the reverse of his. If there was any chance of peace in the summer of 1917 it was more likely to be served by Bethmann's staying in office than by the passing of an ambiguous resolution. But Ludendorff was beyond the Reichstag's reach, and the Kaiser dared not dismiss the one man believed capable of winning the war. Some of the Reichstag members including Erzberger hoped that Bülow would succeed Bethmann; but William II had not forgotten Bülow's behaviour during the *Daily Telegraph* crisis in 1908, and the Austrian government resented Bülow's earlier attempts to buy off Italian hostility at their expense. The intrigue against Bethmann Hollweg thus proved a fruitless as well as a

discreditable episode.[28] Bethmann had prepared the way for his own
fall by helping to put Hindenburg and Ludendorff in the Supreme
Command the year before, a decision which could be justified on military grounds but was politically fatal. Alternative governments, such as
a broad coalition combining annexationists with reformers (as desired
by Stresemann) or one including the Majority socialists and in favour
of a moderate peace (as Groener would have liked) were rejected:
Ludendorff believed he could win the war without making concessions
at home, and that, after victory, there would be no need for them.
If Ludendorff's political philosophy was the price of victory, it was
a price most of the German people were willing to pay.

(iv) MICHAELIS AND HERTLING: THE PENDULUM SWINGS BACK

If the object of the Reichstag peace resolution had been to bring
peace nearer, it failed. The new Chancellor, Michaelis, whose sympathies were Pan-German, was more inclined to listen to the generals
than to the party leaders. It was, however, a slight concession to the
Reichstag that on the resignation of Zimmermann, the Foreign
Secretary who had sent the notorious telegram inviting Mexico to
make war against the United States, the appointment went to Kühlmann, a moderate. Kühlmann was a diplomat, still fairly young, who
had served in the German embassy in London before the war and
played some part in the Anglo-German détente of 1912–14. He was
skilful, conciliatory and free from the illusions which clouded the
judgement of many of Germany's policy-makers. He believed that
Germany would have to give ground in the west in order to obtain
a peace which would leave her with at least some of her gains in the
east. There were two main difficulties: the British insisted on the complete restoration of Belgium, the French on the cession ('de-annexa-
tion') of Alsace-Lorraine. German public opinion was practically solid
in resisting the surrender of Alsace-Lorraine, and the Supreme Command was adamant on the retention of part if not the whole of Belgium. Kühlmann had also to take account of the Committee of Seven,
representing the majority parties in the Reichstag. Formally set up to
advise the government on its reply to the Papal Peace Note of 1
August, the committee was another of the constitutional innovations
of the summer of 1917. The crude annexationism of Hindenburg and
Ludendorff could not be reconciled with the conviction of Scheidemann, the Socialist leader who was a member of the Committee of
Seven, that some concessions were essential in the interests of peace.
The Pope's Note followed informal discussions on the terms of
a possible peace settlement between the Papal Nuncio Pacelli

(the future Pius XII) and the German ministers. The Vatican, which was also in touch with the British government, made it plain in Berlin that no progress could be made unless Germany was prepared to give up Belgium unconditionally. Kühlmann refused to take this step in advance of the proposed negotiations. He was sceptical about the changes of a settlement, if only because – with good reason – he did not believe that the French would give up their claim to Alsace-Lorraine. Also Kühlmann had greater hopes of secret talks with the British government which his friend, the Marquis of Villalobar, the Spanish ambassador at Brussels, was conducting through their mutual friend, Sir William Tyrrell of the Foreign Office. Difficulties however were put in Villalobar's way by the Spanish Foreign Minister, and nothing came of his efforts. Kühlmann did not take the Committee of Seven into his confidence on the Belgian question, and Scheidemann later asserted that it had been duped. Kühlmann suggests in his Memoirs that a premature disclosure of the German government's attitude would have ruined the prospects of his secret diplomacy.[29] He also had to walk warily in his relations with the Supreme Command, which insisted on keeping Liège for Germany and would have liked to annex the Flanders coast. So the Papal peace initiative proved fruitless, and Europe prepared for its fourth war winter.

Michaelis's chancellorship lasted little more than three months. An able and conscientious official who had been Food Controller in Prussia, he was quite unfitted for the post to which he had so unexpectedly been promoted and candidly confessed his ignorance of high-level politics. One of the problems he had to deal with was a minor mutiny in the navy in the summer of 1917. It had been politically motivated in that many of the sailors were known to be in favour of a compromise peace, and some of their leaders had had contacts with members of the Reichstag, particularly, though not exclusively, with Independent socialists. Michaelis, through his Secretary of the Navy von Capelle, accused the Independents in the Reichstag of inciting the sailors to mutiny, but could not substantiate the charge, and in the ensuing debate other parties defended the Independents. Michaelis had lost – or perhaps never won – the confidence of the Reichstag, and his unsuitability was acknowledged. The inter-party committee broke new ground by demanding that the Kaiser dismiss his Chancellor. They also agreed that his successor would have to assent to a four point programme: adhere to the government's letter to Pacelli of 19 September, which (they believed) contained certain assurances about Belgium, reform the Prussian franchise, abolish censorship and army interference in politics, and introduce management–labour councils in industry.[30] The four main parties (National Liberals, Centre, Progressives and Majority socialists) all supported this programme, which reflected in particular the wishes of the Socialists. On these terms Count Hertling, the Prime Minister of Bavaria, was appointed Chancellor in succession to Michaelis, who resigned.

Hertling was a leader of the right wing of the Centre party and a former professor of philosophy. A man of integrity, he was a spent force at the age of seventy-four, and politically a cypher.[31] Offered the chancellorship in July when Bethmann resigned, Hertling had refused it on the grounds of age; now in October, though in bad health and almost blind, he accepted. It was rather like the appointment of the aged Hohenlohe twenty-three years before, but in infinitely graver circumstances. Besides agreeing to the conditions already mentioned, Hertling had to promise autonomy to Alsace-Lorraine, and to appoint as his Vice-Chancellor the Progressive South German parliamentarian von Payer instead of the unpopular right-wing Helfferich. At the same time another Reichstag deputy, the National Liberal Friedberg, was made Prime Minister of Prussia. Both men, in accordance with the constitution, gave up their Reichstag seats. These changes, the setting up of the Committee of Seven, the initiative taken by the Reichstag in ousting Michaelis and the promise made to the parties by Hertling suggested that Germany had entered a transitional stage between constitutional autocracy and a parliamentary regime, and claims to this effect were made by Scheidemann and others. But the difference was more apparent than real. No progress was made on the two vital issues of peace and franchise reform. Hertling had actually disapproved of the peace resolution (he was on bad terms with his radical colleague in the Centre party, Erzberger) and was the last man to stand up to Hindenburg and Ludendorff, whose hopes of a victorious peace he supported. As for Belgium, the government's letter to Pacelli of 19 September had made no firm commitment. Hertling introduced a franchise reform bill into the Prussian *Landtag*, but it was held up by Conservative opposition, which Hertling lacked the strength if not the conviction to overcome until the end of the war when it was too late. He believed that to impose franchise reform on the states would be an unwarrantable violation of their rights, as would the introduction of parliamentary government. Ludendorff's position was actually stronger than in the time of Bethmann Hollweg. The party leaders had made the mistake of not insisting on their own choice of Chancellor. Valentini, the chief of the Kaiser's Civil Cabinet, described the 'parliamentarisation' as a masquerade that would last only a few months – until victory, presumably, gave Ludendorff a free hand at home.[32] As for the Kaiser, his remark to party leaders in July 1918 during a conversation which referred to the Russian Revolution, 'Where the guard steps in, there is no democracy' no doubt expressed his real sentiments.[33]

The formation of a relatively liberal majority in the Reichstag and the peace resolution (even with its annexationist loophole) were enough to alarm the Pan-Germans, who saw a dangerous spirit of defeatism abroad which they were determined to exorcise. Early in September 1917 Tirpitz and his friends, with the benevolent approval of Hindenburg and Ludendorff, founded a new nationalist organisation called the Patriotic Party aimed at rousing support for a victorious (i.e. annexationist) peace and discrediting any idea of compromise. Any peace that fell short of the other ideal would make internal reform inevitable and so destroy the social system which they were fighting to preserve. The temper of the new party can be judged from a pamphlet in which it declared that 'world democracy' was the internal as well as external enemy: 'We are fighting a double war: on fronts in the east and the west, and at home. Those who do not stop the democratic and international efforts on the threshold are working for the enemy . . .'[34] Here was the germ of the 'stab in the back' legend that was to be disseminated a year later as the excuse for losing the war. There were times when Ludendorff admitted that he was more concerned with resisting an internal shift of power than in gaining territory.[35] By the summer of 1918 the Patriotic Party had a million and a quarter members, and its ideas were propagated by officers in the army and navy in the form of 'patriotic instruction'. One of the grievances which lay behind the unrest in the navy was this propaganda, which to the rank and file was a sign that the war was being prolonged in the interests of the Prussian ruling class. Officials and the generals administering the censorship also favoured the nationalists, whereas speeches and articles in favour of a moderate peace were suppressed.

(v) THE DILEMMA OF GERMAN SOCIALISM

'The war', wrote Groener in his diary on 19 October 1916, 'is becoming increasingly a question of the workers.'[36] Groener was one of the few leading generals to realise that, in return for their wartime sacrifices, the workers would expect some redressment of their political grievances, especially of the grossly unequal Prussian franchise. This the Conservatives and Pan-Germans were determined not to concede, if only because they knew that any advance in the direction of democracy would undermine their position. The result was that the Social Democrats had to ask themselves how long they could go on supporting a government which did nothing concrete to meet their wishes for reform and refused to accept their defensive war aims. In 1912 over a third of the electorate had voted for the S.P.D., so that the problem was one of national concern; it did not affect just a few left-wing doctrinaires.

The dilemma was presented, as we have seen, at the very beginning of the war when the Socialists had to decide whether or not to vote for war credits in the Reichstag. Their decision to vote the credits, taken after an agonising re-appraisal, was reached on the assumption that the government meant what it said when it claimed that it had no intention of making conquests, the implication being that if the government changed its mind the S.P.D. would oppose the war. When it became obvious that the government was bent on annexations a split developed inside the S.P.D. as we saw in chapter IV. In March 1916 the dissentients formed the separate parliamentary group known as the Social Democratic *Arbeitsgemeinschaft*. Efforts to heal the breach, notably at an all-Socialist conference held in September 1916, failed. The rebels derided the conformist majority as mere opportunists who had deserted their principles and betrayed the movement. The majority condemned the minority as hopelessly unrealistic and defeatist. In April 1917 the latter set up their own independent party organisation known as the Independent Social Democratic party (U.S.P.D.) which in the summer of 1917 came near to having as many supporters as the parent S.P.D. This process of disintegration of the highly organised S.P.D. was the *Burgfrieden* in reverse, a warning to the government and middle classes of rising discontent and social disunity.

Doubts about the government's war aims and resentment at the lack of reform were also widespread among the Majority Socialists. Yet they continued to vote for war credits. One reason for this was their belief that they were supporting the country not the government. Another was a certain confidence they felt in Bethmann Hollweg and their knowledge that if he fell his successor as Chancellor would almost certainly be less acceptable. As for annexations, the Allies' declared intentions of making territorial gains at the expense of Germany and her allies seemed to prove that the only alternative to backing the war effort was to court a disastrous peace. Basically the S.P.D. was composed of patriots who feared nothing so much as defeat. The Majority socialists also hoped that their patriotism during the war would give them a new status. 'We are defending the fatherland,' Scheidemann told the Reichstag early in 1915, 'in order to possess it.'[37] In October 1917 he told his party that they now had a direct prospect of supremacy in the state: a shift of power had occurred in favour of the proletariat. No doubt there was wishful thinking in this: Scheidemann had to justify to discontented supporters the policy followed since August 1914 and to prevent further loss of adherents to the Independent socialists. But it was reasonable to believe that the three-class franchise would not survive the war and that Germany could not indefinitely withstand the democratic wave then breaking over Europe. Against this argument, it was highly unlikely that if Germany won the war a victorious Ludendorff would introduce popular government. Despite some illusions and not a little opportunism the S.P.D. showed a sense and moderation rare enough in the other parties. It was the only party, apart from the Independents, which took the Reichstag peace resolution seriously enough to refuse to vote for ratification of the treaty of Brest Litovsk even if it did not actually vote against it.[38]

The Independent socialists were, of course, more consistent in their anti-war stand. They were right in suspecting that the government was more annexationist than it publicly admitted, as the Brest Litovsk treaty was to show. The Independents did not, like the Majority, virtually ignore the pre-war policy of the International; they interpreted it as meaning that their duty was to oppose a war of aggression, which this plainly was as far as Germany was concerned. There were two difficulties. One was that the other side also had aggressive aims; the other that aggression tended to be judged in terms of military success, so that if the Allies drove the German army back into Germany, the war would presumably become one of defence for the latter. The more radical Spartacists ridiculed the notion of making support for the war dependent on a fluid military situation, and denied that the war could be justified from any point of view; but they rejected too the concept of national defence, which pre-war socialist policy had accepted. The Independents thus found themselves fighting a war on two fronts, against the nationalist socialists on the right and the doctrinaire internationalists on the left. Their best hope seemed to lie in the activity of similar anti-war groups in other belligerent and neutral countries, such as the British I.L.P. and the Swiss and Italian Socialist parties. Attempts were made to bring the anti-war parties together. The German Independents attended the conferences of Zimmerwald and Kienthal in Switzerland, each of which issued a manifesto denouncing the war. Yet here too ideological differences proved a stumbling block. While the 'centrists' of whom the German Independents were perhaps the most typical stood for constitutional opposition to the war, formed a semi-pacifist platform and sought to rouse support for a democratic peace, the new left, led by Lenin and his Bolsheviks, called for revolutionary action to turn the imperialist war into a civil war. These

differences remained unresolved. As the war lengthened and the lot of
the ordinary citizen became more wretched the mood inside some of
the belligerent countries became subversive. The revolution in Russia
put new hope into the German Independents.

One result of the changes in Russia was a fresh stimulus to peace.
The Petrograd Soviet proclaimed its policy of peace without annexations and indemnities (the Zimmerwald formula), which encouraged
neutral socialists to convene an international socialist peace conference
at Stockholm in the summer of 1917. The conference never met because of boycott by the Allies. But the visit of both German Socialist
parties to Stockholm for talks with the neutrals brought out the difference between the two as far as war aims were concerned. The
Independents were ready to accept far-reaching changes in Central
Europe based on self-determination; their post-war map of Europe
would not have differed greatly from that of the Allied planners. In
spite of this, the German Independents continued to be berated by
Lenin for their pacifism and constitutionalism. The left wing of the
Independents was formed by militant shop stewards, who led the strike
movement which was active in Germany during the last two years of
the war. Apart from them, and from a few firebrand members of the
Reichstag, the Independent socialist party adhered to the traditional
S.P.D. belief in a bloodless revolution, and the use of force was
repugnant to it. Even the left-wing Spartacists were divided in
their attitude to Lenin's use of dictatorship and violence once he
came to power in Russia.[39] Thus the Independents too had their
dilemma: they could neither approve the war nor successfully oppose
it.

Though the Spartacists remained small in numbers they were important in several ways: the purity and fanaticism of their doctrinal
internationalism, their courage in opposing the war at the price of persecution, and above all the personality of their leaders, Karl Liebknecht
and Rosa Luxemburg. Rosa Luxemburg was the most remarkable and
colourful personality in the history of German socialism, to which she
came as an adult recruit from Russian Poland. From the beginning
her hostility to the war was uncompromising, and the Spartacists
worked underground sending out letters and pamphlets as well as
overtly whenever circumstances allowed. They regarded constitutional
opposition including speeches in the Reichstag as useless in wartime,
and came round to the Leninist view that the war could be ended only
by revolution. They agreed with him that there was nothing to be said
for either side, nor any value in a compromise or democratic peace.
Captitalism, which had given birth to the imperialist war, must itself
be destroyed. A new, stronger Socialist International must be created

which would force socialist parties to conform to an internationalist policy in deed as well as word. The Spartacists remained loosely attached to the Independent socialist party for tactical reasons, but poured scorn on the attempt by the latter to find a middle way between support of an aggressive war and the unleashing of premature revolution. Yet the Spartacist cause won few adherents: in a time of fierce nationalism its somewhat abstract internationalism had little appeal, and few German workers were willing to run the risk of defeat for the sake of world revolution. The differences among Spartacists during the last year of the war caused by Lenin's undemocratic and un-Marxist policy in Russia foreshadowed the doctrinal splits of the post-war European left and inside the German Communist party of which the Spartacists were the nucleus.

(vi) 1918, LUDENDORFF'S YEAR

By comparison with the preceding crises the eleven months of Hertling's chancellorship was an uneventful period in German internal politics, except for the strike of January 1918. There was no recurrence of the tension between High Command and Chancellor which had caused the fall of Bethmann Hollweg, though Kühlmann's dismissal as Foreign Secretary in July 1918 showed where the mastery lay. Nor was there any repetition of the breach between Chancellor and Reichstag such as had led to the resignation of Michaelis. Minor as they were, the constitutional innovations of 1917 had temporarily satisfied the demand for change, and the obstruction brought by the Prussian *Landtag* to the franchise reform bill raised little stir, at least on the surface. Men's hopes were fixed once again on winning the war. In the autumn of 1917 Germany's military prospects improved. In Flanders a major British offensive was drowned in a sea of mud. In Italy the Austrians with German help won a crushing victory at Caporetto which, had it been followed up, might have destroyed the Italian army. Russia, increasingly absorbed in her revolutionary struggle, ceased to count as a belligerent. The calculations of the German government in supporting the Russian revolutionary movement, and more specifically in enabling Lenin to return to Russia from Switzerland in April 1917, seemed to have been fully justified when the Bolsheviks seized power in November and declared their intention of ending the war. A Russo-German armistice was signed early in December, and on 22 December peace negotiations between the Bolshevik government and the Central Powers were opened at Brest Litovsk. Ludendorff had already begun the transfer of a million men from the eastern front to the west, where for the first time the number of

German divisions exceeded that of their opponents. Whether the Germans had more troops in the west is doubtful, because the number of men to a division varied between the two armies.[40]

The Brest negotiations, which lasted, with interruptions, for ten weeks, predictably reflected Germany's determination to exploit her victory and Russia's weakness. The German delegation was headed by Richard von Kühlmann, who was a moderate annexationist with few illusions about Germany's prospects. As a man capable of taking long views, he was anxious not to treat Russia in such a way as to blacken Germany's name further in the eyes of neutrals. He also wanted to keep the goodwill of the politicians who had passed the peace resolution of July 1917 though on this point he need not have worried: the Reichstag was as flexible as he was. Kühlmann was accompanied at Brest by General Max Hoffmann, Chief of Staff of the Commander-in-Chief, eastern front, and Germany's shrewdest military brain. The Russians took their stand on the decree *To All!* issued in the first days of the Bolshevik government and calling for a peace without annexations and indemnities – the formula of the Petrograd Soviet and before that of the Zimmerwald Conference. They also demanded self-determination of peoples. The Germans at first accepted this formula, but soon showed that in applying it they meant something other than the Russians expected – a perfunctory consultation of unrepresentative assemblies in territories occupied by the German army. The Pan-Germans rejected even the principle of self-determination, and Kühlmann had to explain that there was no intention of abandoning territory that had been won. The Social Democrats, not to be taken in, accused Kühlmann of cheating. The Germans at Brest took advantage of the refusal of the western Allies to respond to the Russians' appeal for a general peace to declare that they were no longer bound by self-determination. Negotiations became acrimonious as the Russians realised that the peace would be a harsh one. Inside Germany there was a division of opinion over the size of the new 'frontier strip' which was to be annexed from Russian Poland. The Supreme Command wished to extend the area so as to include within Germany between two and three million additional Poles. General Hoffmann managed to persuade the Kaiser that it would be a mistake for him to acquire so many Polish subjects. When Hindenburg and Ludendorff learned this they were so angry that they threatened to resign, whereupon William, as usual, gave way, though not completely. Not only the Foreign Office, but even the Kaiser's civil cabinet felt the wrath of the two demigods as they were called; and Valentini, its head, was forced to resign in favour of von Berg, an ultra-conservative and admirer of Hindenburg. Valentini was blamed for the 'swing to the

2 Imperial Chancellor Bethmann Hollweg, Gottlieb von Jagow (Secretary for Foreign Affairs), Vice-Chancellor Karl Helfferich

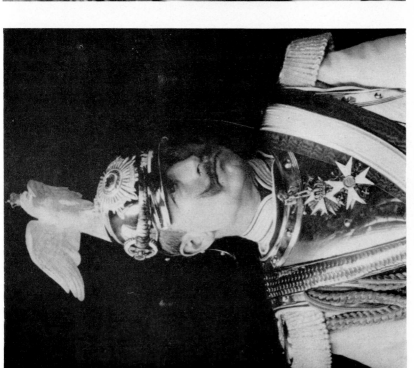

1 Kaiser Wilhelm II

3 Joining up, August 1914

4 Germany's war leaders in 1914

5 The Kaiser in the field, 1916

6 Hindenburg, Wilhelm II, Ludendorff

7 Republican demonstration outside the royal palace, November 1918

8 Revolution, 1918–19

9 The aftermath of war, Berlin, 1919

10 President Ebert at a review on the fifth anniversary of the Weimar constitution, August 1924

12 Gustav Stresemann

11 Thomas Mann

13 The 'Red Front' salutes Thälmann, the Communist leader, May 1926

14 Brüning (right), Curtius (centre) and their advisers in London for a seven-power conference, July 1931

15 Hitler and Hindenburg at Potsdam, March 1933

16 Storm troops at the Bückeberg Harvest Festival, 1934

left' in the government.[41] Hindenburg professed to be devoted to the monarchy: by such acts he was devaluing it.

When the two delegations confronted each other at Brest on 9 January after the first break, Trotsky, a more formidable personality and tougher negotiator than Joffe, was the chief Russian spokesman. He refused to accept the German terms, which amounted virtually to annexation of the occupied territories. Trotsky's hope was to defeat the German militarists by playing for time. While the talks stalled, he used his inflammatory oratory to rouse world opinion to sympathy with the Bolsheviks, appealing especially to the working classes of Germany and Austria-Hungary to follow the Russian example and bring about a revolution in their countries. The Bolsheviks had seen their seizure of power as only the first stage of a European revolution which alone could prevent them from being overwhelmed. Trotsky's appeals, which were heard on the radio and read in the press, did not go unheeded: in the course of January a series of strikes broke out, spreading from Vienna and Budapest to Berlin and other German cities. In Germany alone something like a million men in the engineering industry downed tools in protest against their government's refusal to make a democratic peace with Russia. Other demands by the strikers were for bigger food rations, democratic government, the abolition of martial law and workers' representation at peace negotiations. The strike embarrassed the government but did not interfere with Ludendorff's plans for the offensive or the supply of munitions. It was more embarrassing to the Majority socialists, who could not support it without appearing unpatriotic, but dared not stand aside, partly because they agreed with the objects of the strike, partly because they feared to lose more supporters to the Independent socialists, whose militant shop-steward wing demanded a showdown. The Majority socialist leaders joined the organising committee but did so with the intention of keeping the strike under control and preventing it from escalating, as the extreme left wanted, into an act of political insurrection. The tactic worked, though only just: Ebert himself narrowly missed arrest for making a speech to the strikers in a Berlin park, and was never forgiven for this by the nationalists. The Majority socialists thus anticipated their ambiguous role in the German revolution ten months later, for which the strike was a kind of rehearsal. Yet it is difficult to see what else the S.P.D. could have done. Large numbers of the strike leaders including the militant shop-steward Richard Müller were sent to the front, while Dittmann, the Independent socialist leader, was given a five years' prison sentence for addressing a strike meeting.

The strike had no effect on the negotiations at Brest, where the Germans had strengthened their hand by making a separate peace treaty with an anti-Bolshevik government in the Ukraine, one of the main objects of which was to ensure that Ukrainian corn would be available to replenish the empty granaries of Germany and Austria. The loss of the Ukraine deprived Russia of a high proportion of her industrial and agricultural resources as well as of her population. On 10 February, just after the German-Ukrainian peace treaty was signed, Trotsky made a defiant speech, declaring that the war with Germany was over but that his government would not sign a disgraceful peace, and stalked out of the conference. On the insistence of the Supreme Command, and against Kühlmann's advice, the German government decided to take advantage of the temporary armistice to continue its invasion of Russia. There was no resistance, and in five days the German forces advanced 150 miles, occupying Livonia and Estonia in the north, and the heart of the Ukraine in the south. On 24 February the Bolsheviks acknowledged defeat by accepting the German terms. But Berlin now wanted more. The Russians would have to give up Livonia and Estonia as well as Finland, Courland, Lithuania and Poland, and recognise the independence of the Ukraine. On these condtions peace was signed on 3 March. Lenin had to use all his skill to persuade his colleagues in the Bolshevik party to accept so punitive a treaty, and one which, as appeared later, was to open the way to fresh German penetration and disruption. The survival of the Soviet regime within the new borders which deprived it of three-quarters of Russia's coal and steel seemed very doubtful. In the Reichstag too the treaty was the subject of heated discussion. Some party leaders questioned its compatibility with the peace resolution. The Chancellor declared that the peace resolution was completely and definitely dead.[42] Gröber of the Centre party argued that against a subversive enemy like the Bolsheviks so severe a treaty was justified. Erzberger, the author of the peace resolution if not its actual draftsman, sought to square the circle by maintaining that treaty and resolution were not incompatible provided that the formula of self-determination was applied to the occupied provinces fairly and honestly. This view was disingenuous, for it was obvious that the Supreme Command would not allow self-determination to work where it ran contrary to German interests. Stresemann, of the National Liberal party, who had been a thoroughgoing annexationist, was franker: 'Practically,' he told his colleagues, 'we have brought it to this, that a conclusion of peace in opposition to the peace resolution of 19 July has been agreed to by all the bourgeois parties.'[43] It remained for the Socialists to save whatever shreds of the peace resolution policy remained. For the S.P.D. Scheidemann and David expressed their misgivings about the Russian treaty and warned that it set a dangerous precedent: Germany herself might be faced with the same kind of vindictive peace if she lost the war in the west. Few Majority socialists had the courage to vote against the treaty when the Reichstag voted its ratification; most of them abstained, and left opposition to the Independent socialists. Similarly when, a few weeks later, the separate peace treaty between Germany and defeated Roumania was presented to the Reichstag, it was only the Independent socialists who voted against it.

The peace treaties with Soviet Russia, the Ukraine and Roumania recognised the control which Germany already had over most of Eastern Europe and opened up enticing prospects in many fields. The Bolshevik government was sufficiently under German pressure to sign at the end of August 1918 a supplementary treaty to Brest Litovsk whereby it renounced all claims to sovereignty over Livonia and Estonia, acknowledged the independence of the Caucasian republic of Georgia, and undertook to expel Entente troops from Northern Russia; it also agreed to pay a war indemnity of six billion marks. The unpopularity of the German government in Russia was shown by the murder of its ambassador, Count Mirbach, early in July, and provided an excuse for the German army to seize Petrograd and other important centres had it been ordered to do so. There was no military obstacle. But though anti-Bolshevik sentiment was strong in Berlin, the Foreign Ministry was anxious not to destroy the Soviet regime at least as long as Germany was still at war with the West: certainly the return of a White Russian government would have suited the Germans less because it would not have accepted the Brest treaty. In any case, few expected Lenin and his party to remain in power. Such considerations did not prevent Ludendorff from pursuing plans to set up a Tartar republic in the Crimea, where the presence of German colonists would help to maintain German influence. The supplementary treaty also provided that Russia should sell to Germany 25 per cent of the oil from Baku in the Caucasus, and Ludendorff sent a military mission there, only to find that the Turks had preceded them. In his ambitious schemes to divide Russia politically and exploit it economically Ludendorff anticipated Hitler: it is at this point that the continuity of German aims between the First and Second World Wars is most evident. The rise of Ludendorff and fall of Bethmann Hollweg had signified the growing radicalisation of German policy brought about by the war. Whereas Bethmann Hollweg would probably have made peace on broadly *status quo ante bellum* lines if he had been able to, for Ludendorff only a peace which yielded substantial gains was worth having. In his territorial imperialism no less than in his racial and religious crankiness Ludendorff is the essential link between the age of William II and that of Hitler.[44] But the extension of German power in

Russia, short-lived as it was to be, was bought at a heavy price. A million soldiers were needed to police the vast area between Finland and the Black Sea, who might have turned the scale if they had been on the western front, and the expenditure of political and economic energy was considerable. The results of the much publicised corn forage in the Ukraine were disappointing: only enough was obtained to feed the garrison, and Germany received no oil at all from Baku. Politically the German authorities found themselves at odds with the burgeoning nationalism of the liberated countries, especially in the Baltic states, which showed no desire to play the part of German satellites. Members of the ruling dynasties in the Reich, including the Emperor, were engaged in an unseemly and increasingly unreal wrangle for the crown of Finland and the grand duchies of Courland and Lithuania, Livonia and Estonia; while the rank and file of the German army in the east was exposed to the revolutionary influence of Bolshevism.

Yet it was the western front which held the attention of the world in 1918. In November 1917 Ludendorff had decided on the final offensive there, preparations which had been going on through the winter. The best German troops, including all under the age of thirty-five on the Russian front, had been scraped together for what would be the decisive assault. Special courses were held in offensive tactics for the benefit of troops mainly accustomed to defence. 'We had', wrote Ludendorff, 'to revive in the minds of the fighting forces all those excellent offensive principles which inspired our pre-war regulations.'[45] Emphasis was placed on quick-firing weapons – the light machine gun, the rifle grenade, the trench mortar – and on flexibility and mobility in attack. 'The new German offensive would not be a battering ram, pounding head-on against a wall, but rather like a flood of water, flowing around obstacles, isolating them, and following the path of least resistance deep into the enemy's territory.'[46] Great masses of artillery were accumulated, and troops were trained in the technique of advancing behind a creeping barrage. All these preparations were made with typical thoroughness and in remarkable secrecy.

The 1918 offensive was as much a gamble as the Schlieffen Plan, probably more so. But it presented the only chance of winning the war before Germany's allies collapsed and before American intervention on the western front turned the scale against her. There were other considerations: an offensive was needed to revive morale, both in the army and at home. It does not appear that the alternative policy of seeking a compromise peace with the west while keeping German conquests in the east was seriously considered by Ludendorff, though Hindenburg admitted privately that he could not guarantee the success of the offensive.[47] He afterwards wondered whether Germany would not have been better advised to stay on the defensive in the west while she created her new order in Eastern Europe. Germany already controlled the territory needed for her *Mitteleuropa* plans, but needed time to develop their resources and to build up in Europe and the Near East an economic imperium that would compensate for the failure of her world policy. But the Austrians were doubtful if they could survive another war winter, and the Turks were at the end of their strength. Ludendorff was, in any case, not interested in compromise, as he showed by his refusal to the very end of the war to surrender Belgium, and also by his answer to Prince Max of Baden, who asked him which would happen if the new offensive failed. In that event, Ludendorff cynically replied, Germany must go to her doom.[48]

Prince Max was one of a number of leading civilians who were worried by Ludendorff's plans. Another was Hans Delbrück, the military historian and brother of Clemens von Delbrück, the former Minister of the Interior. Delbrück argued in the periodical *Preussische Jahrbücher* that even if the German army was the best in the world it did not possess a margin of superiority that would enable it to win the war by military means alone.[49] Diplomacy must be brought in: the offer of a moderate settlement (concessions over Belgium) would split the Allies and make England, unwilling to go on fighting for Alsace-Lorraine, ready for peace. Similar arguments were used by members of the Reichstag such as Scheidemann, Erzberger and Friedrich Naumann. Naumann also joined Max Weber, the industrialist Robert Bosch and the trade union leaders Legien and Stegerwald in presenting a memorandum to Ludendorff urging that before the military offensive was launched there should be a 'political offensive' with an offer to restore Belgium. This was also the view of Prince Max, who pressed it on Hertling as well as on Ludendorff. Even Bethmann Hollweg came out of his political limbo to urge on Hertling the advantages of a negotiated peace. But Hertling was not the man to oppose the Supreme Command. Ludendorff assured the Kaiser: 'It will be an immense struggle that will begin at one point, continue at another, and take a long time; it is difficult, but it will be victorious.'[50]

In spite of what Ludendorff told the Kaiser, his only hope of success was to secure a strategic decision by means of his first great blow, delivered by three German armies (the 2nd, 17th and 18th) on a forty-mile front in the Somme valley. This was the sector where the British and French armies joined. An attack in the north would have been more decisive as far as the British were concerned, but Flanders was judged too soggy so early in the year. Moreover a break-through on the Somme offered the prospect of splitting the Allied armies and capturing the important railway junction of Amiens. The German effort was

immense: over 6,400 guns, nearly half the German total on the
western front, took part in the preliminary bombardment. The 18th
Army did better than had been expected, overwhelming the British
5th Army under Gough and making a complete breach in the line; but
the 17th and 18th Armies ran into stiffer opposition and captured less
ground than had been planned. Had the Germans followed up their
initial success by pouring in reinforcements in depth they might have
made the breach permanent, but precious time was lost. The French
(Foch having been hurriedly appointed Commander-in-Chief of the
whole front) threw in reserves, and the defenders rallied and re-
grouped. There were several reasons for the Germans' failure to
exploit their gains: inadequate transport (underfed horses, lack of oil
and petrol), the temptation to troops long deprived of luxuries and
even necessities to plunder supplies of food, drink and clothing left
behind by the British, and lack of reserves both in quantity and
quality. German losses, which were heavy, could not be made good,[51]
whereas once the alarm had been given American divisions arrived on
the western front at an accelerated pace and more quickly than Ludendorff had calculated. It must have been obvious to Ludendorff that the
attempt to win the war by a series of blows extending over several
months offered a diminishing prospect of success.[52] But he refused to
change his plans. A second massive strike against the British in Flanders and aimed at the railway junction of Hazebrouck, 25 miles from
the Channel, followed much the same pattern as the first: territory was
won, prisoners and guns captured, but strategically nothing was
gained. Though the Germans had performed a feat which neither the
French nor the British had been able to achieve in three and a half
years of trench warfare, this was a situation in which anything less
than total success was a failure. In 1914 the German right wing had
been exhausted by weeks of forced marches; in 1918 over much the
same devastated ground the German offensive, despite initial dash
and tactical brilliance, especially in the artillery, showed signs of war-
weariness and lack of stamina.

According to Colonel von Haeften, the representative of the
Supreme Command at the Foreign Office, Ludendorff in his heart of
hearts had ceased to believe in victory by the middle of May 1918;
but he would not call off the offensive. At the end of May the Germans
attacked the French on the ridge in Champagne crossed by the road
named after the daughters of Louis XV, the Chemin des Dames. The
intention was to draw off reserves from the north, where the final
blow (Operation Hagen) was to be struck against the British. The
Champagne attack succeeded beyond expectation, but created another
dangerously extended salient. Once again astride the Marne, the Ger-

man army was now nearer Paris than at any time since September 1914. In the middle of July the French under Foch counter-attacked to such effect that Ludendorff not only had to withdraw behind the Marne but also to abandon his plans for *Hagen*. This was the turning point of the war, and Ludendorff knew now that he could not resume the offensive. 'Disillusionment', he wrote, 'had come.'[53] Publicly however he refused to admit that the war could not be won. He forced the Kaiser to dismiss Kühlmann for declaring in the Reichstag that military measures alone could not bring about peace, and implying that Germany must give up Belgium and seek a compromise with the West. This was strange, considering that Ludendorff had read and approved a memorandum drawn up by Haeften, who was his right-hand man, recommending a 'political offensive' on a grand scale, which implied some concessions over Belgium. Yet Kühlmann was right in thinking that a 'peace offensive' as envisaged by Ludendorff would be seen as a propaganda exercise by the Allies, and he knew that Ludendorff's views on Belgium could not be squared with the Allies' minimum demands. Hertling made little attempt to defend his colleague, who had been in Ludendorff's bad books since their disagreement over the Russian treaty early in the year. Kühlmann had recently put out peace feelers to Britain through Hatzfeldt, the German ambassador at the Hague, and General Smuts, and to the United States through Daniel McCormick, the tractor manufacturer.[54] The majority parties in the Reichstag, whose territorial ambitions had revived with their hopes of victory, gave Kühlmann no support. His successor at the Foreign Office was von Hintze, an admiral who had been in the diplomatic service, and was believed to share the views of the extreme annexationists: in fact, his policy differed little from Kühlmann's. Nor did Ludendorff accept the advice of his subordinate, General von Lossberg, that Germany should return to a strategy of defence and pull the army back to a shorter line running from Antwerp to the Meuse. Political reasons – fear of the impression that would be made at home and abroad – made such a course impossible, Ludendorff explained. According to Rupprecht, the Bavarian Crown Prince who commanded the German army in Flanders, Ludendorff shared his view that decisive victory was impossible, but was waiting for a *deus ex machina* in the shape of an internal collapse of the western powers.[55] It was Germany which was nearing internal collapse, and one reason for the nervous irritability Ludendorff displayed at this time was his fear of revolution at home. Admiral von Müller complained of his frequent fits of violence, and Ludendorff actually underwent a course of treatment with a Berlin nerve specialist, Professor Hochheimer. Rupprecht's attempt to urge Hertling into declaring that Belgium would be given up unconditionally was unsuccessful. Yet by July even the Prussian Crown Prince had come out in favour of Belgian independence.

Then came the sharp defeat of 8 August, when a massive Allied break-through with tanks cast doubts upon the Germans' ability to continue even a defensive war. For the first time German soldiers refused to face the enemy, and there were symptoms of a mutinous spirit which could not be ignored. 'Disastrous news from the Somme,' Müller wrote in his diary, 'the Kaiser was in very low spirits this evening.'[56] Ludendorff concluded: 'Our war machine is no longer efficient.'[57] He blamed defeatism among civilians and the sinister effect of Allied and Bolshevik propaganda. He offered Hindenburg his resignation, which was refused. The Kaiser told his commanders: 'Naturally things can't go on like this indefinitely and we must find a way to end it all.' On 14 August he held a Crown Council at Spa. Ludendorff admitted to the Chancellor that the war could not be won and must be ended by diplomacy, at the same time he gave the impression that successful defence was still possible.[58] The Kaiser proposed that Hintze (who had been privately briefed by Ludendorff on the seriousness of the military situation) should put out peace feelers through the King of Spain or the Queen of the Netherlands, but this was to be done at a 'suitable moment', that is after the next German victory. Such a moment never arrived. Nor was the Supreme Command willing to make the concessions over Belgium that the Allies demanded; and though, under some pressure from the civilians, the German terms were modified, they remained unrealistic in view of Germany's deteriorating fortunes. Thus Hintze's hands were tied, and Hindenburg continued to insist that the German army would be able to stay on French soil and impose its will on the enemy. No clear picture emerged from the Crown Council, and its false optimism was transmitted to the Reichstag representatives when they met Hintze on 21 August.[59] Early in September Hintze learnt that Austria wished to make a separate peace and on 15 September the Austrian Peace Note (for which German consent had not been given) was published. On the western front official reassurances were belied with the abandonment by the German army of all its gains since March. By the end of September its new defensive positions, which were not well prepared, had been breached. There were now over a million and a half American soldiers in France. The crumbling of German power could no longer be concealed. The Turks were defeated in Palestine and Mesopotamia. Bulgaria had collapsed. Ludendorff (a completely broken man, according to von Müller) reached a conclusion which others had reached earlier: an armistice must be sought without delay. Hindenburg concurred. Next day Hintze was informed. He suggested an approach to the American President, to which the Kaiser agreed. It was also decided that a parliamentary regime should be set up under a new Chancellor. Ludendorff was at first unwilling to alter the system of government, but yielded when told that public opinion demanded a change.[60] The idea of a 'revolution from above' was now in the air; it had been suggested, among other things, by Ballin in a memorandum prepared for the Kaiser, and would have the advantage of assuaging discontent at home as well as of placating the democrat Wilson. As far as Ludendorff was concerned there was a special motive: by thrusting power at this time on the left-wing parties he would place on them the odium of making an unpopular peace and exonerate the Supreme Command.[61]

On 2 October a spokesman of the Supreme Command for the first time spoke plainly to the party leaders in the Reichstag. Though some of the better-informed personalities, such as Erzberger, Ballin and the industrialist Stinnes, had already begun to draw their own conclusions, the shock produced by the meeting of 2 October shows how far public opinion had been kept in the dark about the military crisis. It was the Conservative leader, Heydebrand, who reacted most sharply: 'We have been lied to and cheated.' The ten weeks since the defeat on the Marne in the middle of July had been wasted, and the whole country had now to pay the price of Ludendorff's obstinacy and Hertling's complacency.

Germany's first parliamentary government was a hastily contrived compromise. At its head was Prince Max of Baden, heir to his father the Grand Duke of Baden, a man of humane and relatively liberal views but hardly a symbol of democracy; and there were other ministers, such as Solf the new Foreign Secretary, who like Max were not members of the Reichstag. But most of Max's colleagues were parliamentarians, representing the Centre, Progressive and Social Democratic parties. The Conservatives were not included, and after some hesitation the National Liberals stayed out. The cabinet's main tasks were to end the war on the best terms obtainable, and to democratise the governments of Germany and Prussia. This meant making the executive responsible to the legislature, introducing equal suffrage into Prussia, and subordinating the army chiefs to civilian control. The Social Democrats wanted martial law relaxed. They had been in two minds whether to accept the invitation to join the government, and Scheidemann warned against the danger of joining a bankrupt concern. But Ebert persuaded the party that they must put patriotism before self-interest, a decision which, in view of Ludendorff's design to shuffle off responsibility, was to cost them dear. Under great pressure from Ludendorff (who said that the army could not wait twenty-four hours) the government despatched its first message to President Wilson within hours of taking office. It asked for peace on the basis of the Fourteen Points. If Wilson had not already been aware of Germany's plight this gesture would have revealed it, and Ludendorff afterwards regretted the haste with which he had made the cabinet act.[62] Thus began the exchange of Notes across the Atlantic which gradually revealed the outlines of an armistice that could bring little comfort to the German people. Ludendorff's hope that it would be a breathing space so that, if Wilson's terms proved unacceptable, he could regroup his forces and resume the war was frustrated by Wilson's insistence that the German army must retreat to its own frontiers leaving most of its equipment behind. At a war cabinet meeting on 17 October Ludendorff argued that the terms were intolerable and that a fresh effort should be made to carry on the war. The chances of an Allied break-through had diminished, and Germany was now in a position to continue resistance through the winter. But the moral effect of the first message to Wilson could not be reversed, and Ludendorff found himself contradicted by his colleagues in the war cabinet, who knew of the overwhelming desire for peace among the civilians and of the hardships suffered by a population tired of slaughter and worn down by privation.[63] Proposals to call for a fresh popular effort or *levée en masse* fell on deaf ears. Even Wilson's Third Note virtually demanding the deposition of the Kaiser and implying that the change of regime was mere camouflage could not deflect the government from its course, though Hindenburg and Ludendorff made a last gesture of defiance by telling the army that the unconditional surrender which Wilson now required must be rejected. Prince Max, forced to assert his authority against this unconstitutional move, asked for and obtained Ludendorff's dismissal (26 October). Formally Hindenburg should have gone too, but he stayed at his post to allay public anxiety and prevent further deterioration of army morale. Public opinion recognised the significance of Ludendorff's departure. His escape to Sweden in disguise during the German revolution a few weeks later added a cloak and dagger touch to a career which after the pinnacle of military fame was to end in discredit and ridicule.

The Kaiser did not long survive his dictatorial general. Here too outside pressure combined with internal discontent. Abroad William was still blamed for having started the war and instigated German atrocities; he was the victim of his pre-war speeches and postures, and his virtual abnegation of power during the war was scarcely noticed. The switch from autocracy to parliamentary government had come too late and was too obviously calculated to be convincing: hence Wilson's demand for William's abdication. In other circumstances such inter-

ference with Germany's internal affairs might have rallied the nation
in defence of their Emperor, but now the prospect that a Germany
without William II would get a more acceptable peace than otherwise
was enough to turn solid citizens, who were far from being monarchists
or democrats, into advocates of abdication. The mood of Germany in
October 1918, with defeat a certainty and a run on the banks, was
close to panic. In the Berlin factories there was talk of power being
exercised by workers' and soldiers' councils. The Russian Revolution
threw a long shadow.

On 29 October, without consulting Prince Max and against his
wishes, William II left Potsdam for Spa, the town just inside the
Belgian frontier which was now the headquarters of the German army.
This move could be interpreted only as meaning that William, expecting revolution to break out in Germany, was going to shelter from
it among his loyal troops, whom in due course he would lead back
into Germany to defeat the revolutionaries. This was the Kaiser's
'flight to Varennes': not only was it incompatible with his new role
of constitutional monarch in accordance with the reforms so recently
introduced, but it widened the gulf between himself and his subjects and made his abdication almost inevitable. It also added to the
difficulties of Prince Max, whose repeated pleas to William to go
voluntarily went unheeded. Max was under great pressure from the
Majority socialists to insist on abdication. This was not so much because they were republicans (most of the leaders would have been
quite happy for the monarchy to remain) as because in the rising tide
of discontent they feared to lose supporters to the Independent socialists, who were in full cry. William's obstinacy ruined Max's plans for
saving the dynasty by putting on the throne a Hohenzollern grand-
son if not a son: the Crown Prince was not acceptable to the left.
If the Majority socialists left the government it would fall, and there
would be no government to sign the armistice or keep Germany from
falling into revolutionary chaos.[64] Though Prince Max did not manage
to stay in power until the armistice was signed he lasted long enough
to ensure that it would be. Erzberger, one of the new ministers, headed
an armistice delegation which arrived at Compiègne early on 8
November and received the terms from Foch and his colleagues.
They were harsher than the Germans had expected, and Erzberger
had little success in pleading for mitigation. He did however manage
to insert a clause that America and the Allies would contemplate the
feeding of Germany during the armistice period 'as shall be necessary'.
Erzberger had difficulty in communicating with the government in
Berlin and in the end it was the Supreme Command which authorised
him to sign. This was logical enough, for the original decision to ask

for an armistice had been the Supreme Command's; but to the outside world and to the German people it seemed that the responsibility lay with the politicians. The first act of the republican regime was to sign an instrument of surrender, to liquidate the bankrupt estate of which it was the receiver and heir.

Meanwhile the army was continuing its fighting retreat through Belgium and northern France. Many tributes have been paid, by Winston Churchill among others, to its astonishing achievements during the previous four years, when it had won brilliant victories on scores of battlefields and held at bay a coalition of world powers with unlimited resources. Long before the end of the war it was an army of civilians in uniform, for of the original professional force few soldiers, and still fewer officers, had survived. Although Germany had lost the war ideologically, it is difficult to imagine that its military performance would have been more impressive under any other regime. Such a record, reinforced by the stab-in-the-back legend already in circulation, not unnaturally gave rise to the hope that one day the struggle for Germany's ambitions might be renewed in more favourable circumstances. In the meantime the price of defeat would have to be paid.

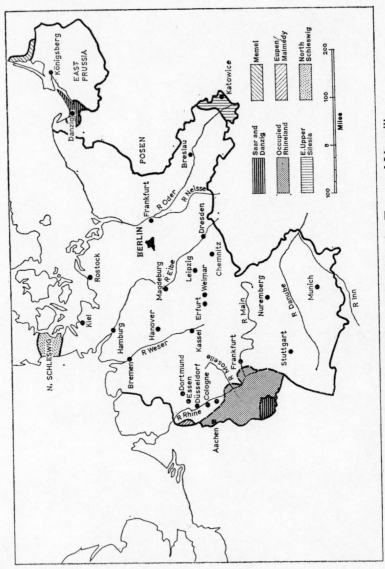

Map 2   The Weimar Republic after the Treaty of Versailles

CHAPTER VI

Neither War nor Peace: The Early Struggles of the Republic

(i) THE 'FROZEN' REVOLUTION

On the same day (28 October) as the Kaiser gave the royal assent to the new constitutional reforms an event occurred which disrupted the smooth transition from authoritarian to parliamentary government. Sailors in the Imperial Navy at Kiel disobeyed orders to put to sea, defied their officers and hoisted the red flag. They believed (with good reason) that the object of the exercise, planned by the Admiralty, was to provoke a suicidal battle with the much stronger British fleet. After being confined to harbour for over four years, and knowing that the war was irretrievably lost and an armistice imminent, the crews refused to sacrifice themselves for a conception of honour they did not share. The Admiralty's decision had been taken without the knowledge or approval of the government, and was a breach of the spirit, if not the letter, of the new democratic regime which put the army and the navy for the first time under a civilian minister. The admirals had misread the temper of their men, which was by now that of the country. Sailors on shore made common cause with those on board, and Kiel was soon in the hands of a sailors' council. Troops sent to restore order went over to the rebels. Two members of the Reichstag (Haussmann, a Progressive, who was a minister in Prince Max's cabinet, and Noske, the right-wing Socialist) who hastened to Kiel to deal with the mutiny came to terms with its leaders, but could not prevent the contagion from spreading along the coast to the ports of Cuxhaven, Bremen and Hamburg and inland to the Ruhr. Groups of sailors commandeered trains and roused the factory workers, who came out on strike and were joined by regiments of the home army. Within a few days practically the whole Reich was in turmoil, proving the truth of the saying of Richard Müller, the leader of the revolutionary shop-stewards, that Germany was a tinder box waiting for a match.

It was a special irony that the revolt began in the navy, which, more than anything else, had symbolised the pride and ambition of the Hohenzollern regime, and that it was taken up by the army which had given Germany the leadership of Europe half a century before. Though the field army continued to hold out against its external enemies, the collapse of the officer's power in the home army meant that no resistance to the revolutionary movement was possible.

Here we are concerned less with the details of the German revolution, than with its general significance as the link between the imperial and republican regimes.[1] Its distinguishing common feature was the emergence in all parts of the country and at all levels of government of hastily elected bodies calling themselves sailors', soldiers' and workers' councils. The councils claimed political power, and exercised it either by deposing existing authorities or by allowing them to function under council supervision. As democratic bodies the councils were broadly representative of both Socialist parties (and in some cases of the Progressives) but the initiative more often than not was taken by Independent socialists. This was natural, not only because the Independents were more radical than the Majority socialists, but because the leaders of the latter could hardly rise against a central government of which they were members. Yet the socialist rank and file had clearly been unimpressed by the October reforms, and shared in the general loss of confidence in the government which was ultimately fatal to Prince Max of Baden's regime, despite his readiness to end the war on terms which amounted to surrender. When President Wilson's Third Note virtually demanded the abdication of the Kaiser, public pressure in favour of this became almost irresistible. Since 29 October William had been at Spa with his generals. His refusal to heed the advice to go 'voluntarily' pressed on him by Prince Max and others, forced the Majority socialists to resign from the cabinet, which in turn obliged Max to hand in his own resignation. By 9 November the only possible government in Berlin was a revolutionary one. Prince Max handed over the chancellorship to Ebert at a time when this seemed a meaningless gesture; for by then there were only two kinds of effective authority in Germany – that of workers' and soldiers' councils, and the still more or less intact power of the generals on the western front. The Kaiser's delayed and reluctant decision to abdicate came too late to influence the course of events in Berlin, where a Republic was proclaimed by Scheidemann. The question now was whether the Republic would be 'bourgeois' or socialist. The other three kings (of Bavaria, Saxony and Württemberg) had lost their thrones, and in Bavaria the Independent Eisner had become the head of a government of workers', soldiers' and farmers' councils. It was even possible that the Reich would fall apart: the unifying forces of the Prussian monarchy and army were no more, and separatist movements in Bavaria, the Rhineland and Silesia were already active. The whole work of Bismarck might be undone.

It was partly by chance that the revolution did not break out in Berlin until 9 November, for Emil Barth, the shop-steward leader who since the January strike had led the 'revolutionary committee', had been very narrowly defeated in a resolution that would have called the factory workers out on a general strike on 4 November.[2] Some of the Independent leaders shared Barth's optimism and impulsiveness; others, like Haase, were cautious. In the end it was the masses themselves who decided when to come out and what form the revolution should take. The morning of 9 November saw processions of factory workers, some armed, streaming from the suburbs into central Berlin, where they were joined by soldiers on foot and in armoured cars and took possession of the public buildings, on which they planted large red flags. The ease with which the capital of the Empire fell, practically without bloodshed, into the hands of workers and soldiers, who proceeded to set up their councils in factories and barracks made a great impression on observers: 'the greatest of all revolutions' was the enthusiastic verdict of Theodor Wolff, editor of the liberal *Berliner Tageblatt*. No one defended the old regime, which seemed discredited beyond recall. Power lay with the left. What would the left do with it? The wartime divisions between Majority and Independent socialists, and between the latter and the Spartacists, remained, though now they turned on divergent attitudes to the revolution instead of on annexations and war credits. The Majority socialist leaders, like Ebert, had not wanted the revolution (though they were resolved to make the best of it) and intended to revert as soon as possible to a parliamentary regime by convening a constituent assembly. The Independent socialists, however, wished to postpone the election of a constituent assembly until after the revolution had been consolidated, by which they meant starting to socialise the economy and 'democratising' the army and civil service. Even if, as seemed not unlikely, the constituent assembly returned a Socialist majority, the Independents knew that it could not be so revolutionary as the workers' and soldiers' councils, which represented primarily the wage-earners. Subject to an agreement on this point, the Independents were prepared to co-operate with the Majority socialists, whereas the Spartacists were not. The Spartacists, represented by Liebknecht, who had recently been released from prison, wanted a regime of councils on the Russian model. He rejected an offer by Ebert to join a new, all-Socialist government, and saw Ebert as a German Kerensky who would soon be overthrown by the Spartacists as the counterpart of the Bolsheviks. On somewhat equivocal terms the Independents joined the Majority socialists in a new six-man cabinet (the People's Delegates) which received a mandate to govern from a gathering of 3,000 representatives of workers' and soldiers' councils in Greater Berlin at the Circus Busch in Berlin on 10 November. Besides this cabinet the Circus Busch meeting elected an Executive Council that was likewise composed of representatives of both the main Socialist parties in equal numbers. This, despite its name, was a supervisory body. Germany was *de facto* a council republic. In the eyes of most middle-class people this was practically equivalent to Bolshevism.

That Ebert and Scheidemann were no Bolsheviks was however known to those in authority who had dealt with them, especially in the last crucial days of the war. Among these were Prince Max, who had made Ebert Chancellor by a procedure which, though of doubtful legality, carried weight in circles where workers' councils were anathema, and General Groener, who had replaced Ludendorff as Hindenburg's mentor and virtual head of the German army. It was on 10 November that Groener, in a historic telephone call which established a relationship between the revolutionary government and the Supreme Command, offered the army's help in maintaining Ebert in office in return for preservation of the officer's power of command (then under threat from the soldiers' councils) and a pledge to fight bolshevism and chaos. Ebert accepted. Thus Groener could be reasonably sure of withdrawing his army of three millions intact behind the Rhine as the armistice required, while Ebert had a prospect of armed support should the Spartacists try to overthrow him. But Groener, a far-sighted man, was also thinking of the future: in this way he could preserve the Officers' Corps and the General Staff, and save from the wreck of the imperial regime the most important element for Germany's future. Ebert believed he was acting in the best interests of the Reich by underpinning his regime and averting civil war. But had the Independents known what had passed between him and Groener they would have been furious. To them a pact with the generals was incompatible with loyalty to the revolution.

Although they had been forced into temporary alliance by circumstances (the popular mood demanded an all-Socialist government in November 1918) the Majority and Independent socialists found cooperation increasingly difficult. Their attitudes to the revolution differed fundamentally. Ebert and the S.P.D. leaders wanted to return to parliamentary democracy without delay. Radical changes in the economy could be left to the constituent assembly, which would give them broad-based support. In any case, in the view of Ebert and of many of his colleagues, the whole question should wait until the newly

appointed Socialisation Commission had reported. Haase, the senior
of the three Independent members of the cabinet, and Ebert's opposite
number, wanted to carry on and consolidate the revolution before the
Constituent Assembly (of which he had no great hopes) met, so that it
would be faced with a number of accomplished facts. The impetus in
favour of socialising the economy and 'democratising' the army must
not be lost. The crucial factor here was the date of election of the constituent assembly. Ebert wanted it to be as soon, Haase as late as
possible. The Spartacists rejected it altogether. Ebert agreed, however,
to leave the decision to the congress of workers' and soldiers' councils
which, representing the masses in all parts of Germany not under
foreign occupation, met in Berlin in the middle of December. To the
surprise of many people, the congress voted for an early election (19
January), thus leaving the minimum of time for revolutionary action
under the council regime. This was a blow to the left, one of whose
leaders (Däumig) described it as the suicide of the German revolution.[3]
Yet proletarian dictatorship, though an essential ingredient of the
Marxist programme in Russia, had never been part of the policy of
the German Social Democrats, who believed in a parliamentary regime
and were not likely to abandon it at a time when the only alternative
appeared to be civil war. But as a radical body the congress of councils
agreed with the left in pressing for socialisation of 'ripe' industries and
reform of the army, including the abolition of the officer's power of
command. It was significant that the congress was not prepared to
leave these essentials to the Constituent Assembly, though to couple
them with a vote for an early assembly showed a surprising lack of
realism. Ebert was in a dilemma. He was able to parry the resolution
on socialisation by reference to the Socialisation Commission already
referred to, which would study the facts and make its expert recommendations. But the military resolutions of the congress could not be
side-tracked. Hindenburg and Groener lost no time in expressing their
adamant opposition to the changes proposed and threatened resignation. They regarded this attempt to undermine the power of the
officer as a breach of the agreement with Ebert of 10 November. Ebert
used delaying tactics to pacify the generals: the changes, he explained,
would not apply to the field army. But now the Independent socialists, whose suspicions of Ebert had been roused by an attempted
counter-revolutionary Putsch and by other incidents on 6 December,
had their fears confirmed. They saw Ebert's readiness to compromise
with the generals as part of a sinister pattern of events that culminated
in a tragic-comic episode in Berlin just before Christmas. On 23
December a group of revolutionary sailors from Kiel who were living
in the royal palace, angry because their pay was in arrears, invaded

the Chancellery and declared Ebert and his colleagues their prisoners. Otto Wels, the Socialist commandant of Berlin, had also been seized and was believed to be in danger of execution. Ebert was forced to telephone the army in the middle of the night and ask for help. Next day a force from Potsdam arrived with artillery and started shelling the palace, causing casualties. The sailors eventually accepted a truce, and left. In the meantime the troops had come under the influence of a large crowd which had gathered in the square in front of the palace and openly sided with the sailors. To the Independent socialists this clash was further proof of Ebert's hostility to the revolution, for they were convinced that he had encouraged the army to use excessive force to liberate himself and the hapless Wels, and had used the sailors' foolish escapade as an excuse to crush them. To the military commanders the affair showed that the troops' morale had sunk to a point where the army was no longer a reliable instrument. Each side drew the appropriate conclusions: the Independents resigned from the government and resumed the freedom of opposition, while the generals set their hopes on the recruitment of volunteer units (Freikorps) to curb the insurgent left. It was a paradox that the soldiers, whose entry into Berlin with all their weapons had brought bitter criticism of Ebert from the radicals, in practice simply melted away, anxious to get out of uniform and rejoin their family before Christmas.

The resignation from the cabinet of Haase and his two Independent colleagues, Dittmann and Barth, was the signal for renewed militancy by the left, Spartacists, revolutionary shop-stewards and left-wing Independents, who demanded the overthrow of the Ebert government, which they identified with counter-revolution. The Spartacists now severed the strained ties which had hitherto attached them to the Independent socialists, and, together with two smaller left-wing groups, held a conference at the end of the year at which they formally constituted themselves the German Communist party (K.P.D.). The step marked the rejection by the dogmatists of the divided and (from the revolutionary point of view) compromised Independent socialist party, but the new party also contained a high percentage of irresponsible adventurers and army deserters. It lacked mass support, and represented a further split of the forces of the left. Some of the Spartacist leaders, and some Bolsheviks too, considered the moment to form the new party ill chosen. One sign of its immaturity was the K.P.D.'s decision, against the advice of its most intelligent leader, Rosa Luxemburg, to boycott the election of the Constituent Assembly. Another was its disregard of her warning that the gaining of power, which she declared could only be with the backing of the majority of the people, might be a long process. Rejection of her advice was shown by the so-called Spartacist rising in Berlin which occurred only a few days after the party conference. The rising was triggered off by a decision of the all-S.P.D. Prussian government to dismiss Eichhorn, the chief of police, who was a well-known Independent socialist. This was seen as provocation, and a mammoth protest demonstration in Berlin demanded action. The scene was ironically described in an article which appeared a year later in the Communist *Rote Fahne*:

What was seen that Monday [6 January 1919] in Berlin was probably the greatest proletarian manifestation in history . . . From the statue of Roland to the victory column the proletariat was massed shoulder to shoulder. The crowd extended deep into the Tiergarten. They had brought their weapons and were waving red flags. They were ready to do anything, to give everything, even their lives. It was an army of 200,000 men such as no Ludendorff had ever seen. . . . Then the inconceivable happened. The crowds had been standing in the cold and fog since nine in the morning. And their leaders were sitting – no one knew where – conferring. The fog lifted and the crowd was still waiting. Noon came; the cold and hunger increased. The masses were feverishly impatient. They demanded a deed – even a word – anything to relieve the suspense. But no one knew what to say; for the leaders were conferring. . . . The fog became denser and night began to fall. The people went sadly home. They had hoped to accomplish great things; they had done nothing because their leaders were conferring . . . first in the Royal Stables and then at Police headquarters . . . outside in the Alexanderplatz the proletariat waited, rifle in hand, heavy and light machine guns ready . . . and behind closed doors the leaders conferred. They sat all evening, they sat all night. They were still sitting next day at dawn. The crowd came back once more and gathered along the Siegesallee and the leaders were still in session: they were conferring, conferring, conferring. . . .[4]

In an atmosphere of approaching civil war three men (Liebknecht, Ledebour of the Independent socialists and Scholze of the militant shop-stewards) formed a revolutionary committee which issued a manifesto declaring the Ebert government deposed. Armed Spartacists occupied a number of public buildings. Liebknecht who was notoriously impulsive acted without the authority of his party, while Rosa Luxemburg opposed the rising at first; later she supported it in order not to leave the masses in the lurch – a gesture that sealed her fate. The rising, like the July days in Petrograd in 1917, was more than a demonstration but less than a serious bid for power. The rebels had no proper plan, and reinforcements on which they had counted failed to arrive.

It was an act of desperation, a forlorn attempt to revive the flagging revolution rather than a carefully calculated strategic move. Nevertheless it might have been temporarily successful given the weakness of the government, had Noske, newly appointed chief of defence by Ebert, not called in the Freikorps to their rescue. The Freikorps were units of volunteers organised by senior officers of the old army with a high proportion of young officers and n.c.o.s straight from the front. Their motives varied. They included patriots, idealists, adventurers and mercenaries; many had been brutalised by the war and knew no other trade. Their politics, so far as they were not opportunist, were crudely nationalist, and they needed little inducement to attack the Spartacists in the name of order and fatherland. The Freikorps, with some unacknowledged help from republican forces loyal to the Ebert government, reconquered Berlin. Among the prisoners taken were Liebknecht and Rosa Luxemburg, who were wantonly murdered. These were not the only atrocities committed. Freikorps ruthlessness, and the acts of terror to which it gave rise, alarmed many moderate Socialists as well as Independents.[5] But Ebert and Noske had little choice. Most of the republican guards were politically unreliable and of little military use. The hostility of the Freikorps to democracy as well as to Spartacus was notorious, but all efforts to counter this by recruiting workers to their ranks proved fruitless. The government depended on a force that was basically opposed to the Republic: it was under the bayonets of the Freikorps that the Constituent Assembly was elected and met at Weimar on 5 February. This marked, in a formal sense, the close of the revolutionary period. The regime of People's Delegates and Central (the renamed Executive) Council was at an end. But the revolutionary impulse survived and inspired several desperate rearguard actions. Berlin in March was again the scene of fighting, as Communists and their allies rose and were suppressed by the Freikorps. In several cities and states, including Bremen and Brunswick, left-wing dictatorships were established which had to be crushed by force. The Ruhr and other industrial districts were paralysed by political strikes. A second congress of workers' and soldiers' councils met in April 1919. A number of soldiers' councils lingered on to resist the rehabilitation of the officers' authority, just as some workers' councils rejected the idea that with the return to parliamentary government their political role was played out. Visually and aurally the revolution in Berlin left a confused memory of groups of ragged men brandishing rifles in a most unmilitary fashion or riding on the tops of armoured cars through streets whose baroque monuments were an ironic reminder of past imperial splendours; of sailors enthusiastically plundering the royal palace and getting drunk on the Kaiser's champagne; of red flags fluttering hopefully from public buildings against a leaden sky; of improvised barricades and bullet-swept squares; of hoarse voices singing the International while shivering crowds listened expectantly to the oratory of an uncertain and divided leadership; finally of the rhythmic march and staccato machine-gun fire of the steel-helmeted Freikorps.

The most bizarre and audacious experiment in revolutionary government occurred in Bavaria. Violence broke out in Munich on 21 February, where Eisner, the Bavarian Prime Minister, was murdered by a nationalist student. This was a turning point in the erratic course of the Bavarian revolution. Eisner was in many ways a unique figure among German Socialist leaders of his time.[6] Unlike most of them, he was not a self-taught working man who had diligently climbed his way up the party hierarchy, but a literary critic and political journalist whose socialism owed more to the ethics of Kant than to the economics of Marx. A pre-war revisionist, Eisner was a genuine internationalist, whom hatred of the war and of wartime chauvinism had driven into the Independent socialist party. Imprisoned for having taken part in the January 1918 strike and released in October, he had seized the initiative on 8 November by proclaiming Bavaria a republic and inaugurating a regime of workers' and soldiers' councils. There was a special reason why the revolution broke out so early in Bavaria, which was the first German state to dethrone its monarchy: the population feared that if the war was not ended immediately, the Allies would invade Bavaria through Austria, which had just surrendered. Eisner's impetuousness and Bavarian desire to assert its independence were also factors. The enthusiasm which carried Eisner to the highest post in the revolutionary government was short-lived; the conservative and Catholic character of the majority of Bavarians soon reasserted itself. Unlike Prussia Bavaria had no Junker problem, and its pre-war government as in the other South German states had been relatively liberal. When the Bavarian *Landtag* was re-elected in January 1919 the Independent socialists won only three seats out of 185. Eisner's resignation appeared inevitable, and he was in fact on his way to announce it when he was assassinated. Right-wing socialists and, of course, the middle classes resented his having held power so long, while the extreme left were beginning to lose confidence in him. This was because Eisner tried to get the best of both worlds: he would not, as a democrat, abandon parliament, but as a revolutionary he saw that the vital role had to be played by the workers' councils.[7] He therefore sought to combine both institutions in a way which, if successful, might have changed the course of German history. But Bavaria was hardly the place for such an experiment, if only because of the lack of support for Eisner's party and his equivocal attitude to the councils.

What made him even more unpopular was his decision to publish documents from the Bavarian Foreign Ministry which purported to establish the war guilt of the Hohenzollern government. Eisner believed that, by honestly acknowledging the misdeeds committed in their name, the German people would win the confidence of foreign democrats and obtain a less punitive peace. Indeed, like President Wilson, though on a much smaller scale, Eisner saw himself as helping to inaugurate a new and happier era in international relations. Like Wilson but more decisively, Eisner was repudiated by his countrymen: the Bavarians accepted his criticism of Prussia but resented his being a Jew; the German nationalists rejected him on both counts. The latter furiously denounced Eisner for playing into the hands of Allied chauvinists. The published evidence was in any case too inaccurate and incomplete to carry conviction. Few sympathised with Eisner's unworldly idealism, and the gap between him and the average Bavarian citizen was unbridgeable. His murder sharpened the antagonism between the left- and right-wing socialists and brought Bavaria near to civil war. Eisner's friends resented the S.P.D.'s willingness to compromise with the bourgeois parties and sought revenge for his martyrdom. They were also stimulated by news of the formation of the Third International in Russia and of the setting up of a soviet dictatorship by Bela Kun in Hungary. A new effort must be made in Bavaria to revive the revolution which had fallen so far short of people's hopes.

On 7 April a mixed group of Independent socialists and anarchists seized power in Munich and proclaimed a council dictatorship.[8] Hoffmann, the S.P.D. leader who had been Prime Minister since Eisner's death, fled with his government to conservative Bamberg in North Bavaria. The new rulers in Munich were mainly young intellectuals, including Landauer a distinguished Shakespeare scholar, Toller a budding playwright, and Mühsam the editor of a literary magazine. All three were well-known in Schwabing, the artists' quarter of Munich. Like Eisner they were utopians and humanitarians. But the new government also included eccentrics such as Franz Lipp the 'foreign minister' (who sent crazy telegrams to foreign governments) and Silvio Gsell, the 'finance minister' who was a currency crank. The regime lasted a week. As a political experiment it was grotesque and even farcical; in the light of the fate suffered by its leaders it was tragic. The Communist party which though small contained a number of tough young men mainly of Russian-Jewish origin despised the Landauer-Toller group as starry-eyed and dilettante. On 13 April after a rising of the garrison inspired by the Hoffmann government, the Communists themselves seized power, deposed the 'anarchists' and proclaimed a second council republic much closer to the Russian model. The new bosses, Leviné and Levien, set about confiscating food and arms, censoring the press, organising a red army and taking hostages, though performance lagged behind intention. Such measures roused the hostility of the population, especially the farmers. Armed opposition gathered inside Bavaria and further north, as Noske prepared to send in the Freikorps to restore the authority of the Hoffmann government. After resisting as best they could, the leaders of the Munich soviet were killed or arrested: Leviné was executed and Landauer too was put to death while a prisoner. The red dictatorship was followed by a white terror in which hundreds lost their lives. The revolution, which had few roots in Bavaria, had been thoroughly discredited, first by association with cranks and unpractical idealists, later with an even less representative alien minority.[9] In the atmosphere of reaction that followed, right-wing nationalism and antisemitism flourished in Munich as nowhere else in Germany, and it was no accident that Bavaria was the seed-bed of the National Socialist movement.

The Munich soviet was the last of the shortlived left-wing dictatorships thrown up by the German revolution. Order reigned again in the Reich, enforced in the name of the constitutional Republic by the army with the help of martial law. In the summer of 1919 men could look back at the preceding period and see how little had been achieved. The genuine revolutionaries in Germany, who included many ordinary citizens as well as radical leaders, had hoped for three main changes: the democratisation of German society as well as of the formal structure of government; the socialisation of key industries; and the transformation of the army into a militia run on egalitarian lines. None of these aims had been realised. Politically the revolution, described by Rathenau as 'frozen', had ended in its own negation, a return to the parliamentary regime which was already assured in October 1918. The Constituent Assembly was a revived Reichstag with a doubled electorate, and the substitution of a republic for a monarchy would have come with or without the upheaval of November. The temporary rule of workers' and soldiers' councils had made little difference to the balance of forces in Germany. The pillars of the Wilhelmine regime, the bureaucracy, the Junkers, the army, the great industrialists, the judges were still standing, though now more often in opposition to than behind the government. In a country with a weak parliamentary tradition whose Reichstag had failed to meet the challenge of the war, the councils were an improvised but potentially effective exercise in democracy, and one which, eagerly seized, might have established the Republic on firmer foundations, especially in rural areas. But when some of the councils took the initiative by asserting their authority against reactionary officials in the more 'feudal' districts of Prussia, Ebert showed little understanding. He and his S.P.D. colleagues saw only two long-term alternatives: a council dictatorship, which the vast majority of the population rejected, or parliamentary government in which there would be no political role for the workers' councils.[10] This judgement was basically sound, yet the haste with which Ebert pressed for the election of a constituent assembly suggests an almost exaggerated reluctance to take advantage of workers' councils even in the transitional period before the assembly met. In Prussia only three out of 48 provincial governors (*Regierungsräte* and *Oberregierungsräte*) and one head of a rural district (*Landrat*) belonged to the S.P.D.[11] The failure of the Socialist government to insure against the sabotage of its own policies by hostile administrators contrasts significantly with the purge of officials that took place after von Papen's *coup d'état* in Prussia in July 1932, when 91 per cent of the provincial governors and 73 per cent of the rural district heads were dismissed. There were, indeed, practical reasons for avoiding change in 1918–19. It was feared that any purge of officials would create chaos and lead to the breakdown of food distribution. Later the impulse for reform was too feeble to overcome resistance. Yet the fact remains that the opportunity passed of imposing a new spirit on the German and Prussian administration, and the councils, which might have been the instrument for this, were discarded. A short-term relief had been bought at a heavy long-term price. Soon liberals as well as socialists complained that the democratic regime was being undermined by monarchist officials; and Preuss, the father of the Weimar constitution, was afterwards to attribute the main weakness of the Republic to the disparity between a reformed system of government and an unreformed administration.[12]

As for the second revolutionary objective, socialisation, laws were passed in March 1919 to bring the coal and potash industries under public ownership. But little real change was made, and the bureaucratic boards created by the government failed to meet the demand of the left for some form of workers' control. Even the experts on the Socialisation Commission were divided on how to proceed. Other industries remained in private hands, and in a coalition government radical plans for economic reform were unacceptable. The Centre partners of the S.P.D. forced the rejection of far-reaching proposals made by Wissell, the Socialist Minister of Economics in Scheidemann's government. But there was a further reason for the slow progress made in implementing a policy which the party had been advocating for half a century. It was a general belief, shared by many Independent as well as Majority socialists, that a time when industry was run down and lacked capital, coal and raw materials, was unsuitable for extending public ownership, which was conceived as appropriate only in a period of plenty. How can we socialise, Eisner asked, when there is scarcely anything to be socialised?[13] According to Marx, capitalism would break down when it was producing more goods than society was able to consume: this was the opposite of Germany's situation. Land reform too, was ruled out on practical grounds: it was feared that the break-up of the Junker estates would reduce the harvest and jeopardise the food supply. Here too there was, understandably, no readiness to sacrifice current needs for long-term advantage.

The third socialist aim, the transformation of the army into a militia, was highly utopian in a country like Germany, with its military tradition and subject to external pressures that kept alive a fierce nationalism. Since the workers would not go into uniform to defend the government, the government depended on the Freikorps to protect it against the extreme left. The ethos of the Freikorps was the exact opposite of that of a citizen army. The Freikorps revived militarism, created a counter-revolutionary atmosphere and profoundly influenced the spirit of the new *Reichswehr* by which many of them were absorbed. Lüttwitz, a senior army general who a few months later was to rise against the government, could write to the Minister of Defence, Noske, in September 1919: 'Today, too, the army is the foundation of state power.'[14] On 9 November, exactly a year after the revolution, officer's shoulder badges were reintroduced into the army – a change trivial in itself, but symbolic of the reassertion of traditional values. Thus the wheel had come full circle.

Yet it would be wrong to conclude that no important changes occurred during the revolutionary period. In the early autumn of 1918, when Germany's defeat seemed certain and signs of unrest alarmed the propertied classes, a number of Ruhr industrialists met in the Stahlhof at Düsseldorf and decided to strike a bargain with the trade unions, whose standing and importance had risen considerably during the war.[15] The negotiations lasted several weeks and led to an agreement which was signed on 15 November and endorsed by the People's Delegates who in the meantime had come to power. It dealt with such matters as demobilisation, unemployment pay, special recognition of the General Trade Unions to the exclusion of the 'yellow' Christian and liberal or Hirsch-Duncker unions, and workers' representation at all levels of industry to negotiate with the employers on wage rates and similar subjects. For the first time the eight hour day, a long-standing demand, was granted. The unions had won much of what they wanted. The employers too could feel some satisfaction, for they believed that they had staved off the threat of large-scale nationalisation. During the revolution the trade union leaders, in accordance with their traditional policy of moderation, supported the S.P.D. against the Independent socialists and showed no enthusiasm for workers' councils, which they saw as diminishing their own role. Thus the unions entered the democratic era enhanced in prestige and power, and the employers were no longer, as in pre-war days, masters in their own house. The trade unions, like the S.P.D. were part of the Weimar establishment, with which the surviving monarchist forces co-existed in uneasy rivalry. The former opposition was now in power; the former rulers were in opposition. But this was an opposition which had powerful support in high places.

The failure of the revolution left wounds which remained unhealed. The Communists never forgave the S.P.D. leaders for the murder of Rosa Luxemburg and Karl Liebknecht, though the crime was committed without the knowledge of those in power; where Ebert and his colleagues were culpable was in mismanaging the trial of the murderers, who received absurdly light sentences or escaped justice altogether. More generally, of course, the S.P.D. was blamed for letting loose a Frankenstein's monster in the shape of the Freikorps. The S.P.D. blamed the Communists and their allies for trying to overthrow the democratic republic. The gulf between the two Socialist parties widened. The Independents, exasperated by the triumph of counter-revolution, and at the helplessness of the moderate socialists to check it, moved in desperation further to the left.

Impressed by Lenin's successful use of the Russian soviets, and convinced that only a proletarian dictatorship could carry out a genuinely revolutionary policy, the Independents turned their backs on parliamentary democracy and demanded government by workers' councils. They prepared for a new 9 November that never came, and so were drawn into the orbit of the Third International, a process that culminated in the party's historic split in October 1920 when about 300,000 or rather more than a third of the total membership joined the Communist party, which hitherto had been a small, divided sect. As for the political right, it continued to view the improvised Republic with hatred and contempt, irresponsibly blaming the Socialists for the stab in the back which allegedly had lost Germany the war and forced her to sign the shameful peace treaty, and looking back nostalgically to the vanished Empire. Thus from the beginning the Weimar Republic was assailed by irreconcilable enemies at both ends of the political spectrum.

(ii) VERSAILLES: ILLUSORY PEACE

In spite of the revolution, the new government elected at Weimar had a familiar look. It was a reconstructed coalition of the parties that had been in power in October 1918: the Social Democrats, Democrats (the re-named Progressives), and the Centre. Any chance of an all-Socialist government (which had seemed a probability in the heady days of November) was ruled out by the failure of the combined Socialist vote to reach a majority, but would in any case have been rejected by the Independent socialists, whose dislike of the Majority socialists had been raised to bitter enmity by the January bloodshed. Instead, the S.P.D. had to turn to the Democrats, who were ready to accept a measure of socialisation, and the Centre. There was much to be said for sharing with other parties the burden of governing a deeply divided country and of signing a peace treaty which was bound to be harsh and unpopular. As the largest of the three parties the S.P.D. had seven out of thirteen ministerial posts, including the premiership (Scheidemann) and the ministries of economics, labour and defence. Socialist influence was also seen in the election of Ebert as President under the provisional constitution, though he had already given proof of his aversion to radical change, and was to take an increasingly non-partisan view of his presidential responsibilities. Erzberger of the Centre party became Minister of Finance: he was the most influential of the 'bourgeois' ministers and his tax reforms which put more financial control in the hands of the central government enabled it to balance the federal budget. The only non-party man in the cabinet was Count Brockdorff-Rantzau, the Foreign Minister, who kept the post to which he had been appointed by the People's Delegates in December in succession to Solf. Brockdorff, a Junker by birth, was an independent-minded diplomat who saw the need to come to terms with the new forces of democracy and socialism; he was one of the few well-known patricians willing to serve the Republic. A critic of the Kaiser, as German ambassador in Denmark during the war he had worked closely with Danish Socialist ministers, and also with German Social Democrats in such tasks as the promotion of revolution in Russia. The People's party (the re-named National Liberals) and the Nationalists (the re-named Conservatives) remained in opposition. Both were monarchist. But these two parties received less than two votes out of every ten votes cast, so that the republican government appeared to stand on a firm popular basis. Much of this support however was short-lived. Having boycotted the elections to the National Assembly the small Communist party was unrepresented, but exercised considerable influence outside in encouraging the rearguard struggles of council dictatorships and political strikes.

The new regime started in crisis and gloom. The Republic seemed grey and shabby after the plumes and pageantry of the Empire. Yet the Empire had left a fearful legacy:

> Two million dead, millions of widows, orphans and wounded: the economy prostrate after four years of war – underfed children lying in paper shirts in their beds, metal turned into ammunition down to the last door knob – people bled white through hunger and undernourishment, now joined by millions of more or less brutalised soldiers, flooding in from the front lines, asking for bread and work. And, into the bargain, a government in debt beyond its assets and with its currency failing. The men who were to pick up the reins of government faced a tremendous, thankless task.[16]

It was difficult to know where to begin. Production could not recover without coal and raw materials (which could be paid for only by exports) and without more food for the workers (the Allied blockade, though mitigated, was still officially in force). Large areas of Germany were under foreign military occupation, and 800,000 prisoners of war had not yet returned. The government's obvious weakness in face of large-scale strikes and recurrent revolutionary outbreaks made foreign observers doubt its ability to survive. Its continuing reliance on the Freikorps to suppress its enemies not only caused fresh bitterness on the extreme left but roused justified misgivings among moderate Socialists at the revival of militarism and the government's failure to master the anti-democratic forces in German society.

During the six months between the signing of the armistice and the presentation of the peace terms the Germans had put their trust in Wilson's Fourteen Points which, though objectionable in many respects, were at least a guarantee against their enemies' more extreme demands. 'The German people', wrote an American observer in May 1919, 'had been led to believe that Germany had been unluckily beaten after a fine and clean fight owing to the ruinous effect of the blockade on the home morale and perhaps too far-reaching plans of her leaders, but that happily President Wilson could be appealed to, and would arrange a compromise peace satisfactory to Germany.'[17] The democratic politicians hoped that their country's adoption of Wilsonian principles would favourably impress the Allies, and that liberal and labour opinion in Britain and America would act as a curb on French and (to a lesser extent) British revenge-seeking. In both hopes they were disappointed. The Allies saw the new regime in Berlin less as proof of a change of heart than as what the *Times* called scene-shifting and Lloyd George a dummy façade. More than that was needed to convince the world that Germany had abandoned aggressive habits. For if the old rulers had relinquished power at a moment of their choice to escape the consequences of defeat, might they not take it back again whenever it suited them? It was all very well for the Americans in their simplicity to equate democracy with goodness and autocracy with evil; the less gullible French knew that national characteristics are not easily changed by ideology, and that support for German expansion had not come only from the Kaiser and his paladins. Indeed it was argued by Marshall Foch that Germany's republican regime, thanks to greater centralisation, the closer relationship between government and people and the survival of militarism, would prove stronger and more dangerous than the monarchy.[18] In England liberal idealism made little headway against the chauvinism which, with the war still fresh in everyone's mind, was given a new lease of life by the 'Hang the Kaiser' propaganda that characterised the election campaign at the end of 1918. Lloyd George, demagogue as well as statesman, had to take such sentiments into account if he was to stay in power. His own second thoughts on the peace treaty, designed to make it less unpalatable in Germany, were to come too late to make much difference. Nor was Wilson's position free from ambiguity. As his confidant House told the Allied ministers on 29 October 1918, the President had 'insisted on Germany's accepting all his speeches, and from these you could establish almost any point that anyone wished against Germany'.[19] Yet the United States' rejection of the peace treaty brought no benefit to the Germans: on the contrary, its main effect was to confirm French intransigence based on fear and to reduce American influence on post-war diplomacy.

So the presentation of the Allies' peace terms on 7 May 1919 had a devastating effect. The treaty exceeded the gloomiest expectations. Some loss of territory (Alsace-Lorraine, North Schleswig, Posen) had been foreseen as inevitable, but the severance of East Prussia from the Reich by a 'Polish Corridor' and the loss to Poland of the rich industrial province of Upper Silesia were shocks for which few were prepared. Germany was to lose 12 per cent of her population and 13 per cent of her territory, including three-quarters of her iron ore and a fifth of her coal. The Saar valley with its coal was to be French for fifteen years, with a plebiscite at the end to decide its future. The Rhineland was to be under Allied military occupation for a similar period. None of Germany's colonies was to be restored. Germany with her allies was branded with the guilt of having caused the war, and an unspecified number of war leaders beginning with the ex-Kaiser were to be tried for war crimes. Germany was to pay reparations in cash of an amount to be fixed which would certainly be enormous, and substantial reparations in kind. She was to disarm drastically. She was not to be admitted for the time being to the League of Nations. As an outcast and sinner she was first to give proof of repentance and good behaviour. The treaty thus combined largely justified territorial changes with punitive clauses reflecting wartime passions and intended to diminish Germany's power (to make up, the Germans felt, for their excess of population over France). A case could be made for every clause of the treaty, but the cumulative effect was overwhelming. Lloyd George himself did not believe that Germany would sign. Most Germans, who were unaware of the sense of outrage prevalent in Allied countries, resented the high moral tone of the treaty, in which vindictiveness appeared clothed in the language of self-righteousness.

It was a foregone conclusion that the treaty would be condemned by all sections of German society. Scheidemann, the Prime Minister, voiced public indignation when he told a special session of the Constituent Assembly held at the University of Berlin that the treaty was a 'death plan' which would make the German people slaves and helots. The hand that signed such a document, declared Scheidemann, would wither. The Germans were given three weeks in which to submit in writing their observations. The Allies received a torrent of protest Notes in which each offending paragraph of the treaty was attacked in passionately argued, heavily documented memoranda. But little impression was made, though Lloyd George, who had earlier feared that a too severe treaty would drive Germany into bolshevism, and was also influenced by the more detached Smuts, was now in favour of concessions. But Wilson, wary of Clemenceau, impatient with a colleague who sought to undo his own handiwork, and unwilling to revive past quarrels, refused to give way on any major point except one: a plebiscite would decide the fate of Upper Silesia. The Germans had counted on more concessions. Scheidemann, committed to reject the treaty, resigned. The third party in the government coalition, the Democrats, also left office, as did Brockdorff-Rantzau the Foreign Minister. Both the Centre party and the Social Democrats were split. Erzberger, a pragmatic politician and irrepressible optimist, pleaded that acceptance of the treaty was the lesser evil. When President Ebert consulted the army he was told by Groener that if Germany refused to sign and the French made good their threat to occupy the whole of Germany no effective resistance would be possible. Ebert and the Defence Minister, Noske, reluctantly came round to the same view as Erzberger. As the Allied ultimatum ran out a new government was hastily got together with Bauer and Hermann Müller, both Socialists, as Prime Minister and Foreign Minister respectively. They made a new attempt to have the 'shame paragraphs' – those dealing with war guilt and war crimes – eliminated before signature. The Allies, sincerely convinced of German war guilt and made more resentful by the scuttling of the German fleet at Scapa Flow, refused to give way. The treaty was finally passed in the Constituent Assembly because the right-wing parties, which were loudest in condemning the treaty but the least willing to take power, abstained from voting against it. The German delegates who made the final, Canossa-like journey to Versailles to sign the treaty stated that they did so under duress and recognised no moral obligation to adhere to it. Indeed as far as reparations were concerned they did not believe fulfilment was possible. As Erzberger said at the time: 'Adversity knows no dishonesty.' It the treaty were rejected and the war was resumed, Germany would suffer complete military occupation, economic hardship would increase immeasurably and the Reich would probably break up. For Germany it was Hobson's choice; but from the beginning the 'policy of fulfilment' inevitably contained an element of duplicity. It was a tactical necessity, no more, and evasion became a mark of patriotism. In extracting the republicans' signature to the treaty, the Allies had practically forced them to sign the death-warrant of German democracy. Nor did public resentment lessen with time: subsequent events, notably the occupation of the Ruhr, exacerbated it. Ten years after the signing of the Versailles treaty a German pastor (who was no nationalist) declared: 'This war educated our German people to peace, this peace has educated it to war.'[20]

German criticisms of the treaty were innumerable: it was imposed, not negotiated; it contradicted the Fourteen Points; it contained territorial injustices, including the ban on union with Austria, incompatible with its own principle of self-determination; it spelled economic ruin; the German people were being unfairly punished for the real or alleged sins of their former rulers; their national pride was insulted. Some of these grievances had less substance than others: Germany's rapid if short-lived economic recovery after 1924 (and her later ability to wage a second war) proved that the economic harm had been exaggerated. No Germans at the time, and few Englishmen ten years later, would admit that Versailles was a just peace; but even if it had been just, it was not wise. It brought disillusion not merely to the German people but to many others, who deplored the failure of Wilsonian idealism to substitute a genuinely international order for the balance of power based on rival blocs. Behind the façade of the League, the old self-seeking diplomacy continued. What was not realised by the Allies at the time was that the treaty would relatively soon become an embarrassment to them because they would lack the will to enforce it. There was hardly any trace of the wisdom and longsightedness which a hundred years before the authors of the Vienna peace settlement had shown in their dealings with defeated France, summarised in Castlereagh's declaration that his aim was not to collect trophies but to bring the world back to peaceful habits. In 1919 there had to be trophies to compensate for the infinitely greater suffering and to honour the secret commitments to allies. Propaganda had done its work too well: Germany was seen, especially in France, as uniquely evil, the source of all wrong and suffering.[21] There was little awareness of the war as a European civil war, or understanding that injury done to Germany could recoil on other nations. As George Kennan has written of the First World War: 'Both sides underestimated the seriousness of the damage they were doing to themselves – to their own spirit and their own physical substance – in this long debauch of hatred and bloodshed.'[22]

The Versailles treaty gave rise to three main problems. One was German disarmament. On the naval side this was a comparatively simple affair, though not without drama: at Scapa Flow, where the Imperial Navy had sailed for internment, its crews, in a final gesture of defiance, had scuttled their ships before the startled British could stop them. The treaty left Germany a modest fleet of six battleships and six light cruisers, with a dozen each of destroyers and torpedo boats but no submarines. German military disarmament, and the second problem, the future of Upper Silesia, are considered later in this chapter. The third problem, reparations, was the most intractable, and the enmity it caused was largely responsible for preventing any approach to reconciliation between France and Germany until seven years after the armistice.

The German government's belief that, even with goodwill, it would not be able to meet its reparations commitments soon received powerful support from an unexpected quarter – King's College, Cambridge, where John Maynard Keynes, having resigned as financial adviser to the British Treasury, wrote his persuasive essay *The Economic Consequences of the Peace*. That there should be disagreement about the total of reparations was inevitable: any assessment depended on imponderables and assumptions, including the pace and extent of Germany's economic recovery. The Allies were concerned with what Germany ought to pay having regard to the damage they had suffered; and her original obligation to pay compensation had now been inflated by the inclusion of pensions and separation allowances – an addition to which the Germans justifiably but fruitlessly objected. Keynes made his own estimate of what Germany could pay, which differed widely from what the Allies counted on getting. One thing was certain. With a depleted gold reserve, with her colonies, foreign investments and merchant navy lost or confiscated, Germany's only hope of paying lay in a favourable trade balance. But this in turn depended on a considerable expansion of German exports. How was this to be achieved in view of the loss of iron and coal under the treaty and the high cost (for a devalued currency) of imported raw materials? Experience was to show that the Allies would not allow in a flood of German goods in competition with their own. There was no prospect at the time of an American loan to Germany. France, who feared a prosperous Germany even more than an impoverished one, would do nothing to restore the Reich's economy. With her own budget unbalanced, her devastated provinces and her large debt to America, she would insist on a strict fulfilment of Germany's payments.

Britain, from the German point of view, seemed more hopeful. Among the public there was a good deal of support for Keynes, in which moral and political arguments were mixed with economic. Idealists were disillusioned that the post-war world fell so far short of the utopia for which they believed Wilson stood and for which so many lives had been sacrificed. Was the new French hegemony compatible with the Fourteen Points and League of Nations? Was it not self-defeating to heap humiliations and burdens on a German democracy that might founder under the strain? As for the economic aspect, the revival of Germany was needed for the recovery of Europe and the reduction of British unemployment, even for the prompt payment of reparations. Hence the British government gave only lukewarm support to the French use of sanctions for reparations defaults, and later disapproved of the occupation of the Ruhr, which was in any case of doubtful legality. When in 1924 Ramsay Macdonald became the first Labour Prime Minister of Great Britain, revision of Versailles even became British official policy.[23] But he was not in office long, and when the Conservatives came back Austen Chamberlain, the Foreign Secretary, declared his purpose to be to uphold the peace treaties as the basis of public law in Europe. Maintenance of the Entente with France, said the francophile Chamberlain, would be the cardinal object of his policy. In short, Germany's attempts to exploit Anglo-French differences brought no immediate gain. The British, among whom mistrust of Germany was still strong, were less perturbed than the Germans expected at French predominance in Europe (which damaged no vital British interest); they realised that the French obsession with security was partly a consequence of their (and the American) refusal to guarantee the new French frontier. Feeling slightly guilty in their isolation the British would criticise France but not act to stop her even when, as in the case of the Ruhr occupation, British trading interests were adversely affected.

(iii) WEIMAR: DEMOCRACY ON TRIAL

Less than five weeks after the agonising vote on the peace treaty, the National Assembly approved the new constitution which had been in gestation since February. For the first time in their history the German people had the chance of building an entirely new political structure: the dynasties which had stood in the way in 1848 no longer existed. Hugo Preuss, the main author of the document, was a professor of constitutional law and a member of the Democratic party. His object was to give Germany a constitution that would completely embody the liberal ideals in which he and a minority of the German people passionately believed. Preuss would have liked to abandon the federal system for a unitary one, as traditionally desired by the left, but had to meet the objections of the South German states, which wished to preserve as much as possible of their independence. The central government was however assigned more power than before, notably over finance, and the states had to give up their separate armies and foreign ministries, which even under the imperial regime had become an anomaly. Prussia, though still by far the largest state, lost its predominance with the disappearance of the *Bundesrat*, and inside Prussia the Junkers lost their monopoly of power with the abolition of the three-class franchise. Thus the state which during the Second Empire had been the heart and soul of conservatism now became the stronghold of republicanism and socialism, and the previous tension between a relatively liberal Reich and a reactionary Prussia was eliminated. The new constitution was a parliamentary democracy in which power rested in the Reichstag, elected by citizens of both sexes over the age of twenty. To ensure complete parity between votes proportional representation was introduced. For the first time there was a fully fledged Reich cabinet. A second legislative chamber representing the states, called the *Reichsrat* (successor of the former *Bundesrat*), was made subordinate to the Reichstag. The powers of the President were widely drawn: he was to be elected not by parliament, as in France, but by the nation, as in America, though unlike the American President he was not to be head of the executive. He was, however, to command the armed forces and had power to dissolve the Reichstag. A special feature of the constitution was the authority given to the President in Article 48 to suspend civil rights and to use the armed forces to enforce his decisions in case of emergency.[24] As if to redress the balance, another clause provided that a referendum could be held either by wish of the President or at the request of a tenth of the electorate. Finally, the constitution contained a list of basic rights and duties. Everything seemed provided for. Germany had the freest and fairest system of government in the world.

The new constitution was thus a compromise between federal and unitary conceptions of the state. It was also a half-way house between conservative liberalism of the kind represented by Stresemann of the People's party, who had welcomed parliamentary rule but deplored the republic, and the Independent socialists, for whom it was bourgeois and capitalist. To satisfy the left, there were clauses permitting socialisation, emphasising the social responsibilities of private wealth, and establishing a Reich Economic Council. This was to be a kind of economic parliament, consisting of business and professional representatives, with power to initiate and review social and economic legislation. Linked to it was to be a network of works councils whose composition and functions were the subject of a separate and bitterly controversial law. The establishment in the constitution of economic and works councils was a legacy of the revolution, an attempt to salvage the council idea and meet the demand of the radicals for some kind of economic democracy. But in practice little use was made of the Reich Economic Council, nor did the works councils fulfil the hopes of their sponsors.[25] The radicals felt cheated: hence their opposition to the Works Councils bill that led to fresh bloodshed in front of the Reichstag in January 1920. The Independent socialists, together with the Nationalists and the People's party, voted against the constitution, which was supported only by the now unpopular Weimar coalition, instead of resting on a general consensus.

It would be unreasonable to put the blame for the failure of German democracy between 1919 and 1933 on the constitution, though certain shortcomings were revealed in its working. Proportional representation meant in practice that candidates for the Reichstag were elected from a central list of names put up by the parties and not by a given constituency, so that parliamentarians had no personal relationship with their electors. This made it difficult for the parliamentary system to develop grass roots. It has often been said that the system encouraged the growth of small parties – twenty-seven contested the general election of 1932, though only fifteen were actually represented in the Reichstag.[26] And even the existence of six major parties (Nationalists, People's Party, Democrats, Centre, Social Democrats and Communists) made it difficult to form strong governments; coalitions, often weak and shortlived, were the order of the day. Yet this had been the basic party pattern under the Empire: the parties reflected political divisions within the electorate rather than any feature peculiar to the new constitution. More serious were the special powers given to the President under Article 48. The object was to strengthen the executive at a time when civil war and separatism threatened the state; and in a country used to authoritarian government it was reasonable to make the President more than a rubber stamp. While Ebert was President he took no undue advantage of his position: the real mistake, which the authors of the 1919 constitution could not foresee, was the choice of Hindenburg as Ebert's successor. The constitution was too theoretically perfect for those who had to work it; it demanded too much from a politically immature and ideologically divided people. Preuss himself in one of the debates on the new constitution referred to the Germans' inability to shake off their political timidity and deference to authority, and he later admitted that democracy did not suit the German character.[27] The ban on honours, for example, intended to promote a sense of equality, was a psychological mistake, which helped to make the Republic, in the words of a British observer, 'neither picturesque nor inspiring'.[28] Yet in the circumstances in which Germany found itself after 1930 it is unlikely that any constitution would have worked: both Nazis and Communists were anti-parliamentary on principle, and the Conservatives at best lukewarm. The experience of the Weimar constitution exemplifies the dictum that the best is often the enemy of the good.

(iv) THE ARMY AND THE REPUBLIC: THE KAPP PUTSCH

The revival of German militarism after the cataclysm of defeat and revolution occurred with remarkable speed. At the end of the war revulsion against militarism was widespread and genuine among the German population, and the whole revolutionary movement had a pronounced anti-militarist character. This was shown in many ways: in the attacks on officers, the rejection of army discipline, the anti-authoritarianism of soldiers' councils, the massive support for radical reform of the army at the first congress of soldiers' and workers' councils, the unwillingness of men to serve even in a *red* army. When during the early days of November Hermann Müller, one of the leading Majority socialists, saw officers allowing their swords to be seized and their shoulder badges torn off without resistance, it seemed to him that Prussian militarism had come to its dying hour.[29] The values and traditions which, in Prussia since Frederick the Great, in Germany since Bismarck, had been revered by civilian and soldier alike, were now derided. Even Hindenburg, the embodiment of Prussia's military virtues, was forced to bow to the new spirit by accepting *Vertrauensräte* (councils of picked men, trusted by their officers, with limited powers) in the field army as an inoculation (as he put it) against the more radical alternative of soldiers' councils which had already undermined the home army. To the dismay of their commanders the troops who had defended Germany for over four years against the strongest coalition known to history were now incapable of protecting the Ebert government against a disorganised band of revolutionary sailors. There seemed no future for what Groener called the 'best and strongest element of old Prussia' – the army. Then came the dramatic reversal of fortune early in 1919 with the appointment of Noske as local Commander-in-Chief, the rise of the Freikorps, phoenix-like, from the ashes of the Imperial army, and their victory over the left-wing rebels in Berlin and other cities. The Freikorps rejected the concept of a citizen army as advocated by the Socialists, and had no use for soldiers' councils. Noske too considered them an obstacle to efficiency. On 19 January a decree issued by the Ministry of War recognised soldiers' councils but limited their functions to such matters as soldiers' welfare. In the new army, known as the Provisional Reichswehr, which was established by a vote of the Constituent Assembly on 6 March, the officers were given full power of command and soldiers' councils were replaced by *Vertrauensräte*.[30] The Freikorps formed the basis of the *Reichswehr*, which thus from the beginning acquired an anti-republican spirit. Most of the senior officers adhered to the Prussian military tradition in which they had been brought up. An exception was Colonel Walther Reinhardt, the Minister of War and head of the Army Command, whose efforts to inculcate understanding for the new regime met little success. Whether younger officers of the new *Reichswehr* were conservatives or shared the right-wing radicalism of the Freikorps made little difference: they were united in their contempt for democracy and for the politicians in charge of the 'Jewish Republic'.

The peace treaty put a new strain on relations between the government and the army, despite the fact that the former decided to sign only after being assured by the Supreme Command that no other course was possible. First, the reduction of the army from its current size of about 400,000 to 200,000 by 30 September 1919 and 100,000 by 31 March 1920 roused a storm of indignation. How could such a force, deprived of all tanks, aircraft and heavy guns, protect Upper Silesia against the Poles and suppress the separatists and revolutionaries who in their various ways threatened to dismember the Reich? Personal interests were also involved. Officers and men faced the loss of their professional career with bleak prospects of earning a living in the shrunken economy and alien environment of the Republic With this drastic cutting down of the size of the army went the abolition of the General Staff and of the Supreme Command, the institutions which had made the army great. Then came the demands in the treaty for the trial on charges of war crimes of Germany's former leaders, starting with the Kaiser and including all the best known generals. These conditions were felt to be insulting. Finally, the German army was to withdraw completely from the Baltic provinces (formerly Russian, now in process of re-organisation as the three new republics of Estonia, Latvia and Lithuania) where, under the command of General von der Goltz, it had been allowed to remain since the armistice, fighting against the Bolsheviks. This was part of the Allied policy of a *cordon sanitaire* against revolutionary Russia. Since the days of the Teutonic Knights Germans had had a mystic attachment to the *Baltikum*, where German landowners formed the upper class. Now members of the Freikorps flocked to the Baltic to join von der Goltz: some wished to settle there and start a new life, others hoped to annex the territory to Germany or even to use it as a springboard for a march on Berlin. These ambitions could all be pursued under the banner of anti-Bolshevism. But the Bolsheviks, distracted by their civil war, ceased to be a threat, and the new Baltic states rejected German tutelage. The Allies wanted the Germans out, and so, with bitterness in their hearts, von der Goltz and his volunteers returned to the Reich, where they remained a source of unrest. The republican government was relieved that the Baltic adventure was over, for it had failed to control the troops on the spot while having to take the blame for their misbehaviour. The weakness of Berlin's authority over the troops was evident.

It was not only the Freikorps from the Baltic who found the idea of a march on Berlin attractive. Among the senior generals who reacted indignantly to the government's decision to sign the peace treaty was General von Lüttwitz, a man of reactionary views who was in command of Berlin and district. On 26 July 1919 Lüttwitz and a number of generals agreed to put certain demands to the government, including non-compliance with the military clauses of the treaty, failing which they would seek to set up a military dictatorship. Thus was hatched the plot which led to the abortive Putsch of March 1920. On 21 August Lüttwitz met Kapp, a civil servant from East Prussia who during the war had supported the rabidly annexationist Fatherland Front and been among the implacable opponents of Bethmann Hollweg. During the heart-searching that had preceded the final decision on the treaty some of the military commanders had looked to Noske as a possible dictator: he and Ebert were the only Socialist leaders in whom the army had confidence, but this confidence waned when Noske reluctantly came round to the view that the treaty must be signed. In left-wing circles, criticism was fierce: Noske was blamed for his tough and sometimes brutal measures against the Communists and for turning a blind eye to Freikorps excesses. Noske knew he had lost the confidence of the left (including many in the S.P.D.) but believed he had won that of the generals. The Kapp Putsch was to disillusion him. In a Note of 3 February 1920 the Allies demanded the surrender for war crimes trials of nearly 900 leaders of the old regime. The German people were united in seeing in this move an act of revenge, not even-handed justice, and the Allies accepted a proposal that the trials should take place in German courts. This was equivalent to de-valuing the whole procedure. But the sop to German pride could not prevent excitement in army circles from reaching boiling point.

Rumours of a military Putsch had been circulating for some time, and Noske had received warnings but took no special precautions. Matters were brought to a head by an order to General Lüttwitz, that forces under his command, including a naval brigade commanded by a Captain Ehrhardt, should be disbanded. Lüttwitz not only rejected the order but made counter-demands on Ebert and Noske, including the replacement of the War Minister, Reinhardt, and a new general election. This was rank insubordination, and Lüttwitz was relieved of his command. But he refused to give it up, and, with his fellow-conspirators Kapp and others, managed to evade arrest. Ehrhardt sent an ultimatum to the government in similar terms to those of Lüttwitz, and marched on Berlin. The government was faced with a choice: to abandon the capital; to stay and negotiate with Kapp; or to resist by force. Ebert and Noske held a council with senior officers including Reinhardt and Seeckt (head of the *Truppenamt*) in the middle of the night. It became clear that the *Reichswehr* (which was split three ways in its attitude) would not fire on *Reichswehr* and in any case the government did not want bloodshed. Since it was not prepared to negotiate, the only course was flight. Ehrhardt occupied Berlin and declared that he and Kapp had formed a new government. The trade unions answered with a general strike, in which white collar employees and civil servants as well as industrial workers took part, and against which the new 'regime' was powerless. After five days Kapp and Lüttwitz acknowledged defeat, and the lawful government returned from Stuttgart, where it had taken refuge. This was a victory for the republican forces, some of whom were determined to make full use of it. The unions issued a nine point declaration which put forward radical demands including the dissolution of counter-revolutionary army units.[31] Only a government pledged to this would receive their support. Bauer (the Chancellor) and Noske, discredited by the Putsch, resigned, and Legien, who for thirty years had been chairman of the free trade unions and was the hero of the hour, was offered the chancellorship. He refused. Another much discussed possibility was the inclusion in the governing coalition of the Independent socialists, whose suspicions of the right wing of the S.P.D. had been amply vindicated. But they or rather their left wing could not bring themselves to collaborate with the Majority socialists, and so the old coalition was reformed, with Hermann Müller as Chancellor. He promised to suppress disloyal elements with an 'iron broom'.[32] In fact little was done to punish the Kapp rebels, still less to discipline those in the army who, like Seeckt, had adopted a wait and see attitude. On the contrary, when Reinhardt, following the resignation of Noske, resigned as head of the Army Command, Seeckt, a traditionalist, was appointed to his post. As he was given increased powers, Seeckt had a stronger position than his predecessor.[33] Thus republican influence in the army was diminished; while Gessler, who succeeded Noske as Minister of Defence, was a less assertive personality. During his easy-going regime the army under Seeckt became a state within a state.

In some parts of Germany the Kapp Putsch was the signal for left-wing forces to revive the revolution and seize power. In the Ruhr a 'red army' occupied the industrial towns in opposition to General von Watter, the commanding general, whose sympathies lay with Kapp. Despite S.P.D. attempts to bring about a compromise (the Bielefeld Agreement of 21 March) fighting flared up again in the Ruhr, and ended with the *Reichswehr* in control. In Bavaria, too, where the Socialists resigned from the government because the latter was compromised with pro-Kapp forces, the balance of power swung to the right. This was indeed the general outcome throughout Germany, as the election results of June 1920 showed. The middle classes had drawn the wrong conclusion from the Kapp affair, and instead of rallying to the moderate parties and supporting those who had been loyal to the Republic they gave their votes to the still officially monarchist People's party, whose attitude to Kapp had been equivocal. The working classes showed their lack of confidence in the S.P.D. by supporting the Independents, whose membership in the Reichstag jumped from 22 to 81. In a sense the S.P.D. deserved their defeat, for they had made little use of their opportunities. Hermann Müller, of whom much was expected, had not kept his promise to the trade unions to purge the army, civil service and economy of reactionaries; and after the elections the Socialists were no longer in power. By an ironical paradox the left-wing victory over Kapp rebounded to the advantage of the right. But there was a lesson also for the nationalists. The failure of the Putsch signified that the masses could not be won for restoration of the old order, which was what Kapp and Lüttwitz stood for: any future bid for power by the extreme right would have at least to use the language of socialism. Hitler knew this: the party's name, the National Socialist German Workers' party, was designed to steal left-wing thunder.

The Allied efforts to disarm – in a wider sense, to demilitarise Germany – which had provoked the Kapp Putsch, continued. All Freikorps were ordered to be dissolved by the end of May 1920. There was, predictably, much resistance, and the Freikorps went under-ground or retired to Bavaria, where a right-wing government gave them asylum in defiance of the order from Berlin. Polish threats against the eastern frontier up to the final decision on Upper Silesia, and French encroachments in the west for breaches of the treaty kept alive a resentful spirit and led to the formation of illegal volunteer units known as the Black *Reichswehr*. The threat of Communism was used to justify the existence of a Home Guard or *Einwohnerwehr*, consisting of middle-class citizens, especially in Bavaria. They too were in viola-tion of Versailles, though Lord d'Abernon, the British ambassador in Berlin, thought the demand for their disbandment 'almost insane'.[34] They finally disappeared in 1921. The Allies were also suspicious of nationalist ex-servicemen's organisations like the *Stahlhelm*, which took part in para-military activities, and later played an important role in right-wing politics. Less obvious were the hidden stocks of arms and equipment in various parts of Germany, about which the civilian authorities, especially if they were known to be socialists or pacifists, were not informed. There were many ways of evading the treaty: dis-guised training of pilots for a future air force; the survival within a permitted *Truppenamt* of a camouflaged skeleton general staff; secret work on gun and tank design by Krupp; the making and testing of forbidden weapons by foreign firms in such countries as Holland, Sweden, Finland, Spain and Turkey, with the help of German money, experts and know-how; the special co-operation with the Red Army which developed after Rapallo for the manufacture of weapons and training in their use. Some at least of the republican Chancellors were aware of these activities. Some of these violations of the treaty were known to the Inter-Allied Control Commission on Disarmament, which frequently warned the Allied governments. But after 1924, when relations between Germany and her ex-enemies improved, such warnings were little heeded, especially in England.[35] It is hard to say how far the Commission itself was hoodwinked, how far it deliberately averted its eyes to avoid difficulty or embarrassment. Stresemann, the German Foreign Minister, kept pressing for the withdrawal of the Commission, which finally left Germany in January 1927. By then the limited production of forbidden arms had begun in Germany. The

Commission's inability to complete its task illustrates the impossibility of disarming a well organised and determined nation against its will without total occupation. As for the Germans, they waited sceptically for the Allies to put into effect their own disarmament which, according to the treaty, was to follow that of Germany.

(v) REPARATIONS, INFLATION, THE RUHR CRISIS

Germany's economic recovery after the war and the defeat was slow and painful. Besides the problems of readjustment from war to peace, shortage of manpower and a swollen internal debt common to all belligerent nations, she faced special difficulties caused by the loss of territory, including agricultural and mineral assets, the surrender of rolling stock and other material under the armistice, and the loss of earnings consequent upon the confiscation of her merchant navy and overseas investments. Her factories and transport system were run down, and the shortage of raw materials could not be made good by additional imports. Not surprisingly, German industrial production failed to regain its pre-war level. In 1920, for example, only three quarters as much coal was produced as in 1913, and less than half as much raw steel.[36] Handicapped by lack of manure and fertiliser, agricultural output also fell far short of its pre-war figures. The government had greatly increased liabilities and less revenue with which to meet them. Despite Erzberger's fiscal reforms, by which the Reich government acquired adequate powers of taxation, a capital levy and a forced loan, the budget remained unbalanced. Indeed, between 1920 and 1923 the government's expenditure was never less than twice its income, and usually much more.[37] The deficits were covered by floating debts – in other words by the printing press.[38] Industrialists as well as the government took advantage of easy credit. The presentation in May 1921 of the final bill for reparations, at the unrealistic total of 132 milliard gold marks, put an intolerable strain on a weak economy and a tottering currency.[39] Since any recovery would demonstrably improve Germany's capacity to pay, there was no incentive to adopt the harsh financial discipline that alone could have stopped inflation. In 1923, when France occupied the Ruhr, German coal and steel production came to little more than a third of their pre-war totals, and the national income was barely a half. These figures indicate a serious deterioration in the standard of living. During the five post-war years the greater part of the population continued to suffer from shortage and rising prices. Hunger was widespread.[40] Inflation was not new in 1923; already in July 1922 the mark was worth less than a hundreth of its 1914 value. But after the beginning of the Ruhr occupation it got completely out of hand, with results that exceeded the wildest fantasy.

The general election of June 1920 caused a shift of power to the right. The new Chancellor, Fehrenbach, was a Catholic and a leader of the Centre party. For the first time the People's party (D.V.P.), which was financed by heavy industry and drew its main support from the Protestant middle classes, joined the government. Thus the new coalition was more broadly based and less vulnerable to attacks from the extreme right, which had hitherto identified the Republic with 'Marxism'. The Social Democrats tolerated the government, i.e. abstained from voting against it in the Reichstag, which was the condition of its survival. But socialist influence counted for less than in the preceding twenty months when the S.P.D. had been in power. Stresemann, who, though not a member of the cabinet, had emerged as the strong man of the People's party, reassured his anxious supporters in December 1920: 'The time for a socialist Germany is past.'[41] The government's chief concern was the interminable wrangles with the Allies over reparations and other obligations of the peace treaty.

In July 1920 the German ministers were summoned to a conference at Spa where the Allies made demands for reparations in kind (mainly coal) and asked awkward questions about disarmament. The Germans at first adopted a defiant attitude, but gave way when the Allies threatened to occupy additional territory if their claims were not met. In the following year the Reparations Commission set up to draw up the final total reached the end of its almost impossible task. By then the atmosphere, already bitter, had been worsened by a new quarrel over the value of reparations in kind so far delivered. It was also alleged that Germany was deliberately delaying the trial of 'war criminals' to which she was committed. In reprisal for these shortcomings, the Allies occupied three towns in the Ruhr; Düsseldorf, Duisburg and Ruhrort. When the reparations bill was seen to amount to a sum three times what Keynes had suggested as reasonable, it came as a fatal blow to the struggling Fehrenbach government.

Fehrenbach's successor, Wirth, was a younger man and belonged to the left wing of the Centre. He formed a government which included the Socialists and Democrats but not the People's party: thus the Weimar coalition was re-formed. For the first time Stresemann made a bid for the chancellorship which might have succeeded had he received more promptly assurances from the British government about reparations and Upper Silesia. As the Germans knew, the British were uneasy about the use of sanctions to enforce the treaty, nor did they see eye to eye with the French over the Silesian question. It had been agreed at Versailles that the future of Upper Silesia, a German province which was also claimed by Poland, should be settled by a plebiscite. The area was industrially of great value, and before the war had provided a fifth of Germany's coal supplies. The plebiscite was held in March 1921, and resulted in a split vote, about three-fifths of the electorate opting for Germany. The intermingling of peoples in the towns as well as the countryside made it impossible to draw a frontier acceptable to both sides; and the committee of the League of Nations charged with this task was accused of partiality by both Berlin and Warsaw. The Germans were bitterly disappointed when the largely German town of Kattowitz and at least three-quarters of the coal mines and iron ore reserves were assigned to Poland. The resulting popular indignation ruined an attempt by Rathenau, Wirth's Minister of Reconstruction, to take some of the acrimony out of Franco-German relations by reaching agreement with his French opposite number Loucheur over reparations due to France. To make the immediate payment of $250 million demanded by the Allies, the German government had had to sell marks on the foreign exchanges, with the result that the value of the mark fell by four-fifths between May and September 1921. It was to avert a further catastrophic decline that Rathenau hit on the idea of transferring some of the reparations from currency to goods, and this was the main feature of his understanding with Loucheur. But before it could be put into effect it was overtaken by events, including the replacement of Briand as French Foreign Minister by Poincaré, the spokesman of implacable French nationalism who would admit no deviation from the letter of the law. A more militant note was now struck in Paris. The Reparations Commission had granted Germany postponement of the reparations payments due in January and February 1922, but in return required the Berlin government to raise more revenue by taxation in order to meet its debts. This was too much even for such 'fulfilment' politicians as Wirth and Rathenau, and they refused. Rathenau, in whom Wirth had great faith, was made German Foreign Minister at the end of January.

Meanwhile Lloyd George had been working on the more constructive idea of calling a European conference to revive international trade and restore the economic links broken by the war. This grand design required the participation of Germany, which in pre-war days had been such a good customer of Great Britain, but also of Soviet Russia, whose return to the concert of Europe the conference, to take place at Genoa, was supposed to mark. More specifically, Lloyd George hoped to do a deal with the Soviets over Russia's pre-revolution debts. Treating Russia as a vast, under-developed country, his idea was that Germany should be encouraged to use her organising skill to unlock Russia's resources; and with the wealth so created she would be able to pay reparations, so that everyone would benefit. But the French refused to be drawn on reparations, while to the Russians the spectacle of German or other western capitalists exploiting their potential was even less attractive. Yet the Soviet government badly needed a western loan; and if the West's demands proved totally unacceptable, they could always turn to Germany, with whom secret bi-lateral talks were held immediately before the Genoa conference. At Genoa the German delegation was headed by Rathenau, the Russian by Chicherin, the Soviet Commissar for Foreign Affairs. A large part of the proceedings consisted of Anglo-Russian negotiations on Russia's pre-war and wartime debts, and on compensation for British owners of nationalised property since the revolution. In these talks Germany naturally had no share, but their outcome was uncertain, and the Germans' fear was that agreement might be reached at their expense. They therefore after initial hesitation accepted a Russian offer to meet in private and sign the draft of the Russo-German treaty that had been discussed by them in Berlin a few weeks before. This was the treaty of Rapallo which was to raise such a storm. Russia renounced all claims for German reparations (reserved by Article 116 of the Versailles treaty) and Germany gave up all claims for pre-war debts or loss of property caused by the revolution, provided Russia did not meet similar demands by any third country. Poincaré, who had refused to attend the Genoa conference, saw in the Rapallo agreement a sinister plot against the peace settlement. The British thought Rathenau guilty of treachery and the *Times* fulminated against the 'open defiance' and 'studied insult to the Entente powers'.[42] If so, it was a defiance which the West had provoked. Article 116 virtually forced Germany to seek a settlement with Russia in order to escape the possible addition of Russian reparations to an already intolerable burden, while Rathenau's attempts to reach an understanding with the British were thwarted when his urgent messages mysteriously failed to reach Lloyd George or were ignored by him.

The immediate effect of Rapallo, as Rathenau had foreseen, was a stiffening of the British attitude and a less sympathetic hearing for the German case in London as well as in Paris. Though the short-term gain and relief to Germany could not be denied – politically as well as economically she was now in a stronger position *vis-à-vis* the West – a price had to be paid. The revival of France's fears for her security paved the way for the return to power of the intransigent Poincaré: as Lloyd George said later, 'If there had been no Rapallo there would have been no Ruhr.'[43] Moreover the basic dilemma of reparations remained: if Germany sold marks to pay her debts her currency collapsed; if she sold goods, her competitors objected to her under-cutting in their markets. The moment had not yet come when the United States would regard Germany as a profitable field of investment, though American bankers had already begun to show an interest. In the long run, Rathenau could only stoically hope that reason and moderation would prevail. There was little sign of those qualities inside Germany, where Rathenau's critics grew bolder; and on 24 June he was shot dead by nationalist and anti-semitic youths in broad daylight near his home in west Berlin. With all his ambiguities (some imposed by circumstances, some inherent in his character) Rathenau had a vision and intellectual capacity such as few of the Weimar politicians possessed, and the nation could ill spare his talents and resourcefulness.[44] Even in a society inured to violence his murder created a sensation, and led to a closing of republican ranks. However, the blow was against the man rather than the policy: anti-communist as the German right was, it was not blind to the advantages of friendship with Russia, and the *Reichswehr* positively favoured it. Shortly after Rapallo was signed, German-Soviet relations entered a new phase with the arrival in Moscow of Count Brockdorff-Rantzau as German ambassador. He was soon on very friendly terms with Chicherin, with whom he had much in common. Both were diplomats of aristocratic birth and bohemian tastes who had thrown in their lot with left-wing governments. Both were convinced of the benefits of co-operation between their two countries. As Lenin observed in December 1920, Russia wanted revolution and Germany wanted revenge.[45] This gave them, at least in the short run, a joint platform against a Europe dominated by the Versailles powers and conservative social forces.

In one sense Rapallo was an accident. Both by inclination and for practical financial reasons Rathenau was a westerner, and would never have come to an understanding with the Russians had he not suspected that the West was about to make a deal with them which would have been detrimental to Germany. Rathenau could not know that the suspicion was unfounded. Yet in another sense Rapallo was a logical consequence of the mutual needs of the two 'pariah' powers. Russia, excluded from Europe by the Versailles treaty, condemned it as emphatically as Germany. As Chicherin said, the two under-privileged nations were natural partners;[46] both sought an end of isolation in each other's company. Germany, exploited by reparations and impoverished by the treaty, was seen in Russia as a semi-colonial country with whom Soviet Russia, the friend of all the oppressed, had a natural sympathy, and in whose survival she had an obvious interest, if only to counterbalance French predominance. Seeckt was not wrong in describing Rapallo as the first attempt by republican Germany to

conduct an active foreign policy. It was the most significant visible link
in the chain of Russo-German relations as it re-formed after the Bolshevik revolution and the German defeat.

The German revolution had proved a great disappointment to the
Russians, and there was a marked lack of cordiality between the two
regimes in the immediate post-war period. The Soviets resented the
refusal of the Ebert-Haase government in November 1918 to re-admit
Joffé, the Russian ambassador who had been expelled in the last days
of Prince Max's government for subversive activity. They also took
umbrage at the German refusal to accept their offer of food, and
more generally at the failure to develop a revolutionary foreign policy.
A high-powered Russian delegation invited by the Berlin workers' and
soldiers' councils to attend their first congress was turned back by the
German government: only the elusive Radek slipped through the net.
German attempts to earn favour in the West by presenting themselves
as a bulwark against Bolshevism, and the continued occupation by
German forces of large areas of former Russian territory, allowed by
the armistice, could only add to Russian disillusion. The Germans on
their side resented Soviet encouragement to the Spartacists to overthrow the Ebert-Haase government in favour of Liebknecht, and
feared that closer relations with the Bolsheviks would drag Germany
into a disastrous revolutionary war against the West: Germany was in
no condition to fight, and Russia, preoccupied with civil war, was in no
position to help. The Soviet leaders somewhat unwillingly concluded
that Germany was not as ripe for revolution as they had assumed, and
that co-operation even with a 'social-patriotic' or bourgeois government in Berlin had its uses. Until 1923 at least there seemed a chance
that the German Communist party, on which Russian hopes mainly
depended, might come to power. After October 1920, when the
hitherto tiny K.P.D. absorbed the left wing of the Independent Social
Democratic party, it began to acquire the numbers needed to enable
it to compete with the other mass parties, while striving to keep the
hard-line policy laid down at the second conference of the Third
International. Meanwhile the Soviet government showed interest in
re-establishing the diplomatic and other links with Germany disrupted
at the end of the war; what Moscow most feared was that Germany
might pass completely into the western camp, though Poincaré's intransigence made this unlikely. What above all brought Russia and
Germany together was their common hatred of Poland, a symbol of
French ascendancy and of the *cordon sanitaire* against Bolshevism.
During the Russo-Polish war of 1920 the Germans hoped for a Russian victory that would restore the 1914 frontier between the two
countries. There was tremendous excitement in Germany when the

Bolshevik army reached the suburbs of Warsaw, and a sharp impetus was given to the 'National Bolshevik' movement consisting of right-wing people who wished Germany to align herself with Soviet Russia despite ideological differences. But after the 'miracle on the Vistula' it was the Red Army's turn to retreat, and, abandoning areas claimed as ethnically Russian, it had to accept a frontier with Poland which left Russia, like Germany, a revisionist power. Few Germans accepted the Polish Corridor as permanent. So good a democrat as Chancellor Wirth could tell Brockdorff-Rantzau in the spring of 1922: 'Poland must be eliminated... On this point I am in full agreement with the military, especially with General von Seeckt.'[47] In a memorandum on German foreign policy Seeckt was equally frank: 'Poland's existence is intolerable, incompatible with the survival of Germany. It must disappear through its own internal weakness and through Russia with our help.'[48] Germany relied on Russia to prevent a possible Polish attack at an awkward moment such as occurred more than once in 1923,[49] while the Russians' main fear was that Germany might be used as the springboard for a combined attack on the Soviet Union.

Trade and arms were other fields in which Germany and Russia had common interests. At a time when German exports met difficulty in western markets, industrialists, diplomats and many others were impressed with the vast possibilities offered to German goods and German skill in the under-developed economy of Russia. For their part the Russians were enthusiastic about the advantages to be gained from German know-how, technology and organisation. A trade treaty between the two countries was signed in May 1921. About the same time the question of military collaboration was broached. The Russians wanted German help in rebuilding their armaments industry, the Germans a way of evading Versailles. Here too the aims of both co-incided. Secret negotiations were opened between the *Reichswehr* and representatives of the Soviet army. German firms were invited to Russia to manufacture and test aeroplanes, tanks, poison gas, heavy guns and other weapons forbidden by treaty. A Russian base was made available where German pilots and air staff could be trained; this was to prove of great importance for the future *Luftwaffe*. How confidential relations between the two sides became is shown by the fact that Russian officers were permitted to take part in secret training programmes for staff officers in Berlin and even to see the organisational plans for illegal rearmament. Politically all this was for the Germans a matter of great delicacy, and elaborate steps were taken to camouflage it. It was important to keep the facts not only from foreign observers, such as the Disarmament Commission, but also from left-wing and pacifist politicians likely to make trouble in parliament or in the press. For this reason even the President, though constitutionally head of the armed forces, was not informed.[50] But Russia was far from being the only country in which arms were manufactured for Germany as a way of evading the peace treaty. Nor was a pro-Russian policy favoured by the majority of German politicians. It was largely a reaction to disenchantment with the West over reparations and Upper Silesia. Germans knew that it was the West which could provide the loans, raw materials and food they needed. In principle, too, the two parties which dominated the politics of the early Weimar Republic, the Socialists and the Catholics, were western in outlook; inherited dislike of Russian 'barbarism' mingled with a fear of Bolshevism kept alive by the quasi-revolutionary activities of the increasingly Russian-controlled German Communist party. Germans after the war looked to America, which had rejected the treaty of Versailles, as a balancing factor in world politics and the power which could rescue Germany from her economic plight, but under President Harding the United States reverted to isolationism. Not until late in 1923 did American diplomacy intervene to break the deadlock in German-Allied relations.

Before this improvement came, the Weimar regime had to undergo its longest and most dangerous crisis. Rathenau's murder, by the same 'patriotic' terrorist group (Organisation Consul) as had assassinated Erzberger the year before, caused a wave of alarm and weakened the mark on the foreign exchanges. It was a brutal reminder of the precariousness of the Republic and the ruthlessness of its internal enemies. The Chancellor, repeating a phrase used earlier by Scheidemann, told the Reichstag: 'The enemy stands on the right.' The trade unions declared a twenty-four hours general strike, and a law for the protection of the constitution was hurriedly passed. The rump Independent socialist party, whose left wing had gone over to the Communists in October 1920, re-joined the S.P.D., a gesture of support for parliamentary democracy. A German request for a temporary moratorium on reparations was turned down by the French, despite its having been approved by a committee of financial experts from several countries. To strengthen the government, Wirth invited the Socialists to enter a reconstructed ministry. Influenced by the enlarged left wing however, they refused to co-operate with the People's party, whose social policy they distrusted. In November 1922, having failed to meet reparations demands and stabilise the mark, Wirth resigned. There followed, for the first time under the Republic, a nominally non-party but in fact right-wing government consisting mainly of business executives, headed by Cuno, managing director of Germany's largest shipping company. The politicians had failed: now it was up to the businessmen to succeed.

The showdown with France which the advent of Poincaré had fore-shadowed was at hand (January 1923). Poincaré was convinced that Germany could pay reparations if she wanted to, just as she could sta-bilise the mark if she exercised the necessary financial discipline. He was bent on obtaining 'productive guarantees' i.e. physical control of German coal in the Ruhr. The German government had long since ceased to balance its budget: 90 per cent of expenditure was met from the floating debt. It could have made a more determined effort to pay reparations just as it could have ended inflation (as it was to do shortly), though given the intensity of feelings about reparations, it is far from certain that a democratic German government could have done so. In any case the Germans claimed to have paid in reparations vastly more than the sum accepted as paid by the Reparations Com-mission. But the French too acted in bad faith: Poincaré's real object was to use German defaults, however trivial, as a pretext for sanctions. By occupying the Ruhr, France could weaken the German economy and perhaps even detach the Ruhr from the Reich, in much the same way as she encouraged – unsuccessfully – separatist movements in the Rhineland and Palatinate. France would gain more security, and there would be some compensation for the failure of Britain and America to guarantee the new French frontier. Lloyd George once said that the French could never decide whether they preferred repara-tions or the pleasure of trampling on Germany.[51] Poincaré decided to have both. On 11th January, after Germany had failed to deliver the specified number of telegraph poles, the French army, supported by the Belgians but with British disapproval, occupied the Ruhr, which they proceeded to cut off from the rest of the Reich.

The German government replied with a declaration of passive resistance. All co-operation with the occupying forces was refused: miners and railwaymen went on strike, civil servants refused to obey French orders. Inevitably tempers rose and resistance at times became active. Clashes occurred between French troops and workers, notably at the Krupp works in Essen, where thirteen people were killed and fifty-two wounded by French gunfire. Gustav Krupp, the head of the firm, was charged with inciting a riot and given a fine of 100 million marks and fifteen years' imprisonment by a military court.[52] Acts of sabotage against the French were punished with prison sentences. Prominent citizens were arrested and kept as hostages. The best known saboteur or freedom fighter was Schlageter, a former Freikorps man who became a national hero after his execution by a French firing squad near Düsseldorf in May 1923. Throughout Germany anti-French feeling reached a new intensity and Krupp, the archetype of a great industrialist, became a martyr to people of every class and party.

Outraged patriotism combined with the desperation caused by run-away inflation gave a new stimulus to political extremism. For the first time Hitler's N.S.D.A.P. was active outside its native Bavaria. Yet passive resistance did not work. Sullenly many colliers returned to the pits and produced coal. Miners and engineers arrived from France. The Reich government had to provide for the tens of thousands of workless and their families, to look after the 150,000 or so expelled from the Ruhr, and to replace the missing Ruhr coal with costly foreign imports. By the summer of 1923 passive resistance was costing the government 40 million gold marks a day. On the foreign exchanges the mark continued to plummet, so that by the middle of August it took nearly three million marks to buy one dollar. Paper money no longer had any practical use, and became too bulky to carry. The collapse of the value of money created a crazy world in which financial transactions became a nightmare of uncertainty, for towards the end of the inflation the value of the mark was falling by the hour. A story typical of the period is of a woman who left outside a shop a basket full of bank notes; when she returned the notes were still there but the basket had been stolen.[53] For the price of a single egg in 1923 one could, five years earlier, have bought five hundred milliard eggs. There was a wild scramble to buy goods, or for those who could afford it, land and property. Ordinary people resorted to barter to satisfy their daily needs. Firms printed their own currency notes which were used as wages. Germany had reached a state in which no society could survive. In the Ruhr 132 people had been killed in clashes, and there was talk of a special currency being introduced. The longer the deadlock continued, the more bankrupt Germany would become and the greater the risk that the Ruhr would be lost.

It was at this crucial juncture that Stresemann became Chancellor in place of the disheartened Cuno. Stresemann's first priority, on which everything else depended, was to stabilise the mark. But this could be done only by ending the costly policy of passive resistance, a step which he took on 26 September. It was an act of enormous courage, for it meant, at least on paper, capitulating to Poincaré and provoking the wrath of the Nationalists. A new bank was set up to issue, in carefully controlled amounts, a new currency known as the Rentenmark, based on real assets. This gradually replaced the old mark, which ceased to be printed: in its final stages it had been worth less than a four billionth of a dollar. Government expenditure was drastically cut and steps were taken to balance the budget. Credit was curtailed. Responsibility for the operation was entrusted to Dr Hjalmar Schacht, a member of the board of directors of one of Germany's largest banks, who was made Currency Commissioner with special

powers. In December 1923, Schacht became President of the Reichsbank, in succession to Havenstein, whose policy of printing unlimited
paper money had proved so disastrous. The success of currency reform
was the work of Schacht but also of two Ministers of Finance: Hilferding who drew up the plans and his successor Luther who carried
them out.

The Rentenmark was not long in proving itself. This was remarkable
considering the circumstances of its origin. For it was during the
autumn of 1923 that the republican regime faced its gravest ordeal
since Spartacus and Kapp. The threat came from several quarters.
There was a revolt from inside when a Major Buchrucker tried to start
a Putsch in the name of the 'Black *Reichswehr*' but failed to win support and was disowned by Seeckt. Bavaria presented a special challenge. There a right-wing government headed by Kahr (behind which
sheltered a number of extreme nationalist and racialist groups, including Hitler's N.S.D.A.P.) established a dictatorship and declared a state
of emergency. This was an act of open defiance against the Reich
government. The Bavarian *Reichswehr* commander, Lossow, declared
that he was no longer under the orders of the Commander-in-Chief,
Seeckt. In Berlin Chancellor Stresemann reacted by proclaiming a
state of emergency throughout Germany and conferring special powers
on the Minister of Defence, Gessler, but he did not actually intervene
in Bavaria, preferring to wait for the rebels' next move. On the borders of Bavaria, in 'Red Saxony' there was the opposite problem: a
coalition of Socialists and Communists threatened a revolution from
the left. The Saxon government was not popular in military quarters
in Berlin because it had exposed the activities of the Black *Reichswehr*
into which Seeckt did not wish civilians, especially Socialists, to pry.
The formation by the Communists of a proletarian militia in Saxony,
though intended for defence, was seen, in conjunction with the revolutionary strategy of the Third International, as the first stage of a
Communist bid for power in Germany. There was also the danger that
Bavarian forces might intervene in Saxony to 'restore order'. The
Reich government accordingly sent its own troops in to depose the
Saxon government, though this action could not be justified constitutionally. In doing so it lost the support of the Socialists, who contrasted
the iron hand shown to the left in Saxony with the velvet glove applied
to the right-wing rebels in Bavaria. The situation was particularly
embarrassing for Seeckt, who, as at the time of Kapp, was anxious
that *Reichswehr* should not have to fire on *Reichswehr*. Though not
sympathetic to Bavarian separatism, Seeckt shared the right-wing
sentiments of Kahr and Lossow and their critical attitude to Stresemann. The Bavarian crisis came to a head when the Nazis staged their

Beerhall Putsch in Munich late on 8 November. The first news reaching Berlin suggested that Hitler, backed by the Bavarian *Reichswehr*, was about to march on the capital; and, as at the time of Kapp, the cabinet held an emergency midnight meeting. Ebert this time transferred his presidential powers over the army direct to the Chief of the Army Command, Seeckt, who thus became, temporarily, a constitutionally appointed military dictator. But at the last minute Kahr and Lossow withdrew their support from Hitler, who was forced to 'go it alone'. When he and his followers, accompanied by Ludendorff, staged a march through the centre of Munich on the following day they met unexpected opposition: the Bavarian police had, in the end, done their duty. Hitler's hysteria and impatience had discredited him in the eyes of his sympathisers in the Kahr regime and saved the Berlin government from a head-on collision with the Bavarian authorities. Henceforth Bavaria ceased to be the thorn in the side of the Reich which it had been in the first five years of the Republic, and German unity had been preserved. But Hitler and his colleagues continued to benefit from the leniency of the Bavarian authorities.

The loss of S.P.D. support forced Stresemann to resign. There were other reasons besides the Bavaria-Saxony problem for the Socialists' discontent. They feared, with good reason, that as part of the austerity campaign to stabilise the mark, the eight-hour day, granted in 1918, would be withdrawn. They were also disheartened because Poincaré had made no positive response to Stresemann's calling off of passive resistance in the Ruhr. The S.P.D. refused to join the next government, headed by the Centre leader Marx, which thus consisted of middle-class parties only (Centre, Democrats and Stresemann's D.V.P.). Marx, a banker of moderate views, had the sense to keep Stresemann as Foreign Minister, the post he occupied till his death six years later. Stresemann's chancellorship, though brief, had laid the foundations of recovery. Inflation had been ended, the Ruhr deadlock loosened. Despite the absence of a gesture from Poincaré Stresemann continued to seek a solution of the Ruhr and reparations problems. His efforts met a response from the British and American governments, which sent representatives to an international committee appointed to look into the whole reparations question. Its chairman was C. G. Dawes, an American businessman, and it held its first meeting in January 1924. 1923 had been make or break year for the Republic; largely thanks to Stresemann, it had survived. But despite the apparent recovery of the next few years, the multiple crisis was to exact its price.

Inflation was a traumatic experience for the German people, an unprecedented financial catastrophe which became a major tragedy.

Its disruptive effect on the normal processes of life can hardly be exaggerated. It struck a nation already demoralised and disorientated, for it came as the culmination of a nine-year period that included the war, the revolution, the Kapp Putsch, and the occupation of the Ruhr. It coincided with the feverish mood of a post-war society that had thrown off the restraints of the past and was indulging in every kind of pleasure and vice.[54] In Berlin and other big cities there was an orgy of dancing, gambling, drinking and sexual debauch, and much dabbling in occultism and in exotic new cults such as Dada and *Nacktkultur*. The gaiety was a reaction to the past but also concealed anxiety about the future, and behind it was a grim background of poverty, unemployment and suppressed revolt. Inflation was afterwards remembered as the time when foreigners lived in luxury hotels for next to nothing under the eyes of half-starved Germans; when the streets were studded with mendicant ex-servicemen, often disabled; when children were sent begging or stealing to get money to buy food for their families; when the birth rate went down and the death and abortion rates went up; when there was a sharp increase in tuberculosis and rickets among young schoolchildren; when the poor queued up at soup kitchens and impoverished rentiers sold their possessions for food. In these and other ways the physical effects of inflation could be measured; its psychological effects, harder to assess, were not less significant. The loss of their savings dealt the middle classes a tremendous moral and material blow, and shattered their confidence, never very great, in the Republic. From the ranks of the disinherited bourgeoisie much future support for Hitler was to come. Those living on fixed incomes and pensions, including over a million war widows, were the chief sufferers. The only gainers were speculators, businessmen who took advantage of cheap credit to buy up factories and create new industrial concentrations: of these Hugo Stinnes, the iron and coal magnate, was the most notorious. While some of the rich became richer, many who had been comfortably off became in an economic sense proletarians. Thus inflation widened the differences and sharpened the tensions in German society. And though the Ruhr occupation tended to draw the people together in an anti-French front, the crises in Bavaria, Saxony and elsewhere showed the danger of political extremism.

In German eyes the blame for inflation lay with the Allies, whose reparations imposed an impossible financial burden. (The extent to which this was true is discussed elsewhere, see p. 248.) Reparations were in fact only one of several causes of inflation, the others being the failure of the German government to balance its budget, the policy of easy credit followed by the business world as well as by the govern-

'I'm just praying that we shall get to the stage where potatoes and small beer are Sunday fare.' (Comment by a profiteer, using a quotation from Schiller's *Räuber*, on the effects of inflation.)

(Drawing by Georg Grosz, 1922)

ment, and the reckless issue of paper money – long before the Ruhr occupation – by the *Reichsbank*. In 1923 less than 10 per cent of the budget was covered by revenue; the rest was provided by the printing presses, which worked day and night to supply vast quantities of increasingly worthless notes, the sheer physical weight of which created further difficulties. As a technical problem inflation was little understood at the time by so-called experts; and in the confused and highly charged political atmosphere it was easy to overlook the sins of the German government and to see Poincaré as a Shylock who demanded both his bond and his pound of flesh. Having decided not to pay the full total of reparations if they could avoid it, the Germans had no incentive to put their financial house in order since to do so would be to weaken their case.

The multiple crisis of 1923 was also a test of the new friendship between Germany and Russia established at Rapallo. In the early 1920s Soviet foreign policy oscillated uneasily between two contradictory aims: security for Russia, which presupposed good relations with capitalist states, and world revolution, which meant supporting the various Communist parties in their struggle for power. Nowhere was this contradiction more glaring than in Germany, Russia's only friend in a hostile Europe but also the country with the largest Communist membership. The German republican government was too weak and too friendless to object to the obvious ambiguity of Soviet policy; while the Russians knew that arms supplied by them to the *Reichswehr* might be used against the German proletariat. Seeckt,[55] the head of the *Reichswehr* and the most influential proponent of a pro-Russian orientation, valued Soviet support in foreign policy and Soviet collaboration in the military field too highly to be deflected by the activities of a Communist party to which as a German conservative he was obviously diametrically opposed. So long as the German Communist party remained only a potential threat, Russo-German relations were little affected by it. But the French march into the Ruhr combined with the misery produced by inflation to threaten the whole political order and created a potentially revolutionary situation. The Communists had to decide how to react.[56] The party's right wing believed that the national struggle against the French should take precedence over the internal struggle against the Cuno government and its policy of passive resistance. The left wing, more predictably, while sharing the anti-French sentiments of the whole country, saw in Cuno a class enemy who must be opposed. There was division too among Communists in Moscow, where the German turmoil was watched with intense interest and some anxiety. The Soviet government, made indecisive by Lenin's fatal illness, inclined to caution because it feared that a Germany in chaos would give the French an opportunity to advance further into Central Europe and so nearer Russia: even a Communist Germany would be no barrier. In the Marxist terms appropriate to the Third International, Germany was a semi-colonial country exploited by Entente capitalists, and therefore even the German bourgeoisie in resisting the French were playing an objectively revolutionary role. There was also the need for the K.P.D., which had only thirteen members in the Reichstag, to win more support, and this could be done by raising the banner of patriotism. Radek, who knew Germany better than any of the other Soviet leaders, made a speech extolling Schlageter, the Ruhr resistance fighter shot by the French. But after the fall of Cuno, fear of chaos following the failure of passive resistance, and distrust of Stresemann as a 'westerner' led to the triumph in Moscow of the revolutionary group, who encouraged the German Communists to make a bid for power. This was indeed the desire of the left wing of the K.P.D. who, as so often before, overestimated the support they would get from the working classes and even (less plausibly) from inside the army.[57] The existence of the Communist-Socialist coalition government in Saxony was also a hopeful sign. But when left-wing resistance in Saxony crumbled against the *Reichswehr*, the projected rising was called off except in Hamburg where the counter-order failed to arrive. The Hamburg revolt, in October 1923, was the last attempt by the Communists to seize power during the Weimar Republic. The half-hearted Putsch infuriated Brockdorff-Rantzau and embarrassed Chicherin. Yet though something of the old cordiality was henceforth missing in Russo-German relations, the basic friendship continued because it was needed. Only Stresemann's policy of *rapprochement* with the West gradually reduced Germany's dependence on her jealous ally; and even then Russian goodwill was judged necessary to hold Poland in check.

(vi) CULTURE IN THE REPUBLIC: ART, POLITICS AND THE INTELLECTUALS

One of the first acts of the provisional government of November 1918 was to abolish the censorship. Although censorship was brought back later, the gesture was symbolic of the newly proclaimed principle of complete artistic freedom. Writers and dramatists whose work had been banned or not performed under the monarchy now came into their own. This was particularly true of the expressionist playwrights whose work was a protest against the values and conventions of a world which, it was too readily assumed, had collapsed in the revolutionary wave that ended the war. The patriotic emotions and expectations roused in August 1914 had long since turned to disillusion as the true nature of the war was realised, and defeat made the experience more bitter. The utopian hopes unleashed by the Russian Revolution among progressives gave rise to another illusion: that a new age was dawning in which there would be no violence or power politics, no capitalism or class rule. Anarchic rejection of all forms of government mingled with vague slogans of eternal peace and the brotherhood of mankind. René Schickelé, the pacifist Alsatian poet, expressed his rapture: 'The new world has begun; it is here . . . the 9th November was the most beautiful day.'[58]

The same mood of vague uplift and unbounded optimism was expressed in some lines written by the editor of an expressionist anthology, who imagined the masses (a typical abstraction) 'feeling with confident joy the gradual fusion of the individual in an increasingly jubilant humanity'. Toller, the young playwright whom the war had made a pacifist, enthused in a play called *Die Wandlung* (Transformation) about the high arched doors of Humanity's cathedral, 'opening to admit the youth of every nation, striding in flames to the luminous crystal shrine within'.[59] There could hardly have been a sharper contrast than between such dreams and the shabby, hungry, hate-filled reality that was post-war Germany. This was the world depicted by Georg Grosz, the radical satirist, whose savage drawings show limbless ex-servicemen begging in the streets while lewd profiteers gorge themselves in restaurants and the Freikorps are busy shooting down bewildered proletarians. Even during the more stable period after 1924 Grosz seems to have had little faith in the Republic's ability to survive. Themes of lust and violence are prominent also in the paintings of Max Beckmann, a visionary realist, whose work reflects profound spiritual disturbance as well as an awareness of social ills. The Expressionism which was characteristic of so much German art and literature in the second decade of the century was the appropriate idiom for an age of violence. It has even been described as 'less a style than a cry of anguish'.[60] Many of the plays written during or immediately after the war, such as Kaiser's *Gas* and Toller's *Man and the Masses* were directly inspired by their authors' experience of the trenches or the revolution.

Taking their cue from the soldiers and workers, in November 1918 many of Germany's leading painters, sculptors, architects and art specialists combined to form an Artists' Council, whose programme, signed by over a hundred well-known names, demanded a new deal for the arts.[61] Left-wing intellectuals naturally supported the revolution, notably in Bavaria, where Kurt Eisner, the Independent socialist Prime Minister, was better known as a man of letters than as a working politician. Writers and scholars were particularly prominent in the first

short-lived Munich soviet in April 1919. Although that was a disastrous fiasco, and the revolutionary euphoria soon evaporated, the
alliance between the progressive intelligentsia and the left-wing parties
lasted nearly as long as the Republic, many of whose artistic achievements were made possible by the patronage of liberal and socialist
public authorities. Just as the early turmoil of the new regime gave
way to relative stability a few years later, so the chiliastic visions and
extravagant imagery were succeeded by the more restrained mood and
idiom of the *Neue Sachlichkeit* or New Objectivity. This was a term
used, apparently, for the first time by the director of the Mannheim Art
Gallery to describe an exhibition he organised in 1925.[62] After the
Wagnerian motifs of the Wilhelmine era, the Republic evolved its own
style – avant-garde, precise and functional. Painting, while becoming
more down to earth, continued its preoccupation with social criticism,
as for example in the work of Otto Dix, who started as an Expressionist
and was responsible for some of the most powerful anti-war statements
in modern art. And just as the end of the Republic was heralded by
the collapse of the parliamentary system, so the aesthetic values of
Weimar came under increasing attack from the cultural counter-
revolutionaries led by the Nazi publicist Alfred Rosenberg and his
'Militant Association for German Culture'. Despite, or perhaps because
of the political tension from which it was never entirely free, the
period was one of 'creativity in the midst of suffering'.[63] And brief
though the life of the Republic was, it gave the world an astonishing
number of masterpieces in many fields: Thomas Mann's *Magic Mountain*, Arnold Zweig's *Case of Sergeant Grischa*, and Döblin's
Alexanderplatz among the novels; the paintings of Paul Klee and the
sculpture of Barlach; the Brecht-Weill *Threepenny Opera*; *The Cabinet
of Dr. Caligari* and *The Blue Angel* among the films; the caricatures of
Georg Grosz; Max Reinhardt's productions at the Deutsches Theater,
Berlin. Germany, especially Berlin, became the European centre of
the modern movement in the arts, a power-house of new ideas and a
workshop for fascinating experiments. In retrospect much of Weimar
culture seems to share the feverish and evanescent quality of its politics,
to be an all too brief efflorescence between the holocaust of the First
World War and the barbarity of the Third Reich.

The Weimar spirit, it has been observed, was born before the Weimar Republic.[64] This is one way of indicating that the artistic break
between the old and the new occurred long before the political –
somewhere about the turn of the century, in fact, or even a few years
earlier. Something was said in the first chapter of this book about the
artists' revolt against the official taste of Wilhelmine Germany, the
search for new forms and techniques, and the evolution of a new style
by a number of forward-looking young architects. The war and its

outcome gave a fresh stimulus to these trends. Defeat was even seen by some as a judgement on imperial art as well as on imperial statesmanship. The revolutionary mood demanded artistic radicalism. Walter Gropius, chairman of the Workers' Council for Art, founded the Bauhaus at Weimar in April 1919. This project, which political opposition forced him to move to Dessau in 1925 (hence its usual name of Dessauer Bauhaus) was probably the most influential of all the republic's cultural achievements.[65] There is no better illustration of the Weimar spirit. It was a pioneer workshop, a social and aesthetic cooperative, and a training school all in one. Its reputation was worldwide. Gropius attracted as his colleagues a number of gifted artists, craftsmen and teachers including names already or soon to be famous such as Mies von der Rohe, Feininger, Marcks, Bruno Taut, Schlemmer, Kandinsky, Mendelssohn and Moholy-Nagy. Gropius insisted that arts and crafts be practised together, and he saw no essential difference between the two. Another of his beliefs was that there must be no barrier between art and industry, beauty and utility. Unlike William Morris, the men of the Bauhaus fully accepted the central place of the machine in modern civilisation, and subjects taught there included architecture, pottery, and ceramics, weaving, metal-work, furniture design and carpentry, typography, stage design, choreography and music. The impulse given by the Bauhaus was fruitful in many directions. 'What we approached in practice was the common citizenship of all forms of creative work, and their logical interdependence on one another in the modern world' was how Gropius himself put it.[66] For him and his colleagues the Bauhaus was the prototype of a new society, in which ethical ideals were fused with a revitalised aesthetic. It was a vision which contrasted dramatically with the political and economic realities of a society divided, impoverished and struggling for survival. In 1932, by which time Gropius and several others of its most gifted artists had left it, the Bauhaus was forced by political pressure to move to Berlin. When the Nazis came to power they closed it down as a hotbed of 'cultural Bolshevism'.

There was one social group whose loyalty the Republic needed but never won: the left-wing literary intellectuals. Unlike the architects and artists, who found scope for their talents in the impressive town-planning schemes and garden suburbs sponsored by local authorities with borrowed money and in the patronage of Germany's many provincial museums, the writers often felt frustrated and neglected. Those who had hailed the German revolution as the start of a new age soon discovered their mistake. Almost from the beginning the Republic was on the defensive. It lacked prestige. It could not even protect its own leaders from assassination or effectively punish their murderers. The radical intellectuals, of whom perhaps Tucholsky was the most outspoken, despised the Social Democrats for their timidity and willingness to compromise (this word nearly always has a disparaging connotation in Germany, suggesting an abandonment of principles). Such criticism was often grossly unfair. Ebert, for example, may have deserved the reproach of having 'betrayed' socialism, like many other socialist leaders in difficult circumstances, but he was far from being the sybaritic and complacent substitute-emperor suggested by Grosz's caricatures. Indeed, the very modesty in which Ebert and his wife lived, while appropriate for a socialist president of a defeated and penurious country, added to the drabness which was one reason for the Republic's unpopularity. Yet when Ebert was succeeded by the venerable Hindenburg, republicans saw this as further evidence of the Republic's lack of confidence in itself. In theory the radicals preferred the Communists, who had not diluted their Marxism with bourgeois democracy; but increasingly they distrusted the Communist party as a tool of Moscow, whose revolutionary postures were quite unsuited to German conditions. Moreover Communist *Realpolitik*, exemplified by the arms deal between *Reichswehr* and Red Army, inspired distrust among those who were pacifists.

By 1930 the 'conservative revolution' was in full swing, and in January 1932 Tucholsky warned of the 'tribal fires of immolation' – a remarkable prophecy of the public burning of his own and other books in May 1933, perhaps too of the Reichstag fire which inaugurated the Nazi terror.[67] Tucholsky himself in his short and stormy career illustrates the dilemma of a rebel who felt passionately about politics but was too independent to fit into any of the existing parties and whose work was a generalised revolt against the Germany in which he had grown up – a country, as he saw it, whose middle class was hopelessly arrogant and mercenary, yet subservient towards authority, a society blighted by militarism.[68] In contrast to the majority of Germans of all parties who condemned the Versailles treaty, Tucholsky found merit in it for one reason – that it imposed demilitarisation. Thus Tucholsky's abrasive satire was a red rag to the nationalists. Though Tucholsky was in some ways untypical – a caricature of the 'rootless intellectual' denounced by the Nazis – it was significant that both he and Maximilian Harden (who was nearly murdered by thugs) preferred to live outside Germany, which became a dangerous place for radicals, especially if like these two they were also Jewish. Life had been safer for them under the Empire.

Tucholsky and other intellectuals of his type have been criticised, not without reason, on the ground that the main result of their undiscriminating and ceaseless attacks on the Republic was to help the cause of its enemies. With all its weakness and compromises the Weimar regime was for any independent artist or writer clearly preferable to the alternative of Hitler's Third Reich or even to the less probable alternative of a Communist Germany. Provocative insults against all that the nationalists held sacred were hardly likely to persuade them of the error of their ways or to make 'republicans by common sense' out of convinced monarchists in the right wing circles which played a significant part in Hitler's rise to power. At the first International Dada Fair, for example, held in Berlin in the summer of 1920, the central hall was dominated by the stuffed effigy of a German officer with a pig's head which was suspended from the ceiling and bore the caption 'Hanged by the Revolution'.[69] This was the work of Georg Grosz and his friends, who were fined for slandering the army. In their wholesale rejection of Weimar Germany as an inadequate society, in jeering where they might have helped, such critics unwittingly contributed to the tragedy which engulfed both it and them. To their opponents their work, which often showed great talent, was simply a manifestation of republican decadence.

Another shortcoming of the Republic was its failure to attract youth, as Thomas Mann admitted in a public speech in 1922 urging young people to give it their support. The general hostility in schools and universities was symptomatic. The anti-republican sentiments of the older generation of teachers and parents were obviously one adverse influence. Another was that of history and other textbooks, some of which propagated the stab in the back legend and belief in Germany's racial superiority. The desire to avenge the detested peace treaty led easily to a contempt for the regime which had signed it. By 1930 both parliamentary democracy and reform socialism seemed out of date and incapable of solving the problems of the depression. The S.P.D. was palpably an ageing party. The Nazis could present themselves as the party of youth, with the confidence and dynamism of men unhindered by the fears and inhibitions of middle age. And Germany was presented as the youngest, and therefore the most vigorous, of the great powers. Nearly all the Nazi leaders were young men.

The republican leaders had more success in restoring Germany's image abroad. The literary counterpart to the Locarno spirit in literature was the spate of books carrying a message of pacifism and international goodwill. In 1928 Erich Maria Remarque published his *All Quiet on the Western Front*, the first and in some ways still the most memorable of the many anti-war novels which appeared almost simultaneously in many countries. It was followed by Ludwig Renn's *War* and by Arnold Zweig's remarkable trilogy, *The Case of Sergeant Grischa, Young Woman of 1914* and *Education before Verdun*. A generation which had not experienced the war, as well as one which had been deluded by official propaganda, now saw it with disenchanted eyes. The peace-loving, democratic Germany of the later

1920s had many foreign admirers; it became a mecca for avant-garde artists and left-wing writers. Rilke and Brecht were influences on the most original of the rising young English poets, W. H. Auden, who, like many of his Oxford contemporaries, spent some time in the Weimar Republic absorbing a new style of life and politics. Another member of the same group who found the air of Germany congenial was Stephen Spender, whose autobiography, *World within World*, gives a vivid picture of Hamburg at the beginning of the depression as seen by a sensitive young poet. Spender found a peculiar fascination in the quality of life in a country so different from England and France: whose young generation, in their worship of nature and cult of *Modernismus*, had neither possessions nor a sense of guilt, and whose almost obsessive love of peace, born of hunger and inflation, was like a too beautiful dream interrupted by a barbarian awakening. Though the verse plays written by Auden and Spender in the thirties owed less to the influence of the German expressionist drama than has sometimes been suggested, there are resemblances between the two both in spiritual outlook and in technique. Auden's co-author in several of his best poems and plays was Christopher Isherwood, whose two novels of pre-Hitler Berlin, *Mr. Norris changes Trains* and *Goodbye to Berlin*, are brilliantly evocative of the period. Unlike the deeply committed Spender, Isherwood preserved an attitude of ironic detachment, observing human beings like insects under a microscope; but both writers felt and conveyed a sense of impending doom. It is hardly an exaggeration to say that a whole generation of British students and intellectuals came under the spell of republican Germany, which attracted sympathy for its struggle against odds and as the victim of an unjust treaty, but also for its tolerance, originality and devotion to hopeful new causes. 'Weimar represented to us', wrote one of those admirers later, 'all those experiments, in literature, in the theatre, in music, in education and not least in sexual morals which we would have liked to attempt in our own country but were so patently impossible in face of the passive and infuriating stupidity of the British middle classes.'[70] To this list might be added the bold new architecture, with its clean lines and shining glass and concrete, to be seen not only in the famous Bauhaus, but in many other buildings and settlements, of which the Weissenhof Estate in Stuttgart was one of the most notable. Weimar Germany was the permissive and progressive society, and Berlin with its depravity and dynamism seemed to combine the qualities of Babylon and New York.

German films, too, were much esteemed abroad, like the Soviet films which they in some ways resembled. The German cinema was outstanding for its brilliant camera work, its use of lighting and handling of crowd scenes, and for the symbolism which contributed so significantly to the expressionist and psychological films in which Germany excelled. The macabre and the morbid were favourite themes, and producers treated with unusual frankness men's private fantasies and the social problems they revealed. Not only the celebrated *Cabinet of Dr. Caligari* (the first expressionist film) but also, for example, *Dr. Mabuse, The Gambler* and its sequel *The Testament of Dr. Mabuse*, deal with lust for power, hypnosis, crime and insanity. Even the 1916 thriller, *Homunculus* is the story of an artificial man who, lacking the power to love and be loved, and rejected by the world, takes a terrible revenge. Obsessed by hatred, he becomes the dictator of a large country, incites the workers to rebel, and then shoots them down; he starts a world war and is finally killed by lightning.[71] Another technically interesting Weimar film was *Metropolis*, a commonplace story set in a monster city dominated by skyscrapers and moloch-like machines: the pervading symbolism is typical of the expressionist cinema. A very different but equally memorable film of the period is *The Blue Angel*, based on a much earlier novel about a provincial schoolmaster by Heinrich Mann, *Professor Unrath*. The theme, the downfall and degradation of a respectable middle-aged man at the hands or rather legs of a beautiful vamp, is presented with almost unbearable intensity. Marlene Dietrich's acrid yet sentimental songs, sung in a mysteriously husky voice, have the same haunting quality as Kurt Weill's in the Brecht-Weill *Threepenny Opera*. The latter was filmed by G. W. Pabst in a version disapproved of by Brecht, who complained that sentiment was allowed to blunt the edge of the Marxist moral. Several remarkable films made towards the end of the Weimar period are concerned, like the anti-war novels that everyone was reading, with the reconciliation of peoples. One was *Kameradschaft*, also by Pabst, a moving story based on an actual occurrence of German miners going to the rescue of their French comrades struck by an explosion deep under the Franco-German frontier. The film suggests the proletarian solidarity of both groups, and was well received in France. Another Pabst film with a similar message was a study of trench warfare in 1918 entitled *Westfront*. The film ends with a French and a German soldier, each lying wounded in a ruined church converted into a field hospital, groping for each other's hand in a final gesture of understanding. As there is not enough chloroform left for amputation, the German soldier dies. Here too a realistic theme was handled with sensitivity and imagination. Films of this kind were anathema to the Nazis who in 1931 forced the authorities to withdraw the Hollywood-made film version of Remarque's *All Quiet on the Western Front* by creating disturbances in the Berlin cinema where it was being shown. It was also symptomatic of the changing climate in the German cinema that one of the last films to be made under the Republic

The early Weimar Republic as seen by Georg Grosz

was *Morgenrot* (Dawn), a story of the U-boats during the First World War. *Morgenrot* had its first night in Berlin on the day after Hitler came to power, and he and members of his cabinet were present. The dawn of the film's title was thus also that of the Third Reich, and its blood-red colour was reflected in the Reichstag fire then and in Hitler's funeral pyre twelve years later. Yet even the last years of Weimar saw the appearance of *Girls in Uniform*, an anti-militarist study of a school in Potsdam for the daughters of Prussian officers. An outstanding documentary film of the republican period was *Berlin, Symphony of a Great City*, an impressionistic study of a day in the life of the German capital.

If most of Germany's intellectuals viewed the Republic with indifference or dislike, there was one notable exception – Thomas Mann. His position as Germany's leading novelist had been sealed with the award of the Nobel Prize for literature. As we have seen, during the war Mann had championed Germany as the embodiment of aristocratic and spiritual values against the shallow and materialistic West. 'I record my deep conviction', he had written, 'that the German people will never be able to love political democracy . . . and that the much decried authoritarian state is the form of state most suitable for the German people.'[72] With his patrician tastes and ironic detachment, Mann had little in common with the democratic politicians. He deliberately rejected the role, assumed by his radical brother Heinrich, of *Zivilisationsliterat*. Yet events such as the murder of Rathenau forced Mann to the realisation that, imperfect as the Republic was, it alone stood between Germany and savagery. Late in 1930, after the disastrous election of that year, Mann again made an eloquent plea for men of goodwill to rally to the rescue of the threatened Republic, without which, he was convinced, there would be neither decency nor peace. Mann had been a defender of the *Bürger*, the responsible middle-class citizen who represented so much that was good in the European past, but he now saw that the German Republic rested on the support of the Socialists; it was they who had backed Stresemann and really believed in the democracy to which the middle classes, especially the Protestants, had so equivocal an attitude. But by now it was too late: the Socialists had left the government and the Nazis were the second largest party in the Reichstag. Thomas Mann was abroad when Hitler came to power, and on the advice of his friends he did not return to Germany. He was the most distinguished of many literary exiles, representing the independent intellectual tradition which Hitler sought to crush in his brutalised Reich. The old German dichotomy of force and spirit was back in its most acute form. When the Dean of the Philosophy Faculty at Bonn University informed Mann that his honorary doctorate at Bonn had been annulled (Mann, like many others, was also deprived of German citizenship) he received a dignified reply that has become a classic. In his diary Mann described the Germans as an 'unhappy, isolated, confused people, seduced by wild and stupid adventurers whom they take for mythical heroes'.[73]

The case of Germany's other most famous writer, Bertolt Brecht, was significantly different.[74] Brecht belonged to a younger generation than Mann, and was still at school when the First World War began. Towards the end of the war he was called up and worked as a nursing orderly in a military hospital at Augsburg, his home town. The experience of tending the mutilated made an indelible impression on him, and inspired one of his most biting satires, a ballad set to music called *The Legend of the Dead Soldier*. In this he imagines the Kaiser, in his desperate search for cannon fodder, ordering a dead soldier to be exhumed and sent to the front after a padre has dowsed him with incense to overcome the stench. The war and his own temperament made Brecht a rebel against convention and hypocrisy as well as against militarism. His first play, *Drums in the Night*, is the story of a soldier who returns home after the war to find his fiancée engaged to someone else: the political theme comes in mainly as background, with Spartacist gunfire in the streets symbolising the revolution. Another early play, *Baal*, is full of violent language and exotic imagery: it suggests that man is a creature who acts entirely by blind instinct in a meaningless universe. The manner is expressionist and there are strong echoes of Rimbaud. Other Brecht plays of the twenties are set in an India obviously derived from Kipling and in a highly fanciful America conceived in terms of the Wild West and Al Capone. Already in *Mann ist Mann* Brecht explores the problem of human personality and suggests that a human being can be taken to pieces and put together like a machine. Though it is often overlaid with cynicism, there is a deep vein of compassion in Brecht, and at the same time a preoccupation with the 'circumstances' that make people what they are. His radicalism could not be satisfied by a republic so obviously a compromise, and one in which real power so often lay in the hands of its enemies. The answer seemed to lie in Marxism. Marx's social message is supposed to be conveyed in Brecht's adaptation of Gay's *The Beggar's Opera*, which he and Weill, the composer, called *The Threepenny Opera*, but it is presented in such attractive wrappings that the impact is lost: the beggars are as improbable as the highwaymen, and the audience is entertained, not revolutionised. So Brecht tried a new technique. The result was a group of didactic plays written mostly in the early 1930s, in which the language is pruned and austere, the treatment formal and highly stylised and the message presented with a direct simplicity that cannot be misunderstood. Such plays are dramatic parables. Characters, wearing masks (a device borrowed from the Japanese No theatre) stand for types, not individuals. As in Greek tragedy, the chorus plays an important part, commenting on the action and explaining it to the audience. The play in which these methods are used pointedly to illustrate a political moral is *Die Massnahme* (1930), usually translated as *The Disciplinary Measure*. Four Comintern agents set out on a mission to China. One of them jeopardises their illegal work because he is unable to suppress his private feelings of sympathy towards workers in revolt whom the Comintern decides not to support. (The analogy with Soviet policy in China in 1927 is striking.) In the end he sees and confesses his error and with his own consent is duly 'liquidated' by his three colleagues, an action endorsed by the party. This, the chorus says, is justified because the party is always right and the individual member must subordinate himself to it. In joining it he becomes 'a name, without a mother, a blank sheet on which the revolution writes its orders'. The message is summed up in lines which deserve quoting:

> Whoever fights for Communism
> Must be able to fight and not to fight
> To tell the truth and not to tell the truth
> To perform services and to refuse services
> To keep promises and not to keep promises
> To court danger and to avoid danger
> To be known and to be unknown
> Whoever fights for Communism
> Has of all the virtues only one:
> That he fights for Communism.[75]

Brecht recognised the paradox that those who wish to transform society cannot keep their own hands clean. 'What vileness would you not commit to exterminate vileness?' asks the control chorus, representing the Party, 'Submerge in the filth, embrace the butcher, but change the world: it needs it.' Against violence, Brecht insists elsewhere, only violence helps, even though force debases those who use it. Brecht's justification of the classic Communist party purge was uncannily prophetic: only five years later Stalin was liquidating the élite of the Old Bolsheviks by terrorising them into making false confessions and convicting them at show trials. In much the same way, Brecht's reconstruction of a human being in *Mann ist Mann* is a remarkable anticipation of the brain-washing techniques subsequently used by totalitarian regimes. Seen in this light, Brecht appears as a literary Stalinist. It would be untrue to say that he betrayed the Weimar Republic, for he never really believed in it, though unlike many critics, Brecht's strictures did not become less sharp as the Republic entered its more stable period. But it can be said that in postulating the infallibility of a party he was guilty of what Julien Benda called the 'trahison des clercs', the apostasy of intellectuals. In the *Massnahme* Brecht makes the chorus sing the praises of the party, as opposed to the individual:

> The individual has two eyes
> The party has a thousand eyes
> The party sees seven states
> The individual sees one city
> The individual has his hour
> But the party has many hours.
> The individual can be destroyed
> But the party cannot be destroyed
> For it is the advance guard of the masses
> And leads its struggle
> With the methods of the Marxist classics, created
> Out of knowledge of reality.[76]

It is ironical that when Brecht was writing this paean of the party as the embodiment of the collective wisdom of progressive humanity, Russia, the only country where the party was in power, was entirely ruled by one arbitrary despot. Another successful didactic play, though in a more conventional form, was Brecht's adaptation of Gorki's novel *Mother*, which Brecht dramatised and whose story he extended from the revolution of 1905 to that of 1917. He used again the 'epic' technique of short, episodic scenes interspersed with songs by the chorus, with slides, caricatures and documentary material to give background, using a method first pioneered by Piscator, the producer of left-wing political plays in the Berlin *Volksbühne*.

Brecht had to leave Germany when Hitler came to power and began a life of exile that took him in turn to Denmark, Finland and finally California, where he spent most of the war. His later plays are less doctrinaire than the didactic ones, richer in content and with a mellower outlook: the subtlety and humour of life are conveyed, the social message is balanced by lyricism, reason by instinct. The cynicism remains, as does the peasant slyness that made Brecht admire Schweik, the legendary Bohemian soldier who ultimately turns the tables on authority by pretending to obey it. In Brecht's work the sceptic and the believer, the puritan and the sensualist, the sentimentalist and the intellectual remain at odds with each other, and much of the fascination of his work arises from their creative tension. The last stage of his career, which began with his return to Germany in 1949 as a resident of East Berlin, was outwardly the most successful. With his own playhouse, his own company and unlimited financial backing from the East German state, he was able to produce his own and other plays with a full use of his dramatic technique in a way which fascinated audiences and transformed the art of the theatre. The paradox was that in the Soviet Union, and in all the satellite countries except East Germany, Brecht was condemned as a formalist and his work was not performed. However heretical his aesthetic, it was politically useful to the Communists in that his theatre was a magnet to the avant-garde of the West, and his *Ensemble*, which made many foreign tours, was the best visiting card which the D.D.R. could have had. Yet there is some evidence that Brecht realised the falsity of his position, and that he felt guilty at times about his failure to criticise wrongs and oppression in the East German state. How far, in his willingness to conform, Brecht compromised his own integrity is a matter on which it is difficult to reach a conclusion. In so far as he was opposed to the regime he cynically allowed himself to be misrepresented, but he regarded any form of communism as a lesser evil than the liberal but allegedly unregenerate capitalism of West Germany.[77]

'To work, Germany!'

After the lie of war guilt, the burden of war debts (a comment, using an untranslatable pun, on reparations at the time of the Young Plan)
(*Simplicissimus*, 1929)

CHAPTER VII

The Weimar Republic: From Recovery to Collapse

(i) ECONOMIC CONVALESCENCE: THE DANCE ON THE VOLCANO

As we have seen, the German government recognised late in 1923 that the key to liberation of the Ruhr and to economic recovery was stabilisation of the mark. Once this had been achieved, the way was clear for the adoption of the Dawes Plan. The *Rentenmark*, successfully established in the autumn of 1923 in place of the worthless paper mark at the rate of one to a billion, was itself superseded in the following year by a new *Reichsmark*. The Rentenmark was based on land and industrial assets, the new Reichsmark on gold. The Dawes Agreement, signed in August 1924, put reparations on a fresh, if temporary footing which removed many of its objectionable features. The new settlement was negotiated, not imposed. Annual payments were to be in German currency, thus eliminating the danger that they would cause a new devaluation of the mark. A special fund, drawn from taxation and from other sources, was earmarked for the annuities, which ceased for the time being to be a bone of contention between the German political parties. To supervise these arrangements an American agent, Parker Gilbert, was appointed, with a general power of control over the *Reichsbank* and German railways. There was no question of any future default leading to sanctions by the creditors in the style of the French seizure of the Ruhr. Germany received a loan of 800 million dollars, mostly from America, which enabled her to re-equip her industries and to become again a formidable competitor. The loan was a sign that the outside world again had confidence in Germany, where the high rate of interest – a legacy of the inflation – was a further inducement to foreign investors.

The recovery was general. Coal and iron output, thanks to the introducing of mass production methods, rationalisation and scientific management on the American model, more than doubled, and

by 1928 had exceeded that of 1913. Exports rose, and they too easily
surpassed the pre-war total, though not until 1929 did they catch up
with imports.[1] Germany continued to live beyond her means, thanks
to foreign credits. Government revenue went up, and the budget
was balanced. Real wages tended to lag behind in the general rise,
but by 1928 the average working man was better off than he had
been under the Kaiser. It was not so much that earnings were higher
as that hours were shorter and conditions of work easier, insurance
more complete (in 1926 unemployment was added to health and
accident insurance) and housing had improved, especially in the big
cities. The inflow of new capital enabled local authorities to undertake ambitious re-housing projects and to build new schools, hospitals
and swimming pools. Much of the new spending was extravagant and
economically unproductive. In these and other ways, such as the use
of compulsory arbitration to settle labour disputes and the extension
of public ownership to gas and electricity companies, the economic
policy of the Republic reflected socialist influence. By way of contrast,
the concentration of industry by cartels and mergers continued: in
1925 the giant chemical combine *I.G. Farben* came into existence,
and in 1926 the steel mammoth *Vereinigte Stahlwerke*. The middle
classes, stripped of their savings by inflation and demoralised by that
shattering experience, felt squeezed between the massive 'Marxist'
proletariat with its unions and left-wing parties on the one hand and
the giant industrial concerns on the other. Between cartel-fixed prices
and rigid labour costs the small entrepreneur found it hard to make a
living. Yet rationalisation was a doubtful boon to the workers too
since labour-saving machinery, while raising productivity, reduced the
number of jobs: even in January 1928, the peak year, unemployment
stood at 1·8 million.

Whereas until 1923 Germany paid reparations from her own resources, from 1924 onwards she financed them from foreign loans, a
step made inevitable by the unwillingness of her creditors to accept the
transfer of goods. Between 1924 and 1931 Germany borrowed over
twice as much as she paid out.[2] This might be justified as long as the
boom lasted, though there was always an element of risk in basing the
new prosperity on such a high proportion (about half) of short-term
loans. In November 1928 Stresemann issued a prophetic warning:
'The economic position is only flourishing on the surface. Germany
is in fact dancing on a volcano. If the short term credits are called in
a large section of our economy would collapse.'[3] His advice, like the
similar advice of Schacht, was ignored. Whereas up to 1923 excessive
spending had simply increased inflation, thereafter it simply added to
foreign indebtedness. The German public, having some incentive to

save, had again begun to invest, but not to the extent required by the economy, and quite a lot of the new capital was invested abroad. The process of carefree borrowing was abruptly ended by the Wall Street crash of October 1929 which started the great depression. By then a new arrangement had been found for reparations – the Young Plan. It was a recognition of the danger of unrestricted borrowing as well as a wish to establish reparations on a permanent footing that caused new proposals to be put forward at a further conference of Germany's creditors presided over by an American banker, Owen D. Young. Relations between Germany and her ex-enemies had lost some of their former acerbity, though the French remained suspicious of any move that might enable Germany to evade her obligations, and no-body now expected her to pay the original demand of 132 milliard gold marks. The Young Plan, signed in Paris in June 1929, made certain important changes. Annual payments were to be reduced at first, then to rise gradually up to 1966, and finally taper off until the last payment of 1988. The new total came to 37 milliard gold marks, less than a third of the original, and was about what Keynes had suggested as reasonable in 1919.[4] Allied control over the German economy was abolished, and reparations were henceforth to be paid into a new institution, the Bank of International Settlements. The amounts due could be reduced in case of emergency or if America cancelled part of the inter-allied war debt: thus for the first time the connection between reparations and war debts was formally ack-nowledged. These concessions were designed to make the Young Plan acceptable to German opinion. But the Nationalist party under its new chairman Hugenberg denounced it bitterly in a campaign in which the Stahlhelm and the Nazis vociferously joined. It was un-realistic of the latter to suppose that Germany would be allowed to stop paying reparations altogether. Yet it was no doubt equally un-realistic of the Allies to imagine that two generations of Germans would be willing to pay for a war for which a diminishing proportion of the population felt any responsibility. Schacht, who had helped to negotiate the settlement, resigned as President of the *Reichsbank* when the German government waived its claims to compensation for German property in the territory ceded to Poland. By then (March 1930) the devastating effects of the American crash were showing in the German economy, which had structural weaknesses of its own and already the year before had displayed signs of a downturn and a rise of unemployment. The crisis that was to destroy the Republic was the direct cause of the fall of the last parliamentary govern-ment. Even without reparations the system would not have survived, but Hugenberg and Hitler naturally blamed reparations for Germany's economic ills and so propagated the idea among ordinary people that prosperity and 'fulfilment' were incompatible.

In view of the part played by reparations in fanning the flames of nationalism it is worth while considering just how big a burden they represented to the economy and the taxpayer. The initial bill for 132 milliard gold marks certainly far exceeded anything that impoverished post-war Germany was capable of paying at the time or in the foreseeable future. By 1924, when both sides had been disillusioned by the Ruhr occupation and the passions of war had begun to cool, annual reparations payments were reduced to a manageable size. In 1928/9, when the Dawes Plan was still in force, reparations accounted for 12·4 per cent of all government expenditure and 3·4 per cent of the national income.[5] Of every ten marks earned by a German individual or company in 1928, 2·73 marks was paid to the state in taxes, of which 34 pfennings represented reparations.[6] In a buoyant year like 1928 the internal weight of reparations could hardly be described an exorbitant. As for the external burden – the transfer abroad of 3·4 per cent of the national wealth – this was equivalent to less than 6 per cent of German exports. It was far outweighed by the loan of foreign capital, which without reparations would not have arrived in such quantities.[7] Although those who paid reparations and those who received foreign credits were not the same people, the benefits of the borrowed capital were felt throughout the economy. Taking all these factors into account, it cannot be said that reparations acted as a significant brake on recovery or appreciably lowered the German standard of living. The objection to reparations was one of principle, linked as they were in the public mind with the shameful war guilt clause in the treaty and with the mortgaging of the German economy under Dawes (a diminution of sovereignty). Although in detail the Young Plan differed from Dawes, the objections remained. And though the payments were not one of the main causes of the depression, they had a contributory effect in that by obliging Germany to borrow heavily they made her especially vulnerable to the American withdrawal of capital in and after October 1929: they also, though not they alone, prevented Brüning from reflating in 1930–2 had he wished to do so. In Hitler's hands reparations became a stick with which to beat the Republic as well as to indict the French. Reparations remained a burning issue in German politics until 1932, though no payments were actually made after the Hoover Moratorium of June 1931. When the Lausanne conference in June 1932 abolished reparations except for one final lump sum which was never paid, the news came too late to save the foundering Republic.

(ii) THE ARMY AND THE REPUBLIC: SEECKT

With Seeckt as head of the Army Command the *Reichswehr* had a new master, and one who was not slow to mould it to his own ideas. He kept a tighter grip on the military establishment than his liberal-minded predecessor, Reinhardt, had done, and at the same time exercised more political influence. Seeckt was also lucky in having in Gessler, the Minister of Defence who succeeded Noske, an easy-going man who made little attempt to interfere with the army. Seeckt combined the traditional virtues of the Prussian officer with others less common.[8] The son of a general, he had a distinguished war record and had been the main planner of the breakthrough at Gorlice in May 1915 which had led to Russia's greatest defeat. But Seeckt was far from being a narrow specialist; he was a cultivated man of the world with a powerful brain and a good deal of subtlety. In the words of the British ambassador, he had a broader mind than was expected in so tight a uniform. Like all Prussian officers of his generation, he was brought up as a monarchist. But he was too intelligent to wish to turn the clock back as Kapp and Lüttwitz had tried to do in March 1920. A slim, elegant figure, with shrewd eyes behind the characteristic monocle, Seeckt looked every inch what he was – a dedicated staff officer, but he was also in his way a visionary. Seeckt and his ideas were the essential link between the Kaiser's army and Hitler's *Wehrmacht*. His contribution was twofold. First, since the Allies (against the advice of Foch) had insisted on Germany's peace-time army being professional, not conscript, Seeckt, making a virtue of a necessity, turned the *Reichswehr* into the best trained army in Europe within the limitations – disregarded where possible – imposed by the peace treaty. It became a corps of qualified instructors and leaders that would be the nucleus of the mass army of the future. 'We want to keep the sword sharp and the shield shining', Seeckt told his troops at the end of 1920.[9] With such restricted numbers he was able to pick his men very carefully. A gifted organiser and strict discipli-narian, Seeckt had no use for the harebrained adventures of the Frei-korps, nor on the other hand did he make any effort to recruit men of republican sympathies. It was not the least of the Republic's many ironies that the proportion of officers' sons and men of aristocratic birth actually rose, so that the new army was more socially exclusive than the army of William II. Secondly, it was Seeckt who reintro-duced into military strategy the concept of mobility which had been largely abandoned during the costly and futile trench warfare of 1914–18. Against superior numbers only a highly trained professional army, using superior skill and re-discovering the vital element of surprise, would be able to achieve the breakthrough needed to win a war. Though Seeckt did not grasp the value of armour, he set German military thinking and planning on the lines that were to lead to the spectacular military successes of 1939–40.

Officially the Seeckt policy was one of isolation from politics. This was a reaction against the experience of the Kapp Putsch, but also owed something to the traditional German distrust of politics as divisive. Officers and men were not allowed to belong to political parties or even to professional associations with party affiliations, nor did they have a vote. The soldier was both less and more than a citizen. The army was to be an independent force, loyal to the state, which was permanent, rather than to the Republic which, with its weak and short-lived governments, was viewed as temporary. Yet Seeckt's claim that in his day the army played a non-political role is not borne out by the facts. His own strongly held convictions were bound to make him sympathise with the nationalist right and to be suspicious of the Social Democrats with their pacifist inclinations and disregard of what for Seeckt was Germany's vital interest – a strong army. And Seeckt's attachment to the secret military agreement with Soviet Russia had obvious implications for German foreign policy and caused Stresemann some embarrassment.[10] Seeckt showed partisanship in criticising Stresemann for his western orientation and lukewarm attitude to Russia. Nor can Seeckt be said to have taken a non-political attitude towards the challenges of 1923. Yet, undeniably, times were exceptional. The Weimar Republic was far from being a normal regime. In no less than nine of its fourteen years there was a state of civil or military emergency.[11] The Republic began in turmoil. It continued with a series of Putsches and sporadic outbreaks of civil war until the multiple crisis of 1923, which it survived with difficulty. Its last three years were marked by constitutional breakdown and growing violence. The larger parties had private armies: the republicans the *Reichsbanner*, the Nazis the S.A. and the Communists the Red Front. There was fighting on the Polish border in 1921 and fear, however ill-founded, of a renewed Polish attack remained a background influence in the critical period preceding Hitler's assumption of power. The passive resistance in the Ruhr in 1923 caused well over a hundred deaths and disrupted the lives and livelihoods of millions. In unoccupied Germany the murder of republican politicians was carried out with impunity by terrorist groups such as Organisation Consul, which had close links with the Freikorps. Of the 376 political murders committed between 1918 and 1922, 354 were against the left.[12] The judiciary, heavily biased towards the right, added to the imbalance. Like most other pillars of the establishment in Weimar Germany, the army never developed any attachment to the Republic: it would, in any case, have been difficult for it to integrate with a society itself so divided.[13] The army never forgot the original terms of its agreement with the Republic: in the Ebert-Groener pact it had negotiated as an equal, its allegiance was conditional. Seeckt, for example, could write in his Memoirs: 'What do I demand of the army? Loyalty to the state. What do I demand of the state? Loyalty to the army.'[14]

Seeckt's greatest test came in the autumn of 1923, when the Reich government was faced simultaneously with the French army in the Ruhr, the final crazy whirligig of inflation, a right-wing *Reichswehr*-supported dictatorship in Bavaria and a Communist-Socialist government in Saxony. Stresemann, the Chancellor, asked Seeckt for his support. Seeckt promised this only if Stresemann acted in what he (Seeckt) construed as the national interest. The general seemed to be making himself the arbiter of Germany, and was known to have the ambition of becoming Chancellor himself.[15] Hitler's abortive Putsch in Munich, which at first had the backing of the local *Reichswehr*, forced President Ebert to give Seeckt special emergency powers against the rebellious officers in Bavaria. This meant that Seeckt had been shrewdly used by Ebert to protect the Republic. When the crisis was over the special powers were withdrawn and Seeckt reverted to his former position. The chancellorship had not come his way; but with the approaching end of Ebert's term of office he might aspire to the presidency. Ebert's premature death in February 1925 led to a presidential election before Seeckt expected it, and when the time came no one supported his candidacy. With the economy recovering and Stresemann's foreign policy beginning to show results, Seeckt's ideas carried less appeal, especially as those who desired a military figure at the top now had one in President Hindenburg. Hindenburg naturally had a much closer relation with the army than Ebert, and this was another reason for the waning of Seeckt's star. When late in 1926 Seeckt was criticised in the Reichstag for having invited the Crown Prince (who was still a red rag to the left) to attend army manoeuvres, Hindenburg, who thought Seeckt arrogant, refused to intervene on his behalf, and Gessler, often criticised for giving way to Seeckt, this time stood his ground and dismissed him. Seeckt had put his stamp on the new army. He had shown great ingenuity in evading the treaty, especially in the thorough training of what was, in disguise, a general staff. He had promoted the understanding with Russia and with other neutral countries that had provided opportunities for the manufacture and testing of forbidden weapons. Seeckt's highly specialised army was a cadre for future expansion; it had more officers and n.c.o.'s than an army of its size needed, just as its expenditure was suspiciously high. Seeckt's importance in reviving the idea of a war of movement in which lightning attack by armour combined with air power would play the decisive part has already been referred to.[16] It is significant too that the cordial relations between *Reichswehr* and Red Army established under Seeckt continued until after Hitler was in power, and were abandoned, on the German side, with reluctance.

Seeckt's successor was Heye, a general without pronounced political opinions, so that Gessler as Minister of Defence was able to exert more influence. But not for long: in 1928 Gessler himself was implicated in a scandal involving the use of defence funds in a speculation intended to augment the secret military budget. The venture failed and Gessler had to go. The new Minister of Defence was Groener, who, after serving as Minister of Transport between 1920 and 1923, had been in retirement. The appointment of a general instead of a parliamentarian as Minister of Defence was a reversion to the tradition of the Empire, a symptom, as Hindenburg's election had been, of restoration. Yet in many ways Groener seemed an ideal choice. Besides enjoying the confidence of Hindenburg – an essential qualification – his relations with the Socialists were good. Groener also believed that he could rely on Schleicher, his protégé in the Defence Ministry who now emerged as the main political influence in the army and had the President's ear. Groener played a leading part in persuading the government against left-wing opposition and at a time of financial stringency to lay down the two battle-cruisers ('pocket battleships') which became a symbol of Germany's will to re-arm. When Brüning succeeded Hermann Müller as Chancellor in 1930 Groener remained in his post: like Hindenburg, a link with the imperial past, but, unlike him, loyal to the Republic.

(iii) STRESEMANN: THE NATIONALIST AS REALIST

Stresemann's courage in calling off passive resistance in the Ruhr brought its reward, though not immediately. The Dawes Committee appointed to look into the whole question of reparations issued its report in April 1924. Its recommendations, the most important of which was the new method of fixing and paying reparations, were accepted by Stresemann, who insisted, however, that no settlement could be made until the French agreed to leave the Ruhr. This Poincaré refused to do: only by maintaining physical possession of the coalfields could France be sure of obtaining her due. But a general election in France in May brought defeat for Poincaré, whose policy had weakened the franc and isolated his country. Herriot, the new Prime Minister, was a radical-socialist who intended to pursue a conciliatory policy. He accepted the Dawes Plan. But would Germany? For a general election there in June 1924, the first since 1920, had brought heavy gains for the extreme right and left, both of which rejected the Dawes terms. The Communists, who had 62 seats in the new Reichstag, automatically opposed any arrangement that brought Germany into closer relations with the West, while the Nationalists, whose representation had risen from 66 to 96, kept up their campaign against the policy of fulfilment. They were now noisily reinforced by 32 members of the Reichstag belonging to the para-Nazi Racialist (*Völkisch*) parties. These changes reflected the multiple crisis of 1923, which was bound to reduce the popularity of the parties in power – the original Weimar coalition of Socialists, Democrats and Centre, to which the People's party under Stresemann's influence loosely adhered. But the two-thirds majority which the Dawes treaty needed to pass the Reichstag could not be produced by these parties alone. Stresemann managed to persuade about half the Nationalist deputies to support the government, and the treaty went through. It was a hard struggle, for the Nationalists denounced the part of the settlement which provided for foreign supervision of the German economy in the interests of the reparations creditors as a 'second Versailles'. This was the debit side: on the credit side, the advantages to Germany were substantial – reparations became for the first time a manageable burden, the foreign loan provided much needed capital investment for the economy, the Ruhr was freed, and with the end of the Ruhr occupation the French-supported separatist movement in the Rhineland collapsed. Almost miraculously the Republic had survived the assaults of its external and internal enemies and preserved the unity of the Reich. Germany's relations with her creditors had at least taken a turn for the better, and economic recovery was under way. Another general election in December 1924 showed some recognition of this improvement by the electorate. The moderate parties regained lost ground, and though the Nationalist vote increased, both Nazis and Communists suffered a setback. Stresemann had won a limited vote of confidence. Another hopeful sign was that the government formed early in 1925 by Chancellor Luther included for the first time several Nationalists. If the latter party could be won for the Republic as Stresemann's People's party appeared to have been, the Republic's prospects would improve. Yet the right wing of the Nationalists, who found a new leader in Hugenberg, remained in implacable opposition to the democratic state.

The Republic suffered an irreparable loss in February 1925 when

President Ebert died, after an illness brought on by a vicious defamatory campaign launched by his nationalist enemies. The choice of his successor was obviously of great significance for the future of the Republic. As none of the five candidates who stood received the necessary majority, a second ballot was held. This time the two main candidates were Marx, the ex-Chancellor and Centre leader, who was nominated by the republican parties, and Hindenburg, the retired Field-Marshal and war hero, who was put forward by the right-wing parties organised as a *Bürgerblock*. The result was a win for Hindenburg by a narrow majority. Had the Communists not insisted on putting up their own candidate (Thälmann) or had the Bavarian People's party not preferred the Protestant Hindenburg to the Catholic Marx, Marx would have won. A further irony was that the original first choice of the republican parties was Gessler, the Minister of Defence, whose candidature was vetoed by Stresemann on the grounds that he would be unacceptable to foreign opinion. Hindenburg's installation could be understood in one of two ways. It might mark the reconciliation of two epochs, the acceptance of Weimar Germany by the hitherto contemptuous Nationalists and old school conservatives. On the other hand, it could signify an attempt to turn the clock back, a restorative gesture that was a snub to the Republic. Events soon showed that the second interpretation was right. Hindenburg, at the age of 78, was too old to change.[17] Even in the reign of William II he had seemed to belong to an earlier age, a survivor of the days of William I and Bismarck, who had fought in the campaigns of 1866 and 1870 and was already retired in 1914. With a reputation for disinterested patriotism and olympian wisdom which the last phase of his career was sadly to belie, Hindenburg was already more a myth than a man, the embodiment of a fading charisma. His election as president was thus both odd and ominous. He was still a devoted monarchist. He was not equipped for the kind of responsibility he was called upon to bear, and for which he himself, it must be said, had shown no ambition. His presidency was symptomatic of the Republic's loss of confidence in itself. Abroad, it was seen by many as proof that the 'old Adam' in Germany was staging a come-back.

Stresemann, who had at first opposed Hindenburg's candidature, knew better than most that Germany had a long way to go before regaining the trust of her former enemies.[18] Their suspicions had in fact been revived by reports from the Inter-Allied Control Commission that the disarmament clauses of the peace treaty were being constantly infringed. Evasion took many forms, including the illegal stockpiling of arms, the manufacture and use of prohibited weapons, the secret training of men, the illegal fortification of towns such as Königsberg near the eastern frontier, and the secret military agreements with Soviet Russia. Para-military formations existed under a variety of names: Labour Commandos or Black *Reichswehr*, *Einwohnerwehr* or Home Guard, *Arbeitsgemeinschaften* or working groups, *Schutzpolizei* or militarised police. Austen Chamberlain, the new British Foreign Secretary, was believed to be contemplating a pact with France which would make it harder for Germany to recover the Rhineland at an early date. To forestall such a move Stresemann revived a suggestion made earlier by Cuno for a mutual defence pact covering the new Franco-German frontier. The British responded to the idea, which was embodied a few months later in the treaty of Locarno. Britain and Italy joined France, Belgium and Germany. Germany relinquished the hope – wholly theoretical – of recovering Alsace-Lorraine, in return for an assurance that there would be no recurrence of the Ruhr occupation, while France's need for security was met by an international guarantee. For the first time Germany was treated as an equal partner. Austen Chamberlain described Locarno as the real dividing line between the years of war and those of peace. It had taken nearly seven years to reach this point, and during that period the seeds of the next war had been sown. In the genial climate of Locarno there seemed the chance of a more promising harvest. There was much talk of the 'Locarno spirit', and something approaching friendship developed between Stresemann and his opposite number, the French Foreign Minister Briand. Germany was invited to join the League of Nations. Many Germans did not welcome this suggestion. It would be humiliating to join what had long been condemned as a victors' club, and would amount to another endorsement of the detested peace treaty. It was also clear to those Germans who had originally been enthusiasts for the League idea that the League as it existed was not so much a substitute for discredited power politics as a façade behind which they could be pursued with more respectability. But Stresemann, while under no illusions, was aware of the many advantages which League membership would confer. Not the least was that the League presented a unique platform from which to influence world opinion. Stresemann insisted, however, that if Germany joined the League, as a great power she must have a seat on the Council. For this he had to wait until a vacancy was found. The wrangling and delay were further grist to the mill of Stresemann's enemies. Another difficulty was the effect of League membership on Germany's relations with Russia. The Soviet leaders had never liked the League, and they watched its activities with suspicion. They were afraid of a war in which the capitalist countries, invoking sanctions, would use Germany as a springboard against Russia. Recognising this fear, Stresemann made it a condition of League membership that Germany would not be expected to take action under Article XVI (the sanctions clause): in case of a war between Russia and Poland, French troops going to help the Poles would not be allowed to cross German soil. This proviso was accepted, and Russo-German relations remained correct if not cordial. The year after Locarno Stresemann signed in Berlin a new treaty with Russia by which, if either country became involved in war through the aggression of a third country, the other would remain neutral; and the Russians were promised that, should the League initiate an anti-Soviet move, Germany would oppose it. The good understanding established at Rapallo was to continue, and Stresemann had taken care to balance his *rapprochement* with the West with a reassuring gesture to the East. France and Britain were still sufficiently suspicious of Soviet Russia to resent the treaty of Berlin, which they considered contrary to the spirit of Locarno. At Geneva, the headquarters of the League of Nations, the Germans still felt themselves treated as second-class citizens by the majority of countries: a notable exception was Soviet Russia which, though not yet a member of the League, was represented on the Preparatory Disarmament Commission that was followed by the full Disarmament Conference of 1932. The German delegates were on cordial terms with the Russian delegates, one of whom was Maxim Litvinov, the later Commissar for Foreign Affairs.[19] With the doubtful exception of Italy, Russia was, after Germany, the only major revisionist power.

What Stresemann liked about the Locarno pact was its limited regional character. It applied only to Germany's western frontier, and it significantly followed the rejection by the British government of a draft treaty, known as the Geneva Protocol, which would have committed all League members to a general guarantee of the *status quo*. Stresemann never disguised the fact that he was unwilling to underwrite Germany's eastern frontier. Recovery of the Polish Corridor and rectification of the border in Upper Silesia were regarded by him as the minimum changes required. In this respect he was the spokesman of German majority opinion. This does not mean that he was planning to fight Poland – he seems to have felt, probably without much justification, that economic pressure could make the Poles agree to frontier revision – but it implied that sooner or later a Polish-German confrontation was inevitable, and there is some evidence that Stresemann accepted that war might be needed in the last resort.[20] The Poles were in no mood to yield to German demands, and had a defence pact with France which was renewed in 1925. But as time went on, and Franco-German relations improved, the French guarantee to Poland lost some of its credibility.[21] This was a development which Stresemann himself did not live to see, but it followed logically from French pre-occupation with a purely defensive strategy (the 'Maginot mentality') combined with British indifference to Eastern Europe.

One immediate consequence of Locarno was the evacuation of the Cologne area of the Rhineland. A year later (January 1927) the Inter-Allied Control Commission also withdrew – a further success for Stresemann, and one not foreseen in the peace treaty. All future super-vision of German armaments was entrusted to the Council of the League of Nations. But this was no longer treated as a matter of gravity. The Commission had continued to provide evidence of secret re-arming by the *Reichswehr*, but its final report of 500 pages was quietly shelved. The Allied governments (especially the British) did not want to spoil the new harmony by bringing up such a controversial subject – Stresemann had been both evasive and indignant in answer to previous questions about breaches of the treaty – and his denials of connivance at what the *Reichswehr* was doing were readily believed. Stresemann even pressed Briand to complete the evacuation of the Rhineland, but this was more than French opinion would grant at the time. Occupation of the Rhine was France's only guarantee of repara-tions. Briand himself was remarkably conciliatory and suggested, with-out consulting the Belgians, that the latter should return Eupen and Malmédy to Germany. In Germany, however, political stabilisation and economic improvement brought some reward in the 1928 general election to the democratic parties. The Socialists, who – ironically, in view of Stresemann's known anti-socialism – were the main supporters of his foreign policy, had their best result since 1919, emerging with 152 seats in the Reichstag (a gain of 21) while the Nationalists (D.N.V.P.) went down from 103 to 78. There were some disquieting features: the Democratic party continued its sad decline; the People's party, convulsed by internal strife, did badly despite Stresemann's successes; and the Communist party vote went up. For the first time since 1920 a Social Democrat (Hermann Müller) became Chancellor in a cabinet drawn from the S.P.D., Democrats, Centre and People's party. Stresemann remained in office, but his health was breaking down. Worn out by over-work and hostile abuse, he died at the age of 51 in October 1929, the same month as the Wall Street crash that ended Germany's brittle prosperity.[22] His last success, gained at The Hague that summer, had been to persuade the French to evacuate the Rhineland by 30 June 1930, five years before the date set in the treaty. It made no impression on the Nationalists and their Nazi allies, who preferred the easy emotional satisfaction of denouncing the French to the less gratifying task of reasoning with them, and could not give credit to the government without destroying their own case.

Stresemann's death was a turning point, not because his policy was exhausted but because he had no successor. None of the later republican foreign ministers combined his unflagging pursuit of national aims with the diplomatic skill that won foreign confidence and had earned him, with the other authors of Locarno, the award of the Nobel Peace Prize. His achievement, though incomplete, was remarkable, considering the magnitude of the difficulties and the paucity of his resources. His basic belief that the key to liberation from Versailles lay in improving relations with the West was certainly correct: no *rapprochement* with Russia – a state which, because of its revolutionary ambitions, Stresemann viewed with distrust – could reduce Germany's dependence on France and to a lesser extent on England. To come to terms with the West, Germany had to accept what the Nationalists considered intolerable humiliations, such as the abandonment of passive resistance in the Ruhr, or the enforcement, if often more in form than in substance, of the disarmament clauses of the treaty. Stresemann, often against his own feelings, had to use the language of moderation and conciliation. There were a few hopes and fears that he could build on: British fear of communism, at times British dislike of French hegemony, could be invoked to condone this or that breach of the treaty. Another approach was the appeal to Wilsonian idealism, to self-determination and justice. Germany could become the champion of the weak and have-not states against the rich and powerful. Stresemann was advised by the German minister in Berne to play this part at the League, and to embarrass the Allies with demands based on progressive principles. This was not an easy role for a man who was a conservative at heart. There was moreover enough evidence of the survival in Germany of militarism and chauvinism to make the country's new liberal image unconvincing. One symptom of this was the rise of Hugenberg, the millionaire industrialist and newspaper proprietor, who in 1928 got himself elected chairman of the Nationalist party.[23] Hugenberg was an ambitious demagogue who wanted a government of the right. He now joined forces with Hitler, the leader of what was still a small and fairly obscure party, in a nation-wide referendum campaign against the Young Plan which collected over five million signatures and exacerbated the passions which Stresemann was trying to allay. By swinging the D.N.V.P. to the right, too, Hugenberg was heading it away from collaboration with the Weimar parties in which it had briefly engaged during the coalitions of 1925 and 1927. He was thus able to frustrate Stresemann's hopes of broadening the basis of government and thrusting responsibility onto its critics. Just as in 1920 the Independent socialists had refused on principle to join a coalition that included nonsocialists, so after 1929 the Nationalists boycotted a coalition that included republicans.

Stresemann's reputation has changed in recent years, as evidence suppressed or unavailable during his lifetime has come to light. Though his underlying nationalism is now unquestionable, in the eyes of contemporary critics he was the successor of Erzberger, Wirth and Rathenau, the fulfilment politician who, despite his earlier record as annexationist and friend of Ludendorff, had become indentified with appeasement and shameful compromise. Lacking subtlety and patience, they failed to see that his purpose was the same as theirs – revision of the treaty – and that he was using the only methods appropriate to the situation in which Germany found herself. Like Bethmann Hollweg during the war, he had to word his public utterances in such a way as to satisfy both his friends and critics, some of the latter being in his own party. Stresemann could not tell the world that his aim was to incorporate Austria, annex the Polish Corridor and absorb into the Reich other territories with a German population, though privately he admitted these things, as he did his intention to 'play it craftily' (*finassieren*). As Foreign Minister of a country which had recently joined the League of Nations, he denied press reports of secret German rearmament of which he was certainly aware. His reconciliation with France, genuine as far as it went, must be seen in relation to his general policy. His attitude was that of a realist: Alsace-Lorraine could not be recovered, the eastern territories might. He was at best a European as far as the West was concerned, and even then not in the sense of an Adenauer desiring integration. Stresemann and Briand meant different things when they talked about Europe. For Stresemann it would be a continent in which Germany, freed from the trammels of Versailles, would play a part justified by her size and importance, automatically putting France in the shade, and in the absence of a strong Russia assuming predominance in Eastern Europe. For Briand Europe must be a political system in which French security, and therefore French hegemony, was perpetuated. Stresemann had learnt with the years that politics must be pragmatic; just as he had become a republican by common sense, so he knew by experience that a diplomatic war of attrition against the treaty of Versailles was more likely to be effective than impulsive attacks which would win applause at home but alarm public opinion abroad and so prove self-defeating. Unfortunately, the time at his disposal was too short to convert the majority of his fellow countrymen to this belief, or perhaps it would be truer to say that Europe as a whole (France as well as Germany) was not yet ripe for the idea of co-operation in which Stresemann and Briand both believed. There

was little backing for the project of a 'united states of Europe' advocated at Geneva by Briand and supported by the dying Stresemann,
and the onset of the great depression brought a sharp revival of
economic nationalism.

(iv) CONSTITUTIONAL DICTATORSHIP: BRÜNING

The 34 months that passed between Germany's last parliamentary
cabinet (the coalition headed by the socialist Hermann Müller) and
Hitler's assumption of power were a period marked, even by Weimar
standards, by an unusual degree of turmoil, confusion and intrigue.
In this twilight of the Republic, which imperceptibly became the dawn
of the Third Reich, politics had a murky and often desperate character. It is difficult to discern any clear theme except one: a prolonged
and ultimately fruitless search for a government that would be
authoritarian but not National Socialist, and popular without being
parliamentary. Events were shaped by four interlocking factors. The
first was a growing rejection of Weimar democracy by the moderate
as well as the extreme right. In party terms the right-wing trend was
shown in the choice of Hugenberg and Kaas as heads of the Nationalist and Centre party respectively, and also in the loss of votes by the
middle parties in the 1928 general election. For some time there had
been a similar movement among intellectuals, economists and publicists that has been described as a conservative revolution. It was a
mood engendered by the 'cultural despair' which had become
characteristic of the right-wing intelligentsia: it went back ultimately
to Schopenhauer and Nietzsche, but defeat had deepened the sense of
pessimism, and the writings of Spengler had popularised it.[24] Such
thinking had an influential platform in the newly founded periodical
Die Tat, whose editor, Hans Zehrer, wrote: 'These times long for
authority, they are tired of liberal ideals.'[25] The Industrialists' Association (*Reichsverband der deutschen Industrie*) referred already in 1929
to a deep longing throughout the nation for achievement and
authority and suggested that there was a widespread desire for
stronger government.[26] Such sentiments are reminiscent even in their
wording of the disillusion that followed the failure of German liberalism in 1848. And just as the new authoritarian regime that began in
1862 could not be just a return to the pre-1848 order, so the conservative revolutionaries of 1930 knew that there could be no mere restoration of the Wilhelmine regime. Society had become less hierarchic
and more egalitarian. The Right, wrote Möller van den Bruck as early
as 1923, was beginning to recognise the pressure and weight of the
masses.[27] None of the conservative revolutionaries had more influence

than Möller van den Bruck himself, the author of an essay entitled *The Right of Young Nations* and best remembered for his book *The Third Reich*, which supplied Hitler with a name for his regime and popularised the basic ideas on which it was founded – contempt for liberalism, rejection of Marxism in favour of a 'true' or German socialism, the need to expand, the right to a share of world power of which Germany had been robbed by defeat and treachery, anti-semitism. Möller, like Hitler, decried the party system, and by 1930 the increasing vogue of an authoritarian state played into Hitler's hands. Too few people realised that a state above parties, as the Nazis promised, would in fact be a one-party state. But the rejection of a western-type parliamentary regime can be seen as an internal counterpart to the repudiation of the 'fulfilment policy' demanded by the Nationalists. Wirth, the former Chancellor, told the Reichstag in 1930: 'Parliamentarianism is not sick because it is threatened by dictatorship; it is threatened by dictatorship because it is sick.'[28] A common wave of revolt united the enemies of Versailles and democracy. By 1930 there was a third discredited force: capitalism. Millions of middle- and working-class Germans, like millions of similar people everywhere, wanted a radical change in the economic system. There was a paradox here, hardly realised at the time by most people, in that for Germany capitalism in its true sense had almost ceased to exist. Yet the fixed prices, wages and other rigidities built into the system, by preventing the self-adjusting mechanisms from functioning, brought serious disadvantages to the less organised – mostly middle class – sections of society.

This brings us to the second major influence: the great depression. At its worst it caused the unemployment of almost one in three of the male working population. It underlay the cabinet crisis of March 1930 which was to have such fateful consequences. The capitalists too were tired of weak government and compromise. The cabinet split, which was basically a dispute between free enterprise and welfare socialism, encouraged businessmen in the belief that only an authoritarian regime could save them, while hunger and despair drove millions of voters to support the Nazi and Communist parties.[29] The situation demanded stronger measures and a more imaginative approach than any chancellor could muster, and the one economic specialist who might have rescued the economy, Schacht, had joined the opposition. The breakdown of capitalism in the eyes of the far left proved that the workers were paying the price for the failure of the 1918 revolution. To the middle classes, including such disparate social groups as farmers, small businessmen, artisans, white-collar workers, technicians, officials, professional men and students, communism offered no salvation; nor did *laissez-faire* economics. A third way must be found. Some conservatives advocated a corporative state. This came near Hitler's ideas. Hitler shrewdly linked the economic grievance with the political: Germany's financial difficulties were ultimately due to Versailles. A vote against 'fulfilment' was a vote against poverty.

Thirdly, the breakdown of the parliamentary regime forced the President to play a more active part. Even at the time of his election in 1925 the aged Field-Marshal had been little more than a dignified figure-head, a symbol of past glories placed somewhat incongruously on the sober structure of republican politics. So long as the system worked, as it did until March 1930, Hindenburg could rely on the rules of the constitution and his own common sense to keep out of trouble. But by then he was in his eighty-third year, physically and mentally exhausted, hardly able to grasp, still less to solve a political crisis for which he had neither training nor aptitude. He leaned increasingly on his advisers, who played on his weakness and prejudices. To most Germans Hindenburg with his square head and massive frame was the incarnation of steadfastness. He also had a reputation for loyalty, though at more than one crisis in his life he had forced his deputy, Groener, to take unpopular decisions, and to Brüning he was to show conspicuous lack of appreciation. His solidity had for some time been hardly distinguishable from inertia; the inertia now became a senile torpor.[30] When he did make a decision, he was not so much exercising an independent judgement as reacting to suggestions made by his son, his secretary or other members of his 'camarilla' such as Schleicher, and he used his presidential powers to undermine the constitution they were supposed to protect.

The fourth factor in the situation was the army. During the Seeckt era that followed the Kapp Putsch the army had kept in the background. But it remained a state within a state, a potential *deus ex machina*. Its attitude during a crisis would depend on that of the government. No one doubted that, if necessary, the army would defend the state against a Putsch by the Communists; but the experience of 1920 and 1923 suggested that its loyalty against a Putsch from the right was more questionable. The rise of Hitler created fresh uncertainty. That the new mass movement had some influence on the army was shown when three young officers were convicted of high treason in 1930 for spreading Nazi propaganda. Even the senior officers, though like most of the upper classes they regarded Hitler as a vulgar upstart, shared his 'national' objectives and appreciated the 'patriotic and military spirit' permeating the Nazi movement.[31] The generals did not like the idea that they might have to take sides against Hitler in a civil war, nor were they keen on a pre-emptive strike. Nevertheless, if the Nazis started rioting, the army was prepared to retaliate. As Germany stumbled down the slippery slope from parliamentary government to presidential dictatorship, the army leaders saw themselves as arbiters of the country's fate. 'In the political developments in Germany not a stone must be moved any longer without the word of the *Reichswehr* being thrown decisively into the struggle,' declared Groener, in the autumn of 1930.[32] As Minister of Defence he intended that word to be his own. But Hindenburg, indifferent to or unversed as he might be in political complexities, never forgot that he was Commander-in-Chief of the armed forces, and the army remained dear to his heart. Unexpectedly however the main threat to Groener came from his resourceful and ambitious protégé, Schleicher, who became head of the newly created political department of the Ministry of Defence and thus the *Reichswehr*'s spokesman on political matters. Schleicher had great influence with Hindenburg, with whose son he had served in the Foot Guards, while Groener, partly for personal reasons (a marriage of which Hindenburg disapproved), partly because of his republican sympathies, lost the President's favour. And whereas Groener was genuinely worried by the rise of the Nazis, Schleicher saw in them a useful antidote to the Communists, while believing that he could tame them by including them in a coalition. This was also the aim of von Papen, whom Schleicher persuaded Hindenburg to appoint as Chancellor after Brüning (also a Schleicher nominee) had fallen under the old man's displeasure. Papen and Schleicher both had difficulty in governing because neither had the support of the Reichstag. Since they were unwilling to seek the co-operation of the Social Democrats, they were forced to turn to Hitler, whose price they refused to pay. Papen's ultimate capitulation marked, though this was not realised at the time, the end of army independence.

The fall of the Republic was a gradual process. Six crucial stages can be identified. The first was the break-up of the coalition government headed by Hermann Müller in March 1930, which followed a dispute inside the cabinet about the financing of a deficit in the unemployment insurance fund. This was a direct result of the economic crisis: the total of workless had swollen to about two and a half million, over twice as many as was assumed by the insurance scheme. To balance the fund, the Finance Minister proposed a rise in the weekly contributions paid by employers and employees from $3\frac{1}{2}$ per cent to 4 per cent, instead of the alternative, naturally opposed by the Socialists, of reducing relief; there was also to be a government subsidy to the fund. The People's party, representing business interests, persuaded the minister to limit the proposed rise to $3\frac{3}{4}$ per cent, but this modification was unacceptable to one of the four S.P.D. members of the government. Müller himself was in favour of the compromise, as was Hilferding, the party's economic expert, but his parliamentary party, under trade union pressure, voted for its rejection. An old and sick man, Müller resigned, and so dissolved the coalition. At another critical juncture in the life of the Republic – the aftermath of the Kapp Putsch – it had been Müller's fate to be Chancellor. Then he had failed to bridle the forces of reaction; now he was unable to persuade his party colleagues whose short-sighted intransigence made them reject the only course that might have preserved the parliamentary regime. Among the Socialists traditional dislike of compromise and fear of losing votes to the Communists prevailed; on the right there was a growing impatience with party rule which welcomed the opportunity of ousting the S.P.D. and establishing a government based on the authority of the president. It was later clear to all socialists, and indeed to all democrats, that 27 March, the date of Müller's resignation, was the black day of the Weimar Republic, the first ominous step towards one-party dictatorship. At the time, of course, the S.P.D.'s decision was not seen in this light, especially as the party still ruled (with the Centre) in Prussia; for many the resignation was a shrewd tactical move which would saddle the other parties with responsibility for unpopular decisions.

The new Chancellor was Heinrich Brüning, chairman of the Centre parliamentary party in the Reichstag. He represented a new generation and was widely hailed as the man of the future, raising hopes soon to be disappointed. His excellent war record endeared him to Hindenburg, and his unimpeachable patriotism was a useful asset against the super-patriots on the right. An austere Catholic and dedicated public servant, Brüning combined social sympathies and trade union experience with authoritarian leanings which appealed to the increasing number of people who, dismayed by parliamentary squabbles, wished for a government 'independent' of the Reichstag. In practice this meant a right-wing government, but the paradox was that the electorate did not vote for the traditional right-wing parties – hence the weakness of successive governments during this transitional period. Brüning wanted a government of the Bismarckian type, but even Bismarck would have found it hard to govern with nearly a third of the labour force out of work. The new cabinet included all the parties in the previous cabinet except the S.P.D.; it was thus based mainly on the Centre and People's party – together a parliamentary minority – with the Socialists 'tolerating' it (especially after the general election of September 1930), and the Nationalists and Communists in opposition. Brüning's immediate task was to solve the budget problem that had defeated his predecessor. Public finance was hopelessly in deficit with falling revenue on the one hand, rising expenses on the other. Acting according to the orthodox financial wisdom of his time, and mindful of the horrors of inflation, Brüning had no remedy for the depression except deflation. Government expenditure (including salaries and wages but excluding military expenditure)[33] was cut, taxes increased, and unemployment insurance contributions raised to $4\frac{1}{2}$ per cent. So unpopular a budget failed to get through the Reichstag, and Brüning had to ask the President to promulgate it by using his emergency powers under Article 48 of the constitution. In doing so Brüning disregarded an S.P.D. offer of co-operation. When the Reichstag, acting within its powers, passed a motion condemning government by Emergency Decree, Brüning dissolved it. This was a tactical mistake, and marks the second stage in the republic's decline. Brüning's hope of winning a parliamentary majority proved a catastrophic miscalculation. Austerity and deflation had antagonised most sections of the population. Salaries, wages and pensions had been reduced, while the fall in prices hit producers including the farmers.

The dominating feature of the new Reichstag was the strength of the National Socialists, who had risen from 12 members to 107. Their behaviour in the House was described by the British ambassador as 'really insolent'. For the next two and a half years the vital question in German politics was how to carry on the government without admitting the Nazis to power. Hitler felt bold enough to demand a seat in the cabinet: Hindenburg refused.[34] The new Nazi supporters came largely from the unemployed (many of whom also swelled the Communist vote), but partly too from the liberal parties and the Nationalists, and also from a rural population suffering from the collapse of food prices. Some of these categories overlapped. The continued decline of the Democrats and People's party was predictable: the former, had been losing ground ever since 1919, while Stresemann's largely unacknowledged success in foreign affairs had failed to rally his own party behind his policy. Hugenberg's Nationalists, who had made the running for Hitler at the time of the campaign against the Young Plan and had subsequently split, lost 1·9 million votes. Despite the depression, which forced millions of people to live at barely subsistence level, Hitler won remarkably little support from the left, whose total votes fell by only 4 per cent; and what the Socialists lost the Communists gained. The Centre actually won six seats to bring its total in the Reichstag to 68. Thus both Catholic and 'Marxist' voters showed, as they were to do until March 1933, a consistent resistance to Nazi blandishments. But Brüning's task as

Chancellor was now more difficult because the Reichstag was more adverse; he thus became increasingly dependent on Hindenberg, whose palace was a centre of backstairs intrigue, mainly adverse to Brüning.

In the winter that followed the general election of September 1930 the economic situation went from bad to worse, as political fears added to the atmosphere of crisis. A flight of foreign and German (Jewish and liberal) capital created a balance of payments problem. One way of alleviating it was to invoke the clauses of the Young Plan which provided for a partial suspension of payment in special circumstances. Such a move would bring political prestige at home as well as financial relief. But reparations were in practice linked to war debts and thus involved all the major western countries. In December 1930 Brüning suggested to the American government an international conference to discuss reparations, war debts and the general economic emergency.[35] (Disarmament, another subject on which Germany felt aggrieved, was also to be discussed.) Brüning could reasonably argue that the Young Plan's obligations had been entered into when the German economy was in better shape, and that times had changed. Like Stresemann before him, he counted on Germany's creditors being forced to help her by self-interest.[36] There was also some disposition on the part of foreign governments to make concessions to Brüning, who was seen as the only barrier to a Nationalist or Nazi government. But Brüning upset a delicate situation by declaring that the German and Austrian governments proposed to form a customs union. The news was badly received abroad, especially in France, and helped to reduce confidence in the mark. The failure in May 1931 of the *Creditanstalt*, the largest Austrian bank, led to a further outflow of gold and foreign currency from Germany.[37] The French offered the Reich a loan, in which Britain and the United States would join, in return for an assurance that Germany would take no step likely to disturb peace, would renounce the proposed *Anschluss* with Austria, and would not increase expenditure on arms. Brüning declined the offer: not only were the political conditions unacceptable, but he wished to avoid further indebtedness.

What Brüning really wanted was an end of reparations without strings. What he got was a breathing space. In June 1931 President Hoover declared a year's moratorium on reparations and war debts. The British approved; the French, who had not been consulted, demurred. They finally agreed after insisting on conditions – including a slowing down of rearmament – which the Germans resented. The delay reduced the value of the declaration, and the run on the mark continued, accelerated by the failure in July of the *Darmstädter und National-Bank*. Brüning had to ask the American banks for a new loan. With the run-down of gold the mark was in danger. Standstill agreements were signed to prevent the further loss of credits. In rather similar circumstances about the same time the British government went off gold and let the pound be devalued. Germany should have devalued the mark, but desisted out of fear of inflation: besides, she had undertaken in the Young Plan to preserve the currency. Meanwhile the projected Austro-German customs union came to nothing. Its significance was mainly political. The more unpopular Brüning's austerity measures made him at home, the more he needed to win prestige abroad. In the auction for nationalist favour, he could always be outbid by the Nazis, but by scoring a success might win credit from the moderates. Brüning was inevitably influenced by the mood of patriotic indignation kept alive by provocative demonstrations denouncing this or that part of the Versailles treaty.[38] A customs union with Austria might be followed by a political union (though this was expressly forbidden in the treaty) and was widely desired in both countries. It was a blow against 'fulfilment' and so revisionist. But the French put heavy financial pressure on Austria, the weaker partner, by withdrawing credits; and the narrowly adverse decision by the Court of International Justice, to which the matter had been referred, came as little more than a formality. Brüning's government had miscalculated both its own strength and the force of foreign reaction. The result was a diplomatic defeat. To please Hindenburg, Curtius, the Foreign Minister, and Wirth, another left-wing member of the Centre, were dropped from the cabinet. To mark their disapproval of Brüning, the Nationalists, Stahlhelm and Nazis joined in a demonstrative rally at Bad Harzburg that anticipated their later coalition. The attempt to revise Versailles peacefully had failed; therefore other methods must be used. Brüning went doggedly on, using the President's emergency powers against a largely hostile Reichstag, in which the new Nazi members voiced their contempt for the man whom the Communists dubbed the 'hunger Chancellor'.[39] It is hardly fair to blame Brüning for sticking to his deflationary policy despite its obvious unpopularity because he really had no choice.[40] Reflation at the time would have worsened Germany's precarious trade balance and in Brüning's view would have caused a loss of confidence in the mark. She would thus have become still more dependent on foreign loans.[41] This, in the circumstances, would have meant borrowing from France, the country with the highest gold reserves, with political strings unacceptable to German public opinion and probably fatal to Brüning's survival as Chancellor. French intransigence was, if anything, stiffened by a declaration by Brüning in January 1932 that Germany would pay no more reparations. The fear in Paris was that the money so saved would be spent on armaments:

it was noted that financial stringency did not hold up the building of a second 'pocket battleship', despite Socialist and Communist opposition.

In April 1932 Hindenburg was re-elected President. In a four-cornered fight with three rivals in the first ballot – Hitler, Düsterberg of the Stahlhelm and Thälmann the Communist – he narrowly failed to win outright. In a straight fight with Hitler in the second ballot Hindenburg won by six million votes – a clear lead, but Hitler had nearly 37 per cent of the votes cast. More disturbing for Brüning was the Nazis' success in the election of a new Prussian *Landtag* which occurred in the same month. They displaced the Social Democrats as the largest party, and indeed now held this position in every state except Bavaria. In the early days of the N.S.D.A.P. its strength had lain in Bavaria; now its main support came from the north and east where traditional Nationalism, radicalised by the agricultural depression, was turning to National Socialism. Groener, pressed by some of the state governments to curb the Nazis, whose violence was a menace to public order, persuaded Hindenburg to sign a decree banning the S.A. and S.S. Hindenburg acted with reluctance, though he owed his re-election to the republican vote. Schleicher, who at first supported the ban, now changed sides. He met Hitler twice to discuss the terms on which, in return for withdrawal of the ban, the latter would call off his hostility to the government under another chancellor. First Groener was dismissed, ostensibly in response to army pressure. Then Hindenburg was easily persuaded by Schleicher that Brüning must go, and acted on this advice, which coincided with his own sentiments. A contributory factor was a plan Brüning put forward for settling unemployed people on bankrupt estates in East Prussia, a project which to the President's conservative mind savoured of 'agrarian Bolshevism'. While Hindenburg's sudden dismissal of Brüning, who had worked indefatigably for his re-election as President, will always remain a classical example of political ingratitude, Hindenburg appears to have thought that he had done Brüning a favour by agreeing to stand. It was especially bitter that Brüning, whose policy had been to strengthen the President's position, who had persuaded Hindenburg to be a candidate against his will and had rallied mass support behind him, should now be offhandedly, almost contemptuously, discarded. There is no doubt that the old man deeply resented his new dependence on the left-wing electorate, and that he blamed Brüning for it. Hindenburg's toleration of Schleicher's intrigues against the Chancellor also shows him in an unfavourable light. Ironically, despite his success in winning a vote of confidence in the last important Reichstag debate of his ministry, Brüning now reaped

Germania

'Nothing to put on, but perpetually worried about the latest fashion in hats' (a reference to the plethora of political parties during the last phase of the Weimar Republic)

(*Simplicissimus*, 1932)

the consequences of reliance on the 'weak and apathetic octogenarian' (Dorpalen) whose confidence he had lost. A tense, sensitive man, courageous but opinionated, Brüning lacked political flair and judgement and popular appeal. He fell between two stools: while he rejected co-operation with the Socialists whose opposition to the 'pocket battle-ships' he deplored, at the same time he was abandoned by the right whose monarchist aspirations he shared and whose authoritarianism he tried to make his own. Towards Hindenburg he was too deferential, speaking as Captain to Field-Marshal rather than as Chancellor to President. Brüning was well aware of the extent to which Hindenburg's mental faculties had declined and realised that he had become the unconscious tool of irresponsible men. Brüning's decision that everything must be done to keep Hindenburg in office thus appears in retrospect a grave mistake, of which he was only the first victim. The absence of an alternative candidate who could command even as much support as Brüning was itself symptomatic of the malaise of the Republic.

Brüning subsequently claimed that he had to leave office when only a hundred yards short of his goal. Elections in France had just brought a left-wing government to power that was willing to pursue a less unyielding policy towards Germany. The British government evidently assumed that no reparations would be paid that year. Had Brüning stayed in power he, not von Papen, would have represented Germany at the Reparations Conference that met at Lausanne in the summer of 1932 and virtually abolished them. Yet Papen got no credit for this from the Nazis, who would never admit that any policy but their own could benefit Germany, nor is there much reason to think that Brüning would have fared any better. Even France's reluctant acknowledgement in December 1932 of Germany's equality of rights in armaments did not save the tottering Schleicher government. Brüning's failure to deal with the economic crisis, particularly with mass unemployment, was the main reason for his loss of support in the country, which in turn reduced his usefulness to Hindenburg. His rebuff over the *Anschluss* with Austria overshadowed his partial success in gaining a financial respite from England and America. Yet his resentment at not being allowed to complete the reparations policy of which he had borne the brunt and to negotiate a new agreement on armaments (the Disarmament Conference had begun at Geneva in February 1932) was understandable. Despite his limitations Brüning's abrupt, almost brutal dismissal was undeserved. If he had not proved the strong man desired by Schleicher, no one had done more than Schleicher to undermine his authority. Brüning's fall was the third crucial turning point on the road to the Third Reich.

(v) PSEUDO-CONSTITUTIONAL DICTATORSHIP: FROM PAPEN TO SCHLEICHER

Franz von Papen, whom Hindenburg made Chancellor in place of Brüning, came from a Westphalian landed family. As a boy he had been a page at the Imperial court, and later become a notable amateur jockey. He had joined the cavalry and served on the General Staff. Although he had for some years represented the Centre, or rather its right wing, in the Prussian *Landtag*, he was hardly known to the general public, and remained politically a lightweight. 'No German Chancellor was ever chosen more frivolously.'[42] With his charm, agrarian background and aristocratic connections, he appealed to Hindenburg's monarchist heart; and Hindenburg's confidence was his main political asset. The fact that during the war Papen, who had been German military attaché in Washington, had been expelled from America for acts of sabotage, was hardly a recommendation at a time when Germany depended on America for credits, but did not worry Hindenburg. In the Reichstag Papen had even less support than his predecessor, for the Centre party, understandably resentful at the manner of Brüning's dismissal, expelled Papen from its ranks, and the Socialists were now in open opposition. Schleicher, who had 'made' Papen, was rewarded with the Ministry of Defence in place of Groener who, identified with the discredited parliamentary regime and now out of favour with Hindenburg, had actually been dismissed while Brüning was still in office. In composition and social outlook the new cabinet was more like a revived cabinet of the Hohenzollern Empire, though with less popular backing. There was a curious contrast between the 'cabinet of barons' as it was dubbed and the nature of the problems with which it was called upon to deal. An advanced industrial society was facing the worst breakdown in its history. In 1932 the national income was three fifths of what it had been in 1928, industrial production was less than three fifths, and exports less than half. Over six million people were officially out of work; the real number was probably even higher. At Krupp's only 18,000 of a labour force of 49,000 were working and they only for three days a week: a mere quarter of the plant's capacity was being utilised.[43] In this situation the choice of a Papen government seemed grotesquely irresponsible; if it suited Hindenburg, who even appears to have had his doubts about his new Chancellor, it lacked the support of 90 per cent of the electorate.[44]

If von Papen had any contribution to make, it was in the sphere of foreign policy, particularly in Franco-German relations. Through the family of his wife, who came from the Saar, he had links with French industrialists; and through the Church, of which he was a prominent lay member, he was in touch with influential French Catholics. His fluent French was another asset. He was also lucky in that the new government in Paris with which he had to deal was a radical socialist coalition disposed to treat German grievances in a conciliatory way. Herriot, the Prime Minister, was the heir of Briand (who died that year) and thus of the 'Locarno spirit'. The Lausanne conference on reparations reduced the amount due from 35 to 3 milliard marks, which was never in fact paid; and, encouraged by the British, the French were cautiously edging their way to a formula which would meet German wishes on the vexed question of armaments. Proposals for a general Franco-German understanding made by Papen to Herriot at Lausanne, which in other circumstances might have borne fruit, were overshadowed by French fears of Germany's new militancy and repeated breaches of the peace treaty.[45] For France, the arms issue was indissolubly connected with security. On paper the heavily armed French army was still so much stronger than anything which Germany could put into the field that French fears appeared groundless, at least in the foreseeable future. But already the French government was beginning to lose faith in the alliances with its smaller European allies.[46]

One of Papen's first measures was to lift the ban on the S.A. and S.S. which had angered the Nazis, whom he wished to 'tame'. This was the signal for the resumption of street fighting: Nazis and Communists met in violent clashes, and hardly a day passed without bloodshed. The victims were often innocent bystanders. Using the cynical argument that the Prussian government was incapable of keeping order, Papen dismissed it, and appointed himself Reich Commissioner for Prussia, an office unknown to the constitution. The two key ministers affected were Braun, the Prime Minister, and Severing of the Interior. Both were Socialists. Prussia had been a stronghold of socialism and republicanism since the fall of the Empire, and its bloodless surrender to a *coup d'état* of more than doubtful legality was a heavy moral and material blow to what remained of the Weimar regime. It was the fourth step in Hitler's advance to power. The Socialist ministers have been much criticised for not resisting. Circumstances were against them. The army, giving moral support to Papen, occupied strategic points in Berlin and a state of siege was declared.[47] Braun, who was unwell, was absent from his office on the fatal 20 July attending to a sick wife. He and his party, depressed by losses in the recent Prussian elections, had no stomach for a fight, which they knew they could not win: the republican Iron

Front was no match for the Prussian police (who should have been on their side) and Schleicher's *Reichswehr*. Since the Prussian elections in April the Braun-Severing government had been a caretaker administration, lacking majority support – but Papen was in a similar position. In contrast to the situation at the time of the Kapp Putsch, the Socialists could not count on the trade unions, which were in a far from militant mood, and could hardly declare a general strike at a time of high unemployment.[48] The S.P.D., peace-loving and law-abiding, contented themselves with challenging the validity of Papen's action in the Reich Supreme Court, whose verdict, largely favourable to the S.P.D. was delivered three months later but had no practical significance. It was argued on the left that Papen was better than Hitler; but by destroying the Republic Papen was doing Hitler's work for him. That the Socialists forfeited some popularity through their almost fatalistic attitude is shown by the Communist gains at their expense in the next two general elections.

The mood of resignation was general. An English observer had noticed it while Brüning was still in power:

There was a sensation of doom to be felt in the Berlin streets . . . the feeling of unrest went deeper than any crisis. It was a permanent unrest, the result of nothing being fixed or settled. The Brüning regime was neither democracy nor dictatorship, socialism or conservatism, it represented no class or group, only a common fear of the overwhelming disorder, which formed a kind of rallying place of frightened people. It was the *Weimardaemmerung*. Tugged by forces within and without, by foreign powers and moneylenders, industrialist plotters, embittered generals, impoverished landed gentry, potential dictators, refugees from Eastern Europe, it reeled from crisis to crisis within a permanent crisis.[49]

There was little to suggest that Papen could allay the anxieties or master the situation. At loggerheads with the Reichstag, he had to ask Hindenburg to dissolve it and order new elections. These were a disaster: the Nazi mandates rose from 107 to 220; the slide of the middle-class parties (except the Centre) continued; the Communists won 12 seats to make their total 89. The extremist gains were the fifth stage in the transition to full dictatorship. Papen's bargaining strength was much reduced, that of the Nazis enhanced. When the President saw Hitler after the election the latter, as leader of the largest party, demanded to be Chancellor, and refused an offer of the vice-chancellorship. But Hindenburg was not yet willing to appoint Hitler (the 'Bohemian corporal') to the highest post, and Papen carried on. In the Reichstag, where Göring had displaced the Socialist

Löbe as President (Speaker), the Nazi deputies yelled and jeered at Papen, who so far from getting a vote of confidence was publicly humiliated. He was also worried lest the Centre strike a bargain with the Nazis, for he knew that secret talks were going on between the two. Again he asked Hindenburg for a dissolution order. Again the German people went to the polls. This time the result showed a significant fall – the first – in the Nazi vote. Many interpreted this as a sign that Hitler had passed his zenith. Goebbels, his propaganda chief, was in despair. The country's economic situation was slightly less bleak. Papen's reflationary measures, such as tax remission certificates, a public works programme and reduced rates of interest on agricultural mortgages, were beginning to take effect.[50] The Nationalists, the only party of any size to support Papen, had won back an encouraging proportion of votes. But over nine-tenths of the Reichstag were still unwilling to co-operate with Papen, who resigned. Hindenburg again saw Hitler and offered him the chancellorship in a coalition government. Again Hitler rejected the conditions. If Papen could govern by presidential decree, why could he not have the same privilege?

Faced with deadlock Papen asked Hindenburg to prorogue the Reichstag indefinitely. Schleicher now intervened, warning the President that such a course would lead to civil war. If it was Hindenburg's intention to make Papen a dictator with army support, that support would not be given to a Chancellor who was repudiated by the overwhelming majority of the nation. If, in consequence, the S.A. and S.S. rose against the government, the army could not be relied on to suppress them.[51] An unexpected if short-lived alliance between Nazis and Communists (who now had 100 seats in the Reichstag) in a transport strike in Berlin underlined the gravity of Schleicher's warning. In this dilemma Hindenburg turned to Schleicher and asked him to form a government. Schleicher, unlike Papen, was fertile in ideas. He counted as a 'social general', a man who was anxious to come to terms with the trade unions and left-wing Nazis. Hitler was even offered the vice-chancellorship, but refused. In the event, Schleicher's cabinet differed little in composition from his predecessor's.

The last phase of the dying Republic was the most feverish: the web of intrigue thickened, rumours multiplied, and the Nazis redoubled their frenetic efforts to impress the electorate. Schleicher became the victim of his own tortuous methods, used now by Papen, the protégé who had become his rival. At first Schleicher had certain advantages: less hostility from the left, more support in the Reichstag. But he had lost the confidence of the army. He tried to break up the Nazi party by detaching the Gregor Strasser wing, but the manoeuvre failed when Strasser hesitated and Hitler promptly denounced him.

Nor was Schleicher successful in coming to an agreement with the trade unions that would have separated them from the S.P.D.[52] While his wooing of the left brought no reward, it caused some alarm among employers on the right, and even induced a swing to Hitler. Above all, Papen who, Schleicher hoped, would leave Berlin after losing office, remained there and still paid frequent visits to his friend Hindenburg.

Early in January Papen met Hitler in the house of Schröder, a Cologne banker. The business world had shown an increasing tendency to support Hitler since the Communist gains in the last two Reichstag elections. Hitler badly needed its financial help, for the S.A. alone cost him at least a million marks a day and the expenses of recent elections had amounted to 50 million marks.[53] Plans were made for a Hitler-Papen government to succeed Schleicher. The Nationalists and Stahlhelm were persuaded to take part to give it ballast and respectability. There was hard bargaining: Hitler made promises he did not intend to keep, Papen insisted on safeguards he would never be able to enforce. Meanwhile Schleicher had been criticised by the President for not providing enough subsidies to keep solvent the estates of bankrupt East Prussian landowners, a cause (as had been shown during Brüning's Chancellorship) dear to the heart of Hindenburg, who himself had been presented with an estate at Neudeck in his East Prussian homeland. Unable to secure the co-operation of the Reichstag, Schleicher asked Hindenburg to dissolve it and to give him special powers to govern without it. Hindenburg refused, reminding Schleicher that he had refused a similar request from Papen for the same reason – fear of civil war. Had Schleicher been content with dissolution, he might have stayed in office; in the event he resigned, carrying on until a successor could be found. His main anxiety was lest Papen succeed him. He hoped to remain as Minister of Defence. As late as 26 January Hindenburg told Hammerstein, the Chief of the Army Command, that he had no intention of making Hitler Chancellor.[54] But in the next two or three days he changed his mind. Papen and other advisers persuaded him that the next government must include Hitler. Time was short, for it was due to be formed before the next meeting of the Reichstag on 31 January. A rumour circulating in Berlin that Schleicher was planning a Putsch against the President's advisers with the help of the Potsdam garrison – almost certainly intended to forestall the appointment of Papen not Hitler as Chancellor – caused the anti-Schleicher group to hasten their plans and resolved the doubts in Hindenburg's mind.[55] The first step was to appoint a new Defence Minister in place of Schleicher. Hindenburg's choice fell on General von Blomberg, who had represented the *Reichswehr* at the Geneva Disarmament Conference and happened to be sympathetic to the Nazis. His inclusion would guarantee the loyalty of the army to the incoming government. He was sworn in before the new Chancellor. Until the last moment it was not clear whether that would be Papen or Hitler. In the event Hitler won. The new cabinet included three Nazis and ten Conservatives (Nationalists and Stahlhelm). Hugenberg, the Nationalist leader, became Minister of Economics and Agriculture. Misleadingly, the new government was seen as a triumph for Hugenberg rather than for Hitler, whose radicalism would be 'contained' by his Conservative colleagues. Schleicher's fall was the sixth and final turning point in the transition from democracy to dictatorship.

Even allowing for age and infirmity, Hindenburg showed a remarkable lack of loyalty to Schleicher, as he had to Brüning, though Schleicher could hardly complain in view of his own record of intrigue. Once he had lost Hindenburg's confidence his days were numbered, for, like Papen, he had too narrow a political base from which to operate. As for the army, the generals were increasingly convinced that only a regime founded on mass support could govern Germany, and that this could be found only in the N.S.D.A.P. Many of the officers were in any case pro-Nazi. All the actors in the drama were 'drawn towards Hitler as the moth is drawn to a flame in which it will ultimately perish'.[56] Though few dates in modern history so obviously mark the end of an epoch as 30 January 1933, this was not generally realised at the time. The piecemeal destruction of the Weimar Republic had been going on for so long that its end hardly came as a shock. The safeguards, such as the large non-Nazi majority in the cabinet and Hitler's promise to maintain the constitution, seemed reassuring. It was also assumed that the responsibility of power would have a sobering influence. On the extreme left the stereotyped Communist view prevailed that a Nazi government could not last long because Hitler was bound to fail. Kautsky, still revered as a sage and mentor in the S.P.D., predicted even after the election of March 1933 that Hitler would be abandoned by his supporters as soon as his inability and unwillingness to live up to his demagogic promises became evident.[57]

Hitler's coming to power had such disastrous consequences that the question why it was allowed to happen has never ceased to be debated. The immediate reasons for it have been indicated: at that particular moment there seemed no practical alternative to admitting the Nazis to the government. The political deadlock was itself proof of the Republic's failure. Otto Braun, in his Memoirs, lays the blame on Versailles and Moscow.[58] This is too simple an explanation and overlooks the strength of those trends in German society which favoured authoritarian government if not dictatorship. It is true that Allied, especially French, statesmen have much to answer for. Their humiliation of the representatives of democratic Germany at Versailles and after, their Shylockian approach to the reparations problem, the tragic shortsightedness with which they continued to treat the men of Weimar faced with appalling problems – all this built up a fund of resentment in Germany which Hitler needed simply to exploit. By 1932, partly as a result of the revisionist campaign against the peace treaty by German scholars and publicists, but partly through the influence of Keynes, British opinion had become very critical of Versailles; and even in France there was a disposition to accept some change as inevitable. But this loss of faith in the moral validity and political wisdom of Versailles came too late (since it coincided with the beginning of the depression) to reverse the revanchist wave in Germany.[59] Whether Stresemann, who did not live to see the fruits of his labours lost, could have stemmed the tide, is a matter of conjecture but perhaps unlikely. As for Moscow, the German Communist party not only refused any co-operation between Communists and Social Democrats that could have given the left a strength it lacked, but continued to insist that the bourgeois capitalist Republic was not worth saving. The S.P.D. was far from blameless: it was a party of compromises, tarnished with the brutality of the Freikorps in the early days of the Republic, lacking in youth and vigour, defensive in mentality. But the Communists, as they later admitted, underrated the danger presented by Hitler.[60] As in France at the climax of the Dreyfus Affair, revolutionary dogma inhibited Marxists from rallying to the republic to protect human rights against the forces of reaction. Men who could describe the German Socialists as social fascists and view Hitler's regime as a transitory phenomenon that would pave the way to their own seizure of power clearly had little grasp of reality.

Yet much as Allied myopia and Communist miscalculations contributed to the weakness of the Weimar regime, they alone cannot account for its fall. An essential factor was the survival of anti-republican and anti-democratic forces in all walks of life: in universities, schools, newspaper offices and board-rooms as well as in the army, the civil service, the judiciary and the churches. In this sense the fall of the Republic was due to the hostility of the right rather than the sins of omission of the left.[61] The more conservative middle classes, the citizens of property and education as the phrase went, resented both their loss of wealth through war and inflation and their decline in status. For them the Republic meant western-type liberalism or Marxist socialism – both un-German creeds, repugnant to their beliefs and traditions. To the Protestant majority the infusion of a Catholic element in the ruling coalition did little to sweeten the pill. Hence there was no development of a stratum of conservative republicans such as Weimar politics badly needed. Stresemann, the monarchist who came to terms with the Republic, attempted to lead the way, but few followed him. The lower middle class – a term covering a wide range of occupations and interests – was also impoverished, not only by the war and its consequences, but by rapid economic change, and, of course, by the great depression. Hitler, wrote Schacht, could play like a virtuoso on the well-tempered piano of lower-middle-class hearts.[62] Broadly speaking, middle-class Germans of all kinds tended to hold certain beliefs which, over and above their economic and social grievances, alienated them from the Republic. First, they did not like the idea of party government, for this involved the conflict they sought to avoid: the state should represent the national interest and be above parties, as it had been under the Empire. They quite over-looked the extent to which, from the days of Bismarck onwards, the Imperial government had in fact been both partisan and polemical. Secondly, they blamed the Republic for the corruption and sordid bargaining associated with party politics. This again was a naïve view, which overlooked the amount of political horse-trading, and the very grave scandals such as that involving Philipp Eulenburg, which had taken place during the reign of William II. Thirdly, the Weimar regime failed to satisfy people's psychological needs. The Republic of reason made little or no appeal to the political romanticism either of the older generation who could remember a glamorous past or of the young who wanted a Utopia to look forward to. The sense of togetherness that Germans had experienced at the time of unification and again in August 1914 was lost under the Republic, and it was this which Hitler, more stridently than the Kaiser, evoked in his propa-ganda.[63] Liberalism, never very robust in Germany, had virtually disappeared from the middle classes by 1932. By then, Hitler had won the vote of a substantial proportion of the working class, or at least of the third or so who were unemployed. This support, unlike much of his middle-class support, was not a hangover from the Empire, a vague sympathy for authoritarian or proto-Nazi ideas; it was simply a desperate response to a desperate situation. The Republic had always had many enemies and in adversity its fair-weather friends deserted it.

There has long been a general belief, not only in Marxist circles, that German capitalists played a key part in helping Hitler come to power through their financial support at crucial moments in his career. In the early days in Munich money had been provided by the Bechstein family, and later individual industrialists such as Kirdorf,

Flick and Thyssen made donations. Hitler's speech to the *Industrie-Club* at Düsseldorf on 27 January 1932 is usually seen as a milestone in this process, since so great was the impression it made that large sums thereafter flowed into the Nazi coffers which helped to defray the heavy expenses of the presidential, Reichstag and *Landtag* elections of that year.[64] The speech itself was one of Hitler's best, playing on the fear of communism to which the big Ruhr employers were naturally highly susceptible, and stressing the need for authoritarian leadership in politics as well as industry. This was language they understood and approved. Nevertheless, the notion that from then on German industry was committed to back Hitler in his struggle for power is considerably exaggerated. The evidence of Thyssen, who claims in his book *I paid Hitler* that heavy industry provided the Nazis with about two million marks a year, apart from contributions by individual firms to particular party manifestations, must be regarded as suspect.[65] Some of the contributors were anxious to insure themselves against a Hitler government rather than to promote one. Moreover, the significance of such subsidies as Hitler received has a much less sinister significance when it is remembered that it was a general practice of industrialists to support financially all the major right-wing parties; and that in the presidential and the two Reichstag elections of 1932 big business was overwhelmingly behind Hindenburg and Papen respectively.[66] Within the business world the main support for Hitler came from the small and middle-sized firms, themselves victims of the depression. Indeed, the business community shared the very general illusion as late as 30 January 1933 that in a Hitler-Papen government it was Papen who would call the tune.[67] The responsibility of businessmen for the Nazi regime was thus mainly indirect: by subsidising Papen they were helping the man who speculated on putting Hitler in power on his own terms. Yet how much choice did Papen have? The problem after Hitler's overwhelming electoral victory in July 1932 was how to keep him out of power, not how to put him in, and this was a problem to which no one, including the Centre, knew the answer. Once Hitler was in power, industrialists had few hesitations in opening their purses, and even Gustav Krupp von Bohlen and Halbach, who hitherto had opposed Hitler, contributed a million marks to the N.S.D.A.P. fund for the March general election.[68] Other industrialists gave a further two million. Thus it was above all in the consolidation of power rather than in its acquisition that Hitler profited from big business.

The political combination that made Hitler's advance to the chancellorship possible was the alliance between the Nationalists and the Nazis which began with the campaign against the Young Plan and was confirmed by the Harzburg Front in October 1931. Both sides had much in common: hatred of Versailles, rejection of parliamentary government, the desire for a strong policy at home and abroad. What men like Hugenberg, Papen and Schleicher failed to grasp was that there would be no place for themselves (except as tolerated hangers-on) in Hitler's totalitarian Reich, that he was not a man with whom genuine co-operation or compromise was possible. Hugenberg was still a monarchist, but the restoration of a regime like that of William II was no longer a practical possibility. The Nazis had never hidden their belief in methods of violence, but even the devoutly Catholic Papen did not object to Hitler's defence of the storm-troopers who murdered Potempa, a Communist miner, in September 1932. Papen's opportunism, of which this was only one example, saved his own skin at incalculable cost to others.

Despite the support, variously motivated, which Hitler received from many quarters, he would never have become Chancellor had his opponents combined against him. The Republic rested essentially on the Socialist-Catholic coalition in which the Socialists were the senior partners even though they had fewer years in power at Reich level. The S.P.D. was in a dilemma: as a government party it wanted to make a success of the basically capitalist economy, as a Socialist party it was committed to its overthrow. A trade union leader asked his fellow socialists in 1931: 'Are we sitting at the sickbed of capitalism, not only . . . as doctors who want to save the patient, but also as cheerful heirs who cannot wait for the end and want to hasten it with poison?'[69] In practice, despite its doctrinaire inheritance and the Marxist phraseology of its programme, the party stood for nothing more revolutionary than a welfare state and a conciliatory foreign policy. Even during the 1920s the S.P.D. had given little sign of a passionate desire to lead the German people to the promised land of socialism. After 1930 it earned unpopularity by helping to keep Brüning in power, without producing a policy of its own that offered a convincing alternative to deflation. But as internationalists the Socialists could be denounced for betraying the nation, while the Communists accused them of selling out to the capitalists. A dispirited party, its leaders worn out by the turmoil of fourteen years, few of which had been without a crisis of one sort or another, the Social Democrats lacked self-confidence and, as their capitulation on 20 July showed, toughness. Nor were the trade unions, their closest allies, in fighting mood. As for the para-military defence force of the Socialists and trade unionists known as the Iron Front, it was far from formidable despite the size of its rallies, at which 150,000 might be present. A contemporary journalist described them:

In this vast army, the battalions of strong young men, the daring youngsters with muscles of steel and a determined spirit, were only a minority. So many ... bore the marks of the long privation of the economic crisis; hunger and cold, the unending search for work, the misery of homelessness or of fusty 'lodgings for single men' had robbed them of vitality and courage.[70]

Many of Hitler's storm troops had been through similar experiences, but they were more aggressive in temperament as well as more fanatical in belief. The German Socialists were products of the enlightenment, who trusted in reason not force, and unlike the S.A. were bad haters. The bellicose, vengeful mood of the Nazi ranks was absent from their democratic opponents. At bottom, the Socialists displayed the same lack of will to power as had prevented them from taking advantage of the revolution of 1918. They had always seen the Republic as a second best; at most a half-way house on the road to socialism. Lacking in new ideas, they had no master plan for recovery from the depression that hit them like a tidal wave.

As for the Centre party, its primary loyalty was to the Roman Catholic Church. Its support of the Republic was equivocal, especially under the leadership of Monsignor Kaas, whose authoritarian sympathies agreed with those of the Vatican.[71] Many Catholics had never been happy about their co-operation with the Socialists and hankered as Brüning did after an understanding with the right-wing parties in which the latter showed little interest: Hugenberg was very anti-Catholic. Though nothing came of them, negotiations between the Centre and the Nazis were held in the late summer of 1932 when together they commanded a majority in the Reichstag. In his New Year address for 1933 Kaas called for a 'saviour', adding, 'It is frankly all the same who leads Germany. The important thing is not who he is but what he can do.'[72] This cry from the heart suggested a certain despair and bewilderment but also an admission that had the Centre been in power it would hardly have known what to do with it. If this was the attitude of one who was a party leader and prelate, it is hardly surprising that the ordinary man should accept Hitler as the strong man whom Germany needed. Hitler's claim to stand for 'positive Christianity' overcame many scruples. Even in the election of March 1933, when the meaning of National Socialism was becoming plain and the rule of law was already undermined, the Centre campaigned against Marxism, liberalism and godlessness rather than against Nazism. In return for not obstructing Hitler's monopolisation of power, the Centre obtained a Concordat which he proceeded to break whenever it suited him to do so. But the experience of the Centre during the whole period 1918–33 indicates the anomaly of its position. There had been some justification for a specifically Catholic party during the Bismarck period because of the *Kulturkampf*; but during the Republic the Protestant bias in government almost disappeared. So far as there was need for a Christian party it was for one which combined Catholics and Protestants as the C.D.U. has done since 1945. The Centre suffered from a sectarianism that limited its basis of support and blinkered its political judgement. Still less for Catholics than for Socialists was the Republic a cause worth sacrificing oneself for.

The only middle-class party that was firmly committed to parliamentary democracy was the State party, as the Democrats had significantly re-named themselves in 1930. This third member of the Weimar coalition had been losing ground almost since its foundation. But in the deepening crisis and against the demand for strong leadership liberalism made no appeal; and the 74 members of the first republican Reichstag had dwindled to 2 by November 1932. The People's party, which Stresemann had tried to keep on a liberal course, took a turn to the right after his death under the influence of the businessmen who seized control, but failed to regain popularity: its representation in the November 1932 Reichstag was 11, exactly half of what it had been in January 1919. Its decline epitomised that of the Republic.

CHAPTER VIII

Hitler's Rise to Power

(i) FROM DRUMMER TO DICTATOR

'The irony of history', wrote Engels in a famous passage, 'turns everything upside down.' The First World War, according to Allied claims
at the time, was fought to make the world safe for democracy. Yet
it was followed during the twenty years of uneasy peace, by the rise,
in one European country after another, of popular dictatorships. Most
of these can be loosely but conveniently described as Fascist. As had
happened in 1848, popular government produced an alliance, followed
by a clash between liberalism and nationalism from which nationalism
emerged victorious. Mussolini, the first of the new style dictators and
in many ways their exemplar, spoke with contempt of the 'putrefying
corpse' of freedom, and as early as April 1922 (six months before he
came to power) announced that his party, the *Fascisti*, would make
an end of the liberal state.[1] As a system of ideas Fascism is hard to
define because it lacked clarity and coherence especially in Germany
where it bore many traces of political romanticism. But as a political
movement, embodied in parties or groups struggling for or holding
power, it had certain easily recognisable characteristics: nationalism,
xenophobia, glorification of the state; a preference for the peasant
and small businessman against both big business and the consumer;
adulation of an authoritarian and preferably charismatic leader;
exultation of instinct over reason; a cult of dynamism and militarism;
regressive social attitudes (for example towards the emancipation of
women); anti-semitism. Fascist ideology appears towards the end of
the nineteenth century as a reaction against the ideology and social
forces released by the French and industrial revolutions: liberalism,
parliamentary democracy, egalitarianism, urbanisation, socialism,
pacifism. It was inspired by the fashionable contemporary doctrine
of Social Darwinism, with lurid echoes of Nietzsche's *Will to Power*.
In its opposition to left-wing progressives, Fascism had much in
common with conservatism, but it differed from the latter in being
more aggressively nationalist and demagogic and less traditionalist,
and in canalising the specific discontents of social groups squeezed

between the pressures of large-scale capitalism and organised labour. Although Fascism was a universal phenomenon – some of its features can be found, for example, in the American Populist movement as well as in such later figures as Huey Long and Father Coughlin – it flourished particularly in countries suffering from humiliation or defeat (France after 1871, Italy and Germany after 1918) or severe economic depression (most of Europe in the 1930s) and among communities threatened with loss of status or impoverishment (the German minority in Austria-Hungary before 1914, large sections of the middle and lower middle classes during the Weimar Republic). The small shopkeeper undercut by the chain or department store, the bankrupt farmer faced with eviction from his land, the rentier whose savings had been destroyed by inflation, the craftsman displaced by the machine – it was to these groups, victims of technological change and financial crisis – that Fascism in Germany appealed. Unlike the Socialists, whose utopia lay in the future, such people looked back nostalgically to the past, and saw in the stability and prosperity of the Hohenzollern era almost a golden age. The First World War with its chauvinism and violence, and still more the ensuing defeat and revolution with its threat of Bolshevism, created conditions very favourable to the growth of Fascism. National Socialism, the German form of Fascism, began as a protest movement of those who refused to accept defeat and the post-war Republic. Another symptom of that protest was the survival of para-military forces in a compulsorily disarmed Reich. It was no accident that Hitler began his political career as the protégé of an army without whose moral and material help he might never have emerged from obscurity, and that his movement grew up in a city (Munich) which was over-reacting against the trauma of revolution. But if Nazism was a product of the same kind of social forces as gave rise to Fascism elsewhere, it reflected specific authoritarian and racial trends in German thinking as well as the prejudices, ambitions and personality of Adolf Hitler.

Though many of Hitler's followers were driven into his camp by defeat and despair, his own ideology was formed before 1914 (when he was already 25) amid the ethnic and social conflicts of the declining Austro-Hungarian Monarchy. The multi-racial Empire had narrowly escaped disruption during the revolution of 1848, in which one nationality had fought against another and the Monarchy had survived (with Russian help) by exploiting these divisions. Many people doubted whether it would outlast the death of the Emperor Francis Joseph, who was 70 in 1900. In the Austrian provinces the privileged German minority watched with alarm as the dynasty made one concession after another to the Slavs, especially to the Czechs, the majority people in Bohemia and Moravia. The rise of Pan-Germanism under Schoenerer in the last decades of the nineteenth century mirrored the Germans' fear of submergence in a Slav sea. In an age of dynamic nationalism the dynastic idea had no appeal, and democracy would destroy German predominance in the Empire. Racial tensions were exacerbated by the effects of Jewish emancipation. Vienna, the capital of the Empire, was a brilliant cosmopolitan society in which the Jews played a part quite disproportionate to their numbers: while forming just over 8 per cent of the population they accounted for about one-third of the university students, and industry and trade were to an overwhelming extent in Jewish hands.[2] In literature, the theatre and the press Jews occupied the highest positions. The reaction to this trend was the formation of a Christian Social party, one of whose leaders, Dr Karl Lueger, was for many years a popular mayor of Vienna and practised a mild kind of anti-semitism. Fear of and contempt for the Slavs, envy and resentment of the Jews, disdain for the Empire's policy of evading rather than solving its problems, admiration for the powerful and successful German Reich – these crude but potent emotions formed the climate of the political and social milieu into which Adolf Hitler was born in April 1889.

His father was a customs official at Braunau on the river Inn, the boundary between Austria and Bavaria, itself the symbol of a division which the young Hitler, following his Pan-German mentors, soon learned to resent. The story of his youth is told, not always accurately, in his autobiography *Mein Kampf*. He left school at the age of sixteen without the school-leaving certificate which for most Austrian boys was the passport to a career. His father had died two years before, his mother was to die two years later. Thus he was an orphan at the age of eighteen. But as a minor he received a small state pension, to which was added his share of the family estate.[3] He was not, therefore, the poverty-stricken youth which his domicile in the Men's Home in Vienna (to which he had moved from Linz, his second home) suggests. It seems certain that his failure to learn a trade or profession, or even to acquire a regular job, left him unsettled and insecure. His boyish dream was to become an architect, and he was bitterly disappointed when his application for a place in the Vienna Academy of Fine Arts was twice rejected. The enthusiasm for architecture which Hitler continued to show till the end of his life proves that this ambition was a genuine one, and its frustration had incalculable consequences. It can hardly be doubted that, had he been accepted as an architectural student in Vienna, he would never have become a fanatical rebel and street corner politician. For the time being he had to content himself with making drawings or paintings of well-known buildings or views and selling them to dealers, thus earning enough for his modest needs. This was his only occupation during the six years (1907–13) he spent in Vienna, except for a short time, probably in 1909, when he worked as a builder's labourer. Whether his refusal to join a trade union while in this occupation was due to inherited middle-class pride or because the unions were too closely identified with Social Democracy is uncertain,[4] and perhaps hardly matters. Socialism was anathema to Hitler because its Marxist creed denied his basic beliefs. Also, as he noticed, many of its leaders were Jews. Jews were particularly conspicuous among the 'promiscuous swarm of foreign people' battening on the old seed-bed of German culture – Vienna. There for the first time Hitler saw orthodox Jews from Galicia and other provinces of the Monarchy in their traditional garb, and was horrified. By the time he left Vienna he was a confirmed Pan-German, a sworn enemy of democracy and socialism, and on the way to becoming a pathological anti-semite. His hand-to-mouth existence was due to character as well as to circumstances. He enjoyed being a freelance and disliked regular hours. A dreamer, he lived in a fantasy world of Wagnerian heroes and sub-human, Jewish villains. Not until the outbreak of the First World War did he discover a purpose in life. By then he had moved from Vienna to Munich, probably to avoid military service under the Habsburgs. In Germany he felt different. In August 1914 he enthusiastically volunteered for the Bavarian army, and spent the next four years on the western front.

Hitler was a surprisingly good soldier, though he was never promoted. He gained several awards for valour, including the Iron Cross, First Class, a rare distinction for a corporal. He was wounded twice, and the armistice found him in a hospital in Pomerania, recovering from blindness caused by gas. Though the comradeship of the trenches was congenial to him after his rather aimless pre-war life, Hitler remained, in contrast to his fellow-soldiers, a tense, withdrawn and somewhat eccentric figure. Germany's defeat confirmed his conspiratorial explanation of history: she had been betrayed by Jews and Marxists, the 'scum' who were now in power. The German revolution drove the lesson home, especially in Bavaria, where Eisner's regime made many enemies, and the subsequent soviet dictatorship left an abiding fear of Bolshevism. There the counter-revolution was more firmly established than in any other German state, and henceforth the Bavarian government reflected in greater or less degree the phobias and prejudices of a conservative and Catholic population.[5] Dislike of 'red' Berlin was added to traditional anti-Prussian feeling. It was in Bavaria that, thanks to the complicity of reactionary legal and police officials, murderers of republican politicians like Erzberger were able to escape justice. Right-wing extremist groups flourished in Munich. Among them was a tiny and obscure body known as the German Workers' Party. This had come into existence during the war to support the policy of annexations advocated by the Fatherland Party of Tirpitz and Ludendorff. It was the nucleus of the later N.S.D.A.P.[6]

Hitler returned to Bavaria in November 1919. He was in Munich during the short but violent soviet experiment, when, according to his own account, he had to defend himself against soldiers who came to arrest him. (According to another account, he was actually arrested by the Freikorps as a suspected 'red'.) Whichever version is correct, there is no doubt that the experience deepened his hatred of communists and Jews. Like many other ex-soldiers, he felt a stranger in a new and alien world. Fortunately for Hitler the army still had a use for him. He became a political instructor in a demobilisation centre. His task was to counteract the influence of the soldiers' councils which had sprung up during the revolution, and more generally to combat the spread among the troops of liberal, socialist and pacifist ideas. The local army commanders had no sympathy for the Republic, and the Bavarian Socialist government was too weak, or perhaps too uninformed, to prevent public funds from being spent in this way. In using the Freikorps to suppress the Spartacists the Reich government had unwittingly given a licence to counter-revolution. The new job suited Hitler, who found the soldiers responsive to his harsh but pungent oratory, and the officers valued him. In the course of his duties he came in touch with the German Workers' party, and in September 1919 he joined it. According to *Mein Kampf* he had decided, while still in the military hospital, to become a full-time politician. And so when, on 31 March 1920, he was discharged from the army, he devoted himself to the party. A month before it had adopted a new name, the National Socialist German Workers' party, and a programme in Twenty-Five Points. Hitler was the chief propagandist, the drummer who became the bandmaster. The programme was mostly the work of another early member, an engineer named Gottfried Feder, and embodied his revolutionary and somewhat cranky economic ideas. Proclaiming the slogan 'Public interest before self-interest' it demanded agrarian reform; the expropriation of land needed for social purposes; the abolition of ground rent and of unearned income, including interest; the public ownership of banks and department stores, and state participation in the profits of large enterprises. This was a radical programme, designed to appeal to the under-privileged in an impoverished country. Though much of the socialism was middle class rather than working class in character, the prohibition of interest was a death blow to the rentier. Few of these demands were new: for example the motto 'Public interest before self-interest' had figured in a book entitled *National Socialism* by a Bohemian German named Rudolf Jung published in 1918. Many of the early Nazis such as Gregor Strasser considered themselves members of a left-wing party, and took the anti-capitalist line seriously; but it is unlikely that Hitler ever did. He certainly did not later; in May 1930 he told Otto Strasser, Gregor's brother, that the workers had no right to displace the capitalists, for the latter had proved by their success that they belonged to a higher race.[7] He was worried by the impoverishment of the middle class, and wanted to see wealth spread more evenly.[8] The socialism in the programme was primarily a sop to the masses, for whom Hitler always had contempt, a way of competing for their favour with the Marxist parties. But it was also a vague symbol of the social equality which the Nazis practised as well as preached. Hitler's main concern was with the four points which stood at the head of the programme and called for self-determination for all men of German blood, annulment of the treaties of Versailles and St Germain, 'living space' for Germany's surplus population, and the exclusion of Jews from civil rights. These formed the theme of most of Hitler's speeches. Social reform was important mainly because it would make more palatable the expansionist foreign policy which was his real aim. In any case, the programme was meant to be a general prospectus, not a precise blueprint to be scrutinised or defended in detail. As the years passed and Hitler's leadership of the party became more firmly established, the party programme meant as much or as little as he intended: the real programme was Hitler. There was no hint in the Twenty-Five Points on how the party proposed to gain power. Hitler despised the Reichstag as a 'talking shop' and no attempt was made at the time by members of the Nazi party to enter it or any of the state parliaments.

Indignation over the peace treaty, political turmoil (the Kapp Putsch) and the industrial unrest continued to favour the growth of the N.S.D.A.P. and similar parties. Hitler's audiences grew in size. They consisted mostly of students, officers, soldiers and businessmen, but, according to some contemporary accounts, did not include many workers.[9] Yet an original list of 193 members has survived showing a fair cross section of the Munich population, with artisans or working-class people forming about a quarter.[10] By the end of 1920 the party had acquired its own newspaper (not yet a daily) the *Völkischer Beobachter*. Its first editor was Dietrich Eckart, a bohemian poet and dramatist, who bought it with the aid of funds supplied from the *Reichswehr* by General von Epp, who was a party member.[11] Eckart not only influenced Hitler's ideas but introduced him to people of stan-

ding in the social and artistic life of Munich whom he would not have
otherwise met, such as Hanfstaengel, the Harvard-educated art publisher, and Frau Bechstein of the well-known piano firm. Thus his
influence widened. Another important development was that of the
S.A. (Storm Troops), a strong-arm squad originally formed to protect
Hitler's meetings and beat up left-wing opponents in the beer hall
brawls which were a common feature of Munich politics. The S.A.
(whose brown shirts, copied from Mussolini's blackshirts, were introduced later) were largely recruited from the Freikorps who in many
ways were their forerunners. They were men who, in the words of
their chronicler Ernst von Salomon, would always have an unbounded
contempt for human life. The first commander of the S.A., Klintsch,
was a serving officer in the army, under whose orders it came for
military purposes. The *Reichswehr* regarded the S.A. as a useful
auxiliary force, especially after the Bavarian *Einwohnerwehr* (Home
Guard) was dissolved under Allied pressure in June 1921. The S.A. in
fact took part, with other para-military formations, in the defence of
Upper Silesia against the Poles. The man who more than any other
was responsible for launching and sustaining the S.A. was Captain
Röhm, a staff officer with Epp, who, having joined the N.S.D.A.P. at
an early date, placed his considerable organisational talents at Hitler's
disposal, and found the money and weapons for training the force.
Heiden, one of Hitler's earliest biographers, described Röhm as the
'all-powerful liaison man' between the S.A. and the army. Hitler thus
owed much of his early success to Röhm, though this did not prevent
him from murdering Röhm later when the latter had become an embarrassment. Röhm himself embodied the qualities – restlessness, blind
dynamism, brutality, lust for adventure – which characterised the
Freikorps. His was the tragedy of a generation of the uprooted:
men whose sole formative experience had been the war, whose only
wish was to perpetuate the values of the trenches. Without the
existence of thousands like Röhm, ex-soldiers who could not adjust to
the humdrum life of peace, neither the mental and moral climate of
the Weimar Republic nor the rise of National Socialism can be understood.[12]

1922 was a year of varying fortune for Hitler, who after a dramatic
reorganisation of the party in July 1921 became its official leader. As
an Austrian subject he narrowly escaped expulsion from Bavaria by
the Minister of the Interior, Schweyer, who was aware of the dangers
inherent in the Nazi movement. Hitler actually spent a month in
prison that summer, serving a sentence received the year before for
breaking up a meeting of the Bavarian League. On the credit side
the Nazis gained publicity and prestige from taking part in a German

Nationalist rally at Coburg in October – one of their first demonstrations outside Bavaria. The same month brought news of Mussolini's successful 'march on Rome', which Hitler took as a considerable encouragement to his own ambitions. Three months later the French and Belgians marched into the Ruhr and provoked the most serious crisis since Kapp. The Reich government's difficulties were Hitler's opportunities. Far from responding to the Chancellor's appeal for a united front against the French, Hitler continued his personal vendetta against the government in both Berlin and Munich: the civil war had precedence over the national one. His conspicuous refusal to denounce the French at this time has led to the suggestion that he may have been in receipt of French funds, but this is mere speculation, for which there is no solid evidence. Certainly Poincaré was his unwitting ally.

At the end of January 1923 the Nazi party held its first full-scale conference, in the course of which colours were presented to the S.A. after a march through the streets of Munich. It was characteristic of the ambiguous situation that the Bavarian government wished to ban the public ceremony, which was illegal under the state of emergency proclaimed shortly before, but was dissuaded from doing so by Hitler's friends in the *Reichswehr*, who foresaw that the S.A. might prove useful in case a policy of active resistance was adopted in the Ruhr.[13] Encouraged by this success, Hitler proceeded to a further trial of strength with the Bavarian government. On 1 May, Labour Day, the trade unions were, as usual, to march through the streets in a peaceful demonstration. Hitler, having tried and failed to get the government to ban the march, decided to use the S.A. to break it up by force. Arms for the purpose were lent by the army, whose barracks were conveniently close. Although the Nazis failed to prevent the May Day rally, Hitler and his friends had been guilty of a breach of the peace. There was plenty of evidence had the government wished to convict him. Plans for prosecution were considered but not proceeded with: Gürtner, the Bavarian Minister of Justice, was a German nationalist who looked favourably on Hitler, and later as Reich Minister of Justice was to shield him on other occasions. (Earlier Pöhner, the chief of police in Munich, had made no secret of his sympathy for the Nazis.) With the backing of such men and of Lossow, the *Reichswehr* commander in Bavaria, it was not difficult for Hitler to defy the civil authorities with impunity, though Röhm had to resign from the army. How far the Bavarian government's own aspirations coincided with Hitler's was to be shown by the events of 1923.

Ever since the Socialists left the Bavarian cabinet after the Kapp Putsch, Bavaria and the Reich had been on a collision course.

Ostensibly the differences arose from conflicting interpretations of the Weimar constitution. Having lost some of their cherished rights in 1919, the Bavarians clung all the more closely to those that remained. But the real issue was political not legal. The Reich government was republican and democratic. That of Bavaria was authoritarian with strong monarchist leanings. It tried in vain to keep the *Einwohner-wehr*, and rejected the law for the protection of the constitution passed by the Reichstag after the assassination of Rathenau. A compromise was eventually reached whereby the implementation of the law was left to the Bavarians. Ironically it was over this that the Bavarian Minister of Justice resigned, Gürtner being his successor. Thus Bavaria's stand in favour of its historic independence played straight into the hands of the Nationalists and Nazis, who enjoyed a protection denied to them elsewhere. Hitler himself was quite indifferent to Bavarian grievances, which were useful to him only so far as they weakened the authority and popularity of the regime in Berlin. He wished to gain power in Bavaria as a stepping-stone to power over the whole of Germany.

The survival of the Republic appeared very doubtful in September 1923 when Stresemann was bitterly criticised for calling off passive resistance in the Ruhr and inflation had reached its last and giddiest stage. The Communists were preparing to seize power, and in the Palatinate the French-backed separatist movement was gaining ground. Even the imperturbable Seeckt was thinking in terms of a right-wing dictatorship. A big anti-republican rally was held at Nuremberg on the anniversary of the battle of Sedan (2 September) in which the 'patriotic associations' including the S.A. took part. Among the invited guests were generals, admirals and members of former royal houses. Some senior government officials were also present. Altogether about 100,000 people heard Hitler speak.

On the day that Stresemann called off the passive resistance in the Ruhr, Kahr, the former Bavarian Prime Minister and a recognised strong man, was brought back as State Commissioner with dictatorial powers. The Berlin government replied by declaring a state of emergency throughout the Reich and conferring special powers on Lossow to deal with the crisis in Bavaria. Lossow's military superior, Seeckt, was the subject of a vitriolic attack in Hitler's *Völkischer Beobachter*, which suggested that he was planning to make himself a dictator. Gessler, the *Reichswehr* minister in Berlin, ordered the paper to be banned. Kahr refused. Gessler then demanded Lossow's resignation. Kahr rejected this, claiming that Lossow was his subordinate. There was now an open breach between the two governments. With many other problems on its hands, the Reich cabinet was unwilling, and perhaps unable, to take a firm line with the rebellious Bavarians. In Munich the 'patriotic associations', impatient for action, were talking of a seizure of power in Bavaria that would be the prelude to a similar move in Berlin, where they would instal their own kind of regime, much more extreme than anything envisaged by Seeckt or even by Kahr. On 24 October Lossow told the patriotic associations that they could expect to march on Berlin in three weeks.[14] But Kahr was urged by Seeckt to show restraint and not to intervene in Saxony and Thuringia, where a Socialist-Communist coalition had come to power. The fear in Berlin was that the Bavarian *Reichswehr* and 'patriots' would occupy Saxony and Thuringia on their way north to Prussia. The central government's intervention in the two 'red' provinces forestalled such a step. While Kahr and Lossow waited for Berlin's next move against Bavaria, Hitler, encouraged by Ludendorff, decided to strike. The date chosen was 9 November, fifth anniversary of the detested revolution of 1918 and the day after an important patriotic gathering which Kahr was to address.

The story of the abortive Munich Putsch, which first brought Hitler into the headlines of the world's press, is well-known and can be briefly summarised. A large patriotic gathering met in the *Bürger-bräukeller* on the evening of 8 November to hear Kahr speak. The Bavarian Prime Minister, the police chief (Colonel von Seisser) and other members of the government and officials were present. In the middle of the proceedings Hitler, whose storm-troops had surrounded the hall, burst in, brandishing a revolver. Mounting the rostrum, he fired shots at the ceiling and announced that the governments in Munich and Berlin had been overthrown and that a new 'National Republic' was being formed. In Bavaria he himself would lead the new regime, with Kahr as Regent and Pöhner as Prime Minister. At Reich level Ludendorff was to be given command of the army with Lossow as Minister of Defence and Seisser as Minister of Police. Temporarily stunned by this irruption, Kahr, Lossow and Seisser (the 'triumvirate') retired to a backroom where they agreed, at pistol point, to Hitler's plans. In the meantime Ludendorff, still a legendary figure, arrived on the scene and, overcoming his surprise, gave Hitler his backing. News of the Putsch was flashed to all wireless stations and appeared in the early morning edition of the Munich newspapers. But in the course of the night the 'triumvirate', having returned to their offices and learnt that their colleagues were opposed to the whole enterprise, decided not to take any further part in it. News that Seeckt had been given plenary powers by the Reich government influenced their decision. Though Röhm occupied Army Headquarters in Munich, most public buildings remained in the hands of the government. By midday the press carried the news that the Putsch had failed. Ludendorff, apparently unaware of this, and convinced that the army would not oppose a march on Berlin, persuaded Hitler to hold a demonstration in Munich to rally support. On its way to the Ministry of War in the centre of Munich the procession of 2,000–3,000 Nazis found the way blocked by police. A shot was fired, followed by a hail of bullets, and altogether 19 people (16 Nazis and 3 policemen) lost their lives. Ludendorff, marching at the head of the column, was not fired on, but was taken prisoner. Hitler, dragged to the ground when the man next to him was killed, fell and broke a bone in his shoulder. He fled and was captured two days later. Among the other wounded was Göring, the former air ace who had commanded the S.A. since March 1923. He escaped to Austria. Röhm at Army H.Q. capitulated.

In a situation full of ambiguities the most intriguing question was the extent to which Kahr and Lossow were accomplices with Hitler up to their last minute withdrawal. They had acted unconstitutionally towards the Reich government, and their hesitations about a march on Berlin were purely tactical, though the kind of dictatorship they wanted would not have satisfied Hitler. Lossow declared that he would march if he had a 51 per cent chance of success, and Kahr's attitude, though more cautious, was basically similar.[15] Although the two men were not involved in the charge of high treason that faced Hitler, they were both discredited. They had failed to stop Hitler's obvious preparations for the Putsch, and the assertion that their temporary assent to Hitler's plans was only the result of duress was widely disbelieved. Kahr resigned, and Lossow, who had disobeyed his military superiors before the Putsch, was dismissed. Kahr's belief that he could make use of Hitler without destroying his own position was typical of the approach of many conservatives. Nine years later Papen was to make a similar mistake, with more serious consequences. Kahr was to pay for his 'treachery' with his life in the blood purge of June 1934.

The trial of the accused Nazis took place in February and March 1924. Hitler accepted responsibility for what had happened, thus attracting the limelight to himself, but he also drew attention to the share of Kahr, Lossow and Seisser, thus embarrassing the judges and influencing them in favour of leniency. In defending himself he seized the opportunity to make political speeches which were listened to respectfully by a court whose members were openly biased in his favour. His rousing oratory, defiant, not apologetic, was addressed to a wider audience:

The army we have formed is growing from day to day . . . I nurse the proud hope that one day the hour will come when these rough companies will grow to battalions, the battalions to regiments, the regiments to divisions, when the old cockade will be taken from the mud, when the old flags will wave again, when there will be a reconciliation at that last great divine judgement which we are prepared to face . . . For it is not you, gentlemen, who will pass judgement on us. That judgement is spoken by the eternal court of history . . . You may pronounce us guilty a thousand times over, but the goddess of the eternal court of history will smile and tear to shreds the brief of the State Prosecutor and the sentence of this court. For she acquits us.[16]

Though Hitler was not acquitted by the court which gave him such a sympathetic hearing, its sentence of five years' detention was in the circumstances mild enough; and in the event he served only nine months of it. Even the *Bayerischer Kurier* complained of the one-sidedness of the trial and described the day on which sentence was passed as a black day for Bavarian justice.[17] In prison Hitler was treated almost as an honoured guest, and given every facility for writing his memoirs. Without the nine months in Landsberg fortress, the world might never have had *Mein Kampf*. Thus Hitler used the failure of his Putsch to lay the foundations of later success.

A new phase began with Hitler's release from goal in December 1924. One of his first acts was to assure the Bavarian Prime Minister, Held, of his peaceful intentions, a gesture signifying the abandonment of violent tactics. The reward was not long in coming: in February 1925 the ban on the N.S.D.A.P., imposed after the events of November 1923, was lifted. The party was to operate within the framework of the constitution. This had two main implications. The first was that the S.A., hitherto a dependency of the *Reichswehr*, now became an integral part of the party. Röhm, who disagreed with the new policy, resigned and departed for South America. The S.A. was reorganised under a new commander, a former Freikorps man named Pfeffer von Salomon. The other change was the decision to stand for parliament, which was taken by Hitler with considerable reluctance and against the wishes of many of his followers. The years 1925-6 were marked by a general debate inside and on the fringes of the party on aims and methods. Gregor Strasser, the most influential man in the N.S.D.A.P. after Hitler and Gauleiter of Lower Bavaria, had opened a headquarters at Elberfeld in Westphalia which was drawing support from industrial workers and youthful elements who, like Strasser himself, took the socialism in the official programme seriously.[18] They wished to divide up the large estates, especially those east of the river Elbe, and to nationalise the shares of large industrial firms. In foreign policy the left-wing Nazi supporters favoured an alliance with Soviet Russia against the capitalist West – a policy advocated since 1919 by the group of Russian-orientated nationalists known as National Bolsheviks. There were, indeed, some Bolshevik leaders who saw the Nazis as a left-wing party and wished to go half way to meet them: Radek in 1923 had spoken in favour of a Communist-Nazi alliance against the French and praised the spirit of the S.A. But Hitler, influenced by the rabidly anti-Bolshevik Rosenberg, a Baltic German refugee who was the party's leading ideologist, insisted that 'Marxism' was the main enemy, whether in its virulently Leninist form as in Russia or in the mildly reformist S.P.D. Hitler was successful in imposing his authority and views on his colleagues, and among those who came over to his side was Goebbels, hitherto a radical, but, like many others, primarily an opportunist. Though the disgruntled radicals remained within the party, giving rise to later revolts that culminated in the alleged Röhm plot of 1934, it was becoming plain that existing institutions, including capitalism, had little to fear from Nazism.[19] In 1926 Hitler began a series of addresses to employers and businessmen aimed at winning recognition as well as financial support.[20]

The years 1925-9 are usually described as the quiet period of the Nazi movement as they were of the Weimar Republic. Hitler himself was banned from public speaking in Bavaria until 1928, in Prussia until 1929. Yet despite this major handicap, and the absence of conditions favourable to right-wing extremism the party grew. Membership (55,000 at the time of the 1923 Putsch) rose from 27,000 in 1925 to 109,000 in 1928 and 210,000 in March 1930. For the first time the Nazis began to gain ground in North Germany, where Gregor Strasser was the main representative. But Strasser was soon overshadowed by the man who in 1925 became his private secretary, Joseph Goebbels, and went on to become a propagandist of genius. A Rhineland journalist, of a Catholic lower-middle-class family, Goebbels combined mental and literary gifts with a mellifluous voice and an oratorical skill which made him a much more attractive speaker than Hitler.

Goebbels was the ablest and most intelligent of the Nazi leaders, a cynic among the credulous, an intellectual with a Latin lucidity among the half-educated cranks and crude practitioners of violence.[21] He was an interesting psychological type, a complex personality whose extreme malevolence can hardly be accounted for by physical deformity or frustrated ambition. Dwarfish in size, Goebbels walked with a limp because on one leg, which was shorter than the other, he wore a surgical boot. Yet this handicap did not debar him from a successful career at school or from winning a scholarship to Heidelberg University (where he sat at the feet of the distinguished Jewish professor Gundolf), nor did it deprive him of other satisfactions, such as success with women, even if it explains his misanthropy and somewhat precocious mental development. Like many another aspiring author (not only in the Weimar Republic) he spent several years writing unperformed plays and unpublished articles: on one occasion he applied for but failed to get a job on the liberal *Berliner Tageblatt*, whose editor was a Jew. Goebbels was an angry young man who started on the political left and might just as easily have become as rabid a Communist as he was a Nazi. This early radicalism never completely left him, and it was characteristic that he continued to take an interest in the modern paintings that Hitler found decadent. Had his literary talents been greater, he might have become one of the Republic's rebellious journalists, perhaps a sort of Tucholsky of the right. In the event he found his métier in propaganda, an art in which he excelled. He had a strong political sense and a flair for exploiting new techniques. It was he who persuaded Hitler to use an aeroplane in his whirlwind presidential campaign in 1932, and he brilliantly exploited the mass media in the service of the party. Superficially fanatical, he remained at heart detached, watching public reactions like an impresario. He was the Iago of the Nazi movement, a sophisticated manipulator whose contempt for humanity equalled Hitler's. His anti-semitism has been described as half pathologically genuine and half calculated, and if one can imagine Hitler abandoning anti-semitism, Goebbels would have dropped it without hesitation.[22] In 1927 Goebbels started a daily newspaper in Berlin, *Der Angriff*, which was the North German counterpart of the Munich *Völkischer Beobachter*. His first great test came when he was made Gauleiter (party chief) in Berlin. It was a tough assignment, for Berlin, with its huge working-class population, was 'red', though divided between Communists and Social Democrats. As a man who loved to shock the bourgeoisie, Goebbels was good at making anti-capitalist speeches, and he borrowed the methods of his Marxist opponents such as the use of party cells in factories to break the monopoly of the left. The S.A. courageously made provocative marches through solidly proletarian districts such as Wedding and Neukölln to show the swastika. In 1929 Goebbels was promoted to be propaganda chief of the N.S.D.A.P. Together with 11 other Nazis he was elected to the Reichstag in the general election of 1928. He did not even bother to disguise the fact that he was using the democratic constitution in order to destroy it. 'We come as enemies! Like the wolf tearing into the flock of sheep, that is how we come' he wrote in an article published on 30 April 1928.

In 1929 events began to move in the Nazis' favour. Hugenberg, the new leader of the Nationalist party, invited Hitler to join him in a nation-wide campaign against the Young Plan. Thanks to his dominating position in the press and film world Hugenberg was able to give the Nazi party more influence than it had ever had before. Though the campaign failed, it was excellent publicity for Hitler, who gained respectability by association with an established patriotic party that had strong middle-class backing. The Nazi vote rose in state elections, especially in country districts, and in 1930 for the first time a Nazi parliamentarian became a minister (Frick in Thuringia). Stresemann's death weakened the forces of moderation, and the economic depression was grist to Hitler's mill. The Reichstag election of September 1930 boosted the number of Nazis in the chamber from a mere 12 to 107; overnight they became the second largest political party. Their gains were largely at the expense of the Nationalists, whose tactics had boomeranged. The chancellorship appeared almost within Hitler's grasp. In October 1931, at his first meeting with President Hindenburg he asked for it and was given a brusque refusal. But henceforth no government of the right − and given the hostility between S.P.D. and K.P.D., no government of the left was a practical possibility − could ignore a party as large as Hitler's. In the 1932 presidential election and the following Reichstag election in July the Nazis gained 37 per cent of the total vote. After Papen and Schleicher had both failed to stay in power because the basis of their support was too narrow, Hitler had his chance. Hindenburg, under the influence of the plausible Papen, swallowed his objection to the 'Bohemian corporal' and allowed him to become Chancellor under safeguards which soon proved worthless. It is often said that Hitler came to power legally. This is true in a formal sense. It is not the whole truth. The Weimar constitution had already been violated in spirit by the virtual supersession of the Reichstag for nearly three years and the excessive use of Emergency Decrees (60 were issued in 1932 compared with 5 laws).[28] Secondly, Papen's dismissal of the Socialist ministers in Prussia in July 1932 was unconstitutional in the letter as well as in the spirit. Thirdly, by 1932 Germany had become a country in which intimidation was a normal occurrence and political murder a weekly if not a daily event. In such an atmosphere the Nazis had an advantage which the moderate parties lacked. Hitler himself declared many times before 30 January 1933 that if his party won the struggle for power it would be thanks to the S.A.

'Germany, wake up!'

'No need to shout so loud, you young people! I haven't been able to sleep
since 1914.' (The average German citizen is unimpressed by the propaganda of Hitler's storm troops.)

(*Simplicissimus*, 1932)

By 1930 the S.A. had grown to a force of about 100,000. Röhm was recalled from South America to be its commander. With unemployed men flocking to join it the number rose by 1933 to about 300,000. By June 1934 it was over four million. The storm-troopers in their brown shirts with swastika armbands were a familiar sight in every German town, where they marched with huge swastika banners preceded by bands, bawling out their songs, and intimidating their opponents. At Nazi meetings they set the stage and created the atmosphere. The hypnotic rhythm of marching feet and the intoxicating blare of martial music roused the emotions of the audience long before the speeches began. The excitement when Hitler entered the hall where he was to speak was extraordinary. Suddenly, after hours of mounting tension, the applause would rise to a crescendo of *Sieg Heils*, the lights would go out, and a hush would fall. Then, brilliantly picked out by searchlights against a wall of darkness, a small but familiar figure would pour out his impassioned oratory, and the harsh, vibrant voice would preach the by now familiar gospel of salvation from the twin evils of Marxism and Versailles. The key to Hitler's success as a speaker was his *rapport* with the audience rather than what he said.[24] If the S.A. was the mass movement, who filled the streets and fought the reds, the élite force was the S.S. The S.S., who wore black shirts, began in 1923 as Hitler's personal bodyguard. Revived with the party in 1925, the S.S. as late as 1929 consisted of only 280 men.[25] But in that year an otherwise undistinguished poultry farmer named Heinrich Himmler became its commander with the title of *Reichsführer*. He greatly enlarged the S.S., which by January 1933 had 52,000 members. Nominally the S.S. was still subordinate to the S.A., but was developing into its most dangerous rival, as the events of June 1934 were to show. An offshoot of the S.S. was the Security Service (*Sicherheitsdienst*) whose head, an ex-naval officer named Heydrich, was to rival Himmler in his fanatical cruelty in days to come. Once Hitler was in power, these forces were able to use his authority to establish a reign of terror.

By the time of Hitler's chancellorship the Nazis had developed a whole network of formations which enabled them to influence every aspect of German life. Young people were trained and indoctrinated from the age of six in the Hitler Youth (for boys) and *Bund Deutscher Mädchen* (for girls). Having absorbed most of the pre-1933 youth organisations, the Hitler Youth by the beginning of 1934 had risen to a total of 3·6 million. There were associations of Nazi doctors, lawyers, teachers and women. Special attention had been paid to farmers, and the main farmers' organisation, the *Reichslandbund*, had been virtually taken over by the N.S.D.A.P. It was not difficult for the

N.S.D.A.P. to infiltrate and control a white-collar union such as the National Association of Commercial Employees or D.H.V. More remarkable was the success of the party in penetrating the ranks of the workers and founding their own trade union, the N.S.B.O., which by January 1933 had almost a million members.[26] Thus the socialist unions were being challenged on their own ground. The other political parties had similar organisations: the Centre its *People's League for Catholic Germany*, its youth groups and trade unions; both Social Democrats and Communists a whole range of welfare, sporting and educational bodies, such as the Socialist *Workers' Youth* or the Communist *Rote Hilfe*. Most parties had para-military organisations, each of which paraded in a kind of uniform: the republicans their *Reichsbanner*, the Communists their *Red Front*. The *Reichsbanner* had little training and was inclined to be pacifist in outlook, so that in 1931 an attempt was made to produce a reorganised and more militant republican defence force known as the Iron Front. But it proved no match for the S.A. When Hitler became Chancellor the number of Nazi associations multiplied, and by 1945 there were over fifty of various kinds, ranging from the party itself (about 8 million members was the peak figure) to the Association of German Hunters.

(ii) THE NAZI REVOLUTION

At the trial of young army officers charged with high treason on account of their Nazi activities in October 1930, Hitler, who gave evidence, told the Supreme Court: 'Once we possess the constitutional right to do so, we shall cast the state in the form which we consider right.'[27] This amounted to an assertion that, though the Nazis intended to come to power legally, when in power they would manipulate the law to suit themselves. This is precisely what happened after 30 January 1933. At first the odds seemed unfavourable to Hitler, who had a share of power, not a monopoly. Only three of the eleven-man cabinet were Nazis: Hitler as Chancellor, Frick as Minister of the Interior, and Göring as Minister without Portfolio. Göring was also Minister of the Interior in Prussia. The other eight ministers belonged to the Nationalist party or the Stahlhelm. Papen reassured one of his friends: 'Don't worry. In two months we'll have pushed Hitler so far into the corner that he'll be squeaking.'[28] The 'containment' of Hitler appeared guaranteed, not only by the cabinet majority, but also by the constitution and the President who had sworn to uphold it. In theory the new government could be defeated in the Reichstag – hence Hitler's determination to dissolve the latter. His aim of eliminating first his enemies and then his unsuspecting allies, and concentrating all power in his own hands, was accomplished within six months. The 42 per cent or so of the electorate represented by the government had to be turned into a working majority. Hitler made sure that, before the election, he had enough of the resources of the state – control of the police, influence over the press and broadcasting – to bring about the desired result. He also continued to use the Emergency Decrees by which Germany had been governed since 1931. Clause 48 of the constitution, originally intended to save democracy in a crisis, became the means of its destruction. Hitler on taking office actually declared that his aim was to return to normal legislation through the Reichstag. What he destroyed was not parliamentary government but the rule of law.

It was not difficult to persuade Hindenburg to dissolve the Reichstag once Hugenberg had withdrawn his objections in return for a promise that, however the election turned out, his own place in the cabinet was safe. This was one of many promises to be broken by Hitler after it had served his purpose. The Nazi propaganda machine which, under the direction of Goebbels, had made possible Hitler's past success, again went into top gear, rousing, cajoling and bamboozling the electorate. Less than a week after the formation of the new government an Emergency Decree 'for the protection of the German people', which significantly had been drafted in Schleicher's time, authorised the Minister of the Interior (Frick) and the Police (in Prussia under Göring) to ban all public meetings and publications dangerous to security. It was followed almost immediately by another Emergency Decree which completed the destruction of Prussian independence begun by Papen's coup of July 1932, and appointed Papen Special Commissioner for Prussia. In practice this power was exercised by Göring, soon (11 April) to become Prussian Prime Minister. Göring dismissed republican police officials and replaced them with Nazis. The Prussian civil service was similarly purged. 40,000 S.A. and S.S. men were drafted into the police as auxiliaries, and the force was ordered to use its firearms ruthlessly in case of resistance. The Nazis were now in a position to use governmental authority and their own physical force to terrorise their opponents. Hitler claimed to be saving Germany from communism. The event which made his claim plausible was the Reichstag fire.

The Communists' reaction to Hitler's chancellorship was verbal defiance and an appeal for a general strike, but the trade unions did not respond. The Social Democrats declared that Red Berlin would never become the capital of a Fascist Reich, but even now common danger could not force the two left-wing parties to co-operate. Twice in February police raided the K.P.D. headquarters in Berlin, but found little incriminating evidence, though the files they confiscated helped them to identify and shortly afterwards seize leading party members. Then on 27 February a young Dutch psychopath named van der Lubbe set fire to the Reichstag. The Nazis claimed that van der Lubbe, who was a communist with anarchist leanings, had been instigated by the German Communist party in what was to be the signal for a general rising. In view of the rapid build-up of intimidation by the Nazis and their influence over the news media, it was a brave man who rejected this explanation of the origin of the fire, especially as the obvious culprit was wrongly assumed to be incapable of starting it on his own. Outside Germany the extraordinary propaganda value of the fire to the Nazis, occurring as it did just before a vital general election, seemed proof enough that they must have been its authors. This view, confirmed by a 'trial' held in London a few months later, was generally accepted in Germany after the Second World War. Then in 1962 Fritz Tobias, a journalist who carried out extensive research into the fire, wrote a book proving that it too was a myth and that van der Lubbe had in fact set fire to the Reichstag without help from the Nazis or anyone else.[29] Though incomplete and conflicting evidence leaves many questions unanswered, the political significance of the affair is not in doubt. While Hitler and his colleagues were genuinely surprised by the fire, they at once showed diabolical skill in exploiting the mood of alarm and indignation. All-out measures against the 'red peril' now seemed justified. There was little general realisation at the time that despite its six million voters and militant language the German Communist party was really an impotent giant. It was immediately outlawed and 4,000 of its leaders were arrested and interned. A few managed to emigrate or go into hiding in Germany; among the latter was Walther Ulbricht, who escaped abroad later. Communist buildings were seized and newspapers banned. In the general onslaught against Marxists, left-wing Catholics as well as Socialists were vilified and attacked. A new Emergency Decree authorised the police to arrest anyone, search his house and confiscate his possessions. The Reich government was also empowered to take over any state government deemed incapable of maintaining public order. Germany had become a police state. The weapon sanctioned for use against the Communists was soon to be turned against anyone who was not a National Socialist. In this atmosphere of panic the German people went to the polls in what was to be the last general election for thirteen years. The crisis sparked off by the Reichstag fire marks the emergence of Hitler as a 'power-intoxicated' dictator.

The Nationalist and Stahlhelm leaders, Hugenberg and Düsterberg, joined Papen in a so-called Black-White-Red Fighting Front which invoked the name and prestige of Hindenburg, who had again become the symbol of the right. The Nazis used their alliance with these much decried reactionaries to proclaim a common patriotic platform which it was the duty of all right-thinking Germans to support. Despite the deluge of propaganda and an exceptionally heavy poll, the government parties gained only a bare majority, 51.8 per cent, of which the Nazi share was 43.9 per cent. Though narrow, this margin of victory was enough. In the new Reichstag the Nazis with 287 seats instead of 207 actually had a working majority because the Communists, who in spite of persecution had won 81 seats, were debarred from sitting. Some of the Social Democrats had also been arrested or were too scared to attend. The electorate was divided into two almost equal halves between the Nazis and Nationalists on the one side and all the other parties on the other. In practice the advantage lay with the Nazis, since, even had the Communists not been proscribed, a working alliance between them and the democratic parties was hardly conceivable. Still, it was significant that not all Goebbels' frenzied efforts had succeeded in wringing a majority from an electorate deafened by propaganda but still remarkably independent in the polling booth.

But Goebbels (appointed Minister of Propaganda and Public Enlightenment on 13 March) knew how to use a unique opportunity presented by the opening of the new Reichstag at Potsdam on 21 March. It was a scene which dramatically symbolised the arrival of the Nazi state, known henceforth as the Third Reich – a title which established it as the successor of the Second Empire of still glorious memory and, more remotely, of the medieval Empire founded by Charlemagne. At a brilliantly stage-managed ceremony in the Potsdam garrison church, above the grave of Frederick the Great and in the presence of a distinguished congregation including the ex-Crown Prince, generals and ambassadors, Hindenburg and Hitler made speeches and solemnly shook hands. The unlamented Weimar Republic was officially dead and buried. The guardians of the Prussian tradition – the royal house, the army, the Lutheran Church, the President – had given their blessings to the upstart from the back streets of Vienna who now ruled in Berlin as their recognised heir. No doubt Hindenburg, too old to grasp the full significance of the revolution to which he had given his approval, saw the Nazi regime as a half-way house to a restored monarchy, though he can have had few illusions about that by the time of his death a year later. But for millions of Germans the demagogic outsider, who still looked ill at ease in the conventional top hot and morning coat, had become a respectable and even dignified figure. It was also a brilliant military occasion. In the bright spring sunshine bands played and uniforms glittered as thousands of *Reichswehr* and Stahlhelm, S.A. and S.S. marched through swastika-bedecked streets to the cheers of crowds which had not seen such a colourful parade since the fall of the Empire. Foreigners too were impressed. Throughout Germany, as Hitler boasted, order reigned. On the surface unity and harmony were complete. Apart from attacks on Jews and other known non-Nazis, violence had been banished to the concentration camps and improvised prisons (such as the Columbia House in the middle of Berlin) where tens of thousands of political prisoners were held by the S.A. and S.S. and interrogated, often under torture. A dozen or so camps, including the notorious Oranienburg and Dachau, were set up at this time, and Frick declared on 8 March that 100,000 enemies of the regime had been arrested.[30] When the new Reichstag met at the Kroll Opera House in Berlin it was surrounded by men in unifrom and looked like a barracks. Hitler himself appeared in the brown shirt of the S.A.

Two days later Hitler took advantage of the prevailing mood to present the Reichstag with an Enabling Bill. This measure, cynically described as 'for the relief of people and Reich', authorised the government to pass laws without the Reichstag. It thus made any fresh issue of Emergency Decrees unnecessary. As an amendment to the constitution (really its annulment) it needed a two-thirds majority. To be sure of this, Hitler had to buy off opposition. The key party was the Centre, for the Socialists were unlikely to yield. Hitler had never disguised his dislike of political Catholicism; and the new leader of the Centre, Monsignor Kaas, was more interested in the rights of the Church than in the fate of his party, though in the view of many Catholics the one depended on the other. Hitler made vague but reassuring promises to both churches which disposed them to a favourable attitude, and he was known to be considering a Concordat with the Pope. A minority in the Centre, headed by Brüning, saw the danger of accepting the Enabling Bill and wished to oppose it, but was overruled. The smaller parties, also divided and aware of their impotence, resignedly voted, like the Centre, for the bill. Heuss, the future West German President, tried to persuade the handful of State party deputies (formerly Democrats) to make a stand, but he too failed to convince his colleagues. The bill contained certain safeguards, but there was no guarantee that Hitler would observe them if it suited him not to. The only party which voted against the Enabling Bill was the Social Democrats, for whom Otto Wels made a defiant and courageous speech. It was a belated gesture by a party which even after 30 January had seen in Hugenberg, the 'capitalist', a greater danger than Hitler. In passing the bill the Reichstag was giving up its powers and accepting its future role of a rubber stamp. The parties were signing their own death warrants. Had the Centre opposed the bill, Hitler would have lacked his two-thirds majority; and while he would certainly have forced the bill through by one means or another, a reaction of this kind would have done something to bolster the sagging morale of the non-Nazi half of the population and have invalidated Hitler's claim to represent the whole German people.

Hitler's pledge to observe state rights had already been broken by Emergency Decree. He now went a step further. On the pretext of suppressing disorder (in fact fomented by the Nazis themselves) he appointed Reich Commissioners in all states except Prussia (where the police had already been nazified by Göring). In January only four of Germany's twenty-one states had Nazi governments. By April all had. The last state to submit was, appropriately, Bavaria, where Hitler's old patron, General von Epp, now chief of police, seized power from the Bavarian People's party. And just as the Reich government no longer depended on the Reichstag, so the state governments ceased to depend on their *Landtage*. The process of centralisation was completed by a law passed early in 1934 which abolished all state rights and parliaments. Already in the spring of 1933 special governors (often party officials) using the powers already exercised by the Reich Commissioners had been set up to enforce the subordination of the states to the capital. In Prussia Gauleiters or S.A. leaders became provincial governors. Nazi mayors took power in all the larger towns. The elective principle was abandoned in favour of the leadership principle propounded in *Mein Kampf*. Later, judges as well as civil servants had to swear an oath of loyalty to Hitler. Thus a combination of legality, pseudo-legality and physical force had transformed the face of Germany.

There was now no place for any parties except the N.S.D.A.P., and their liquidation began. Like the Communists, the Socialists watched helplessly while their leaders were arrested and interned, their offices occupied, their funds seized and their press banned. There was no question of resistance. The moment for that, if it ever existed, had passed, especially for a party like S.P.D. which was wedded to legal methods. Some prominent Socialists escaped abroad, mainly to Prague, where Stampfer, the editor of *Vorwaerts*, set up a *Neuer Vorwaerts* and helped to form a new executive committee. Others stayed in Germany, hoping vainly that in return for good behaviour some kind of constitutional opposition would still be permitted. Some, like Keil of Stuttgart, were content to receive a pension from the Nazi government, others like Schumacher, the future leader, preferred the rigours of a concentration camp to compliance or exile. The S.P.D. made the humiliating concession of resigning from the Second International and most of its members voted for Hitler in the foreign policy debate in the Reichstag on 17 May. None of these gestures turned Hitler's wrath. On 21 June all activities of the S.P.D. ceased to be legal, and soon afterwards the party was formally dissolved.[31] The others followed suit. The Centre, which had preserved its strength and integrity throughout the Republic and had even emerged relatively unscathed from the March election, now went to pieces.[32] Kaas left for Rome to discuss the proposed Concordat and never came back. Brüning, who succeeded him as leader, had more backbone but was powerless. A year later he had to emigrate to save his life. Early in July the Centre and its Bavarian counterpart, the Bavarian People's party, accepted dissolution with a docility which astonished even Hitler.[33] The remaining parties passed through a similar phase of demoralisation and disintegration before they too ceased to exist. Even the Nationalists, with whose aid Hitler had climbed to power, were not spared. Hugenberg resigned, a disillusioned man. On the very first day of the Hitler government he had confessed to a friend: 'Yesterday I committed the worst folly of my life: I became an ally of the greatest demagogue in world history.' His role was now played out.[34] None but Nazis remained in the cabinet. Henceforth Nationalist members of the Reichstag sat as members of the N.S.D.A.P. and the Stahlhelm was virtually absorbed in the S.A. On 7 July Hitler could boast: 'The party has become the state.'[35] The formal unity of party and state was proclaimed by a law passed in December 1933, and was symbolised by the entry of Hess, Hitler's deputy as party leader, into the cabinet.

This unity was not in fact complete. Relations between the party and the state had never been worked out in theory, nor were their respective spheres ever clearly defined. The two power structures remained, with Hitler presiding arbitrarily over both, as he did over the army, though increasingly the state became an executive machine of the N.S.D.A.P. Despite the purge of civil servants obnoxious to the Nazis, some sectors of the public service, notably the Foreign Ministry and the higher ranks of the army, remained comparatively immune from or even opposed to Nazi influence. But these too were in time brought under control. Sometimes party organisations, like the *Büro Ribbentrop*, set themselves up as rivals to state departments. Germany was divided into 38 *Gaue* (districts), a total which rose to 45 as a result of annexations before and during the war. Sometimes the same man was state or provincial governor and regional party boss

(*Gauleiter*). Nazis of long standing ('old fighters') were rewarded
with responsible posts in central and local government, while many
established bureaucrats joined the party to further their careers. By
1937 86 per cent of all officials in Prussia, and 63 per cent of those
elsewhere, belonged to the N.S.D.A.P.[36] By 1938 non-Nazis like
Schacht, the Minister of Economics, and Neurath, the Foreign
Minister, had been displaced from key positions in favour of party
favourites. Yet within the party, behind the façade of total conformity,
fierce conflict remained. Among leading Nazis the struggle for power
or for influence over the Führer – often the same thing – led to bitter
rivalry: Himmler against Röhm, Rosenberg against Goebbels, Göring
against the generals, the generals against the Ministry of Economics,
later Speer against Göring, Himmler against Bormann, Speer against
Sauckel, to mention only some of the more important. Underlying
these personal animosities lay a basic feud between the party ideolo-
gists (who still took seriously the revolutionary slogans of the 1920s)
and the pragmatists or technocrats (who wanted efficiency and a quiet
life). The jealousies tended to become fiercer with the passing of time
and as the conquest of much of Europe offered new opportunities for
empire-building. During the war the S.S., both through its hold on
the police and as a result of its power in the occupied countries,
became the most formidable of the contending forces within the
Reich. So far from the dictatorship imposing unity, it is best described
in the words of a German journalist at the time as a system of
'authoritarian anarchy'.[37] Certainly the totalitarianism of Nazi Germany was far from complete by comparison with other models, notably
the Soviet Union. It depended on the will of one man, who was
arbitrary, moody and often inconsistent. He made no attempt to
resolve the discords among his immediate followers, probably seeing
in them the best guarantee of his own continued supremacy.

Like the parties, the trade unions too surrendered without a
struggle. The depression had depleted their numbers (though they
still had four million members), reduced their funds and lowered their
morale. Their leaders realised that, once Hitler had come to power
legally, it was too late for any organised resistance. But by co-operating
with the new regime the unions hoped to avert the worst. After the
election of 5 March the chairman of the largest trade union organisation, the A.D.G.B., wrote to Hitler assuring him that the unions
would not cause him any trouble.[38] In a gesture of appeasement the
A.D.G.B. cut its traditional links with the S.P.D. and declared its
political neutrality. But neutrality did not satisfy Hitler. Early in April
the union leaders began to negotiate for a merger of all trade unions –
Christian and liberal as well as socialist – under Nazi leadership, and

actually dismissed those of their colleagues who were unacceptable to the new regime.[39] On 1 May 1933 the former Social Democratic unions took part in the traditional Labour Day parade which now for the first time was taken over by the Nazis and made into a national festival under the sign of the swastika. The demonstration was meant to illustrate the new unity between the party and organised labour, just as the Day of Potsdam illustrated its unity with Old Prussia. But submissiveness failed to save the unions, who stood by passively while next day their premises and their assets were confiscated. The destruction of the unions was breath-taking in its audacity and simplicity. 'German syndicalism', wrote a foreign observer, 'disappeared as though through a trap-door.'[40] With the working-class organisations dissolved, the government announced the setting up of a Labour Front to which all engaged in industry and trade, employers and workpeople, would belong. It would symbolise the classless society, the *Volksgemeinschaft*. The Labour Front was meant to signify the end of the class war, but also to be an agent of the National Socialist party and a means of popular indoctrination.

Thus all the safeguards which, it had been assumed, would hold Hitler in check had proved worthless. The Reichstag and the parties had given up without a struggle. The President, whose political grasp, never very strong, was now intercepted by periods of blankness, had failed to preserve the rule of law, or even the decencies of civilised life.[41] Hindenburg had always leaned heavily on his advisers: Ludendorff during the war, Groener at the time of revolution, Papen in the last months of Weimar, now his secretary Meissner and his son Oskar. It seems that little or nothing was done to alert the old man – lethargic by nature, and now with his faculties failing – to the dangers inherent in Hitler's assumption of unprecedented power. The *Reichsrat*, the senior legislative body with the special duty of safeguarding state rights, and the Supreme Court, arbiter of the constitution, had both allowed themselves to be brushed aside. Papen, who at first had been present at Hitler's meetings with Hindenburg at the latter's wish, ceased to attend, and indeed was quite powerless to resist the Nazi onslaught. Hardly a voice or hand was raised when thousands of Jews, socialists, pacifists, liberals and others were dismissed from the civil service, the universities and schools, the professions of law, medicine and journalism, from theatres and orchestras, when Jewish shops were boycotted and their owners publicly humiliated and robbed, when innocent people were assaulted by the S.A., arrested and held without trial. The lawyers, hoping, like so many others, to avert the worst by meeting Hitler halfway, acquiesced in the distortion of the law to justify Nazi malpractices and had to accept the setting up of special

courts to try political offenders. The new law of treason was drafted
in such a way as to make it an offence to pass on any information
which the government considered against the public interest, and the
number of prosecutions for high treason rose from 268 in 1932 to over
11,000 in 1933, of which over 9,500 ended in sentences.[42] Despite the
special courts for political offenders the Gestapo did not hesitate to
arrest and intern people on its own authority.

The absence of public reaction to such lawlessness and inhumanity
would be easier to account for if the anti-Nazi vote had not been so
large in the March general election. Half of the population had
apparently capitulated almost overnight. Was this result due to lack
of foresight, to opportunism, cowardice or self-deception? Was it a
case of mass suggestion or public hysteria under the impact of a
propaganda campaign of unprecedented intensity? No doubt all these
factors were involved. The readiness with which the bulk of the German people adjusted themselves to Hitler's dictatorship suggests a deeper
explanation than mere susceptibility to propaganda or even intimidation. It indicates a psychological predisposition that was more than willing to respond to the highly emotional appeal of a charismatic leader.[43]
The national revival proclaimed by the Nazis produced a mood like that
engendered by the Kaiser's one nation speech at the beginning of the
First World War. By identifying National Socialism with Germany
Hitler could call on people's deepest loyalties, could present himself as
the embodiment of authority and unity as none of the republican
leaders had been able to do: Hindenburg, the surrogate emperor, was
too old and too out of touch to rouse any enthusiasm among the young.
For the older generation it was almost as if the days of the monarchy
had returned – yet a monarchy with a difference. There had been
nothing in the days of the Hohenzollerns to match the enthusiasm, the
egalitarian togetherness of the Nuremberg party rallies. Germans are an
idealistic people, and Hitler offered them a cause which was also a
cure. The jobless, the uprooted, those to whom Weimar had become
synonymous with despair, responded. Millions were willing to support
any government that would give them work and hope for the future:
constitutional safeguards meant little or nothing to them. In his *Song
of the S.A. Man* Brecht expresses the reactions of many an unemployed man who fell in behind Hitler because he was willing to go
anywhere to escape from his miserable lot.[44]

> My belly rumbled with hunger,
> I fainted and went to bed,
> Then I heard in my ears a shouting –
> 'Germany, awake!', it said.

And I saw so many marching
To the Third Reich, they cried;
I had nothing to lose and nowhere to go,
So I joined them and marched beside.

To such men, the daily meal provided by the S.A. was a far from
negligible benefit. It was a common belief, from Communists on the
left to Nationalists on the right, that Hitler's government would not
last long, or at least that the terror would be temporary (as he
promised). Middle-class and professional people, who also suffered
from a high rate of unemployment, saw a choice only between Nazism
and Communism. They naturally felt that the former was the lesser
evil. To many in the less powerful or influential social groups, who
derived little benefit from the existing economic system and had nothing to hope for from the projected Marxist millennium, Hitler
offered both material advantages and psychological satisfaction. The
popularity of National Socialism cannot be understood unless it is
seen as a movement of liberation, and not only in the sense of emancipation from a detested peace treaty.[45] Most of the non-political, the
silent majority who in November 1918 had accepted the Republic as
an accomplished fact, now came to terms with the Nazi dictatorship
in the same fatalistic spirit, though in many cases with considerably
more enthusiasm. Hitler would end the economic crisis and destroy
Versailles. If in the process some people got hurt, was the price not
worth paying? Was not the Nazi revolution bound to give rise to
some regrettable excesses like every other revolution in history? Such
attitudes are understandable, yet they contained much wishful thinking. Few saw or wanted to see the nihilism in the National Socialist
movement, the cynicism in Hitler himself, in Goebbels and in many
others. Perhaps the first event which opened men's eyes to the real
nature of the regime was the Röhm affair of June 1934, which was
also its first serious crisis.

(iii) THE SHOWDOWN WITH RÖHM

There comes a time in all revolutions when disagreement breaks out
among the revolutionaries. The leaders, having achieved their immediate aims, wish to consolidate and enjoy their gains, while their
more radical rivals, still struggling for power, insist on a further turn
of the revolutionary wheel. In the eyes of the radicals the moderates
are opportunists if not traitors; in the eyes of the moderates the
radicals are fanatics or utopians. Behind the ideological catch-words
lie personal rivalries. Such a situation existed in Germany at the end

of 1933. The Nazi leaders were tasting the fruits of power; they sat in the government, directed civil servants, humiliated their opponents, developed their economic policy, but they also adapted themselves to the realities in which they found themselves. There remained the vast army of rank and file party members and the storm-troopers, most of whom were still insufficiently rewarded for their contribution to the Nazi victory. Their dissatisfaction made them a danger to Hitler. He was now more concerned with government and foreign policy than with the fulfilment of the vaguely radical aspirations of his left-wing followers. He knew that the civil servants wanted the country to settle down, and he wished to show the world that the new Germany was a land of peace and order. He had no intention of allowing the S.A. to let loose a second wave of revolution. In a speech on 7 July he warned the state governors that the time had come to call a halt to party excesses: 'The revolution is not a permanent state of affairs . . . The stream of revolution that has been released must be guided to secure the bedrock of evolution.'[46] And he spoke equally bluntly to the leaders of the S.A. and S.S.: 'I will suppress every attempt to disturb the existing order as ruthlessly as I will deal with the so-called second revolution.'[47] Röhm, Chief of Staff of the S.A., rejected this view. The revolution, he complained to his senior colleagues, had fallen into stagnation, and the S.A. and S.S. might sink into mere propaganda bodies. To imagine that order was the citizen's first duty was to betray the cause, and the struggle must be continued.

Differences between Hitler and the S.A. widened after Hitler's assumption of power. While up to then all storm-troopers belonged to the N.S.D.A.P., by the summer of 1934, when the S.A. numbered four and a half million, only about a quarter were party members. Their loyalty was doubtful, and their lack of a definite role made them restless. Though in December 1933 Röhm became a minister in the cabinet, he had no executive power and felt frustrated. His ambition had been to become Minister of War. The S.A. chiefs would have liked to run the army, with the much smaller *Reichswehr* absorbed in what Röhm called the 'brown flood' of the S.A. 'I regard the *Reichswehr*', he wrote to one of his senior officers, 'only as a training school for the German people . . . the conduct of war and therefore of mobilisation too in future is the task of the S.A.'[48] To subordinate the highly professional army to the semi-trained mass of brownshirts was quite contrary to Hitler's plans. Hindenburg, whose attachment to the *Reichswehr* was exceeded only by his veneration for the monarchy, would have vetoed it. Nor did Hitler himself believe that the stormtroops were capable of playing the part assigned to the army. The *Reichswehr*, with its expertise and proud traditions,

was indispensable. Hitler knew that the generals had no love for the
S.A., and that once conscription was introduced the latter would
be superfluous.[49] There was another consideration: Hitler was soon
to offer the western powers a reduction of the S.A. as a contribution
to disarmament and proof of his sincerity. For all these reasons, a
showdown between Hitler and Röhm was becoming inevitable.

On New Year's Day 1934 Hitler publicly thanked Röhm for his
'imperishable services' to the Nazi movement and the German people,
but relations between them became increasingly strained. In an
address to his Gauleiters on 2 February Hitler again emphasised that
the revolution was over and that stability was now the party's duty.
All internal quarrels must be set aside in the interest of unity:
'Especially for reasons of foreign policy it is necessary to have the
whole nation hypnotically behind us. . . .'[50] On 28 February Hitler
persuaded Röhm to sign an agreement with Blomberg which stated
that the *Reichswehr* Ministry bore sole responsibility for national
defence and left only training functions to the S.A. Röhm did not
hide his annoyance, and told his followers privately that he did not
intend to keep the agreement. This was reported to Hitler, whose reaction was: 'We must allow this affair to ripen fully.'[51] He made his
preparations for the expected Putsch. Himmler, the head of the S.S.,
was put in charge of Göring's political police, the Gestapo. The S.S.
were to be the executioners in the forthcoming purge. But the army,
the main immediate beneficiary, was to provide arms, barracks and
transport. Blomberg urged Hitler to act, promising that the army of
the future would be a National Socialist one. Hitler knew that time
was short, for he wanted to settle accounts with Röhm before the
approaching death of Hindenburg. He may also have been stung into
action by a speech made by Vice-Chancellor von Papen at Marburg
on 17 June attacking Nazi lawlessness and warning against a second
wave of revolution. This was a reminder that the regime had critics
on the right as well as on the left.

Early in June Hitler, after summoning Röhm for a long conference,
ordered the S.A. to go on leave for the whole of July. Röhm himself
was given sick leave to attend a sanatorium for treatment of a painful nervous malady. The future of the S.A. was to be discussed at a
meeting of senior S.A. officers at Bad Wiessee in Southern Bavaria.
Suddenly, at the end of June, Hitler struck. He himself arrested Röhm
and others in their Bad Wiessee hotel. Similar arrests of S.A. leaders
took place in other parts of Germany, especially in Berlin and Silesia.
The victims were usually taken to a barracks or prison and executed
summarily. Röhm himself, understandably bewildered by the whole
action, was shot in a Munich prison after refusing to commit suicide.

Hitler took advantage of the opportunity to settle a number of grudges with past and present political opponents of all shades. Those murdered included Kahr, the former Special Commissioner for Bavaria who had 'betrayed' Hitler in November 1923; Schleicher and his wife, accused posthumously of plotting with Röhm and with the French ambassador François-Poncet; Gregor Strasser, with whom Hitler had broken in December 1932; Klausener, a well-known Catholic leader and civil servant; and Papen's legal adviser, Edgar Jung, also a Catholic and the author of the Marburg speech. Hitler admitted to 77 deaths; the exact number is not known, but was certainly much bigger. According to the Ministry of Justice, the total was 207.[52] The S.A. was also disarmed. Papen himself had a narrow escape, which he owed to the friendship of Hindenburg or the intervention of Göring, or possibly to the fact that he was Vice-Chancellor. The army made no effort to save Schleicher or his fellow officer von Bredow; though the Officers' Corps was furious, it was powerless because Blomberg believed Hitler's story of a conspiracy with François-Poncet. Nor did the Roman Catholic Church protest at the murder of Klausener and Jung. The jurists abjectly accepted Hitler's claim that on 30 June he had acted as the supreme judge of the German nation against a National-Bolshevik rising, and an article in the *Deutsche Juristenzeitung* of 1 August 1934 carried the cynical title: 'The *Führer* protects the law.' The allegation that Röhm was about to lead a revolt against Hitler was virtually disproved by his behaviour just before the purge, and no serious evidence incriminating him was ever produced. Yet in a more general sense Röhm and his S.A. did represent a genuine threat to Hitler's regime. Henceforth German law was the will of the Führer. The claims of the S.A. were disposed of for ever, but the forces of order, which had defeated them, were in the hands of a gangster. Many Germans were now disillusioned about the Third Reich, but too frightened to act or speak against it. The real victors were the S.S., who were now placed directly under Hitler. Two years later the S.S. leader, Himmler, was put in charge of all the police in Germany. Hitler had promised the army that it would be the sole bearer of arms, but in time the S.S. was to become a more dangerous rival to the army than the S.A. and to achieve the kind of dominance Röhm had only dreamt of.

Five weeks after the bloodbath Hindenburg died. The weary old man, belying his earlier reputation for solidarity of character, had proved a bitter disappointment to the millions of republicans who had voted for him in April 1932 as the last safeguard against dictatorship. He had made his peace with Hitler and accepted the latter's version of events, including justification of the murders of 30 June 1934.

Occasionally he protested – against the persecution of Jewish ex-soldiers, the excesses of German Christians or a move to make the pro-Nazi Reichenau Minister of War – but on the whole he played his allotted part in the general *Gleichschaltung*. Within twenty-four hours of his death Hitler had persuaded the generals to swear an oath of unconditional obedience to himself. Hindenburg's last wishes were embodied in an official testament which was made public, and in a private letter to Hitler which was not. In the latter he had urged restoration of the monarchy, but at a time of Hitler's choosing.[53] According to Hindenburg's son Oskar, his father's wish was for Hitler to be his immediate successor as head of state. Hindenburg's funeral on the site of the battle of Tannenberg was one of those military displays in which the Third Reich excelled. The spirit of Prussia's military past was invoked and the triumphs of the First World War were recalled. Scarred and bemedalled veterans in spiked helmets rubbed shoulders with blue-uniformed youths who were pilots of the still unofficial *Luftwaffe*. In his funeral oration Hitler consigned the departed hero (who was a devout Christian) to the glories of Valhalla. He also described him as the lord protector of the National Socialist revolution, though Hindenburg had long since ceased to protect anything. Hitler announced that in future he would be taking over the powers but not the title of president: he would be known as *Führer* and Chancellor. The change was approved by a plebiscite which gave him 84·6 per cent of the votes, a slightly lower proportion than in the plebiscite of the year before, but enough for his purpose.[54] He repeated his promise that the revolution was over. All civil servants as well as officers and soldiers had to take an oath of personal loyalty to Hitler, whose orders were declared to override all legal authority. Conscientious people were in a dilemma: to oppose Hitler was to commit perjury. The cheering majority observed that, at the party's sixth annual rally at Nuremberg in September 1934, the S.A., S.S. and Hitler Youth were joined by the Labour Front and the army in an impressive demonstration of national solidarity.[55] Much of the success of the regime in identifying Germany with National Socialism was due to Goebbels, who manipulated public opinion with all the techniques at his command. An outstanding broadcaster, he could be described as the Mephistopheles of the microphone.

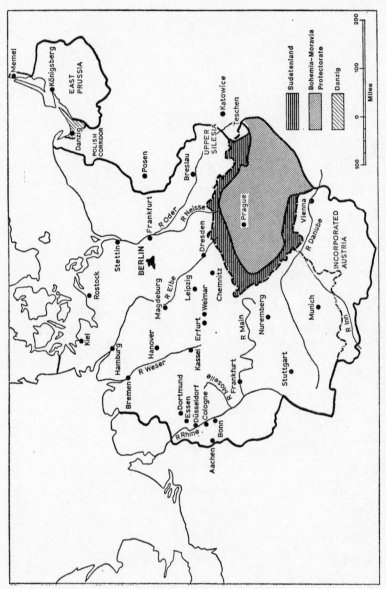

Map 3 Nazi Germany on the eve of the Second World War

CHAPTER IX

The Third Reich: Peace (1933-9)

Hitler's coming to power was watched by Germany's neighbours with obvious concern. His foreign policy had three main objects: to destroy the treaty of Versailles; to enlarge the Reich by the incorporation of Austria and other German-speaking territories such as the Sudetenland; and to conquer land and resources (*Lebensraum*) capable of supporting a larger population.[1] The Germans were constantly reminded that they were the only great nation without an empire, a hemmed-in *Volk ohne Raum*. These aims had all been made public in Hitler's writings and speeches, as well as in the programme of the N.S.D.A.P. Unlike William II, his primary interest was continental, not world policy: as befitted a man born in the centre of Europe, he showed little enthusiasm for seapower, and not much more for colonies. Whereas William had sought *Lebensraum* overseas, Hitler pursued it in Eastern Europe, and he combined it with a racial policy more extreme than that of the Pan-German League in its heyday. How were these objectives to be gained? Germany in 1933 was still disarmed and vulnerable to the threat of preventive war; though not without friends, she lacked allies; and she was still surrounded by the French girdle of defensive alliances as well as subject to the security guarantees (for what they were worth) of the League of Nations. In *Mein Kampf* Hitler had assumed the permanent hostility of France (the hereditary foe but also the guardian of the Versailles system and a 'negroid' society) and of Soviet Russia (the main ideological enemy and the prospective source of *Lebensraum*). Italy and Britain were to be Germany's allies in her attempt to recover her position as the greatest European power. The Europe of 1933 did not differ very significantly from Hitler's postulates. Though no formal Anglo-German alliance existed, there was in England a growing willingness to revise the now discredited peace treaty and to meet German grievances wherever possible. Until it was alienated by Hitler's domestic policy, the British left, and progressive opinion generally, was distinctly pro-German and critical of the French. Even the Permanent Under-Secretary of State in the Foreign Office, Sir Robert Vansittart, proposed as early as 1931 abrogation of the military and naval clauses of the treaty of Versailles.[2] It had been clear for a long time that England would not undertake any military action to uphold the *status quo* in Eastern Europe. Even in France, where Hitler's assumption of power could only confirm traditional mistrust of Germany, there was a feeling that some concessions over the Polish Corridor were becoming inevitable, coupled with an increasing reluctance to honour the military commitments to France's East European partners that alone made the system credible. Italy, where Mussolini saw the Nazi regime as a flattering imitation of his own, was revisionist, provided that her protégé Austria and the mainly Austrian province of South Tyrol were left alone; and when in May 1933 Mussolini actually proposed a four-power pact his intention was to divert German expansion in another direction – hence the opposition of France and her allies. Soviet Russia, isolated and embroiled in Stalin's five-year plan and its agrarian revolution, wanted nothing so much as to be left in peace. Stalin himself was quite prepared to continue the Rapallo policy of friendship with Germany despite the brutal destruction of the German Communist party, the largest outside Russia, and the breaking off of the special ties between the Red Army and the *Reichswehr*. In May 1933 the treaty of Berlin which Germany and the Soviet Union had signed in 1926, was renewed by mutual agreement. The decision to end this relationship was Hitler's own: several of the leading generals, including Blomberg, Brauchitsch and Keitel, had visited Russia, and would have been willing to continue the Seeckt policy of collaboration.

The search for security, the main theme of European diplomacy since Versailles, went on. Disarmament was still on the agenda: having disarmed Germany, and given a vague promise in the peace treaty to follow suit, the former Allies could hardly reject pressure by Germany to organise the disarmament conference which they had long talked about. Financial stringency too demanded it. Neither treaty revision nor the level of armaments could be considered in isolation from each other: Churchill in the 1920s had said that the redress of the grievances of the vanquished should precede the disarmament of the victors. The Germans, resenting France's refusal to disarm, claimed equality in the arms field, a claim accepted in theory in 1932 (with great reluctance on the French part) but difficult to put into practice. The French, mindful of Germany's demographic and economic superiority, were naturally loth to lose their advantage in weapons, while no one outside the Reich wanted Germany to arm up to the French level. The second Disarmament conference at Geneva in

February 1933 wrestled for months with this problem without finding a solution. The British proposed that the French army be reduced to 200,000 and the German army raised to that figure. Neither government would accept. One of the difficulties was that German military preparedness could not be assessed only in terms of the regular army: hundreds of thousands of young Germans were being given some military training in the S.A., S.S., Hitler Youth and various 'Defence Sport' associations.[3] Hitler, preoccupied with the consolidation of power at home and anxious to forestall the threat of a preventive war, proclaimed his peaceful intentions in a Reichstag speech that was a masterpiece of persuasiveness. Germany, he told the world on 17 May 1933, would act strictly within the framework of existing treaties, and was willing to forswear the use of aggressive weapons and even to wait five years before attaining complete equality in arms with France. By the autumn of 1933, the Nazi revolution completed, he felt bolder. If Germany stayed at the Disarmament conference her rearmament programme, already under way, would come under international scrutiny. This could not be allowed. In October Hitler announced that Germany would leave both the Disarmament conference and the League of Nations. It was a daring gesture, which incidentally killed Mussolini's four-power pact. Previous German governments, while having few illusions about the League, had valued it as a platform from which to influence world opinion. Hitler showed his indifference, even his contempt, for such things. Every German government since Versailles, however much lip-service it had paid to fulfilment, had been revisionist at heart: given the depth of German resentment at the treaty, and the widespread if mistaken belief that Germany's economic woes were also due to it, no other attitude would have been possible. But the republican ministers had sought to bring about changes by diplomacy, propaganda and eventual economic pressure. Hitler's method was force or the threat of it. He was willing to let Germany become more isolated if that was the price of ultimate success; and he used foreign criticism to strengthen his grip on the nation. A plebiscite to approve Germany's departure from the League gave Hitler 87.8 per cent favourable votes, his greatest electoral success hitherto. He had another weapon not possessed by his republican predecessors: the agitation of the Nazis and their allies in the German *irredenta* – Austria, the Saar, Danzig, Memel, the Sudetenland. The party had its own Foreign Organisation (A.O.), which sent its agents abroad to make contact with pro-Nazi elements and was later given disciplinary powers over all Germans living outside the Reich. The scope of this task was enormous, for there were twenty-seven millions of Germans in this category, and besides Austria and Czechoslovakia, there were few countries in East and South-East Europe which did not have substantial settlements of Germans, most of which had been there for centuries. The Foreign Ministry, to which in theory the A.O. was subordinate, was often embarrassed by its activities. In addition there was the *Büro Ribbentrop*, a special office for the man who soon emerged as Hitler's favourite party diplomat and was a serious rival to the established professionals of the Foreign Ministry. In Danzig the local Nazis gained control of the Senate, and in Austria Hitler's party representative Habicht started a campaign of intimidation and violence against the government. In the Saar too the Nazis beat the nationalist drum to great effect.

Hitler's first year of power was marked by one surprise: the Non-Aggression pact with Poland signed in January 1934. In view of Germany's often expressed denunciation of the frontier with Poland – the Corridor and the special status of Danzig were especially resented – an agreement with the firmly anti-revisionist Polish government was a shock for public opinion everywhere. Yet talks between the two governments began in the early summer of 1933, and led to the agreement, which was supposed to last ten years (it actually lasted six). It was a tactical move for both sides, neither of which had any illusions about the other. It did not commit the Germans to recognition of the disputed frontier; but it averted a dangerous deterioration of German-Polish relations, and it banished the spectre of a preventive war for which the Poles had tried unsuccessfully to enlist French support at the start of Hitler's regime. Poland, beginning to realise that she could not count on France in a crisis, felt safer and more independent for the time being. The treaty marked the new realism that was to characterise the diplomacy of the thirties. The Poles remained linked by treaty with France; and Beck, the Foreign Minister, went to Moscow to negotiate a non-aggression pact with Soviet Russia, a reassuring gesture for Paris. Nevertheless for the Germans (and not only for them) the Polish treaty represented the beginning of a breach in the French alliance structure and seemed even to indicate possible future co-operation between Germany and Poland against the Soviets. It turned Hitler's attention to other objectives: as the Polish leader, Pilsudski, is said to have remarked, his country was relegated from Germany's hors d'oeuvres to the dessert.[4] This was the end of Germany's special relationship with Russia, and led the French to reconsider the attractions of a Soviet alliance.

On the first page of *Mein Kampf* Hitler had demanded the union of Austria with Germany. Post-war Austria was an unhappy and unbalanced country. Her economy, which had never recovered from the break-up of the Habsburg Empire, was kept solvent by repeated loans from the League of Nations. Externally she had been forced to accept the unwelcome patronage of Mussolini. Her impoverished population was bitterly divided between Catholics (middle class and peasant) and socialists (working class and Viennese) with a growing third force, the Nazis, who profited by these differences. Under these strains parliamentary democracy had broken down. Dollfuss, the head of an authoritarian Catholic government, suppressed the Socialists by force and established a dictatorship. Hitler had tried to ruin Dollfuss by imposing a ban on German tourists to Austria. In the summer of 1934 the Nazis believed that their time had come. After a reign of terror instigated from Germany, a *coup d'état* was staged in the heart of Vienna and Dollfuss was murdered. Mussolini reacted sharply by sending troops to the Brenner Pass and warning Hitler not to intervene. Schuschnigg, a colleague of Dollfuss, succeeded him as Austrian Chancellor and, with the help of the police and army, defeated the Nazi attempt to seize power. Hitler had to disavow his subordinates. He had met Mussolini for the first time – at Venice – only a few weeks before, but had failed to grasp his determination not to let Austria go. Papen, whose presence Hitler no longer desired in Germany, was sent as ambassador to Vienna where he could use his old-world charm to repair the damage. Hitler now knew that to succeed in Austria he must (as earlier in Germany) use legal or semi-legal methods. The *Anschluss* had to wait for a more favourable opportunity.

After the Austrian fiasco Hitler needed a success. He found it six months later in the Saar, where the plebiscite provided for by the peace treaty to determine the territory's future was held in January 1935. Under the League of Nations regime, which had lasted fifteen years, the Saar had been economically part of France, so that its inhabitants had been spared the inflation and other vicissitudes experienced by the Germans. The Saar population was Catholic and largely working class as well as solidly German by speech. Unlike the Reich Germans the Saarlanders had access to information about the Nazi territory and knew what had happened to the Socialist and Centre parties as well as to the trade unions and other free institutions. Nevertheless they voted overwhelmingly for return to Germany. The plebiscite proved the power of nationalism. It was one of Hitler's most striking electoral victories, gained in the face of democratic opposition and under international auspices. It added greatly to his prestige. With the Saar and its mines back in the Reich, he could safely risk another act of defiance.

The French, however, had not been inactive. Faced with a resurgent Germany, and being somewhat doubtful of Poland, they turned to their traditional ally, Russia. Russia, with Litvinov in charge of foreign relations, was co-operative. France proposed an Eastern Locarno, in which she and Russia would guarantee Germany's eastern frontiers. Germany rejected this out of hand, but also did the Poles, fearful of a Russian guarantee that might result in a loss of their independence. The Soviets now realised that Germany, not France, represented a threat, and they hastened to proclaim the need for collective security, even joining the League of Nations which they had previously decried. But in October 1934 Barthou, the French Foreign Minister who had taken the initiative in this policy, was murdered in Marseilles with King Alexander of Yugoslavia. The inadequate security arrangements and the neglect of the dying Barthou did much to discredit the French police (who some months before were involved in the Stavisky scandal) and lowered French prestige in Yugoslavia. Laval, Barthou's successor, preferred an alliance with Italy to one with Russia. This suited the British government, which did not favour a *rapprochement* with Moscow, but whose attitude to Germany was seen to be hardening when details of secret German rearmament were revealed in a Defence White Paper. A few days later Hitler announced that Germany would have its own air force. Most observers knew that an unofficial, scarcely disguised air force already existed. Hitler went on to reintroduce conscription and to order expansion of the army to 36 divisions, equivalent to at least 550,000 men. The military clauses of Versailles were a dead letter. This was too much even for Mussolini. He met the French and British ministers at Stresa in North Italy to discuss a common anti-revisionist policy. Mussolini had already decided to conquer Abyssinia, the independent African state which the Italians had tried but failed to annex in 1896. Though the British had some idea of what was on foot, they refrained from raising the issue at Stresa in order not to upset the tripartite harmony. This was a mistake, with dire consequences. Mussolini left the conference with the impression that the Abyssinian question might be settled in Italy's favour without a war, and that Britain would not oppose his plans, though to have condoned an act of aggression by one League member against another would have made nonsense of the British government's pro-Geneva policy. The French, less principled and more pragmatic, were ready to compromise with Italy at Abyssinia's expense in return for Italian support against Germany. Meanwhile the British, showing that they too could be pragmatic, had made a separate naval agreement with Germany. This could be justified on the ground that it helped to avert the fierce naval building rivalry which had been the major cause of Anglo-German hostility before the 1914 war. But as a unilateral breach of the peace treaty it aroused great distrust in Paris. Mussolini went on with his plans, and in October 1935 the invasion of Abyssinia began. The League, under British pressure, voted for sanctions against Italy. The Stresa front was in ruins. The British government's repudiation of the Hoare-Laval plan, in response to public pressure, put a new strain on Anglo-French relations. Mussolini became entirely dependent on Germany economically as well as diplomatically, and could no longer oppose Hitler's plans. The Abyssinian war had ended German isolation. The French played the Russian card. A Franco-Russian security pact 'within the League of Nations' was signed, and followed by a similar pact between Russia and Czechoslovakia. Hitler had revived the encirclement which had proved fatal to the Wilhelmine Empire – but more in appearance than in reality. The French were soon seen to be dragging their feet over the Russian treaty, which their parliament did not ratify until March 1936. It was obvious that the French contemplated the prospect of another war with extreme distaste, and that the Soviet alliance was widely unpopular in France, not only on the extreme right.

By then Hitler was ready for his next gamble, the reoccupation of the Rhineland. Like the other anti-Versailles measures, this was a calculated risk. Hitler knew that his troops were half-trained and under-equipped. French opposition west of the Rhine, where most of the demilitarised zone lay, was more than a possibility. If it occurred, the German soldiers had orders to make a fighting retreat back across the Rhine.[5] The French however stayed in their Maginot Line, though Hitler's action had in fact been foreseen by the French government. The generals were reluctant to order the general mobilisation which, they declared, would have been necessary in case of an armed clash. The German march-in was a breach of Locarno, the treaty which Hitler had not so far denounced, as well as of Versailles. The French ministers, divided and irresolute, consulted the British, who advised them against any military action. This gave France an excuse to do nothing. The Council of the League declared Germany guilty, but verbal condemnation especially in such moderate terms did not worry Hitler, who softened foreign reaction by offering to negotiate a new peace treaty to last twenty-five years. Since failing to prevent Italy's conquest of Abyssinia (following its earlier failure to stop Japan in Manchuria) the League had anyway lost much of its credit. By reoccupying the Rhineland, Hitler had won a moral as well as a strategic victory. He had discerned the weakness of the western democracies: behind the speeches and high-flown phrases, the mixture of guilt, pacifism, wishful thinking and lethargy which made them incapable of action. French foreign policy was weakened by internal divisions, exacerbated by the Stavisky affair, the threat to parliamentary government presented by the Fascist leagues, and class antagonism. In Britain the Peace Ballot movement was at its height when Hitler offered a new non-aggression pact to replace Locarno and even suggested that Germany might rejoin the League. But such gestures could not disguise the fact that the western democracies had suffered a defeat. Once the Rhineland was re-fortified, France could no longer invade Germany with impunity if Germany attacked Poland or Czechoslovakia. Thus neither of these two countries could attach so much importance as in the past to French aid. This lesson had, in fact, already been implicit in France's obsession with defence as well as in the loosening of her eastern alliances: the Maginot Line begun in 1929 was evidence that in case of war France expected her junior ally to take the offensive. But the events of March 1936 made this brutally clear. They also showed that France would not take any military step without British support, even though, except in the air, French military superiority over Germany was still overwhelming. In dealing with his foreign opponents as with his domestic ones, Hitler relied on a failure of nerve to bring about capitulation. At home he capitalised on the popularity of regaining full sovereignty on the Rhine by holding a plebiscite which gave him 99 per cent of the votes. Negotiations between Germany and the West languished, and no agreement was reached.

1936 continued to be a successful year for Hitler. In August the Olympic Games were held in Berlin in a comparatively relaxed atmosphere. Antisemitic signs were temporarily removed from public places, though the year before the Nuremberg laws had deprived Jews of full citizenship and prohibited marriage between Jews and Aryans. A temporary halt was called to the harrying of the churches, and the number of prisoners in concentration camps was down to about a third of what it had been in July 1933.[6] Foreign visitors to the Games were impressed by the handsome new stadium and beguiled by the hospitality and pageantry which the rulers of the Third Reich were past-masters at displaying. Goebbels gave a particularly sumptuous party for 3,000 guests at his romantic villa on Peacock Island in one of the Berlin lakes. Nor was it only to see the athletics that foreigners visited Germany that year. Lloyd George was but one of the distinguished guests who made the pilgrimage to Berchtesgaden and came away full of admiration. (A year later the Duke and Duchess of Windsor were to make a much publicised call on Hitler.) Outside Germany events combined to favour Hitler's purposes. No sooner had Italy conquered Abyssinia than a civil war broke out in Spain which also helped to distract attention from what many people were beginning to call the German menace, and to sow fresh discord between the powers. While Italy intervened heavily on the side of the rebel forces, led by General Franco, the British and French followed a hesitant and largely ineffective policy of non-intervention. Germany helped Franco (a potential ally against France) and used Spain as a testing ground for new aircraft. Russia despatched military advisers and supplies to the Spanish government, in which democrats, communists and anarchists formed a somewhat incongruous coalition. The Spanish government thus became dependent on Russian help: this, and the part played by the International Brigade (in which left-wing intellectuals from many countries fought) identified the republican cause with communism, and enabled Franco to represent himself as the saviour of western civilisation. In France the effect of the Spanish imbroglio was to sharpen antagonisms between right and left. Despite its pacifism, the French left, which came to power in April 1936 under the Socialist Premier Blum, would have liked to help the Spanish republicans for patriotic as well as ideological reasons. But the right passionately favoured Franco. Blum, whose Popular Front government was supported by the Communists, was pledged to a programme of overdue but controversial social reform. Right-wing opposition to these reforms, as well as fear of Russian influence in Spain and dislike of the Soviet alliance, led to the cry of 'Better Hitler than Blum'. France's technological backwardness, defeatism and political confusion could no longer be disguised. Hitler was quick to draw the conclusion: the French were too divided and disorganised to be capable of fighting a war. German hopes were raised by Belgium's decision to abandon alliance with France in favour of neutrality. In Italy Mussolini, estranged from the western democracies by the policy of sanctions, gave fresh proof of his admiration for Hitler by proclaiming, in November 1936, a Rome-Berlin Axis. Japan, where the military party had come to power, was preparing for an attack on China, and signed the Anti-Comintern pact with Germany which Italy was to join a year later. Russia faced a prospect of war on two fronts. Mussolini, making a virtue of a necessity, no longer intended to prevent a German takeover of Austria when the time was ripe. A 'Gentleman's Agreement' between Hitler and Schuschnigg left Austrian independence ostensibly intact; but secret clauses provided that *inter alia* Austrian crypto-Nazis, members of the 'national opposition', should join the government. This was the policy of undermining from within. Schuschnigg's regime lacked appeal. The Socialists had been antagonised by the fighting of February 1934, when the workers' flats had been shelled on Dollfuss's orders. The independence for which Schuschnigg stood was not backed by credible international guarantees, and nationalism pointed to union with Germany. The Austrian economy remained precarious, and few European cities had more hungry children begging for food outside smart restaurants than Vienna.

There was, however, one disappointment for Hitler during this period. Like William II, though in a very different way, he had a love-hate relationship with England, or rather an attitude compounded of admiration and envy. The 'touching solicitude' which he at times showed for the welfare of the British Empire was probably genuine.[7] In the first years of the Nazi regime hopes of detaching England from France ran high. The British Foreign Secretary, Sir John Simon, lacked a clear-cut policy. The Anglo-German naval agreement was hailed in Berlin as an indication that, in return for German renunciation of a big navy policy, the British would not obstruct German plans in Central Europe. Ribbentrop, the Führer's roving ambassador extraordinary, who had negotiated the treaty on the German side, was given the London embassy in August 1936. A wine-merchant who had become wealthy by marriage, Ribbentrop was a rather late recruit to the N.S.D.A.P. and one whose abilities Hitler greatly overrated. Apart from speaking English well (he had spent some years in Canada) Ribbentrop had few qualifications for a post requiring exceptional tact and skill, and he entirely misjudged the temper of the British people. Eden was now Foreign Secretary. Basing his policy on the League of Nations and alignment with France, he was wary of German approaches, and was identified with the sanctions policy against Italy. But Ribbentrop had influential friends and acquaintances. Among them was Mrs Simpson, with whom the new King, Edward VIII, was already in love. Edward was known to be well-disposed to the Germans. His abdication in December 1936 ended hopes that the influence of the crown would be used to steer Britain on a pro-German course. Ribbentrop himself, by his brash and overweening behaviour, did much to cause ill-will. Despite his failure in London, in February 1938 he was promoted to the post of Foreign Minister in place of the career diplomat von Neurath, who was soon to become Protector of Bohemia and Moravia. Ribbentrop continued to shower Hitler with advice on how to handle the British. Ciano compared his feelings for England with those of a woman for a faithless lover. After his return to Berlin he often took a more jaundiced view of Anglo-German relations than was warranted, especially in view of Neville Chamberlain's genuine desire to come to terms. By 1939, Ribbentrop could be described as the leader of the war party at Hitler's court.

In 1937, too, circumstances played into Hitler's hand. The Spanish civil war continued to deadlock western diplomacy and divide public opinion. Whichever side won, Spain would not be a democracy. With Chamberlain as British Prime Minister in place of Baldwin after May 1937 the outlook for Germany was distinctly favourable. Chamberlain had energy and a sense of urgency. An obstinate man of strong opinions, he was convinced that war could be averted if the just grievances of the have-not powers, Germany and Italy, were redressed. It was a humane as well as a rational approach to the situation. Unfortunately it came too late. Hitler despised both qualities. His confidence was bolstered by a visit to Germany by Mussolini, who was enthusiastically welcomed and came away with an indelible impression of German strength. Japan invaded China, but also started an undeclared war against Soviet Russia. Russia itself was paralysed by Stalin's purges, which cut swathes through the higher ranks of the Communist party and the Red Army; and when the Commander-in-Chief of the latter, Tukhachevsky, was shot for allegedly conspiring with Nazi Germany, outside confidence in Russia sank to a very low level. At a time when western capitalism had broken down and Marx's predictions seemed to be coming true there was growing sympathy for Soviet Russia, especially among intellectuals. But the spectacle of the heirs of the revolution exterminating their colleagues after trials which were a parody of justice was hardly an advertisement for Communism. Chamberlain did not believe that Russia had a constructive part to play in Europe. Lord Halifax, Lord Privy Seal and soon to be Foreign Secretary, agreed with Chamberlain. In November 1937 he visited Hitler at Berchtesgaden and in the course of a long conversation mentioned 'possible alterations in the European order which might be destined to come about with the passage of time. Amongst these questions were Danzig, Austria and Czechoslovakia. England was concerned that any alterations should come in the course of peaceful evolution and without methods likely to cause far-reaching disturbances. which neither the Chancellor nor other countries desired.'[8] The four great powers of Western Europe, Halifax suggested, must together create the basis upon which a lasting European peace would be built. Though Russia was, with France, a guarantor of Czechoslovakia, she was clearly excluded from the Big Four. Such hints of territorial change, which Hitler could interpret as an invitation to stir up trouble in the areas concerned, embarrassed Eden, the Foreign Secretary, who was to resign four months later. British policy spoke with two voices, or at least with two different emphases. This was made even more apparent by the uncritically pro-German attitude of the new British ambassador in Berlin, Sir Nevile Henderson. But from Paris, too, clear indications reached Hitler that

France would not oppose peaceful changes in Austria and Czechoslovakia: a reorientation of French policy in Central Europe was,
said the French Premier Chautemps, entirely open to discussion.[9]

Shortly before Halifax's visit Hitler had held a conference with
the heads of the armed forces which contained an explicit statement
of his aims. Its importance is shown by the fact that Hitler wished it to
be regarded as his last will and testament in case of his death.[10] Germany needed living space. Two 'hate-inspired' antagonists, France
and Britain, barred the way. There were three possibilities. Germany
could wait until 1943/45, by which time her armaments programme
would be complete: any delay beyond that point would be to her
disadvantage. This was the long-term prospect. But favourable opportunities might occur much sooner. France might be paralysed by civil
war, or weakened by war with Italy. In either of these cases Germany
should act against Austria and Czechoslovakia, in the latter case with
lightning speed. Britain almost certainly, and probably France as
well had in fact written off the Czechs. Hitler thus implied that it
might be safe for Germany to invade Czechoslovakia even if France
was not incapable of action, since the risk of war on two fronts was
so small. Seven weeks after this conference, the minutes of which (the
Hossbach Memorandum) were to be much quoted at the Nuremberg
Trials after the Second World War, new mobilisation orders were
issued to the army and air force. Plans for a campaign on two fronts
(Operation Red against France, Operation Green against Czechoslovakia) remained, but with a significant shift: the latter now had
priority. Hitler had realised that he could safely commit a higher
proportion of his resources to the Czech front, and he may have
sensed that this might even increase the chances of western military
inactivity in case of war. The 'Hossbach conference' has been described as 'the point at which the latent expansionism of the Third
Reich ceased to be latent and became explicit'.[11] It was important in
another way too. As a result of the doubts and objections voiced by
his generals Hitler decided on changes in the High Command.

Before Hitler became Chancellor the attitude of the army had been
one of the imponderables, but since he did so legally, there was no
question of a military counter-move. During the chancellorship of
Schleicher, the most politically-minded general, Germany seemed
close to a military dictatorship, but by the time he left office Schleicher
had lost the army's confidence. The next War Minister, Blomberg, who
was appointed before Hitler himself, soon showed that he was only
too willing to fall in with the Führer's wishes, more from uncritical
enthusiasm than from specifically Nazi convictions. Blomberg was
also made Commander-in-Chief of the *Wehrmacht*, a new post which

signified that the three fighting services were to be co-ordinated under a single authority.[12] The handshake between Hitler and Field-Marshal Hindenburg at Potsdam on 21 March symbolised the armed forces' acceptance of the new order. In June Blomberg told his divisional and corps commanders that they must serve the National Socialist movement with complete devotion, and he furthered the dissemination in the army of Nazi propaganda.[13] The 'non-political' attitude of the Seeckt era was a thing of the past. There was indeed much common ground between Hitler and the generals. Both were in favour of a larger *Reichswehr*, one based on conscription and free to use the weapons of its choice without regard to the Versailles treaty. Both wished to restore German power. The generals welcomed the improved status of the army and its larger share of national resources after the lean years of the Republic. Nor were they averse to an authoritarian type of government. But what the generals, with their monarchist sympathies, envisaged was a return to something like the relationship between army and government which they had known under the Empire, with the army freed from parliamentary control. Among the younger officers, even the aristocratic ones, there was a good deal of support for Hitler, who was a man of their generation. The one very senior officer who was known to dislike the Nazis was General von Hammerstein, Chief of the Army Command, who conveniently retired at the end of 1933. In his place Hitler wished to put von Reichenau, whose pro-Nazi views were well-known, but Hindenburg, exercising his prerogative as Chief of the Armed Services, used one of his rare vetoes. In the end the post went to Fritsch, a very capable staff officer but also a man of conservative opinions and often at loggerheads with Blomberg. Shortly after Fritsch's appointment Hitler addressed leading officers of the *Reichswehr* and S.A., telling them that the army must be expanded 'at full strength' and that, if *Lebensraum*, vital for German prosperity, was to be won, they must be prepared for a war of defence in five years, an offensive war in eight.[14]

An early example of *Reichswehr* collaboration with Hitler was in the preparations, made in conjunction with the S.S., for the S.A. purge of 30 June 1934. The army chiefs thus helped Hitler to destroy the threat to themselves presented by Röhm, though not without cost to their honour: they connived at murder and afterwards failed to protest publicly against the killing of their colleagues Schleicher and Bredow. The purge was also seen in the army as a private feud between Hitler and the S.A., though Beck, the Chief of Staff, was upset by it and developed a distrust of Hitler which caused his resignation four years later. Hitler's abortive attempt to seize Austria through the murder of Dollfuss soon afterwards showed how far the kind of impromptu risk he was willing to take differed from the well-laid plans favoured by the General Staff. Hindenburg's death gave Hitler the opportunity to claim his reward for the elimination of Röhm: henceforth every officer and man had to take a personal oath of loyalty to Hitler as Commander-in-Chief as well as Führer. This greatly strengthened Hitler's moral hold, and thereafter there could be no presidential brake, however ineffective, on his arbitrary actions. The generals were relieved that in the Röhm affair the conservative elements had triumphed over the radicals. They did not understand that the army had lost its boasted independence, and that the real victors had been the even more fanatical S.S. The armed forces adopted the swastika as their flag, and in future took part in the annual party rally at Nuremberg, the greatest emotional event of the Nazi year. Yet Hitler did not take the generals into his confidence: his announcement of conscription in March 1935 came as a surprise to them, and they would have preferred a slower and surer expansion. Quality was sacrificed to quantity, and the new flood of recruits included a high proportion who had been members of the Hitler Youth. The Officers' Corps lost its exclusive character, and the generals were no longer masters of their own house. The re-occupation of the Rhineland was ordered – again at very short notice – against the advice of the Chiefs of Staff, who were appalled at the risk of provoking a war with France for which Germany was far from ready. But since Hitler's bluff worked and their fears proved unfounded, his reputation rose and theirs fell. They appeared as craven, he as an infallible genius. Even those who did not share the ideology of Nazism admired his nerve and intuition. By now he had lost his earlier awe of the generals, while his distrust of them as an aristocratic caste remained. His plans as revealed at the 'Hossbach conference' in November 1937 roused their objections, which in sum amounted to the very reasonable assertion that Germany was not strong enough to go to war with France and Britain as well as with Czechoslovakia. Even Blomberg, who had earlier opposed increased participation in the Spanish civil war, did not give the Führer unqualified support. His removal was therefore decided on, a step which Hitler could justify on the grounds that he had just taken, as his second wife, a woman who had been a prostitute. Such a marriage (though ironically Hitler had been present at the wedding) was incompatible with the standing of a Prussian officer, let alone a Field-Marshal. Next Fritsch, whose disagreement with Hitler's plans was more decided, was ousted from his post on a trumped-up charge of homosexuality. This move was inspired by Himmler, who was anxious lest Fritsch succeed Blomberg as War Minister, and it was significant that three months after Fritsch's fall the

Waffen S.S. was formally declared an 'independent sword-bearer', ranking equally with the *Reichswehr*.[15] (The *Waffen S.S.*, the S.S.'s own armed force, was an élite body steeped in Nazi ideology, originally intended for internal use and now given permanent status. By the end of the Second World War it numbered nearly a million and had recruits from many countries). Thirteen high-ranking generals were retired and 44 posted, a purge which gives some indication of the extent to which Hitler had failed to carry the army with him. Hitler did not appoint a successor to Blomberg, but became his own Minister of War and Head of the High Command of the armed forces (O.K.W.). Keitel, hitherto a little known figure, became his deputy as Chief of Staff, with Jodl as Chief of Operations, the most important of the four departments into which the O.K.W. was divided. Brauchitsch was made Chief of the Army Command. The army had forfeited the status of which it had been so proud during the era of Seeckt, for the O.K.W. was little more than a secretariat through which Hitler exercised his power of command.

These changes heralded the strike at Austria which Hitler had long contemplated. It was alleged that the agreement of 1936 with the Austrian government had not been honoured by Schuschnigg, who was summoned to Berchtesgaden to hear complaints. He was told to appoint a Nazi as his Minister of the Interior. Pressure from Germany mounted. Schuschnigg announced that a plebiscite would be held as a vote of confidence in his government. This Hitler was determined to prevent. At the last moment Schuschnigg agreed to postpone it, and resigned. The Austrian President Miklas refused to appoint as his successor the Nazi candidate Seyss-Inquart, who thereupon declared himself Chancellor. German troops crossed the border into Austria, and the *Anschluss* was an accomplished fact. Hitler drove triumphantly into Linz and on to Vienna. His success was hardly the constitutional affair he had intended. Otherwise his expectations were fulfilled, even over-fulfilled, since he had not originally envisaged the complete absorption of Austria in the Reich. No one came to the rescue of the small Republic, whose union with Germany was approved in a plebiscite by 99 per cent of the population. In a formal sense Austria had been violated; but the enthusiasm with which the German troops were received – as in the Rhineland two years before with flowers and cheers – suggested that the victim had been far from unwilling. Mussolini, bowing to the inevitable, gave no sign of disapproval.

The annexation of Austria automatically put Czechoslovakia at the head of Hitler's 'shopping list'. As an Austrian and Pan-German he had always disliked the Czechs and had naturally resented the decision of the peace-makers in 1919 to include the Sudeten Germans, as the German-speaking inhabitants of Bohemia and Moravia were usually if inaccurately known, in the multi-national Czechoslovak Republic instead of in Austria. There were many outside as well as inside Germany who had doubted the wisdom of this decision, including Masaryk, the first Czech President; but it was believed that to divide the provinces along the language border would be to deprive the new state of defensible frontiers and a viable economy. Geography and history seemed to have predestined Bohemia to remain a unity. More than a quarter of the population of Czechoslovakia consisted of minorities – Germans, Hungarians, Ruthenians and Poles. There was one German for every two Czechs; and if the Slovaks were counted as a separate people, the Czechs were a minority in the country which they alone effectively ruled. Though the Germans, unlike the Slovaks, were not a *state people*, they were better treated than most minorities in that part of Europe, and they shared fully in the country's genuine parliamentary democracy. In the twenties signs of reconciliation between Czechs and Germans, who differed in language rather than in race, appeared, and there were German ministers in the Prague government. But in the 1930s relations deteriorated. This was partly due to the stimulus given by Hitler, once in power, to the Nazi party in the Sudeten districts, where the main parties hitherto had been agrarian and socialist. But it was also caused by the industrial depression, which resulted in disproportionately high unemployment in the German districts. The Germans were convinced that they were discriminated against in appointments to the civil service, and now they felt economically ruined. The Czechs favoured their own people, while many Germans had never bothered to learn Czech. Such grievances, and encouragement from the Nazis in Germany, explains the rapid rise of Konrad Henlein, the gymnastics teacher who as head of the local Nazis captured 70 per cent of the German vote in 1935.[16] The Czechs incurred Hitler's wrath by their defence treaty with Russia. Czechoslovakia, he complained, was an outpost of Bolshevism and a base for air attacks on Germany. Henlein (who received a modest subsidy from Hitler) became more exacting in his demands for a greater measure of autonomy, and the Czechs were asked by their friends, especially the British, to agree. Hitler's Austrian triumph caused great excitement among the Sudetens, and rallies were held at which shouts were heard of 'Ein Volk, ein Reich, ein Führer'. On 28 March, a fortnight after entering Vienna, Hitler met Henlein and told him that in his supposedly bona fide negotiations with the Czechs he must always ask for more than they were willing to give. On 24 April 1938 Henlein presented Prague with a list of demands which, if accepted, would have destroyed Czechslovakia's independence.

Faced with an approaching crisis, the French and British governments had to decide what to do. The French obligations were clear on paper: they were to come to the help of Czechoslovakia, if she was attacked, and Russia would follow suit. The French were desperately anxious to avoid war, and realised the practical difficulties of providing military aid. It was obvious that France would fight only if England did too. England, consistently with her general policy of not guaranteeing any frontiers east of the Rhine, did not intend to fight for Czechoslovakia, though she would not allow France to be defeated. Chamberlain myopically described Czechoslovakia as 'a far-away country of which we know nothing'; this was his way of saying that it was not a vital British interest. There was also a good deal of sympathy for Henlein, who visited England more than once and made a favourable impression on Chamberlain and others. Suddenly, on 20 May, for reasons which have never been fully elucidated, the Czechs, believing that Germany was about to attack them, mobilised. France and Britain warned Hitler that they would stand by the Czechs. Hitler was furious at being thus publicly humiliated; besides, the rumour of German mobilisation had been false. At the end of May Hitler signed new plans for an attack on Czechoslovakia, which it was his unalterable decision to smash. The Czech problem, he wrote, must be solved by force not later than 1 October.[17] The western powers did not of course know Hitler's timetable, but they realised that time was running out and redoubled their efforts to find a solution. This meant pressing Prague to make concessions and urging Berlin to show restraint, with more emphasis on the former. In August Chamberlain persuaded the Czech President, Benes, to accept Lord Runciman, a respected Liberal peer, as a one man arbitrator and investigator. Runciman reported in favour of a federal Czechoslovakia with maximum freedom for the Germans. His recommendations were not welcome to Benes, who nevertheless accepted them to show goodwill and retain western support. But the question was whether Hitler – not Henlein – was interested in any compromise.

One consequence of Hitler's order to destroy Czechoslovakia by 1 October was a fresh quarrel with his generals. Beck, the army Chief of Staff, did not share the belief that the Czechs could be eliminated by a lightning blow, and he argued stubbornly that to try it would be to precipitate a general war which Germany would not win. He saw, too, that more than military issues were involved.[18] Even Brauchitsch believed that a general war would be the end of German culture. But an attempt by Beck to persuade Brauchitsch to join in a collective protest by the generals failed. Brauchitsch was a man of honourable character, but no fighter when it came to a clash with Hitler, and by allowing his Chief of Staff to go he weakened his own position. Beck's independence of mind cost him his post, which he left at the end of August. Thereafter he was one of the leaders of the opposition to Hitler inside Germany, and was one of the first to be executed after 20 July 1944. His successor as Chief of Staff, General Halder, shared Beck's misgivings but kept them to himself; he rarely questioned Hitler's decisions except on technical grounds.[19] Even on technical grounds the generals' scepticism was well founded. Germany's prospective enemies had unlimited resources, and, unlike the Maginot Line, the West Wall was far from complete. Hitler had the better intuition: morale was a military factor, and the French, who had the means of fighting, lacked the will. Henceforth the relationship between Hitler and his generals was one of suspicion and tension, a foretaste of the wholesale sackings that were to take place during the Russian campaign as well as of the anti-Hitler conspiracy in which so many senior officers took part.

On 12 September, in the heady atmosphere of the Nuremberg Party Rally, Hitler made a speech denouncing the Czechs for their treatment of the Sudeten Germans, and containing vague threats. Disturbances broke out in the Sudeten districts. Three days later Chamberlain, fulfilling a plan which had been in his mind for some days, flew to Berchtesgaden to meet Hitler and find out his intentions. He was told that the German lands would have to be ceded to the Reich: no other solution would be acceptable. Hitler appealed to the principle of self-determination which the western democracies had championed at Versailles. Chamberlain promised to consult his colleagues and allies, and asked Hitler in the meantime to abstain from the use of force. When the German terms were discussed with the French it was decided that they should be sent to the Czechs with a recommendation for acceptance. Benes, yielding to 'unheard-of pressure' reluctantly acquiesced, and Chamberlain went back to Germany to give Hitler the answer. This time they met at Godesberg. But now Hitler wanted more. Encouraged by the Germans, the Hungarian and Polish governments demanded areas of Czechoslovakia inhabited by their people, while the Slovaks were pressing for full self-government. Czechoslovakia was on the verge of falling apart. If the transfers were not made by 28 September, Hitler declared, he would invade. This was more than Chamberlain would stomach. Again the French were consulted: the meeting broke up indecisively. The French showed a resolution in London which they lacked in Paris. The Godesberg terms were transmitted to Prague, where rejec-

tion of them was certain. The Czechs mobilised. The British called up
the Home Fleet and dug shelters in the London parks. Chamberlain
promised France support if she went to war, and war seemed a certainty
within days if not hours. Sir Horace Wilson was sent to Hitler to make
a final appeal for reason. But Hitler seemed unmoved. The French and
British still hoped for an escape from their dilemma. It was provided
by Mussolini, who, prompted by the British ambassador in Rome,
proposed a four-power conference in Munich the following day (29
September). When the four heads of government (Chamberlain,
Daladier, Hitler and Mussolini) met they had little difficulty in agreeing on terms which, so far as the transfer of territory was concerned,
hardly differed from the Godesberg demands. Areas containing more
than 50 per cent German-speaking people were to be evacuated by
the Czechs in stages. In disputed districts there would be a referendum under an International Commission, including a Czech
representative, which was also responsible for drawing up the boundaries of the rump state. Mussolini, ostensibly acting as mediator,
spoke from a brief prepared for him by the German Foreign Ministry.
Thus was signed the treaty of Munich, one of Hitler's greatest triumphs. The Europe of Versailles was buried, and the balance of power
had moved decisively in Germany's favour.

The Czechs had been let down by their allies: 'We have double-
crossed the Czechs for our own security' was the City of London's
gibe, and the Czechs' disillusion with the West set them on a pro-
Russian orientation which was to have unhappy consequences. Hitler
had used Hungarian and Polish revisionism as well as Slovak nationalism to destroy the state he hated – Versailles was, in part, employed
against itself. The Franco-Russian alliance remained on paper, though
as it lacked military clauses it was from the German point of view
fairly innocuous. Hitler was the unchallenged master of Central
Europe. British acknowledgement of this was, in German eyes, implicit
in the Anglo-German Peace Declaration which Chamberlain had persuaded Hitler to sign.[20] Benes, unwilling to play the part of a German
satellite, went into exile. Nor were Czechs the only victims. Socialists,
liberals and Jews in the Sudeten districts became the object of Hitler's persecution or escaped abroad as best they could, following in the
footsteps of earlier refugees from Vienna. The flourishing Jewish
intelligentsia in Prague, which had long been a mainstay of German
culture, ceased to exist. In Russia, isolated and aggrieved, the psychological foundations for the following year's Nazi-Soviet Pact had been
laid. One of the unanswered questions of the Sudeten crisis was
whether, had war broken out, the Soviets would have fulfilled their
treaty obligations to aid Czechoslovakia provided France did so first.

Soviet spokesmen and historians have always maintained that their country intended to stand by the Czechs, and there is a good deal of evidence to support this view.[21] The Soviet reaction to Hitler's seizure of Austria had been to propose consultation with the western powers 'to check the development of aggression', an initiative rejected by the British government. On 21 September Litvinov, the Soviet Foreign Minister, told the League of Nations: 'We intend to fulfill our obligations . . . by the ways open to us,' and he suggested staff talks with France. Two days later the Soviet government formally warned Poland not to send troops into Czechoslovakia. Dr Hodza, the Czechoslovak Prime Minister until that date, declared later that Russia meant to help the Czechs even if the French deserted them.[22] Nevertheless, there is some reason to think that the Soviets may have been bluffing. They may have suspected that the French would not fight when it came to the crunch. A more important consideration was the difficulty or virtual impossibility of aiding a state with which they had no common frontier. Neither Poland nor Roumania was willing for Soviet troops to cross their country, and Roumania opposed the passage of Soviet aircraft through her airspace.[23] Mountains and lack of railways in the area between Slovakia and the Soviet border would in any case have made Russian intervention extremely slow and ineffective, even if Polish and Roumanian objections had been overruled. Litvinov's language to the League on 21 September shows that he was aware of this. It can be inferred that since any aid given by the Soviet Union would have been partial and indirect it could not have been decisive. As the crisis ended without putting the Soviets to the test, they, in contrast to France and Britain, emerged from it without loss of face, though the subsequent destruction of Czechoslovakia reduced the Soviet Union's sense of security. Possible Russian intervention was not a deterrent for Germany. On 30 May 1938 Weizsäcker wrote: 'Russia hardly exists in our calculation today.'[24] Hitler, with his generally contemptuous view of the Soviets, was unlikely to take their warnings more seriously than the head of his Foreign Ministry.

Chamberlain's defence of Munich used four arguments. The first was that the handover of territory was peaceful and not violent, the second that he won time to rearm, the third that German gains were justified by self-determination, the fourth that public opinion, especially in the dominions, would not have supported him in going to war. Hitler could and did use time (at first) more effectively than Chamberlain, so that this argument was double-edged. Chamberlain believed that by remedying Germany's just grievances he was eliminating the reasons for Hitler to break the peace. Thus Munich for the

British was a mixture of high-minded and self-regarding motives: desire to right a wrong, and fear of war. Admittedly British armaments hardly permitted her to fight since her cities were vulnerable from the air, but the arms level depended on public opinion. A democratic country will not devote a sufficient proportion of its resources to armaments unless it believes that there is no acceptable alternative.[25] As far as Hitler was concerned, his policy should have been to lull British suspicions that he was not interested in self-determination except when it worked in Germany's favour. Danzig, not Prague, should have been his next objective since in Danzig he had a good case, while he continued his attempts to divide France from Britain. Instead Hitler took the line of least military resistance (Prague) and ignored the predictable outcry. His contempt for Chamberlain blurred his judgement.

An unforeseen effect of the Sudeten crisis was to dishearten the German opposition to Hitler. Despite the removal of Blomberg and Fritsch and the resignation of Beck, the remaining generals (Jodl noted in his diary) had neither confidence nor discipline because they could not recognise the Führer's genius.[26] Indeed, Beck's example had encouraged the spirit of resistance among his former colleagues. Halder, his successor as army Chief of Staff, was one of several senior officers who shared in a conspiracy that had been started by Admiral Canaris and Colonel Oster of the army's Counter-Intelligence service. Even Brauchitsch, the army's new Commander-in-Chief, agreed to co-operate though he never did so. The intention was to arrest Hitler as soon as the final order for the invasion of Czechoslovakia had been issued, and to put him on trial. At the same time a special envoy, von Kleist-Schmenzin, had been sent to London on 18 August to warn the British government of Hitler's intentions and to urge it to stand firm.[27] Kleist saw Chamberlain and Halifax as well as Churchill and Sir Robert Vansittart, who was now less influential as diplomatic adviser but had outspokenly advocated a hard line towards Hitler when head of the Foreign Office. Shortly afterwards Theodor Kordt, the German chargé d'affaires in London, brought an urgent message to the British government from his brother in the German Foreign Ministry (A.A.) and approved by Weizsäcker, the senior State Secretary, that the attack on Czechoslovakia was expected by 1 October and again urging no concessions to Hitler. Kordt's argument was summarised in one sentence: 'In the present situation we must prefer even the temporary encirclement of National Socialist Germany to the certainty of a Second World War which might mean the end of western civilisation.'[28] But this mission was no more successful than its predecessor. The British listened politely but would not commit themselves. By this time (5 September) Chamberlain was already thinking of meeting Hitler, who, he was convinced, had the support of the overwhelming majority of the German population. On the British side scepticism about the ability of the generals and diplomats to accomplish their aims was reinforced by traditional distrust of the military and Junker milieu to which the conspirators belonged. Chamberlain, like many better informed people, did not perceive that the situation created by the Nazi regime raised moral and ideological issues that transcended national boundaries. The western capitulation at Munich cut the ground from under the conspirators' feet, though whether, had Chamberlain not gone to see Hitler, the latter would have been overthrown is something which cannot be proved and may well be doubted. Inside Germany Hitler now appeared as a man of peace as well as victor. The officers concerned in the plot were discouraged and many were posted. Hitler's popularity soared. Brauchitsch, despite his contacts with the opposition paid fulsome tribute to 'Adolf Hitler, our inspired leader, who ... has built and secured for us the new Greater German Reich ... Above and beyond all classes and divisions a new unique fellowship of the nation has been created to which we, People, Armed Forces and Party, all belong.'[29] While many Germans rejoiced that war had been averted and perhaps believed that the western forces were incapable of making a firm stand, others saw that war had been merely postponed. Among these was Goerdeler, a former Lord Mayor of Leipzig and Price Commissioner for the Reich, who was the leader of the civilian opposition to Hitler. 'By shrinking from a risk', Goerdeler wrote in a letter to America, 'Chamberlain has made war inevitable.'[30]

Like other ambitious rulers, Hitler could not rest on his achievements. The obvious distaste for war shown by the German public before and during the Munich conference and its relief when peace was saved did not deter Hitler from planning further moves that kept Europe on tenterhooks. The full fruits of Munich had still to be reaped. Once Polish and Hungarian as well as German claims had been met, Czecho-Slovakia (the hyphen emphasised the new autonomy of the Slovaks) was too powerless to have any genuine independence. The international guarantee to the Czechs on which the West had insisted turned out to be without practical value. The Germans, masters of the Danube valley, assigned the southern fringe of Slovakia to Hungary, but not the whole. Slovak airfields, said Göring as head of the Luftwaffe, might be useful to Germany in case of a war against the East.[31] Hitler patronised Tiso, the priest who was leader of the Slovak autonomy party; and when the Prague government, trying to re-assert its authority, occupied Bratislava and deposed Tiso, the latter appealed to Hitler for help. Bowing to German pressure, a Slovak parliament declared Slovakia independent, and under a new government headed by Tiso the country entered on its new course as a German satellite with its foreign and defence policy controlled from Berlin. Hungary was, however, allowed to incorporate Ruthenia, the small easternmost province of Czechoslovakia that was inhabited by people of Ukrainian stock and could have served as the spring-board for an attempt to detach the Ukraine from the Soviet Union. (An earlier offer of Ruthenia to Poland in return for Danzig and a corridor across the Corridor had been rejected.)[32] It thus seems that Hitler had no immediate plans for war with Russia. Instead he summoned to Berlin the elderly President of 'Czechia' and his Foreign Minister Chvalkovsky, and bullied them into surrendering their country. German troops marched in to Prague, where Hitler pro-claimed that Bohemia and Moravia were a German Protectorate. Czechoslovakia had ceased to exist. Without a shot Germany had acquired the industrial, financial and military resources of a small but well equipped state which occupied a key position on the Euro-pean chessboard. Country after country in South East Europe recognised the shift in the balance of power and hastened to make its peace with Hitler. German economic penetration increased, and soon quantities of Roumanian oil and wheat were on their way to the Reich. It was, in effect, a revival of the *Mitteleuropa* of the First World War. Hitler had passed from the gathering in of the German tribes to the conquest of *Lebensraum*. Mussolini, jealous of his rival's success, did his best to emulate Hitler by attacking Albania in April 1939, and to gratify him by signing the Pact of Steel the following month. Italy, it appeared, would march with Germany in all circum-stances. Italian demands for Tunis, Corsica and Nice worried the French, and suggested that Italy and France had moved nearer a state of war. This fitted in admirably with Hitler's plans.

The German occupation of Prague produced a sharp reaction, especially in Britain. Chamberlain, remembering Hitler's earlier assurance that he did not want to rule over Czechs, was stung by his bad faith. The policy of appeasement was now under attack. The relief felt at the time of Munich had given way to a new and deeper anxiety, accompanied by a growing sense of guilt as the human as well as the material cost of the defeat was counted, Hitler's failure to respond to Chamberlain's friendly approaches created a bad im-pression. Even a man as confident in his own judgement as Chamber-lain could not ignore the new mood. Rumours ran of an imminent German attack on Poland or Roumania. Britain, Chamberlain warned, would fight rather than make any more concessions. Within days he had offered Poland a defence pact, which was followed by similar pledges to Roumania and Greece. The threat to Poland was not new. On 24 October 1938 Hitler demanded the return to Germany of Danzig and a motorway and railway across the Polish Corridor. Though these claims were rejected by the Poles, they were presented again when Beck visited Germany in January 1939. The British government felt obliged to step in, for the Franco-Polish alliance was virtually dead, and it was obvious that France would not fight without England. France, Chamberlain told the Poles, participated in the British guarantee. This was a disappointment to the Germans, who hoped that they had persuaded the French to abandon the role of policeman in Eastern Europe.[33] In December Ribbentrop had visited Paris and signed a treaty in which Hitler renounced any claims to Alsace-Lorraine; he thus guaranteed France against his own aggression. In return he expected a free hand east of the Rhine. If France could be neutralised England would be militarily powerless, since France was her continental sword. Then came the seizure of Prague, of which Hitler boasted that in two weeks no one would speak of it any more.[34] This was his most serious miscalculation to date. Prague revived the 'encirclement' which Munich had temporarily destroyed.

Since Munich, when Poland had shared in the spoils, German-Polish relations had been curiously ambiguous. On the one hand the Poles rejected Hitler's demands and were worried by his threats; they were also piqued by his refusal to establish a common frontier between Poland and Hungary after the break-up of Czechoslovakia. On the other hand, the Germans still hoped that Poland, with her anti-communist sympathies, might join the Anti-Comintern Pact, and her known 'aspirations towards the Soviet Ukraine and a connection with the Black Sea'[35] could make her an ally of Germany against Russia. The immediate problem was Danzig and the Corridor. Fears of a German Putsch in Danzig rose after Hitler had ordered his forces to occupy Memel, the formerly German port ceded in 1919 to Lithuania, on 23 March. The Reich press published ominous reports alleging the maltreatment of the German minority in Poland, and Beck ordered partial mobilisation of the Polish army as a warning. On 25 March Hitler issued a directive to the *Reichswehr*: though he did not wish to solve the Danzig problem by force, plans for war with Poland must be considered. If war came, Poland must be so crushed that she would cease to be a political factor for decades. On 3 April, when the British undertaking to Poland had become known, Hitler ordered definite plans for the invasion of Poland (Operation White). Living space, not Danzig, was his real objective, he told his generals on 23 April.[36] The German frontier was to be pushed back to approximately

its 1914 limits, and within the regained area the Polish population
was to be evacuated and re-settled. On 28 April Hitler denounced
both the Non-Aggression pact with Poland and the Anglo-German
naval treaty.

Chamberlain's promise to Poland was novel in that for the first
time Britain guaranteed a state in Eastern Europe. It was also remarkable since the definition of what constituted an attack on their independence (their frontiers were not guaranteed) was left to the Poles.
The British had signed a blank cheque – blank in a double sense, for
they promised military aid which they did not possess. Thus as a deterrent it was ineffective. The Germans knew of British unpreparedness,
and they observed the half-heartedness with which in the summer of
1939 the pact began to be implemented. Hitler, according to Weizsäcker, dismissed the British guarantee as bluff.[37] If it is a sound rule for
a country never to let its political commitments outrun its military capabilities, that rule was ignored by the authors of the Anglo-Polish treaty.
Neither then or afterwards did the Poles receive the help which alone
could have preserved their independence. The pact had the character
of a hasty improvisation by a government caught off balance by an
external threat and reacting to a public outcry. Chamberlain, sceptical
of Soviet help, despite the Anglo-French negotiations with Russia
which had begun in Moscow, continued to seek agreement with
Germany. In a broadcast speech on 29 June Halifax hinted at a
settlement of Germany's colonial claims if the German government
showed a new spirit. It still seemed not beyond the wit of man to find a
formula for Danzig, where fresh tension arose when the Poles accused
the German Senate of importing arms. 'I doubt' (wrote Chamberlain
in July) 'if any solution, short of war, is practicable at present, but if
dictators could have a modicum of patience, I can imagine that a
way could be found of meeting German claims while still safeguarding Poland's independence and economic security.'[38] The British
government's attitude to Hitler was in effect: We do not mind your
taking Danzig (which everyone knew to be an almost wholly German
city) provided you do so without starting a war. But Danzig was
rightly seen as the symbol of a much larger issue. When R. S. Hudson,
Parliamentary Secretary of State at the Ministry of Overseas Trade,
invited a senior official of Göring's Economic Ministry, H. Wohltat, to
hold talks on trade and colonies, a far-reaching Anglo-German agreement was foreshadowed. It was then that Sir Horace Wilson, Chamberlain's confidant, who also took part in the discussions, suggested
the signing of a non-aggression pact which, if accepted by Germany,
would enable England to get rid of her commitments to Poland.[39] The
thinking of Dirksen, the German ambassador in London, ran on

similar lines: he hoped for a settlement that would 'chemically dissolve' the Danzig problem and enable the British gradually to withdraw from their Polish pledge. He also informed his government that such a pact would be judged in London incompatible with the simultaneous pursuit of an 'encirclement policy'.[40] But Hitler was not impressed. He knew that the French and British were negotiating in Moscow for a treaty with the Soviets, and had decided to get in first. His main object was to prevent the revival of the Triple Entente. His means was the Nazi-Soviet Non-Aggression pact. This was preceded by trade talks and by a series of soundings and feelers. The pact was signed on 23 August following a decision by Hitler late in July; the Russian decision to negotiate was probably made between 10 and 21 July.[41] Ever since a speech by Stalin on 10 March there had been indications (including the replacement of the pro-western Litvinov by Molotov as Foreign Minister) that the Russians, despite their earlier talk of collective security, might after all come to terms with Germany. The significance of Hitler's resolve to let Hungary have Ruthenia did not go unnoticed in Moscow, and Japan's expansion in the Far East was another reason for Russia to seek good relations on her western border. The complete about-turn in Hitler's foreign policy left many Germans, including members of the Nazi party, bewildered and bitter; but as Ribbentrop observed at the time, dictators do not have to take into account 'fluctuating public opinion'. Hitler's impatience, and his fear of a possible settlement between Russia and the West, enabled Stalin to drive a hard bargain. News of the pact naturally put an end to the West's negotiations with the Soviet Union, which had dragged on most of the summer. Failure to reach agreement was due to several reasons, the main one being the impossibility of reconciling military aid with the Poles' refusal to admit the Red Army to their soil.

Hitler almost certainly assumed that his pact with Stalin would deter France and Britain from honouring their pledge to Poland. For what he could not possibly know was that by a secret stipulation in the Anglo-Polish treaty the British guarantee applied only in case of a German violation of Poland and not in case of violation by the Soviet Union: it must therefore have appeared to him that Britain and France had only the choice between neutrality and war on Poland's behalf against both Germany and Russia. Even when the British and French governments actually declared war, Hitler, despite his obvious disappointment, stuck to his plans: as he told Brauchitsch on 28 August, 'If I am pushed to it I shall wage a two-front war'.[42] His generals had warned him that, to avoid the season of rain and mud, the last date for starting a campaign in Poland was 1 September. In public Beck, encouraged by western backing, but also reflecting the mood of his country,[43] took a firm stand: Danzig had become a symbol of Polish independence, and Polish rights would not be abandoned – it was a question of honour. In private he continued to seek a compromise. According to the German ambassador in Warsaw, he even expressed doubts of the wisdom of the British alliance, and hankered after an understanding with Germany,[44] though he also assured Potemkin, the deputy Russian Foreign Minister, that Poland would not be a party to any combination with Germany against Russia.[45] Polish efforts to interest Hitler in a projected Polish-German condominium for Danzig evoked no response.[46] Once he had decided to come to terms with the Soviet Union, he was less interested in anything the Poles could offer. Far-sighted observers had long foreseen a fourth partition of Poland as a consequence of the failure of Russia and the West to agree, but the secret protocol of the Nazi-Soviet pact provided also for the division of Eastern Europe into German and Russian spheres of influence. Finland, Estonia and Latvia, as well as eastern Poland, were to be in the Russian sphere, Lithuania, western and central Poland in the German. Russia was to have a free hand in Bessarabia, and Germany expressed her disinterestedness in the Balkans. The pact made it impossible for the western powers to reconstruct Versailles Poland, and Hitler hoped that, with Stalin as his accomplice and Poland conquered and divided, they would recognise the new order as irrevocable. Yet there was a final hesitation. Orders to invade Poland on 26 August were countermanded hours before the attack was due to start. Hitler was disturbed by the British government's formal ratification of its treaty with Poland, and by a message from Mussolini that Italy was not ready for war and would not take part if it broke out. News of Japanese disapproval of the Nazi-Soviet pact, which shocked Tokyo, came as a further unpleasant surprise. Hitler decided to give negotiations one more chance. This time a Swedish businessman sponsored by Göring, Birger Dahlerus, acted as intermediary between Berlin and London. The British government still believed that a compromise over Danzig and the Corridor was possible, but the Polish government showed scepticism. In the event not enough time was left to work out an agreement when Hitler's deadline of 1 September was reached. On that day the Second World War began.

For over six years Hitler had gambled successfully. He had taken great risks and won great triumphs. Beginning with few assets and facing formidable obstacles, he had built up, using at first a mixture of bluff and psychological warfare, a position of strength (modified in Russia's favour by the pact of 23 August) such as Germany had not had, especially in the eastern half of Europe, since the days of

Brest Litovsk. The Europe of Versailles had gone: France was reduced almost to the status of a second rank power, a half-willing accomplice in Hitler's purpose, her former allies at Hitler's mercy; Britain still half inclined to accept a compromise over Danzig, a somewhat reluctant convert to her new containment policy in Eastern Europe. Had Hitler had the patience, had he made a conciliatory gesture towards the conquered Czechs, he could have lulled the fears of the western democracies, which still faced the prospect of war with extreme aversion.[47] As Weizsäcker had written in a memorandum on 10 November 1937: 'From England we want colonies and freedom of action in the East, from us England wants military quiescence, particularly in the West.'[48] But patience was lacking. The seizure of Prague made it virtually certain that war could not be confined to Eastern Europe, and the invasion of Poland finally confirmed it.

(ii) THE NAZI ECONOMY: GUNS, BUTTER AND AUTARKY

Apart from agriculture, Hitler's economic policy reflected practical needs rather than ideology, and bore little trace of the radical slogans, such as abolition of the 'slavery of interest' and denunciation of 'predatory' as opposed to 'productive' capital, which had featured in the party's programme and propaganda. Since its re-foundation in 1925 the N.S.D.A.P. had been gradually but unmistakeably shedding this heritage, and the two leaders who took it seriously, Gottfried Feder and Gregor Strasser, had lost all their influence by the time they were expelled from the party at the end of 1932. Hitler had long been anxious to allay the fears of the capitalists, not only because he needed their financial support, but because he could hardly become Chancellor without the goodwill of the parties with which they were associated. For much the same reasons he refused to annoy President Hindenburg, as Brüning and Schleicher had done, by supporting land reform or criticising the subsidies paid by a hard-pressed Treasury to the bankrupt landowners of East Prussia. Yet as a politician Hitler was sufficiently aware of the importance of left-wing support to refuse to show his hand, at least before the crucial election of 5 March. Once the election had been won and the Enabling Act passed, he could deal with the economy as he pleased. It was soon evident that there were to be no great structural changes: Schmitt, who succeeded Hugenberg as Minister of Economics in June 1933, told leading industrialists that Hitler did not intend to carry out a programme of socialisation.[49] Nevertheless, the German economy, which even in the heyday of liberalism had been far from laissez-faire, by the 1930s was subject to further restrictions. Prices, salaries, wages, rents and rates of interest had to be approved by the government. Industry was organised on both a territorial and a functional basis, and the National Union of German Industry, which represented heavy and light industry, dealt with general questions of economic policy and provided advice on the formation and working of cartels. It was not difficult for the Nazi government to take over this organisation and use it for their purposes. The Corporate State, however, which Mussolini claimed to have created in Italy, never became a reality in Germany despite the support it received from some members of the Nazi party.

The most urgent task before Hitler, as before any Chancellor, was the reduction of unemployment. Brüning and Papen had tried to do this by launching a programme of public works and providing financial inducements to businessmen to invest capital and employ labour. This policy was continued and greatly expanded by the Nazis, who added projects of their own, such as the building of motorways, soon followed by that of barracks, airfields and frontier defences as the rearmament drive got under way. Cheap and mobile labour for these enterprises was provided by the National Labour Service, begun in 1933 on a voluntary basis and made compulsory two years later. All men between the ages of 18 and 25 had to spend six months in it, after which they proceeded to their military training. All married women between the ages of 17 and 25 also had to do Labour Service, usually in agriculture or domestic work, but in war work after 1939. Firms were urged to employ as many people as possible and to use human labour rather than machines; also in accordance with Nazi philosophy, men in preference to women, until later wartime shortage of manpower forced a reversal of this policy. The new arms factories, and those producing the new synthetic substitutes for imports, also added to the demand for labour, while from 1935 onwards conscription and the Labour Service withdrew hundreds of thousands of young men from the labour market. The stimulus given by these measures was felt throughout the economy. Hitler was fortunate too in that by the time he came to power the trade cycle had already begun recovery from its nadir in the summer of 1932. During his first year in office, unemployment fell from 6 to 3·77 million, industrial production rose by 13 per cent and agricultural income by 20 per cent.[50] By 1938 the number of unemployed was only 400,000, industrial output had nearly doubled and the national income had risen by 87 per cent.[51] Germany's problem now was a shortage of labour: ironically, the 'nation without space' had vacancies for half a million workers. The difficulty was alleviated by the 'repatriation' of ethnic Germans from outside the Reich, a process greatly accelerated by the Nazi-Soviet pact of 1939. But more important was the influx of foreign workers, chiefly from Eastern Europe, who by the summer of 1939 numbered some 300,000. This total was greatly augmented during the war years by millions of foreigners recruited from prisoners of war and from the population of the occupied or friendly countries. In 1937 real wages passed the previous best level, that of 1928. Output of consumer goods lagged behind that of production goods (whether the latter were for military or civilian use), and much of the newly created purchasing power remained unabsorbed. Prices rose, and the boom created fears of a flight from the mark. The memory of inflation was still vivid, and to no one more than Dr Schacht, the former President of the *Reichsbank* who was recalled to his old job by Hitler in March 1933 and became Minister of Economics in July 1934. Schacht knew that Hitler and his colleagues had no understanding of how the economy worked and saw it as his task to curb excess government spending and to prevent the wilder Nazi schemes from leading to a fresh monetary crisis. Schacht himself, to whom much of the credit for the recovery from inflation at the end of 1923 was due, was regarded as a pillar of economic orthodoxy and his joining the government gave it an aura of respectability and stability. His hope of imposing restraint on the government had little chance of success, given the nature of the Nazi leaders and their ambitions. Schacht was however a man of great resource. One of his innovations was a method of financing public expenditure without printing more banknotes (the fatal mistake during the inflation of 1923) or weakening the government's credit. Contractors were paid with bills, issued by a financial agency known somewhat cryptically as the Metallurgical Research Commission, which were accepted by the *Reichsbank* and thus became a negotiable form of currency. The Mefo bills, as they were called, were renewable for periods up to five years; by the time they matured, public revenue was expected to have increased enough to meet them. In this way it was possible for Germany's internal national debt to rise more than threefold between 1933 and 1939 and for the budget, unpublished after 1935, to remain unbalanced, without a flight from the mark. Control of prices was tightened by a special Price Commissioner. Schacht realised that Hitler intended to use increased revenue not to pay off debts but to step up arms expenditure and he was worried by the diversion of raw materials from exports to armaments. The appointment of Göring as Controller of the Four Year Plan in 1936 with authority over raw materials and foreign exchange robbed Schacht of most of his effectiveness, and henceforth the rate of rearmament proceeded more rapidly with scant regard for Schacht's warnings. He resigned, first as Minister of

Economics, later (January 1939) as President of the *Reichsbank*. It was a victory for the Party and for Göring in particular over the traditionalists. Schacht's disappearance also marked the end of the influence of the big capitalists over the Nazi regime. By this time it was clear that the solution of Germany's debt problem was to be through the annexation of foreign territory. Schacht was now disillusioned. Yet, wittingly or not, he had served Hitler well. His public career, which was to end in the dock at Nuremberg, exemplified the tragedy of an able and ambitious man who, having at first supported Hitler for patriotic reasons realised too late that his masters were criminals.

Had Hitler's aim been simply to restore prosperity he would, of course, have adopted a consumer-oriented investment policy and have tried to restore Germany's foreign trade, which had fallen by about two-thirds since the boom year 1928. But his main objective, as he told Göring when inaugurating the Four Year Plan, was to make the Reich self-sufficient in food and raw materials, while the army was to be ready for war by the end of the same period. Hitler remembered Germany's vulnerability to blockade in the First World War, and was determined that this experience should not be repeated. Göring was told to do the impossible, but, as he himself once said, 'If the Führer wishes it, then two times two makes five.'[52] This remark not only sheds light on Hitler's psychology but suggests the reason for his ultimate failure in a refusal to come to terms with reality. Nevertheless Germany's dependence on agricultural imports fell from 25 per cent to 15 per cent between 1933 and 1939, a significant achievement even if the result was often a stodgy and unbalanced diet. By the time the Second World War broke out she was virtually self sufficient in bread, potatoes, sugar, milk, meat and coarse vegetables.[53] A similar degree of self-sufficiency in other sectors of the economy proved unattainable despite strenuous efforts. Though her scientists developed with varying degrees of success oil from coal, wool from cellulose and artificial rubber from a mixture of coal and lime, the country's requirements could never be wholly met from these new sources. Among indispensable materials, for example, was high grade iron ore imported from Sweden for the making of steel. Germany's own iron ore deposits, which were much inferior in quality, were processed at Göring's new publicly-owned steel plant at Wattenstedt-Salzgitter, with disappointing results. Nevertheless steel output rose from 7·2 million tons in 1932 to 19·2 million tons in 1937.[54] Essential imports continued to be financed, though with difficulty, and the purchase of scrap material, copper, tin and nickel actually increased. Germany had negligible gold and currency reserves, so that the only way of paying for imports was by exports. Here she faced two special difficulties: several of her customers and rivals, such as Britain and U.S.A., had made themselves more competitive by devaluing their currencies, and they had introduced or raised tariffs to protect their own industries. German trade was also hit by an American boycott of German goods in retaliation for Hitler's treatment of the Jews. The Germans, fearful of inflation, refused to devalue the mark, but they subsidised exports to help their trade balance, which came to much the same thing. No capital was allowed to leave the Reich, and foreign creditors watched impotently while the interest or amortisation payments due to them were placed in blocked accounts to be spent only in Germany. As far as possible trade between Germany and other countries was conducted by bilateral clearing agreements, in which the value of the mark varied according to circumstances. Sometimes barter was resorted to. Strict control was kept over imports, and increasingly only countries which bought from Germany could sell to her. The result was a shift of German trade away from traditional western markets to new ones in the Balkans, the Near East and Latin America.[55] Small countries such as Yugoslavia and Greece were forced to take German exports irrespective of suitability because Germany bought a high proportion of their agricultural produce. This made them more susceptible to political pressure, and Nazi trade policy was one factor which helped to break up the French system of alliances in Eastern Europe. An unexpected but general revival of world trade in 1937 also enabled Germany to raise both exports and imports quite substantially. Politics too came to the aid of economics, as when the seizure of Austria and Czechoslovakia added financial assets, valuable raw materials and industrial plant to the economy of the Reich. Hitler's goal of autarky was to be reached by the conquest of living space: as he said in September 1936: 'If we had at our disposal the Urals, with their incalculable wealth of raw materials, and the forests of Siberia and the unending wheatfields of the Ukraine, our country would swim in plenty.'[56] The *Reichsbank* also gained financially from the plunder of Jewish property, especially after the Pogrom of 9 November 1938 – the *Kristalnacht* or night of broken glass – when, over and above loss of life and heavy material damage, a fine of a milliard marks was imposed on the Jewish community in retaliation for the murder of a German diplomat in Paris. Nevertheless Göring did not succeed in making Germany independent of the outside world, and when the Second World War began her reserves of oil, copper, rubber, aluminium, and other raw materials were quite inadequate.[57] Only her new trade treaty with Russia, the product of the

Nazi-Soviet Non-Aggression Pact, was to give her some immunity against the British blockade.

As has been said, the Nazis did little to implement their proclaimed economic principles. Even the middle-class socialism of their programme, exemplified by the closure or nationalisation of department stores in the interest of small shopkeepers, was in practice ignored. Party zealots succeeded in getting some big stores closed (many of them were Jewish-owned and would have suffered anyway), but when the result was found to be a rise in prices and loss of employment, the policy was tacitly abandoned.[58] Though the small retailer was not unimportant politically, he counted for less in the fulfilment of Hitler's plans than the industrialists and the wage earners. These were the two main groups that had to be placated. The small businessman and the craftsman were progressively eliminated. In Berlin alone 10,000 shops and stores had been shut down, largely owing to the shortage of goods, by November 1939, and the introduction of war rationing accelerated this process.[59] Though the Nazi leaders were nostalgically attached to those groups who were threatened by the impersonal forces of progress and technology, in practice they had to allow these forces free play in order both to raise the standard of living and to construct their war machine. Redundant small shopkeepers were a useful source of manpower for the armaments industry, as the *Schwarze Korps* (the organ of the S.S.) took pleasure in pointing out.[60] The cavalier treatment of the lower middle classes by the Nazi regime contrasted sadly with their successful wooing by Hitler before he came to power.[61]

The keynote of Nazi policy towards the economy, as everywhere else, was *Gleichschaltung* or regimentation. There had to be one association each of industrialists, merchants and craftsmen, just as there had to be one of clerical and manual workers. Finally they were all grouped together in a single mammoth organisation, the German Labour Front, which, as we have seen, was meant to symbolise the end of class war and the integration of both sides of industry under the party in the 'folk community'. A law passed early in 1934 made the leadership principle binding in industry as well as in politics. This suited paternal employers such as Gustav Krupp, who was chairman of the Reich Association of German Industry, and whom Hitler appointed to a new post, Head of German Industry, in May 1933. Like the generals, the leading manufacturers felt immediate benefit from Hitler's coming to power (more orders, greater factory discipline), but in course of time they too realised that they had lost their independence. The employer or managing director was designated 'leader' in each factory or workshop, with the employees as his 'followers'. In place of the democratically elected workers' council of Weimar days, a council of trustees was set up in every business employing more than twenty people to represent the workers. It was elected by secret ballot from names drawn up by the management in consultation with a shop-steward appointed by the Labour Front. The council of trustees was empowered to 'advise' the management, but any disputes had to be referred to the local trustee of labour, who was an official of the Ministry of Labour in charge of a large area. He had wide-ranging powers over such matters as wages, hours of work and the election of the councils of trustees. There was some rivalry between him and the Labour Front, which, besides having its representative in the factory in the person of a shop-steward, exercised a general control over all aspects of employment: hiring and firing, workmen's compensation and insurance, care for the elderly and the disabled. With a staff totalling 30,000 and a revenue twice that of the N.S.D.A.P., the Labour Front was a powerful body, which was liable to intervene at any time to inspect, negotiate or investigate complaints.[62]

One of the most important activities of the Labour Front was the organisation for welfare and leisure known as Strength through Joy. This was the counterpart of Mussolini's *Dopo Lavoro*, but a good deal more ambitious. Strength through Joy, a name which gave rise to a good deal of mockery, enabled millions of wage-earners to do many things which they had never done before, such as going to the theatre, attending subsidised concerts, visiting art galleries, sailing or playing tennis, enjoying cut price holidays or taking part in cruises in the Baltic, Mediterranean and elsewhere. By 1939 some fifty-five million people (often, in fact, the same people several times) had shared in these recreations, which they could never have afforded on their own.[63] This was one of the most popular and successful aspects of the regime. Another organisation, known as Beauty of Labour, did much to improve lay-out and conditions of work in factories, including canteens, washing and changing rooms and sports grounds. The masses were looked after paternally, but propaganda was never absent, and discipline was there when needed. 'Every worker,' ran the slogan, 'must regard himself as a soldier in the economy'.[64] As the economy moved towards full employment, with shortages of skilled labour at many points and firms bidding against each other with a promise of higher wages, industrial discipline tended to break down. The government passed a number of restrictive measures. Every employee had to have a work book or labour pass. People were debarred from moving into big cities and were assigned to industries short of labour, such as agriculture, or to work of national importance like the Hermann

Göring steelworks or the Siegfried Line. Carpenters, masons and later on all building workers were bound to their jobs.[65] Ley, the head of the Labour Front, boasted in 1938: 'There are no private citizens any more.'[66] Yet the government, mindful of the need for a contented labour force, was both hesitant and inconsistent in applying its own rules.[67] Capital was easier to control than labour, and a discontented capitalist was hardly a political danger. The government used its powers to regulate cartels, prohibit and direct investments, and to allocate raw materials. By 1939 over a third of the national income consisted of goods and services ordered by the state.

Schacht claimed that both the public and private economies were centralised and rigidly concentrated, thanks to the power of the authoritarian state. Yet the unity imposed on the economy was more apparent than real. Within the party and governmental ruling élite there was anything but harmony. Apart from the rivalry between Schacht and Göring which ended with the latter's victory, there was a continuous feud between Göring and General Thomas, head of the Economic and Armaments Department of the O.K.W. in what Thomas's secretary described as a 'confusion of competencies'.[68] Inadequate supplies of steel and other materials, of transport and labour were competed for by four rival organisations: Göring's Four Year Plan office, Thomas in the O.K.W., Funk's Ministry of Economics, and the Organisation Todt which was responsible for building the new motor roads, the fortifications in the west and many other projects. Hitler wished to rearm Germany, satisfy the consumer, and launch an almost incredibly ambitious building programme in Berlin and other cities all at the same time. 'The myriad organisations,' concludes one recent investigator, 'regulating the German economy issued such a flood of orders, such a variety and diversity of provisions and amendments controlling production, that by 1939 nobody could make head or tail of it at all.'[69] Thomas himself later testified: 'In Hitler's so-called leadership state there subsisted in economic affairs a complete absence of leadership, and an indescribable duplication of effort and working at cross purposes; for Hitler shut his eyes to the need for long-term planning.'[70] Even by the end of the war, as Speer found after he had taken the place of Todt as Minister of Armaments, there was still a good deal of slack and waste in the German economy. Only 45 per cent of German women were employed in the armed forces or the economy, compared with 61 per cent in Britain, and Germany still had over a million domestic servants.[71] Luxury projects for the private gratification of Nazi leaders were still being worked on. Nevertheless with all its inadequacies the Nazi economy provided the means by which the German army conquered most of Europe. Despite his lack of understanding of economics, Hitler had grasped the elementary truth that labour and material resources are there to be used. It was only after *Blitzkrieg* tactics failed in Russia that Germany was forced against her will to fight the war of attrition for which her system of government was unsuitable and her means insufficient.

This very brief summary of the Nazi economy suggests two questions. The first is: Given the priority of guns to butter proclaimed by Göring, how did the consumer fare? The second is: Given the direction of labour and the prohibition of strikes, how did the workers react?

That the consumer came off second-best is clear from the lag, already referred to, between the output of production goods, which more than doubled between 1933 and 1939, and that of consumer goods, which rose by less than a half.[72] Less wheat and rye were actually being produced in 1938 than five years earlier, and the number of cattle and hogs was also down, mainly because of drastic cuts in fodder imports. Milk production was marginally up, but the shortage of fats remained, despite a doubling of the use of fertilisers. The only significant rises were in potatoes and sugar beet, especially the latter. Thus the average citizen did not have a much greater choice of diet than before, though he probably ate more calories. Where he gained was in housing and consumer durables. Though a large backlog in housing, inherited from the past, remained, between 1933 and 1939 the average rate of house or flat building was 100,000 a year more than during the Weimar Republic.[73] The output of radios and furniture went up substantially, and firms dealing in such goods as confectionery, spirits and shoes also experienced boom conditions. By 1938 twice as many automobiles were being manufactured as in 1929, the last of the pre-depression years.[74] Taxes were high, though certain groups, such as newly married couples, got more relief, and the rise in the birth rate suggested a more optimistic outlook among the population. Still, the Third Reich was an economy in which a high proportion of output went to the state, which meant, increasingly, to the armed forces. In 1939 only 63 per cent of Germany's net national product was spent on personal consumption, compared with 79 per cent in Britain and France.[75] The cost of living, as official statistics admitted, increased by 7·2 per cent (11·5 per cent in the case of food) between 1933 and 1937, but weekly real earnings rose considerably more.[76] Up to 1936 it was possible to satisfy both civilian and military needs by re-activating those parts of the economy which had lain idle: after that date the one group could grow only at the expense of the other. The real pay-off for the German consumer came with the exploitation of the occupied countries from 1938 onwards. But even when the Second World War began, Hitler was loth to make demands on civilians which would reduce his popularity. The result was that even at the beginning of 1942 consumer production in Germany was running at only 3 per cent below pre-war level.[77]

There has been some argument among historians over the extent to which the Nazi economy was a war economy. Allied Intelligence at the time exaggerated the scale of German rearmament, which was far from being as complete as appeared from the outside, just as it was less rationally organised than its opponents believed.[78] Though German military expenditure rose steadily between 1933 and 1939, it did not accelerate during the first years of the war, and did not reach its peak until 1943-4. As late as 1940 Germany spent proportionately less on her armed forces than did Britain, which had started the race later but made a great spurt in 1939-40.[79] Germany spent 1 per cent of her gross national product on military expenditure in 1932, 6 per cent in 1934, 13 per cent in 1936 and 27 per cent in 1938. During the same period British military expenditure rose from 2 per cent of the gross national product to 7 per cent. By 1943 the British proportion was 56 per cent compared with Germany's 61 per cent. Thus in the pre-war years the German economy's commitment to war was far from total, and as we have seen in some ways, such as the use of women, even during the war it fell far short of the British war effort, as Speer complained at the time.[80] Germany's lead before 1939 was substantial, but she had started from a lower base. Her advantage in 1940 was that her weapons were more modern rather than more numerous. The fact that Hitler's readiness for war was exaggerated by his prospective enemies was a psychological point in his favour. Up to 1942 his armaments were in width not depth, and contained serious gaps, due mainly to shortage of raw materials, but also because he assumed that Germany was adequately equipped for his purpose, which was not a long war (that he knew he could not win), but a series of short strikes. He calculated that each conquest would provide a breathing space and yield new plunder that would make good Germany's deficiencies. Less than three weeks before the Polish campaign began General Thomas of the O.K.W. warned Hitler that Germany lacked the economic means to fight a war that was not local and temporary. Yet Hitler's gamble succeeded, and only in the later stages of the war did the German consumer really suffer. Even then his hardships were caused by Allied bombing rather than by a shortage of food, fuel and clothing such as had made civilian life almost intolerable during the years of the First World War. And only after the shock of the first Russian winter of 1941/2 did Hitler agree to arm in depth and to abandon the assumptions of his *Blitzkrieg* strategy.[81]

The attitude of the working classes to the Nazi regime presents something of a paradox. Hitler had dissolved their parties, persecuted their leaders, suppressed their unions, and destroyed their democratic rights. The reasons for their lack of resistance have already been discussed. Effective opposition was in any case impossible after March 1933. But there was little sign of that intense hostility to Fascism on the part of the wage-earners which might have been expected. This was partly because demoralisation and disorientation were not confined to the middle classes, but had spread to the political left and its supporters. Several other factors have also to be borne in mind. By 1934 about a third of the members of the N.S.D.A.P. belonged to the working classes, so that there was a partial identification between the two.[82] Through the N.S.B.O. (the Nazi factory organisation) the party had won a foothold in many factories as the Nationalists and People's parties had never done. The radical image produced by Hitler's denunciation of reaction and early anti-capitalist propaganda survived into the period when he was in power. Secondly, what reconciled the Nazi regime to millions was that it provided them with jobs. The unemployed (many of whom joined the S.A. for want of an alternative) regained a living wage and self-respect. And though the share of wages in the national income actually fell between 1933 and 1939, this was largely disguised by an average annual increase of 2·8 per cent in real wages during that period.[83] No previous government had mastered the economic crisis. Hitler, in his own way, did. Thirdly, the workers, like other classes, responded to the appeal to nationalism, and approved of Hitler's onslaught on the treaty of Versailles. Fourthly, although the Nazis were not socialists, they were in their own sense egalitarians. Few of the party bosses came from the ranks of the traditional power-holders, and most of them displayed an anti-aristocratic bias which gave them common ground with the under-privileged. In the Third Reich, the employer was relieved of pressure from the defunct trade unions, but he was far from being the master in his own house that he had been before 1914. As we have seen, capital was subject to control, and dividends were restricted. It was made clear that the right to property depended on service to the new state.[84] The nobility of all forms of labour was more than a slogan. Classlessness was practised as well as preached. In the party organisations young men of every background mixed on equal terms, and the highest positions were open to all. A prince might be a Gauleiter's secretary or chauffeur to a party bigwig. The old snobbery between the man of university education, the *Akademiker*, and the masses was broken down, as was the barrier between the office staff and those on the factory floor.[85] It was symptomatic that secondary and primary school teachers all belonged, for the first time, to a single body, the National Socialist Teachers' Association, which included 97 per cent of the profession. In the new *Reichswehr* too a more friendly and relaxed relation existed between officers and men, in contrast to the tensions of the old Imperial army. Ironically, something was accomplished which the revolution of 1918 had tried but failed to achieve. The Weimar Republic had sought to make a subject into a citizen; Hitler succeeded in making him into a 'comrade' (*Volksgenosse*) and in generating a genuine collective enthusiasm over the new togetherness.[86] Fourthly, workers in Germany tended to be less resentful of authoritarian management than those of many other countries. In the firm of Krupp for example, labour relations were remarkably good despite or perhaps because of the paternalistic attitude of the management; loyalty to the firm and the family was strong whatever the form of government. Management was expected to show, and usually did show, a high degree of competence and responsibility, and these qualities were reflected in the workpeople. Finally, the welfare side of the Nazi regime must not be overlooked.[87] Though wages remained low, there was a modest rise in the standard of living, partly in money, partly in social services. Priority was given to low rent housing. Besides Strength through Joy, a Winter Relief organisation and the institution of a one dish meal on Sundays to raise funds for the needy were held up as laudable examples of 'German socialism'. This 'nationalisation of charity' was important too as a means of transferring relief expenditure from the Treasury to the general public. Hitler's promise of a Volkswagen for all at the price of a thousand marks also had its propaganda value, even if its fulfilment had to wait until the Third Reich lay in ruins.

One sector of the economy has still to be considered: agriculture. Here the ideology of the N.S.D.A.P. played a larger part than in industry, though the results were often the opposite of what was intended. The rural population was seen as a racial élite, whose preservation was essential; the townspeople, by contrast, had been contaminated by miscegenation and industrialisation. The army had always drawn its best recruits from the countryside, and Hitler expected the farmers to be the main settlers and propagators of German *Kultur* in the lands to be occupied and colonised. As food producers, too, the farmers played a vital role. The Nazis had long looked to the farming community for support and had infiltrated their organisations. Glorification of the land and its cultivators was expressed in the cult of blood and the soil which featured prominently in Hitler's propaganda. Its main exponent was Walther Darré, the party's agrarian expert, who succeeded Hugenberg as Minister of Agriculture in June 1933. Like a surprisingly high proportion of Nazi leaders

(Rosenberg and Hess were other examples) Darré was born outside Germany: his birthplace was the Argentine, and he later went to school in Wimbledon. Darré's beliefs were summed up in the title of a book he published in 1929: *The Farmers as the Life-Source of the Nordic Race.* He was the principal author of the Hereditary Farms Act which gave security of tenure to occupiers of holdings of between 20 and 310 acres, which accounted for about a third of Germany's agricultural land. Many farmers, hit by the catastrophic fall in prices, had been heavily mortgaged and finally forced to sell up. In 1931 alone some three million acres had come under the hammer. The protection now given to the farmer against the mortgagor and the creditor was therefore welcome. Yet, in some cases, a farmer might wish to sell a farm but be debarred from doing so because it could not pass into the possession of anyone else (except his children). Darré's policy was thus a mixed blessing: the price paid for increased security was stagnation in an industry that needed change and modernisation.

The outbreak of war in September 1939 emphasised the difference between theory and practice, which had been growing since 1936. Increased demands for labour by industry made the slogan of 'Back to the Land' impracticable. The earlier promise of land reform, meaning the break-up of big estates (mainly east of the river Elbe) and their distribution in small holdings to the landless had not been fulfilled, though this had been an essential part of Darré's programme. On the contrary, estates which had been on the verge of bankruptcy in 1933 prospered from the monopoly of cereal and potato production they had enjoyed since.[88] Moreover, so much space was needed for motorways, military training grounds, airfields, etc. that fewer farms came into existence under Hitler's regime than during the Weimar Republic. It is estimated that nearly a million people left the land between 1933 and 1938, while some towns, notably those with important chemical factories, doubled their population.[89] Paradoxically the effect of National Socialism was to foster urbanisation because Hitler's plans of conquest made this inevitable. Where the German farmer did benefit was in the higher prices obtained for his products. Food prices had sunk catastrophically during the depression, though in Germany they remained, as before, above the world level. There, as elsewhere, the remedy was found in the setting up of producers' associations (marketing boards) whose function was to fix prices, regulate supplies and organise selling. In Germany control went so far as to prescribe the charges for each process involved in the production of bread, starting with a fixed quota for each crop, with severe penalties for non-fulfilment. During Hitler's first year of power the average price of foodstuffs went up by 25 per cent, some items, such as fats, rising by as much as 40-50 per cent.[90] This was hard on the consumers, who were unlikely to be consoled by Goebbels' remark that they could always manage without butter, but not without guns. Help was given to farmers in other ways, too: through tax reductions, lowering of rates of interest, and extra labour provided by the Labour Service at harvest time and for land improvement schemes. Nevertheless, during the Third Reich the rise in agricultural incomes failed to keep pace with that in other sectors of the economy.[91] The policy of expansion which Hitler pursued required an economy very different from the rural idyll of Darré's dreams. Yet the Nazis were successful in their other aim of increasing the proportion of food grown in Germany, even if some variety was lost. Because of this and of an efficient rationing system, the German population did not experience the shortage of food it had known in 1916-18. The intake of the average civilian remained at or near 2,700 calories a day for most of the war; even during the winter of 1944-5 it was about 2,450.[92] The German standard of living was bolstered by food imports, including loot, from occupied countries, and prisoners of war and forced civilian labour took the place of conscripted land workers. By the end of the war, about one in ten of those working on German farms was a foreigner.

(iii) CULTURAL DICTATORSHIP: THE MOBILISATION OF A NATION

At the Reich Party Congress in 1933 Hitler announced a somewhat cumbrous slogan: 'Through ideological renewal and the consequent racial purification to find a new style of life, culture and art'.[93] The new style was soon revealed: in many ways, it was the revival of an old style or rather several old styles. Goebbels had already begun to mould German society to the Führer's will. All writers, artists and journalists had to belong to a Reich Chamber of Culture which consisted of seven sections covering the fields of literature, the press, radio the theatre, music, painting and sculpture, and the cinema. The whole organisation was presided over by Goebbels himself, and was thus closely associated with the Ministry of Propaganda. Hitler had often expressed his contempt for intellectuals, who were described in Nazi writings as bloodless and rootless, and he complained that people had too much education. The Nazi movement was a reaction against modernism and an attempt to rehabilitate primitive values. In place of reason and experiment it exalted feeling and tradition. It was anti-urban and anti-industrial, glorifying the countryman, and saw the 'asphalt culture' of big cities as a pernicious influence like Jewish intellectualism or negro music. Apart from architecture, in which practical considerations tended to prevail over theory, Nazi culture showed remarkable consistency between theory and practice. It did more than reject the standards of Weimar: it denied those of the European civilisation of which Germany was a part. In this sense it is true that the cultural revolution proclaimed by Goebbels was more complete than the political.

Most of Germany's creative writers during the Republic had been progressive in politics, and belonged to or sympathised with the artistic avant-garde. Many had contributed to the *Weltbühne*, the leading left-wing weekly which was the champion of every radical cause from pacifism and socialism to sexual freedom and reform of the blasphemy laws. All these causes were anathema to Hitler. They were part of the 'cultural Bolshevism' he was never tired of denouncing, inseparably connected with the 'corrosive poison' of Jewry. For left-wing intellectuals (many of whom were Jews or had Jewish wives) the Third Reich offered only the choice between emigration and a concentration camp. During the first few weeks of the regime some 250 writers and artists left Germany in protest. Few well-known names were missing from the list of emigrants which included Thomas Mann and his brother Heinrich, Werfel, Wassermann, Feuchtwanger, Brecht, Stefan Zweig, Arnold Zweig, Zuckmayer, Ludwig Renn and Remarque, as well as distinguished painters, architects, musicians and scholars. They were the first of many exiles in what was to be one of the most productive diasporas of modern times. Scattered representatives of a humane tradition (very few were hardline communists) now branded as un-German, they found new homes – often with difficulty – in different corners of the world between São Paolo and Stockholm, California and Tel Aviv. A few, depressed beyond endurance by the worsening news from Germany and the later horrors of the Second World War, took their own lives. Some ultimately returned to a Germany they hardly recognised. Most stayed to plant the seeds of Weimar culture in the lands that gave them asylum, often with more far-reaching results than if they had never left home. The loss to Germany of so much talent cannot be measured.

Though such a high proportion of the German intelligentsia chose freedom and exile, there were a few notable exceptions. Among them was Gerhart Hauptmann, the veteran playwright whose early ties had been with the socialists and who had been especially honoured by the Republic. Hauptmann offered Hitler his enthusiastic support. So did Heidegger, the philosopher, who as Principal of Freiburg University told his students: 'The Führer, himself and alone, is the present and future reality of Germany and its laws.' Richard Strauss, the composer, became the first President of the Reich Chamber of Music.[94]

Paul Hindemith, by contrast, as a foremost composer of modern music, which was condemned, emigrated in 1934. One of the leading avant-garde poets, Gottfried Benn, whose work reflected the cultural pessimism fashionable during the Weimar period, hailed the Third Reich as 'a new vision of the birth of man', an outburst of uncritical admiration that its author soon bitterly regretted.[95]

Of well-known writers who stayed in Germany Ricarda Huch, the much respected elderly novelist whose views were far from left wing, resigned from the Prussian Academy of Arts in protest against Nazi intolerance. It was a rare gesture. More common was retreat into silence, the 'inner emigration' from which they were to emerge in 1945, less compromised than their collaborating colleagues, but also with a feeling, not always admitted, that they might have shown more courage. On a popular level there were the outpourings of party devotees such as Anne Marie Koeppen, who addressed the Führer with quasi-religious reverence in verses which contain the following typical lines: 'Thou art present in the growth of the ears of corn, in the song of children, in the movement of the plough, in the sound of the scythe . . . When our children utter thy name it sounds like the joyful song of the lark . . . Thou hast taken their hearts into thy hands and mouldest them with true mastery.'[96] Oddly enough, the novel which in some ways is most typical of the Third Reich was published some nine years earlier. This was Hans Grimm's *Volk ohne Raum*, the story of a young German who had emigrated, as Grimm himself had done, to South Africa, where he had fought with the Boers against the British and had been interned. Later in German South West Africa, he had again fallen foul of the British, and had ultimately returned to a Germany stripped of its colonies, impoverished and overcrowded within its shrunken borders. Half a million copies of this book had been sold by the outbreak of the Second World War, and it was undoubtedly influential in spreading the belief that Germany must expand to live, and that only British jealousy combined with Jewish machinations and unpatriotic Marxism, stood in her way.

Just as the conservative revolutionaries of the Weimar Republic had first hailed Hitler as Germany's saviour and later realised their mistake, so many of the intellectuals who had opposed or been indifferent to the Republic underwent their own form of disillusionment with the Third Reich. Stefan Georg, the symbolist poet whose aristocratic tastes and romantic cult of leadership marked him as a natural sympathiser with an authoritarian kind of government, showed his antipathy by retiring to Switzerland, where he soon afterwards died. Georg's aesthetic ideals were in fact to inspire Stauffenberg and other members of the anti-Nazi movement, men who in their student days had come under the influence of the 'Georg Circle' that attracted many of the more ardent spirits in the literary and academic world. A distinguished writer who had done a good deal to prepare the ground for National Socialism, though he never became a party member, was Ernst Jünger, whose reputation was based on his novels of the First World War in which he had served with shock troops and won the highest military award.[97] Jünger was hailed as the spokesman of the front line generation which had sacrificed everything and gained nothing in spite of its heroism. Not only did Jünger denounce Weimar democracy and nihilistically laud the 'high treason of the spirit', but his vision of a hierarchic militarist state run by an élite of workers or technocrats and soldiers came near to Nazi ideals if not to Nazi practice. In a different vein, Jünger's beautifully written allegorical On the Marble Cliffs, completed just before the outbreak of war in 1939, was an attack on the National Socialist regime. Jünger had the bizarre distinction of being banned by Hitler before the end of the war and then of having his work forbidden by the British occupation authorities just after it – at the same time as his books were being printed in London. The paradox illustrates the ambiguity of Jünger's position: while he was in the broad sense a spiritual forerunner of the Third Reich, he never actually compromised with Hitler in power, and he emerged from the war and postwar years with a reputation for independence and integrity enjoyed by few of his colleagues. Another writer who shared many of Jünger's assumptions and ideas was Oswald Spengler, the historian, whose monumental Decline of the West earned him the mantle of a somewhat gloomy prophet. His Prussianism and Socialism, published in 1920, extolled German socialism as opposed to Marxism, and his advocacy of authoritarian rule, praise of war and passionate nationalism placed him too among the leaders of 'intellectual anti-intellectualism'. Yet in a book published soon after Hitler came to power Spengler expressed his doubt and disapproval in suitably veiled language, while for their part the Nazis snubbed this exponent of cultural pessimism who died in 1936.

The élite that presided over Nazi culture between 1933 and 1945 was hardly impressive, though among the academics were two Nobel Prize winners.[98] The task of the intellectual was to be an ideological soldier, to disseminate the Nazi view of the world. The duty of the artist was to serve the race: his function was biological rather than aesthetic. Scientific objectivity and art for art's sake were out of date, relics of a discredited liberalism, while criticism was identified with subversion, the product of an unhealthy individualism. Modern art was condemned, whether in the form of expressionist or abstract painting and sculpture, twelve-tone music or the psychological novel. Anything in this category was forbidden to be shown, played or published. A total of nearly 16,000 objects, including prints and drawings, was removed from German museums. Many of them were sold by auction in Switzerland. Work by foreign as well as German artists was confiscated.[99] Offending artists were in some cases forbidden even to paint. There was a complete ban on Jewish artists and composers, past and present. A selection of condemned paintings, hung in such a way as to appear ridiculous, and including many inferior works, was displayed in Munich as an exhibition of Degenerate Art in 1937. Oddly enough, the largest number were by Emil Nolde, the Expressionist painter from Schleswig Holstein who in earlier days had been a member of the Nazi party. To point the contrast, another exhibition was arranged which consisted of works approved of by the Führer. This was shown in the House of German Art, a neo-classical building designed by Troost, at the time Hitler's favourite architect. Apart from a few portraits of generals and Nazi heroes and scenes from the First World War, it contained mainly neo-romantic landscapes or idyllic peasant studies in a naturalistic nineteenth-century manner. Hitler's taste was for traditional subjects, competently painted in a cosy style with a kitschy quality such as could be found on the walls of any lower middle-class home. There was nothing sinister about this, but the escapist significance is obvious. To judge from the triptych of semi-draped nudes that hung above the mantlepiece of his Munich house, he also liked mildly erotic art of a conventional kind. His own early drawings were faithful copies of buildings that reveal a talent for draughtsmanship but little imaginative power; according to Speer, his later pen sketches were more distinctive and self-assured. It was architecture that really excited him. Ever since his failure to enter an architectural career he had been obsessed with building and town planning. Despite all his other preoccupations Hitler found time to take a lively interest in the plans for rebuilding Berlin and other cities drawn up at his wish by Speer, the gifted young architect who succeeded Troost as his personal architect and was made General Inspector of Buildings in 1937. Speer had already impressed Hitler by his ability to achieve dramatic effects. In the Nuremberg stadium, designed by Speer for the annual party rallies, a hundred and thirty searchlights, with beams reaching to a height of 20 to 25 thousand feet, created what Speer himself described as the first 'luminescent architecture of this type', a structural interplay of light which struck the British ambassador Sir Nevile Henderson as 'a cathedral of ice'.[100] Like other dictators, but even more so, Hitler required architecture to give visual expression to his dreams of greatness. In conformity with his megalomania, Speer's plans for Berlin had to be on a monumental scale. The city's population was to be doubled and its centre rebuilt with a huge avenue running through it to connect a triumphal arch into which the Paris Arc de Triomphe could have fitted 49 times, with a domed Assembly Hall having a volume sixteen times that of St Peter's, Rome, and capable of holding 150,000 people.[101] Speer's style was modernised classical or Nordic heroic which, to please Hitler, became increasingly ornate and gilded as the Third Reich evolved its own Empire idiom. Domestic architecture, by contrast, generally was encouraged to use traditional models, with the high-gabled detached single-family house superseding the flat-roofed block of flats favoured by the republic's architects. Thatch and half-timbering were also brought back in, for example, youth hostels. Yet despite the regime's known preference for archaic and rural styles, most of the architecture of the time was functional, and owed more to modern influences and techniques than was admitted.[102] The building programme in its eclecticism mirrored the division of opinion among the Nazi leaders, notably between the two cultural rivals Rosenberg and Goebbels (whose novel *Michael*, published in 1929, praised Expressionism). Many of the military and industrial buildings, social centres, schools, stadia and even churches were good of their kind, whether (as usually) neo-classical or neo-Gothic. Just as in the economy practical needs overrode ideology, so in architecture the need for urban renewal and the exigencies of war forced the adoption of a more contemporary style than the blood and soil zealots approved. Public monuments could be in the Greek style because the Ancient Greeks had been a Nordic people.

In the theatre the Third Reich brought changes in the type of play performed rather than in dramatic technique. The demand was for historical plays with a strongly nationalist flavour usually taken from the heroic past, Frederick the Great and the First World War being favourite themes. One of the first plays to be performed after 30 January 1933 was Hanns Johst's drama about Schlageter, the martyr of the Franco-German clash in the Ruhr in 1923, who was acclaimed the last soldier of the First World War and the first of the Third Reich. It is significant that in an earlier play by the same author, *Prophets*, whose subject was Martin Luther, some of the Jewish characters are portrayed as usurers and blasphemers and their murder is advocated, apparently with the author's approval. Johst, who had begun as an expressionist writer, became President of the Reich Chamber of Literature. He wished the theatre to become a cult. It did so most of all through a theatrical innovation which was very characteristic of the Third Reich: the open-air performance in a specially built amphitheatre of a *Thing* play (*Thing* was the old Germanic word for an open-air court of justice). This was usually the dramatic treatment of a patriotic or party theme involving much use of comment and choruses and with the audience joining in the singing. As a popular art form in which drama, music and architecture were combined the *Thing* play had a powerful propaganda value.

Similar trends dominated the German cinema after 1933.[103] Much of the talent that produced the great pioneering films of the republic left Germany for Hollywood or other centres in or before 1933. Of the Nazi film-makers Leni Riefenstahl, already well-known as an actress and producer of films on mountain themes, stood out with *Triumph of the Will*, a memorable study of the Nationalist Socialist party rally at Nuremberg in 1934, which received prizes in Venice and Paris as well as in Berlin.[104] Other films glorifying Hitler's achievements were *Baptism of Fire*, showing the part played by the *Luftwaffe* in the conquest of Poland, and *Victory in the West*, whose subject was the campaign of 1940, both largely made from newsreels. Goebbels, with his flair for publicity, was quick to grasp the importance of the cinema as a means of indoctrination. Emphasis was placed on films that furthered Nazi ideology. Here again heroic themes from the past such as the Seven Years' War and the First World War were favoured, but blood and the soil were also prominent. In the glorification of the German race the farmer and soldier (often the one became the other) held pride of place. The villain was inevitably a Jew if not a Slav. Goebbels ordered anti-semitic films such as *Jew Süss*, a travesty of Feuchtwanger's novel about eighteenth-century Württemberg, and distributed it not only in Germany but also in occupied countries to prepare people for pogroms or deportations of Jews. A cleverly made 'documentary' with the same purpose was *The Eternal Jew*, a composition which made vicious use of photographs taken in the Polish 'ghettos'. Other films with a political purpose had as their subject euthanasia, this time to influence public opinion in favour of the killing of the disabled and insane. *Ohm Krüger* was an anti-British film about the South African war which was partly scripted by Goebbels; it showed harrowing scenes in the concentration camps set up by the British for Boer women and children. Another historical film made late in the war was *Kolberg*, a spectacular costume production depicting the defence of the Baltic port against the French under Napoleon. Its objective was to bolster morale and encourage last ditch resistance, and significantly its first showing was to the beleaguered German garrison at Brest in 1944. Goebbels was, however, shrewd enough to realise that most people object to a constant diet of indoctrination, and the great majority of films made during the Third Reich were in fact purely for entertainment.

In putting into effect their educational programme the leaders were able, here as in other fields, to exploit long-standing resentments and current discontents. Many, probably the majority of university professors, had a negative attitude to the Republic. Accustomed to the hierarchical structure of the Empire, they were ill at ease in a democratic society. During the war a significant proportion of them supported the Pan-German demands for maximum annexations, and later they were critical of both the policy of fulfilment and the parliamentary regime. Their views inevitably influenced the students, who had their own reasons for dissatisfaction. A quarter of the university students were the sons of middle-grade civil servants, people who resented their loss of status since the fall of the Monarchy.

Lack of scholarships made it possible for only a small proportion of working-class boys to attend the university, so that the democratic leaven was small. The corporations to which about half the students belonged were racialist (*völkisch*) and expansionist (Pan-German) in outlook, a trend which was encouraged by the presence of German-speaking students from Austria and Bohemia. Many students were influenced by the nationalism they had acquired while serving as part-time volunteers in the *Reichswehr* in the early years of the republic. The Nazi slogans of youth and dynamism, combined with contempt for bourgeois ideals, attracted a generation that felt frustrated and responded readily to the 'heroic urge' of which the historian Meinecke spoke in 1925. The financial crisis after 1929 reduced the number of jobs available to those leaving the university and added to the already numerous white-collar proletariat. In 1931 a university-educated professional class of 300,000 to 330,000 was faced with 148,000 new graduates seeking entry.[105] By then the National Socialist Students' Association had won a majority in the general Students' Union, while the proportion of university teachers sympathetic to the Nazi cause was also high.[106] In May 1933 students took part enthusiastically in the ceremonial burning of 'un-German' books on the opera square in Berlin, while in the same month a collective statement by the professors expressed confidence in the government. The dismissal of Jewish and left-wing lecturers from the universities left vacancies that ranged from a tiny percentage in Tübingen and Rostock to nearly a third in Berlin and Frankfurt.[107] The number of students also fell markedly, from 116,000 in 1932–4 to 67,000 in 1936–7.[108] There were several causes including the expulsion of Jews, the introduction of a *numerus clausus* for women and the lower birth rate during the First World War. But the basic reason was the Nazis' discouragement of intellectual pursuits. University syllabuses and curricula soon reflected the new policy. The aim was described as 'the creation of a new type of student . . . a new type of university teacher and the formation of a new concept of learning'.[109] Liberal ideas and cosmopolitan influences were out. Promotion went to the new racial and political élite. Lecturers were encouraged to serve in the S.A., membership of which was compulsory for students. A book on the reform of universities described them as 'intellectual frontier forces' and military qualities were prized above academic.[110] New courses in 'racial science' and defence studies were introduced: in the latter every discipline was studied in relation to its use in war – there was war chemistry, war mathematics, war philosophy and so on. 'Aryan physics' was advocated by a Nobel Prize winner as an alternative to the 'Jewish physics' of Einstein. (Incidentally, Nazi disdain for research by Jewish physicists was one reason for Germany's failure to develop an atomic bomb before America.) In the fields of biology, ethnology and eugenics the new teaching often had grotesque results. A Bavarian Minister of Education told Munich professors that what mattered was not what was true but what was meaningful for National Socialism.[111] The absence of protests against the moral capitulation and intellectual absurdity implicit in this and similar statements reflected no credit on the German academic world and caused much later embarrassment. In extenuation it may be said that some intellectuals in other countries have on occasion been guilty of similar aberrations without being exposed to the same pressures as their German colleagues; and that equally craven examples can be found in the history of the other totalitarian regimes. Yet no other regime has resulted in such sinister perversion of the fruits of knowledge and science.

The same concern with indoctrination of the young and the training of a new élite for their role in a Nazi-dominated Europe was shown in the schools policy. Baldur von Schirach, the Reich Youth Leader, declared in 1936 that the youth leader and educator of the future would be a priest of the National Socialist faith and an officer in the party's service.[112] The vast majority of teachers belonged to the Nazi Teachers' Association. Emphasis was placed on physical training and on fitness as a prerequisite of military efficiency. Besides exercising its influence over the existing schools, the regime set up new schools of its own for children specially chosen for their leadership qualities and racial purity. One type of establishment was the *Napola* (National Political Education Institution), a boarding school for future officers with a syllabus biased in favour of military training and instruction in party ideology. As relatively conservative institutions the *Napolas* were deliberately modelled on the English public schools, and no doubt some of their practices, though few of their ethics, would have been approved of by Dr Arnold. Children entered the school at the age of ten, and fees were paid according to the parents' means. Altogether 43 Napolas were established in Greater Germany, including three for girls. Another type of school, also designed to produce a new governing class, but with a later admission age and a more radical stress on party and race, was the Adolf Hitler school, which was actually run by the party not the Ministry of Education. The crown of the edifice was the *Ordensburg*, a kind of residential university for older boys who had already done their military and labour service and were destined for high positions in the party hierarchy. The name recalled the fortresses – notably the well-known castle in West Prussia – built by the Teutonic Knights against the Slavs during the Middle Ages and was symbolic of the new racial superiority proclaimed by Hitler. Hitler himself, in language recalling Nietzsche, said of these *Ordensburgen*: 'My pedagogy is hard . . . In my fortress of the Teutonic Order a youth will grow up before whom the world will tremble. I want a violent, domineering, undismayed, cruel youth. . . . It must bear pain. There must be nothing weak and gentle about it. The free splendid beast of prey must once more flash from its eyes. . . .'[113]

For inculcating the broad mass of German youth with Nazi ideas the principal means remained the Hitler Youth, to which boys were admitted at the age of ten, after a preparatory stage in the *Jungvolk*, and where they remained until they were eighteen. Girls had their counterpart, the B.D.M. Membership of the Hitler Youth rose from nearly 110,000 at the end of 1932 to three and a half million in 1934 and about six million in 1936.[114] Under its young leader, Baldur von Schirach, who was 26 in 1933, it acquired a monopoly of all youth work, taking over the organisations run by the churches and the political parties. Military training was an important part of its activity, and by 1938 about 320,000 young Germans were organised in various air, naval or motorised units serving the needs of the armed forces. More than most Nazi organisations, the Hitler Youth drew on strong roots in German society – the revolt of the young against their elders, the desire for adventure and 'dynamism', the search for a faith, the longing for a future less drab and uncertain than the republic appeared able to provide. The cult of youth was a common phenomenon in inter-war Europe, especially in the Fascist movement that appeared in nearly every country. Germany, with its pre-war *Wandervögel*, had been the first country to experience the conflict of generations and the rejection of official values by the young in favour of a misty romanticism. During the Weimar Republic these ideals, radicalised by the war and the post-war turmoil, survived in the non-political but vaguely nationalist youth groups (*Bündische Jugend*) from which many of the Hitler Youth were recruited. Some of the pre-war youth leaders, like Wyneken, supported the Republic as a liberating force for the individual oppressed by conformism, but this was a minority voice. The emotional pull of the N.S.D.A.P., proclaimed by Schirach to be the party of youth, proved stronger.

National Socialism was a substitute religion. Although its ideology fed on many sources and answered a widely felt need, it depended in the last resort on the will and fanaticism of its founder, Adolf Hitler. No explanation of Hitler's success can ignore his neurotic personality, which presented different facets to different people. In Hitler creative and destructive impulses were inextricably mixed. To many, especially outside Germany, it has seemed almost incredible that a man so commonplace, so warped in his thinking and savagely vindictive in his purposes, should have captivated a great nation and been an object of hero-worship to millions of intelligent people. Nor was it only Germans who felt Hitler's fascination: foreign visitors too fell under his spell. Winston Churchill was not one of those who made the pilgrimage to Berchtesgaden, or ignored the seriousness of German rearmament, but in an essay published in 1937 in *Great Contemporaries* he expressed admiration for Hitler. Apart from the eyes, Hitler's mediocre appearance did not suggest any outstanding qualities, good or bad: he was almost Chaplin's little man, the victim of circumstances, the average obscure citizen, the anonymous face in a city crowd. This was an advantage, for it meant that the masses could identify themselves with him. But appearances were deceptive. Hitler had remarkable abilities: psychological astuteness, an untrained but penetrating mind, organising skill, strategic flair, formidable will power, a retentive memory, especially for military details, and a mesmerism that many people found irresistible. He worked by intuition rather than by logic, and was often erratic, moody and petty. But he stuck remorselessly to his basic ideas. As a speaker he could be calm and persuasive as well as – in his rabble-rousing style – obsessive and vituperative. On occasion, especially in the company of individuals, he was relaxed, even charming, free from tension and hysteria. With Speer, for example, his 'fellow artist' he could talk as an equal and be innocently enthusiastic about his building projects. But faced with a crowd Hitler could be a man possessed. His gifts were dangerous because they were harnessed to an immoderate lust for power and a malevolence that bordered on the insane. He could not have done what he did if he had not struck responsive chords among the German people. The supreme demagogue of recent, perhaps of all history, he appealed to the instincts of greed and envy which lie in everyone, and which were particularly easy to arouse in a nation which believed that it had been cheated and had certainly suffered and been humiliated. Hitler expressed the collective resentments and neurosis of a people in confusion and despair, but he was also the healer, the 'greatest psychotherapist of a nation' in the words of a contemporary British psychologist.[115] He was the spellbinder who fulfilled the prophecy of his fellow Austrian, the poet Hofmannsthal: 'Politics is magic. He who knows how to summon the forces of the deep, him people will follow.'[116] In a Central Europe divided by past hatreds and still smarting from war and civil war, he had his chance. In the end he pulled down the pillars of the civilisation he claimed to be saving. So far as his aims were nationalist he acted with brutal consistency. Believing that only the fittest survive and that one country's gain must be at the expense of its rivals, he sought to give Germany, whose national destiny was still unfulfilled, the dominant place on the continent of which she was the centre. The conquest of living space was, on certain assumptions, a rational objective, more rational indeed than the pre-war pursuit of colonies of little economic value and hard to defend, though whether the conquest and colonisation of so vast a country as Russia would in any circumstances have been a practical proposition is a moot point. The destruction of European Jewry, Hitler's second major aim, was a different matter. That at the height of a world war he could divert scarce resources to the massacre of defenceless women and children is a measure of the abnormality that lay at the heart of the Nazi movement. Rauschning, the one time Nazi leader in Danzig who knew Hitler well, called National Socialism the revolution of destruction because of its inner core of nihilism. Yet the fact remains that Hitler largely accomplished his second purpose and missed the first by only a narrow margin. Over a quarter of a century later his achievement, in terms of both its magnitude and its inhumanity, is still astonishing. According to Speer, who knew Hitler as well as anyone in his years of power and decline, Hitler privately admitted that much of his own *Mein Kampf* was out of date, and even ridiculed the extravagances of his more extreme followers like Himmler. If the later Hitler was indeed such a sceptic he was like the founder of a false religion who loses faith in it but is unable or unwilling to stop the demonic forces he has unleashed.

(iv) HITLER AND THE CHURCHES: HYPHENATED CHRISTIANITY AND RELUCTANT RESISTANCE

Relations between the Nazi government and the churches followed a tortuous course, oscillating between co-operation on the one hand and persecution and resistance on the other. Intimidation would be succeeded by détente, which in turn would give way to tension. The totalitarian claims of the regime gradually forced the Christian leaders into a conflict which most of them would gladly have avoided. Even so, they were slow to grasp the nature and magnitude of the threat, and the issue between the two sides was never fully joined.[117] For this there were at least four reasons. In the first place there was, especially among Protestants, much initial goodwill towards Hitler, and politically a good deal of common ground between him and the churches. In both confessions there was little enthusiasm for Weimar democracy, a readiness to accept his claim to have saved Germany from communism and 'Marxist materialism' and approval of the aims if not the means of his foreign policy. By the time the church leaders realised that Hitler did not keep his promises and that he was bringing disaster on Germany, it was too late: the compromises had already been made. Even then, there was more awareness of the doctrinal and institutional challenge presented by Nazism than of its moral implications. Not until well on in the war was the full iniquity of the regime revealed in its wholesale murder of cripples, gypsies and Jews, and by that time other emotions, such as wartime patriotism and – after June 1941 – anti-Bolshevism affected church attitudes. The Vatican, which was naturally the main outside influence on German Catholics, in its anxiety to avoid a break with Hitler, preferred prevarication to plain speaking, and allowed the moral issue to be obfuscated by 'reasons of state'. Secondly, neither Church, particularly the Evangelical, was emotionally prepared or intellectually equipped to resist Hitler's inroads. There was in Germany no theology or tradition of tyrannicide. Thirdly, Hitler himself used shrewd tactics, and refrained from provoking the churches too far. As an ambitious politician before 1933 he was too astute to quarrel with the organised Christian bodies to which 95 per cent of the population belonged. Once in power he disarmed Catholic fears by signing a Concordat with Rome, and exploited the right-wing sympathies of the Evangelicals in much the same way as he used the German Nationalist party which most of the pastors supported. Fourthly, the two confessions did not present a united front, and the Evangelicals especially were divided among themselves. The Führer wished the churches to become his 'spiritual sword',[118] and had no desire to start a new

Kulturkampf or to make enemies inside the churches gratuitously. He needed, especially after the outbreak of war, a united nation, and commanded that no further action be taken against the churches while the war lasted. It was Protestants and Catholics who voted, worked and fought for him: even among the S.S. nearly a quarter were Catholic. Like Napoleon, Hitler valued religion as a social cement. In private, as he told his confidant Rauschning, he believed that religion was dying out: the masses would never go back to it. Despite his criticism of the Roman Catholic Church in *Mein Kampf*, he had considerable respect for it as an institution whose hierarchical organisation and power of survival impressed him, but he despised the Protestant clergy for their submissiveness.[119] Had Hitler won the Second World War, there is little doubt that he would have dealt with the churches much more drastically. Yet at the time he not only resisted the extremists' demand for the replacement of Christianity by a Nordic religion based on blood, race and soil, but he refused to separate Church and State. Still, Hitler's compromise was not a bad one from his point of view: he had persuaded or forced a supposedly Christian nation to submit to his authority and become an accomplice in his crimes, yet the Pope never excommunicated him (though many rulers had in the past been excommunicated for relatively trifling offences) and the German churches went on praying for the success of his arms. It must have seemed to Hitler that what people believed was unimportant so long as they obeyed his orders.

The two Churches had played very different parts in German history since unification. Hitler's accession to power seemed to present more of a threat to the Catholics than to the Protestants. Nominally a Catholic, Hitler inherited a double tradition of anti-Romanism: partly from the Austrian Pan-Germans, whose 'Break with Rome' slogan had coloured his earliest political beliefs; partly because since Bismarck's *Kulturkampf* Catholics had been suspected of divided loyalties. A party under clerical influence like the Centre was always liable to the charge of ultramontanism. Liberals as well as Nazis objected to any confessional party. The notion that German Catholics, who formed perhaps two-fifths of the total population, were less patriotic than the others died hard, despite the war record of Catholics in every field, including propaganda, where the Centre leader Erzberger had used his considerable influence at Rome and elsewhere to further the German cause. Even in 1933 many German Catholics seemed to feel the need to prove their loyalty by supporting Hitler. It is true that the bishops were aware of the paganism in the Nazi movement and ideology, and at first took up an attitude of reserve. In February 1931 the Bavarian bishops issued a declaration condemning five major errors of National Socialism, including the exaltation of race over religion and the rejection of the Old Testament, and concluded: 'What National Socialism describes as Christianity is not the Christianity of Christ.'[120] On 18 March 1933 Cardinal Bertram told Papen that the Catholic Church opposed the Nazi revolution because, among other things, if the Nazi party succeeded in getting total power, the outlook for Catholics would be extremely gloomy.[121] Ten days later however the hierarchy virtually made an about-turn. Hitler was now dangling a Concordat before them, as a *quid pro quo* for the Centre's acceptance of the Enabling Bill. Some of the Catholic laity, too, sided with Hitler in asserting that fidelity to the church was apostasy to the nation. And in the Reichstag Hitler referred to the churches in laudatory terms. 'Positive Christianity' had been specifically proclaimed as a Nazi aim in the party's original programme. Now Hitler spoke of co-operation and promised that the churches' influence in education and other spheres would not be diminished. At a conference at Fulda on 28 March the Catholic bishops formally withdrew their earlier warnings against National Socialism. Hitler personally assured Berning, the Bishop of Osnabrück, that the freedom and rights of both Churches would be protected, and Berning promised that his Church would serve the new state with 'ardent love' and with all its power.[122] This was at a time when many Catholics, as well as a much greater number of non-Catholics, had been attacked by S.A. or S.S. hooligans; but such incidents were seen by the bishops as a deplorable but passing phase at a time of political upheaval. Their hopes were fixed on the Concordat, which was signed on 29 July and caused great satisfaction on both sides. For years a Reich Concordat had been talked about, but a majority for it in the Reichstag had been lacking. What neither the Empire nor the Republic had managed to achieve had been accomplished by the National Socialists in a few months. The Roman Church was promised freedom to continue its activities, to maintain denominational schools, to keep up its organisations and to publish its pastoral letters. Hitler had with the minimum of trouble eliminated the Centre party, the 'political Catholicism' which he resented; and the Concordat, the first international treaty signed by his government, gave him prestige and respectability in the eyes of the outside world.

The attitude of the Catholic hierarchy cannot be understood without some reference to the background. The Church had no commitment to democracy: and it watched the destruction of the Weimar regime with little or no regret. As the Papacy had shown eleven years earlier in its attitude to Mussolini, and more recently in its Encyclical *Quadragesimo Anno*, it preferred an authoritarian to a liberal regime, even if (as in the case of the Italian *Popolari*) the liberals were confessed Catholics. Intellectually the Church was still unreconciled to the ideas of 1789 for which the Weimar Republic stood. Though the Centre party had played an active parliamentary role and formed coalition governments with the Socialists and the Democratic party, and though some of its leaders, such as Erzberger, had been convinced democrats, the party had been moving, under the leadership of Mgr. Kaas, in an authoritarian direction. Kaas himself was more concerned to safeguard the rights of the Church than to champion civil liberties or even to preserve the Centre party, which, as we have seen, was sacrificed with little compunction. Another sign of the times was the formation in June 1933 of a conservative Catholic organisation called 'Cross and Eagle' whose patron was von Papen. The Church had not fared badly under the Republic, of which the Centre had willy-nilly been a founding member; but many Catholics had not been happy at sharing power with an officially atheist party (the S.P.D.) nor did they approve the permissive moral climate of Weimar – the sexual and artistic licence, the tolerance of blasphemy and pornography, the weakening of traditional *mores*. The main concern of Brüning, the last Centre Chancellor, had been to find on the political right an alternative partner to the Socialists. Even Brüning had been willing to form a government with Hitler. The Catholics knew that Hitler was a wild man, but he might not stay in power long, and they believed that the responsibility of office, especially with the Papal Chamberlain von Papen at his side, would sober him. Despite undoubted excesses – priests had been assaulted and arrested, Catholic youth organisations closed down and about 3,000 Catholics imprisoned during the early months of the Third Reich[123] – the Concordat was worth paying a high price for, at least in the eyes of the Vatican which Hitler treated with circumspection. How high, no one then foresaw.

The tensions that arose between the Nazi regime and the Evangelicals were initially of a different kind, though in time a broad similarity of experience developed between the two Churches. The Evangelicals had certain advantages the Catholics lacked: their close ties with the Prussian establishment freed them from any suspicion of deficiency in patriotism, and ensured them of support in high places – the presidential palace, the upper reaches of the civil service, the army, the law courts. At the same time, they were also more vulnerable. Three hundred years of close dependence on the temporal power had made the Lutherans, in the words of Bishop Dibelius, more like a department of ecclesiastical affairs than a church.[124] In November

1918 they too were identified with the Monarchy to find easy adjustment to the Republic or even acceptance within it. Legally, they had none of the protection offered by a Concordat. They had no organisational unity, and it was not difficult for a dictator to play off one independent bishop against another. Of the twenty-eight churches some were Lutheran, a few Calvinist (Reformed) and the largest, the Old Prussian Union, a combination of the two. Doctrinally, too, the Protestants did not speak with one voice. Traditional certainties had been eroded, first by the rational theology of the late nineteenth century associated with the name of Harnack, later by the iconoclasm that was a product of the 1914 war. The new secularised theology was often far from proof against Nazi ideas. The Weimar Republic found the Lutheran clergy disorientated and uncertain. The fall of the monarchy had broken the historic link between throne and altar and created new difficulties: education had become more secular, and in other ways too the pastor was no longer so welcome or accepted a figure in German society. The political collapse was even felt to be a blow against the Reformation. Nationalism (*Volkstum*) tended to become a kind of substitute for the vanished monarchy, and there was a tendency to give religious sanction to the ideology of nationalism and even to National Socialism.[125] It was symptomatic that the Evangelical authorities actually instituted an annual Sunday of mourning in protest against the treaty of Versailles. Materially times were hard: most clergy received lower pay than other kinds of employee, and some actually died of want.[126] Church life was at a low ebb, and 1933 was the first year for some years when the number of people who left the Church did not increase.[127] Hitler's reassuring words and gestures when he came to power encouraged the hope that there would be a religious revival. Few churchmen had any political objection to his regime. Lastly, the orthodox interpretation of St Paul's advice in Romans 13 predisposed both Catholics and Protestants to obey the secular power under all circumstances. As a Lutheran pastor put it in 1934: 'As Christians we honour every authority, even a debased authority.'[128] Only under the unprecedented pressures imposed by Hitler did the Lutheran Church feel its way, slowly and painfully, to a more critical attitude. It was not easy for churchmen of that tradition to break their oath to a ruler even if his name was Hitler, especially during a war when such an act might bring about Germany's defeat. Like other institutions, too, the Lutheran Church contained a fair proportion of opportunists who were quite willing to come to terms with the new masters.

An immediate danger for the Protestants was the dilution of Christian doctrine by a small but growing group known as the

German Christians, who had been active before Hitler came to power, and whose influence in the Lutheran Church spread after January 1933. Broadly the German Christians sought to reconcile their faith with National Socialism by playing down the Jewish origins of Christianity and making Jesus Christ into an Aryan hero. In the state of Thuringia, for example, where the German Christians were dominant, the Old Testament was dropped from the schools' religious syllabus. About a third of the Lutheran clergy appeared to give some support to this movement, which offered Hitler the chance of dominating the Church from within. As the slogan proclaimed, there was one people, one Reich, one Führer – why not also one Church? Hitler's professed desire for a united Evangelical Church may have been genuine: on this point he disagreed with his more radical followers such as Rosenberg and Bormann. He decided to impose unity on the Lutherans by creating a new post, that of Reich Bishop, and nominating for it an army chaplain of German Christian sympathies named Müller. The non-Prussian churches, however, resented the threat to their independence. Moreover, Müller was, both personally and theologically, unacceptable to most of his colleagues, who preferred an alternative candidate, Bodelschwingh, the well-known and respected head of a home for epileptics founded by his father. Under official pressure Bodelschwingh's election was declared invalid, and he resigned. In a new election which was rigged, Müller had enough support from the laity to win, but he lacked authority and soon retired from the scene. Nevertheless, some of the twenty-eight provincial churches had allowed themselves to be integrated into the new National Church and their leaders had been deprived of their offices. Opposition to Hitler's plan to dominate the Church was marked by the formation in September 1933 of a Pastors' Emergency League whose moving spirit was Martin Niemöller, a former submarine commander. The object of the League, whose declaration has been described as the first important document of large-scale church opposition, was to protect Biblical Christianity against the new idolatry of race and nationalism. By the beginning of 1934 over 7,000 clergy out of a total of about 16,250 had joined the League, which was the nucleus of the so-called Confessional Church. German Protestantism was now in schism.

The German Christian movement, though it lasted till the end of the Third Reich, was soon a declining force. As its true character was recognised, an increasing number of clergy turned away from it, and its adherents split up into more or less radical groups at odds with each other. Hitler saw that it was too extreme to suit his purpose, and abandoned it, together with the hapless Bishop Müller, who later committed suicide. Foreign criticism of Nazi attacks on the churches also had a restraining effect. In May 1934 an opposition Synod of Lutherans and Calvinists at Barmen reaffirmed their adherence to the historic Gospel and rejected the Nazi attempt to pervert doctrine. 'We reject', declared the signatories, 'the false doctrine that the state ... should become the single and totalitarian order of human life, thus fulfilling the Church's mission as well.'[129] For the Lutherans, with their traditional reverence for the state, this was a bold statement and implied a rejection of the view that 'politics do not concern the Church'. The Nazis accused the Confessional Church of high treason.[130] The proposed exclusion of Christians of Jewish origin was also successfully resisted, though only at the price of a compromise: it was understood that they would not undertake any ecclesiastical duties. The co-operation of both Protestant confessions was a significant reaction to a common threat, and Barth, the distinguished Calvinist theologian who from the first took an unequivocal stand against Hitler, helped to stiffen the Lutherans' attitude. In the following year the Confessional clergy of the Old Prussian Union issued a warning: 'We see our people threatened by a deadly danger. The danger consists of a new religion – the religion of blood, race and nationalism.'[131] Hitler now tried a new tactic. The unification of the Protestant Church, which Müller had failed to bring about, was to be accomplished through Kerrl, hitherto Prussian Minister of Justice, who was given the new office of Reich Minister for Church Affairs. But Kerrl too, though he tried for some years, was unsuccessful and antagonised both the Confessional wing and the German Christians. His plans for electing a new general synod had to be abandoned when it appeared that the results might be unpalatable to the government. Hitler had to content himself with taking punitive measures against the leaders of the Confessional Church, some of whom were arrested by the Gestapo in a Berlin church in 1937. Among the 800 churchmen seized that year was Niemöller, whose determined stand was the more remarkable because he had in the past voted for the Nazis and sent Hitler a telegram of congratulation when Germany left the League of Nations. Freed in March 1938 by a court order, Niemöller was arrested a day later by the Gestapo and sent first to Sachsenhausen and later to Dachau. For the outside world, where the Confessional Church had many friends (including the Bishop of Chichester, who was to meet Bonhoeffer and other representatives of the German resistance during the war) as well as inside Germany Niemöller was the symbol of martyrdom and the conscience of German Christianity.[132]

Without Niemöller's leadership the opposition leaders among the Lutheran clergy found it hard to keep up morale in face of a campaign of harassment, in which Himmler, head of the S.S. and Gestapo, joined. The 800,000 organised Protestant youth were forcibly merged in the Hitler Youth. Church taxes were cut by a fifth and church property was taken over by the state. The clergy were hindered in their pastoral duties and in freedom of speech, and were in constant danger of being denounced and dismissed. They received little support from their congregations:[133] as in other spheres, the German resistance was the movement of a dedicated minority. A courageous stand was taken by Bishops Wurm of Württemberg and Dibelius of Brandenburg, but most of the clergy took up a middle position, rejecting the German Christians but also unwilling to identify themselves with the Niemöller wing. They sought a compromise with the state that would leave them in peace. Typical of this large centre group was Marahrens, Bishop of Hanover, who ordered all his pastors to swear an oath of personal allegiance to Hitler. Yet Dibelius too had not been free from this kind of ambivalence. While in a sermon at Potsdam on 21 March 1933 he had warned a largely Nazi congregation against identifying public office with private and arbitrary power, less than three weeks later he had broadcast to America a defence of the Nazi boycott of Jews.[134] In the later thirties Nazi pressure, helped by Hitler's success in Austria and Czechoslovakia, continually increased. Only about 250 Lutheran clergy, including bishops, joined the N.S.D.A.P., but some belonged to the S.A. or S.S. Some churches, such as Brunswick Cathedral, became Nazi shrines, and Nazi forms of baptism and weddings were introduced. The annual harvest festival ceremony at Bückeburg, the climax of the year for farmers, was a pagan affair; and a German Farmers' calendar for 1935 showed the Christian festivals replaced by dates from the Nazi Pantheon – Christmas Eve was given over to the celebration of the birth of Baldur, guardian of light, and Good Friday was remembered for the 4,500 Saxons slaughtered by Charlemagne.[135] Theological faculties were suppressed and by 1939 the percentage of German university students reading theology had fallen since 1933 from 6 per cent to 2 per cent. In one year alone, over 100,000 people left the Roman Catholic Church.

The story of the Catholic Church from the summer of 1933 onwards is one of growing disillusion. The Concordat had hardly been signed before it was violated, and Nazi leaders were soon denouncing it as out of date. The work of Caritas, the main Catholic charitable organisation, was hampered, denominational schools were attacked, seminars deprived of funds, monks and nuns maliciously defamed, and the Catholic press banned. Later during the war a large number of monasteries and other church property were seized by the state.

Rosenberg, the main exponent of neo-paganism, and author of *The Myth of the Twentieth Century* (which was placed on the Index) was appointed head of the party's ideological training. This book contained a violent and often scurrilous attack on the Church: the Pope for example was described as a big witch-doctor. In March 1937 Pius XI broke silence. His Encyclical, *With Burning Anxiety*, issued with the support of the German bishops, accused the Nazi government of breach of faith, and denounced the Nazi idolatry of race and blood. Hitler banned the Encyclical, but could not prevent its being read from every Catholic pulpit. He was reported to be thinking of abrogating parts of the Concordat.[136] By September 1939 some hundreds of priests had been arrested and sent to concentration camps. Yet some ambiguity in the Church's attitude remained. Hardly one Catholic priest joined the N.S.D.A.P. Nevertheless the annexation of Austria and destruction of Czechoslovakia were welcomed, and the Führer's fiftieth birthday, 20 April 1939, was celebrated with the ringing of church bells and the holding of special services and prayers.[137] Cardinal Bertram sent a telegram of good wishes. On the day Germany attacked Poland, Monsignor Rarkowski, Chaplain General to the *Wehrmacht*, urged the troops to follow the 'shining example of a true fighter, our Führer and Supreme Commander, the first and bravest soldier of the Greater German Reich'.[138] Hitler, to avoid needless antagonism, ordered no further action to be taken against the churches for the duration of the war. Similar restraint (which was often breached) was not applied to the countries conquered and occupied by Hitler's armies, such as Poland, where persecution of Christians as well as of Jews reached a scale unknown in Germany. In the Warthegau, as the former province of Posen was now known, there was, the German Catholic bishops complained, 'an almost complete suppression of the Christian religion'. Yet when Hitler launched his attack on Russia in June 1941 the Council of the German Evangelical Church sent a telegram assuring him of their 'unshakeable loyalty'.[139] Even Niemöller offered in September 1941 to rejoin the navy.

It was above all to the moral problems confronting them – the Nazi destruction of human rights, the contempt for human life – that the churches were slow to react. They did not condemn the blood purge of June 1934 although several well-known Catholic laymen were among those murdered. Nor was there any denunciation of anti-semitism, which, beginning with the boycott of Jewish shops and dismissal of Jews from all important posts, went on to enact the Nuremberg laws of 1935 and reached its pre-war climax in the Pogrom of 9 November 1938 with a wholesale burning of synagogues.

Thousands of Jews were attacked and thrown into concentration camps. The churches, it seemed, were only concerned for the security of their own 'non-aryan' members, unlike Bonhoeffer, who as early as April 1933 declared that it was the Church's duty to help the victims of any social order, whether they were Christians or not.[140] The first major example of a Catholic prelate taking a stand against murder was when von Galen, Bishop of Münster, denounced the so-called euthanasia campaign which led to the killing by gas or injection of about 70,000 people deemed unworthy of survival. (Many were weak, old or mentally deficient; not all were incurable.) The protest of Galen and others had some effect: euthanasia was not abandoned, but its operation was transferred to Poland, where its victims could be disposed of with less publicity. The technique of gassing was soon to be applied on a much larger scale to the Jews. Denunciation by the churches of the 'final solution' of the Jewish problem were rare, though in October 1943 the Prussian synod of the Confessional Church declared that the state had no right to take human life, except in self-defence: every life, including that of the people of Israel, was sacred to God.[141] It does not appear that this protest had any effect on those engaged in the murderous work. There were individual heroes such as Provost Lichtenberg of St Hedwig's Catholic cathedral in Berlin, who prayed publicly for the deported Jews; after serving a term of imprisonment he was re-arrested and died on his way to Dachau. Provost Grüber, a Protestant, set up a committee in Berlin to help Jewish Christians emigrate and to rescue abandoned Jewish children until he too was stopped by the Gestapo and imprisoned. A Jesuit, Father Delp, paid with his life for taking an active part in the Kreisau resistance circle. But such acts of courage were exceptional. The Vatican never abandoned its efforts to find a *modus vivendi* with the Nazi leaders. Whereas Pius XI had been openly critical of Nazi attacks on the Church and the Gospel and might have broken with Hitler if he had lived longer, Cardinal Pacelli, who succeeded him as Pius XII in March 1939, had a different approach. He combined the traditional prejudices of a conservative prelate with illusions about the true nature of National Socialism, as Brüning found when as Reich Chancellor he discussed German politics with Pacelli, then Cardinal Secretary of State, during a visit to Rome.[142]

Pius XII's role is and probably always will be the subject of controversy. With his complex character and habitual caution he liked to keep his options open. He had spent many years as Papal Nuncio in Germany, where he had acquired a genuine liking for the people which led him at times to make statements showing uncritical support for the Third Reich and even personal regard for Hitler.[143] Admittedly his sincere desire to end a war which he wholly deplored made him encourage the conservative opposition in Germany and even to act as an intermediary in the peace feelers between the latter and the British government which took place in the winter of 1939-40, and involved among others Joseph Müller, a Catholic lawyer who represented Cardinal Faulhaber of Munich. As Papal Secretary of State Pius XII had been closely associated with the Encyclical *With Burning Anxiety* issued by his predecessor. Yet despite Hitler's attacks on the Church, Pius regarded Soviet Russia as the main threat to Christendom. Anxious – probably excessively so – not to lose the support of the forty million German Catholics or to compromise the neutrality of the Vatican, he would neither proclaim a crusade against Nazism nor specifically condemn evil deeds committed by Germans. Though he denounced the invasion of Belgium and Holland, he appeared inexplicably indifferent to the fate of the Catholic population in occupied countries, especially in Poland, from which he received reports of the horrifying persecution in the Warthegau province and elsewhere. Nor did he react as many people hoped to the atrocities against the Jews. In this case at least it is hardly conceivable that his intervention would have made the situation worse, as Pius was alleged to fear, and possible that it might have made even Hitler recoil, as did Cardinal von Galen's sermons against euthanasia. The Catholic hierarchy in Germany, who were themselves divided in their attitude to the Nazi regime, received little support from Rome in so far as they tried to resist Hitler, and the Pope's refusal to condemn Nazi crimes put him in a morally false position. In June 1945, looking back on the 'satanic spectre' of National Socialism, Pius described it as 'arrogant apostasy from Jesus Christ, the denial of His doctrine, and of His work of redemption, the cult of violence, the idolatry of race and blood, the overthrow of human liberty and dignity'.[144] These were strong words, which contrasted with the pained restraint of the Vatican's official pronouncements over the years, but they could not efface the memory of his 'prudent silence' (a phrase he himself used in a letter to the German Archbishop Frings) or make up for the many missed opportunities. The German Catholic bishops, in a declaration issued at Fulda in August 1945, admitted that many Catholics had committed crimes and helped others to do so while the Evangelical Church started the post-war epoch with a collective confession of guilt. 'We accuse ourselves', ran part of a statement issued by the Confessional Church and other Protestant groups meeting at Treysa in August 1945, 'of not having professed more courageously, believed more gladly and loved more intensely.'[145] Both confessions were faced with their greatest crisis since the wars of religion.

If the Third Reich was an ordeal from which the churches emerged with little credit, it was one for which they were completely unprepared. They expected it to be like authoritarian regimes of the past; they did not realise that it would be a unique experience, one which demanded agonising decisions, self-sacrifice and even martyrdom. The Lutherans were torn between political sympathies and theological beliefs that were often tinged with nationalism or opportunism: the result was the hyphenated Christianity of which Barth complained, or the hybrid ideology of a 'German Christian'. The Catholics, though more cohesive and less isolated from the outside world, were also favourable to 'strong government', and the ambiguous silence of Pius XII did nothing to strengthen their resistance. They too had their pro-Nazis, like Abbot Schachleiter, and their politicians, like von Papen, who played Hitler's game. Both churches tried to combine loyalty to Hitler as head of state with defence of the historic Gospel and of their traditional structure. Neither responded to the challenge presented by the Nazi regime, which required German churchmen to act with a radicalism of which few were capable. It was Bonhoeffer's greatness that he saw this clearly, so that he, the outstanding theologian of his generation, also became its martyr. He was the patriot who desired his country's defeat, the pacifist who approved the use of violence. It was fitting that this outstanding example of Christian witness should have been made against a regime responsible for so much evil and from within a Church often criticised for its subservience to the state. As human institutions the churches reflected a community that, despite its military strength and technological progressiveness, was politically immature, credulous and narrow, with a very undeveloped sense of individual responsibility. The leaders were too concerned to keep their flocks intact and bring them through the storm, unmindful of their duty to those in distress outside their ranks. There was, as one historian has observed, something wanting about a Catholic episcopate which excluded men from the sacraments for duelling or agreeing to have their bodies cremated but not for murder.[146] Those who had strained at the gnat had swallowed the camel.

CHAPTER X

The Third Reich: War

(i) THE EARLY TRIUMPHS

The German conquest of Poland was accomplished in four weeks, but the decisive blows all fell within a matter of days. Taken by surprise, with their mobilisation incomplete, and faced by an enemy superior in every department of war except courage, the Polish armies were rapidly outmanoeuvred, surrounded and overwhelmed. The Germans struck from three directions: East Prussia in the north, Pomerania and Silesia in the west, and Slovakia in the south. The Polish air force was eliminated during the first forty-eight hours when its machines were destroyed on the ground, and Polish cavalry proved helpless against armoured divisions backed by fast-moving heavy artillery, bombers and dive bombers. The Polish infantry lacked the mobility needed to counter penetration in depth. Poland's western allies had expected her to hold out through the winter, and they might conceivably have done so had the French, as the Poles expected, attacked the thinly held German line in the west. The Russians were also taken aback by the speed of the German onslaught, and on 17 September the Red Army, in accordance with the secret protocol of 23 August, marched into the eastern Polish provinces. This was the final blow to the Polish hopes of further resistance, and unexpected by the local population, who imagined that the Russians had come to help them against the Germans. Hitler had urged Stalin to intervene without delay in order to shorten the campaign, and Stalin did so with alacrity from fear that the Germans, who were already over a hundred miles east of the agreed partition line in places, might stay where they were. On 28 September, the day when Warsaw surrendered after a savage bombardment from the air, Ribbentrop was again in Moscow, where a further treaty, signed by him and Molotov, made certain territorial changes in the secret protocol: most of Lithuania was now allocated to the Russian sphere of influence, and Germany in return received a larger share of central Poland, including the province of Lublin. The revised frontier coincided to some extent with the Curzon Line of 1920, but with modifications in favour of Russia, which thus acquired a large slice of ethnic Polish territory. Of Poland's 36 million inhabitants, 24 were now on the German side, 12 on the Russian. The German area was sub-divided into two: a western half, including but exceeding the territory that had been German before 1914, was annexed to the Reich, while the rest was treated as a colony to be exploited under a German governor. It was known as the Government General. With Russian encouragement, the Germans thus abandoned their earlier idea of leaving a small, nominally independent rump Poland which would have been a magnet for Polish nationalism. The provinces occupied by the Red Army were simply annexed to the soviet republics of White Russia and the Ukraine respectively, except for the Vilna district which reverted to Lithuania. The new order in Poland was a pointer to Hitler's general plans and purposes, and its implications were of wider significance.

First, there were the military lessons of the campaign. The success of the German High Command showed that a strategic revolution had taken place since the First World War, though the beginnings of the change could be traced back to Ludendorff's surprise tactics in March 1918. Mobility had overcome attrition. Tanks moving at high speed and supported by mechanised infantry and aircraft were able to make penetrations in depth that rendered obsolete the 1914–18 conception of trench warfare. Obvious though this was in retrospect, it made little impression at the time on the Allied generals, who clung to the argument that the Germans would not be able to use in the west the tactics they had employed with such effect in Poland. Nor was much attention paid to the German use of fifth columnists drawn from the million or so *Volksdeutsche* in Poland. Thus the shattering experience of the Poles did nothing to shake the complacency of the French and British leaders, while it gave Hitler's newly blooded but half-trained troops much needed confidence.

Secondly, the Polish campaign exposed the half-heartedness with which the French conducted a war on which they had embarked with obvious reluctance. Gamelin, the French Commander-in-Chief, had promised his Polish opposite number to take the offensive within fifteen days of a German attack on Poland. When hostilities started, the Germans had only eight active and twenty-six reserve divisions on the whole of the western front from Aachen to Basle. The troops were untrained and unready for battle, and had no tanks and very little ammunition. The defence line, known as the West Wall or Siegfried Line, had been hastily improvised and was far from impregnable. Facing it were between sixty and seventy French divisions with a huge preponderance of artillery, so that a determined French attack could have broken through and reached the Rhine in a fortnight with little difficulty. But France had a 'slow motion' army, and much of the artillery had to be brought out of storage at a somewhat leisurely pace. There was no movement except a much publicised French advance into the Saar which involved no real penetration of the German defence system, and even this limited territorial gain was soon abandoned. Gamelin tried to excuse himself in a letter to the Polish Prime Minister Rydz-Smigly asserting that the Germans in the west were well prepared for defence and that a considerable part of the German air force was present in support: the truth was that all the flying units of the *Luftwaffe* were then in Poland.[1] The supreme importance attached to the supposedly impregnable Maginot Line in French military thinking implied a defensive strategy, and it was an unstated but inescapable consequence that France expected her East European allies to be able to defend themselves. Like the British, the French were determined not to waste lives in the prodigal fashion of the First World War. They were also waiting for the British, represented at first by only four divisions on the western front, to take over a larger share. If the British military effort at the beginning of the war was minimal, in the air and at sea it was the British alone who were active against Germany. The events of September confirmed Hitler in his belief that the French were pacifists at heart and that their army was suffering from lack of confidence and low morale. It was characteristic of the 'phoney war' that a British offer to bomb targets in Germany was rejected by the French, who feared reprisals on their poorly defended cities.

Thirdly, the new partition of Poland and the concomitant division of Eastern Europe between Russia and Germany created a new balance of power which was at least as advantageous to Stalin as to Hitler. For in breaking down the door which barred their own eastward expansion, the Nazis automatically opened the way to the Soviets' expansion westward. The power vacuum created by the collapse of Poland had to be shared, whereas that caused by the destruction of Czechoslovakia had been monopolised by Germany. German influence in the Balkans had been growing since 1936. But in the Nazi-Soviet pact of August 1939 Hitler promised political disinterestedness in the Balkans and specifically recognised Russia's interests in Bessarabia, the former Russian province annexed in 1919 by Roumania. As the entire Baltic region had been assigned to Russia, Soviet influence was now predominant from Finland to the Black Sea. Before the end of 1939 the Russians were in partial military occupation of the three Baltic republics of Esthonia, Latvia and Lithuania, while Germany's triumph in the west in the summer of 1940 was quickly followed by their formal incorporation in the

U.S.S.R. By then the Soviets had not only Bessarabia, but also North Bukovina, the Roumanian, formerly Austrian province which had never belonged to Russia. Another more immediate consequence of the Russo-German deal was the evacuation of people of German descent from the Russian sphere and their resettlement within the enlarged Reich. Hundreds of thousands of people whose families had lived for centuries in the *Baltikum* or in Eastern Poland, Bessarabia and Bukovina, were uprooted and found themselves refugees: later they were joined by others from Slovakia, Yugoslavia and the South Tyrol. By 1941 some 600,000 Germans had been displaced in this way, and the problem of expellees thus began in 1939, not in 1945.[2] More disadvantageous to Hitler's future plans was the extension of Soviet power across lands earmarked for German conquest as living space. In other ways Hitler gained from his *rapprochement* with Stalin. Russia gave moral support to the 'peace offensive' launched by the Nazis after the subjugation of Poland, and – equally significant for propaganda purposes – the Communist parties of the world, including those of France and Britain, denounced the war as imperialist. Through the increase of trade between Germany and Russia the former acquired stocks of food and raw materials which largely offset the effect of the British blockade. Without these imports from the Soviet Union, the German economy could not have lasted for more than nine to twelve months. Grain, soya beans, milk products, fats, oil and rubber were among the commodities received from Russia or via Russia from the Far and Middle East.[3] Further, the naval co-operation between the German and Russian navies that followed the Non-Aggression pact strengthened Hitler in one element, the sea, where he was most vulnerable. Germans supplied Russia with naval equipment and training facilities; in return they received harbour facilities in Murmansk and elsewhere which enabled German vessels to escape the clutches of the British navy and to play a part later in the conquest of Norway.[4]

Fourthly, the setting up of Hitler's new order in Poland showed the ruthlessness with which his policy of racial superiority over the Slavs and other subject races was being implemented. Already in January 1939 he had told a group of senior officers that he intended to re-model Europe on racial lines, and as early as 1928 he had written of the Poles that they must be sterilised or removed from their land.[5] In October 1939 German military rule in Poland was superseded by a civilian government headed by Governor Frank, the most prominent of the Nazi lawyers. Hitler's instructions to Frank are worth quoting: he was 'to assume the administration of the conquered territories with the special order ruthlessly to exploit this region as a war zone and object of plunder, to reduce it, as it were, to a heap of rubble in its economic, social, cultural and political structure'.[6] All Poles between the ages of 14 and 60 were made liable to compulsory labour service. At the same time Himmler moved in as head of the S.S. to terrorise the population and to arrange the exchange of populations in the interests of the master race. The deportation of Poles and Jews from areas reserved for Germans went on during the exceptionally severe winter of 1939/40 in conditions of appalling hardship. Acting on Hitler's orders, Himmler set to work systematically to destroy the Polish intelligentsia and upper class. All universities and most secondary schools were closed down, and nearly all the professors and lecturers at Cracow University were deported to Sachsenhausen concentration camp, from which few returned alive. No higher education than that provided by a four-class primary school was to be allowed for the non-German population. 'The aim of this primary school should be solely to teach the pupil how to count up to a maximum of 500, how to write his name, how it is God's command that he should be obedient to the Germans, honourable, industrious and brave. I regard reading as unnecessary.'[7] If the measures laid down were carried out, Himmler boasted, in ten years the population of the Government General would consist of 'a remnant of substandard beings ... a leaderless labour force'. The destruction of the Polish nation was further attempted by carrying off to Germany any children considered racially valuable, who were then distributed to childless S.S. families to be brought up as Germans. The Jews were to be completely eliminated: as a first step they were herded into ghettos and concentration camps. As the war proceeded it became clear that their fate was to be not deportation (though the Polish camps themselves served as a deportation area for much of Europe) but death. Even before the conquest of Poland was complete, massacring and 'liquidation' of the inhabitants began. On 8 September S.S. commanders were reported to be boasting of shooting 200 Poles a day, and in the first month of German rule the victims numbered some tens of thousands.[8] In one diocese alone nearly a third of the 690 priests were executed, and this was only the preliminary to a harsh persecution of the Catholic Church. Reprisals were savage: on one occasion after the killing of a German policeman by two Polish criminals, 170 Polish citizens were shot.[9] On 21 November a German general wrote indignantly to his wife about the misery in Warsaw where 'elegant ladies of three or four months before are reduced to selling themselves to common soldiers for a loaf of army bread' and continued: 'The wildest fantasy of atrocity propaganda is feeble in comparison with what an organised gang of murderers, robbers and plunderers is doing there . . . I am ashamed to be a German. This minority, which . . . is besmirching the German name, will be the disaster of the German people if we do not put a spoke in their wheel.'[10] This critic (Blaskowitz) was transferred to the west. There were many in the army who were embarrassed by the barbarity of the S.S. but there were also those who excused it. Reichenau, who was himself anti-S.S., defended the massacre of Jews in Russia in 1941 on the grounds that it constituted a 'severe but justified atonement required from the Jewish sub-humans'.[11]

Before invading Poland Hitler had declared that even if the western powers did not go to war, once Poland was defeated they would accept the accomplished fact and be ready for peace. He soon put his theory to the test in a peace offer issued in October. If they would recognise the new settlement in Eastern Europe he would guarantee their frontiers, though he would expect some colonial concessions. Chamberlain replied that peace could be made only if Germany first gave proof of her peaceful intentions by restoring Poland and Czechoslovakia. Hitler's offer may have been bluff, intended only as propaganda, but it was perfectly consistent with his repeated assertion that he had no quarrel with France and Britain if they would give him a free hand in Eastern Europe. He must have realised the futility of the gesture, for before Chamberlain's answer arrived he had ordered his generals to plan an offensive in the west, known as Operation Yellow. He even wished to launch it that autumn despite the doubts of the generals, who did not believe that they were strong enough to beat the French. Taunted by Hitler with timidity, they felt deep unease about where he was leading them, and Brauchitsch actually offered his resignation, which was refused.[12] Hitler had several reasons for striking quickly: he did not want to get involved in a long war, for he knew that time was not on his side; he feared that the Allies, by occupying Belgium, would threaten the Ruhr; and he needed air bases in Western Europe in order to get to grips with England. Operation Yellow had to be postponed repeatedly because of insufficient preparations and bad weather, but also because of the generals' delaying tactics. Finally it was put off until the spring. On 8 November Hitler had one of his many escapes, when a bomb went off in the *Bürgerbräukeller* in Munich where he made a speech in celebration of the Putsch of 1923. He left the hall before the explosion, which killed seven and injured sixty-three of the party's 'old fighters'. He professed to see in this the hand of British Intelligence, but the plot was actually the work of a communist sympathiser, a carpenter named Elser, who was picked up by the Gestapo and eventually executed.

The Russians were not at ease over the pact with Hitler, and they even suspected that his peace overtures might lead to an end of the war and so make possible that combination of capitalist powers which they had always feared. They wanted to strengthen their defences, and having secured military bases in the Baltic republics, proceeded to make demands on Finland. The Finns were required to cede territory along the border opposite Leningrad, in exchange for Russian land further north. They refused. The Russians launched an attack on Finland which was expected to bring the Finns quickly to heel. Instead the Finns, despite great inferiority in numbers and equipment, held out stubbornly and inflicted on the Russian invaders losses exceeding the total of their own army at the beginning of the war. A four months' winter campaign ended in a peace by which Finland yielded strategic territory, including the Viborg Peninsula and several islands, but kept her independence. Sympathy for Finland during the war was general and was shared by Germany's ally Italy. The Soviet Union was expelled from the League of Nations. Many European countries, including neutrals, sent supplies to Finland. France and Britain, especially France, talked of military intervention. Their motives were mixed. They hoped, by getting a foothold in Scandinavia, to cut off the supply of Swedish iron ore on which Germany depended, and the French were anxious to divert German arms away from themselves. Had the western powers actually gone to war to help Finland they would have made an enemy of Russia with consequences that could only have benefited Germany. In the event the Finns, understandably doubtful of the promptness and effectiveness of Allied help, made the best terms they could with the Russians, who were glad to be relieved of an embarrassing situation. The Soviets' dismal military performance (though only a fraction of their total strength was mobilised) did nothing to raise the prestige of the Red Army from the depths to which it had fallen during Stalin's great purge, of which an extraordinarily high proportion of senior officers had been victims. It was easily overlooked that the terrain with its numerous lakes and large forests was unusually favourable to the defence.

The attention on the Baltic and Scandinavia focused by the Finnish war had further consequences. As in the First World War, the British attached great importance to the blockade of Germany, which was enforced by a real but invisible barrier across the Channel but also across the three hundred miles of sea dividing Scotland from Norway. One important gap in the blockade was the inability to deny Germany the Swedish iron ore which provided three-quarters of her needs. During the winter this iron ore travelled by train from Sweden to the

Norwegian port of Narvik, from where it went to Germany by ship in Norwegian territorial waters. The British Admiralty was keen to intercept this traffic, but the government was unwilling to commit a flagrant breach of the neutrality which both Norway and Sweden naturally wished to preserve. In fact neither the British nor the Germans showed much regard for Norwegian rights. Early in January 1940 the British accused the Germans of torpedoing their ships in Norwegian waters, and in the following month men from a British destroyer boarded a German naval tanker, the *Altmark*, to set free some British sailors who were prisoners of war. The Norwegians stood by, helpless; Hitler believed them to be in collusion with the Royal Navy. But iron ore was not the sole reason for Hitler's interest in Norway. If he occupied that country he would not only outflank the blockade but would also possess useful harbours and bases for naval and air operations against England. He was encouraged to plan an invasion of Norway by the former Norwegian War Minister and Fascist leader, Quisling, who was friendly to the Nazis. On a visit to Germany Quisling urged Hitler to act before the British did, and suggested that there was widespread support in the Norwegian forces for a *coup d'état* led by himself. Hitler ordered plans for the occupation of Norway and Denmark (Operation Weser). When in March 1940 the Finnish war was over, the chances of Allied intervention in Scandinavia were reduced, but pressure for action in Norway remained strong on both sides of the North Sea. The British Admiralty, with Churchill in the lead, announced that it would lay mines in Norwegian waters. On 8 April Hitler, who had less to lose in the eyes of the neutrals, got his blow in first. Operation Weser, which began on 9 April, was an ambitious exercise because it depended for success on a combination of naval, air and land forces in a vast area where British naval superiority might be decisive. It was the first joint services operation planned and executed by the O.K.W. But speed and ruthlessness paid off, as they had in Poland, and the Germans achieved surprise by the unexpectedly bold scale of their attack. Though the Allies made several successful landings in Norway, the whole country eventually fell to Hitler's forces. The victory was a narrow one, clinched only by Allied withdrawals after the fall of France. The Germans suffered the destruction or damage of half their surface fleet, a loss they could ill afford when soon afterwards the invasion of England became a possibility. British naval losses were also heavy as the Admiralty had underestimated the effect of air power on shipping. Once France was won, Hitler had less need of Norway, but when Operation Weser was planned he could not foresee the completeness of his victory in the west. The occupation

of Norway and Denmark from now till the end of the war tied down
thousands of German soldiers who could have been more usefully
employed elsewhere. But Hitler dared not risk losing the Swedish ore,
and feared that an Allied occupation of Norway would cancel
Germany's advantages in possessing the Channel coast. Still, the
British, by occupying Iceland and the Faroe Islands, could continue
to deny access to the Atlantic of German ships, and the blockade of the
Reich went on.

While the future of Norway still hung in the balance, the German
offensive in the west received its final preparations. But the plan was
no longer Operation Yellow. That had been discarded in favour of a
much bolder and more original scheme known as Operation Sicklethrust. This was based on a strategy proposed by von Manstein, Chief
of Staff to the commander of the Central Army Group on the western
front, von Rundstedt, and submitted to Hitler in a series of
memoranda bearing Rundstedt's signature. Operation Yellow had envisaged an enveloping movement from the north sweeping through
Holland and Belgium, designed to separate the French and British
armies and reach the Channel. Like the Schlieffen Plan, it carried
the main punch on the extreme right, but it also had less promise of
success: it lacked the element of surprise, its right wing was not powerful enough to deliver the knock-out blow, and it could not assume,
as Schlieffen did, that the French would expend much of their
strength on a fruitless offensive in Alsace. Manstein's brainwave was
to shift the centre of gravity of the attack from the extreme right to
the centre (the Meuse valley) where he believed that a strategic break-
through was possible despite the natural obstacles presented by the
Ardennes mountains. Manstein received powerful support from
Guderian, the army's chief tank expert, who agreed that tanks could
operate in the Ardennes but insisted that the central thrust must be
made strong enough to resist Allied flank attacks and penetrate to the
estuary of the Somme. Curiously enough, this thinking coincided with
that of Hitler, who some months before, in October 1939, had
suggested the Ardennes as the choice for the offensive. But many
senior officers, including Halder the Chief of Staff, were sceptical.
Manstein was posted to a command in the east, and Operation
Yellow, though modified, remained in force. On 9 January however
a staff officer of the German air force carrying the complete operational plan for the invasion of Holland and Belgium made a forced
landing near a Belgian village and was unable to destroy his documents
in time. Enough half-burned fragments remained to alert the Belgian
authorities, who passed the information on to the French. Hitler's
reaction was to call off Operation Yellow altogether and to set his

staff to work on the Manstein plan which he now presented as his own. The crossing of the Meuse near Sedan became the crucial manoeuvre, with the attack in the north as a massive feint, intended to lure the Allied armies forward into a trap. The centre received the bulk of the armour (seven divisions) with a corresponding weight of guns and motorised infantry. Had all the armour employed been arranged in a single column, it would have stretched from Aachen to Königsberg in East Prussia.

Since the preceding September the number of German divisions had risen from 107 to 155, including ten armoured divisions compared with seven. Facing them the Allies had 137 divisions (128 French and 9 British), of which less than four were armoured and three lightly mechanised. The Germans had 2,574 tanks and about 4,300 aircraft, the Allies 3,254 tanks and about 2,800 aircraft (of which 650 were reserved for the defence of the British Isles). Thus the Allies had more tanks, but neutralised this advantage by having them mostly distributed throughout the army instead of being concentrated, as on the German side. For it was the tactical use of tanks, not their numbers, that was to prove decisive, and the German tanks had the advantage in speed.[13] In the air the Germans still had a favourable margin, as a result of their earlier start in the arms race of the later 1930s, but it was a diminishing asset, for by 1940 Britain was producing more aircraft than Germany. In quality too, especially as regards fighter planes, the British had the upper hand. Tactically the Germans had learnt to use their air force more effectively by integrating it with their ground troops in a way unfamiliar to their opponents. Air bombing had largely taken the place of the artillery barrage of the First World War. Nevertheless, despite certain advantages enjoyed by the Germans, on paper their army was in many ways weaker than the French. For example, in the five years since the reintroduction of conscription in Germany it had been possible to train fully only one officer in six,[14] whereas in France intensive training had been carried on ever since the previous war. But France paid a price for this continuity in that, in conjunction with other qualities, it bred a cautious conservatism that was to prove no match for the new dynamism of the *Wehrmacht*. Too much of French military thinking was geared to the experience of 1914–18, and too much of French strength was embodied in or tied to the static steel and concrete of the Maginot Line.

Operation Sicklethrust began on the morning of 10 May with a spectacular invasion of the Low Countries. The Dutch, attacked from the air, by parachute and by tanks, were bewildered and stunned. They surrendered in five days at a cost to the Germans of 2,000 killed and 2,800 wounded. The Belgian army, larger than the Dutch and with more time to mobilise, held out until 28 May. Gamelin, the Allied Commander-in-Chief, reacted as the Germans hoped by sending strong reinforcements, including two-thirds of his armour and most of his reserves, to the threatened north. In the apparently uneventful central sector the German armoured divisions advanced without opposition through Luxembourg to the valley of the Meuse near Sedan. There, just inside the French frontier, they managed to cross the river at three points. This was the vital lunge. The French, aware of their danger too late, counter-attacked west of the Meuse without success. Six days after the beginning of their offensive the Germans found the road to the west open. Having pierced the French defences, which were often inadequately fortified and half-heartedly defended, the German tanks poured through the gaps and fanned out to form a wider corridor, closely followed by mechanised infantry and with protection and support from bombers and Stukas. The thrust divided the Allied forces, and Gamelin's whole strategy collapsed. Isolated attacks on the German flanks by French tanks (de Gaulle near Laon) and British tanks near Arras scored local gains but could not stem the rush of German armour, which covered the 200 miles from the Meuse to the Channel in ten days. In complete disarray, the French High Command (where Weygand, recalled from Syria, replaced the discredited Gamelin) could only improvise under conditions which exposed the limitation of its thinking and practice. A month before the world had believed that the French army was the strongest in Europe; now it was obvious to everyone that its generalship was unimaginative and complacent, its staffwork incompetent, its training out of date and its morale abysmal. Vital bridges were not blown up, important messages were lost or not acted on. Defence was handicapped by the flood of refugees who choked the roads leading to the front, while rumours, often wildly exaggerated, of fifth columnists and saboteurs added to the sense of defeat. Though in Hitler's racial cosmogony the French had a relatively high place, their behaviour confirmed his low opinion of the French fighting spirit. Perhaps for reasons of cultural snobbery he never envisaged colonising France, though its countryside was less populated than many of the overcrowded rural areas of Eastern Europe. Hitler's victory was so overwhelming that it was easy to overlook the element of luck which turned the scale at crucial moments, just as, in his Russian campaign, the narrow margin between success and defeat is easily ignored.

The French débâcle and the consequent surrender of the Belgian army put the small British army on the spot. Lord Gort, the commander, had fallen back with his Allies until he found himself penned in along the Franco-Belgian border. Embarkation seemed to offer the only way out, and the British made for Dunkirk, whose steadily shrinking perimeter offered little resistance to German pressure. On 26 May Hitler issued a historic order to his armoured divisions to halt outside Dunkirk instead of capturing it. Thus the British had the time to make good their escape, thanks to a remarkable rescue operation mounted by thousands of ships, large and small. This decision was the Germans' first mistake in the campaign, but a serious one. The reasons for it have been much discussed. Hitler may have been acting on the advice of Rundstedt who believed that his armour needed rest and repairs, and both perhaps over-estimated the effort of which the French were still capable. Keitel and Jodl may have given similar advice.[15] Hitler was also influenced by Göring, who wanted his *Luftwaffe* to have the honour of destroying Dunkirk. It is possible, even probable, that Hitler allowed the British to get away because he did not wish to prejudice the chances of a compromise peace. Whatever his motives, the result was that a force of about 350,000, including 100,000 Frenchmen, embarked from the Dunkirk beaches, without of course their guns and equipment. The cloudy weather, which handicapped air attacks, was another factor that helped the defence. More important at the time in Hitler's eyes was no doubt the final battle for France further south. Having lost half their air force, the French offered little sustained resistance. On 10 June their government left Paris which, in contrast to 1914, they decided not to defend. The appointment of the aged Marshal Pétain in place of Reynaud as French Prime Minister was a sign that the 'softs' had defeated the 'hards' in the French cabinet. The stage was now set for France's capitulation. A Franco-German armistice was signed in the railway carriage at Compiègne where nearly twenty-two years before Germany had signed the armistice that ended the First World War. Hitler had won his long desired revenge. Much of the satisfaction was psychological. The north and west regions of France were to be occupied by the Germans and to form part of Hitler's new economic empire, and French prisoners of war, numbering nearly two million, were to be held for the time being. Germany's *de facto* annexation of Alsace-Lorraine also began. For the rest Hitler showed that his object was less to crush France than to make sure that she could be of no more use as England's ally. By treating her with relative leniency, he hoped to lay hands on her navy (which was in various North African ports) and to dissuade her colonies from throwing in their lot with the Free French movement now beginning under de Gaulle. Judged by the standards of 1914–18, Hitler's victory had been cheap. The Germans had lost 27,000 killed, 18,000 missing and

11,000 wounded. Berlin was given its first victory parade through
the Brandenburg Gate since 1871, and Hitler created twelve new field-
marshals. It was noticeable however that there was still, as in September 1939, a marked lack of enthusiasm for the war among the
German population, though Hitler stood at the peak of his reputation.
Keitel described him as the greatest commander of all time. His
intuition had triumphed where the generals' professional judgement
had wavered. Henceforth opposition to him would be even more
difficult.

(ii) 1940–1: THE YEAR OF TRANSITION

The year that passed between the overthrow of France and the
invasion of Russia was for Hitler a time of waiting, probing and
preparation: first waiting for England to acknowledge defeat, then
trying to subjugate her from Germany's new position of strength in
Europe, and meanwhile preparing for the conquest and colonisation
of Russia on which his heart was set. The battles that were fought,
on land at sea and in the air, were all part of his general strategy, and
were important to him only so far as they served this long-term
purpose. In his inability to understand why the British refused to
come to terms with him, Hitler failed to recognise that their object
was as much to preserve the European balance of power as to protect
their empire – indeed, it was for continental rather than imperial
reasons that England had gone to war in 1914. Nor did he grasp the
effect on the British government of a public opinion horrified by
the Nazis' domestic as well as foreign policy. The significance of the
change from Chamberlain's premiership to Churchill's was also at
first underrated in Berlin. During the phoney war period secret
exploratory peace talks had been held between the British government
and the German opposition under the auspices of the Vatican, but
with Churchill any such negotiations were ruled out. The British
saw that victory had consolidated Hitler's hold on Germany, and in
England guilt feelings about Versailles were buried with the discredited policy of appeasement.

Hitler's unexpectedly quick and complete victory over France
created more problems than it solved. He found himself having to
reconcile the conflicting interests of his allies (Italy and other signatories of the Tripartite Pact) and of the neutrals whom he hoped to
use, Spain being the outstanding example. So far as continuing the
war with England was concerned, Hitler had more than one option.
The most obvious, but also the most hazardous, was the invasion and
occupation of the island. Apart from the serious military risks involved,

there were good reasons for Hitler's reluctance to take this course. He had never intended to incorporate the British Isles in his New Order; the living space he sought was entirely in Eastern Europe. All he now desired from Britain was her neutrality. He was no doubt sincere when he declared that he had no wish to destroy the British Empire and that the main beneficiaries of its break-up would be America and Japan. Ultimately he wanted Germany to become a world power, but only after his continental supremacy had been achieved. There were also practical considerations. If England were under German occupation, her government, with the support of her navy, would almost certainly carry on hostilities from Canada, and thus extend the war which Hitler was anxious to conclude. Now that the British had been expelled from the Continent and their trade was threatened by a German occupation from Norway to the Pyrenees, Hitler expected them to draw the necessary consequences and sue for peace. The terms would have been, as before, recognition of Germany's domination in Europe and perhaps, if only for reasons of prestige, the return of some former German colonies. Why, he reasoned, should England insist on holding out, since without a continental ally she could never re-conquer the Continent? 'The Führer', wrote Halder in his diary for 13 July 1940, 'is greatly puzzled by Britain's persistent unwillingness to make peace.'[16] Churchill's growling defiance, and his cabinet's rejection of Germany's 'final' peace terms, convinced Hitler that plans for invasion of the truculent island must be proceeded with. With some reluctance he gave orders for Operation Sealion. It was a project to which neither he nor his generals had given much thought, though the naval staff had been working on it since the previous November. But the plans were not ready, and the British had been allowed to escape at Dunkirk. Hitler knew that the twenty-six picked divisions held ready for invasion would be able to defeat a British army deprived of tanks, guns, motor vehicles and ammunition. After the evacuation of Dunkirk, scarcely enough equipment remained for two divisions; and even though by August some twenty-six British divisions had been formed, only fourteen of them were adequately armed.[17] The problem was not so much how to land the German troops in the first place as how to keep them supplied against opposition from a powerful navy and an efficient air force. 'Crossing the Channel appears very hazardous to the Führer', noted Halder after a conference with Hitler on 21 July.[18] Raeder, who commanded the navy, was frankly sceptical about the whole enterprise, and insisted that if it was to have any chance of success, air mastery must be won first. But this would be far from easy. The *Luftwaffe* could neutralise the R.A.F. over the Channel, but the

German navy would not be a match for the Home Fleet. Torpedoes, mines and shore batteries would make it difficult for the Germans to control even a section of the Channel. There were also the unfamiliar hazards of tides and weather. The only barges available for carrying troops would not be able to move at more than three knots, and heavy losses must be expected.[19] Nor had German troops been trained in amphibious warfare. As in the invasion of Norway, co-operation of all three services was essential, but this time basic agreement was lacking. The army stressed the need for invading on a broad front between Ramsgate and Lyme Regis, while the navy insisted that only a narrow sea corridor could be held. The air force overrated its chances of success and underrated the British output of fighter planes. The element of surprise was lacking. Preparations went on, but the doubts remained, and Hitler shared them. Considering that when the Allies landed in Normandy in 1944 they had not only naval and air supremacy but also used five thousand ships and four thousand ship-to-shore craft, one can hardly describe Hitler's hesitations as unjustified. Though much of his success throughout his career was due to a readiness to take risks, this was one gamble he refused.

On 13 August the *Luftwaffe* started an all-out offensive over England. The main targets were airfields, aircraft factories and ports. British Fighter Command, using the new Spitfire planes, put up unexpectedly tough resistance, and thanks to the new invention of radar, the scattered defenders were able to make up for lack of numbers by concentrating against the raiders. Reacting to relatively heavy losses, Göring switched his attack to industrial towns and to London in the hope of destroying civilian morale as well as crippling docks and factories. The effect, however, was to make the British people more unyielding, and readier to accept the blood, sweat, toil and tears promised by Churchill, while Göring's change of targets relieved the pressure on those who had been guarding the airfields, so that the advantage gained by the initial attacks was not pressed home. By 15 September, the climax of the attack on London, the operation had evidently failed. The task assigned to the *Luftwaffe* had been beyond its powers: it had been built as an auxiliary of the ground forces, not as a long-range bombing fleet, and its fighters could not give it the necessary protection.[20] The British fighter pilots were more thoroughly trained and had better aircraft. By mid-September too the R.A.F. had destroyed 12 per cent of the Germans' invasion barges in continental ports. Another unfavourable factor for Hitler was the unseasonably bad weather in the late summer. The date of invasion had to be postponed several times; finally on 12 October it was put off until the spring – which meant in fact its abandonment.

Operation Sealion was largely, but not entirely, an act of bluff on Hitler's part, an exercise in psychological warfare. First the threat to invade, then the 'softening up' by the *Luftwaffe*, were intended to bring the British to a point at which actual invasion would be unnecessary.[21] For weeks before the project was shelved Hitler had been giving thought to alternative plans, including an attack on Russia. At the beginning of October the Chief of Staff of the German Air Force drew up a discouraging balance sheet: since the start of the air war against England Germany had lost 350 fighter aircraft out of 950, and 300 bombers out of 1,100.[22] The loss of trained pilots was equally serious, for, unlike the British pilots shot down, if they survived it was usually as prisoners. These figures were an under-estimate. During the period 1 July – 30 September the number of German aircraft destroyed or damaged beyond repair came to 1,389, compared with a corresponding British total of 792.[23] The Chief of Air Staff's conclusion from his incomplete statistics was that to defeat England Germany needed an air force four times as big, and that for the Reich to fight a war on two fronts would be impossible. His unpalatable advice was not heeded by the Führer.

Hitler's wariness in regard to England was justified, for her position was stronger than it looked. Unready as she had been for invasion in June, by September she had thrown aside the lethargy of the phoney war period and no invasion then would have been a walk-over. An early sign of the confidence of the Churchill government was its decision to respond to the Italian declaration of war by sending a powerful naval squadron to Gibraltar. From there the force exercised control of the western Mediterranean abandoned by the French, kept a vigilant eye on French warships in French and North African ports, and protected British shipping in the eastern Atlantic. In August the British cabinet felt bold enough to despatch half its available tanks to reinforce its army in Egypt. Thanks to the close understanding established between Churchill and Roosevelt, substantial arms shipments, including half a million rifles, 80,000 machine guns and tommy guns and 900 field guns, had reached Britain from America in the course of July.[24] In September Congress ratified Roosevelt's pledge to hand over 50 United States destroyers in return for the lease of Caribbean bases. They helped to fill gaps in the Atlantic convoys caused by the concentration of British naval vessels for the expected invasion.

If England could not be invaded, she might be coerced into surrender by blockade. On 17 August Hitler declared the British Isles a blockaded area, a threat he was unable to make good because at that date Germany possessed fewer U-boats than she had had a year before.

18 A parade in Nuremberg during the Nazi Party Rally, 1938

17 Hitler, Papen and Blomberg, 1934

19 Ribbentrop signs the Nazi-Soviet Non-Aggression Pact, August 1939

20 The Place de la Concorde, Paris, 1940

22 Unter den Linden, Berlin, summer 1945

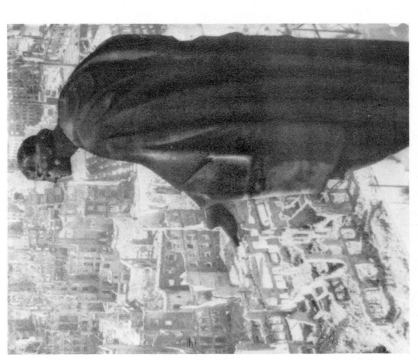

21 Dresden after the bombing, February 1945

23 Scrounging for food, 1945

24 Digging potatoes near the Soviet war memorial, with the ruins of
the Reichstag behind

25 Otto Grotewohl, Wilhelm Pieck, Walter Ulbricht

26 The Brandenburg Gate, Berlin, during the East German rising,
    June 1953

28 Chancellor Brandt with Professor Karl Schiller, his Minister of Economics and Finance, 1969

27 Churchill and Adenauer, 1951

29 Flight from East Berlin, 1961

30 Wedding at the Wall, 1969

31 West Berlin, 1965, with the Europa Centre and the rebuilt Kaiser Wilhelm Memorial Church

32 New housing in East Berlin, with statue of Lenin, 1971

At the beginning of the war she had 57, of which only 22 were equipped for the Atlantic run, and before 1941 she never had more than fifteen operating at any one time.[25] Like other lessons of the First World War, the experience of the submarine campaign was vividly in Hitler's mind. He knew that any intensification of U-boat warfare would involve attacks on American shipping and so make more likely American intervention. He also knew that the United States was already far from neutral: the revision of the Neutrality Act in November 1939 by the 'Cash and Carry' law worked wholly in favour of the Allies, and Roosevelt's help to Britain in the summer of 1940 tilted the balance still further. Roosevelt's re-election in the autumn of 1940 enabled him to press this policy with more vigour, and meanwhile a formidable rearmament programme was under way in the United States. While he had no illusions about America, Hitler's policy was to avoid provoking her as far as possible even to the extent of not reacting to American provocation of Germany, at least until such time as the Reich would be militarily and economically invulnerable. It was with the object of intimidating the United States that Hitler signed the Tripartite Pact of September 1940 with Italy and Japan, by which Japan undertook to fight if any of the signatory powers was attacked by a fourth power, meaning America. When in April 1941 Matsuoka, the Japanese Foreign Minister, visited Berlin, the Germans did their best to persuade him to expand southwards to Singapore and so to goad the United States into a war in the Pacific. Roosevelt had however already persuaded Congress to pass the Two Ocean Navy Bill which was to prepare America for a simultaneous war against both Japan and Germany. Hitler continued his efforts after the signing of the Tripartite Pact to induce Japan to become a belligerent, but Japanese policy, reflecting divisions within the government, was ambiguous and hesitant. Ribbentrop went so far as to tell Matsuoka in May 1941 that American rearmament was 'the greatest bluff in the history of the world', a typical piece of braggadocio, though in that year the United States produced more aircraft than Germany.[26]

It was on the Mediterranean, not the Atlantic, that Hitler's gaze was fixed during the last months of 1940. If England could not be invaded she might be ruined through loss of her trade and possessions in the Mediterranean. Italy had been at war since 10 June; to her must be added Spain and, if possible, France in an anti-British coalition that would seize Gibralter and turn the Mediterranean into an Axis lake. One advantage of this strategy was that it need not embroil Germany with America. Another was that the capture of Gibraltar would make possible Axis penetration of North Africa, where both Spain and Italy had ambitions and Germany had visions of a new African empire based on her former colonies of Togo and the Cameroons. Hitler wanted Africa for raw materials, not for settlement, he told Suñer, the Spanish Foreign Minister, adding that for settlement Germany had enough land in Europe.[27] Italy's central position in the Mediterranean was ideal for seizing Malta and sinking British ships bound for Egypt, so compelling the British government to send reinforcements for the Middle East round the much longer Cape of Good Hope route. In the Arab lands bordering the eastern Mediterranean Germany could exploit the prevailing discontents and present herself as the deliverer from French and British imperialism and Zionism. Yet none of these hopes was realised. Spain refused to commit herself, Italy's military achievements were in inverse ratio to her ambitions, and her territorial claims proved an embarrassment to her ally. Egypt for example had no wish to exchange British tutelage for Italian. Finally, Hitler's strategy in the Mediterranean was handicapped by its lack of priority compared with his other plans, notably the invasion of Russia. He was unwilling to commit more than a small proportion of his resources to it despite the cheap victories to be had there. Apart from Hitler's difficulties with Italy, he faced the problems of a land power trying to fight a war that had become largely maritime in character. Even success in the Libyan campaign depended on mastery of the sea across which supplies had to be carried.

In the immediate aftermath of his triumph over France, the outlook for Hitler seemed bright. In June Franco told him that Spain intended to enter the war 'after a short preparation of public opinion'.[28] In return Spain expected to receive Gibraltar, the whole of Morocco, and additional territory in Guinea and West Africa. This put Hitler on the spot. If he gave way to Spanish demands he could not treat France with the leniency needed to prevent the French navy and empire from going over to the British and de Gaulle. When, in September 1940, Hitler called on Franco to declare war on England the response was cool. Franco now insisted that economic aid must also be part of the bargain. This was one of the subjects which Hitler and Franco discussed when they met at Hendaye on 23 October. The Führer was subjected by his fellow dictator to a searching cross-examination of a kind he was not used to. Spain (where the Franco regime had hardly had time to consolidate after the civil war) was still exhausted, and her economy depended on imports, especially on food from North America. If she became a belligerent she would lose this and much else besides: essential raw materials would be cut off, and the British would seize Spain's Atlantic colonies. Fulsome as Franco was in his professions of loyalty to the Axis, which had helped him to win the civil war, he shrewdly resisted Hitler's pressure and evaded any promise to go to war by a given date. By the end of 1940 he saw that the Axis had suffered reverses in the Balkans and in Libya. Since Spain remained obstinately neutral, the German plan for capturing Gibraltar was shelved indefinitely. Yet had Spain entered the war, it would have been a far from unmixed blessing for the Germans, who would have had to stretch their resources to protect the long and vulnerable Iberian coastline as well as to bolster the shaky Spanish economy.

After his unsatisfactory interview with Franco, Hitler met Pétain, the new French Head of State. Pétain's policy was one of wait and see, while his Foreign Minister, Laval, was openly in favour of collaboration with Germany. Like Franco, Pétain refused to declare war on England. Hitler's dilemma was that on the one hand he needed to use France as an asset in the continuing struggle with England, while on the other if he pressed the French too hard he would turn their neutrality into hostility. Both Italy and Spain wished to make territorial gains at French expense, while France could be compensated only at the cost of the British Empire. In Vichy the wrangle between the collaborationists and the *attentistes* went on, and though the latter were soon successful in ousting Laval, his successor, Admiral Darlan, was prepared to go along with Hitler for reasons of opportunism. England's defeat was still taken for granted. But Hitler was cautious. He wrote to Mussolini on 5 December: 'We are not absolutely sure of the attitude of the government of Vichy. . . . The slightest false move may bring about a rupture between North and West Africa and Vichy which would offer Great Britain an operational base extremely dangerous for us.'[29] There was a moment after France's defeat when a genuine Franco-German reconciliation seemed possible. The German occupiers showed a respect for human life and property that was in marked contrast to their conduct in Poland: even looting during the 1940 campaign was severely punished. French resentment against England, already strong in some quarters, was fanned by the destruction of the French navy at Mers el Kebir, on Churchill's reluctant orders, to prevent its falling into German hands. But though the terms of the Franco-German armistice were relatively mild, the *de facto* annexation by Germany of Alsace-Lorraine began, and about 100,000 French people were expelled from the two provinces. Moreover the German occupation cost the French taxpayer 20 million marks a day. The French also resented Italy's claims against them, which Hitler tried to curb. The Vichy government was susceptible to American influence, which was hostile to the Axis. In the long run France would collaborate with Hitler only as long as he was successful; and Pétain managed to come to an informal agreement with the

British government behind Laval's back whereby each side undertook not to attack the other.

If neither Franco's Spain nor Pétain's France played the role which
Hitler desired, it was his Italian ally which proved the greatest disappointment. On paper Italy was impressive: her air force contained
about 3,300 planes, of which a third were up to date, and her navy
outnumbered the British Mediterranean fleet.[30] The Italian army of
215,000 under Graziani in Libya was four times the size of the British
Empire force opposing it. But the impression of strength given by these
statistics was misleading. The Italian army was short of tanks and
motor vehicles and many of its guns were antiquated; the navy lacked
fuel oil and had an inferiority complex which made it loth to challenge
the British. Only two of the six Italian battleships were ready for
action. Though Mussolini declared war at a moment when the British
were fully occupied at home, he failed to seize Malta, inadequately
defended as it then was, or to cut off British ships bound for Malta
and Egypt. In November 1940 the Royal Navy's Air Arm attacked the
Italian naval base at Taranto, sinking three battleships and damaging
two cruisers. Wavell's desert offensive the following month pushed
Graziani's forces back several hundred miles into Libya and took
130,000 prisoners. Indeed, had the advance not been curtailed by the
Churchill government's decision to send an expeditionary force to help
the Greeks, the North African campaign might have ended in the
spring of 1941 instead of two years later. Hitler posted a squadron of
the *Luftwaffe* to Sicily to reinforce his ally, and in February 1941
General Rommel arrived in Libya with an armoured force, nucleus of
the Afrika Korps. Mussolini, who at first had refused German help,
now pleaded for it. The attack on Greece which he had launched,
without consulting Hitler, at the end of October 1940, had turned
out a complete fiasco. Hitler was understandably annoyed, for the
new front in the Balkans enabled the British (who had guaranteed
Greek independence) to intervene. Their small army in Greece was to
be the linchpin of an anti-Axis alliance, and they occupied airfields in
Crete and other islands from which they could bomb the Roumanian
oilfields. And since the Italians, so far from defeating the Greeks, were
driven back into Albania, Hitler was obliged to send German troops
into Greece to turn the defenders' flank. Affairs in Yugoslavia reached
a crisis. For some time past the pro-Axis government in Belgrade had
been under heavy pressure to join the Tripartite Pact, to which Hungary, Roumania, Bulgaria and Slovakia already belonged. On 25
March the Yugoslavs decided on this step. But two days later an
officers' *coup d'état* put in power a nationalist government that concluded a treaty of friendship with Soviet Russia. Hitler decided to

occupy Yugoslavia as well as Greece, and both countries were overrun
in a short victorious campaign, German troops entering Greece from
Yugoslavia and also from Bulgaria. The British evacuation of Greece
was followed in May 1941 by the German capture of Crete, an airborne operation which involved heavy casualties on both sides. There
was no question now of Mussolini waging the 'parallel war' in the
Mediterranean of which he had boasted: Italy's military as well as
economic dependence on Germany was obvious, and without German
backing the Italians would be driven out of North Africa. Henceforth
Italy was a satellite rather than an ally. Hitler had no illusions: he
trusted no one in Italy except Mussolini, whose infatuation with the
Führer was shared by few of his compatriots. Possession of Crete gave
the *Luftwaffe* a valuable base for the air battles over land and sea
that helped to decide the war in Libya, and balanced the Italian naval
defeat off Cape Matapan (Greece) in March 1941, in which the
Italian navy lost three cruisers and two destroyers. Yet Hitler never
took full advantage of his opportunities in the Mediterranean, as his
naval advisers urged. In 1940–1 German forces could have seized
Malta or Gibraltar, or driven the British out of Egypt, but even many
months before the Russian campaign began he saw the Mediterranean
theatre of war as auxiliary to his main purpose. Had he decided to
exploit the various possibilities there, with all their strategic and
economic consequences, Hitler would have radically changed the
character of the war, though hardly its final outcome. For any
southward extension of German power would have evoked a reaction
in America, and in particular German control of French colonial
territory on the Atlantic coast of Africa would have added to the
reasons which made the United States' full intervention in the war
sooner or later inevitable.[31]

(iii) THE MEDITERRANEAN AND THE ATLANTIC

Rommel's appearance in Libya opened a new phase in the campaign
without altering its limited strategic character: for though in British
eyes the war in the Western Desert was of vital importance, both to
hold the Middle East and as the beginning of an attempt to knock
Italy out of the war, for Germany it was primarily a diversion of resources to shore up the Italians. Rommel, who quickly added to the
reputation he had already won through his exploits in France, lost
little time in launching an offensive. Taking advantage of the militarily
unwise British decision to help Greece, he recovered Cyrenaica and
advanced to the Egyptian frontier. He might indeed have gone further
had he had the necessary reinforcements, and had the British garrison

in the port of Tobruk not managed to hold out. But Hitler was now preoccupied with the war in Russia; and he calculated that after his victory there, he could gather the spoils of the Middle East at his leisure. There was talk in German military circles of a thrust from the Caucasus into Iraq. From Hitler's point of view the pro-Axis rising led by Rashid Ali in Baghdad in April 1941 was premature: the Germans sent a few aircraft, but such half-hearted support could not save the rebels, who were defeated by the end of May. Rashid Ali's bid for power was the most overt expression of the nationalist feeling that simmered just below the surface of Arab politics in those years. To seal off Iraq, the British occupied Vichy-held Syria, a move which strengthened their position in the Eastern Mediterranean and enabled them to put pressure on Turkey. Yet despite the departure of some of Rommel's air squadrons for the Russian front, the second half of 1941 saw the fortunes of war swing in his favour. Thanks to the transfer of 26 German submarines from the Atlantic to the Mediterranean British shipping losses rose, and an aircraft carrier and a battleship were sunk. Italian frogmen also damaged two battleships in Alexandria harbour. Japan's entry into the war in December caused a dispersal of British naval strength, and two divisions with much equipment left Egypt for the Far East. Although Auchinleck, who had succeeded Wavell as British Commander-in-Chief, Middle East had started an offensive a few weeks earlier, much of the ground won was lost when Rommel counter-attacked in January. In the spring of 1942 the front again solidified on a line running from Gazala to Bir Hacheim in eastern Cyrenaica. The pause in the fighting was short-lived as both sides prepared to attack again. The British Eighth Army planned to strike first, but Rommel was quicker off the mark. His offensive before the end of May overran the British positions and carried him back over the Egyptian frontier. The Eighth Army's retreat, which brought the fall of Tobruk despite its abundant supplies of food and fuel after little resistance, was a shattering blow to Allied morale. An atmosphere of defeatism settled on Cairo, where the wildest rumours found ready credence. The departure of the British fleet from Alexandria for the Red Sea, and the smoke of burning documents over official buildings in Cairo seemed to presage the abandonment of Egypt to Rommel, whose prowess was now a legend. Auchinleck, who had taken over direct command of the Eighth Army, made a stand at El Alamein, little more than a point on the map and only sixty miles west of Alexandria. It was a good choice, because two ridges gave the defence the advantage of height, while to the south the Qattara depression prevented it from being outflanked. For the moment Rommel was unable to continue his pursuit owing to the exhaustion of his troops and shortage of fuel. British air mastery had caused severe losses of Axis tankers in the central Mediterranean, and the Axis was paying heavily for its failure to capture Malta. But in Italy, where the desire to occupy Egypt had always been stronger than in Germany, hopes ran high, and Mussolini arrived in Libya in preparation for a triumphant entry into Cairo. It was hardly realised at the time that the check to Rommel in July, known as the first battle of Alamein, was probably the decisive turning point.[32]

At the end of August Rommel resumed the offensive, but this time the Eighth Army, now commanded by Montgomery, resisted strongly and he could make no headway. Though Churchill continued to urge attack at the earliest possible moment, Montgomery, unlike his less fortunate predecessors, could afford to wait until he was ready. Massive reinforcements arrived through the Suez Canal. By 23 October, when the historic second battle of Alamein began, he had three times as many troops as Rommel, six times as many tanks fit for action (including some of the new Shermans from America) and three times the number of serviceable aircraft.[33] Thanks to this material superiority, but also to a feeling of confidence generated by Montgomery's highly professional approach, the British went into battle with a belief in victory that proved justified. Rommel was again handicapped by lack of fuel and of air support. Hitherto he had shown superior generalship, and the German tank repair service, for example, was better than the British. But Montgomery's skill and methodical use of greater resources turned the scale, and despite initial orders from Hitler to stand firm, the Afrika Korps was soon in full retreat, leaving behind most of its armour. Meanwhile American and British forces had landed in Morocco and Algeria, so that when Rommel, abandoning Libya, crossed the frontier into Tunis, he was faced with another Allied army advancing from the west. Although Hitler sent three divisions to Tunis as reinforcements, the Axis armies were ultimately surrounded and obliged to surrender. By May 1943 the North African campaign was over and more than 150,000 German and Italian soldiers had passed into captivity.[34] This reinforcement of an untenable position was one of Hitler's worst errors of judgement and the loss of troops made it harder for him to defend Southern Europe. The irony was that if Rommel had had four more German divisions at the beginning of 1942 he might well have reached Cairo and the Suez Canal.[35] While he never had more than about 12 divisions of which not quite five were German, against the Russians two hundred divisions were deployed: the disparity in number marks the difference in priority as well as in size between the two fronts.[36] The desert war stood out among the campaigns of the Second World War: it involved almost no damage to non-belligerents and was conducted on comparatively civilised lines. In some ways fighting in the desert resembled naval warfare, with groups of tanks instead of battleships and the sand almost as featureless as the sea. There were no atrocities, and the fact that a captured general might be asked to dine with his captor, as von Thoma was by Montgomery, preserved a flavour of old-fashioned chivalry. All this was a far cry from the wholesale extermination and racial fanaticism that characterised the war in Russia, and even from the destruction suffered by civilians in normal land campaigns.

One reason for the German reluctance to commit more resources to the desert war was the realisation that whatever its outcome it could not be decisive in the struggle against England. From that point of view the battle of the Atlantic was much more significant. The British government knew that the Atlantic was crucial. Here the vital weapon for Germany was the U-boat: the loss in December 1939 of the pocket battleship *Graf Spee* showed the limitations of surface vessels against British sea-power. Admiral Dönitz, commander of the submarine arm of the German navy, had urged Hitler at the beginning of the war to give absolute priority to the building of U-boats, and stated that a hundred was the lowest number needed to be in operation at any one time. This meant trebling the existing total. Hitler never really accepted this case. Admittedly in August 1940 he declared a total blockade of the British Isles, but he lacked the means to enforce it, and it amounted to little more than a psychological move in the war of nerves by which Hitler hoped to impose a settlement.[37] He also ordered a stepping up of the submarine building programme in June 1940, the results of which would, however, not be seen before the following year. Basically Hitler had two reasons for not giving submarines the absolute priority for which Dönitz asked. One was his fear of provoking America to declare war; and though he saw this as in the long run inevitable, he wished to postpone it as far as possible. Secondly, since Hitler's first priority was the conquest of Russia, the sea war with Britain was for him an irritating irrelevance, whatever his ultimate hopes of an overseas empire. The naval building programme approved by Hitler in the spring of 1940 was not to be complete until 1946 at the earliest:[38] Germany had become involved in war with England long before he was ready, and to this extent his whole strategic design was upset. From the start of the war he was forced to improvise. Not until the spring of 1943 were U-boats given priority over other weapons, and by then Hitler knew that the war was lost.[39] And though Dönitz was convinced that the Atlantic was the essential theatre of war, his superior Raeder, who was Commander-in-Chief of the German Navy until Dönitz succeeded him in January 1943, wished to concentrate on the Mediterranean, and tried in vain to persuade Hitler not to invade Russia before the subjugation of Britain.

The German offensive in the Atlantic reached its first climax in 1941, when a number of surface vessels, including two battle cruisers, the *Scharnhorst* and the *Gneisenau*, and a pocket battleship, the *Scheer*, sailed out to aid the rising number of submarines. They were soon joined by the newly launched battleship, *Bismarck*, and a cruiser, the *Prinz Eugen*. In the second quarter of the year one-and-three-quarter million tons of British, Allied and neutral shipping was sunk, a monthly average not far short of the level of April 1917. Yet seen against this figure of 30·5 million tons, the total of British imports that year, it is less impressive.[40] During the second half of 1941 sinkings fell away again (157,000 tons in October). On the British side better air protection and reconaissance, stronger escorts for convoys, better anti-aircraft guns and growing American participation at the western end of the routes and near Iceland were the main reasons for the reduced losses. For the Germans the transfer of U-boats to the Mediterranean and the diversion of aircraft to Russia made a difference, especially as there was no German equivalent to the Fleet Air Arm. The *Bismarck*, having made its way into the Atlantic round the north of Iceland, was pursued by numerous British ships, crippled and finally sunk off Brest in May 1941, after an engagement in which the British battleship *Hood* was destroyed. The *Scharnhorst* and the *Gneisenau* (the former damaged) took refuge in Brest harbour before making a successful dash through the English Channel to the North Sea in February 1942. The *Gneisenau* was later put out of action by bombers in Kiel. The *Prinz Eugen*, which was used against British convoys to Murmansk, was finally torpedoed in Norway. Except for the raiding vessels on the Murmansk route, which were based on Norway, German surface ships were withdrawn from the oceans early in 1943.

America's full entry into the war at the end of 1941 gave a new dimension to the battle of the Atlantic. Hitherto U-boats had not attacked American ships in the western Atlantic, the so-called U.S. defence zone. Now U-boats concentrated in packs along the American east coast and in the Caribbean with devastating results. Having built 300 submarines in 1941, the Germans could deploy over a hundred at a time in the Atlantic, and with improved methods: U-boats hunted in packs, and could re-fuel from under-water supply craft. To escape under-water detection devices they attacked convoys at night on the surface. By the end of 1941 164 U-boats were operating in the Atlantic.[41] Even this number could have been exceeded had preparations for the land war in Russia not competed with shipyards for labour and materials. In June 1942 Allied sinkings exceeded 800,000 tons, mainly near the United States' eastern seaboard. The American landings in North Africa in November of that year provided the U-boats with another heavy toll. As Americans reduced the risks to their coastal shipping by means of convoys, the U-boats moved to mid-Atlantic where Allied aircraft could not be so effective. Had the U-boat command not been obliged by Hitler to divert a proportion of its vessels to the Arctic to attack enemy convoys to Russia and to Norway (where Hitler expected an invasion), it might have forced the British into surrender by the destruction of essential imports. But Hitler had too many irons in the fire; and in the long run America's almost unlimited capacity to build ships and replace losses was bound to tell. By March 1943, when the battle of the Atlantic reached its third and final climax, over half a million tons of shipping was sunk there in a single month, four-fifths of it in convoy. But just when it appeared that the convoy system had been mastered, the Allies came back with a combination of improved radar, high-frequency direction finders, more escort carriers, anti-submarine vessels and long range aircraft. The Germans' biggest handicap continued to be the lack of air reconnaissance and protection. So high a proportion of U-boats was destroyed in the next few weeks that on 24 May Dönitz ordered their total withdrawal from the North Atlantic. They remained active elsewhere, and the output of U-boats went on rising, despite heavy bombing. The new method of manufacture, introduced by Speer, was to build the U-boats at inland factories and take them in sections to the coast for assembling.[42] The total built in 1944 was almost as large as in 1942, and in March 1945 Germany still had a fleet of 463. Dönitz had persuaded Hitler to build no more big surface vessels after 1943. Further research into submarine design and performance produced larger models and new devices, including an electric submarine fitted with an air tube (the *Schnorchel*) which enabled it to take in air and recharge its batteries while submerged. But many of these improvements were still in the trial stage, and they had little effect on the war. The U-boats caused no significant damage to the Allied landings in Normandy in 1944. Other inventions, such as a new type of pressure-operated mine, had more success, but on a limited scale. Though U-boat sinkings around the British Isles and in many other parts of the world continued until the end of the war, performance per U-boat in 1944–5 compared very unfavourably with what a much smaller fleet had achieved in 1917–18, and by 1943 was already less than a quarter of what it had been in 1940.[43] The law of diminishing returns more than offset the increased building programme.

(iv) BARBAROSSA

On 18 December 1940 Hitler signed the directive for the attack on Russia (Operation Barbarossa) launched six months later. It was not a sudden decision: the idea of invading Russia had never been absent from his mind, even during the ambiguous honeymoon of the Nazi-Soviet Non-Aggression Pact. Indeed, Hitler had specifically referred to it at a conference of his commanding generals on 22 August 1939 when Ribbentrop was already on his way to Moscow. The pact was in many ways unnatural, a tactical, temporary move dictated by unforeseen circumstances – the Anglo-French guarantee to Poland – and never really accepted by the party leaders (Ribbentrop was a notable exception) or popular among the German people. Apart from the Jews, Bolshevism was Hitler's greatest bugbear; and the Soviet Union symbolised both, for in his distorted vision Russia notwithstanding the rise of Stalin (whom he admired) was under the yoke of a Jewish oligarchy. The central theme of *Mein Kampf*, suggested by the slavo-phobia of Hitler's early environment and Germany's lack of colonies, was that the Reich could find in under-populated and under-developed Russia – and only there – the space and resources she needed to become an independent world power. Thus Barbarossa marked a return to Hitler's original strategy; this, not the war 'forced' on him by the West was the war he had always meant to fight.[44] There were also practical reasons for his choice. As long as England remained an enemy there was always the risk, exemplified by the Cripps mission to Russia in the summer of 1940, of an Anglo-Russian alliance. Russia might replace France as England's 'continental sword'. And even if this did not happen Russia was an uncomfortable neighbour. Political motives were as important to Hitler as economic, perhaps more important. The hard bargaining which had preceded the Nazi-Soviet Pact had disclosed some of Stalin's ambitions; the Soviet moves after the fall of France revealed more. Stalin absorbed the three Baltic states, demanded fresh concessions from Finland, and, as we noticed earlier in this chapter, annexed the provinces of Bessarabia and North Bukovina. In self-defence Finland and Roumania looked to Germany for support. Hitler guaranteed Roumania (whose defence treaty with Britain had obviously become inoperative) on condition that she yielded territory to Hungary (Transylvania) and Bulgaria (Dobrudja) – another 'revision' of the 1919 peace treaties.

German troops entered Roumania, where King Carol abdicated and a Fascist dictator, General Antonescu, seized power. The Finns received arms from Germany, ostensibly to defend themselves against a British attack, in reality against Russia, and a German force arrived in Finland. The German stake in Finland was economic as well as strategic: the nickel mines at Petsamo were an important source, coveted too by the Soviets. On 26 October Russian troops occupied the Kilia Islands in the Danube Delta and so gained control of the river traffic. They were thus able to put pressure on Roumania. The next Russian demand was for South Bukovina, which was equivalent to requiring Germany to cancel its guarantee of Roumania. This was obviously unacceptable to Berlin. The Soviets also made clear their interest in Bulgaria and Turkey. In the Non-Aggression pact of August 1939 Germany had recognised the Balkans as a Russian sphere of influence, but this no longer suited Hitler. He needed Roumania because it supplied over a fifth of Germany's oil. The dangers arising from Mussolini's war in Greece provided a further reason for Germany to control the Balkans.

It was to try and persuade the Russians to adjust to the new situation that Hitler invited Molotov, the Russian Foreign Minister, to visit Berlin in November 1940. Since July, if not before, Hitler's mind had been moving towards a military solution of the Russian problem: troops had been transferred to the eastern frontier and a build-up of transport and supply facilities for a Russian campaign begun. Indeed he had spoken of invading Russia that summer before his generals had persuaded him that it was too late in the season, whereupon the project was postponed to the following spring. Meanwhile, and without prejudice to the military plans, forceful diplomacy might help by deflecting Russian attention away from areas where her interests clashed with Germany's. The Russians might be induced to join the Tripartite Pact of Germany, Italy and Japan, which would make an Anglo-Russian *rapprochement* less likely. It was even more important to head Russia away from the Balkans towards the Persian Gulf and Indian Ocean.[45] Ribbentrop talked airily of the liquidation of the British Empire and suggested a carve-up of the world among the 'new nations', again with the secondary motive of driving a wedge between Russia and Britain. But Molotov was shrewd and realistic, as he showed by his searching questions and sceptical attitude to Ribbentrop's glib assurances. Neither side was willing to allow the other a free hand in the Balkans. On Turkey both countries agreed that the Montreux treaty should be revised in favour of the free passage of warships through the Straits, but Russia wished to underpin a new settlement with Turkey by a pact with Bulgaria. The talks thus failed to reconcile Russo-German differences, and Hitler can hardly have been surprised or even disappointed, for on the very day of Molotov's arrival in Berlin he ordered preparations for the invasion of Russia to continue. A new Russo-German economic treaty was, however, signed in January 1941, which was considered satisfactory by the Germans, but it was significant that Hitler forbade publication of its terms to the German press.[46] Something was done to offset the economic consequences of a breach with Russia (of which General Thomas of the Economic and Armaments section of the O.K.W. warned the Führer) by arranging for rubber and other vital materials brought to Germany by the Trans-Siberian railway to come by sea. Most of the generals were uneasy about starting a war with Russia before Britain was defeated, though few doubted that the *Blitzkrieg* tactics which had been so successful in France would work in Russia. Thus Barbarossa met little of the resistance with which the army chiefs had tried to talk Hitler out of an offensive in the west. The Führer's prestige and that of his *Wehrmacht* were at their zenith. Whereas against England Germany was fighting with weapons (navy, air force, economic blockade) in which she was usually inferior and at best on equal terms, against Russia she had the apparently invincible army that would otherwise be 'wasted'. Even in retrospect it can hardly be said that Hitler was wrong to attack Russia from a strictly military point of view. His fault lay in doing so before Germany had acquired the superiority in arms production and was prepared for the kind of war imposed by Russian conditions. Whether the Nazis could ever have found a political solution is another question and, in the light of what happened, improbable.

While the military planning of Barbarossa went on smoothly, political preparations ran into difficulties. Finland and Roumania, which both had obvious reasons for desiring Russia's defeat, promised military support and the use of their territory as a base for the offensive. But the Balkan situation was worrying. The disastrous war launched by Italy in Greece opened the door to British intervention, with the implied threat that the R.A.F. might bomb the Roumanian oilfields. Nor could the Axis tolerate an Italian defeat. Hitler decided to step in and invade Greece from Bulgaria, whose king, Boris, was his admirer and had served in the German army in the First World War. There remained Yugoslavia, where, as we have seen, an anti-Axis government came to power at the end of March 1941 and signed a treaty of friendship with the Soviet Union. Hitler was furious, and next day his troops entered Yugoslavia, which capitulated within eight days. It was a model *Blitzkrieg* – short, cheap, decisive – and cost Germany only 151 dead and 392 wounded in return for 344,000

Yugoslav prisoners. German troops also entered Greece from Yugoslavia. With the subsequent expulsion of the British from the Greek mainland and islands, including Crete, Hitler had made sure of his right flank, though the starting date of Barbarossa had to be put back by five weeks. The postponement, however, did not seem of great significance, since Russian resistance to the German war machine was not expected to last more than a few weeks. This was also the expectation in other countries. The late spring that year would in any case have made earlier operations in Russia hazardous. Meanwhile the Soviet government, alarmed by Hitler's swift success and warned from several quarters of his intentions, did everything possible to conciliate him: deliveries of materials were speeded up, a dispute on the northern section of the Russo-German frontier was settled in Germany's favour, and even the Finns and Roumanians felt the change in Moscow's mood. Soviet recognition was withdrawn from the governments of the countries under German occupation. Stalin's assumption of the premiership (chairmanship of the Council of People's Commissars) was also a gesture in support of continued co-operation with Germany, a point underlined by his demonstrative friendliness to the German military attaché when both met at the Moscow station to see off the Japanese Foreign Minister, Matsuoka, after negotiation of the Russo-Japanese Neutrality Pact. (Incidentally this Pact went against Hitler's wishes, a sign that Germany had little influence on Japanese policy. The Germans would have liked the Japanese to make their main military effort against Russia: instead, the Japanese, to the surprise of Berlin, launched their attack on Pearl Harbor. Despite their formal alliance, there was no real co-ordination of plans between Germany and Japan.) The situation was ripe for a new political settlement with Russia if Hitler had desired it. But having decided to attack he would not be deterred. Rather than bargain for a larger sphere of influence or more favourable terms of trade, he would conquer Russia and help himself. Outwardly Stalin went on behaving as if he gave no heed to the warnings: despite explicit information about German troop movements near the Russian border supplied by the British government, TASS, the Soviet News Agency, reported as late as 14 June that rumours that Germany was about to invade Russia were without foundation.

Hitler's orders for Barbarossa were for the 'destruction of the bulk of the Soviet Army located in western Russia by bold operations involving deep penetrations by armoured spearheads' and the reaching of a line from Archangel on the Arctic Sea to Astrakhan on the Caspian by the autumn. This is not the place to chronicle the four-year campaign on which the fate of the Nazi Reich depended. At first all went according to plan: deploying about 3·2 million men the Germans made rapid progress in a series of pincer movements, taking vast numbers of prisoners who were surrounded almost before they had a chance to fight. In July the war seemed as good as won; by the 17th of that month Smolensk, less than two hundred miles from Moscow, was in German hands. In August the army Chief of Staff, Halder, was not so sure. Already 360 Russian divisions had been identified instead of the 200 expected.[47] The Russian reserves appeared inexhaustible. They needed to be: by the middle of October the number of Russian prisoners exceeded three million. But the intention of destroying the entire Soviet army west of the Dnieper had not been fulfilled, and the autumn rains were beginning to turn the whole country into a morass. The advance on Moscow began under great difficulty. Winter set in unexpectedly early that year and was the most severe for over a century. Tanks, motor vehicles and fuel froze up, and among the troops there were over 100,000 cases of frostbite. The army was paralysed, but Hitler refused to withdraw it into winter quarters. In December the Russians, equipped for such conditions and using warmly clad troops from Siberia, launched a successful counter-attack. By the end of the year the Germans had been thrown back from Moscow, and one in five of their army was a casualty. These losses were never entirely made good, and despite subsequent reinforcements and replacements the moral effect of that nightmare winter remained.[48]

The Germans had to wait until the following summer to launch their next offensive, for which the main targets were the industries of the Donetz basin and the oilfields of the Caucasus. In the north, Leningrad was to be captured and a junction made with the Finnish army. Hitler's forces crossed the Don, completed the conquest of the Crimea and advanced into the western Caucasus. They also crossed the Volga, thus cutting off Moscow from its oil supplies, and reached Stalingrad, the key town in the Volga valley. 'The Russian is finished' Hitler told Halder in July, and Halder agreed.[49] Unaware of Russia's formidable reserves, Hitler had visions of a southward sweep to Astrakhan and Baku, but also of a northward thrust to take Moscow in the rear: Stalingrad would thus be a sheet-anchor to protect the flank of the Caucasian armies but also the springboard for these other more ambitious operations. There was some misunderstanding between Hitler and his generals on military objectives, and Hitler's decision to hold the highly exposed city of Stalingrad at a time when a concentration of Russian strength made it almost untenable led to a fresh dispute with Halder, who no longer had the Führer's confidence. In the event the German Sixth Army was trapped when the

Stalingrad salient was surrounded by five Russian armies and forced to surrender. Over 200,000 German troops were dead or prisoners; few of the latter ever returned home. The German forces in the Caucasus were nearly cut off and retreated with considerable difficulty. After this disaster the strategic offensive passed to the Russians, who increasingly had the advantage in men and material. Stalingrad is usually considered the turning point of the war, especially as its investment coincided with the battle of Alamein. But the most critical time for the Red Army had been in the autumn of 1941, when the German thrust was still unblunted and America's entry into the war had not swung the global balance of power in favour of the Allies. If Stalingrad was in some ways a freak – one of the reasons for it was the failure of Germany's Roumanian and Italian allies, another the failure of the *Luftwaffe* to deliver promised supplies – the Kursk tank battle in July 1943 was a fair trial of strength between two well-equipped and well-matched antagonists which ended disastrously for the Germans. This was the third great crisis of the *Wehrmacht* in Russia, and after it the Germans knew, even if Hitler would not admit, that they had lost the war. By October 1943 two and a half million German soldiers were facing a Red Army of five and a half millions.[50]

Military historians will continue to debate the reasons for the failure of Barbarossa and the allocation of blame between Hitler and his generals. The Führer's pathological suspicion of them was shown by his unceasing criticism, his taunts, and the ease and frequency with which they were dismissed. In sacking his best commanders he defeated his own long-term aims. Brauchitsch was driven to resign in December 1941; Bock, leading the Central Army Group, and Guderian, Germany's best tank general, were replaced in the same month, as was von Rundstedt, who had played a big part in the defeat of France and was later to be recalled as Commander-in-Chief in the West. Halder was dismissed in September 1942 after warning Hitler, in vain, of the risks involved at Stalingrad, while Manstein, one of the ablest German generals and author of the plan which had defeated France, was relieved of his command in March 1944. Hitler had the dislike of a self-made dictator for a traditional military caste. In their eyes he remained an inspired corporal whose genius was inseparable from a vulgar fanaticism and an alarming unpredictability. Most of the generals led double lives: obeying the Führer, often with obvious unwillingness, to his face, while confiding their fears and doubts to their diaries or to colleagues who, like themselves, belonged to a greater or less extent to the secret opposition. Both in their post-war interrogations and their memoirs, they naturally blamed Hitler for what went wrong.

Each side was a scapegoat for the other. Hitler's case inevitably tends to go by default. Yet his responsibility is indisputable. It was he who decided on Barbarossa, prescribed the way it was to be fought, and directed it. After Brauchitsch went, Hitler was not only Commander-in-Chief but also acted as commander of one or other army groups, and interfered in operational detail to an extent which the men on the spot found infuriating. It was Hitler who, in August 1941, decided against giving priority to the capture of Moscow as the generals wanted, but insisted on a simultaneous attempt to seize Leningrad and occupy the Crimea. The result was a failure which might have been avoided with different priorities. Similarly it was Hitler's under-estimate of Russian strength and his obsession with the symbolic value of Stalingrad which led to the catastrophe of 1942–3. In both cases a too ambitious strategy led to an over-extension of resources, aggravated by a refusal to give ground in order to save lives. In the Stalingrad case, an army group which originally occupied a front of 800 kilometres was expected to hold a line of over 4,000 kilometres at a time when Germany had already suffered 1·3 million casualties.[51] It was Hitler too who, out of fear of appearing weak, refused to abandon any of the territory conquered in 1942 in preparation for the coming winter. And in the summer of 1943, when a successful defence of the Reich was not beyond Germany's capacity, it was Hitler who, against the advice of Guderian and other tank generals, insisted on attacking in a position (the Kursk salient) where the Russians were well prepared and where their superior gunpower proved decisive. Like Ludendorff, Hitler was not interested in a compromise peace. With few exceptions, of which his caution in invading England in 1940 is perhaps the most notable, he gambled for the highest stakes. Too late he found that he had miscalculated the military strength and even the economic and organisational efficiency of the Soviets. German Intelligence was badly informed about the number and quality of Russian tanks and artillery. Russia's recuperative powers also exceeded expectations. In 1942 despite huge losses of plant and territory, she produced twice as much industrial output as in 1940, and the transfer of factories from the west to sites east of the Urals was a remarkable achievement. Neither Hitler nor his advisers had foreseen the catastrophic effects on a mechanised army of vast distances, bad roads or none, swamps and forests, or correctly assessed the logistic problems involved. Maps proved inadequate and misleading. Tracked vehicles quickly wore out, wheeled vehicles were confined to the inadequate roads and even there got bogged down in bad weather. It was hard to keep up the supply of spare parts. Climate as well as geography presented unforeseen difficulties.[52] The failure to arm in depth now exacted its price.

Moreover the country was too big for the Germans to occupy physically the space between their armies. In these by-passed areas, which were often heavily forested, large bands of partisans carried out continuous sabotage, supplied intelligence information to the Red Army and effectively controlled the countryside. In 1942 partisans kept busy about 10 per cent of the German army in Russia, and in the following year they occupied some 200,000 square kilometres behind the German lines.[53] Partisan warfare had a considerable moral as well as material effect on both sides. The Germans had underestimated the skill and tenacity of the ordinary Russian soldier, who proved a more formidable opponent than the *moujik* of the First World War, and his ability to fight in arctic conditions when the German soldier was glad if he could keep himself alive. Underlying this false idea of the value of the Red Army was Hitler's contempt for Bolshevism, coupled with his low opinion of all Slavs. Not least of the reasons for the success of the Russian army was the support given by the *Ossoviakhim,* a para-military organisation run by the Communist party which had some 36 million members.

Almost as fatal as the military miscalculations was the political strategy, which sprang from the same false assumptions and prejudices. The Russians were officially described as sub-human, and the war was stated, before Barbarossa began, to be one of extermination.[54] The intention was to divide European Russia into several dependencies which were to be run for the benefit of Germany, with displacement of population to make room for German and other West European settlers.[55] There were in theory two ways in which Russia could be split up and weakened politically. One was to exploit the antagonism between the Russians and the minority nationalities, the Balts, Poles, Georgians, Armenians and Turkoman peoples of Central Asia, nearly all of whom had been forced into the Russian Empire against their will. And even within the Russian population the differences between Great Russians as the predominant majority and White Russians or Ukrainians gave opportunities to a would-be conqueror, which the Germans had taken advantage of in 1918. Rosenberg, the Nazi 'philosopher' who became Minister for the Occupied Eastern Territories wished to use this strategy, but Hitler was not interested in liberating minority peoples or in bargaining with Ukrainian separatists, as the Kaiser's government had done, despite the initial welcome of bread and salt to the German troops by many Ukrainian peasants. The other possible approach was to profit by the unpopularity of the Communist regime, and particularly of Stalin, among many sections of the population including the peasants, whose memories of compulsory collectivisation, famine and terror were still fresh. Yet this policy too was rejected. Despite partial de-collectivisation of farm land, no serious attempt was made to offer a regime less oppressive than Stalin's or to win the goodwill of his numerous victims. For Hitler Russia with all its population was just an object for exploitation and the pre-destined *Lebensraum* for Germany. He wanted territory vacant or with a helot population, a colony for the production of raw materials and not an industrial competitor with Germany. As Göring once admitted, tens of millions of people in the industrial areas of Russia would become redundant and would have to die or emigrate to Siberia.[56] Only very late in the war, when it was already lost, did Hitler agree to make use of the anti-Communists from Russia who, as prisoners of war or auxiliary workers, were prepared to fight for him. Most of these belonged to the minority nationalities who had their own reasons to collaborate with the Germans. Others did so to escape starvation. By the last winter of the war 800,000 Soviet citizens were wearing German uniform. Among these was the captured General Vlassov, who, the son of a peasant and ethnically a Russian, had served for 24 years in the Red Army, been a member of the Communist party since 1930 and received the Order of Lenin.[57] It was conditions of life under Stalin and particularly the wholesale purge of the Red Army in the 1930s which made him offer his services to Germany. He was eventually made head of a shadow Russian government, a shadowy counterpart indeed to Stalin's Free German Committee in Moscow, though the proportion of anti-Stalinists in Russia was probably higher than that of anti-Nazis in Germany, and Vlassov was finally given command of his own army in an already collapsing Reich. But by then the Red Army had re-established its grip over the Russian population and made any response to Vlassov's appeals impossible, even had the crimes committed by Hitler's forces in Russia not blackened the German name beyond redemption.

From the very beginning the war in Russia had a ferocity unknown in the campaigns in western Europe. The fighting was savage, and so was the occupation. In a notorious decree Hitler ordered the shooting out of hand of all Jews and Commissars, the latter term being interpreted to mean not only officials of the Communist party but anyone connected with it. Mass executions were carried out by special squads of the S.D. (Security Service), a part of Himmler's S.S. empire, under the command of Reinhold Heydrich, the later 'Deputy Protector of the Czech state', who rivalled Himmler in cold-blooded cruelty. An order on martial law deprived the local population of any legal rights in cases of crimes committed against them by the German army. Prisoners were often shot, many starved or died of overwork in Germany. Captured partisans, against whom Hitler ordered unusual severity, were also murdered *en masse*, and thousands of people were executed as partisans who had not even been armed.[58] Reprisals for sabotage were ordered at the rate of 50 or 100 Russians for every one German killed. The total number of deaths in the Russian campaign, military and civilian, has been estimated at 17 million, of whom 12 million belonged to the Soviet Union.[59] This, like the working to death of prisoners of war, was one form of the economic exploitation of the *Ostraum*. Other methods included the removal of physical assets and raw materials – factories, railways, food and livestock. The murder of civilians, including 1·7 million Jews, deprived the German occupying forces of much needed labour power: it was difficult, at times, even to get a pair of boots mended. Such atrocities put new life into the Russian resistance, which rivalled that of the Nazis in its fanaticism and at times in its savagery. The primitive toughness of the Russian soldier was steeled by the unceasing pressure of the party, represented by the ubiquitous commissars or the broadcast voice of Stalin himself. The appeal now was to patriotism, not to ideology: the heroes held up to admiration were the generals who had defeated Napoleon, not the discredited men (Trotsky and Tukhachevsky) who had created the Red Army. Persecution of the churches ceased. And even had the Russian soldier not been hard by nature and training, the war gave him no alternative but to fight on even against hopeless odds. If he became a prisoner of war and ultimately returned to Russia, he would face a further term of imprisonment: in Stalin's eyes a prisoner, even a wounded one, was assumed to be a man who had chosen surrender to a heroic death. Not that his chances of survival were good: of about five and three quarter million Russian prisoners of war, close on four million died in captivity.

Another aspect of war with Russia was its propaganda value as a crusade against Bolshevism. The Nazi-Soviet pact had caused the Nazis some embarrassment by forcing them to soft-pedal the antisoviet theme for nearly two years. But after June 1941 Germany could again be presented as the defender of European civilisation against Bolshevik barbarism. Like anti-semitism, anti-communism was an effective slogan, especially in Eastern Europe. Almost all European nations took some military part in the Russian campaign: Finnish, Hungarian, Slovak, Italian and Roumanian units were later joined by volunteers from Spain, Belgium, France, Holland and Norway. Even the *Waffen S.S.* was opened, as the exigencies of war undermined racial principles, to Balts, Ukrainians, Russians, Caucasians, Balkan Moslems and other lesser races once the supply of Nordics proved inadequate.[60] Altogether about 200,000 non-Germans served in the *Waffen S.S.* in the course of the war. As defeat in the east loomed nearer, Goebbels dwelt increasingly on the horrors that would befall Europe if the Red Army was victorious. Yet Hitler did nothing to ensure that the western armies would overrun Germany before the Russians and may even not have desired it.

Although Hitler liked to think of Russia as Germany's India, empire-building or colonisation is too constructive a term to describe his policy, especially the attempt to enforce his racial ideas on a scale commensurate with his insensate ambitions. It was an arena where the feuds and rivalries of the party leaders were fought out with no holds barred, where second- and third-rate bosses could exercise the arbitrary power and indulge the epicene appetites of a degenerate Roman Emperor, where fantasy became reality and lust for violence could be sated unchecked by higher authority and uncensored by public opinion. Use was not made of Germany's real Russian specialists and ablest administrators. Corruption, abuse and personal enrichment were the order of the day. During the First World War Germany's dynastic rulers had competed for titles in the East; now it was the turn of the Gauleiters to play the role of grand dukes. Like Kipling's 'East of Suez', this was territory where the Ten Commandments did not apply, where, despite sporadic efforts by the army to observe the decencies of civilised warfare, morality ceased to count. Even Rosenberg, the head of the Ministry for Eastern Territories, a Baltic German who hated Russians and had taught Hitler much of his anti-Bolshevism, was appalled by the behaviour of his nominal subordinates. The area was divided into three provinces, whose governors were subject to Rosenberg in theory rather than in fact.[61] In the north, Ostland included the three Baltic states (Lithuania, Latvia and Esthonia) under Reich Commissioner Lohse, a former Gauleiter of Schleswig-Holstein; to the east White Russia, so far as it was not under military control, was placed under a separate General Commissioner named Kube; to the south the Ukraine was assigned to Reich Commissioner Koch, a former Gauleiter of East Prussia who had once been a railway booking clerk. Koch's satrapy was by far the largest and most important. He was entirely devoid of the mysticism and sentimentality felt by many Germans, whose image of Russia was based on an adolescent enthusiasm for the novels of Dostoevsky. Koch had no time for the Slav soul, but treated his Ukrainian subjects as niggers, to be handled with a mixture of cheap tobacco, vodka and the whip. Koch summarised his views in a speech at Kiev on 5 March 1943: 'We are a race of masters who must always remember that the humblest German worker is racially and biologically a thousand times more valuable than the population here.'[62] Rosenberg's attempts to curb Koch's brutality failed because Koch had Hitler's support. On other counts however Koch gave the Führer less satisfaction. As the chief exploitation area, the Ukraine was expected to yield rich tribute, especially of agricultural produce. Despite a partial return to private farming, the results were disappointing. The German army lived off the land, but the population of the Reich received little benefit: the Ukraine, it has been estimated, contributed only about 5 per cent of Germany's annual food consumption.[63] Indeed, altogether Germany probably gained less from the Russian economy than if she had continued peaceful trading under the treaties of 1939-41. It has been calculated that the occupied eastern territories supplied the Reich with only one-seventh of what it obtained from France.[64] The Russian economy was systematically devastated by the war and the policy of scorched earth practised by both sides. Another difficulty was shortage of labour. During the latter part of the war Sauckel, the Nazi Commissioner for Labour, recruited millions of foreign workers for the Reich to take the place of conscripted Germans in industry and agriculture. The demand was increased by Speer's augmented arms programme. Russia, like other occupied countries, was combed for forced labour, and some 2·8 million civilians (men, women and children) were deported to work in Germany. To escape this fate vast numbers of Russians fled to the forests to join the partisans. Thus one type of exploitation clashed with another, and savagery in one direction exacerbated difficulties elsewhere. All the rival bosses competed for Hitler's favour. Sauckel was working against Koch, Koch was at loggerheads with Rosenberg, the S.S. was murdering people whom the army would have liked to employ, and the whole Nazi policy was in contradiction to the view of the 'Russian experts' in the Foreign Office and the army who favoured discriminating between pro- and anti-Stalinists and urged that 'Russia could be conquered only by Russians'. As the case of Vlassov shows, only tardily and reluctantly did Hitler agree to wage political warfare. His own approach to the Russian problem was brutally simple, and when that failed it was too late for political finesse to succeed. It was symptomatic that Hitler showed no interest in suggestions made by the Russians in favour of a separate peace.[65] In the final stages of the war his hopes were fixed, with the parallel of the Seven Years' War always in mind, on a collapse of the 'unnatural alliance' of Russia and the Anglo-Saxons which he had provoked. But shaky as the alliance was, it held out until Hitler's defeat, and not even the first skirmishes of the cold war could save the Reich from the vengeance of its enemies, of whom the Russians were inevitably the most implacable.

Although the many contradictions in Hitler's eastern policy stemmed

The Victor at the Conference

'I've defeated my friends, all I need now is to defeat my enemies.' (A comment on Stalin's conference with Churchill and Roosevelt at Teheran) (*Simplicissimus*, 1943)

from the incompatibility of ultimate aims with the demands of war, they also reflected a basic clash within the Nazi hierarchy. Even Hitler could not and probably did not wish to eradicate the sordid personal rivalries of his satraps. The Nazi conquest and occupation of Russia was never complete, and therefore the long-term plans were never put into effect. But enough happened in Russia to suggest that no solution of Hitler's would have worked. He offered death to the ruling minority, slavery and exploitation to the rest. Even if Hitler had avoided those military mistakes which cost him the campaign and perhaps the war, it is hard to imagine how the Nazis could have imposed a viable political settlement over so vast a territory. Against endemic revolt German resources would have been stretched to breaking point and Hitler might well have tried genocide on a larger scale. But even that might have been beyond him in view of the numbers and area involved.

(v) THE GERMAN RESISTANCE

The German Resistance was a tragedy within a tragedy. Over a quarter of a century later it remains a controversial matter, not only because many aspects have never been cleared up (few participants survived) but also because of wide differences in evaluation and interpretation. At the time of the 20 July plot against Hitler Allied commentators tended to play it down. Churchill described it as the leaders of the Nazi Reich destroying each other, though in a more informed later judgement he paid tribute to the conspirators. It was noted that the attempt failed, that some of those involved were opportunists, and that nearly all were senior officers or officials and therefore assumed to be militarists and nationalists. Outside opinion had hardly expected the main opposition to Hitler to come from the heart of his war machine; and those many people in England and elsewhere who believed that their main enemy was Prussian or German militarism rather than National Socialism would have been surprised to learn how far some of the military leaders detested the party ideology. Yet the Allied governments were informed of the nature and extent of the German underground from their numerous contacts with its members. Allen Welsh Dulles, who was in charge of the American Office of Strategic Studies in Europe from 1942 to the end of the war, with an office in Switzerland, was in continuous touch with various anti-Hitler groups and actually visited Berlin several times during that period. He knew their aims and something of their plans. But the British and American governments, in contrast to the Russians, for reasons which are discussed below, showed little inclination to encourage German resistance, and thus by implication accepted the identification of the German people with Hitler on which Goebbels insisted. Few historians would now endorse an earlier verdict that the main objective of the conspirators against Hitler was a German victory and failing that their own insurance against defeat.[66] The sincerity and courage of these men and their idealism are now generally acknowledged, even if few of them were democrats in the western sense and many were old-fashioned nationalists. There was no single ideology underlying the German resistance, just as there was none within the anti-Hitler coalition, but a determination in both cases to get rid of his tyranny. The 20 July was more than just a military plot, and the decision to overthrow Hitler was taken long before the war was known to be lost. Gustav Dahrendorf, one of the few survivors among the socialists, wrote later: 'The revolutionary coup of 20 July should not be considered a badly executed undertaking on the part of officers who had given up all hope and sought to escape from an exigency. Neither was it an attempt by grumbling reactionary militarists to cut the bond which tied them to Fascism. . . . There was only one aim, to remove Fascism and end the war.'[67] At this, its climax, the opposition actually became what it had long been on the verge of becoming – resistance. If outside Germany people were slow to appreciate the significance of the resistance, within the country there has been since 1945 a natural inclination to uncritical admiration of all its aspects because of its symbolic importance: like the Dreyfus Affair in a very different context, it raised fundamental moral issues, and became a kind of touch-stone of integrity. Recent studies by German historians show the development of a more discriminating and dispassionate approach to what is still a sensitive subject.

The first opposition groups inside the Third Reich sprang, as might be expected, from the Socialists and Communists who (apart from the Jews) had been the chief victims of Hitler's revolution. Among the younger Social Democrats there had for some time been dissatisfaction with the leadership of the party, particularly over its rather defeatist attitude to the Nazis in the period preceding and following Hitler's assumption of power. One sign of this discontent in the last years of Weimar was the emergence of a left-wing offshoot, the Socialist Workers' party. Hitler's success seemed to prove the militants right, and there was a predisposition among them to heal the breach with the Communists which had harmed them both and fatally weakened the anti-fascist cause. Yet this was easier said than done. The long mutual hostility of the two left-wing parties made co-operation difficult even when common persecution might have brought them together, and Socialist suspicion of the Communists was kept alive by the Stalinist regime with its purges and show trials. Proletarian dictatorship remained the Communist objective even after the adoption of the Popular Front policy.[68] The most notable of the new underground groups was *New Beginning*, a movement that took its name from a pamphlet by a German exile published at Karlsbad (Karlovy Vary) in 1933 which sought to revive the revolutionary spirit that the S.P.D. had patently lacked. *New Beginning* co-operated with another group called the *Popular Front*, which also included former parliamentarians and trade unionists. Underground work in Germany was difficult and dangerous. Hitler's aggressive foreign policy was popular, as was his abolition of unemployment. The Gestapo was vigilant, and anyone could be an informer. The police terror was greater there than in most of the countries later occupied. A Gestapo report found after the war records that in 1936 alone there were 11,687 arrests for spreading illegal socialist propaganda, 17,108 trials and 1,643,000 leaflets confiscated, figures which suggest a remarkable level of activity at a time when some illegal groups, such as the Red Shock troops, had already been discovered and destroyed.[69] From Prague the executive committee of the S.P.D. supplied money, machines for clandestine printing, information and assistance to the families of imprisoned party members. It also helped to smuggle imperilled party members and Jews out of Germany. But all this became more hazardous when the committee had to move to Paris after Munich. By 1938 *New Beginning* had been suppressed. Meanwhile the German Communist party too had been taking stock. It had been misguided and myopic in its unceasing attacks on the Social Democrats as 'Social Fascists' and its readiness, as in November 1932, to make a tactical alliance with the Nazis. Stalin now tardily proclaimed the policy of the Popular Front, to which the German Communist party in exile, like every other member party of the Third International, had to conform. At a special conference of the K.P.D. held outside Moscow in October 1935 – called the 'Brussels conference' to fool the Gestapo – it was admitted that there had been mistakes. The Nazi-Soviet Pact of 1939 caused a good deal of ideological confusion, but the *linientreue* Ulbricht declared that it was the Anglo-French war bloc which wanted to fight the Soviet Union.[70] The pact did not lift the ban on Communists in Germany, though it saved them from execution if they were caught. Communist underground cells existed throughout the war despite the success of the Gestapo in infiltrating their ranks, and more Communists suffered than members of any other party. The most successful Communist underground organisation was of a different kind. This was the so-called *Rote Kapelle*, which after the invasion of Russia acted as an intelligence agency for the

Red Army. It consisted mainly of serving officers and intellectuals, and was led by a Lieutenant Schulze-Boysen of the Air Ministry, who oddly enough was a great-nephew of Tirpitz. This was a spying organisation rather than a resistance group of the usual type, but it had its utopians who believed that they were working for an ideal communism.

Apart from the left, opposition to Hitler came from three directions. The first was the General Staff. As we have seen, a memorandum by Beck, the army Chief of Staff, in the summer of 1938, had argued that Hitler was leading Germany into a disastrous war. Plans were made to depose and imprison or execute him. It was probably the first time in Prussian history that generals had plotted against the civilian power, and it was particularly significant because the whole notion of conspiracy was incompatible with the traditionally sacred officer's oath. But desperate situations, as Beck realised, require desperate remedies. Though Beck's courage led to his dismissal, his fears were shared in greater or lesser degree by Halder, his successor as army Chief of Staff, and by a number of other senior officers, civil servants and diplomats. Hitler's success at Munich deflated opposition hopes, and the outbreak of war a year later made conspiracy more difficult. Halder vacillated and complained that Brauchitsch, his immediate senior as army Commander-in-Chief, would not commit himself against Hitler. Many generals were willing to jump on the bandwagon once the Führer was dead, but in 1940 his reputation soared to new heights. Of the many civilians who sympathised with Beck the most determined was Gördeler, a well-known public man who had been Lord Mayor of Leipzig and Reich Price Controller in the governments of Brüning and Hitler. Gördeler gave up this post in 1935 to return to Leipzig, but resigned as mayor in the following year when the Nazis removed the statue of Mendelssohn from outside the Leipzig concert hall. A man of ability and probity, Gördeler was a rather austere representative of that upper middle class which had never really thrown in its lot with the Weimar Republic. His associates included Ulrich von Hassell, German ambassador in Rome from 1932 to 1937, Weizsäcker and the Kordt brothers in the Foreign Ministry and – though they parted later – Popitz, a former Prussian Minister of Finance. These men all belonged to the political right, and tended to draw their inspiration and ideas from the past.[71] One of Gördeler's heroes was Stein, the Prussian reformer at the beginning of the nineteenth century. Like most of the Conservative opposition during the Weimar Republic they preferred an authoritarian form of government based, as the Kaiser's had been, on the rule of law and an acknowledgement of the Christian ethic. Their ideas on foreign policy were also rather old-fashioned and mildly Pan-German.

They assumed that Germany would continue to be the leading power in Europe within the frontiers of 1939 if not those of 1940. Because Gördeler and his friends wished to restore the former eastern border, eliminate French influence in Eastern Europe and absorb into the Reich German-occupied territory that had formerly been part of the Habsburg Monarchy, it is sometimes suggested that there was little to choose between them and Hitler, who also wanted these things. Such a view overlooks the all-important difference that while for Beck, Gördeler and their associates these were final objectives, for Hitler they were merely the first step towards his major purpose, the conquest and colonisation of Russia. As Hugh Trevor-Roper has pointed out, it was impossible for geographical reasons for Hitler to attain his larger aims without first fulfilling their narrower ones: to reach Russia, he had first to occupy or neutralise the lands lying between Germany and the Soviet border.[72] A German did not have to be a Nazi or even a nationalist to desire frontier revision with Poland on grounds of self-determination or the *Anschluss* with Austria (originally a socialist demand) or even – on certain assumptions – the annexation of the Sudeten territories. The expanded Germany of which the conservative opposition dreamed was the completion of Bismarck's work in the new circumstances created by the First World War. Hitler of course respected none of Bismarck's limits and thus destroyed what remained of his Europe as well as that of Versailles.

The second source of opposition to the Nazi regime was also inside the establishment: it was the Military Intelligence Department of the O.K.W. (Combined Services) known as the *Abwehr*. This organisation had recruited a good many people – lawyers, businessmen and land-owners – who were anti-Nazi as was its head, the cunning and resourceful Admiral Canaris. His deputy, General Oster, was even more committed to the anti-Hitler cause and belonged to the inner circle of the conspiracy. The *Abwehr* occupied a key position in the secret plans because under its auspices members of the underground could go abroad and meet representatives of foreign countries including those with which Germany was at war. Thanks to the *Abwehr*, Schlabren-dorff was able to warn Churchill shortly before the outbreak of war of the Nazi-Soviet Pact and the impending attack on Poland; Gördeler informed the Swedish government through the banking family of Wallenberg of his plan to overthrow Hitler; and Bonhoeffer managed to meet his old friend George Bell, the Bishop of Chichester, in Sweden with proposals which the bishop passed on to the British government. Under *Abwehr* cover the Catholic lawyer Joseph Müller carried on confidential discussions with a representative of the British government at the Vatican in the winter of 1939-40, and Gisevius and other trusted persons met and talked to Allen Welsh Dulles. Unfortunately for the *Abwehr*, two of its agents in Turkey defected to the Allies in 1943, and the Gestapo became suspicious. Himmler who, unknown to Hitler, had already had secret talks with members of the German underground, was able to annex the *Abwehr* to his empire, and Canaris, Oster and many of their colleagues were arrested before their plans matured and were later executed.

Bonhoeffer was only one of a number of distinguished people who belonged to the third and most remarkable strand in the German opposition: the group associated with Count Helmut James von Moltke and named after his estate at Kreisau in Silesia. Its meetings, which took place in Berlin as well as at Kreisau, brought together a fascinating collection of gifted men from the most diverse backgrounds: noblemen, officers, lawyers, socialists, trade unionists, churchmen. Moltke himself, a landowner by birth and a jurist by training, was a man of radical sympathies, wide social connections (his mother was the daughter of a South African judge) and force of character. He was incidentally a nephew of the Moltke of Bismarck's day. Resembling him in many ways was Adam Trott zu Solz, another man of charm, intelligence and good looks, also coming from a family with a tradition of public service and Anglo-Saxon ties (his father had been a Prussian Minister of Education, his grandmother was American).[73] Trott had been a Rhodes scholar at Oxford and had many friends in England and America. His visits to England in the summer of 1939 and to America later that year (where he talked to Roosevelt) were arranged by the anti-Nazi group in the Foreign Ministry in which he was employed. Trott was a scholar and man of the world, a devotee of Hegel and a student of Marx. Less intellectual, but with an equally strong streak of idealism and integrity was Count Claus von Stauffenberg, a regular soldier who joined the conspiracy only in 1943, the year in which he became Chief of Staff to the commander of the General Army (i.e. the Reserve) in Berlin.[74] Despite the loss of an eye, his right hand and two fingers of his left hand while fighting in North Africa, Stauffenberg was the man finally chosen to assassinate Hitler. The most important members of the Kreisau circle (in which aristocrats and socialists far outnumbered representatives of the middle class) were two leading Social Democrats, Wilhelm Leuschner and Julius Leber. Leuschner, a former minister in Hesse, had been deputy head of the General Trade Unions, while Leber had been a member of the Reichstag and was considered one of the ablest leaders of his party. Both men had been in Hitler's concentration camps. Bonhoeffer, the theologian whose stand against Hitler had from the first been unequivocal, belonged to the circle, as did Father Delp, a Jesuit in

Munich. All these men passionately desired a complete break with Nazism and a return to legality and morality, and all were prepared to pay a price. They were motivated by strong convictions, which enabled them to live dangerously and to die bravely. Most of them were convinced if unconventional Christians. Politically they were well to the left of the Beck-Gördeler group, and were more anti-fascist than anti-communist. They had no wish to restore the Weimar system but envisaged a social order that would combine the decentralisation of power with a socialist concern for welfare and the diffusion of wealth. The intention was for a broadly based government to take over when Hitler had gone, with the army being ordered to obey the new regime. The scheme was Operation Valkyrie, and its first draft was produced in 1942. A new Germany was to take its place in a new united Europe. The Kreisau circle did not share Beck-Gördeler illusions about the future role of Germany or their residual great-power nationalism. They recognised that their country would have to pay for Hitler's crimes and aggression, and would certainly not be allowed to keep the frontiers of 1939 or even those of 1937. But that, to Moltke, was not important. 'For us', he wrote in 1942, 'post-war Europe is less a question of frontiers and soldiers, of top-heavy organisations and grandiose plans, than of how the image of man can be re-established in the hearts of our fellow-citizens.'[75] And Trott no doubt shared the sentiment expressed in a letter to him from an English friend: 'For us, nationalism is an illusion for the masses.'[76] It was in accord with this outlook that the Kreisau group sought contact with resistance forces outside Germany. Nor were their efforts entirely unsuccessful: in several occupied West European countries they managed, with the help of local resistance units, to prevent the taking and illegal detention of hostages and the massacre of Jews. Differences between the Beck-Gördeler group and that of Kreisau did not debar them from co-operating in plans for a post-Hitler government in which Beck was to be Head of State, Gördeler Chancellor, Leuschner Vice-Chancellor and Field-Marshal von Witzleben, another initiate, Commander-in-Chief of the army. Leber was to be Minister of the Interior.

From the beginning the conspirators were dogged by misfortune. After 1942 Hitler rarely left his headquarters in the forests of East Prussia and was scarcely seen in public. In March 1943 two attempts on his life were made by friends of Stauffenberg: the first time a couple of bombs in the aircraft in which Hitler was travelling failed to explode, on the second occasion a time bomb carried into an exhibition hall visited by Hitler proved useless because he unexpectedly left the hall before the explosion was due. Chance does not wholly account for these and several other failures to destroy the tyrant. The Führer was heavily guarded, and his personal magnetism still worked: even his enemies could not escape it. The plotters delayed too long, and the native hue of resolution was sicklied o'er with the pale cast of hesitation and introspection. The longer they waited the greater the chance of the secret being discovered by the Gestapo, and the less meaningful the act would be as the Reich faced defeat on two fronts. Besides the *Abwehr* chiefs, by the summer of 1944 Moltke and Bonhoeffer were in gaol. On 4 July Leber was arrested after he had arranged to meet a group of Communists, one of whom turned out to be a Gestapo agent. Gördeler had to go into hiding. The Russians were in East Prussia and the Anglo-American forces in Normandy. The war was lost, as even those generals who were not in the conspiracy realised. One of the first tasks of the projected new government would have been to make peace with the western governments by offering them an unopposed run to Berlin. Whether such an offer would have been accepted is another matter. Since the Casablanca conference of January 1943 Churchill and Roosevelt had been committed to a policy of unconditional surrender. Even before Casablanca they were unwilling to give any direct encouragement to the German resistance, as Bonhoeffer found when proposals he transmitted through the Bishop of Chichester evoked no response. There were three main reasons for this negative attitude. The first was scepticism about the opposition leaders' ability to deliver the goods. The second was a determination to forestall any recurrence of the stab in the back legend or of the charge that the Allies had broken their word, as they had been accused of doing after the First World War, if they made any promises to German representatives. The third reason was anxiety to avoid raising Russian suspicions of a secret deal between Germany and the West. The Russians themselves, with fewer inhibitions, seemed not averse to making their own terms even with Hitler, and on Soviet initiative peace talks were held in Stockholm in 1942 and 1943 between a Russian diplomat and a representative of Ribbentrop. And though the Russian motive may have been purely tactical – to force America to pay a higher price for her alliance – Soviet propaganda offered much more hope than that of the West to the German opposition, and indeed to all non-Nazis. Broadcasts by the Free Germany Committee, the body of exiled Communists and prisoners of war formed after Stalingrad, made a point of distinguishing between Hitler and the German people and promised that after the war Germany would be a strong, independent and democratic state, and that no revenge would be taken on the 'seduced and misguided' if in the hour of decision they sided with 'the people'.[77] The German argument to the West was that to abandon unconditional surrender would be to shorten the war and give the Anglo-American forces an advantage over the Russians: the appeal was to self-interest, for it was not expected in Berlin that the Allies would be guided by any sentimentality towards the German people. But London and Washington stuck stonily to their formula, though it could be guessed that once the anti-Nazis managed to seize power in Berlin a more flexible attitude would emerge. It was against this rather hopeless background and in the knowledge that the bargaining power of the German underground was running out that the decision to act was made, though it was far from certain that the plans would work. Even Stauffenberg was doubtful. But Tresckow, a major-general on the eastern front who was heart and soul in the plot, convinced him: 'The assassination must be attempted at all costs. . . . What matters now is ... to prove to the world and for the records of history that the men of the resistance dared to take the decisive step. Compared with this objective, nothing else matters.'[78] This was in accordance with Bonhoeffer's conviction that Germany had a moral duty to get rid of Hitler whatever the price. After Leber's arrest Stauffenberg was asked and agreed to strike the blow despite his physical handicap and the fact that he was now required to play a double part: to direct operations in Berlin as well as to be the assassin at Hitler's headquarters at Rastenburg in East Prussia.

On 18 July Stauffenberg received orders to report to Rastenburg two days later. This, he decided, would be the opportunity: he would leave a bomb in a briefcase under the table of the conference room near Hitler's chair, and then, when the explosion had taken place and Hitler was dead, would return by air to Berlin to take charge of *Valkyrie*. The story of that day (20 July) is well known. Stauffenberg arrived for the conference, which began at 12.30. A few minutes later he excused himself and left the room. Outside he waited to watch the explosion, which occurred about 12.50. The briefcase, resting against the massive leg supporting the table, had inadvertently been pushed to its other side, which was further away from Hitler, who consequently did not feel the full impact of the bomb. Also the wooden walls of the hut allowed much of the blast to escape, as would not have happened in a concrete building. Nevertheless, the explosion appeared to be so complete that when he saw it Stauffenberg assumed that Hitler was among the dead, and returned by air to Berlin, which he reached three hours later. Even though Hitler's injuries were only slight, Valkyrie could still have worked if everyone had played his allotted part. Army headquarters under the new Commander-in-Chief issued orders to all the German armies. In Paris the Military Commander put the S.S. and S.D. under arrest, but it was only there that the conspirators – for a matter of hours – were completely success-ful. Field-Marshal von Kluge, the Commander-in-Chief, Western Europe, was known to be willing to join the conspiracy once it was assured of success, and Rommel, the most popular general in Germany, had promised his support before injury from a British air attack removed him to hospital. But a vital link in the whole chain was missing: the signals officer at Rastenburg (who was in the conspiracy) cut the telephone wires between Hitler's headquarters and the outside world, but was forced to re-connect them two hours later. The result was that when Stauffenberg's men went to arrest General Fromm, commander of the Home Army, the cautious Fromm was able to disprove their statement that Hitler was dead by ringing up Rastenburg, where a shaken and excited Keitel assured him that the Führer was still alive. Fromm then arrested his captors. Similarly Goebbels, by speaking direct to Hitler, was able to convince waverers in Berlin, including the commander of a Guards Regiment who was supposed to arrest him, that the plot had failed, and to threaten reprisals to anyone who supported it. Thus army units were soon in receipt of counter-orders and Operation Valkyrie was dramatically reversed. Beck was allowed to commit suicide, Stauffenberg and three other officers implicated were summarily shot at army headquarters in the Bendlerstrasse. They were the lucky ones: for their colleagues and associates there remained suspense, suffering, public humiliation and a grisly method of execution.

Hitler's vengeance was not confined to the people, numbering perhaps two hundred, who were directly involved in the conspiracy, but extended to anyone suspected of complicity or even sympathy; and the total number of executions between 20 July and the end of the war was about 5,000. Trials, after interrogation involving torture, were held before the People's Court and its sadistic judge, Freisler, who vilified and ridiculed the defendants before sentencing them. Just before taking his own life on 21 July Tresckow had uttered prophetic words: 'Now everyone will turn upon us and cover us with abuse. But I am convinced ... that we have done the right thing. I believe Hitler to be the arch-enemy, not only of Germany, but of the entire world ... Just as God once promised Abraham that He would spare Sodom if only ten just men could be found in the city, I also have reason to hope that, for our sake, He will not destroy Germany. No-one among us can complain about his death, for whoever joined our ranks put on the poisoned shirt of Nessus.'[79] In a farewell letter Gördeler wrote: 'I ask the world to accept our martyrdom as penance for the German people.'[80] The main conspirators were hanged with cords suspended from meat-hooks in Plötzensee Prison in Berlin, and

Hitler had a film made of the executions. This, unlike the film made of the trials before the People's Court, has not survived. The 20 July failed largely for technical reasons. Despite the care and effort put into the preparations, it had an amateur and improvised character. When Stauffenberg saw the explosion he took it for granted that Hitler was dead but did not verify it. More serious was the failure to use the vital two hours and a half between the explosion and the re-opening of Hitler's telephone line. A more imaginative leadership would have seized the Berlin broadcasting station. This was not the meticulous planning one might have expected from the German army. Yet the need for secrecy inevitably imposed great handicaps, and the shortage of leaders after the many arrests placed too heavy a burden on Stauffenberg. The conspirators had delayed too long and placed themselves at a psychological and practical disadvantage.

Despite its failure the 20 July had a positive as well as a negative significance. Hitler's survival meant of course that the war went on for the best part of a year, with the loss of millions of lives and the further destruction of the moral and material substance of Europe. Moreover, the German élite which had been planning to take power on Hitler's overthrow was virtually wiped out, and the final collapse of the Third Reich found no shadow cabinet waiting in the wings. Almost the entire opposition, both conservatives and radicals, perished in its gaols by the time the war ended. Thus the break with the past in 1945 was more complete than it would have been otherwise. The death of the men of July implied the end of an attempt to work out a 'German way' in politics, the collapse of romantic ideas of a 'German mission' cherished by Gördeler and others who sought a kind of state based on neither western nor eastern models.[81] The attempt on Hitler's life can also be seen as the last political act of the Prussian ruling class before such of them as survived the two world wars saw Prussia itself disappear from the map. Few outside Germany, or even inside it, would have predicted that the blow for human rights against arbitrary power would be struck by noblemen and generals. It was in many cases an act of expiation for the help given to Hitler in his climb to power. The men of the resistance had few illusions left by 1944. They knew that they were a small minority who, unlike their opposite numbers in other countries, could count neither on the support of their fellow citizens nor on moral and material help from the Allies who, it was fairly obvious, regarded the German opposition as an embarrassment rather than an asset. Not all were consistent or heroic; some made pitiable attempts at their trial to prove their loyalty to Hitler. There had always been some time-servers: even Himmler tried at one stage to join the opposition. But there were moments when the issues at stake emerged with clarity, as when Count Peter Yorck von Wartenburg told Freisler, the President of the People's Court: 'The decisive factor . . . is the totalitarian claim of the state on the individual which forces him to renounce his moral and religious obligations to God.' There is no question here of calculation or expediency.[82] The words of one of the last letters written by Moltke before his execution have a similar ring of truth: 'I stood before Freisler, not as a Protestant, nor yet as a landowner, nor yet as a Prussian, nor yet again as a German, but as a Christian and absolutely nothing else.'[83] And a sentence from Tresckow's memorable farewell message to Schlabrendorff already quoted is equally unambiguous: 'The worth of a man is certain only if he is prepared to sacrifice his life for his convictions.' It was the fate of such men to die as traitors in the eyes of their countrymen, as Hitler's accomplices in those of the outside world.

It was in this stand for right and legality, irrespective of success or failure, that the positive significance of the German resistance lies. This was its legacy to posterity. It did something to salvage Germany's self-respect at a time when its name was branded with untold infamy. The next generation could look back upon a few genuine heroes and martyrs in the recent past, even if the glory of the few contrasted with the shame of the many. The Federal Republic, by honouring the memory of the resistance, has helped Germany's rehabilitation and its relations with the rest of the world. The men of 20 July also formed a link with the past, not so much with the Weimar Republic which few of them admired as with the older and decent traditions of past centuries, the Germany of Luther and Kant, Stein and Humboldt. Important as the 20 July movement was, it would be wrong to overlook the numerous obscure and isolated individuals, many of them young, who in one way or another – listening to foreign radio stations, painting up subversive slogans or distributing home-made leaflets – registered their protest and often paid for it with their lives. Among students the most notable group was the 'White Rose' group in Munich, whose leaders Hans and Sophie Scholl had the courage to scatter from a university balcony handbills containing such slogans as 'Our people are rising against the enslavement of Europe by National Socialism'. Arrested by the Gestapo, they were promptly executed together with the professor of philosophy who had aided them. Today they too have a place of honour in the pantheon of the resistance.

(vi) THE HOME FRONT: SPEER AND HIMMLER

Apart from Hitler, two names stand out during the last years of the Third Reich: Speer and Himmler. Speer, who became Minister of Armaments in February 1942, was mainly responsible for the spectacular increase in weapons of all kinds which enabled Germany to survive so long against a vastly superior coalition. A technocrat of genius, Speer pursued rational goals in a rational way.[84] He successfully transformed an economy still largely geared to production for peace into one that met the demands of total war. Himmler by contrast, who took Hitler's 'philosophy' more seriously than his master, embodied all that was most morbid and obsessional in National Socialism. As the radicalising pressures of war concentrated on Speer the power of an economic dictator, so the expansion of German rule over Europe made Himmler the arbiter of life and death for millions of Hitler's conquered subjects. With the terrifying logic of a crank and the impersonal pedantry of a bureaucrat, Himmler, the head of the S.S., tried to build his Nordic utopia on the bones and ashes of such of the lesser races as were not required to work in Speer's factories or in other sectors of the Nazi economy. Each man represented an essential element in the Third Reich, made his own contribution to its unique mixture of reason and madness. It was Himmler who transposed Hitler's racial fantasies into the instruments of torture and death – the electric barbed wire, the whip, the gibbet, the gas chamber – but without the normal and efficient Speer his opportunities would have been greatly curtailed. Complementary as the two men were, they were also rivals inasmuch as Himmler, controller of a vast organisation with its own economic activities, competed with Speer for labour and other scarce resources.

Until the end of 1941 Hitler still believed that the war could be won without any radical change in armaments policy. (In terms of economic warfare, 1940–1 was the wasted year whose inactivity may have cost Germany the war.) The Russian campaign began as a *Blitzkrieg* on a bigger scale. So certain of victory was Hitler in July 1941 that he actually ordered a reduction in the production of weapons, munitions and aircraft.[85] But by the beginning of the following winter unexpectedly heavy losses of equipment in Russia forced him to make a reappraisal. Plans for 1942 accordingly provided for an increase of guns and weapons of nearly every calibre, though even at the end of that year Germany was producing less munitions than in 1918. The minister chiefly responsible for the new programme was Fritz Todt, the engineer who, as Inspector General of Roads, had built the famous motorways, the West Wall or Siegfried Line, and part of the Atlantic defences. When Todt died as the result of an air crash in rather mysterious circumstances in February 1942, Hitler appointed Speer his successor. It was a far from obvious choice, since Speer, though known to be the Führer's favourite architect, was neither an industrialist nor a gunsmith. He had however been in charge of construction work for the armed forces since the beginning of the war, and Hitler shrewdly judged that his abilities could be applied to a wider sphere. At first the new minister's powers were limited. War production was an arena where there were still four other competitors: the Four Year Plan Office under Göring, who was also head of the *Luftwaffe;* the Economics and Armaments section of the O.K.W. under General Thomas; the Ministry of Economics under Funk; and the Ministry of Labour under Seldte. Gradually, thanks to his friendship with Hitler and his acknowledged efficiency, Speer wrested more power into his own hands at the expense of his chief rivals, Göring and Thomas. Göring, who in the early years of the Third Reich had been Number Two to Hitler had lost much of his prestige and was to lose more. In contrast to Göring's boastful promises, the *Luftwaffe* failed to conquer England, relieve Stalingrad or protect German cities from mass air attack. In everything except physique, Göring by 1942 was a deflated figure, whose self-indulgence and grotesque exhibitionism contrasted sharply with the mood of a country fighting for its life. Thomas was a man of foresight, who as early as May 1939 had urged the need to prepare for a long war.[86] Accused of defeatism, he failed to get on with Speer, who accomplished what Thomas had long desired – armament in depth – but with different methods. Thomas resigned in January 1943 and by January 1944 Speer had acquired control of arms production for all three fighting services. His success in stepping up output was phenomenal, though some of the credit should go to his predecessor Todt.

Speer took up the slack in the economy and cut out waste. He economised in the use of raw materials, eased bottlenecks, reduced delays, introduced time and motion study and arranged for closer co-operation between manufacturers. The results were soon apparent. In January 1943 more Tiger tanks were produced than in the whole of 1941, and by 1944 tank production, measured by weight, was seven times what it had been three years before. Aircraft production rose from 9,540 front line planes in 1941 to 34,350 in 1944.[87] Total munitions output trebled in the same period. These increases were achieved with a relatively small rise in the consumption of steel and an even more modest expansion in the numbers employed.[88] Yet though the productivity of labour rose, the demand for it continued to exceed the supply. It was to solve this problem that Sauckel, the Gauleiter of Thuringia, in March 1942 was appointed Commissioner for Labour with the special task of recruiting workers from outside Germany. Of the three main sources of supply, occupied, friendly and neutral countries, it was the occupied which provided the largest number. By the end of the war over eight million foreigners were working in German farms and factories, or about one in five of the total labour force. Nearly two million were prisoners of war, the majority of the remainder were deportees, some were taken from concentration camps. The methods of recruitment were especially brutal in Poland and Russia, from which most of the civilian workers came, and it was the *Ostarbeiter* who suffered chiefly from bad housing, under-feeding and general exploitation. Later in the war shortage of manpower led to the use of concentration camp labour in industry, and many a Jew owed his survival to this shift in priorities. In October 1944 at the synthetic petrol plant owned by the I.G. Farben Company at Auschwitz, over a quarter of the labour force consisted of prisoners from the nearby concentration camp.[89] Similar pressures brought about some improvement in the treatment of the despised East Europeans, who were becoming impossible to replace.[90] After 1943 foreign workers were the backbone of the mining, steel and chemical industries. In his decisions on the use of imported labour Speer frequently disagreed with Sauckel, who refused to give way to his senior colleague. Again there was a clash of personalities between the educated and well-to-do Speer and Sauckel, the Nazi boss of humble birth who resented Speer's favoured position and, like most of its left wing, took the party's radical ideology seriously. Unencumbered by racial or social prejudices, Speer was mainly preoccupied with making good certain key deficiencies in the economy. It was no good expanding the output of tanks and aeroplanes if they were immobilised by lack of fuel, as not infrequently happened in the last year of the war in consequence of Allied bombing and the loss of Roumania. Shortage of petroleum, which prevented German pilots from being adequately trained, was mainly responsible for the ineffective defence offered by fighter aircraft against Allied raids in and after 1944, despite an impressive increase in the number of aeroplanes.

Intensive bombing of Germany began in 1942: the old Hansa city of Lübeck burned in March, Cologne experienced its first thousand bomber raid in May. In June it was the turn of Essen and Bremen. At the beginning of the war the British had been reluctant bombers, scrupulous, even squeamish about attacking any non-military target. By 1942 there were few doubts inside the Churchill government, and the public, from which protests would have come, was misled by euphemistic assurances. The argument now turned on whether selection bombing, aimed at precise targets known to be of vital importance, such as oil refineries and U-boat pens, or area bombing, which meant generalised attacks on towns, would be more effective. The Americans favoured the first, the British, whose Bomber Command after February 1942 was in charge of Arthur Harris, the second. The Churchill-Roosevelt conference at Casablanca in January 1943 sanctioned area bombing as an alternative to continued attacks on special targets. Selection bombing was more difficult because the targets were hard to find, especially at night, hard to hit, and heavily defended by anti-aircraft fire and fighter planes. It was believed that the destruction of Germany's largest towns would cause vast disruption, interfere with production, shatter civilian morale and even possibly lead to an internal revolt. These expectations were not fulfilled, as the raids of 1943 showed despite their ferocity. First the Ruhr was heavily attacked. Then in the last week of July a series of raids on Hamburg wrought immense damage, in which the incendiary bombs gave rise to fire storms with temperatures of 1000° centigrade and created scenes of unprecedented horror. 50,000 people lost their lives, 900,000 were made homeless, and three-quarters of Hamburg was destroyed. Yet five months later Hamburg's production was 80 per cent of its normal level.[91] In November it was the turn of Berlin. Here even less accuracy was possible because the weather was cloudy and the defence stronger. Whole areas of the city were flattened, and a total of about 50,000 people were killed in these and similar raids up to the end of the war. Yet in April 1945 65 per cent of the Berlin factories were still working.[92] No doubt the city bombing affected the economy in many ways: it made people late for work, reduced their efficiency and caused a diversion of labour from war production to clear streets and railway lines and repair vital public services. But civilian morale (as earlier in Britain) was only toughened, and the determination to hold out, already consolidated by the Allied demand for unconditional surrender, was strengthened. Goebbels was quick to exploit this mood. In a speech at the Berlin Sports Palace in February 1943, soon after the news of Stalingrad had been made public, he appealed to his audience for a fanatical commitment to a life and death struggle. The disaster was not hushed up – three days' mourning were in fact ordered – but Goebbels insisted that the heroic sacrifice had not been in vain, and that the German people had been 'inwardly very profoundly purified by the tragic blow of fate'.[93] Using bad news to revive morale, like Churchill after Dunkirk, Goebbels spoke eloquently of looking into the hard and pitiless face of war, and of Germany defiantly saving Europe from Bolshevism. The audience responded by re-affirming their loyalty to the Führer (who of course was not to blame) and their confidence in ultimate victory. The keynote of the new propaganda campaign was Germany as the defender of Europe against Bolsheviks and plutocrats. But, as Roosevelt observed, it was a fortress without a roof.

Allied bombing in the first half of 1944 was directed primarily at targets in France, in preparation for the Normandy landings. Once these had taken place, the emphasis was switched backed to Germany, where bombers accompanied by improved long-range fighters (the American Mustangs) were able to penetrate more deeply and to pinpoint their objectives more accurately. There was greater concentration on synthetic oil plants and ball-bearing factories and less area bombing. Speer countered by organising quick repairs after raids, and, wherever possible, by dispersing plant. But even he could not decentralise the mines and steelworks of the Ruhr or make good the loss of oil, which almost forced Germany to give up the fight in the autumn of 1944. It was then (September) that the total of German armaments production reached its peak, three times what it had been in 1941.[94] Even in January 1945 over four times as many tanks were turned out as four years earlier, but to little purpose. With the loss of Silesia and the Ruhr by the end of March, the army was no longer in a position to continue the war, as Speer told Hitler. For some months he had been doing his best to nullify the scorched earth order issued by Hitler the preceding September, during the German army's retreat in the west, according to which everything of value was to be made useless. It would be a mistake, Speer warned the Führer, to destroy assets which might still be recaptured, an argument which could hardly be used after January 1945. Speer used his influence with the Gauleiters, army commanders and civil servants to substitute temporary paralysis for irrevocable destruction.[95] The amount of wilful damage which Speer was able to prevent in the occupied countries and in Germany is incalculable. He was the only minister who had the courage to tell Hitler that the war was lost and who threatened to resign when Hitler re-issued in more drastic terms the destruction order of the previous autumn. He spent the last weeks of the Third Reich thinking out ways of circumventing or sabotaging this decree and of killing the tyrant whom he had served.

In the summer of 1944 Allied air mastery enabled British and American pilots to bomb Germany almost at will, and to resume the daylight raids which had been temporarily abandoned in favour of night attacks. Yet as post-war surveys of German industry showed, much less damage was done than had been supposed. The claims of the 'bomber school' of which Air Vice-Marshal Harris was the out-

standing protagonist were seen to have been exaggerated, particularly
as far as area bombing was concerned. Speer afterwards admitted that
a rapid repetition of the type of attack on Hamburg on another six
German cities would have crippled the will to go on producing armaments and thus presumably have ended the war. But a similar result
might have been achieved at less cost to both sides by more sustained
concentration on vital targets, such as synthetic oil plants, with the
help of the precision bombing technique that had been developed during the war. It has been claimed that the Allies' mass air raids were
not wanton or undiscriminating.[96] This claim cannot be sustained. It
was often, as at Hamburg, the inner suburbs with their dense working-
class population which received the heaviest punishment, while the
factories, situated on the outskirts, escaped comparatively lightly. In
the carpet bombing, schools, hospitals and churches were inevitably
hit. The most flagrant example of unnecessary destruction was Dresden, the attack on which with high explosives and incendiary bombs
had no military or strategic justification.[97] The best estimate put the
number of lives lost at 135,000, a much higher figure than the immediate death roll at Hiroshima. Asphyxiation and burning were the main
causes of death, and the majority of victims were not found or if
found not recognisable. Misgivings in Allied countries about the wholesale slaughter of German civilians were countered by references to the
Nazi practice of genocide against Jews and Slavs, yet it would have
been more to the point to bomb the concentration camps. The British
government, caught up in its own double-think on terror bombing,
could not entirely hide its embarrassment, and six weeks later Churchill
in an official minute described the destruction of Dresden as 'a serious
query against the conduct of Allied bombing', though he based his
doubts on practical grounds – Germany must not be utterly ruined
before it was occupied.[98] The physical annihilation of German cities
was a terrifying object lesson, a visible sign of the retribution which
the crimes of its leaders had brought on the heads of their people.
Every town of over 100,000 (and many below that number) was over
50 per cent destroyed; in many cases the percentage of ruined buildings was three-quarters or more. Mountains of rubble, concealing
their dead, and giving out an acrid smell, especially in hot weather,
dominated Germany's urban landscape for years after the end of the
Third Reich, a grisly reminder of its cost to humanity.

It was characteristic of Hitler's regime that although he was Chancellor, Head of State and Commander-in-Chief of the armed forces, it
was by his party title of Führer that he preferred to be called and to
exercise power. Many aspects of his policy, such as the racial and demographic programme and the running of concentration camps, were

more approriately carried out by the Nazis' own fanatically trained and ruthless force, the S.S., than by the state. The S.S. was the party élite in action. Himmler, its leader, rose with it to become the boss of a many-sided organisation whose main object, apart from terrorising enemies of the regime, was the 'purification' of the German race and the extirpation of lesser breeds as a source of biological infection.[99] There was nothing in Himmler's early life to suggest the monster he later became or to explain why he became it. His background was respectable – middle-class, Bavarian, Catholic – indeed, more than respectable, for his father had been tutor to the Bavarian royal family. Perhaps, as has been suggested, the authoritarian streak in the family – his father had been a headmaster, his grandfather a commandant of police – left young Himmler with a desire to dominate or be dominated; but there were thousands of other young men, not only in Germany, with similar antecedents who did not share Himmler's obsessions. More significant was Himmler's eccentricity, shown in a preoccupation with the shapes of skulls, runes and occultism, which in normal circumstances would have made him a harmless crank. But Weimar Germany, especially Bavaria in the early 1920s, was hardly a normal country. Himmler was not a sadist, and his personality was quiet, even timid, in contrast to the tough public image. He struck people as prim and dull. Physically, for one who believed so fanatically in racial superiority, Himmler was unimpressive, with poor eyesight, a receding chin and sloping shoulders. For Hitler he was useful because of his organising ability and doglike devotion. Only in such a regime would such a man become a mass murderer; only on the orders of such a leader would his warped mentality have produced such fearful consequences.

An early associate of Hitler in Munich, and a participant in the Putsch of 9 November 1923, Himmler became secretary to Gregor Strasser in 1925 and four years later was appointed head of the S.S. with the imposing title of *Reichsführer*. In April 1933 Hitler made him chief of police in Bavaria, and a year later he held a similar position in every German state, including Prussia, where, under the premiership of Göring, he had charge of the political police or Gestapo. In 1934 Himmler played a key part, with the assistance of the army, in the downfall of Röhm and of the rival S.A. It was the S.S. which provided the firing squads and emerged as the victor, as the army later found to its cost. In 1936 Himmler became head of the first united German police force, a consequence of Hitler's policy of centralisation, with purely nominal subordination to the Reich Minister of the Interior. In strengthening and extending his empire, Himmler was assisted by an able and ambitious subordinate named Heydrich

who was soon to carve out a domain for himself, becoming head of the
Gestapo and also of the Nazi party's own secret service or S.D. Heydrich was as ruthless as Himmler without his crankiness, and he was
to be in charge of the mass execution of Jews and other unwanted
peoples in Eastern Europe by the Special Commandos (*Einsatzgrup-
pen*). It was Heydrich who was in charge of the notorious conference
at Wannsee in January 1942 at which plans were drawn up for the
'final solution' of the Jewish question. Later that year Heydrich, who
had become Acting Protector of Bohemia and Moravia, was assassinated
by Czech patriots flown in from London. In 1938 Himmler had been
active in the intrigues which led to the dismissal of Fritsch as Commander-in-Chief of the army. In this shift of power which marked a further
significant loss of independence by the generals, the S.S. was again the
beneficiary. The *Waffen S.S.*, the élite military force which had been
set up originally for internal purposes, was now placed on a permanent
footing and given equal status with the army. By the end of the war it
had enlisted (allowing for losses) some 900,000 men, including many
non-Germans and, as we have seen, even non-Nordics.

The outbreak of war in September 1939 led to a great increase in
Himmler's responsibilities. After the conquest of Poland he became
head of a new organisation for strengthening German nationhood. It
was he who gave orders for the expulsion of Poles and Jews from
areas earmarked for German settlement, and for re-settling in the
Reich Germans transferred from the Russian sphere of influence as
defined between Hitler and Stalin. German designs for the *Ostraum*
required the use of land without its inhabitants, and as early as January 1941, with the conquest of Russia in prospect, Himmler told an S.S.
colleague, von dem Bach-Zelewski, that Hitler's plans for the East
necessitated the elimination of some 30 million Slavs.[100] Himmler
organised the concentration camps where thousands of mass executions
took place every day. No one did more to carry out the 'final
solution' of the Jewish problem: in Auschwitz alone over 800,000
men, women and children were put to death in gas chambers. The
total number of the Nazis' Jewish victims was between five and six
million: the exact figure will never be known. Torture was a regular
feature of the camps, and one of Himmler's favourite pursuits was the
use of prisoners for medical and other experiments that often involved sterilisation, injection with gangrene poisoning or freezing to
death. Though Himmler himself was so squeamish that he could not
bear the sight of torture or execution, he treated the whole exercise
with clinical detachment: it was a job to be done, and there was no
room for sentimentality. Reports of the killings were couched in cold
bureaucratic language as if they were recording the destruction of

vermin – which was precisely what, for Himmler, they were doing. The anti-semitic Nazi film 'The Eternal Jew' made a direct comparison between Jews and rats, and Himmler was only drawing the consequences. One of his most notorious speeches was his address to S.S. leaders at Posen in October 1943, in which he declared his utter indifference to the fate of Russians and Czechs, and the need to exterminate the Jewish people, while the executioners themselves must remain 'decent' and 'idealistic'. This illustrated the perversion of values for which the S.S. stood. By the end of 1943 most of Poland's three million Jews were dead. The last great wave of persecution was the deportation and gassing, in the summer of 1944, of Jews from Hungary. But by then Himmler was having second thoughts about completing the racial programme of a Jew-free Europe. He was tempted to use the opportunity to strike a bargain with the Allies for the exchange of Hungarian Jews for lorries or a cash payment, and he feared the retribution which would follow Germany's now inevitable defeat. Already the Russians were in Poland and advancing on Hungary, and the time had come to evacuate all the concentration camps in the occupied East as well as those beyond Germany's western frontier. The gas chambers in Auschwitz ceased to function in October, and by January 1945 most of the surviving prisoners had been transfered to concentration camps within the Reich. The official number of such prisoners in January 1945 was 714,211, of whom rather more than half a million were men and the rest women.[101]

In 1943 Himmler succeeded Frick as Reich Minister of the Interior, and early in 1944 he gained control of the Counter-Intelligence organisation, whose two heads, Canaris and Oster, were deeply involved in the conspiracy against Hitler. The failure of the attempted assassination on 20 July 1944 made Hitler more suspicious than ever of the army, and therefore more dependent on the S.S. Himmler was given command of the Home Army in place of the compromised General Fromm. Later in the year his military ambition was further gratified when he was put in charge of an army in the field. But the result of this appointment was in fact to reduce Himmler's importance, because henceforth he saw less of Hitler (who remained in East Prussia) and as a fighting general Himmler was not a success. He himself, as early as 1942, had become highly critical of Hitler's handling of the war. Through his Finnish masseur, Kersten, Himmler made contact with an American who was Roosevelt's special envoy. His peace feelers with the Americans, like his flirtation with the German resistance, was an insurance against defeat. This did not prevent Himmler from savagely joining in the reprisals against anyone connected with the conspiracy of 20 July after its failure. He seized the opportunity to expand the economic organisation of the S.S., which included a wide range of profitable activities, from mining and quarrying to armaments, foodstuffs and textiles. The special characteristic was the use of slave labour from prisoner of war and concentration camps. Even racial policy had to give way to the exigencies of total war, though the conditions in which many of the prisoners worked amounted to a slower form of extermination. Already by 1942 some 175,000 prisoners were working for the S.S. building programme alone.[102] Among the projects manned by S.S. labour was the Rocket Experimental Station at Peenemünde on the Baltic, from which the V1s and V2s, Hitler's last secret weapons, were launched against England and other selected sites in North West Europe. As an economic empire builder, Himmler frequently clashed with Speer, who resented both his demands for and inefficient use of dwindling manpower and materials.[103]

Powerful as Himmler was, in the last year of the Third Reich he was eclipsed by Martin Bormann. Bormann was the successor of Rudolf Hess, who, as Hitler's deputy, had flown to Scotland shortly before the German attack on Russia in a dramatic but forlorn attempt to make the peace with Britain which Hitler (on his own terms) had consistently sought. Bormann, a brutal and dominating personality, resembled Hess only in his devotion to his master, from whom he derived all his power. He became head of Hitler's Chancellery, which meant that all the Gauleiters and party officials were responsible to him, and was also Hitler's secretary. An ideological fanatic as well as a much feared bureaucrat, Bormann was one of the most implacable enemies of Christianity. Goebbels despised him as a 'primitive OGPU type', but was also afraid of a man so close to the Führer.[104] Finally, Goebbels himself was the only one of the original Nazi Big Three to emerge from the last phase of the Third Reich with an enhanced reputation. It was he, not the absent Hitler, who visited the dazed inhabitants of bombed cities and comforted them with promises of retribution (the V1 and V2 attacks on England), whose morale-raising speeches helped Speer to increase war production to unprecedented heights despite the devastation, who conjured up what his enemies called 'strength through fear' by painting blood-curdling pictures of what would happen if Germany lost the war. The more hopeless Germany's military prospects became, the more Goebbels clung to the hope of a political solution – the breakdown of the unnatural alliance between the western powers and Soviet Russia. In vain he warned the former of the danger to them and their democracy if the Communists conquered Central Europe. In his ambivalent attitude towards East and West Goebbels was typical of many Nazi leaders. Drawn to the West by cultural and ethnic ties, despising but fearing the Russians, they felt more than a sneaking sympathy for Stalin, and knew that at a pinch they could do a deal with him (as they had in August 1939) in a way impossible in the case of Britain and America. So no decisive steps were in fact taken by the German leadership to make the war end favourably for either the Russians or the Anglo-Americans. Although Goebbels' last pronouncement on 24 April 1945 was a reaffirmation of the anti-Bolshevik crusade which Hitler had often proclaimed, nothing concrete was done to make it easier for the West to forestall the Red Army. The one miracle that could still save Nazi Germany, an East-West split, could be brought about only by the collapse of the Reich and the creation of a power vacuum in the heart of Europe.

Goebbels himself did as much as anyone to prolong the Third Reich's resistance against the enemies who closed in on all sides. After the 20 July plot, which Goebbels helped to foil, he was appointed Minister for Total Warfare with new powers, including the direction of labour. Sauckel was deposed as special Commissioner for Labour, because his last recruitment drives had failed: as Germany's defeat appeared inevitable, it was increasingly harder to cajole or pressurise the inhabitants of the rapidly diminishing occupied territories. Nor had the further mobilisation of German man- and woman-power ordered by Hitler in January 1943 on the eve of the Stalingrad surrender brought the expected results. Of the three million women not then engaged in warwork it is estimated that not more than half a million were actually recruited. As late as 1944 Germany had 1·38 million domestic servants, only 13 per cent fewer than in 1939.[105] Goebbels carried out a final, drastic comb-out of German manpower, and all males between the ages of 16 and 60, including untrained schoolboys and veterans of the First World War, were drafted into the Home Guard or *Volkssturm*. Hitler even permitted the call-up of women up to the age of fifty for national defence. The switch of labour from industry to the forces had an adverse effect on production, which was already reduced by air raids. Theatres, cabarets and all places of entertainment were closed, no more fiction was allowed to be published, the number of newspapers was curtailed.[106] All except a few orchestras and schools of music were disbanded, and the artists sent to the army or munition factories. These measures could not stave off defeat, but they matched the mood of a country facing a fearful nemesis. The winter of 1944–5 was to be the worst in Germany's history.

(vii) FROM FORTRESS EUROPE TO THE FALL OF BERLIN

The Anglo-American decision to launch a campaign on the Italian mainland after expelling the Axis from North Africa was made at the Casablanca conference in January 1943. It was clear by then that the promised second front, the invasion of Northern France, could not begin until the summer of 1944. Meanwhile use must be made of the substantial Allied forces in the Mediterranean. Churchill was keen on going into Italy for a number of reasons: it would knock her out of the war; from Italian airfields targets in Roumania (the oilfields) and Central Europe could be bombed; Italy could be the springboard for a landing in the Balkans in support of the Yugoslav partisans and ultimately for a thrust through Slovenia into the Danube valley; Turkey might be induced to enter the war; the Italian front would divert and absorb German troops from other fronts and help to relieve the pressure on Russia. The Americans were less happy about the choice of Italy, which they feared would interfere with the build-up for the real second front and prove an unprofitable sideshow. They were also suspicious of intervention in the Balkans as a political move on Churchill's part that could not be militarily justified. Stalin, of course, cordially agreed with them. Churchill however had his way; and while the Allied troops were still engaged in the conquest of Sicily news reached them of the overthrow of Mussolini. They were unable to take full advantage of this, largely owing to shortage of equipment caused by America's commitments to the war against Japan; and though Badoglio managed to surrender secretly to the Allies and to escape, with the Italian royal family, to behind the Allied lines in South Italy, the Germans soon had a tight grip on Rome and reinforced their position north of Naples. Thereupon a campaign of attrition began, which was to last until the end of the war, as the Germans were slowly forced back from one fortified line to another. The Italian theatre of war was never intended to be decisive. It succeeded in its limited aim of holding down a number of German divisions, though fewer than there were in the Balkans. But it had not been expected that the conquest of Italy would prove so laborious and slow: indeed it was originally supposed to be complete by 1 June 1944. Churchill's warning against 'crawling up the leg of Italy like a harvest bug' proved unhappily prophetic. Allied mistakes, such as the failure to exploit the Anzio bridgehead and the futile if heroic attack on Monte Cassino, were one reason for the delay. As always, German resistance was skilful and tough, and full advantage was taken of the good defensive nature of the Apennines. Churchill's oft-quoted aphorism about the soft under-belly of the Axis was apt if applied to the Italian attitude to the war, but very misleading as a physical description of the country. A further handicap to Allied progress in Italy was the transfer of troops and equipment earmarked for the landings in France. As a result, despite the far from unexpected defection of his ally, Hitler was able to hold his enemies on the periphery of Fortress Europe and far from its vital centres.

At the Teheran conference in November 1943, attended by Churchill, Roosevelt and Stalin, Stalin was promised that the Anglo-American assault on France would be made early in June 1944. The operation was preceded by intense bombardment of French railways, bridges and airfields so as to isolate the invasion zones from the rest of the country. The Allies' mastery of the air also enabled them to examine and photograph Hitler's Atlantic Wall, which was far too long to be strong everywhere. The bombing was spread over a very wide area, and was particularly heavy in the Pas de Calais, where the Germans expected the landings, though Hitler had a hunch that they would be in Normandy. Elaborate precautions had been taken in other ways to deceive the German defenders, who were faced with the choice of dispersing their troops along the whole coast, as Rommel advocated, or keeping the armour in reserve for dispatch to the coast when the alarm was given, as Rundstedt preferred. Both courses were risky: in the first case the necessary strength would be missing, in the second the loss of time would be fatal. In the end Hitler came down on Rundstedt's side, though the stationing of most of the German armour in the Pas de Calais represented a compromise. In the event, the German tanks were prevented from reaching the Norman landing beaches in time by the Allied destruction of the bridges over the Seine. As Rommel, who commanded the German troops in Northern France, had foreseen, the first twenty-four hours of invasion were decisive. On 6 June the British and Americans landed 135,000 men, a force too well armed and entrenched to be pushed into the sea by local defence forces and too rapidly reinforced to be crushed by German armour when it arrived. A month later there were a million Allied troops in France, with over half a million tons of supplies. In the latter part of July the attempt on Hitler's life, in which Rommel was involved, had a temporarily stunning effect on the German commanders. Rommel himself, wounded by an Allied air attack, was soon after compelled by Hitler to commit suicide.

Once the Allies captured the port of Cherbourg, the break-out from the Cotentin Peninsula and coastal areas of Normandy began. It soon developed great momentum, and though pockets of German resistance remained in several Channel ports and other strong points, most of France was liberated in a matter of weeks. Paris fell on 24 August, by which time the American, British and French landings on the Riviera had carried the South against almost negligible opposition. In the North, Montgomery drove into Belgium and Holland, liberating Brussels and Antwerp at the beginning of September. But German troops held out longer on the Scheldt estuary, denying the Allies the use of the port of Antwerp until the 26 November. Nevertheless, before its retreating forces could re-group along its frontier the Reich lay wide open to invasion. The Americans were already pressing on the frontier at Aachen and further south in the Saar and Alsace, and a determined thrust, according to the later statements of German generals, could have ended the war by Christmas. But to achieve this the broad front approach favoured by Eisenhower would have had to give way to a narrow break-through as advocated by Montgomery, the British commander in the Low Countries, who wished to cross the Rhine north of Duisburg and outflank the Ruhr. Using similar arguments, Patton, the most dynamic American general and commander of the right wing, urged an all-out effort there, though none of the South German targets had the same economic importance as the Ruhr. By the time Eisenhower was convinced of the need to change his strategy, it was too late to concentrate the resources required, though he allowed Montgomery to launch a parachute attack on the Lower Rhine at Arnhem, which if successful could have opened the way to an invasion of North West Germany.[107] The gamble did not come off for a number of reasons, the most important being that the men were dropped too far from their target, and by October it was clear that the war was going to last through the winter. Meanwhile the Germans had rapidly consolidated their defences, while the Allies' speed of movement was hindered by difficulties of supply. Communications were bad (the obverse side of their own saturation bombing), lack of ports, especially Antwerp, was a handicap, and too little use was made of aircraft to fly fuel to forward positions. Basically, the Allies were unprepared for such swift success by the end of August, and their planning was not sufficiently flexible or imaginative to take advantage of it. Eisenhower, the Commander-in-Chief, was conscious of the need to show impartiality between generals of different nationalities and was understandably reluctant to impose his views on men with far more military experience than himself. With his cautious and conciliatory nature, he was the ideal chairman of a military committee, not the man to seize unforeseen opportunities.

Another factor that favoured the defence was the weather, though it could also help the attack, as was shown when the German counter-offensive in the Ardennes in the middle of December made good use of the prevailing fog. This was Hitler's final fling, using up his last reserves in an attempt to cut the Allied front in the Ardennes and re-capture Antwerp. The battle was fought over much the same ground as Operation Sicklethrust of 1940, but in very different circumstances. It was unexpected by the Allies, who were thrown off balance. But though the Germans gained ground, they just failed to reach the Meuse, and Allied reinforcements combined with air mastery brought the advance to a halt. Its effect was to hold up the invasion of Germany from the west by several weeks, but at the cost of Germany's eastern front, where lack of reserves made it impossible to stem the Russian tide that swept irresistibly forward.

It had also been agreed at Teheran that the Russians would start an offensive to coincide with the Normandy landings. By the end of 1943 they had re-captured two-thirds of the territory lost since 1941, and their front line ran west of Smolensk and Kiev. Their progress after the summer of 1944 was rapid. Striking in turn from north to south, the Red Army knocked Finland out of the war, relieved Lenin-grad, recovered White Russia, Esthonia, Latvia, eastern Poland and the western Ukraine. By October 1944 it was on the borders of East Prussia, and had cut off a German army in Courland which Hitler had forbidden to retreat. But it was further south that the Russians made the most spectacular gains. Having entered Roumania, they deprived Germany of her sole remaining source of natural oil, and initiated the series of political upheavals which caused Roumania, and later Bulgaria and Hungary, to change sides and declare war on Ger-many under anti-Fascist governments dependent on the Soviet Union. Yugoslavia, which Tito's partisans had liberated with little help from outside, was also about to join Stalin's camp. In Greece, from which the German forces were hastily withdrawn, the British were in pre-carious occupation, for the chances of a take-over by local Communist forces were good and a civil war followed the expulsion of the Ger-mans. The Russians had also fought their way into the eastern pro-vinces of Czechoslovakia. By this time the Germans had savagely suppressed the heroic and tragic rising in Warsaw, Stalin's negative reaction to which has been described as 'the most arrogant and most unmistakeable demonstration of the Soviet determination to control Eastern Europe in the post-war period'.[108] It was against this back-ground of expanding Soviet power that Churchill, who was in Mos-cow in October, made his famous, or notorious, offer to Stalin to divide the Balkans into Russian and British spheres of influence. This foray into the discredited methods of the old diplomacy seems to have been regarded by Stalin as perfectly natural: no one had practised *Real-politik* more successfully than he, and the Balkan agreement (to which he adhered just as long as it suited him) was only part of his total demand. His insistence on annexing what had been Eastern Poland forced the western powers to offer the Poles German territory up to the rivers Oder and Neisse (without specifying which river Neisse was meant), with the consequent expulsion of its inhabitants. It was the *Drang nach Osten* in reverse. At the beginning of 1945 the Red Army, now greatly superior to the Germans in numbers and armaments, was still east of the line Königsberg-Warsaw-Cracow. By the beginning of February it had reached the river Oder, about fifty miles from Berlin, and had occupied Silesia, Germany's sole undamaged industrial district. Despite the bitter weather millions of refugees were now on the move, thronging the roads to the west with their pitiful possessions and hampering the defence, fleeing from a Red Army whose reputation for pillage and rape ran before it like the warning of a plague. Dresden was full of refugees when it was obliterated on 14 February. Budapest had fallen to the Russians three days before, but Vienna held out until 6 April. By the third week in February the Germans had managed to stabilise the much shortened eastern front with the aid of reinforcements from the west and the home reserve, so that in the end it was the Anglo-Americans who first penetrated into the heart of Germany.

A report by the Internal Intelligence Service of the Reich Security Department dated 6 March painted a frank and gloomy picture: 'Since the Soviet break-through every member of the community knows that we are facing the greatest national catastrophe...'[109] People were suffering severely from the bombing terror, food was running short, defeatism was general. 'Confidence in the leadership has recently plummeted ... There is pronounced fear of the Soviets. The people's attitude towards the British and Americans is one of critical appraisal ...' Whether or not Hitler saw this report he ignored its implications, though the following weeks saw a steady deterioration in Germany's position. By the end of March the Allies were across the Rhine at several points, and the Ruhr was about to be encircled. Yet Hitler insisted on repeating his scorched earth orders: from railway engines to electric cables, from bridges to broadcasting stations, nothing was to be left. Speer knew that the population could not survive without water, gas, electricity, food, factories and farm animals, yet all these things were supposed to be destroyed. When at the risk of his life he dared to remonstrate with Hitler and tell him that the war was lost, he received the reply:'If the war is lost, the people will be lost too. This fate is inevitable.'[110] The good had fallen, Hitler declared, only the mediocre remained, and there was no need to worry about them. By being defeated, the Germans had shown themselves weaker than the 'stronger eastern people' to whom the future of Europe belonged. Thus, as the end approached, Hitler remained true to the Social Darwinism with which he had started, and acknowledged that the master race had failed in its great test. And as Speer was no longer trustworthy, Hitler entrusted the demolition programme to the Gauleiters. But when Speer made a scene and affirmed his loyalty, Hitler allowed him to issue the implementation instructions for the decrees. In one way and another Speer managed to sabotage these instructions. He managed, for example, to get arms and explosives concentrated in army hands so as to prevent their use by party fanatics. Hitler's lust for destruction was not confined to material objects. Only with difficulty did his advisers dissuade him from denouncing the Geneva Convention, as Goebbels suggested in February 1945, which would have permitted the shooting of all captured enemy airmen out of hand and the use of new poison gases. It was Goebbels, too, who after the death of Roosevelt on 12 April exclaimed: 'The perverse coalition between plutocracy and Bolshevism is breaking down.'[111]

But the coalition, perverse or not, outlasted the Nazi regime. In the course of the month the Anglo-American forces penetrated deep into Germany, and on 25 April the Americans joined hands with the Russians at Torgau on the Elbe. With the British at Wismar on the Baltic (forestalling a Russian occupation of Denmark) and the Americans in Saxony, by the time hostilities ended the western armies were in occupation of much of the territory assigned at the Yalta conference to the Russian zone of occupation. The much rumoured Alpine defence redoubt in Bavaria did not materialise, nor did the youthful guerilla organisation known as the Werewolves do more than minor damage. Hitler still professed to believe that the Red Army was at the end of its resources, while prophesying in his last order of the day that if the Bolsheviks overran Germany, old people and children would be murdered, women and girls used as prostitutes and the remainder of the population transported to Siberia. The warning was hardly necessary, for the main preoccupation of most Germans in the last weeks of the war was to make sure that when the end came they would be under Western not Russian occupation. Here and there refusal by a local Nazi boss to surrender caused unnecessary destruction, as happened for example in the historic city of Hildesheim, whose Romanesque churches were pulverised from the air. When on 12 April the first American troops reached the Elbe at Magdeburg, they were less than sixty miles from Berlin, which they could have reached before the Russians. This had originally been Eisenhower's intention. Now however he ordered the units to make for Dresden, where they would meet the Red Army. Though this decision upset Churchill, who had counted on Berlin falling to the West, Eisenhower justified his change of plans on military grounds, particularly on the need for a strong build-up further south to meet expected German resistance. As a soldier Eisenhower professed to be unconcerned with politics, but in any case he was only reflecting the views of a President who showed little awareness of the significance which capture of the capitals of Central Europe would have for the post-war balance of power.[112] For similar reasons Eisenhower readily complied with a Russian wish that his forces, which had crossed the Czechoslovak frontier at the beginning of May, should halt on the line Karlsbad-Pilsen-Budweis instead of advancing on and capturing Prague. The Russians quickly made their own plans to seize Berlin.

The last act in Hitler's personal melodrama was played out in a Berlin made almost unrecognisable by Allied air raids and Russian shelling, and whose inhabitants lived like troglodytes in cellars and air raid shelters, short of food, water, heat and light. By this time Hitler was little more than a shadow of his former self. Despite cuts and burns the only permanent injury caused by the attempt on his life was to his ears. But a general deterioration of his health had begun long before. A detailed medical report on him in 1942, which was in the possession of Himmler, referred to insomnia, dizziness and severe headache, and suggested that Hitler was suffering from a progressive paralysis which would ultimately affect his mind. There was a 'chronic degeneration of the nervous system'.[113] Göring remarked in 1943 that in three and a half years of war Hitler seemed to have aged fifteen years. His way of life, with overwork, very little sleep, no exercise and heavy doses of drugs supplied by his doctor, Morell, exacerbated the symptoms of decline. By the spring of 1945 Hitler was described by one of his generals as a 'walking corpse' with a puffy and colourless face, listless eyes, trembling hands, a stooping back and a shuffling gait with a dragging left leg. Yet his will power was still immense: between long periods of torpor he would at times flash with the old fire and silence his obsequious attendants with a nervous outburst. His shrinking band of courtiers took more liberties than before, as he planned imaginary victories and issued orders to non-existent armies, but they still feared his wrath. As late as 28 April he was still ordering 'traitors' to be shot. The final assault by the Red Army began on 16 April. Hitler at last admitted that the war was lost, but decided to stay in Berlin and direct its defence from his underground shelter or bunker in the Chancellery garden. By 25 April the city had been completely surrounded by the Russians, who fought their way into the centre through streets which were littered with the dead and dying. The Wilhelmstrasse, where the Chancellery was situated, was under fire.

Among the scenes of apocalyptic horror one may stand for many: S.S. men blew up a four-mile tunnel under an arm of the river Spree and the Landwehr Canal. The inrush of water trapped the thousands of civilians who were sheltering there and also, since the tunnel happened to be a railway link, four hospital trains of wounded men.[114] Apart from Goebbels and Bormann, who stayed with Hitler to the end, most of the Nazi leaders had escaped to the west. A few, like Göring, sought refuge in Bavaria, more, like Himmler, in Schleswig-Holstein. Both men tried, without the Führer's authority, to make a separate peace, Göring by a direct approach to the Americans, Himmler by negotiating with the West through Count Bernadotte of the Swedish Red Cross. The Allies stuck grimly to their resolve to accept nothing less than complete and simultaneous surrender to them and the Russians.

Hitler's fury when he heard of the 'treachery' of Göring and Himmler was expressed in his decision to exclude them from the succession as laid down in his will. This will, drawn up on the night of 29-30 April, was Hitler's last political act. It was preceded by his midnight marriage to Eva Braun, his companion of many years, who did not wish to survive him. The ritual death of both was now prepared and orders issued. At 3.30 on the afternoon of 30 April Hitler gave his wife poison and shot himself. Both bodies were soused in petrol and set alight. The flesh was consumed, but not the skeletons, which were buried in a nearby crater. Although the Russians, who arrived on the scene two days later, have never publicly revealed the facts, they are known to have disinterred the bodies and, after identification, to have secretly removed them to an unknown destination, probably in Russia.[115] Goebbels followed the Führer's example of self-immolation a day later after trying unsuccessfully to negotiate an armistice with the local Russian commander. Having poisoned his wife and six children, he shot himself; the bodies, charred rather than burnt, afterwards disappeared. The rest of the party in the bunker tried as best they could to make their way to the west through the Russian lines. Among those who almost certainly failed to get through was Bormann, who was probably shot in the back near a bridge over the Spree.[116] On 1 May Goebbels and Bormann sent a message to Grand Admiral Dönitz that Hitler was dead and that he had been appointed Reich President under the will. The appointments of Goebbels as Chancellor and Bormann as Party Minister lapsed with their deaths. No new Führer was named: constitutionally, Germany reverted to the situation before the death of Hindenburg. It was equally characteristic that the will ended with an appeal to continue the war and to uphold the racial laws in their full rigour and mercilessly resist the 'poisoner of all nations, international Jewry'. The obsession remained to the end. Hitler's last anxieties were not about the western powers which in two world wars had frustrated German ambitions, or about the Russians beginning to wreak a terrible vengeance for their own immeasurable suffering, but the spectre of the homeless but ubiquitous Jew, whom he discerned behind them all.

Map 4   Germany since 1949

CHAPTER XI

The Occupation Regime

(i) THE BREAKDOWN OF FOUR POWER CONTROL

Between the suicide of Hitler and the beginning of Allied Military
Government in Germany there occurred the unscheduled interlude
known as the 23 days of the Dönitz regime. Grand Admiral Dönitz,
head of the navy and one of the few senior officers who had not quar-
relled with Hitler, had been appointed Chancellor under the latter's
will, which also named other members of the Dönitz cabinet.
Dönitz himself had taken refuge at Flensburg on the Danish border,
and was at first given *de facto* recognition by the British and Americans. His main concern was to end the fighting in the west immediately,
while postponing as long as possible the surrender of the German
forces in the east so as to give them and the mass of refugees fleeing
from the Russians time to move far enough west to be within the
British or American sphere when the armistice lines were finally drawn.
In this aim he was only partially successful: Eisenhower would not
risk a breach with the Russians. After the German armies in North
West Europe and elsewhere had, with Dönitz's authority, surrendered
to Montgomery on Lüneburg Heath, the final surrender of all the
armed forces to the four victors took place in formal ceremonies at
Rheims and at Karlshorst, the Berlin suburb where the Russians set
up their headquarters. The war was over. Germany lay prostrate under
the conqueror's feet, stunned and crushed. The victory could not have
been more complete; in the words of the last communiqué of the
O.K.W., issued on 9 May, it was the darkest hour in German history.
Some doubted whether the country would ever revive. Though it had
taken the combined resources of three world powers to defeat the Reich,
as an independent unit it had ceased to exist and its population was
entirely at the mercy of its occupiers. Dönitz's other aim was to preserve the semblance of a central German government into the post-war
period, but it was not to be. When on 23 May Dönitz was arrested
and treated as a prisoner of war and war criminal, it was little more
than a formality. Dönitz had been of use to the Allies since he had

authorised the surrender and ordered demobilisation of the *Wehrmacht*.[1] But his removal was inevitable, partly because of his Nazi associations, and partly because the Allies wanted a completely free hand in their plans for Germany. Also the Russians would certainly have objected if Dönitz had been kept on as the head of an accredited government.

On 5 June the commanders of the British, American, French and Russian forces, meeting in Berlin, issued a declaration that they had assumed supreme authority in Germany. There was to be no central German government for the time being. Government lay with the Allied Control Council, which was composed of the four commanders themselves, and met for the first time on 30 July.[2] Most of its work was in fact done by its Co-ordinating Committee, which consisted of the four Deputy Military Governors. They were in charge of their respective zones, the borders of which had been fixed in the course of 1944. The exception was the French Zone, which was carved out of the American and British Zones shortly before the end of the war after a decision to make France the fourth occupying power. It was still assumed that, once the war was over, American troops would leave Europe and that a revived France would be needed as a counterpoise to Germany. The French were also assigned a sector of Berlin by the British and Americans, the Russians having refused to yield any of their own territory for this purpose.

What to do with Germany after the war had been long and passionately debated, especially in the Anglo-Saxon countries, and had been the subject of innumerable memoranda and reports. It had been discussed in conferences at Moscow, Teheran, Quebec, Yalta and elsewhere. A European Advisory Commission, consisting of a British, American and Russian representative, had held meetings in London since early in 1944 to study the problem and make recommendations. There was at first a strong inclination, especially among Roosevelt and his advisers, to dismember Germany; with this was coupled the policy of stripping it of heavy industry ('pastoralisation') propounded by Morgenthau, Secretary of the U.S. Treasury, and briefly endorsed by both Roosevelt and Churchill. But by the end of the war the pendulum had swung back in favour of administering Germany on a quadripartite basis. Stalin, to the surprise of many people, declared on 9 May 1945 against partition, and this decision coincided (though for different reasons) with the now prevailing view in London and Washington. Only France disagreed. But her views did not carry much weight and to her chagrin she was not invited to the tripartite conference at Potsdam where the future of Germany was to be decided. In favouring a unified treatment of Germany Stalin had two principal motives. One was political. He wanted to use the central administrative machinery to promote Communist policy in the whole of Germany, and to win popularity for the German Communists by presenting Russia as the champion of their country's legitimate national interests: although the German Fascists were to be punished, the people (who were not to be identified with the Fascists) must be given some encouragement to respond to the Communist cause, especially in view of Russia's heavy claims on German assets. By exercising an influence over the whole of Germany Stalin would be in a stronger position than if he were confined to one zone. The second reason was economic. Russia badly needed reparations, including the transfer of industrial plant as well as of current production. Apart from Silesia, which had gone to Poland, and the Saar, which was earmarked for France, there remained the Ruhr as Germany's sole heavy industrial region. Only through quadripartite agreement could Russia secure a share in the dismantling and output of the Ruhr. Nevertheless the attempt to govern Germany through the Allied Control Council was to prove a failure. Each of the four powers had the right of veto. The French, who did not feel bound by the decisions made at Potsdam, objected to the proposed establishment of all-German departments in the most essential technical and economic fields, although clearly without some such central machinery no quadripartite policy could work. It is unlikely that it would have functioned in any case, given the divergency of aims between the Russians and the western powers, and the French veto, embarrassing at the time, saved an American one later. Moreover to be effective quadripartite rule would have needed the free movement of military government staff between all the zones, and this is something which the Russians would hardly have allowed. Thus, in practice, Germany's zonal borders, originally intended to have a mainly administrative character, soon became political frontiers, especially between East and West.

The Potsdam meeting late in July 1945 was the last of the great wartime conferences, for within a few days of its conclusion the explosion of the first atomic bomb at Hiroshima compelled Japan's surrender. Never again were the Big Three to reach so large a measure of formal unity. But this was possible mainly because fundamental differences were glossed over or hidden behind bland generalities. Since Yalta, much had happened to show the growing divergence between Russian and western views, as Montgomery wrote in his diary in June. The German problem was increasingly being seen in the context of a Europe that was hardening into two hostile camps. The basic disagreement over Poland had nearly caused a split at Yalta and would have done so had Roosevelt not been determined to avoid a breach with Russia at all costs. With his vision of world events increasingly blurred by fatal illness, Roosevelt felt more concern about the dying imperialism of Churchill than about the resurgent imperialism of Stalin, and he saw himself as a mediator between the two. Rather than face the unwelcome implications of Soviet expansionism, his mind was set on bringing the American army home as soon as possible, and on making sure, by territorial and other concessions, that the Soviet Union would take part in the war against Japan (it was not known in February that the atomic bomb would be ready by August). Above all, he wished to persuade Stalin to co-operate in the new plan for a United Nations organisation, which was almost as dear to Roosevelt's heart as the League of Nations had been to Woodrow Wilson's. He was, therefore, prepared to overlook or belittle the gathering signs of Soviet hostility. There was a difference in bargaining positions in that Stalin was basically satisfied with the West's recognition of the new frontiers of Russian power, whereas Roosevelt still felt he had to buy Stalin's goodwill if the Soviet Union was to act as one of the four 'world policemen' of which he had spoken at the Teheran conference.[3] Harry Truman, the new American President, was to display a robust common sense which saved him from Roosevelt's self-deception, but he was still too new in his office and too unfamiliar with the problems to alter the course set by his predecessor. For that reason he rejected Churchill's proposal before Potsdam that the American and British forces, which were at some points over 100 miles deep inside the Soviet Zone, should not withdraw to the zonal borders until the Russians proved more accommodating. The presentation of the western case at Potsdam was probably weakened by the disappearance of Churchill after he lost the British general election, for although Attlee and Bevin, representing the new Labour government, virtually continued Churchill's policy they naturally carried less weight. Subsequently Churchill declared that he would never have accepted the final Potsdam decision over the Polish-German frontier; but it is doubtful whether his continued presence at Potsdam would have made any difference, given the American disinclination to quarrel with the Russians and the physical possession of the disputed territories by Poles and Russians since June.[4] The western powers thus found themselves acquiescing in much they were soon to regret. But it was the last time that the Russians would find the British and Americans so conciliatory; and the actual experience of governing Germany was already breaking up the precarious three-power unity.

The Potsdam conference ruled that Germany must be occupied and disarmed, that National Socialism must be rooted out, that democracy must be established, and that reparations must be paid to the countries overrun and plundered. On two points, demilitarisation and denazification, few major difficulties arose. It was taken for granted that the Germans should have neither army nor armaments in the foreseeable future. And even if denazification was pursued in the different zones with different emphases and interpretations, there was a general determination to make a clean sweep. The Nazis could be identified, if not by their deeds (thousands of the important ones were involved in war crimes) at least by their membership of the party or of one of its many ancillary organisations. There were assumed to be enough non-Nazis in Germany capable of filling the posts of limited responsibility under military government. Democratisation, as soon appeared, was a loaded word. To the western powers it meant freedom, human rights, tolerance, parliamentary rule, free elections, and – especially in the eyes of Frenchmen, and, at first, Americans – a wide measure of decentralisation, the diffusion of power. To the Russians it meant the expropriation of landowners and capitalists and the concentration of power in an authoritarian Communist party acting in the name of the workers and peasants, with single list elections organised to produce the desired result. (It was characteristic that the Russians called their sector of Berlin the democratic sector, in the same way as the Communist states of Eastern Europe were described as people's democracies.) Reparations proved a still more intractable source of dispute. Even at the Yalta conference differences between Russia and the West over Germany's capacity to pay had prevented agreement. This was a question of facts and figures rather than of political semantics. The Russians were naturally determined to squeeze as much as possible out of Germany; and though no final reparations figure was reached at Potsdam, it was agreed that in addition to what she took from her own zone, Russia would receive 25 per cent of reparations in the form of industrial plant from Western Germany. She also claimed reparations in the form of current deliveries. In return, the Russians were to provide food from their zone for the heavily industrialised British Zone. But though the West sent industrial deliveries to the East, the Russians did not reciprocate; they were already busy stripping their zone and transferring factories and equipment to the Soviet Union. In West Berlin alone 380 factories were dismantled before the arrival of the western occupation forces in July 1945. How much valuable equipment reached its ultimate destination and how much lay and rotted in railway sidings because no one knew what to do with it, it is impossible to say.[5] There was another complication. It was recognised at Potsdam that there was a connection between industrial disarmament and the German standard of living: as wealth was transferred from Germany, she would become poorer. It was laid down that the German standard should not be higher than the average standard of living in other European countries – a formula which, while deliberately vague, provided a ceiling but no floor. Security too was involved. Reparations were intended to weaken the German economy as well as to compensate for war damage. The less steel Germany produced, the less capable she would be of waging war. Before 1939 German steel production had been at the annual rate of 19 million tons, of which 9·6 million went on civilian uses.[6] The Allied Control Council, reflecting Russian, French and American views, decided that Germany should not be allowed to produce more than 5·8 million tons of steel a year, with a total capacity of 7·5 million tons. Here was an echo of the 'pastoralisation' policy so recently favoured in Washington. Within her reduced frontiers Germany must export or die, yet her industrial base was being eroded. The Potsdam conference declared that the German people were to be neither enslaved nor destroyed, but its economic policy seemed to imply a level of existence intermediate between living and dying.

For the situation was immeasurably aggravated by the influx of refugees. Here too unilateral action by Russia had prejudged the decision. It had been agreed at Yalta that the Polish eastern border would be approximately along the Curzon Line, and that compensation for Poland would be found in the west at the expense of Germany. Two or three million Poles would move out of the territory recognised as Russian and settle in the ex-German territory, which would reach as far as the rivers Oder and Neisse (whether eastern or western Neisse was not clear – that there were two rivers of that name was a point easily overlooked by the western diplomats). Something like four million Germans would in turn be displaced to make room for the Poles, and re-settled inside Germany. When the western representatives arrived at Potsdam, they found that the forced transfer of population had reached much larger proportions than they had bargained for. The territory under Polish administration had been extended to the western Neisse, embracing a region where over two and a half million Germans had been living, and included the important Silesian capital of Breslau. The Baltic port of Stettin was also claimed by the Poles against American wishes (the British attitude was rather ambivalent).[7] Germany had lost a quarter of her former territory and as the whole region, according to Stalin, had been cleared of Germans, the total of refugees was more like seven or eight million, many of whom had fled to the west.[8] Although Stalin's statement was untrue, there was little that the British and Americans could do, faced with a series of accomplished facts, other than accept the position under protest while insisting that the final delimitation of frontiers would

have to wait for a German peace treaty. They also sanctioned the
gradual expulsion and transfer in 'humane conditions' (which were
largely ignored) of a second great wave – the German minorities in
Czechoslovakia and Hungary, numbering over six and a half million:
again, they were simply recognising a process that had already begun.
During the war the Czech government in exile had obtained Allied
assent to the eviction from Czechoslovakia of the German minority
of over three million, including the socialists and other anti-Nazis.
Altogether post-war Germany had to find room for between twelve
and thirteen million extra people, two thirds of whom settled in the
western zones. In addition, several hundred thousand foreign workers
(Poles, Balts and Ukrainians, now known as Displaced Persons), the
residue of the immense foreign labour force working in the Reich at the
end of the war, refused to be repatriated for political reasons. All these
people had to be fed, and, if possible, employed.[9] A year later myriads
of refugees, clutching what remained of their chattels, were still making
their way to the west in overcrowded trains, sleeping in railway stations
and air raid shelters, pouring into the ruined cities and overflowing
into villages already packed with evacuees. By 1950 one person in four
in Bavaria, and one in three in Lower Saxony was a refugee; in
Schleswig Holstein the proportion was even higher. Friction between
the refugees and the local population was inevitable. One result of the
problem was the formation of a Refugees' and Expellees' party, which
played a not insignificant part in the early history of the Federal
Republic. The assimilation – psychological as well as economic – of
such a vast population naturally took time, and the older refugees
at least for many years refused to abandon the hope of return to their
lost homes, especially as juridically the frontier question was still
undecided. With the flight, often in appalling hardship and involving
the loss of uncounted lives, of the once flourishing and long established
German communities in the countries of Eastern Europe, a chapter of
history came to an end which had lasted the best part of a thousand
years. It was the tragic nemesis of the *Drang nach Osten*, the logical
climax of the struggle between nationalities which had torn the Continent apart in wars of increasing ferocity.

The immediate task of the four Military Governments was to deal
with the economic emergency and to re-create the conditions of civilised life. Railways and bridges had to be repaired, canals cleared, the
harvest got in, public utilities made to work despite lack of fuel, police
appointed, the postal and telephone services restored, schools re-opened.
Local government had to be rebuilt from the beginning, for here too
the collapse had been complete. Mayors had to be chosen for villages
and towns, *Landräte* for rural districts. It was not easy to find people

suitable for these posts. Many of the right age groups had belonged to the N.S.D.A.P. or were compromised in other ways. There was a crippling shortage of men; over three million had been killed in the war, two million were disabled, large numbers lay wounded in hospital, and several million were still held as prisoners outside Germany. The Allies were pledged to the revival of democracy. Political parties were licensed on a zonal basis in the course of 1945. In the Russian Zone the Communist party, whose leader, Ulbricht, had arrived from Moscow with the Red Army on the day after Hitler's suicide, was already engaged in a programme of land reform (breaking up the big estates) and nationalisation of industry. This party was unique in that, unlike the others, it was the voice and arm of the Russian Military Government. There was of course an absolute ban on the revival of National Socialism, but any 'democratic' party was allowed to function, and it was symptomatic that every major party had this word in its title.

The main parties that emerged in the western zones were the Social Democrats, who were trying to pick up the threads again after years of suppression, and the Christian Democratic Union or C.D.U. (In Bavaria, where politics still have a more local flavour, it was called the Christian Social Union or C.S.U. and represented in fact a continuation of the former Bavarian People's party.) In standing for a synthesis of Christian and democratic principles the C.D.U. was the German counterpart to similar parties in France and Italy. It took the place of the Centre party, which experienced a brief revival in Catholic areas but failed to take root. The Centre had lost credit by its failure to resist Hitler during the critical months before and after his assumption of power. Nazi persecution had driven Catholics and Protestants closer together, and in the new ecumenical climate an inter-denominational party, which would not be dominated by the Roman Catholic hierarchy, was called for. It is mainly in its stand on specific issues, such as denominational schools and religious education that the C.D.U. can claim to be a Christian party, especially as the Social Democrats have abandoned their anti-religious attitude. Critics of the C.D.U. have said that the 'C' in its name increasingly stands for Conservative. As originally constituted, the C.D.U. was really a coalition of industrialists and Catholic trade unionists with a good deal of middle-class support. Konrad Adenauer, who emerged as its leader, had been Lord Mayor of Cologne for sixteen years before 1933 and chairman of the Prussian state council, but few people had heard of him outside Germany. The best known name in German politics immediately after the war was that of Kurt Schumacher, the leader of the S.P.D. This party, as before, contained among its leaders both hard-line Marxists and pragmatists, with mass backing from the industrial working class especially in the Protestant parts of the country. Schumacher himself, despite his tactical rigidity and dictatorial manner, was not a doctrinaire, and sought to adopt a basic Marxist approach to a situation which neither Marx nor anyone else had foreseen. The third largest party, still some way behind the big two, was the Free Democratic party or F.D.P. It consisted of an alliance between businessmen and industrialists on the one hand and liberal intellectuals, such as Theodor Heuss, soon to be the Federal Republic's first President, on the other. In one sense the F.D.P. was the successor of Stresemann's People's party, but it also contained quite a lot of ex-Nazis who were somewhat incongruous bedfellows with the liberals, most of whom came from the south-west, where the radical ideas of 1848 had left stronger traces than elsewhere. Of the other parties represented in the first post-war West German parliaments, the Communists at first had a not unimportant following in the industrial districts. But as West Germany became prosperous and Communist policy in East Germany was seen to be wholly subservient to Russian purposes, the K.P.D. lost ground. Most of the millions of Germans who had been in Russia during the war came back with their anti-communist sentiments confirmed, and it was clear that the Communist party would never recapture its mass electorate of Weimar days: even in East Germany it needed artificial help and a shotgun marriage with the Social Democrats to gain a majority. The decision of the Federal Constitutional Court in 1956 to ban the German Communist party, while of doubtful political wisdom, brought no practical change since the party had lost most of its support. At the other end of the political spectrum was the German party or D.P., basically a regional party representing the farmers of Lower Saxony. It was conservative with a quaintly old-world flavour due to its sentimental attachment to the Hanoverian royal house which had been deposed in 1866. The significance of these parties appeared to be limited by the restricted scope of German politics, for up to 1948 the general expectation was that the occupation would go on for at least ten years, and possibly a good deal longer. The Russians spoke of keeping Germany disarmed for the next forty years.

In the Russian Zone the same party labels were used as in the west, but the contents were different: even the permitted 'bourgeois' parties could operate only within circumscribed limits. They all belonged to an Anti-Fascist Front which was headed by the Communists. They were virtually cut off from their West German colleagues. Moreover, although there were coalition governments in each of the five states, it was significant that four out of the five prime ministers together with all or nearly all the ministers of education and the interior were members of the S.E.D. This, the Socialist Unity party, was a new creation, formed by the merging of the Communists and the Social Democrats. Grotewohl, the chairman of the S.P.D. in Berlin, had taken this step under considerable Russian pressure in defiance of the wishes of his colleagues in the western zones, who regarded the S.E.D. as simply the Communist party in a new guise. It was, predictably, an unequal partnership, for although the S.P.D. had been the larger of the two Socialist parties during the Weimar Republic and still was – as the Berlin elections of 1946 showed – it was the other partner who called the tune. Henceforth the S.P.D. was banned in the Russian Zone and also – unofficially – in the Russian sector of Berlin. Behind the democratic façade, what occurred in East Germany was the substitution of one dictatorship for another. The new élite party was given preferential treatment in many ways: it received extra rations and over 90 per cent of all newsprint allocated to the political press.[10] And just as the Nazi party had made use of its mass organisations, such as the S.A., Hitler Youth and Labour Front, to impress the electorate with mammoth demonstrations, so the Communists used their mass organisations, such as the Free German Youth, the Democratic Women's League and the Free German Trade Union Association, to consolidate and demonstrate their power. Block seats were assigned to these bodies in the later East German parliament or *Volkskammer*, thus assuring the ruling Socialist Unity party of a permanent majority.

In the west, it was the Americans who set the pace for political advance. The first post-war local elections were held in 1946; democracy was to be built up from below. By the end of that year the three states of the American Zone (Bavaria, Hesse and Württemberg-Baden) had their own elected parliaments and governments under constitutions which had also been approved by popular vote. Bremen, which was under American occupation, and served as the port for the Zone, joined it as the fourth state in 1947. State elections in the British Zone soon followed. Here, too, there were four states or *Länder* (Schleswig-Holstein, Hamburg, Lower Saxony and North Rhine-Westphalia).[11] Whereas the first two were historic entities, the latter two were made up of what had been Prussian provinces, with the addition, in the case of Lower Saxony, of three small *Länder*. The largest *Land* in population, though not in area, was North Rhine-Westphalia, which contained the Ruhr and Lower Rhine industrial complex. Its population was not far short of fifteen million. The abolition of Prussia, which these changes presupposed, was formally decided early in 1947 by the Allied Control Council. This historic agglomeration of provinces, some Prussian from time immemorial, some acquired as late as the nineteenth century, was irrevocably divided into four sections. East Prussia was divided between Russia and Poland, with Königsberg becoming Kaliningrad. The other eastern provinces, including most of Pomerania, West Prussia, Posen, Upper and Lower Silesia, were allocated to Poland. Brandenburg became, with Saxony, the core of the Russian-occupied Zone of Germany, while the 'new' ex-Prussian provinces west of the Elbe made up the greater part of the British Zone.

Prussia's disappearance from the map had one practical advantage: for the first time no one German state had a disproportionate preponderance. But the event was of much wider significance.[12] Prussia denoted a system of values as much as a territory. Ever since the eighteenth century it had been identified with militarism, and Bismarck's three wars confirmed this reputation. During the First World War Prussia was seen as the dynamic behind German expansionism – a considerable over-simplification. Prussian militarism was a historical fact, but one which had become heavily encrusted with legend. It was not uncommon for Allied propagandists to draw a distinction between a 'good Germany' (of the south and west) and a 'bad Prussia'. The non-military aspects of Prussian civilisation, whether in philosophy or architecture, were ignored, as were the non-Prussian roots of Pan-Germanism, from Arndt and Fichte to Heinrich Class. Yet inside Germany Prussia had become a rallying point for advocates of aggressive nationalism even if, like Treitschke and others, they were not Prussian by birth. It is perhaps not surprising that neither the strength of Social Democracy in Prussia between the wars nor the radicalism of 'Red Berlin' did much to change Prussia's image in the outside world. The problem in the Second World War was not so much militarism as the ideology of National Socialism, the roots of which lay outside rather than inside Prussia, though in England and America there was still a tendency to blame Prussia for the sins of the Third Reich. Yet Hitler himself was an Austrian and most of his leading henchmen came from Bavaria, Saxony or the Rhine. What Hitler did was to take over and use for his own purposes the Prussian myth, and to claim that he was the heir of Frederick the Great and Bismarck. Although much in the Nazi ideology was repugnant to the Prussian tradition, he presented National Socialism as its apotheosis. (Spengler's *Prussianism and Socialism*, published in 1920, was a forerunner.) A tragic by-product of the survival in changed circumstances of the old Prussian stereotype was the failure of Churchill and others during the Second World War to grasp the extent to which opposition to Hitler was a Prussian affair. The 20 July plot was a belated attempt by a group of officers and others to salvage the honour of the Prussian army after its debasement into an instrument of mass murder.[13] Just as, after

1933, church opposition to Hitler had been led by Niemöller, the Prussian officer turned pastor, so after 1945 it was the Prussian socialist, Reuter, who did more than anyone else to rebuild democracy in Berlin and to strengthen the will of the people to maintain their freedom.

The Potsdam conference had recognised that the economic problems of Germany could be solved only if the country was treated as a unity, and had decided to set up central agencies of German officials for finance, transport, communications, industry and foreign trade – all matters of vital concern to the functioning of a highly organised industrial society. Yet these agencies never came into existence, mainly owing to French objections. In practice, each zone went its own way, dealing as best it could with the difficulties inherent in a truncated economy. In order to co-ordinate affairs within their zone, the Americans arranged for regular meetings of the *Land* prime ministers and other ministers in a body known as a *Länderrat*, and in February 1946 they sponsored the first joint conference to prime ministers from their own and the British Zone. The British occupying authorities, while noticeably less eager to foster interzonal activities on the part of the Germans, had their own Zonal Advisory Council at Hamburg which consisted of political and party leaders, officials and trade unionists. In the summer of 1946 British Military Government, frustrated by the grave disadvantages of economic isolation, accepted an American proposal for an economic merger of the two zones, which became effective on 1 January 1947. In retrospect, this move, like earlier moves in the same direction, came to be interpreted as a decision in favour of the partition of Germany, and the Russians certainly saw it in that light, despite the elaborate precautions taken to emphasise the provisional and *ad hoc* nature of the proceedings. In fact the Americans, at least up to 1947, were trying to implement the Potsdam policy, not to evade it: their plans for economic co-ordination, imposed in the first place by sheer necessity, were designed as a step towards the still non-existent central administration of Germany, not as a substitute for it, and ultimately towards the restoration of political unity.[14] In this endeavour the co-operation of both the French and the Russians was invited. Neither accepted: the French because all their efforts were directed against centralisation, the Russians because they were unwilling to follow an American lead. Partly, it appears, through a misunderstanding of the Americans' position, the Russians denounced the latter for sabotaging Potsdam and deliberately splitting Germany – a thesis which soon gained credence from the asperities of the cold war. Though continuing to pay lip-service to Potsdam the Russians had taken many measures in their zone which raised almost insuperable barriers to a uniform treatment of Germany.

While the future of Germany as a nation state became increasingly problematic and controversial, democracy in western Germany began to revive at the grass roots. The results of *Land* and local elections were encouraging. It had been widely expected that the German people, after the Nazi trauma and the shock of defeat, and pre-occupied with pressing material problems, would be apathetic if not cynical towards politics, especially politics under occupation. This was indeed the first impression, but attitudes soon changed. People showed a willingness to vote, and for the moderate parties. There was little sign of extremism. Nearly all the elected state Prime Ministers in the British and American Zones were Christian or Social Democrats. The only exception was Württemberg-Baden, where the government was headed by a Free Democrat. This was Reinhold Maier, one of a number of former parliamentarians who returned to the political arena. The usual pattern of state government was a coalition, which gave stability and helped to reduce party animosity. Only in the French Zone was progress towards self-government deliberately held back. The zone itself was an artificial creation made up of several states, mainly Baden, the Palatinate and southern Württemberg. France's aversion to anything that might conduce to German unity was sometimes carried to absurd lengths, as when the S.P.D. was forced to call itself the S.P.B. (Baden instead of Deutschland). In other respects too the French went their own way. Their German policy, reflecting past fears, was basically a continuation of their age-long attempt to keep Germany weak: the Saar would be annexed by France, the Rhineland and the Ruhr would be detached from the rest of Western Germany, and in what remained the form of government would be one of maximum federalisation. With a large military government staff and their families settled in Baden-Baden, the capital of their zone, the French were in no hurry to align their policy with that of the Anglo-Saxon powers. On some key issues their position was nearer that of the Russians, and there were signs of a Paris-Moscow axis over Germany in contrast to the London-Washington axis, though the Russians were unaware of the extent to which the British and Americans also opposed French demands over the Ruhr and Rhineland. Yet soon the French realised that the balance of power had changed permanently, and they could not ignore the realities of a Europe in which the Red Army was less than a hundred miles from the Rhine. They came to see that a stable and contented Germany was also in their interests, and gradually French resistance to American pressure in favour of tri-zonal co-operation ceased. In return France's western allies gave her a free hand in the Saar, which was treated as no longer part of Germany.

The main reason behind this pressure was Germany's desperate economic situation. Output in 1946 was only a third of the 1936 total. The shortage of food varied in the different zones. It was particularly acute in the highly urbanised British Zone, but also in the French Zone because there the occupiers lived off the land. Conditions in the American Zone were mitigated for many people by the generosity of the occupying army (whose rations were lavish by contemporary European standards) and by the arrival of CARE parcels from the United States (some 16 million of these were sent between 1946 and 1949). Both the British and to a lesser extent the American authorities were worried by the non-arrival of food deliveries from the Russian Zone which were supposed to make possible the balanced economy postulated by the Potsdam conference. The loss of the eastern provinces deprived Germany of her traditional cornlands and even the Russian Zone lacked many essential foodstuffs. The daily ration of 1,550 calories in the British Zone (about half the normal consumption of a west European country) was cut in March 1946 to 1,015 calories. The previous harvest had been below expectations, and the rations could not always be honoured. As Montgomery pointed out in a memorandum to the British government, 1,015 calories was equivalent to slow starvation.[15] An American report found that Hamburg alone had about 10,000 cases of hunger oedema. There were known to be 260,000 cases of tuberculosis in the British Zone and the death rate had risen by more than 50 per cent since 1938.[16] Only 12 per cent of the children in Cologne at the end of 1946 were of normal weight. If the twenty million inhabitants of the British Zone were to have their rations restored to the previous level, food would have to be brought in from outside. Britain herself was short of food, but grain was diverted to Germany at the cost of bread rationing, which even during the war had not been necessary. For the rest, food had to be found overseas. Yet in 1946 less than a third of the cost of imports was balanced by exports. Output of the most important export, coal, had actually fallen after the food cuts, and productivity in the mines was down to less than half the pre-war level.[17] Moreover Germany's prospects of achieving a balance were steadily diminished by Russia's insistence on removing industrial plant as well as current production: the Soviet Union was thus applying those parts of the Potsdam Agreement which suited her and ignoring the others. The result was that, as the Chancellor of the Exchequer told the House of Commons in October 1946, the British were subsidising the German economy;[18] and had they continued to supply the Russian Zone they would have been subsidising the Russians. This could not be allowed to go on. The Americans, though they had no balance of payments problem, also rejected the

Soviets' one-sided implementation of Potsdam. Like the British, they suspended deliveries to the Russian Zone. This gave some relief to the western zones at the cost of worsening relations with Russia, but it was only one of several issues on which East and West were now locked in acrimonious and interminable argument.

Almost as serious as the lack of food, especially during the long and exceptionally hard winter of 1946/47 was the shortage of fuel. The Ruhr was producing little more than a quarter of its pre-war quantity of coal and output would not improve until the miners had better rations. Railway engines, canals and even rivers froze. People cut down trees in city parks and burnt furniture to keep themselves warm, and the railway stations were thronged with children waiting to pilfer coal that fell onto the track. There was also an acute accommodation problem. With six million refugees (a number which was increasing all the time) and five million made homeless through bombing, West Germany was estimated to be short of about six million dwelling units. Tens of thousands of people lived in cellars, in the basements of ruins, in air raid shelters. Much of the best surviving residential housing was requisitioned by the occupation forces and their familes. The shops were empty. It was impossible to buy a reel of cotton, a cake of soap, an electric light bulb or a pane of glass. Apart from the black market, the only means of trading was by barter. Every town had its large notice boards advertising every kind of article for exchange. The black market was dominant. Almost everyone denounced it, but there was hardly anyone who did not make use of it. Even legal denunciations of the black market had to be written on paper obtained from that source, for there was no other; and judges themselves did not scruple to get black market coal. The law of self-preservation was stronger than any legal code. It is estimated that about a third of the consumer goods made by factories found its way to the black market, and the proportion of home-grown food sold there was even greater: considerably less than half of the 1946 harvest was handed over to the authorities for distribution through the ration cards. Since the paper currency was virtually worthless, payment on the black market had to be in cigarettes, though farmers would accept carpets or jewellery in exchange for lard or potatoes.[19] The nominal price of a pound of coffee in Berlin in 1946 was 600 marks, and a pound of butter 300 marks: average wages varied from 200 to 400 marks a month.[20] The source of cigarettes, coffee, chocolate and other luxuries was the occupation forces.[21] A packet of twenty American cigarettes was worth 150 marks or 15 dollars on the black market. A lieutenant who sold his entire cigarette ration could get 12,000 dollars in four months. It is small wonder that the occupation of Germany often had a demoralising effect on the forces themselves. There was practically nothing which cigarettes would not buy, though every time a cigarette changed hands a little of the precious content fell out, and the ultimate consumer – presumably a farmer, perhaps a miner – would certainly not get full weight. A cigarette stub thrown away in the gutter would immediately be pounced on, picked up and carefully preserved. Another familiar sight in those days was of shadowy figures ransacking the dustbins outside military messes for potato peelings or other edible scraps, while hungry workers left their factories to forage on the land. Rubbish dumps were intensively searched for anything of the slightest value. Not since the Thirty Years' War had conditions of life been so miserable. Two years after the war a German exile returning from America painted a gloomy picture of his former fatherland. It was, he wrote,

> a nation irremediably maimed in its biological structure – with a long-term sharp decline of the population inevitable . . . intellectually crippled by the horrors of twelve years of Nazi despotism, by isolation from . . . the outside world . . . morally ruined . . . without food or raw materials . . . a nation whose social fabric has been destroyed by mass flight, mass emigrations, the compulsory mass settlement of strangers . . . in imminent danger of partition between its former Western and Eastern enemies . . . in which there is no guarantee of personal liberty, no habeas corpus and no democracy . . . a country where, amidst hunger and fear, hope has died . . .[22]

Despite some exaggeration, this was broadly a true picture of Germany in 1947. Its gloomiest predictions were not, however, fulfilled. Help was nearer at hand than most people supposed, and Germany was shortly to experience the greatest transformation in its modern history.

(ii) DENAZIFICATION AND THE NUREMBERG TRIALS

One of the most controversial aspects of military government was denazification. The occupying powers had declared many times, and most recently at Potsdam, their intention to destroy National Socialism and eliminate its influence. They were all agreed on that, though, as in other fields, each had its own way of going about it. For if the theory behind the policy was simple, the implementation bristled with difficulties. To begin with, the numbers involved were formidable. There had been eight million members of the Nazi party and an estimated four million belonged to one or other of the affiliated organisations.

The denazification directives ruled that anyone who had been more than a nominal supporter of Nazism would have to be removed from industry, commerce, agriculture and finance as well as from government, education and journalism.[23] (There were not in fact enough qualified people with impeccable political records to take the place of those dismissed: this was one reason why in practice the policy had to be modified.) It was known that not every German was a Nazi, but there seemed no way of telling who was and who was not except by a large-scale inquiry into political attitudes and records. The system used in the British and American Zones was to make almost every adult fill up a questionnaire called a *Fragebogen*. This was a lengthy proforma requiring answers to 131 questions, some of a semi-private nature, and was designed to elicit every scrap of information which might throw light on a person's political past. In the American Zone more than 13 million *Fragebögen* were completed, 3·6 million people were charged, and nearly 800,000 received penalties of varying severity.[24] In the British Zone the numbers of *Fragebögen* were not quite so large, despite its greater population, yet even there 2·1 million people were charged with Nazism, and 156,000 persons were removed from office between May 1945 and September 1946.[25] In the Russian Zone over half a million Nazis or nearly one in thirty of the total population were dismissed, according to official figures. There denazification went by political and economic category rather than by individual conduct. People tended to be penalised if they belonged to suspect classes or groups (landowners, capitalists) which in any case were doomed to liquidation; while ex-Nazis who were willing to work for the new masters were often quite acceptable, and in such a closely supervised authoritarian system were not a security risk, as they might have been in the West.[26] The Russians, more used to purges, were less concerned than the western powers at any lowering of technical or other standards caused by dismissals. In the French Zone less attention was paid to paper directives and the approach was more pragmatic, the difference between Germans and National Socialists being treated as relatively unimportant. The French had some familiarity with the problem through their own experience of collaboration under the Vichy regime; it was also alleged that many members of French Military Government were themselves collaborationists or Fascists.[27] Denazification tended to swing from one extreme to another in the American Zone, where an initial period of witch-hunting was followed by a reversal of policy as embarrassing as it was abrupt. British and American officials soon found themselves faced with vast stacks of *Fragebögen* to be read and evaluated. The Public Safety (police) branch was responsible for this task, yet it was one for which qualifications were often lacking. The British policemen seconded to the Control Commission were no doubt equipped to train the new German police on democratic lines: but few had the linguistic knowledge or familiarity with the political background needed to form a considered judgement on the hundreds of thousands of cases which required special examination. It is small wonder that denazification was soon made a German responsibility, for which special courts of appeal (*Spruchkammern*) were set up, but it was not always easy to find Germans who were suitable and willing to serve. In the American Zone there were at one time 545 tribunals employing a staff of 22,000.[28] Everyone scrutinised had to be placed in one of five catagories: major offender, offender, minor offender, follower, exonerated. Penalties ranged from ten years' imprisonment and forced labour to exclusion from public office, disfranchisement and payment of a fine in the form of a contribution to a fund for the victims of Nazism. Certain categories of people, including very high-ranking party officials, the S.S., S.D. and Gestapo, were subject to automatic arrest and held in camps pending trial. These numbered about 136,000 in the two main western zones in 1945.[29] As we have seen, the total ultimately sentenced varied considerably between one zone and another. Denazification in the west was over by 1950; in the Russian zone it had ended earlier.

The trial of the top party leaders and heads of the regime was conducted on a quadripartite basis at Nuremberg, where a special international court sat from November 1945 to August 1946. The twenty-four accused were tried on one or more of four charges: conspiracy against peace, crimes against peace, violation of the laws and customs of war, crimes against humanity. Twelve received death sentences, seven were given terms of imprisonment and three were acquitted. One man (Ley) took his own life before the trial, another (Göring) after it. Two, Frank, the former governor of Poland, and Baldur von Schirach, the ex-leader of the Hitler Youth, showed contrition. Bormann was sentenced to death *in absentia*. The Nuremberg trials were an innovation in several ways. The victors were sitting in judgement on the vanquished, and provided both prosecutors and judges; and while no one could doubt the appropriateness of demanding retribution for crimes against humanity, the charge of conspiracy to wage war was one which could be brought against other governments than Hitler's; indeed, the British government in 1940 was preparing to invade Norway. Another aspect of the trial which many found objectionable was that the Soviet government, one of the four judges had allegedly committed genocidal crimes like the wholesale murder of Polish officers at Katyn which the Russians unsuccessfully tried to pass off as a Nazi atrocity. Also the methods of justice in Stalin's show trials had not been very different from those of Hitler's People's Court. Moreover, the accused at Nuremberg were being found guilty under a code which had not been drawn up when the crimes were committed. Nevertheless, the Nuremberg trials were generally felt to be justified. There had to be some settlement of accounts for the atrocities committed on so vast a scale and of so barbarous a nature; and the warning to future belligerents was salutary. One important by-product of Nuremberg was the bringing to light of a mass of information about the Third Reich which proved invaluable to historians and filled 42 bulky volumes. It was the first in a long series of trials which involved generals like Manstein charged with mass murder in Russia, industrialists like Alfried Krupp von Bohlen and Halbach (son of Gustav) charged with employing slave labour, S.A. men accused of murdering prisoners, concentration camp guards, doctors in concentration camps who performed medical experiments of ghastly cruelty, and senior officials in the Foreign Ministry and Ministry of Justice who had helped to organise crimes. Altogether about 5,000 people were sentenced, a thousand to death (of whom only 600 were executed) and the rest to prison, from which they were freed by amnesty in the course of the 1950s. With the German recovery of sovereignty responsibility for holding such trials passed to the German authorities. Many suspected war criminals had gone into hiding, some in Germany, others overseas: South America was a favourite destination. Some were traced and brought to trial. The difficulties of catching them are indicated by the fact that a quarter of a century after the end of the war the search for war criminals was still going on and charges were still being brought.

Given the numbers involved and the quantity of data to be processed, denazification was bound to be slow and cumbrous. As General Clay wrote, never before in world history had such a mass undertaking to purge society been attempted.[30] Some objected to it as smacking of collective guilt, which they indignantly repudiated; others criticised denazification as too lenient. Faults were easy to find. The justice meted out was anything but exact, and differed between zone and zone. Many of the Allied officers were personally out of sympathy with the purge, despite the zeal of a minority (often of refugee origin). Refugees usually lacked documents so that their statements could not be corroborated. Although the *Fragebogen* was long and went into what appeared to be unnecessary detail, in some cases it failed to put the pertinent question, for example whether a lawyer had served in one of the Third Reich's special courts. Evaluation of a *Fragebogen* was made more difficult by the addition of bulky supporting documents. A person could have done great service to the Nazi party without having been a member: Heinrich Müller, the Gestapo chief, did not join it until 1939. Conversely a party member might have taken risks to save the lives of Jews or other persecuted persons. As for those who sat on the tribunals, their judgement might easily be affected by personal, political or religious factors, and the opportunities for corruption were obvious. There were examples of denunciations and false depositions. A general criticism was that the small people tended to be penalised while the more important Nazis, who had a better chance of getting away or enjoyed some form of 'protection', escaped justice or were treated lightly. Their cases always took longer to prepare, and they benefited from the growing leniency of the courts. Of the two dangers, that denazification would become a witch hunt and that it would turn into a perfunctory formality if not a farce, the latter was nearer the truth. There was a good deal of whitewashing, and a current joke referred to denazification certificates as Persil vouchers. A caustic critic of the whole process was Ernst von Salomon, one of Germany's most gifted writers, who though a member of the Organisation Consul that had murdered Rathenau and others, never became a Nazi himself. His best-selling novel, *Der Fragebogen*, mocked at the whole denazification procedure as an example of naïve moralism and crude over-simplification. The problem was certainly too complex to be solved by any rule of thumb. In practice too expediency counted for a good deal. There was a strong temptation, not always resisted, to retain specialists whose removal would have brought a loss of efficiency. Further, to leave former active Nazis in posts of responsibility would be to risk sabotage of democracy from within; but to oust them and make them permanently second-class citizens would encourage them to become a subversive element and therefore a source of danger from outside. A compromise had to be found, and with the passing of time a more tolerant attitude could be adopted. Thus a law of 1951 (approved by the occupation authorities) enabled those dismissed from public service and subsequently re-graded as nominal offenders to return to their posts. The alternative of pensioning them off while allowing others to hold their former jobs would have cost a good deal at a time of financial stringency. In the case of the more serious offenders, cold war influences were soon at work. Most Germans refused to believe that those convicted of war crimes, such as Alfried Krupp, would have been amnestied so early in their sentences had the American authorities not wanted to make a gesture to the Germans as their new allies. Such politically motivated clemency did much to confuse the moral issue at stake, and justified a certain cynicism towards the whole procedure. Up to 1947 American Military Government insisted that denazification was a pre-condition of economic recovery; from 1948 onwards the winding up of denazification was declared equally essential.

Despite its obvious inadequacies and contradictions, denazification was an indispensable stage in Germany's new start. It was both a moral imperative and a matter of common sense that the new regime should depend on civil servants, teachers, judges, policemen and journalists who had not actively supported Hitler's ideology. Democracy would never work if the spirit of National Socialism remained. Yet the purge was much less complete than seemed likely at the beginning, especially in the legal profession. Of the 15,000 judges and prosecutors who held office in the Federal Republic in 1950, between two-thirds and three-quarters are estimated to have done so during the Third Reich, and some had certainly been involved in judicial crimes.[31] Even in the Foreign Ministry it was found in 1952 that thirty-nine out of forty senior officials had been Nazis.[32] It was hardly surprising that sometimes the search for war criminals was met with passive resistance on the part of prosecutors and police.[33] Much embarrassment was caused when from time to time, often as the result of information supplied by the East Germans, a high-placed judge or other official was discovered to have an unsavoury record. As late as 1965 the President of the Federal Patents Court in Munich turned out to have sentenced to death a woman in Poland for trying to save the life of an eighteen-months-old Jewish child which was subsequently gassed. The best known, if far from worst case was that of Hans Globke, whom Adenauer kept as his right-hand man despite the fact that Globke had written the legal commentary on the anti-semitic Nuremberg marriage laws of 1935. In the event the retention in office of such people proved morally repugnant rather than politically dangerous, and no doubt many a man who was once a convinced Nazi has served the democratic state faithfully: examples in political life come easily to mind.

Denazification was the substitute for the revolution which Germany never had. It has been argued that it would have been better had the revolution taken place. Should German anti-fascists have dealt with Hitler and his hard core of adherents as the Italian anti-fascists dealt with Mussolini and his entourage? They knew who the worst offenders were and by taking the law into their own hands they could have made a clean sweep and saved the world a lot of trouble. In fact there was no revolutionary mood in Germany at the time. Those (mainly of the upper classes) who might have led a rising had been eliminated in the many arrests which preceded and followed the July 1944 plot. The German population watched with little overt emotion while the Allies liquidated the last vestiges of Hitler's regime. Hitler's mystique did not, for most people, survive his defeat, even if he was more descredited by his failure than by his crimes. The majority of Germans just wanted to forget the recent past and their own part in it: Allied fears of a resistance movement against them proved unfounded. On the contrary: hardly anyone would admit to having been a Nazi in any meaningful sense. This was so well known among the occupation forces that any person who made such a confession was liable to receive ironical congratulations. Many guilt feelings were repressed. At first Allied policy was one of non-fraternisation with the German population. What above all roused opinion against everything German was the discovery and liberation of the concentration camps with their living skeletons, torture chambers, and mass graves. Buchenwald was visited by a British parliamentary delegation. Journalists wrote descriptions of Dachau, Belsen and the other notorious camps. Exhibitions were held, photographs published. The Germans professed to be equally shocked and surprised. They had known of the existence of concentration camps, but not of what went on inside them. This argument was not always credible; for example, the village of Bergen-Belsen lies between the railway station and the camp so that the prisoners going from the one to the other must have been noticed by the villagers. The mayors and other leading citizens of Celle and other towns in the neighbourhood of Belsen were forced by the British authorities to see the horror for themselves. The Americans did the same at Dachau and a film about that camp was forcibly shown to the German public.[34] Later the Nuremberg trials gave world-wide publicity to the incredible details of crimes, which had caused something like twelve million civilian deaths besides those killed as combatants. Yet it should not be forgotten that Hitler's apparatus of terror was originally set up for his fellow countrymen. Some 200,000 Germans (not counting Jews) suffered in Nazi concentration camps.

Denazification was necessarily a negative process. The positive aspect of post-war policy was summed up in the word 're-education'. This had a priggish ring about it, especially when propounded by foreigners in uniform, however well meaning. Yet there could be no doubt that a radical change was needed. Thomas Mann in his novel *Dr. Faustus*, perhaps the most profound response of any writer to the tragedy of National Socialism, depicts Hitler as the devil with whom Germany, like Faust, makes a pledge which leads to perdition. He describes her in the war as 'reeling, a hectic flush on her cheeks, at the height of barren triumphs, about to conquer the world through a pact which she means to keep and had signed with her heart's blood. Today (in 1945) girt round with demons, a hand over one eye and with the other staring into horrors, she plunges from despair to despair . . .' A socialist pamphlet written during the war declared that the re-education of the German people must be the task of Germans.[35] And there were millions of German democrats willing to undertake this. It was not forgotten, even at Nuremberg, that Hitler had come to power on a minority vote: there was no question of indicting the whole nation. Nevertheless it was not possible in the early stages to leave re-education to the Germans. They were too uncertain of themselves and lacked the means. Germany after the war was a cultural as well as a physical desert, cut off from the rest of the world by its former rulers and now shunned as a pariah. It was true that it had a democratic tradition, but the experience of democracy under Weimar had been unhappy, and the precedent was discouraging. German isolation had to be broken down, so far as the meagre funds allowed, by visits to and from foreign countries, by the renewal of contacts at many levels, by the exchange of literature and the gradual resumption of normal relations. Visits were arranged through the occupation authorities with institutions of all kinds: churches, youth organisations, schools, town councils, trade unions. Education Branch of Military Government initiated the new outlook in schools and universities. It was in this field and in local government that the Control Commission did its most constructive work and where – at least in the British Zone – relations of mutual confidence developed between the occupying officials and their German opposite numbers.[36] A search was made for non-Nazi specialists who had been deposed by Hitler and could now be reappointed: thus Adolf Grimme, a Social Democrat who had been Minister of Education in Prussia before 1933, became Minister of Education in Lower Saxony. New textbooks were provided to replace Nazi ones, especially in history. Discussion groups were started and courses were run for teachers, youth workers and others. In England successful courses had been held for prisoners of war at Wilton Park, near Beaconsfield, and elsewhere. Later, the Wilton Park centre moved to new quarters in Sussex and developed as a residential college to which parties of Germans and later other Europeans were invited to study democratic institutions and develop contacts with British people in many fields. Inside Germany newspapers and broadcasting, operating under licence, made a new start. Among the more influential newspapers were Axel Springer's *Die Welt*, published in Hamburg and probably the nearest to a national newspaper in the Federal Republic, and the American-sponsored *Neue Zeitung* in Munich. Publishers reprinted books banned by Hitler, and imported books were in great demand. As newspapers were at first hardly obtainable, information centres where people could sit and read them were opened by Military Government. Some of these were later developed into cultural centres with libraries and other facilities, such as cinemas and exhibition halls, in order to promote Anglo-German and international meetings and exchanges. They were known as *Brücken* (Bridges) and were considered of sufficient value to receive German financial support in later years, while some were taken over by the British Council. The Americans, who launched their re-orientation programme strangely late in the day, had their equivalent in the *America Houses* which were to be found in every sizeable town. The French had their *Maisons de France* which laid less emphasis on the workings of democracy than on art and culture. They were particularly successful in attracting intellectuals and artists. The Russians too did much to woo the intelligentsia, but as the cold war developed their propaganda was increasingly marked by a heavily didactic tone, crude stereotypes and a grossly over-simplified black and white (or red and white) picture of the world. Indoctrination in Communism was explicit in the whole educational programme of their zone, in its entire *Kulturpolitik*. East Berlin had its own Russian centre, later re-named the Central House of German-Soviet Friendship, which presented the Soviet Union as the leader of the world peace movement and mentor of all progressive forces in Germany as well as the champion of the workers and model of socialism. This was the former Prussian Ministry of Finance, an elegant classical building in Unter den Linden, where the usual portraits of Marx and Lenin, garnished with red flags, looked down on an interior of crimson plush and heavy Victorian-like drapery. The East German government made special efforts to influence intellectuals, and all 'progressive' writers were invited to join the Communist-sponsored 'Cultural Association for the Democratic Renewal of Germany' (*Kulturbund*), which also operated in West Germany. By the end of 1946 it had over 60,000 members.[37] It was the anti-fascist front in cultural form. East Berlin also made a point of inviting German writers in exile to return, especially if they had left-wing sympathies. Heinrich Mann was on the point of leaving California for East Berlin (where he was to become President of the East German Writers' Association) when he died. Leon Feuchtwanger expressed sympathy but stayed in America. The significance of Brecht's return to East Berlin in 1949 is discussed elsewhere.

Two well-known German intellectuals made important contributions to the debate on what had gone wrong with Germany and what should be done about it. The first was Meinecke's *The German Catastrophe*, an essay in which the grand old man of German historiography surveyed his country's history since unification. Historical post-mortems after the First World War had usually put the blame on William II, whose irresponsible sabre-rattling had isolated Germany and led her into a disastrous war such as Bismarck would have avoided. Revising his own earlier views, Meinecke concluded in 1945 that the seeds of the future disaster actually lay in the policy of Bismarck, who had imposed on the Reich an authoritarian and militarist structure and mentality, and had kept Germany politically retarded. The re-assessment of recent German history initiated by Meinecke has been going on ever since, with fruitful results. Fritz Fischer with his massive study of German war aims during the First World War has not only added greatly to our knowledge of the subject but has reopened a debate on the origins of the war which many historians had considered closed.[38] What is most significant about this and similar revaluations is not just the new evidence offered and its interpretation but the objectivity shown and the absence of any attempt to whitewash or apologise. The contrast between this attitude – and Fischer at times seems to go out of his way to place the least favourable construction on Bethmann Hollweg – and the defensive approach of many German historians after the First World War is revealing. Indeed, a leading historian, Ludwig Dehio, in an essay published in 1950 admitted that reticence in dealing frankly with pre-1914 German imperialism was due not only to the general belief (far from unique to Germany) that the historian's task was to strengthen national consciousness, but to unwillingness to supply Germany's ex-enemies with compromising or incriminating material. The decline of nationalism since 1945 has thus been of direct benefit to historical scholarship. An equal detachment is also characteristic of the numerous studies of the Nazi regime and of the origins of the Second World War by the younger historians. The other notable contribution to the post-1945 debate was a study of the guilt question by the philosopher Karl Jaspers. He distinguished between criminal guilt (a matter for the courts), moral guilt (a matter for the individual's conscience), metaphysical guilt (which depended on one's beliefs about human existence), and political guilt, which rested on the whole German nation. Jaspers rejected the notion of collective guilt, as currently understood, but said that every citizen who had failed to react against the crimes of the Nazi regime bore some share of responsibility for them. Theodor Heuss coined the phrase 'collective shame' to describe this. It was Heuss too who summed up the situation of his people in 1945 as being simultaneously liberated and destroyed. Re-education was basically an attempt to make sense of the liberation while coming to terms with the other consequences of Adolf Hitler.

(iii) BIZONIA AND THE BERLIN BLOCKADE

1947 was a year of diplomatic revolution. The wartime alliance between Russian and the western powers was in ruins, and nothing of the wartime cameraderie remained. Meetings between East and West foreign ministers failed to reach agreement on the German problem; indeed, the gulf between the two sides actually widened. Hopes of post-war co-operation changed to disillusion. The Allies could no longer disguise from themselves the extent to which they had been duped over Poland. In many parts of the world – the Far East, Persia, Turkey, Greece – Communist forces were pressing forward against weak defences to extend Stalin's empire. In France and Italy large Communist parties were striving for power and threatening industrial sabotage. President Truman pledged support for free peoples resisting subjugation, and accepted responsibility for the defence of Greece and Turkey. In Germany quadripartite policy broke down before it was enunciated: even prior to Potsdam the Russians were treating their zone as their own property and converting it into a satellite. Stalin was putting into practice what he had told Djilas in June 1944: 'This war is not like past wars: whoever occupies a territory also imposes on it his own social system. Everyone imposes on it his own social system as far as his army can reach. It cannot be otherwise.'[39] It was an ironic solution for a Europe which, a quarter of a century before, had been re-modelled on lines of self-determination. In America people were beginning to read the signals: one congressman as early as December 1945 described Russia as 'a predatory aggressor nation which was following the same fateful road of conquest and aggression with which Adolf Hitler set the world on fire'.[40] In Western Germany the continued influx of refugees from the East clearly made it impossible to go on implementing the Potsdam de-industrialisation programme without depressing the standard of living below what was tolerable, and hampering the recovery of the rest of Europe, which, it was now agreed, depended on that of Germany. This was, indeed, the main conclusion of the Hoover Report on the Food Situation in Europe commissioned by President Truman. As Ernest Bevin, the British Foreign Secretary, told the House of Commons: 'We have . . . a major interest in seeing that Germany does not become a permanent distressed area in the centre of Europe, and that the Germans should have a proper and reasonable standard of living.'[41] No one doubted that a German population reduced to misery and despair would be a prey to communism, and there was good reason to believe that this was part of the Russians' design. While the programme of denazification and demilitarisation should continue, the view was now taken that Germany must be allowed to keep enough peaceful industry to pay its own way and contribute to the rebuilding of Europe.

The first public announcement of the new policy came from James

F. Byrnes, the American Secretary of State, in a speech at Stuttgart in September 1946 before a mixed American-German audience. Byrnes made three main points. Firstly, American troops would stay in Europe indefinitely. Secondly, to enable the west German zones to develop a self-sustaining economy steps must be taken to let them function as a single unit. This should be done initially through the merging of the American and British Zones and the setting up of bizonal agencies to carry out a common financial and industrial policy. The level of industry would be adjusted upwards to compensate for the difficulties caused by the collapse of quadripartite policy. Thirdly, Byrnes declared that the German people must be given a greater measure of self-government, and he spoke of their winning back an honourable place among the free and peace-loving nations of the world. At the time they were spoken these were bold words, and they came to the millions of Germans who heard or read them as the first glimmer of dawn after a long, dark night. Their moral impact was incalculable. The British were more cautious than the Americans about restoring German self-government, but even in the British Zone many functions originally performed by Military Government, like public utilities, were already being handed back to the German authorities. Indeed the British Control Commission, which was considerably bigger than the American, began to shed staff almost before it had stopped recruiting it. The British government agreed to co-operate in the formation of a new entity known as Bizonia. Though neither zone was economically viable, the merger helped the British in two respects: it ensured that more food was available from the agricultural south for the industrial north, and also that, to the great relief of the British balance of payments, food imports to Germany would be paid for in American dollars. Bizonia, which came into existence on 1 January 1947 had important implications in the political field. In Frankfurt, its unofficial capital, there was soon in session an elected economic council of 52 (later 104) chosen from members of the eight state parliaments with an executive council as a sort of presiding cabinet. To this was attached a bi-zonal civil service divided into five departments (in effect shadow ministries) for economics, finance, agriculture, post and transport. Although both Social and Christian Democrats were represented on the Economic Council in equal numbers, the Executive Council did not turn out to be the coalition which most people expected. For the S.P.D. Schumacher insisted on boycotting it on the grounds that opposition was preferable to compromise.[42] The executive thus came to consist entirely of Christian Democrats and their allies. Schumacher's decision was a tactical mistake since it enabled his rival, Adenauer, to seize the initiative and shape policy. The Executive Council became in effect the shadow government of the C.D.U. Care was taken to emphasise that the whole structure was provisional, and not an attempt to divide Germany or repudiate the Potsdam agreements. There was no desire, least of all on the German side, to give Russia an excuse for further unilateral acts or for hardening the zonal frontier. It was a rescue operation for a bankrupt economy which had to absorb an unprecedented mass of expellees and refugees, and the western hope was that a prosperous West Germany would act as a magnet to the East – a hope that was to be partially fulfilled in a way not foreseen. There was no deliberate intention to break up Germany. Yet after the failure of the Moscow four-power conference in 1947, to which the internal parallel was the negative outcome of an all-German state prime ministers' meeting at Munich, the growing divergence of the two parts of the country could no longer be ignored. Events strengthened the determination of the American and British governments to proceed with their own plans for the future of Germany. Though both sides continued to profess their attachment to the principle of German unity proclaimed at Potsdam, their actions spoke a different language. The split was particularly sharp in Berlin, where East and West officials were in daily friction and the ingredients of a civil war were already present.

After the hard winter of 1946/47 the West German economy showed a slow improvement. Its productive capacity was greater than outward devastation suggested: even in the much bombed Ruhr it was estimated that only 30 per cent of plant and machinery had been damaged beyond repair.[43] The first Hanover trade fair in August 1947 gave a surprising indication of what could be produced – for export (or the black market); virtually none of the goods displayed could be bought in the shops. In June 1947 Secretary of State Marshall made his famous Harvard speech offering economic help to the war-stricken countries, including Germany. This promised injection of capital was just what the German economy needed, and acted as a psychological boost long before it actually arrived. To prepare the ground it was necessary to strengthen the bi-zonal economic organisation. The Economic Council doubled its numbers and the Executive Council was replaced by a Council of States, while the civil service departments were also expanded. A new director of the Economic Administration was elected – Ludwig Erhard, a professor of economics who had been the first post-war Minister of Economics in Bavaria. The effect of these changes was twofold: the bi-zonal executive was given more authority over the states, while more power passed into its hands from the Allied controllers. A revised Level of Industry Plan raised the permissible ceiling from 50 – 55 per cent to 70 – 75 per cent of the 1938 level. A new institution, the *Bank deutscher Länder*, was set up as the central bank of Western Germany, later re-named the *Deutsche Bundesbank*. In an economic sense Germany was already practising a limited form of self-government, and had acquired a quasi-parliamentary structure that in many ways served as a model for the forthcoming federal republic. The next step was currency reform, which was long overdue, and had been discussed by the occupying powers since 1946. Here, as in other matters, delay was imposed by the inability to reach agreement with the Russians. After the failure of the foreign ministers' meeting in Moscow in December 1947 at which the Russians even raised their terms, the western powers decided to go it alone. Early in 1948 the French agreed at last to merge their zone for economic purposes with the other two western zones, so that 'Bizonia' became 'Trizonia'. Germany formally became a member of the Organisation for European Economic Co-operation set up in Paris to handle Marshall Aid, an important step in her political as well as economic rehabilitation. The reform of currency took place on a Sunday, 20 June. The population was allowed to change only 60 old marks (RM) for the same number of new marks (DM) at the rate of one for one: of these forty could be exchanged at once, the remainder two months later. Savings and bank accounts were subject to a different rate: 6.50 DM for every 100 RM. The bank of issue was the *Bank deutscher Länder*, which was allowed to circulate notes up to the value of 10 milliard new marks. The effect on the economy was electrifying. Next day, as if by magic, astonishing quantities of goods appeared in shop windows, the cigarette lost its value as a substitute currency and with the return of confidence people even began to save.

The point had been reached at which a decision had to be taken about future economic policy. The controlled economy inherited from the Third Reich with rationing and wage and price controls still existed in theory; in practice it had broken down, replaced by the black market. The Social Democrats wished the expansion made possible by currency reform to take place within a centrally planned economy in which these regulations or many of them would remain in force. Any return to unrestrained competition was in their eyes unthinkable. At first the Christian Democrats seemed to share this view, for in its programme drawn up at Ahlen in February 1947 the party declared in favour of nationalising the coal and steel industries. This reflected the thinking of the Christian trade unions which formed the left wing of the C.D.U. and was designed to eliminate the 'danger of state authority succumbing to the unlawful influences of concentrated economic power'.[44] Memories of the great depression and of capitalist support for Hitler combined with post-war radicalism to favour this course. Allied insistence on de-cartelisation reinforced the trend, while leaving open the question whether the alternative to cartels was more public ownership or more competition. Yet by the summer of 1949 the C.D.U. had become, almost as much as the F.D.P., a party of free enterprise. This change was due partly to Adenauer, who, pragmatic though he was on many issues, was consistently antisocialist, but even more to Erhard, who as Director of the Bizonal Economic Administration held one of the most important posts then occupied by a German. The switch in C.D.U. policy was epoch-making. Almost the whole trend of economic thinking and practice since 1914 had been in favour of increasing state control and higher government expenditure. That classical liberalism would enjoy a spectacular revival and that German recovery would become a triumph for free enterprise was a surprise that few would have predicted. Yet in a policy speech made in April 1948 in anticipation of currency reform Erhard announced the end of controls and the adoption of an experiment in freedom. He was convinced that, given adequate incentives, industrial output, financed by Marshall Aid, would expand to meet demand, and he relied on competition, a high degree of unemployment and a tight credit policy to prevent prices from soaring. A similar policy had been successfully tried out in Italy by the Liberal minister Einaudi, and also in post-war Belgium: all the same, it was a daring move on Erhard's part. Immediately after currency reform the statutory limitations on prices and wages were removed, though in practice decontrol came in stages and controls remained for some time to come on such necessities as coal, steel, flour and bread, electric power and housing. Erhard described his system as a *social* market economy (a phrase coined by a professor of economics at Münster University) because public resources were used for social ends. Those who had suffered little materially in the war, for example, paid a special tax to compensate those who had lost everything (the 'equalisation of burdens'). But Erhard insisted that the key to the production of wealth was the maximum use of individual effort and skill, and to encourage this the profit motive had to be recognised and made respectable again. Erhard also saw to it that Marshall Aid was used not to finance a consumer spree, but to rebuild the productive sectors of the economy such as power stations and transport, and to boost exports. Thus the foundations of future prosperity were laid. The rapid progress made by the Federal Republic from June 1948 onwards vindicated Erhard's judgement and faith. Industrial production rose by 50 per cent in the second half of 1948 and by 75 per cent in 1949. Shortages soon disappeared. Food rationing ended while it was still in force in

Britain. The economic miracle soon became a cliché, but is no exaggeration. By 1953 living standards were higher than they had been in 1938. Thanks to the Federal Republic's favourable balance of payments, the mark became one of the soundest currencies in Europe. All this helped to boost German confidence and restore self-respect. The one blot on the economy was the persistent unemployment (two million in 1950) but this was largely due to external factors such as – initially – Allied dismantling, the return of prisoners of war and the continued inflow of refugees. Unemployment fell below 3 per cent for the first time in 1959, and during the sixties was running at less than 1 per cent. A remarkable feature of the German recovery was the speed with which the small businessman, shopkeeper or entrepreneur built up enough capital to expand his business. The people worked hard, and their efforts were rewarded. At first the trade unions were far from happy about the new policy, but they rarely took a militant line, and the co-management legislation (see p. 519) was a substantial concession to left-wing demands. Adenauer's good relations with Hans Boeckler, the chairman of the General Trade Unions, were of some importance, and gradually the Socialists too accepted the neo-liberal economy. Although American Military Government was officially neutral, most Americans concerned with the running of Germany made no secret of their preference for free enterprise. Indeed Washington's intervention was needed to block German plans for nationalising the Ruhr coal industry in 1947, for which there was a majority in the North Rhine-Westphalia parliament, and some backing from the British Labour government. The latter, including the minister for Germany, J. B. Hynd, was naturally inclined to support the German Socialists. But Bevin, the British Foreign Secretary, was far from doctrinaire, and his dependence on American goodwill in many fields led him to accept American leadership in Germany. Apart from Britain's responsibilities as an occupying power in Germany, her mood was rather isolationist: this was reflected in her refusal to take part in the Coal and Steel Community and in the Common Market which developed from it.

The Russians watched the gradual build-up of Western Germany with unconcealed hostility. The soviet-controlled press in Berlin and the eastern zone was already pouring out a stream of anti-American invective, accusing the United States officials, including General Clay, the Military Governor, of imperialism and exploitation.[45] A favourite allegation was that the German forces in the West had never been properly disbanded. The American capital helping West German industry to recover was described as a sinister intervention by Wall Street interests, and the Marshall Plan was condemned as an attempt to turn Germany into an American colony. (In fact Germany received less than half as much as France or Britain per head.) The bombing of Dresden, to which the Russians had certainly not objected at the time, was denounced by S.E.D. propaganda as a horrifying example of Anglo-American imperialism, and political capital was even made out of the trial by a British military court of Field-Marshal Manstein for war crimes committed in Russia.[46] The atmosphere in the Allied Control Council became more and more acrimonious, and this was reflected in the *Kommandantura*, the four-power control body for the city of Berlin. The main difficulty arose from the Russians' insistence on treating Berlin as the capital of their zone and applying to it the same totalitarian methods. Their intention was to establish a Communist dictatorship in the city as well as in the zone and to dominate the municipal government, the *Magistrat*, by a mixture of propaganda and intimidation. The problem for the three western commandants was how to preserve the façade of Allied unity while preventing the Russians from taking over the city against the wishes of its inhabitants. For what the Berliners wanted was clearly shown in the first post-war elections held in October 1946. The result was a decisive victory for the Social Democrats, who received nearly half the votes cast and over twice as many as the Communists (S.E.D.), who came behind the Christian Democrats. This was a great moral blow to the Russians and virtually proved that, had the elections in the Russian Zone been free, they would not have been won by the Communists. The Socialists emerged clearly as the Communists' successful rival, and within the S.P.D. a new personality, Ernst Reuter, stood out as leader of the group most determined to assert its rights. As a socialist and a prisoner of war in Russia during the First World War, Reuter had seen the revolution at first hand and been converted to communism. After returning to Germany, he became general secretary of the K.P.D., but a year later rejoined the Social Democrats. He had experienced the disillusion which drove many left-wing idealists out of the Communist party, whose successive purges discouraged all but the cynics and the opportunists. He played a comparatively minor part in Weimar politics, but rose to be mayor of Magdeburg and in 1932 became a member of the Reichstag. Reuter left Germany when Hitler came to power to take up a teaching post at Istanbul University, where he remained throughout the war. Returning to Berlin in 1946, he quickly saw what was at stake and supplied a leadership his party needed. Knowing their man, the Russians vetoed his appointment as lord mayor, though they had to allow another Social Democrat, Frau Luise Schröder, to hold office. The political division of Berlin now began, inasmuch as the S.P.D., already banned in the Russian Zone, was virtually prevented from functioning in the Russian sector of the city. The city hall, where the *Magistrat* met, was in that sector and therefore subject to every kind of physical and psychological pressure.

When on 20 March 1949 Sokolovsky, the Russian Commander-in-Chief, angrily walked out of the Allied Control Council for the last time, it was a clear sign of impending trouble. Nor was there much doubt as to the form it would take. Berlin was the Allies' Achilles heel. All their supplies came by the rail and road links from western Germany; and there was no written agreement with the Russians about the use of routes, though in the American understanding non-interference with communications with Berlin had been a condition precedent to the withdrawal of Allied troops from the Russian Zone in the summer of 1945.[47] By removing one sleeper from the railway or a single plank from the temporary bridge over the river Elbe the Russians could claim technical reasons for the hold-up of traffic. The harassment of trains and lorries began in the spring of 1948. At first it was a creeping blockade. The immediate subject of dispute was the currency to be used in West Berlin. Since its economy depended on the West, the introduction of the new west mark would have been logical. But the western authorities decided against it to avoid the complication of two currencies circulating in one city. The Russians insisted that all Berlin have the same currency as they were introducing into their zone. The allies were in an impasse; for while they did not want to yield to Russian pressure, they were almost equally unwilling to split the city. One possible solution was to accept the Russian currency provided that the western powers had a share in its issue. This the Russians refused. It was clear that the West could not allow the Russian marks to circulate in their sectors of Berlin, economically because it would place the economy of West Berlin under Russian control, politically because it would symbolise Russian sovereignty over the whole city. The Russians claimed that West Berlin was really a part of their zone, but this was contrary to the original protocol on zonal borders drawn up by the European Advisory Commission in September 1944.[48] Of greater practical importance was the fact that since they had begun their occupation of the twelve West Berlin boroughs in July 1945 the western powers had been responsible for feeding their two million inhabitants. A certain amount of food was imported from the surrounding Russian Zone, and for electricity West Berlin depended on power stations in the eastern sector. Now all this was cut off. The Allied garrisons and Military Governments could if necessary be provisioned by air, but what of the civilian population? When the total blockade of West Berlin began, the city contained food and fuel for six weeks.[49] The decision to risk the blockade instead of giving up Berlin was not an easy one for the western powers to make, for no one knew just how long the city could hold out with the help of airborne supplies. It was a policy that required faith and a strong nerve. The Allies had 6,500 troops in West Berlin against Russian totals of 18,000 in East Berlin and 300,000 in the East Zone.

It was General Clay, encouraged by the American commandant Colonel Howley, and strongly supported by Reuter, soon to be Lord Mayor, who persuaded a hesitating American government to accept the Soviet challenge. Clay realised from a conversation with Sokolovsky soon after the beginning of the blockade that the currency issue was not decisive for the Russians:[50] their real purpose was to make things so uncomfortable for the Allies that they would either withdraw from Berlin or preferably abandon their plans, already taking shape, for a West German government. Berlin was thus a trial of the West's determination to defend its rights, an issue on which more than the future of one city depended. Clay saw the Russian blockade of Berlin as part of a general strategy of aggression: the Communists had seized power in Prague a few weeks before, a threat to Norway was reported, the situation before the Italian general election was critical. If the West gave up Berlin, would it, in the view of repercussions, be able to hold West Germany? Clay's own belief was that the Russians would not push the Berlin quarrel to the point of war; they were testing their opponents to see how far they could go. In his own words:

> The care with which the Russians avoided measures which would have been resisted with force had convinced me that the Soviet government did not want war although it believed that the western allies would yield much of their position rather than risk war.[51]

Clay accordingly proposed to his government the despatch of an armed convoy on the motor road to Berlin equipped with engineering material to overcome any technical difficulties. The proposal was not accepted. What would have happened if it had been, it is impossible to say. The psychological effect of such a move might have induced the Russians to change their tactics. One cannot be sure. In the event, the Americans and British broke the blockade by stepping up air deliveries to West Berlin. The airlift provided a remarkable success. A third airport was built in the French sector, and the amount of freight brought in daily rose as the months went by from a few hundred tons to 8,000 tons. By the end of the blockade, in the spring of 1949, nearly 1,400 aircraft landed in a single day.[52] The worst period was the winter, when coal was very short and the average household had a coal ration of 25 lbs a month and electricity or gas for only two periods of two hours in twenty-four, one of which might be in the middle of the night. People sat shivering in their kitchens by candle light. Trees and furniture were burnt for fuel. Public transport was severely curtailed and many small businesses had to close down. Unemployment rose to 150,000. But morale held, and less than $2\frac{1}{2}$ per cent of West Berlin's inhabitants crossed over to the East to draw the rations offered there.[53] Berliners felt a new pride, and a new solidarity developed between them and the Allies, who were protectors as well as occupiers. A monument was built near the Tempelhof airport to commemorate the 79 pilots and ground staff (American, British and German) who lost their lives in the operation. Berlin was now a symbol of liberty; its inhabitants, wrote Clay, 'had earned their right to freedom; they had atoned for their failure to repudiate Hitler when such repudiation on their part might have stopped his rise to power'.[54] (In fact, even in March 1933 less than one Berliner in three had voted for Hitler, almost the lowest proportion of any large town in Germany.)[55] One inevitable consequence of the blockade was completion of the long threatened split in the city government. The Russians walked out of the *Kommandantura*, and through their henchmen, the S.E.D., they made it impossible for the *Magistrat* to function. The S.P.D. mayor and her colleagues were forced to quit the city hall and take up new headquarters in the town hall of Schöneberg, a borough in the American sector. Reuter replaced Luise Schröder as Lord Mayor of West Berlin, after an election which gave two-thirds of the votes to the S.P.D. (In East Berlin the Lord Mayor's office was held by Friedrich Ebert, the Communist son of the former German President.) In 1950 West Berlin received a new constitution. While legally it remained (as it still is) occupied territory, in practice it had the status of a semi-autonomous city state, and the burgomaster, known henceforth as the Governing Mayor, was more like a prime minister than the head of a municipality.

By the spring of 1949 the Russians showed signs of wanting to call off the blockade, which had failed of its purpose and was damaging the economy of their zone, for the West in retaliation had stopped supplies of coal and steel. After conversations between Russians and Americans in New York, traffic to and from Berlin was allowed through and life in the city gradually returned to what was then normality. With the introduction of the new west mark West Berlin's economy was closely geared to that of West Germany and began to share in its prosperity. Special measures had to be taken to revive industry and trade and reduce unemployment, which had been high: Marshall Aid was used, but also a substantial subsidy from the

Federal Republic was needed. A massive rebuilding programme was soon under way. With the return of confidence Berlin recovered some of its old gaiety and liveliness, and even the Kurfürstendamm regained much of its former glamour. As the frontline city in the cold war, it became a show window of the West with its virtues and defects, but the latter seemed unimportant by comparison with the sense of security and the invigorating effects of economic aid. West Berlin was very conscious of its new role and was for years the only part of the free world which could be visited by people from the other side of the Iron Curtain. The annual cultural festival inaugurated in West Berlin reflected its desire to keep alive its own vigorous artistic traditions as well as to raise morale and impress the outside world. No longer a capital, West Berlin was important as an island of democracy, a haven for refugees (not only from East Germany) a listening post for those studying the Communist world and a centre for broadcasting and propaganda to it. These advantages also made it an important centre for spies of both East and West. The effect of the blockade on the Russians and their East German satellite was to encourage the separate development of the latter, with the status of West Berlin somewhat grudgingly accepted and petty harassment of its communications occurring from time to time. In theory the Communists still favoured a united Germany and denounced western 'separatism'.[56] Grotewohl declared in July 1948: 'Our party [the S.E.D.] with the help of the Soviet Union will unite Germany.' Such appeals never had much credibility; once the West German state was an accomplished fact they had none at all.

Yet for many West Berliners relief over the end of the siege was tinged with disappointment at the failure or inability of the western powers to place the status of West Berlin beyond doubt by making it a part of the emerging Federal Republic. This was actually the solution proposed by Reuter but rejected by the Allies on the grounds that it would have contravened the four-power agreement.[57] The quadripartite policy was now hardly more than a fiction; the only extant examples of it were the Air Safety centre, the Spandau Prison, where those convicted at Nuremberg were serving their sentences, and the Allied right of entry into East Berlin. Still there were advantages in not disturbing Russia's latent rights, as the successful revival of four-power diplomacy leading to the Berlin agreement of 1971 showed. Moreover the alternative policy of incorporating Berlin into West Germany was physically impossible because of its geographical separation by over a hundred miles of hostile territory. Fresh difficulties of access were to arise when the Soviet Union tried to substitute East Germany for itself as the power controlling the traffic routes. There

was no doubt some truth in the accusation made against Adenauer
that he felt little attachment to a city of such different traditions, and
one which politically sided with the opposition. Yet in practice West
Berlin has been treated very much as if it belonged to the Federal
Republic. It is part of the same legal, economic and financial system,
it shares in its social welfare and continues to receive a federal subsidy
which has helped to reduce unemployment. Its trade is almost exclusively with the West. Berlin's representatives have seats (though
without voting rights) in the *Bundestag* and *Bundesrat* at Bonn, and
Berliners have West German passports. The Federal President has an
official residence in West Berlin, and his election has taken place there
in a ceremony intended to symbolise Berlin's importance as Germany's
past and prospective future capital.[58] Berlin's isolation, especially since
the building of the Wall in 1961, has given rise to understandable
pessimism about its future. Each successive change in its status and
every hardening of the division of Germany has lessened the prospect
of its becoming the capital of a reunited Germany, at least in the
forseeable future. In many ways the former world-city has inevitably
acquired something of a provincial character. And although West
Berlin's economic recovery since the blockade has been impressive,
with industrial output rising from 1.8 billion marks in 1950 to 24
billion marks in 1971, for many years it has had an ageing population.
Only since the 1960s has the decline in population been reversed
thanks to an annual immigration which now includes a high proportion of young people under the age of 25.[59] How far the other difficulties of its insular position will be removed by the agreement signed
in 1971 remains to be seen. For three-quarters of a century Berlin was
the capital of the Reich. For another quarter of a century West Berlin
was a beleaguered fortress in the cold war. The role which now seems
indicated for it is that of a meeting place between East and West, a
city of international congresses. Much depends on how the Communist
countries and East Germany in particular actually carry out their
undertakings.

(iv) THE MAKING OF THE FEDERAL REPUBLIC

The Berlin blockade was one of several developments which led the
three western powers to a new initiative in the German question. The
failure of the four-power conference on Germany in London in
December 1947 following the breakdown of earlier talks in Moscow
at last convinced the governments in London, Paris and Washington
that they must act without the Russians if any coherent policy was to
be applied in Germany. Russian purposes were obviously incompatible

with theirs. A meeting in London was held in March 1948 of British, American and French ministers together with representatives of Belgium, Holland and Luxembourg. There it was announced that the basis must be laid for the participation of a democratic Germany in the community of free peoples. This was a diplomatic way of stating the intention to set up a West German state. It was an implicit acknowledgement that the Potsdam agreement was a dead letter. It was still less than three years since the end of the Third Reich, and even two years earlier the idea of re-creating an independent German state so soon would have seemed out of the question. But the cold war had brought about a complete reappraisal of western policy: henceforth it was a matter of propping Germany up rather than holding her down. There was also a growing sense of urgency, especially in Washington. The Truman doctrine of 'containing' Russia meant the strengthening of Western Europe, which implied a reasonably prosperous Germany. A democratic Germany could be integrated into Europe to their mutual benefit. The closing of ranks against the threat from the East was exemplified militarily in the defence treaty of Dunkirk in which seven nations joined, and economically in the Organisation for European Economic Co-operation which combined sixteen nations, including West Germany, in the European Recovery programme. The newly formed Council of Europe meeting at Strasbourg embodied the hopes of many people who desired a closer alignment between national policies and a move towards a united Europe. This ideal had a powerful appeal for many young Germans, who needed a substitute for the discredited gods of nationalism and sought reconciliation with former enemies. The success of the quasi-parliamentary experiment in Bizonia indicated that the Germans were ripe for the next stage on the road to full self-government. On 9 June 1948 the three military governors called upon the ministers of the West German states to convene a constituent assembly.

German reactions were mixed. On the one hand there was a natural wish to throw off Allied tutelage and recover independence; on the other, a reluctance to take steps that might perpetuate the division of their country and prejudice its eventual reunification. There was also some misgiving about the wisdom of accepting the limited sovereignty now offered and some questioning of the validity of a constitution and a state formed under these conditions. But the Russian threat to Berlin and the need to make some political progress, even of a limited kind, removed many doubts. On balance the view prevailed that it would be a mistake to let the opportunity pass. And whereas the Social Democrats led by Schumacher showed the greatest hesitation, it was Reuter of their party who, speaking from his experience in Berlin, reminded them that, whether they liked it or not, the partition of Germany was an accomplished fact. The state Prime Ministers finally told the Allies that they would like a Parliamentary Council (a committee of the state parliaments) to meet and draw up a Basic Law.

The belief was that a decision taken by a parliamentary assembly would be less binding than one supported by a popular referendum, and that a 'Basic Law' would have a less permanent character than a formal constitution. (For similar reasons Bonn, not Frankfurt, the most likely choice, was selected as the capital of the new state.) In the event the difference was one of words only, though the final clause of the Basic Law contained an assurance that it would cease to be in force as soon as the whole German people was in a position to adopt a constitution of its own choice: meanwhile only the Federal Republic was a legally valid German state. Rarely has the French saying 'Nothing lasts as long as the temporary' been more strikingly illustrated than by the history of the Bonn Republic. The Germans' counter-proposals were accepted by the Allies, one of which (the United States) was patently anxious to hasten the birth of a viable West German state. The Parliamentary Council, which consisted of sixty-five members drawn from the *Land* parliaments, met at Bonn on 1 September and proceeded, with the help of various drafting committees, to work out a Basic Law which turned out to be a constitution in all but name, and which significantly gave little indication of the extent to which the German people were still subject to Allied restrictions then, and later under the Occupation Statute.[60] The main argument was between those who favoured a fairly centralised structure, something like a revived Weimar constitution without Prussia, and those who wished the emphasis to be on state rights. The Social Democrats were in the first camp, most of the Christian Democrats in the second. Allied views had also to be taken into account, but here too there were differences. The French were adamant against any return to a powerful central government, while the British, if mainly for economic reasons, preferred centralism. The Americans, with their own federalist tradition, naturally inclined to the federalist solution. The *Länder* were in a strong position because they existed in fact while the central government had still to be created. The result of hard bargaining was a compromise which satisfied all except the most extreme advocates of federalism. The Social Democrats fought successfully for the financial supremacy of the central government, while cultural policy, including education, remained entirely a matter for state governments. The main legislative body under the Basic Law is the Bundestag, which is elected by universal suffrage for a term of four years. It consists of a variable number of deputies (usually slightly below 500), including twenty-two from West Berlin who can speak but not vote, since Berlin is not juridically part of the Federal Republic. The second house or *Bundesrat* represents the *Länder*; its forty-five members, including four non-voting from Berlin, sit as delegates of the state governments, the largest *Länder* having five each and the smallest three. As the members vote *en bloc*, it follows that the political complexion of a *Land* government can influence Federal policy. The Head of State is a President, who holds office for four years and can be re-elected once only. He is elected not by referendum, a method of which the Germans are understandably wary, but by a special electoral college consisting of the entire Bundestag together with another five hundred or so from the state legislatures. One of the President's principal functions is to appoint a Chancellor or Prime Minister who must have the confidence of the Bundestag. The interpretation and enforcement of the Basic Law is the responsibility of the Federal Constitutional Court which sits at Karlsruhe.

The Basic Law was designed in every way to avoid the mistakes of its predecessor, the constitution of 1919. The powers of the President are accordingly strictly limited, though he is more than the figure-head sometimes suggested. Being elected by parliament he could hardly become its rival, as a president by referendum might be. He was not made Commander-in-Chief of the armed forces, which Germany in 1949 did not possess, nor was he entrusted with those emergency powers which had proved so disastrous in the hands of Hindenburg. The Chancellor, by contrast, was endowed with more authority than before, and the Bundestag cannot depose him without at the same time naming his successor. The obvious intention was to strengthen the executive and to avoid those repeated cabinet crises which had brought parliamentary government into disrepute in the time of Weimar. The method of electing members of the federal parliament also differed from what it had been under both Weimar and the Empire. The new system, which was twice modified by law before reaching its present form, is an attempt to combine the advantages of the 'British' practice of voting for a known candidate in a single member constituency with those of proportional representation, whereby each party receives exactly as many seats as its total of votes entitles it to. The objection to making elections purely a matter of party lists is that politics thereby becomes too impersonal – this was felt to be one of the defects in German democracy between 1919 and 1933. Under the Bonn system every elector has two votes, one for a specific candidate, one for a party list, so that half the members of the Bundestag are chosen in one way and half in the other.[61] Another innovation was that any party which failed to win either three seats direct or at least 5 per cent of the total votes cast forfeits its right to be represented, the object being to discourage the proliferation of small parties, again with the Weimar experience very much in mind. Even more significant was the importance attached to the Federal Constitutional Court, which was given greater powers than its ineffective predecessor. This court has the right and duty of pronouncing on the constitutional legality of political parties, it is the highest court of appeal if the legality of an election is challenged, and it has the deciding voice in case of conflict between the two houses of parliament or between the federal government and the states. It has acted with determination against what it judges to be a threat to the rule of law: in 1952 for example it banned the extreme right-wing Socialist Reich party in which former Nazi leaders were prominent, and four years later the German Communist party was similarly declared unconstitutional, though in the 1953 federal election it had not won a single seat. In this and other ways the Federal Constitutional Court has not hesitated to make decisions and challenge the executive; it has taken a bold rather than a narrowly legalistic view of its functions, and has established itself as one of the strongest pillars of the new structure.[62] The rule of law for which it stands is emphasised throughout the Basic Law. Article 1, for example, begins with the assertion: 'The dignity of man is inviolable. To respect and protect it is the duty of all state authority.' Article 3 states that no one may be prejudiced because of his sex, parentage, race, language, homeland and origin, faith, or religious and political opinions. The rights of conscientious objectors to military service are expressly recognised. During the two decades and more for which the basic law has been in force it has worked effectively and on the whole smoothly. Post-war German politics have been characterised by a stability and moderation which have gone far to justify those not very numerous optimists who from the beginning believed that, in spite of all that had happened before 1945, democracy could develop strong roots in Germany. This success owes something of course to the new system's inherent merits but more to the men responsible for working it. Above all it rests on a consensus of opinion such as the Weimar Republic conspicuously lacked.

Germany's first general election since 1933 was held in August 1949, and the Bundestag met for the first time in September. Its immediate task was to elect a government. No party had an absolute majority. The Christian Democrats had the largest number of seats (139) closely followed by the Social Democrats (131). The Free Democrats came third with 52 seats. No other party had more than

17 seats, and the extremists were weak, the Communists mustering 15 and the right-wing splinter group only 5 seats. Adenauer, who had been chairman of the Parliamentary Council and was chairman of the Christian Democratic party, was elected Chancellor by one vote – his own. To govern he needed a coalition. There were two possibilities. One was a government of the right, including the Free Democrats and the much smaller German party; the other was a government of the middle by a coalition with the S.P.D. Many of Adenauer's colleagues favoured the latter course. Through their links with the Christian trade unions they were inclined to a policy of state control rather than free enterprise and many of them were already used to coalition with the Socialists in the state governments. There was also the argument that in Germany's abnormal situation a government of all the talents was called for. Adenauer himself was strongly opposed to a deal with the S.P.D.: his own antipathy to that party stood in the way, and he believed that one reason for the failure of Weimar democracy had been its succession of weak coalition governments based on unsatisfactory compromises. A C.D.U.–S.P.D. government also would leave opposition to the extremists, which would not be healthy for democracy. Moreover, for Adenauer, the convinced Christian, co-operation would not be easy with a party officially professing a materialist philosophy. So a government was formed which included ministers from the Free Democrats and German party as well as the C.D.U., but it was the C.D.U. and particularly its free enterprise wing which had the predominant influence. Erhard, who had guided the economy since the early days of the Bizonal Economic Council, became Economics Minister. The Free Democrats received some satisfaction from this, because Erhard's policy was their own, as they did from the election of Heuss as first President of the German Federal Republic. Blücher, another of their leading men, became Vice-Chancellor. With these decisions taken, Germany was set on the political and economic course she was to follow for the next two decades. It was the beginning of the Adenauer era.

This was a result which could not have been foreseen even two years earlier. It was a severe blow to the Social Democrats and their leader Kurt Schumacher, who had confidently expected to have the leading place in the new republic. Indeed there were good reasons for this belief. The S.P.D. was Germany's oldest and largest political party, with a respected tradition and a nation-wide organisation; its record of opposition to Hitler was better than that of any other party; and the general post-war radical revival in Europe was expected to favour the German Socialists. The Labour government in Britain certainly showed some sympathy for the S.P.D., and according to

Adenauer, some favouritism, though the Americans showed an equal partiality for the C.D.U. It could also be expected that the widespread 'proletarianisation' of German society through the loss of all their possessions by millions of refugees and expellees would benefit a party of the have-nots. Yet events took a different course. Ever since the setting up of the Bizonal Council there had been signs that the Christian Democrats were gaining at the expense of the Socialists, especially in the Catholic districts. The loss of the mainly Protestant East gave the Catholics for the first time a proportion of the population not far short of half. The C.D.U. was helped by the success of Erhard's economic policy and accused the Socialists of waging an obsolete class war. An unexpected bonus for Adenauer was the refugee vote: many of those who had fled from the East had acquired a lasting aversion to any kind of socialism. The rivalry between the two main parties, which was the central theme of German politics from now on, was reflected in the clash of their respective leaders.

Kurt Schumacher, a native of West Prussia, was a symbol of endurance and inflexibility.[63] Having volunteered in the First World War, he was wounded and lost an arm. Demobilised, he joined the Social Democratic party, and tried to infuse into them some of his own militancy. When Hitler, despite these efforts, came to power, Schumacher refused either collaboration or exile, and consequently spent the next ten years in a concentration camp. As a result of his sufferings he subsequently had to have a leg amputated, so that by 1949 he was a double cripple who was able to continue his political career only thanks to heavy reliance on drugs and an indomitable will. Not surprisingly, he was uncompromising and embittered. Everyone admired his courage, but working with him was difficult. He was a man who gave and took hard knocks, often indulging in bitter sarcasm and at times showing arrogance. He carried over into the post-war world a political attitude formed during the Weimar Republic: that was his great misfortune. He knew that one reason for the failure of the Socialists in the past had been their alleged lack of national feeling, and he was determined that this should not be held against them in the future. He felt justified in advocating a hard line with the Allies because, unlike so many Germans, he had nothing to be ashamed of: he had stood up to Hitler when foreign statesmen were courting him, and had paid for it with his health. 'We were in a concentration camp when other countries were making deals with Hitler' was one of his sayings.[64] On another occasion he declared: 'The German people must be imbued with a new national self-confidence, divorced from the offensive arrogance of the past and from the widespread tendency to see every Allied wish as a revelation of Europeanism.'[65] Unlike his colleagues who had lived in exile, he did not realise that in foreign eyes even German Socialists were not guiltless: they had let Hitler come to power, and afterwards voted and fought for him. Opinion in Germany and to a lesser extent in other western countries was moving away from nationalism, which was increasingly seen as out of date, towards international ideals. Both the tragedy of two world wars and the pressure of a powerful and expansive Soviet Union made co-operation between the free countries a necessity. Schumacher was convinced that, if West Germany allowed itself to be too closely tied to the West, its chances of reunification would diminish. He expressed his dislike of what he called the 'class egotism of large-scale capital disguised as internationalism'. Schumacher's views did not go un-challenged in his own party, for Reuter, its other outstanding person-ality, had a more realistic assessment of Soviet objectives, and was broadly in agreement with the Adenauer policy of close alignment with the West in order to counter-balance Russian power. Reuter's posi-tion as mayor of West Berlin made him very conscious of this, but Schumacher's misgivings about reunification were to be vindicated. In later years Reuter's policy was to be continued by his protégé and ultimate successor in Berlin, Willy Brandt. The Adenauer-Schumacher duel was prematurely cut short by the latter's death in 1952, when his tortured body, exhausted by a ceaseless round of speeches and travel-ling, could no longer respond to the demands made on it.

Adenauer too was an authoritarian, but was otherwise very different. He was deeply rooted in the Catholic culture of the Rhine, in contrast to Schumacher who had a lifelong antipathy to the Church of Rome. Born of respectable but modest parents, Adenauer had been trained as a lawyer before entering local government and becoming Lord Mayor of Cologne, one of the largest German cities, at the age of forty-one in 1917. He remained there until the Nazis removed him in 1933. Though he belonged to the generation which had grown up in the days of Germany's imperial splendour, unlike many others he had not been beguiled by Pan-German dreams. Serious, hard-working and a natural politician, Adenauer combined flexibility in tactics with astuteness in judgement. He spent the last years of the war in an internment camp, where he was sent after the plot of 20 July, in which he was not actually involved. This experience, alarming at the time, stood him in good stead after the war. He had not compromised with Hitler. Re-appointed mayor of Cologne by the Americans soon after they captured the city in the spring of 1945, he was dismissed by a British brigadier a few months later for alleged incompetence, and was forbidden to engage in any political activity. The ban was how-ever soon lifted, and this experience too, though humiliating, at least exempted him from the charge of being a tool of the Allies. Moreover his loss of a job enabled him to concentrate on politics.

Few men would have begun a second career as Adenauer did at the age of seventy in such circumstances. He threw himself with zeal into the work of the new Christian Democratic party, and became its first chairman in the British Zone. Like his rival, Schumacher, he was a member of the Zonal Advisory Council. When later he became chairman of the Parliamentary Council, he had at last reached the centre of the political stage and was determined to make the most of it. At a time when many were undecided, he knew his own mind. He also evoked a response. After years of state regimentation, Germans were willing to try a neo-liberal economic policy such as Adenauer favoured. After years of neo-paganism, they were ready to support a party which stood, however vaguely, for Christianity. And after the fanatical nationalism that had ruined Europe, men turned to the international co-operation in which Adenauer believed (though he saw it only in terms of Western Europe). Schuman in France and de Gasperi in Italy were thinking along similar lines and Churchill in his speech at Zürich in September 1946 came out for it strongly. Adenauer had never – remarkably enough – been anti-French, and he was the right man to take advantage of the forthcoming shift in French policy which he did much to make possible. He won French confidence as no previous German Chancellor had done, and he reflected the desire for reconciliation evident on both sides of the Rhine. Though he himself was primarily – at times perhaps exclusively – preoccupied with foreign affairs, much of the popularity of his government was due to the success of the economic policies associated with Erhard. Many people had written off the capitalist system after the catastrophe of the great depression, in which they saw the total crisis of the liberal state, not just the nadir of a particularly severe trade cycle.[66] It turned out to have unexpected powers of recuperation. The economic recovery of West Germany was more convincing than any propaganda. For the first time democracy could be identified with prosperity and also with strong government, for Adenauer ruled as Chancellor with almost patriarchal authority.

There was still a long way to go before the half-fledged Federal Republic of 1949 reached full independence. The Allies had reserved for themselves such important subjects as disarmament, reparations and dismantling, denazification, refugees, war criminals and foreign policy. All this was specified in a document called the Occupation Statute. Yet in the ceremony which marked the formal transfer of power to the Federal government, the new French High Commissioner, François-Poncet, told Adenauer that if everything went well the restrictions would be relaxed by stages. Two still unsolved problems were the Saar and the Ruhr. The French had already annexed the Saar economically, and seemed determined to incorporate it politically. The Ruhr, it had been decided in 1948, was to be ruled by an International Authority which would later include Germans as well as the six other interested powers. This was a compromise the Federal Republic had to accept, as the alternative was the complete detachment of the Ruhr which France had earlier advocated. However distasteful the idea of internationalising the Ruhr might be, it was in conformity with Adenauer's own concept of West European integration. And indeed the Ruhr Authority turned out to be the basis of the Coal and Steel Community, which in turn led to the Common Market.

The new German government had to steer a difficult course between two very different sets of critics. If it seemed to neglect German interests and failed to keep up the pressure for Allied concessions in such matters as dismantling, it would be accused by the large and watchful Socialist opposition of selling out; if it demanded too much too quickly, it would upset public opinion in the Allied countries and revive the latent fears of Germany. In this situation, the understanding that grew up between the Chancellor and the three Allied High Commissioners was useful to both sides: they gave enough ground to enable him to keep his majority in the Bundestag, while they reassured their own governments about the developments in Germany. Adenauer was also fortunate in that the French Foreign Minister at the time, Robert Schuman, spoke German fluently and shared the Chancellor's desire to improve Franco-German relations and to form a European federation. 'The fragmentation of Europe', Adenauer told the press, 'has become an anachronism, a nonsense and an anarchy.'[67]

The list of firms to be dismantled was soon reduced. Originally dismantling was part of demilitarisation, but it was also involved in reparations and restitution. Cases were reported in the press of firms closed down by Allied officers in pursuit of private business interests. Such abuses, while probably not very common, helped to discredit a process which was bitterly resented because of the unemployment it caused. In addition, public opinion in America and England, both of its own accord and under the influence of German protests, soon showed signs of concern about the whole policy. The change in outlook brought about by the Korean war ended dismantling. Some months earlier, Adenauer had agreed that West Germany would join the Ruhr Authority and waived any objection to the Saar joining the Council of Europe (which implied its formal severance from Germany). Germany itself was to become a member of the Council and would be allowed to open consulates in Britain, France and the United States.

These and other decisions were embodied in the Petersberg Agreement of November 1949, which was the first freely negotiated treaty between the Bonn government and its ex-enemies and marked a milestone on the road to full independence. It was followed by a stormy debate in the Bundestag, where the Social Democrats accused Adenauer of having betrayed German interests over the Ruhr and Saar. It was on this occasion that Schumacher described Adenauer as the 'Chancellor of the Allies', a wounding phrase which caused a nation-wide scandal. Schumacher's outburst was understandable but tactically inept. Adenauer survived the taunt, while Schumacher acquired the reputation of a nationalist and a demagogue. The roles of the two parties had been reversed. The right-wing Christian Democrats stood for international understanding and conciliation, the Social Democrats' slogan was Germany first. But the middle classes, who in the past would have responded to Schumacher's oratory, seemed unmoved. Collaboration with the western powers was respectable as 'fulfilment' in the twenties had not been, for in the cold war few Germans were neutral. It was easy to criticise Adenauer but not to envisage an alternative. Schumacher's own foreign policy seemed very negative. He was against Germany's joining the Council of Europe and against the Schuman Plan. He distrusted the 'cartels and clericals' of the countries later to form the Common Market. In practice this meant a policy of isolationism, which for the time being, unlike Adenauer's policy, seemed to bring no dividends.

Much of the old bitterness between France and Germany had vanished during the war. Early in 1950 Schuman paid his first official visit to Bonn, where he had been a student before the First World War, and spoke warmly of the new Franco-German understanding. Whereas in the 1920s Stresemann had never had room for manoeuvre between a France almost neurotically afraid of Germany and a German public opinion dreaming of revenge, in the 1950s Adenauer, who incidentally was born two years before Stresemann, found a willingness to meet on both sides. There was another difference between Stresemann and Adenauer. The former was trying to balance a western against an eastern policy, Locarno with Rapallo. Adenauer hardly had an eastern policy, and his commitment to the West was unqualified. His western partners knew that he was not likely to spring a surprise on them or negotiate a new Rapallo. In a way this knowledge weakened Adenauer's bargaining position, for the western powers did not have to outbid the Russians. But Adenauer was surely right in his judgement that the balance of power in Europe had changed so fundamentally that Germany, divided, truncated, and, until 1955, under occupation, could no longer negotiate on anything like equal terms with the Soviet super-power. A Stresemann-like policy was no longer possible. Yet by gaining the trust of his western partners, Adenauer won back its sovereignty for the larger half of Germany more quickly and smoothly than anyone had dared to hope. There were those like the former Chancellor Brüning, then briefly occupying a chair of political science at Cologne, who criticised Adenauer for not making a serious attempt to reach agreement with the Russians over German reunification before integrating the Federal Republic in the West. This question is discussed in the next chapter. Whether or not Adenauer's scepticism about negotiating with the Soviet Union was justified, his hope that a strengthened western alliance could make its own terms with Russia turned out to be a tragic illusion. Meanwhile his ideal of a united Western Europe is still unrealised.

CHAPTER XII

Adenauer and his Successors

(i) THE DEMOCRACY OF BONN

In September 1951 a conference of Allied ministers in Washington issued a declaration on Germany in which they defined their objective as 'the inclusion of a democratic Germany in a European community on the basis of equal status'.[1] This implied that Germany was to recover full sovereignty and was an indication of the extent to which western governments, especially the American, now saw in Germany a new ally rather than an ex-enemy. Already much had been done since the signing of the Petersberg Agreement to reduce or remove the remaining controls. The Occupation Statute was formally revised in March 1951. Germany again had a Foreign Ministry and diplomatic representation abroad. The western and other nations formally ended the state of war with her, and restrictions on industrial production, including shipbuilding, were lifted. The Federal Republic became a full member of the Council of Europe, and, though she could not belong to the United Nations without raising the awkward question of East German membership, she joined the economic and social agencies of U.N.O. such as the Food and Agriculture and World Health Organisations, the World Bank, the International Labour Office and U.N.E.S.C.O. Both as a democracy on trial and as a newly admitted member of the international community West Germany was making gratifying progress. In June 1950 Adenauer went to Paris to sign the Schuman Plan which put French and German steel and coal production under joint control. This was a constructive step towards the integration of Western Europe on which Adenauer had set his heart, and represented a turning point in the French attitude. Hitherto France had been mainly concerned to extract economic reparation from Germany and to weaken her politically. Now a way appeared of satisfying the French desire for security without denying Germany the equality which was implicit in her new status of partner. Once French and German heavy industry were indissolubly linked together, a future Franco-German war was unthinkable, and France would be sure of getting the Ruhr coal needed for her iron deposits. In 1952 agreement was reached between the Allies to end the occupation regime entirely, and the Federal Republic was recognised as completely sovereign except for certain reserved subjects such as the stationing of foreign troops in Germany, reunification, Berlin, and a final peace settlement with both parts of Germany. Three of these four were matters which the western powers had to keep in their own hands since they also concerned the Soviet Union and were inseparable from the Allies' position as victors of the Second World War. But while negotiations for the winding up of the occupation were going on smoothly, an issue was raised which introduced far-reaching complications and touched deep springs of emotion. It was decided that the new treaty with West Germany should come into force simultaneously with new arrangements for her defence. This meant that in one form or another there was to be again a German army.

The North Atlantic Treaty Organisation (NATO) was formed in April 1949. When its council met in New York in September 1950 to consider the defence of Western Europe its members were deeply influenced by two recent events: the successful testing of Russia's first atomic bomb, and the outbreak of war in Korea, which intensified the cold war. The council decided that Germany could not be defended without the Germans. This was a reasonable, indeed an unavoidable decision, yet it came as a bombshell. The Petersberg Agreement, signed in November 1949, contained a pledge by the Federal Republic 'to endeavour to prevent by all means in its power the re-creation of armed forces of any kind'.[2] The swift reversal of policy naturally caused an uproar. Opposition was vociferous and widespread. In Allied countries the old bogey of German militarism was far from forgotten, especially on the political left, where Adenauer's Catholicism and conservatism made him anyhow suspect. Fears were expressed that a German army would give a new lease of life to the discredited military élite, revive Nazism, encourage dangerous ambitions and sabotage the young democracy of Bonn; it might even provoke the Russians and drag the West into a thermonuclear war. In France the vast majority of the population was opposed to German rearmament on any terms, and in Britain an important section of the Labour party, and large numbers in other parties and in none, had the strongest possible objections. In Germany, though Adenauer himself (as he confidentially told the Allies) accepted the need for an army of some kind and saw that it would give him extra political leverage, the general reaction was unfavourable. The youth, especially those who had been involved in the last war, often when they were still of school age, wished to have nothing more to do with military service. Their own experience and Allied anti-war propaganda had bitten deep. Professional soldiers resented the slur on

the honour of the army implied by the trials of generals as war criminals, and by the revelation of the part played by the military in mass
executions in Russia and elsewhere. There was a good deal of ironic
bitterness at the western powers' abrupt change of policy: they were
accused of enlisting as cannon fodder those to whom they had just been
preaching the evils of militarism. Among the Social Democrats and
an influential wing of the Evangelical Church pacifism was strong;
Niemöller, the leader of Protestant resistance to Hitler, now head of
the Church in Hesse, was wholeheartedly opposed to rearmament, and
Heinemann, Minister of the Interior in Adenauer's cabinet and a leading Protestant layman, shared his misgivings to the point of resigning
when the decision to rearm was taken. But however emotionally objectionable rearmament might be, the question of security could not
be brushed aside. The Russians were striving for nuclear parity with
America and had an overwhelming superiority in conventional forces.
Across the zonal border the East German police was being given military training. The Berlin blockade and the Korean war showed that
the Communists were bent on expansion. Hitherto the western powers
had been solely responsible for defending West Germany's east frontier,
but with the return of German sovereignty other arrangements would
have to be made. The risks must be shared, and the financial burden
too: a Germany relieved of defence expenditure would be too favoured
a competitor in world markets. Adenauer ruled out neutrality, as exposing his country to too many risks, and neutralisation, which would
have required four-power enforcement. Nor would he accept the idea,
advocated by many in France, that German troops would be a kind
of ancillary or second-class force with limited weapons. A German
army must not be discriminated against, though this did not rule out
the scrambling of national armies in a supra-national force.

It was the French Premier, René Pleven, who put forward the proposal for an integrated European army to which Germany would contribute a contingent. A scheme was drawn up for a European Defence
Community and signed by the governments of France, the Benelux
countries and the Federal Republic. It was ratified by the Bundestag.
But the French Prime Minister fell and opposition grew. After long and
passionate debate the Chamber of Deputies rejected the E.D.C. treaty.
In Paris the pressures of the cold war were felt less than in Washington
and memories of the last two wars were more vivid. The French
government was caught between Gaullist nationalism and pro-Soviet
communism. The failure of the project was a setback to those who
believed in the integration of Europe and in Franco-German reconciliation as the heart of it. It was a particularly heavy blow for Adenauer himself, and he needed all his resilience to recover from it. The

British government made a somewhat belated gesture by promising greater participation in the defence of Western Europe for the next fifty years; having helped to allay French fears, France's western partners insisted that Germany be treated as an equal. The Federal Republic was invited to join the Brussels Defence Pact, and in the following year became a member of NATO. In doing so, the government of Bonn formally renounced the use of atomic, biological and chemical weapons and pledged itself not to attempt the unification of Germany by force. Thus although Germany was compelled, by the logic of events, to have her own army, every effort was made to ensure that its relationship to the Republic would be very different from what it had been under Weimar. The soldier was to be a citizen in uniform. There would be none of the blind obedience and harsh discipline, the contempt for civilians, the heel-clicking and goose-stepping of the old-style Prussian barracks. Special care was taken over recruitment. A Personnel Committee, which included democrats of impeccable standing, was set up to examine the credentials of those applying for senior posts. This was essential because all the applicants had served in Hitler's army, though some had been involved in the plot of July 1944. Other precautions included the appointment of a civilian with special powers, known as the Special Commissioner for Defence, whose function it was to look into any complaints brought by soldiers and who was responsible only to the Bundestag. The Bundestag's Defence Committee also kept a close watch on the progress of the army. Leadership was a word which had been debased during the Third Reich, but Count von Baudissin, a general who had supported the July plot, was put in charge of a special department of the Ministry of Defence responsible for training officers and n.c.o.'s in leadership and character training. The problem was to produce an army which would be technically efficient without being militarist, in which a democratic mentality would not exclude professional pride. From the first the new *Bundeswehr*, which came into being in 1955, was extremely sensitive to criticism both at home and abroad. The Russians and their satellites did their best to revive old fears of German militarism, and made the most of the fact that all the new German generals had been in the Nazi *Wehrmacht*. Whether the new citizens' army would show the same fighting qualities as past German armies is a question which has never been answered, and it may be that the test will never come. A current joke in Germany was that the West wanted the German army to be strong enough to resist Russia yet too weak to be a danger to Luxembourg. A war in Germany would be a civil war, and it is hard to say how far this factor would influence the behaviour of the soldiers towards East Germany. It should, however, be recorded that the fears of those who opposed German rearmament in the early 1950s have not been borne out by events: there has been no 're-militarisation', and the army has remained firmly under civilian control. Although by the 1960s the German contribution to NATO was second only to that of the United States, the number of men under arms in the Federal Republic never quite reached the prescribed total of half a million. Conscription, originally fixed at a year, was extended to eighteen months in 1962.[3] More than once economic stringency has caused a reduction of defence expenditure. As a non-nuclear power West Germany has accepted her dependence on America and her loyalty to NATO has been exemplary. Apart from the frontier guards all German forces have been under NATO command. A feature of the late 1960s was the growth of conscientious objection inside as well as outside the army, which is no longer immune, as it was once, to the radical pressures of the outside world. The doubt now is rather of its military qualities. In recent years the number of cases of indiscipline and desertion in the *Bundeswehr* has reached a point where it causes serious concern to the military authorities.[4]

The outstanding feature of the new parliamentary democracy of Bonn was its stability. One symptom of this was the gradual disappearance of small parties. Although in the first Bundestag election in 1949 some fourteen parties competed, only six of them actually won seats. Thereafter, thanks to the electoral law which excluded parties with less than 5 per cent of the total vote from the Bundestag, the number of parties represented actually fell to five in 1953, four in 1957 and three in 1961. The trend was towards a two-party system, as in Britain. Although the third largest party, the Free Democrats, remained a force to be reckoned with (unlike its British analogue, the Liberals, the F.D.P. benefits from the system of proportional representation) it is unlikely ever to rival in size the Christian and Social Democrats, and may in time decline still further. The predominant party during the first twenty years of the second German Republic was Adenauer's C.D.U., which, as we have seen, was at first in partnership with the Free Democrats and the small German party. Adenauer's second government, formed in 1953, was also a coalition, including this time the Refugees' party (B.H.E.) founded in 1950 to represent the millions of Germans expelled from the lost territories and claiming also to speak for those who had fled to the west from the Russian Zone. By 1957 the C.D.U. had so far consolidated its position as to obtain a clear majority, and Adenauer's third cabinet consisted entirely of men of his own party. When in 1961 he fought his fourth general election he had passed his zenith and the C.D.U. lost control of the Bundestag. Another coalition was necessary, again with

the Free Democrats. But the last two years of Adenauer's Chancellorship (1961–3) were less successful. The trouble started in 1959, when
Adenauer was eighty-three. In that year Heuss, the first President of the
Federal Republic, was due to retire, having served the limit of two
terms. Adenauer decided that he would like to become President himself, a less exacting office than that of Chancellor yet one in which he
expected to be able to continue to influence policy especially if, as he
assumed, the Christian Democrats remained in office. Having studied
the Basic Law however he belatedly came to the conclusion that the
President of the Federal Republic does not in fact possess much political power; and he was unhappy at the prospect that Erhard, his
probable successor, would not make a good Chancellor. Adenauer
accordingly changed his mind and decided to run again for Chancellor
in 1961, a decision which was much criticised. It was bound to discredit the dignity of the presidential office, and even his own party
resented Adenauer's vindictiveness towards Erhard and blatant cling-
ing to power. The coalition he formed with the Free Democrats in
1961 ran into difficulties the following year. October 1962 saw the
gravest political crisis the Republic had known. It concerned *Der Spiegel*,
the weekly news magazine which is the German counterpart of *Time*
magazine. Besides reporting news, the *Spiegel* specialised in drawing
attention to abuses and revealing information which, not always for
good reasons, the authorities preferred to keep secret. Recent NATO
manoeuvres indicated that the German army, the *Bundeswehr*, was not
as efficient as it should be, and in an article which provoked a good deal
of attention, the *Spiegel* suggested that excessive reliance on America's
nuclear deterrent had caused the *Bundeswehr* to neglect its conventional weapons, with the result that defences were seriously below par.
The government's reaction was hasty and heavy-handed. The proprietor and defence editor of the *Spiegel* were arrested (the latter in
Spain where he was on holiday) on a charge of high treason and police
broke into the *Spiegel* offices and seized files. The initiator of this arbitrary action was the Minister of Defence, Franz Josef Strauss, the leading
Bavarian Christian Democrat and often spoken of as a possible future
Chancellor. The Minister of Justice, a Free Democrat, was not even informed. The government looked foolish because it was unable to substantiate its charges against the *Spiegel*, and Strauss lied in reply to
embarrassing questions from members of the Bundestag. Since in
defending Strauss Adenauer himself was not entirely truthful and also
made wild accusations, he suffered a further loss of prestige. The Free
Democrats refused to remain in the coalition unless Strauss was
sacked, and Adenauer had to promise that he himself would not
stay in office beyond 1963. His last two years were thus a somewhat

humiliating experience, and by then even his foreign policy, which had been unusually successful in the 1950s, had run into difficulties.

Yet these blots on Adenauer's reputation, in which an inborn tendency to authoritarianism was exacerbated by the petulance of old age, cannot diminish the value of his achievement. He had been Chancellor for fourteen years, as long as the entire Weimar Republic. Under his aegis the German people made an astonishing recovery from the nadir of 1945, the time when, in the words of an inscription on a soldier's grave in the middle of Berlin, it seemed to be *Finis Germaniae*. Germany became politically sane and stable, economically prosperous, she absorbed and assimilated millions of refugees, she regained the respect of the outside world and was re-admitted to the comity of nations. Adenauer was certainly the greatest German statesman since Bismarck, with whom he is often compared. If his achievement was less than Bismarck's it may well be destined to last longer, for he showed more prescience. Any comparison between the two has to take account of their very different circumstances as well as of differences in aims and methods. Whereas Bismarck liked to keep his options open, Adenauer pursued a single objective with single-minded devotion. Yet there were striking resemblances. Both were strong personalities who loved to exercise power and to manipulate men for their purposes; both were inclined to treat political opponents as personal enemies and hostile to the state; both could be unscrupulous and pettily vindictive; both were capable of arrogance;[5] both combined strong religious convictions with a cynicism born of experience; both were more interested in foreign than in domestic affairs, and were pragmatists rather than doctrinaires; both were skilled diplomats, Bismarck by profession, while Adenauer acquired the art (with surprising aptitude) after a lifetime in local government. Both had a gift for reducing complex issues to terms which people easily understood. In some ways Adenauer's task was harder than Bismarck's: he started with fewer assets, and at first he had to play the difficult role of prime minister of an occupied country who often had to pocket his pride and conceal his feelings. Though Adenauer professed democracy and Bismarck did not, Adenauer was hardly a democrat in the Anglo-Saxon sense. He was far more autocratic than the head of a parliamentary government ought to be; he treated his cabinet colleagues as subordinates rather than equals, and at times showed scant respect for the Bundestag. He was particularly secretive about foreign affairs: it was eighteen months for example before the Bundestag was informed that he had offered German divisions to the Allied High Commission in August 1950.[6] 'Chancellor democracy' as it was called, was a cross between a parliamentary and a presidential regime. Yet, it can be argued, it was no bad thing for a nation used to authoritarian government to have firm leadership during the first critical years of its second experiment in democracy. A weak Chancellor would undoubtedly have been less successful in bargaining with the Allies and in regaining foreign confidence, nor would domestic politics have run so smoothly. Despite his pragmatism, there were times when Adenauer held fast to principles despite flexibility in methods. He also had the statesman's ability to distinguish the important from the ephemeral and the trivial. Both these qualities were exemplified by the agreement between the Federal Republic and the state of Israel, with which Adenauer's name will always be linked. The question of compensating Hitler's Jewish victims for their sufferings during the Third Reich was handled by Adenauer himself without even the assent of his cabinet. Though he was normally imperious, on this occasion he showed great patience and understanding in the delicate talks with Jewish representatives which preceded the signing of the treaty. Moreover his decision to pay Israel some £3,000 million, with a further £450 million for Jews in other countries, was taken by Adenauer against the advice of his financial experts. In this and other ways Adenauer's influence exceeded the narrowly political. It affected the style and quality of life in the Federal Republic. It was a strange turn of fate which brought to power a man who in many ways belonged to the almost legendary pre-1914 world: the sober, responsible citizen and provincial lord mayor whose undemonstrative patriotism belonged to the Rhineland rather than the vanished Reich. On his eightieth birthday one of the editors of the *Deutsche Rundschau* wrote of Adenauer: 'Since the German people first received their sovereignty thirty-six years ago, he is the first Chancellor who has fully mastered the technique of legitimate power . . . With Adenauer the civilian spirit of the German bourgeoisie has for the first time attained political success by means of a great parliamentary majority.'[7] He was indeed a patriarchal figure whose very longevity gave a sense of continuity to a disorientated society with a disrupted history. The age of coloured shirts and mass hysteria was (for the time being) over: middle-class values came back into fashion, the bourgeois ceased to be a figure of mockery. Those who had known Weimar Germany found that of Bonn dull by comparison, in the sense that normality is less interesting than disease. Though the Bonn Republic, in its public manifestations deliberately avoided the grandiose and struck the minor key, it gave many ordinary people a well-being and happiness they had hardly known in the stormy years preceding it. Many Germans learnt to appreciate the calm and security in which wounds could heal and a new confidence develop. That this coincided with a similar trend in neighbouring countries facilitated Adenauer's self-appointed task of anchoring Germany firmly in the western community of nations.

No assessment of the first decade of the Federal Republic should overlook the real, if unspectacular contribution of its first President, Theodor Heuss. In 1949 Heuss was the leading Free Democrat in the Bundestag and as an experienced parliamentarian he took a leading part in drafting the Basic Law. Scholar, politician, journalist and author, Heuss had begun his career as a pupil of Friedrich Naumann, and afterwards wrote his biography. He worked on *Die Hilfe*, Naumann's periodical, and was active in the pre-1919 Progressive party before becoming a Democratic member of the Reichstag in 1924. During the Weimar Republic Heuss was director of studies at the *Hochschule für Politik* in Berlin, which in some respects was the German equivalent of the London School of Economics. An undoctrinaire liberal, an intellectual who was shrewd, modest and naturally democratic with a keen sense of humour, Heuss proved an excellent choice for the presidency. He showed wisdom and courage in making often difficult decisions. His non-partisan and tolerant approach to politics made him acceptable to many who found Adenauer too authoritarian or opinionated, and there was widespread support for Heuss when he was elected for a second term of office in 1954. Karl Jaspers once said that what was needed was to breathe life into the formal structure of democracy. No one did more to help this process than Heuss, and much of what is good in the Federal Republic owes its inspiration to him and to his public-spirited wife.

The disappearance of commanding figures always creates a vacuum, and with Adenauer's belated resignation in 1963 a rather unsettled period in German politics began. In retrospect the next six years can be seen as one of transition between the Adenauer era and that of Willy Brandt, who became Chancellor in 1969. Erhard, Adenauer's successor as Chancellor, found himself dealing with a number of difficulties, foreign and domestic, which in the end proved too much for him. He had little political flair, and despite his success as Minister of Economics since 1949, he lacked decisiveness. De Gaulle was now asserting himself against America, and West Germany, as the ally of both America and France, felt pulled in opposite directions. Erhard himself had no doubt that the Federal Republic must stick firmly to the United States, but by now, as a wealthy and stable country, it was no longer the client state it had been in the fifties. Some Germans felt that they were not getting enough consideration from America either in the form of defence costs for American troops in Germany or strategically – President Johnson's shelving of the projected Multilateral Nuclear Force to include Germany was a blow to the

Republic's prestige. Erhard was stung to tell his critics: 'We are not a satellite of Washington.'[8] The German Gaullists on the other hand were attracted by the policy of an independent Europe until they realised that behind this slogan de Gaulle was moving towards neutrality and pursuing French national interests. The break-up of NATO, which France left in 1966, was the last thing most West Germans wanted, and after that enthusiasm for de Gaulle noticeably cooled. At home there was a temporary break in the economic boom, and with rising unemployment the budget that year was in deficit. State elections showed that the Free Democrats, who shared the government coalition with the C.D.U., were losing support, while the right-wing National Democratic party made unexpected gains, which caused unfavourable comment abroad and revived doubts about the durability of German democracy. Although the C.D.U. slightly improved their position in the 1965 Bundestag election, they and the Free Democrats showed little enthusiasm for working together. As a Christian Democrat Erhard had lost the confidence of the majority of that party, and after an adverse parliamentary vote he resigned. In the ensuing reshuffle late in 1966 it was agreed to form a Grand Coalition, that is one between the two largest parties, the Christian and Social Democrats. Such a government, it was thought, was needed to face the problems of reunification and relations with Eastern Europe, which had entered a new phase. The new cabinet consisted of eleven C.D.U. and nine S.P.D. members. K. G. Kiesinger, of the C.D.U. who had been Prime Minister of Württemberg-Baden and specialised in foreign affairs, became Chancellor, while Brandt, mayor of West Berlin and leader of the S.P.D. since 1964, was made Foreign Minister. The new government of all the talents thus contained an ex-Nazi (Kiesinger), a former member of the resistance (Brandt) and an ex-Communist (Wehner). It symbolised a remarkable convergence of policies. The Social Democrats' decision to join this coalition was a turning point in their history and in that of Germany. To understand it we have to take into account changes which followed the death of Schumacher in 1952.

As a party fated to spend the first seventeen years of the Federal Republic in opposition, the Social Democrats had no easy time. They were handicapped by the loss not only of Schumacher in 1952 but of their other outstanding personality, Reuter, the following year. Schumacher's successor as head of the party was Erich Ollenhauer, a rather colourless personality, who as leader of the opposition was no match for Adenauer. The real strength of the party lay less in the rather bureaucratic guidance provided by Bonn than in the well-known and much respected Social Democrats who held power in the large provincial centres – men such as Kaisen, President of the Bremen Senate, Brauer, the Lord Mayor of Hamburg, and Brandt himself, the Governing Mayor of West Berlin. All these men were capable administrators, of broad views and experience, all had gone into exile during the Third Reich, and all were undogmatic socialists. Yet by the end of the 1950s the party was aware of a deepening sense of frustration: it seemed unable to increase its vote beyond the third of the electorate which traditionally supported it -- and which it had actually won as far back as 1912. The long years in the political wilderness were disheartening. The intransigence of Schumacher was increasingly seen to be out of date. New leaders, notably Wehner, one of Brandt's supporters, favoured a more flexible approach, as did Brandt himself. The result was that at a conference at Bad Godesberg in 1959 the S.P.D. adopted a new programme. It declared itself a people's, not a class party, and on economic policy it accepted the formula of as much competition as possible, as much nationalisation as necessary. It thus not only eliminated the remains of its original Marxism, but placed itself only slightly to the left of centre. It also expressly repudiated the old hostility to the churches which had alienated many Christians and made socialism a kind of religious substitute. By this time too the S.P.D. had abandoned its opposition to German rearmament and membership of NATO. Schumacher had been against rearmament and membership of NATO mainly because he judged that they made harder the task of unification: his basic criticism of Adenauer was that the latter put the integration of Western Germany into Western Europe before German national interests. But by 1959 Socialists had fewer illusions about Russia's willingness to permit reunification after two of their leaders had visited Moscow and talked to Khrushchev and other Russian leaders. In any case, the Russian terms had become stiffer. Nor did the hard line followed by the Communist regime in East Berlin encourage S.P.D. hopes. The party had come a long way since the days of Bebel and Ebert, but so had Germany and Europe. The result of these changes was that the gap between the Social and Christian Democrats had narrowed significantly, so that it was not very difficult for them to come to terms in 1966. The S.P.D. was successful in attracting more middle-class followers, and prosperity had given the vast majority of the population a middle-class standard of living. Yet the Grand Coalition was hardly a success. It was hard to combine it with electoral politics, in which members of the same cabinet attacked one another. Inevitably many of the differences between the coalition parties were settled behind the scenes, and the unity was more apparent than real, while the stultification of opposition – represented by a small minority – was seen as a danger to democracy. In the 1969 elections the S.P.D. gained more votes than its C.D.U. rival for the first time, and Brandt became Chancellor in a coalition with the much smaller F.D.P. Several signs were indicative of a new temper and a new stirring in German society. One was the support for Brandt's policy of reconciliation with Communist Eastern Europe. Another was the growth of extra-parliamentary opposition. The price paid by the S.P.D. for moving towards the political centre was the alienation of the radical left, who took up the slogans of the new and not-so-new fashionable paper-back ideologies and called for direct action or what was sometimes described as 'provocative counter-violence'. The New Left captured the main students' union, their representative organisation, and even the Socialist Students' Association ceased to support the S.P.D. 'Left-wing youth' wrote a British observer, 'are anti-America, anti-Bomb, anti-establishment.'[9] This was a trend perceptible in all western countries, but it was particularly significant in the Federal Republic, where moderation and conformity had been the hallmarks of post-war society. After the war young people had been brought up, especially in the former American Zone, to regard America as an ideal country, rich and powerful yet tolerant, the guarantor of liberty and the model of democracy. The Vietnam war and the scandals connected with it, combined with the murderous race riots in American cities, completely spoilt this image. The disillusion was considerable. University students took part in demonstrations which led to bloodshed: that such things could happen in West Berlin was a measure of the change that had come over Germany since the fifties. The best known radical student leader, Rudi Dutschke, was himself a refugee from East Germany, whose revolutionary ideas challenged both the liberal establishment of Bonn and the quasi-Stalinist dictatorship of Pankow.[10] A well-known sociologist described German youth in the 1950s as the 'sceptical generation'. Earlier generations of young people had thrown themselves idealistically into the pre-1914 youth movement, the First World War and the Hitler Youth respectively. Their successors who had experienced the Third Reich were understandably wary and unwilling to commit themselves. They distrusted all authority and were cynical about power. When military service was reintroduced in the mid-1950s, the attitude of many young men was summed up in the catch-phrase 'ohne mich' ('Don't count on me'). In the later 1960s the new wave of radicalism showed that the mood had changed again. Discontent focused on the more obvious grievances or defects of western society, from the discreditable war in Vietnam to the need to reform the hierarchical structure of German universities. But it also arose in part as a reaction against the consumer cult and the satiety of affluence. By 1972 the

radical left, though in a minority, had won control of the student parliaments in twelve of the largest universities, and students had obtained
a share – in some cases equal to that of the academic staff – in the
universities' governing bodies. Thus the radicals are able to influence
curricula and to veto the appointment of lecturers and professors of
whom they disapprove. This endangers the principle of academic freedom, and in the opinion of many university teachers, including those
who are Social Democrats, such power, one-sidedly exercised, represents a greater threat to democratic society than the much publicised
and more spectacular acts of violence.[11] Schools too have been affected
by the rejection of authority which has transformed the teacher-
pupil relationship and undermined traditional discipline.

In contrast to Weimar Germany, right-wing radicalism is less of a
problem in the Federal Republic than a reading of the foreign press
might suggest. Most of the extremists are on the far left. During the
last quarter of a century, many observers have waited for some sign
of a Nazi revival. Such signs as there have been indicate rather a Nazi
survival, which is obviously less significant. Books have been written to
prove either that the Nazis are still in power behind the scenes or that
they are about to stage a comeback. Such fears are not borne out by
the record. There have certainly been some disquieting symptoms,
ranging from the daubing of synagogues and the desecration of Jewish
cemeteries to the retention of former Nazi officials, including those
who committed war crimes, in high office in the Republic. Public
opinion polls at various dates have disclosed the survival of pro-Nazi
attitudes even among the youth. The N.P.D. is generally considered a
neo-Nazi party, and its success in state elections, though limited (it has
never won more than the 9.8 per cent of votes it received in Baden-
Württemberg in April 1968) has been watched with some anxiety.[12]
Anti-N.P.D. demonstrations by young people have been a feature of
German politics, while similar action has been taken to prevent Nazis
from being appointed to important posts. A well-known example was
the protest by Göttingen students in May 1955 against the choice of
Leonhard Schlüter, a publisher of neo-Nazi books, as Minister of Education in Lower Saxony. Schlüter was forced to resign. The teaching of
democracy in citizenship has been carried out with great thoroughness
at many levels. The Protestant Church has made a notable contribution
through the Evangelical Academies, of which there were fifteen in the
Federal Republic and West Berlin by the end of the sixties. These are
adult education centres comparable to the numerous Folk High
Schools which provide a wide range of adult education courses. Radio,
television and the press have done much to enlighten public opinion.
Textbooks have been rewritten. One of the most significant attempts to

eliminate bias and to promote international understanding has been made by Georg Eckert, a professor of history at Brunswick, who has held conferences of teachers from different countries to agree on a common attitude towards controversial events and particularly to eliminate chauvinism from French, German and other textbooks. What is always possible is a revival of German nationalism: this could result from an economic crisis or simply from long pent-up frustration over the division of Germany. A German de Gaulle is by no means unthinkable. Adenauer's hope that German national feeling would be sublimated in European patriotism has not been fulfilled because Europe in that sense hardly exists: even within the Common Market national rivalries and jealousies are far from eliminated. In future Germany may well become more assertive of its national interests, but the resurgence of the old type of highly emotional nationalism seems very improbable. It has little appeal to young people, who are as unlikely to sing '*Die Wacht am Rhein*' as British youth to strike up '*Rule Britannia*'. Master-race doctrines are as out of date as eulogies of the white man's burden. Patriotism was so contaminated during the Third Reich that there is still great uncertainty about it. For some time after the war there was no national anthem, until Heuss proposed that the third verse of '*Deutschland über Alles*' was unobjectionable and could be used. Another example of the moral dilemma is an incident which occurred in November 1966, when a writer named Krämer-Badoni was invited to speak at a ceremony on the day of National Mourning, equivalent to Britain's Remembrance Sunday. He told the assembled audience: 'How, I ask you and myself, should we commemorate the dead of the two world wars? Can we say: They stood at Thermopylae and fought to the last man against the attacking barbarians? We cannot. *We* were the barbarians in the last war.'[13] He went on to speak with great feeling of the millions of people, German and foreign, adults and children, who were murdered in open graves, buried alive, gassed and burnt, and to praise the resistance fighters. It was scarcely surprising that the chairman of the organisation of former prisoners remonstrated: people had come, he declared, to remember their dead sons, not to hear about the Nazis. This is less of a problem for the young generation, who are not so emotionally involved in the war dead as their elders.

Germany is much more detached from its past than France or England, because the year 1945 was such a complete break. In this sense the Federal Republic strikes many visitors as a country cut off from its historical roots, where the newness of most of the buildings symbolises the arrival of a clinically new era. The Federal Republic has been described as a unique combination of a balanced, liberal and internationally minded society with a state weaker and less self-assured than any other, whose style is West European rather than specifically German.[14] Three-quarters of the present German population were born after 1930, which means that they were too young to have any responsibility for what happened before 1945. They are the 'guiltless generation' sometimes referred to. Nevertheless, they are not totally unaware of what went on during the Third Reich, though they may know it from books, newspapers and television rather than from their parents. Another phrase often used is the Overcoming of the Past, which might be paraphrased as the exorcising of the ghosts of Auschwitz and all the other places where the German name was dishonoured. And the youth of Germany are conscious of this legacy, they realise that something of the collective shame of which Heuss spoke remains and will remain for some time to come. But they are also willing to face the past instead of seeking to escape from it, as many people did after 1945 (the '*ohne mich*' generation). Many examples of this could be cited: perhaps the most telling is the interest in Anne Frank, the Jewish girl who was murdered at Belsen after hiding in Amsterdam for years under the German occupation. Her Diary was a best seller, and the play based on it was performed in many theatres and made a deep impression. Young Germans go to the Anne Frank house in Amsterdam, which is kept as a museum, as on a pilgrimage, and there is an Anne Frank village near Wuppertal where young people of many nations meet to promote peace and understanding. In 1957 two thousand young Germans took part in a pilgrimage to Belsen concentration camp organised at the suggestion of Erich Lüth, a Hamburg senator who has done much to bring about a reconciliation between Germans and Jews. Christian-Jewish 'weeks of brotherhood' are held every year in the main cities. The Jewish population of 30,000 or so in the Federal Republic is for the most part elderly, and almost bound to diminish rather than grow in numbers. Links with Israel, however, are likely to develop.

West Germany has come of age.[15] During the post-war years people needed a period of quiet to recover morally as well as physically from the Nazi trauma, and to come to terms with themselves and their recent history. Instead they were drawn with hardly a break into the polemics of the cold war; their ex-enemies thrust weapons into their hands almost before denazification was complete, creating a good deal of confusion. The scramble for possessions and the cult of wealth also distracted people from reflection. As an occupied country the Germans could leave the difficult decisions over reunification and the eastern frontier to their mentors, and faith in America, their powerful defender, was almost unlimited. In the sixties a different atmosphere prevailed. America was still the shield, but no longer the model. The German people really came to grips with the recent past, both in their understanding of the Third Reich and in the decision by the Willy Brandt government to liquidate the vestiges of the war with Poland by recognising the Oder-Neisse frontier. It involved shedding the illusion, dear to many, that the verdict of 1945 was not final, that something might be retrieved from the lost war. The reassessment of recent German history already mentioned shows the same willingness to face facts.

(ii) ECONOMIC TRANSFORMATION: THE MIRACLE AND AFTER

'We have lost our political credit', a German banker was reported as saying, 'our economic credit is all we have left.'[16] In fact the recovery of both kinds of credit went together, though it took less time for the world to acknowledge the Federal Republic as a formidable economic partner than to accept it as an established democracy. Germany's revival as a trading nation was helped by the steady improvement in its foreign relations. The two vital first steps were the currency reform of June 1948 and the credits provided by the European Recovery Programme. The G.A.T.T. treaty signed in 1947 was an important move towards the liberalisation of world trade, and Germany's inclusion in the Organisation for European Economic Co-operation also provided German businessmen with opportunities such as they had not had after the First World War. The European Payments Union which acted as a clearing house also facilitated the exchange of goods. The result was that whereas after 1918 the volume of world trade regained its pre-1914 level only in 1924, by 1950 it had risen far above the level of the 1930s. Already during the occupation regime strenuous efforts were made to revive German exports, since the loss of the eastern territories and the cutting off of the Russian Zone forced the West Germans to find new markets to pay for raw materials from other sources. At first the most important export was coal, which was in heavy demand in other parts of Europe, but soon it became possible to export manufactured goods such as cameras, which meant a better return and more coal available inside Germany. In the years following currency reform unemployment remained high (still over a million in 1955), and prices showed little tendency to rise. Exports were helped by a slight devaluation of the mark in the autumn of 1949. They doubled that year and rose by 74 per cent in 1950, while the Korean war which broke out in June 1950 led to a boom of which Germany took full advantage.[17] Most countries, like the Federal Republic, were short of consumer goods and lacked capital equipment of all kinds. Wartime destruction had created an immense housing

shortage, and the rebuilding of German cities provided jobs and opportunities for investment. Power stations, shipyards, railways and roads
all needed capital and labour. By the middle 1950s over half a million
new dwelling units (mostly flats) were being built every year, and
more than half the West German population now lives in a house
built since 1945. The demand for steel caused production to rise
rapidly, and by 1960 West Germany was producing 50 per cent more
steel than united Germany before the Second World War, and ranked
third among the world's steel producers. By 1958 it had overtaken
Britain as an exporter, and in 1961 over one million German cars
were sold abroad. The Volkswagen works at Wolfsburg was the
largest car factory in Europe, and the Volkswagen itself, modest,
tough and immensely practical, had become a worldwide symbol of
German achievement. For the first time in Germany, the private car
was an article of mass consumption. The mark was revalued by 5 per
cent in 1961, but the favourable balance of payments continued. As
early as 1955 the gross national product of West Germany exceeded
that of the whole country in 1936, though with 75 per cent of the
population and only 53 per cent of the area.[18] The annual growth
rate of the German g.n.p. in the fifties was 7·4 per cent, nearly three
times that of Britain in the same period.[19] By 1963 West Germany's
share of world trade had climbed back to one-fifth, almost exactly as
much as the proportion of undivided Germany in 1929. The standard
of living was transformed. Between 1950 and 1964 consumption per
head trebled, and since 1955 hourly earnings have more than
doubled.[20] For the first time ordinary wage-earners have been able to
afford luxuries. A working-class family which in the early fifties might
spend its holiday on the North Sea, by the end of that decade would
have discovered the Adriatic or the Costa Brava, and by the middle
of the sixties would be thinking in terms of a safari in Kenya. The
annual rate of growth had slowed down but was still between 4 and 5
per cent. The recession in 1966 proved temporary. Despite a further
revaluation of the mark in 1969 the boom continued into the seventies.
Germany was now an expensive country and there was a good deal
of anxiety about inflation. West Germany has by far the strongest
economy in the Common Market and is responsible for about 35 per
cent of its total gross national product. Its volume of trade, inside and
outside the Market, is double that of France. The compulsory break-
up of giant industrial firms after the war, such as Krupp and I.G.
Farben, intended to destroy excessive concentrations of economic
power, seems to have had little effect on output. Later, despite an
anti-cartel law of 1957, economic pressures led to fresh agglomera-
tions in industry, trade, banking and insurance.

The Federal Republic's now legendary economic success owed more to good management than to good luck; above all it was due to the people's resolve to make use of a favourable situation.[21] The post-war market for goods of every kind was almost insatiable, but the significance of the German boom was that it was led by exports. This was possible because domestic consumption was kept down. Profits were ploughed back into the industry rather than distributed as higher dividends or wages. Even before the war a feature of the German economy had been the high percentage of the gross national product spent on capital formation, which the tax system was designed to favour. Between 1948 and 1965 the Germans assigned, relatively, about half as much again for this purpose as did the United Kingdom. Wages and salaries took about 47 per cent of the gross national product compared with a British figure of 58 per cent.[22] The German rate of saving, also fostered by fiscal policy, was high. That, combined with wages tied to productivity and a tight credit policy in the post-war years, helped to peg prices. Management was keen and enterprising and, thanks to the war and dismantling, most of the plant was new. Efficient production was supported by good salesmanship, especially in the export field. Labour was hard-working and co-operative. The great majority of workers had a peaceful temperament and a disciplined and responsible attitude to their job. Unemployment was still high, with refugees constantly adding to the number seeking work. There were many other reasons why the trade unions refrained from pressing unrealistic wage demands. One was fear of inflation, a legacy of the bitter experience of 1923. Another was that since prices remained steady, earnings slowly improved. Rising unequal shares bring more benefit than 'fair shares' that scarcely rise, for only a few years' per capita gain at an average rate of 3 to 5 per cent is worth more to the lower income groups than the redistribution of a stagnant total within a narrow range.[23] The union leaders accepted the need to postpone consumption for the sake of greater productivity, and like their colleagues in the United States they realised that high earnings could come only from high profits. The unions themselves were efficient. They had been revived after the war with Allied encouragement, and the fact that they numbered only sixteen meant that there was no overlapping and little jealousy: demarcation disputes were hardly known, and there were few restrictions of a kind to limit output. Although people remembered the mass unemployment of the early thirties, the greater catastrophes which had occurred since made them little disposed to dwell on past grievances. The line drawn across German history in 1945 put an end to inherited resentments as well as to longstanding traditions.[24] The strike weapon was rarely resorted to – as one trade union leader said, it produces a bad atmosphere, and makes workers lose their zest for their job – and the time lost in stoppages is minimal.[25] Finally, the unions were politically detached, without the close links with the S.P.D. such as the British trade unions have with the Labour Party: they do not, for example, contribute to party funds. In the West German situation the union leaders were often more concerned to fight Communists than capitalists. This does not mean that the unions lacked political objectives. A major one was the policy of co-determination in industry introduced after the war with Allied approval, and later extended.

Hans Böckler, the chairman of the General Trade Union organisation or D.G.B., attached great importance to associating workers with industrial management. It was an idea which had been strongly advocated during the revolution of 1918 as an attempt to introduce economic democracy, and had even been enshrined in a neglected paragraph of the Weimar constitution. It was taken up after the Second World War by the C.D.U. in its Ahlen programme, and Adenauer, who was friendly with Böckler and responsive to similar pressure from the churches, decided to meet the unions on this point.[26] A law in 1951 laid down that in the coal and steel industries half of the supervisory council of each firm was to consist of representatives of its workers. The same principle, somewhat modified, was later extended to the whole of industry by an act of 1952 which said that one-third of the supervisory council of every limited or joint stock company must consist of workers from the shop floor. The system gives the workers a considerable say in such matters as conditions of work, holidays and general welfare, and any decision to close down the works or a part of it has to be referred to the workers' own statutory committee, the *Betriebsrat*. But day to day management continues to be the responsibility of the managerial board, only one member of which, the labour manager, has to be approved by the workers' delegates on the supervisory council. In practice these arrangements make little difference to the running of industry, but the employees obviously have a new status and feel themselves, much more than before, part of the firm which employs them. It is hard to say how far this sense of integration is responsible for the generally excellent labour relations which have characterised the Federal Republic, though undoubtedly it has made a contribution. Partly because of these relations, partly because of the emphasis on capital formation and the ploughing-back of profits, output per hour rose faster in West Germany than in other industrial countries, and during the 1950s the annual increase in labour productivity was three times the British.[27] Between 1950 and 1965 real wages more than doubled, while the

working week was reduced by over 20 per cent. The Common Market
has provided West Germany with new opportunities and new challenges. Well equipped as it was to take advantage of industrial open-
ings, its agriculture, hitherto protected by a tariff, was vulnerable
to competition from countries with a more favourable climate and
soil and a lower standard of living.

The heavily urbanised and economically unbalanced Federal Republic produced a smaller proportion of its food than the old German
Reich. With the return of prosperity and a rising population, German
farmers were less and less able to supply the country's requirements;
food imports on a larger scale than before had to be let in, and the
German producer lost his monopoly of the market. With the Common
Market in mind, the Agricultural Act of 1955 proclaimed the intention
to make German farming fully competitive. This was to be done by
greater competence and adaptability. The first need was to eliminate
the large number of small farms: as late as 1961 a quarter were of
less than five acres each, and by British standards almost two-thirds
were too small to be viable.[28] Many of the holdings were divided into
tiny, scattered strips, which hindered efficient cultivation. The Federal
government instituted a policy of consolidating farms, and the number of really small ones has been halved. Secondly, agriculture has
been mechanised. In 1955 four farms out of five had no tractor. Since
then, with government help, tractors, large numbers of combine
harvesters and milking machines have been introduced. As a result
of these and other changes, including the greater use of fertiliser,
crop yields have risen sharply. West Germany now produces double
the amount of wheat and more than double the amount of barley
grown on the same area in the 1930s.[29] The increase per acre has
been remarkable. Livestock farming has grown in size and importance,
and milk yields per cow are considerably higher. The result is that,
despite the loss of the eastern cornlands, the Federal Republic is now
more self-sufficient in food in some respects than united Germany
was before the Second World War. As a much richer country she is,
of course, well able to import the fats, cheese, fruit and vegetables
needed by a population with a mounting standard of living. This
greatly improved performance by German farmers has been achieved
with a rapidly falling labour force. Whereas up to 1950 rather more
than one German in five worked on the land, the proportion today is
less than one in ten. In 1964 a much smaller number of farm workers
produced 50 per cent more than before the war.[30] It is not too much
to describe these changes as an agrarian revolution.

One of the key factors in the economic miracle of the fifties was
the reservoir of labour represented by the refugees, to which were

added those made redundant by a mechanised agriculture. They enabled industry to expand without wage inflation. The supply of labour was being continually augumented by the influx of people from the Russian Zone (over 3 million between 1949 and 1962), who usually arrived penniless and bewildered, and after being questioned at a reception camp were assigned to one of the West German *Länder*. The refugees were the equivalent of Italy's southern peasants but much better educated and, though at first they were a burden on the economy, they soon proved its greatest asset. Sometimes whole factories came to the West: the Bohemian glass works at Gablonz in Czechoslovakia was expelled with the Sudeten Germans in 1945 and re-established in West Germany, and part of the famous Zeiss optical firm also migrated from Jena to a site in Württemberg. The building of the Berlin Wall put an end to the human flow from the East. But since then German industry has recruited about two million workers from other parts of Europe, mostly Italy, Yugoslavia, Turkey and Greece, and their remittances to their families in these countries are an important debit item in the German balance of payments. But the Federal Republic can well afford it. In the 1960s the size of its trading surplus was actually an embarrassment, and led to the two revaluations of the mark in that decade. While the mark strengthened the dollar weakened, as America's balance of payments went into the red, largely because of the Vietnam war. West Germany had plenty of capital to invest abroad, most of which went to the European and North American economies that were its main trading partners. (For German investment in the developing countries, see Section (iii) of this chapter.) But much remained at home as the rate of interest in Germany was high, and investment at home profitable. If the high rate of 'plough back' was one reason for economic growth, another factor, it is often suggested, was the small proportion of the gross national product spent on defence. It is true that in the ten years after the war West Germany had no army of its own, but it had to pay for occupation costs, which were not light, and since 1955 has continued to contribute a share of the expenses of the British and American forces stationed on German soil, as well as maintaining its own army. During the 1960s German defence expenditure rose steeply.[31] As a non-nuclear power it is, however, free from the heavy research and other costs of maintaining a nuclear capability.

The main credit for Germany's spectacular economic success went to Erhard, who established the policy and presided over its implementation. Erhard himself emphasised his distrust for planning and his belief in making the individual act for himself instead of relying on an all-powerful state. His neo-liberal ideas had been propounded years before by a professor of economics at Freiburg University, Walter Eucken, and, like Eucken, Erhard believed that in the long run political freedom depended on freedom in the economic sphere. Yet Erhard's system was far from being a *laissez-faire* one. The government intervened, for example, to abolish or prevent monopoly, and to encourage investment in sectors of the economy where expansion was urgently needed. As we have seen, fiscal policy was also used to favour production rather than consumption and to stimulate exports. And while the original stress was on the creation of wealth, later much thought was given to its distribution. West Germany is a welfare state, in some respects less so than Britain, in others more so. From the beginning of the social aspects of economic policy were far from neglected, and the large proportion of resources spent on welfare was reflected in the high level of taxation and of insurance contributions. The government did more to direct the economy than is often realised. Besides owning the railway and public utilities it was actually engaged in the production of such things as coal, iron and aluminium, and about half the total capital formation in the Federal Republic is financed, directly or indirectly, from the public purse.[32] When after the war the government found itself faced with the care of millions of war victims, it made special provision for the disabled, widows and orphans. Insurance against sickness, old age and unemployment covers the whole population, though people with incomes above a certain level are allowed to insure through a private company insurance. Insurance payments by employers and employees altogether amount to about 30 per cent of the total wage bill. Pensions are generally higher than in Britain. Children's allowances, hitherto not very common in Germany, were introduced on a large scale in 1954 and subsequently increased. Since 1957 pensions, allowances and other benefits have been geared to the general level of earnings – a 'dynamic' feature which is much valued by the recipients in an age of inflation. Housing, especially at low cost, is a sector where the government has stimulated the supply by providing investment capital at low rates of interest. With its total of over ten million new dwelling units since the war, West Germany has an unequalled record. The trade unions have also made a big contribution here, and as the owners of about 200,000 flats are the largest landlords in Western Germany. Low income families enjoy subsidised rents, but the subsidies are paid to the family not deducted from the rent, so as not to interfere with market forces in housing.[33] But the most unique piece of social legislation in the Federal Republic is the Equalisation of Burdens, whereby those whose property survived the war pay a capital tax of up to 50 per cent into a special fund for refugees and expellees.

The whole transaction is spread over twenty-seven years, to be completed in 1979. Over thirteen million applications for relief under this scheme have been received. Legislation was also passed authorising payment of material compensation to people who were persecuted during the Third Reich, including those who lost their jobs. Three million applications have been filed under this heading, and here too the amount of legal work in presenting and judging such cases is enormous. Both these laws were essential if the Federal Republic was to be accepted at home and abroad as a state standing for justice, and one sincerely trying to make amends for the crimes of its predecessor. The treaty with Israel already referred to was of course even more significant morally. (The East German government, by contrast, has made no such payments on the grounds that it is not in any sense the legal successor of the National Socialist government.) Finally, the Bonn government has done something to distribute wealth more evenly and to create a property-owning democracy by helping the small saver and encouraging wider share ownership. The largest automobile factory, Volkswagen, which belonged to the state, has been sold to private hands; the number of investors in it is said to be over a million and a half. The return to power of the Social Democrats in 1969 gave a new impulse to the government's social and welfare policies. The Minister of Labour, Walter Arendt, was a former chairman of the Miners' Trade Union who did much to extend and improve social insurance, raise pensions and improve the status of the blue-collar worker. Among the main beneficiaries of these changes were the two and a half million war pensioners whose incomes went up by nearly 30 per cent.

The decline and eventual disappearance from the Bundestag of the Refugee Party is the best comment that can be made on the success of the Federal Republic's refugee policy, for it means that the refugees have become socially and psychologically assimilated as well as provided with a livelihood. One consequence of this is that the government can now conduct its *Ostpolitik* without constant adverse pressure from the refugee associations. In recent years the economic problems facing West Germany have been much the same as in other industrial countries. The replacement of coal by oil and atomic energy has made many miners redundant: this was one reason for the bankruptcy of Krupp in 1967. New industries such as electronics have been established. The economy continued its expansion, but by the end of the sixties the long period of price stability was over. Inflation, a word with particularly bitter associations, was now the government's main worry. Demand far exceeded the capacity of industry to supply it. Besides the ordinary inflationary influences of full employment and

booming trade, there was a special factor in the vast amount of
foreign currency held in Germany as a result of its highly favourable
balance of payments. The government took deflationary measures.
It cut back public expenditure, postponed certain promised reforms,
and urged restraint on both sides of industry. The second revaluation
of the mark in October 1969, intended to redress the balance of payments alleviated the problem, but did not solve it. The Federal Bank
was in a dilemma. If it lowered the discount rate to discourage the
influx of foreign capital, the effect was to revive home demand. If it
raised the discount rate to curb domestic spending, it stimulated the
demand represented by excessive loan capital. In either case an unacceptable degree of inflation appeared unavoidable. The weakness
of the dollar increased the desirability of the mark. In the year 1970
alone some 44,000 million dollars entered the Federal Republic,
while wages went up by 16 per cent, the highest rise in any one year
since the Korean war. The official number of unfilled vacancies in
June 1971 was 723,000.[34] In May 1971 the Bonn government, having
failed to persuade its Common Market partners to agree on a common
revaluation of their currencies, decided to go it alone. Though France
did not hide its disapproval, the mark was allowed to float, which
amounted to an unofficial revaluation. In explaining the government's
decision, Chancellor Brandt declared that henceforth he would put
German interests first. It was a sign of increasing toughness, needed to
reassure his supporters at home. For every up-valuation of the mark
had an adverse effect on farmers and businessmen (making imports
cheaper and exports more expensive), and a government with such
a narrow parliamentary majority as Brandt's and an *Ostpolitik* that was
constantly under fire from his opponents could not sacrifice popularity
at home to good neighbourliness abroad. In the past most of Germany's economic problems stemmed from its indebtedness to foreign
creditors; today it is itself a major creditor power and the difficulties
arise largely through the failure of other countries to run their
economies as well as the West German economy is managed. A common criticism of Bonn's economic policy is that it 'imported inflation'.
For the 'over-heating' of Germany's economy caused by an excessive
balance of payments was partly due to the lack of financial discipline
practised by her European trading partners. By having to exchange
sound marks for 'consumptive' lire or French francs, the Germans
complained that they were involuntarily financing Italy's development
programme in its southern provinces and France's ambition to become the world's fourth nuclear power – a phenomenon which politically worked rather to Germany's disadvantage by adding, especially
while de Gaulle was in power, to French intransigence. It has often

been said that the real test of German democracy would be its ability to survive a depression. So far it has not had to face such an ordeal, but it has now established a degree of prosperity which would leave its population well protected against adversity, at least by the standards of the past. It seems reasonable to assume that parliamentary government and the rule of law have put down roots which will not easily be torn up even by an economic gale. Like its Weimar predecessor, the Bonn Republic owes its existence to Allied arms, but unlike the former from the beginning it rested on a consensus which is the only ultimate guarantee of its continued success.

(iii) ADENAUER'S FOREIGN POLICY: FULFILMENT AND FRUSTRATION

During the 1950s Adenauer was able to pursue simultaneously his two objectives of reconciliation with France and close co-operation with America. He did not allow the French rebuff over E.D.C. to put him off course, though it was proof that France was not ready for that scrambling of national sovereignties which many in Germany, especially the youth, saw as the next stage in Europe's evolution. However a degree of internationalism was acceptable even to the French in the shape of the Schuman Plan for the Coal and Steel Community, which came into force in July 1952 and superseded the now superfluous Ruhr Authority. A few years later the six powers which belonged to the Coal and Steel Community (Germany, France, Italy and the Benelux countries) agreed to establish a European Economic Community or Common Market, in which all internal tariff barriers would be gradually abolished. The treaty of Rome, which formalised the arrangements, was signed in March 1957. Thus part of Adenauer's dream was realised, and one of his closest colleagues, Professor Walter Hallstein, became the first President of the E.E.C. Commission, as the executive of the new organisation was called. By that time the last remaining territorial difference between France and Germany had been settled. This concerned the Saar. After 1945 France reasserted the policy of detaching the Saar from Germany and attaching it economically to herself as she had done for fifteen years after the first war. Not only was the Saar with its valuable coal and iron within the French customs union, but after a large pro-French vote in an election held in October 1947 Paris obtained a fifty-year lease on Saar mines. In 1949 the Saar was declared an associate member of the Council of Europe, an indication that its political future was to lie in a somewhat shadowy international status. But the Bundestag passed a resolution that the Saar as German territory could not be alienated without Germany's approval, and even

Adenauer insisted that the last word must be said by the Saar people themselves. It was nevertheless agreed, despite a good deal of dissent in Germany, that the Saar should be internationalised under Western European Union, the re-named and enlarged alliance of the Brussels Pact powers. The Saar was to be the guinea-pig for a French-sponsored experiment in which the French themselves refused to join. The problem was solved however by the people of the Saar, who in a plebiscite held in October 1955 rejected the plan and returned a vote of no confidence in their Prime Minister Hoffmann, whose behaviour had been somewhat highhanded. The result also reflected the growing prosperity and attractiveness of the Federal Republic. Only one practical alternative for the Saar now remained, return to Germany, and this formally took place in 1957, when the Saar became the Republic's tenth *Land*. It was lucky for Adenauer that the plebiscite turned out as it did, for few Germans were willing to give up the Saar, and any other election result would have been suspect. The prevailing view was that only the Federal Parliament, not the government, had authority to renounce German territory. The French accepted the verdict in the knowledge that under the Coal and Steel treaty coal from the Ruhr, which of course was much more important than the Saar, was now freely available to them. A problem which had burdened Franco-German relations for forty years was disposed of.

No such difficulties clouded the relations between Germany and the United States. The 1952 presidential election brought Eisenhower to the White House in place of Truman. The new Secretary of State, succeeding Acheson, was John Foster Dulles. Adenauer's understanding with Acheson had been good; that with Dulles was even better. A special relationship developed between Washington and Bonn, and West Germany began to be spoken of as America's favourite ally. Both saw eye to eye on the cold war, and were inflexibly opposed to Communism. Dulles believed that increased western strength would force Russia to withdraw from the advanced position she occupied in Central Europe in 1945, and he spoke of 'rolling back' Soviet power and liberating the satellite countries, as well as of re-uniting the two parts of Germany. Such talk made it inevitable that Soviet propaganda should depict both Dulles and Adenauer as war-mongers, and strengthened the bonds between both Poland and Czechoslovakia and the Soviet Union. Moreover the Federal Republic refused to recognise the severed eastern territories as lost *de jure*; this was in line with the Potsdam declaration of the western powers that a final decision on the frontier should await the general peace treaty. Since the disputed territories were firmly incorporated in Poland and settled by Poles, it was becoming an increasingly unreal position, though it was left to de Gaulle to declare publicly in 1959 that France for one accepted the Oder-Neisse frontier.

Although the West saw German reunification in terms of Russian withdrawal and frontier revision, the Russians, surprisingly, appear still to have favoured a united Germany provided that their security needs were met. Stalin's domestic policy, in East Germany and the other satellites as well as in Russia itself, was so rigid and repressive that western governments were unaware how flexible he was prepared to be over the German question.[35] It is probable that in the early fifties he had not given up the hope of a Germany tied together in such a way that Communist influence would extend to the West. The ubiquitous Communist propaganda at the time in favour of meetings between East and West Germans was therefore not entirely an exercise in dust-throwing. Quite clearly Moscow (not yet an atomic power) feared a rearmed Western Germany added to NATO, and was prepared to act to forestall it. In November 1950 Otto Grotewohl, Prime Minister of the East German Republic, wrote to Adenauer proposing the setting up of an All-German Constituent Council made up of Germans from both sides in equal numbers.[36] Adenauer refused, on the grounds that the East German government was the cause of the split. It was an essential part of the western case that the regime in East Berlin was a puppet one, imposed by the Soviet authorities, and with no mandate to speak on behalf of the East German population. Hence the Bonn government was the only legal government in Germany, and the East German administration was not a recognised negotiating partner. In any event as neither German state yet had full sovereignty, initiative in the matter of German reunification lay with the occupying powers. Yet when representatives of the four powers met in Paris to discuss a new meeting of foreign ministers they could not even agree on the agenda. On 10 March 1952 however the Soviet government sent a Note to the three western governments proposing an immediate peace treaty with reunited Germany from which all occupation troops would have been withdrawn within a year. Other named conditions were that the new all-German state should have democratic rights and freedom, free activity for political parties (except those hostile to democracy and peace), with its own armed forces but bound not to ally against any of its Second World War enemies. This Note is generally considered to have marked the furthest point ever reached by the Russians in their willingness to meet the West over German unification. It was sent at a time when plans were being made for West Germany to enter the proposed European Defence Community and was obviously designed to prevent German rearmament. In a further Note of 9 April the Soviet government mentioned the possibility of holding free all-German elections, which for the Bonn government was the essential first step. The western reply was not encouraging, and no serious attempt was made to probe Soviet intentions. Certainly no encouragement to do so came from Dr Adenauer, though there were German politicians, including the Free Democrat K. G. Pfleiderer, who advocated a positive reaction to the initiative from Moscow and were prepared to give a lower priority to free elections than most western spokesmen.[37] The Russians soon afterwards reverted to their original position that free elections (in their sense of course) should be held after the conclusion of a peace treaty.

In retrospect, the western failure to respond to the Russian initiative of March 1952 is seen by many as the turning point in the history of the attempt to reunite Germany, the decisive missed opportunity in post-1945 German history. Others believe that there was never any real chance of agreement, only the appearance of one.[38] Since so little is known of Soviet intentions and documentary evidence is lacking, any opinion must be largely conjectural. There are cogent arguments on both sides. In defence of the western attitude it is contended first of all that Stalin would never have permitted free elections in any sense acceptable to the West, for he must have known that a Communist victory in them was out of the question. Therefore, the elections would have had to be rigged. It was significant that when a Commission of the United Nations was especially appointed to investigate the organisation of free all-German elections, it was refused entry into the Soviet Zone. Secondly, there are grounds for doubting whether the neutrality offered by the Soviet Union would have been genuine. The Russians would not have allowed the Communist regimes in their other satellites to fall, therefore Russian troops would have remained on the borders of a united Germany, ready to intervene if its policy turned out to be insufficiently 'peace-loving and democratic', which in fact meant Communist or fellow-travelling. In such circumstances Germany's sovereignty would have been in fact limited, and its economic freedom of movement too might have been restricted. It might have been, at best, a larger Finland in relation to the Soviet Union. Unlike Austria, which regained independence at the price of neutrality, Germany was potentially an economic giant, and in the cold war both sides would inevitably have tried to draw it into their orbit. A third argument against accepting the Russian offer was that it would have meant withdrawal of American forces from a strategic part of Europe and possibly led to further withdrawals elsewhere. The Federal Republic was the linchpin of western defence as it was of western economic recovery. Adenauer agreed. It was not only a question of keeping over fifty million Germans in freedom and security instead of putting seventy million in some kind of political limbo with an uncertain future, but of preserving Western Europe from the fate of Eastern Europe.

On the other hand, to make free elections the pre-condition of any settlement, as the West insisted, was to ignore the Russian need for security and thus to be unrealistic. The fact that the Russians were willing to discuss the modalities of such elections was a sign that some compromise might be possible. This was precisely one of the points which the West ought to have probed as an earnest of Soviet intentions. Just because Russian fear of a rearmed West Germany backed by America was genuine, the price Moscow was prepared to pay might have been higher than the West rather off-handedly assumed. There was also room for discussion on what exactly the Russians meant by neutrality: that they were not willing to see seventy million Germans allied against them was understandable. As for the argument that West Germany naturally formed part of Western Europe, there is some truth in Schumacher's contention that German legitimate interests were being sacrificed to those of her western sponsors – though they might have had to be sacrificed anyway as the price of defeat. Adenauer may have been right in his belief that Russian terms, if fully probed, would have turned out unacceptable, even if the Soviet initiative was more than just an attempt to wreck western solidarity as Adenauer assumed. Where he and many others were mistaken was in supposing that the Dulles policy of 'rolling back' Russian power was feasible. Time was not on the side of the West. Twenty years later, any West German foreign minister who received an offer from Moscow like that of March 1952 would consider himself extremely fortunate.

West Germany thus concentrated on its own consolidation and security, though as we have seen the policy of rearmament was opposed by the S.P.D. and by many individuals or groups in other parties on grounds of pacifism or because they feared that it would perpetuate German disunity. As Gustav Heinemann, who resigned from Adenauer's cabinet on that issue, said later, the so-called policy of strength played the Soviet game, by persuading the West that it need not engage in serious negotiations with the Russians.[39] Public opinion continued to be anxious about the fate of the eighteen million fellow Germans in the Soviet Zone. The steady flow of emigrants from East to West testified to the prevailing discontent and at the same time prevented economic recovery. Stalin's death in March 1953 inspired hopes that it might be easier to do a deal with a more amenable Soviet government. The uncertainty of Russian policy in the following months probably made the West over-confident. The East German rising of June 1953 seemed to indicate that even the hardline

East Berlin regime would have to make concessions. Yet if the rising was a moment of truth for the Communists, it was no less one for the West. For the fact that the western powers could only look on helplessly while Soviet tanks crushed the rebels did much to undermine Dulles' theory that the West would intervene in Eastern Europe. It was to be finally exploded during the outbreaks in Poland and Hungary three years later. Morally the June rising was damaging to the Communists, but to their opponents as well. In terms of power politics it was harmful only to the West, for among its consequences were firstly a tightening of controls and party orthodoxy in East Germany, and secondly a downgrading of the importance of West Berlin. For while West Berlin continued to be a place of escape for refugees from the East, and a show window, listening post and publicity centre for the West (RIAS, the American radio station, had an appreciative audience in East Germany) the day when Berlin would become the capital of a reunited Germany had obviously become more distant. The often used phrase that West Berlin was an outpost of freedom was literally true: Berlin was out on a limb. The building of the Wall eight years later was to make the position even more brutally clear.

So long as the E.D.C. treaty was not ratified by the French, the Russians went on trying to reach agreement over Germany. But a four-power conference held in Berlin in January 1954 brought a settlement no nearer. The western ministers presented the Russians with a timetable for German reunification which began with free elections and ended with a peace treaty; the Russians insisted on proceeding in just the opposite order. The real nub was whether a reunited Germany should or should not belong to NATO. Implicitly throughout and later explicitly, Dulles made it clear that he expected that it would. In March 1954 the Soviet government made what in retrospect seems an astonishing proposal; it offered to join NATO, perhaps in the hope of turning it into the 'new Locarno' for which Churchill appealed in one of his speeches. The summit meeting of the Big Four at Geneva in July of that year was also unproductive as far as Germany was concerned. The Russians sought, now as always, to weaken the western position by sowing doubt between the Allies; this was not very difficult in view of lingering French suspicions of Germany, which were fed by embarrassing revelations about ex-Nazis in high positions in the Federal Republic. Indeed French unwillingness to accept E.D.C. was shown by its final rejection that same month; yet, however illogically, within a year France had agreed to a separate West German army within NATO. East Germany joined the Warsaw Pact, the counterpart to NATO, so that the German policies of both sides became enmeshed in the wider arrangements for European security. At the same time fear of thermonuclear war – the Soviet Union had by now exploded its first atomic bomb – made men less willing to take risks to alter the *status quo*. Both sides now accepted the *de facto* partition of Germany, and diplomatic activity on the general balance between East and West, with Germany taking a lower place on the agenda. For Adenauer one duty remained which he must discharge. Somehow the German prisoners still in the Soviet Union must be freed and repatriated. He decided to go to Russia to plead their case, at the same time hoping to use his influence with the Soviet leaders to break the deadlock on reunification. In August 1955, against the advice of his experts, Adenauer visited Moscow, where he was received with appropriate honours but found the bargaining tough. In order to obtain the release of the prisoners he had to agree to establish diplomatic relations with the Soviet Union, which already had them with East Germany (the D.D.R.). On unification no progress was made. To dissuade other countries from following Russia's example and recognising two German states, the Bonn government announced that it would regard recognition of the D.D.R. by any other country that did not already do so as an unfriendly act. This would keep the D.D.R. for some time, but not for ever, in a kind of diplomatic purdah.

By the end of 1955, with the Federal Republic's sovereignty fully recognised and a settlement of the Saar in sight, Adenauer had obtained from the West as much as the West could give. This was really the limit of his success. The negotiations between the West Germans and their western partners had been long and hard, but despite occasional setbacks, such as France's rejection of E.D.C. and the wrangle over the Saar, both sides could look back on the results with satisfaction. The Germans had achieved a moral and material position in the world unthinkable seven years before, while the Atlantic alliance had a reliable new ally, an asset instead of a liability. The other side of the medal was the diminishing prospect of reunification. For reasons already mentioned – the success of Soviet atomic research, the failure or refusal of the West to intervene in Poland and Hungary in 1956, the growing differences between the two German states with the inevitable effect of accomplished facts on habits of thought, the declining interest in the German question by comparison with the security issue – the Russian attitude hardened. In 1957 the first Sputnik gave spectacular proof of the advances made by Soviet scientists (with the help of 'captured' German scientists) in rocket technology and space research. The West Germans no longer believed that they could be protected by conventional weapons, and the demand grew for nuclear arms. This in turn alarmed the Russians and their allies, and spurred them to put forward proposals for an atom-free zone in Central Europe and for a thinning out of troops. This was the plan named after the Polish Foreign Minister Rapacki, which certainly had Soviet approval. The British government was interested. The American government at first showed reserve but later, when J. F. Kennedy became President, gave the idea serious consideration. The French, never happy at the prospect of a Russo-American deal to which they might not be a party, were sceptical. Adenauer viewed the whole subject of disengagement with distaste. He feared the exposure of West Germany which would follow an American withdrawal, for once the United States forces went back to America the whole balance of power in Europe would change in favour of the Russians. The partial neutralisation for the Federal Republic would, Adenauer believed, disrupt the western alliance and reduce West Germany's leverage in the struggle for unification. Also the Rapacki Plan would involve both German states signing a security pact and thus lead to recognition of the East Berlin regime.

It was a new consciousness of Russian strength coupled with fear of a West Germany provided with nuclear arms which prompted Moscow's next move. Khrushchev, the Communist party secretary who had become head of the Soviet government in March 1958, decided to issue an ultimatum on Berlin, which remained vulnerable because of its geographical isolation. In a speech made, significantly, in the Moscow Sport Palace on 10 November, followed by a Note to the three western powers seventeen days later, he declared that within six months the occupation of Berlin must be ended and the western garrisons must quit the city. The occupation powers still exercised by the Soviets in East Berlin would pass to the East German government and West Berlin would become a free city. Since the routes to and from Berlin would be controlled by the East German (D.D.R.) authorities, the western powers would be forced to recognise it and thus to acknowledge the existence of two German states. This was the greatest challenge to the West since the blockade. America and her allies were uncertain how to react. Dulles was a sick man with only a few months to live. No responsible western statesman was prepared to abandon Berlin, but there was understandable reluctance to become involved in thermonuclear war for the sake of one city, however important. A compromise seemed the only solution. One suggestion, actually proposed by Dulles, was for the West to recognise the D.D.R. officials as 'agents' of the Russians for purposes of traffic to and from West Berlin.[40] This was quite unacceptable to the Bonn government, which, however, had few ideas of its own. The West German interest was really to preserve the *status quo* since any likely change would be for the worse. Adenauer was worried by differences within the western camp. Only de Gaulle, newly come to power in Paris, seemed undaunted by the Russian threat. Macmillan, the British Prime Minister, facing a general election and needing popular support, paid a theatrical visit to Moscow without consulting his NATO allies. His talks with Khrushchev led to no concrete result but helped to tide over the dangerous period when the Soviet ultimatum expired. The Americans came out with a comprehensive plan for German unification in four stages at an international conference at Geneva in May 1959. A feature of this plan, to which the Bonn government had agreed with reluctance, was the co-option of representatives of both German states. But as the Russians rejected the plan *en bloc*, the deadlock remained. The Soviet Union had now completely abandoned the language of Potsdam and manifestly wished to keep Germany divided until such time as reunification could be brought about on its terms. The first step was recognition of the D.D.R., whose 'socialist achievements' must be extended to West Germany. Adenauer's scepticism of the value of East-West meetings on Germany seemed fully justified. But the Americans were still interested in discussing the whole question of security and believed that useful business could be done. In September 1959 Khrushchev visited the United States and had talks with President Eisenhower at Camp David. The tour was a propaganda success for the ebullient Khrushchev, and Eisenhower was less than firm over Berlin. A further and more formal summit meeting between the two men was arranged in Paris the following May. This proved a fiasco, following the capture by the Russians of an American Intelligence pilot intruding on Soviet air space. The local Berlin crisis smouldered on, with harassment of traffic to and from the city by East German border guards, but summit diplomacy helped to reduce its relative importance, and other trouble spots, notably Cuba, stole the limelight. Khrushchev had not carried out his threat, but the threat remained.

Adenauer's last years were marked by conflicting trends in German foreign policy. Circumstances were no longer so favourable as they had been. It was one thing for the Federal Republic to become identified with the West when the West meant Acheson or his successor, Dulles, with whom Adenauer had been linked in friendship as well as identity of view. It was another matter when Kennedy was in power in Washington and when de Gaulle was developing an independent policy which had certain attractions for Germany, but led to Franco-American differences. Kennedy, who entered the White House in January 1961, was anxious to break the deadlock with Russia and end the cold war. Whereas Dulles had spoken of massive retaliation, the new slogans were graduated response, flexible defence and limited engagement. There must be no escalation into war. This meant playing down the German problem. Adenauer thought Kennedy's confidence brash, but as West Germany was wholly dependent on the United States for her security he dared not oppose the young President's search for a settlement with the Soviet Union. In simple terms West Germany, faced by a choice between America and France, was bound to choose America, but the presence of German 'Gaullists' in the Adenauer cabinet was a complicating factor. Kennedy's first and only meeting with Khrushchev at Vienna in June 1961 again appeared to justify Adenauer's pessimism. There was no longer in the western camp the same insistence on free elections before the projected peace treaty or on the freedom of a united Germany to join NATO. This was a concession to realism. But Khrushchev would not abandon his demand for prior recognition of the D.D.R., which he had the temerity to suggest was required by the principle of self-determination. The western view that the D.D.R. was an odious state because it persecuted its own citizens was only confirmed by the building of the Berlin Wall in August 1961. The emotional reaction in West Berlin caused disturbances which nearly got out of hand. The demand (as in June 1953) was for the West to do something, and when nothing happened, people felt understandably bitter. It is hard to say what the West could have done, short of knocking down the Wall, which would have been rebuilt further back if by that time war had not broken out. But neither Allied nor West German Intelligence appeared to have foreseen the Wall at that date, and therefore no countermeasures had been planned. The Allied reaction was in fact slow and uncertain. Kennedy sent General Clay, the hero of the blockade, to address the Berliners and bolster morale, and two years later the President himself visited the city. He made a speech in which he re-affirmed the promise that America would not leave West Berlin and declared that he was proud to be a Berliner, a sentiment which was much applauded. But there is no denying that the Wall was a moral and material defeat for the West. Of the three million people who had moved from East to West Germany in the preceding twelve years, a high proportion had come through Berlin, whose role as the gate to freedom had now virtually ended. Henceforth the only refugees who arrived did so illegally at peril of their lives. The ingenuity and courage shown by those determined to cross the frontier deserve to rank high among the escape epics of the twentieth century, and resulted in the frontier's becoming ever more impenetrable and lethal, with its concrete pill-boxes manned day and night. Tension rose dangerously whenever a refugee was shot while trying to break through into West Berlin, a not infrequent occurrence. Apart from the scores of known victims there were many unknown ones, who fell on the eastern side before they could cross. For Germans at least, the Wall symbolises as nothing else the cold war, and for them it will not be over as long as the Wall stands.

Despite the infamous Wall, the search for a détente went on, and the State Department produced a plan for international control of road and air routes to Berlin under a consortium of thirteen governments. Adenauer disliked the scheme, which among other objectionable features provided for a reduction of the West Berlin garrison to a total of 9,000, and torpedoed it by leaking its contents to the press.[41] His fear was that in their search for agreement with the Russians, the Americans would sell out German interests. The Americans understood German fears, which were no doubt exaggerated, but resented the lack of constructive proposals from Bonn, and there was a crisis in German-American relations when the Federal Republic's ambassador was virtually expelled from Washington. Kennedy's attitude to Russia necessarily stiffened after the Cuban missiles confrontation later that year. Both super-powers recoiled from the brink of war, and the Berlin crisis fizzled out. Yet the Cuban affair, in showing that America and Russia had one supreme interest in common – the avoidance of nuclear conflict – implied that the possibility of a deal between them at the expense of lesser powers such as Germany had increased rather than diminished.

His distrust of Kennedy's policy made Adenauer more receptive than we would otherwise have been to the ideas of de Gaulle, whom he met for the first time shortly after the latter's return to power in May 1958. Despite the obvious differences between the two men, they shared certain basic beliefs and found a good deal of common ground. De Gaulle was as sceptical as Adenauer of the summit diplomacy which many people in England and America were then hailing as almost a panacea for East-West understanding. Adenauer was impressed by de Gaulle's imperviousness to Russian threats and by his tendency to take a hard line over Berlin. De Gaulle needed Adenauer as a partner in his attempt to construct a European policy independent of America. The differences between them was that Adenauer never shared the Frenchman's pathological anti-Americanism or his vision of Europe as a continent dominated by France. Indeed de Gaulle's nationalism was such that he frustrated Adenauer's attempts to develop the institutions of the Common Market towards supra-nationalism. De Gaulle's later decision to take France out of NATO and his blatant attempt to establish an independent French nuclear power were not compatible with German interests and destroyed much of the sympathy which the

General won during a triumphant tour of West Germany during the late summer of 1962, in the course of which he said many things soothing to German self-esteem. Adenauer's flirtation with de Gaulle could not make Germans forget for one moment that their safety depended on American power. But it could remind America that it should not presume too far on German friendship, and there was the prospect that de Gaulle might soften East European hostility to the Federal Republic by his carefully cultivated contacts with the Communist states even if his ideas on German reunification did not coincide with Bonn's. Above all, it ensured a continuation of that Franco-German *rapprochement* which was dear to Adenauer, and which was embodied in the treaty of friendship signed in January 1963 – one of the old Chancellor's last acts. Yet even here there was a flaw, for at the same time de Gaulle vetoed the British application to join the Common Market against the wishes of his partners, including most Germans. In retrospect it is clear that de Gaulle used Adenauer for purposes which brought no benefit to Germany. It has even been suggested (with perhaps excessive subtlety) that de Gaulle's toughness on Berlin and German unification was motivated by a secret French desire to keep Germany divided, since it made less likely a German-Russian understanding.[42] Certainly the Franco-German relationship has worked out rather one-sidedly in favour of France, particularly in matters of economic policy.

Though there were many German 'Gaullists' in the C.D.U., including Adenauer himself and Franz Joseph Strauss, who was Minister of Defence before his resignation over the *Spiegel* affair in 1962, Erhard, the Chancellor after Adenauer, was not among them. He and his Foreign Minister Schröder brought the Federal Republic back on its previous course in line with America, though the old cordiality was not restored. The earlier one-sided relationship had been replaced by one of a more equal character, and Germany's growing wealth enabled her to bear a greater share of the common defence burden. The Americans had tried to satisfy German fears for security and desire of equality of status by proposing a Multilateral Nuclear Force of which Germany would be a partner.[43] The plan was ill received in France and England and had a mixed welcome even in the Federal Republic. In the United States doubts about its military credibility added to the embarrassment caused by hostility to the project in Paris and Moscow. Yet when it was quietly dropped by President Johnson in 1965, the Erhard government felt slighted. As the sixties went on, the United States became increasing absorbed in Vietnam, and West Germany found itself supporting American policy there simply in order to make sure of reciprocal backing over Berlin. This was distressing to many who knew that no German interests were at stake in Vietnam and disap-

proved of what the Americans were doing there. Yet de Gaulle's growing inclination to neutralism tended to leave Germany dangerously
isolated in Europe. No progress was made on the unification issue. On
the contrary, the prospects grew dimmer. Efforts to control the conflict actually made its ultimate solution more remote: a temporary
relief was bought at the cost of a long-term *impasse*. As as recent writer
has commented, the paradox is that 'without an abating of East-
West tensions neither side could afford to allow German unification on
the opponent's terms, yet an East-West détente contained the possibility that the German *status quo* might get not only a tacit but also a
legal blessing'.[44] So long as Khrushchev was in power there was at least
the possibility of a deal between the Soviet Union and the Federal
Republic, especially during the years 1958–62, when Hans Kroll was
ambassador in Moscow. Kroll was successful in getting on unusually
cordial terms with Khrushchev in spite of the 1958 ultimatum and the
Berlin Wall. On several occasions the Russians, already engaged in
inconclusive talks with the Americans, suggested direct talks with the
West Germans, and in some ways, as Kroll writes in his Memoirs,
Adenauer was the right man for Khrushchev to negotiate with.[45] He
alone among German politicians had the authority to make so important and controversial a settlement, he was trusted by the Americans,
and the two men, despite their obvious antipathy, respected each
other, as their meetings in 1955 had shown. Yet in other ways, such as
his one-sidedly western orientation, Adenauer was far from being the
ideal negotiator in Moscow. Kroll himself was an ardent advocate of a
deal with Russia and he suggests that his confidential talks with
Khrushchev laid the foundations of what might have become another
opportunity of bringing about German reunification. Kroll himself went
beyond his brief and was recalled to Bonn. Khrushchev had actually
been invited to visit Bonn when he fell from power in October 1964.
His liking for speculative diplomacy, of which his move towards a deal
with Bonn was an example, was probably one reason for his disgrace.
Certainly his successors in the Kremlin have been altogether more
cautious in their approach to the German problem. Meanwhile the
increasing economic strength and prestige of the D.D.R. have given it
more weight within the East European grouping, though over Berlin,
to judge by the 1971 treaty, the East German government appeared to
have overplayed its hand.

If the Federal government's foreign policy has been mainly concerned, in the first place with its western partners inside and outside
the Common Market, and in the next place with the eastern bloc
and the problem of the D.D.R., there is a third facet which is easily
overlooked: relations with the Third World, particularly the develop-

ing countries of Asia and Africa. As a creditor nation with capital to invest, skills to impart and trade to offer, West Germany is able to play an important part. It was rather slow at first to assume this role as it had fewer connections with countries concerned than Britain and France, and was very conscious of the political and economic risks involved. In 1965 only 9 per cent of its foreign investments and only 3·5 per cent of its foreign trade was in Asia, Africa and South America.[46] In its favour was that as Germany had not been a colonial power since 1919 it was less tarred with the imperialist brush than other powers, and was not involved in the ungratifying colonial wars which in many cases preceded the granting or winning of independence. In recent years Bonn's Ministry for Economic Co-operation has stepped up its contributions, which total over 35 milliard marks altogether since 1950. In 1969 West Germany spent 1·33 per cent of its gross national product on the developing countries, the second highest percentage of any western nation. The aid takes many different forms and has been supplied to 91 countries. Some of the capital is provided by the government, some by private industry; it goes either direct, or is channelled through the Specialised Agencies of the United Nations and other international organisations such as the Asian Development Bank. Germans have built steel works, hydro-electric stations, model farms, dams and irrigation works. They have sent abroad scientists, technicians, teachers, doctors and agricultural advisers. In 1969 over 20,000 persons from the developing countries were being trained in Germany or by Germans in their own homelands for technical or managerial jobs.

Yet in the Third World too the problem of German disunity casts its shadow. Bonn has used its aid programme to induce receiving countries to adhere to the 'Hallstein doctrine' and has cancelled such aid where, as in the case of Egypt in the spring of 1965, the recipient developed cordial relations with the East German rival. It is, paradoxically, with the Arab countries that the Federal Republic has experienced most difficulty. German tourists in the Near East and North Africa during the post-war years found themselves embarrassingly popular, and it was not uncommon for them to be greeted with 'Heil Hitler' by the local inhabitants. The Helwan steelworks near Cairo was built by West Germans. But the West German-Arab honeymoon ended with the Federal Republic's treaty with Israel, and the massive reparations received by the Israelis, which according to the Arabs included American arms, led to the breaking off of diplomatic relations with Bonn by most of the Arab states. The Federal government to its credit continued to fulfil its obligations to Israel in spite of the risk that the Arabs would in retaliation recognise the

D.D.R. In recent years there have been a few signs of improvement between some of the Arab governments and West Germany, though Egypt's growing dependence on the Soviet Union before and after the war of 1967 meant that in Cairo East German influence had supplanted that of the West Germans.

(iv) THE OTHER GERMANY: THE D.D.R. AS A MODEL SATELLITE

The story of the D.D.R. (German Democratic Republic), as the Russian-occupied Zone of Germany has been officially known since 1949, really begins with plans made by the Soviet government and its German collaborators during the war. In July 1943, when it was clear that Hitler's attempt to destroy the Soviet Union had failed, a National Committee for a Free Germany was set up in Moscow. It consisted of German Communists in exile and prominent German prisoners of war, and its object was to encourage resistance to Hitler both inside the German army and among the civilian population. In contrast to western propaganda, which at that stage of the war offered little but unconditional surrender, Free German broadcasts on Moscow radio promised that, if the German people would help Russia overthrow the Nazi regime, they would have a bright future in democracy and independence.[47] A League of German Officers was also formed in 1943 under the chairmanship of General von Seydlitz, a member of an old Prussian family who had been second-in-command to von Paulus at Stalingrad. Paulus himself joined the League after the 20 July plot against Hitler, which the League heartily supported. Besides the broadcasting, the Free Germany Committee published a newspaper called 'Free Germany', which circulated among the tens of thousands of prisoners of war. In this propaganda the emphasis was on German or rather Prussian traditions, and much play was made with such historic names as Yorck (who had made the agreement with Russia against Napoleon at Tauroggen), Scharnhorst and Stein. Little was said about Marx or Communism. It was only later that the Russians, who at the time praised the anti-Hitler conspirators as heroes, discovered that they represented an alliance of reactionary generals and monopoly capitalists in league with British and American imperialism.[48] When the invasion of Germany began in the winter of 1944–5 a manifesto signed by fifty of the eighty captured German generals called upon the German population to end the catastrophic war. Attention now focused on the political tasks ahead, for which a handpicked group of German Communists had been carefully prepared.[49] The senior of them was Wilhelm Pieck, a veteran of the German Socialist movement who had been a founder member of the K.P.D., a companion of Liebknecht

and Rosa Luxemburg during the January 1919 rising, and later a
member of the Reichstag. But the most important was Walther
Ulbricht, a Saxon, and like Pieck originally a carpenter. He too had
been in the German Communist party since its beginning and in the
Reichstag from 1928 to 1933. Whereas Pieck was a rather jovial,
avuncular figure, who, being neither a Marxist theorist nor a faction
leader, had survived the heresy hunts of the twenties with apparent
equanimity, Ulbricht was a younger and much more ruthless personality. He was already seen as the key man in Russia's plans for post-
war Germany. A gifted organiser with an immense capacity for work
and thoroughly trusted by Moscow, he was the party official, the
apparatchik par excellence. On 30 April 1945, before the German surrender, a group of ten men, led by Ulbricht, flew to Germany to take
up their new duties. Making contact with local anti-fascist groups, they
began to revive political life in the Soviet Occupation Zone under
the supervision of the Soviet Military Administration, whose headquarters was in the Berlin suburb of Karlshorst.

The Russian objective in Germany, as defined at the time, differed
little from that of the other occupying powers. Militarism and Nazism
were to be uprooted, democracy established and the bourgeois revolution – overdue since 1848 – completed (as the preliminary to socialisation). This was to be accomplished by a coalition of anti-fascist parties,
bourgeois and working class – a popular front policy brought up to
date. There was no immediate question of a Soviet Germany or of
reviving the hardline Communism of the Weimar period. This was in
conformity with the general Russian strategy at the time in all the
satellites: Czechoslovakia for example was governed by a mixed coalition, and in theory all Germany was still under four-power control. The
Russians were anxious not to antagonise German opinion outside their
Zone as well as inside it. Political moderation was also advisable in view
of the heavy reparations which the Russians were beginning to extract
from the East German economy. In choosing mayors, *Landräte* and
other officials, care was taken not to appoint only Communists. The
first provincial elections, held in 1946, were contested by three parties:
the Socialist Unity party or S.E.D., Liberals and Christian Democrats.
Later two other parties were formed: one for farmers and one, called
the National Democratic party, for ex-Nazis. Thus all acceptable shades
of opinion were catered for. But behind this democratic façade power
was exercised by one party, the S.E.D. This was the result of a merger
between Communists and Social Democrats that took place in April
1946. The Russians naturally wanted the Communist party to hold
power but to do so with the appearance of popular support. If the
Communists could capture the Socialist vote they might get a majority:

in any case, the Socialists had always been a much larger party than the K.P.D. There was a strong feeling among both the left-wing parties that the bitter rivalry which had been so disastrous before 1933 must not continue, and some kind of working agreement was generally favoured. But on what terms? In West Germany and in Berlin, it was realised that the Communists, who initiated the merger, were acting as the instrument of the Russian occupying power. While Grotewohl, the Social Democratic leader in Berlin, was willing to do a deal with Pieck and Ulbricht, the S.P.D. head in West Germany, Kurt Schumacher, was not. Under Russian pressure the deal went through, with Grotewohl and Pieck ostentatiously shaking hands in a much publicised ceremony under the approving photograph of Karl Marx. In theory, within the new combined party, Socialists and Communists had parity of status; in practice it was the Communists who called the tune. But by claiming the allegiance of the millions of previous socialist voters the S.E.D. was able to secure between 44 per cent and 50 per cent of the vote in the election of the first provincial parliaments. (Had the S.P.D. and K.P.D. entered the election separately their combined total would probably have been higher – there were some defections to the middle-class parties.) Although in each of the five provinces (Mecklenburg, Brandenburg, Saxony, Saxony-Anhalt and Thuringia) a coalition government was formed, in every case except one the Prime Minister was a member of the S.E.D., and four out of the five Ministers of the Interior were also S.E.D. In the West Berlin election held at the same time the S.E.D. was heavily defeated by the S.P.D. and even trailed behind the C.D.U.; henceforth the S.P.D. was forbidden to function in East Germany, and great difficulties were put in its way in East Berlin – a breach of the four-power agreement, which the western powers were powerless to prevent.

Meanwhile a major programme of economic change had been launched in the Russian Zone. It began with agriculture. All estates of over a hundred hectares (roughly 240 acres) were broken up and the land divided among small farmers and landless labourers. This was the counterpart to the Bolsheviks' land distribution in 1917, and like it was intended only as a transition stage before collectivisation. (This came in East Germany at the end of the 1950s.) Like the big landowners, but more so, the big capitalists were denounced for having brought Hitler to power; their expropriation without compensation was therefore held to be justified. Industry was nationalised, the banks and insurance companies liquidated. The greater part of trade was also brought under public ownership, with special state-owned shops ('H.O.') for goods not rationed. A central planning board was set up, and price and wage controls continued. The problem of feeding the population was less acute in the Russian Zone than in the heavily urbanised British Zone, and the average East German had slightly more calories than his opposite number in West Germany during the immediate post-war years despite dislocation caused by land reform. There was however no equivalent in the East to the West's spectacular recovery after currency reform in 1948, and rationing in East Germany went on until 1958. Many factors combined to keep the standard of living of the East German population low. The chief was the crippling effect of dismantling and other forms of reparations. Estimates of the cost of dismantling vary considerably: one puts it at about £350 million.[50] The list of objects taken included railway engines, track and workshops, power stations, electricity plant, breweries and optical firms. In the early years of the occupation over a third of current production was removed as reparations. Labour (not only of P.O.Ws) was conscripted by the Russians. In addition, Soviet corporations took over a number of firms or industries and as trading companies bought up a large number of German products from coal to jewellery for sale in the Soviet Union. The total cost of reparations of one kind or another is not known and even the estimates vary enormously. According to one estimate each East German paid in reparations nearly twenty times as much as the average West German (2,500 DM compared with 140 DM); another calculation shows the difference as of the order of 200 to 1.[51] The East German population also had to pay occupation costs, but received of course no equivalent of Marshall Aid. Finally, the East German economy was diverted from its natural markets in West Germany and Western Europe and forced to buy and sell in the less advantageous markets of the communist states, and in particular to sell goods to Russia at unfavourable prices – in effect a disguised form of reparations though one which was shared by the other satellites. It is not surprising that in view of all these handicaps and of the evident prosperity in West Germany, every year a proportion of the East German population decided to migrate across the zonal border. The immeasurably greater freedom in the West and absence of the political pressure which in the East was inescapable were another reason for quitting. Once one member of a family left, his relations tended to follow. In the years 1950 to 1961, before the Berlin Wall was built, the annual number of emigrants from East to West (including West Berlin) never fell below 173,000, and in one year (1953) it reached the total of 408,000.[52] Altogether in little more than a decade the East German population fell from nineteen to seventeen million. This continual drain of manpower, much of it young and skilled, was another heavy burden on the East German economy.

The comparatively lenient policy followed in the first years of occupation, described as the 'German way to socialism', was superseded after 1948 by the transformation of East Germany into a people's democracy or proletarian dictatorship. This again was in line with Soviet policy, which hardened with the growing hostility between the two halves of Europe. The Berlin blockade brought the full rigours of the cold war, and Stalin's denunciation of the 'traitor' Tito created new fears and tensions inside the Communist camp. There were heresy trials in Czechoslovakia. The establishment of the Federal Republic at Bonn was matched by parallel moves in East Berlin. In December 1947 a People's Congress was called to demand an all-German peace treaty. This was supposed to be an all-German body (though few came from the West) representing trade unions, mass organisations and intellectuals as well as political parties. Forty per cent of its members were from the S.E.D. The Congress soon functioned as a quasi-parliament. In 1948 it elected a main committee known as a National Council with three chairmen drawn from the three main parties. In March 1949 this National Council approved a constitution for an independent East German state. Another People's Congress was then elected by a procedure which made the result a foregone conclusion; candidates were chosen from a single list and the usual pressures were applied. A second National Council convened in October 1949 as a temporary parliament, pending the election of a permanent parliament (People's Chamber) a year later. The Russian-occupied Zone was formally proclaimed to be the German Democratic Republic and a government was appointed, with Pieck as President and Grotewohl as Prime Minister. The formal change made little real difference. The Soviet Military Administration was replaced by a Control Commission. The new government had a Foreign Ministry, but outside the eastern bloc it was not recognised, and so far as the Russians gave up their powers they did so to the S.E.D., not to the East German electorate. From the beginning the problem had been how to reconcile the form of democracy with the reality of minority dictatorship in the interests of the occupying power. So far as parliamentary representation was concerned, the solution lay in the mobilising of mass organisations and giving them, as well as the parties, representation in the People's Chamber. These organisations were the Free German Youth, the Communist ('Free') Trade Unions, the Democratic Women's League, the *Kulturbund* and the Association of Victims of Nazism. Since these were all under S.E.D. influence if not actually attached to it, the S.E.D. had a working majority in the Chamber despite having only 25 per cent of the seats. The percentage of seats for each party was worked out beforehand. The parliament is thus a pseudo-parliament, and in any case has no real power.[53] Policy is made by the S.E.D. on the Leninist principle of democratic centralism, which means that important decisions are made by the party's supreme cabinet or Politbüro. Many of its existing leaders, including former Communists as well as Social Democrats, were degraded and expelled. In the harsher political climate several of the middle-class party leaders, such as Jakob Kaiser, a Christian Democrat who had worked with the resistance against Hitler, and Ernst Lemmer, another C.D.U. man who had represented the Democratic party in the Weimar Reichstag, fled to the West after falling foul of the authorities for refusing to take part in the People's Congress. More and more key posts were monopolised by the S.E.D.

The party's new course was laid down at its third congress in July 1950, at which Ulbricht was elected its general secretary. Its task was defined as to direct the activity of the state machine with the help of its members working in that machine. It was to be a governing élite. 'The aim of the party is socialism, which presupposes the political domination of the working class.'[54] Apart from the Leninist reorganisation of the S.E.D., the tougher policy was shown in several ways. The abolition of the five historic *Länder* in favour of a single government area divided into fourteen districts was an act of centralisation that facilitated control from the top. Class concepts were officially applied to the administration of justice. Despite the Soviet Note on German unification of March 1952, and other gestures of that kind, the S.E.D. leaders showed that they were more concerned with consolidating their own power and in deliberately emphasising the difference between East and West Germany. The D.D.R. already had a people's police force equipped with tanks and guns – a militarised force, in fact. There was also a 'sea police' and an 'air police'. Young people were encouraged to join a 'Society for Sport and Technology' whose activities included shooting, gliding, parachuting, navigation and signalling as well as normal sports, games and athletics. As soon as West Germany had her own army, the D.D.R. turned the para-military police force into a National People's Army and joined the Warsaw Pact. At the end of the 1950s a vigorous drive was begun to encourage the 'voluntary' elimination of the private farmer in favour of state farms and co-operatives. By 1963 90 per cent of the land was collectively owned. It was the loss of their holdings which caused many thousands of small farmers to abandon their possessions and seek a new home in the West. Some even committed suicide.

This was the background to the building of the Berlin Wall, which was preceded eight years earlier by the rising of 1953. The unrest which caused the rising arose mainly from continued economic difficulties in a period of political uncertainty. Stalin's death in March

1953 relieved tension all over the Communist world and was the
signal for a more relaxed policy in Russia. Where Moscow led the way,
East Berlin must follow. The demand was heard for a new course,
what was later known as destalinisation. Discontent was general. There
was a shortage of food and other consumer goods caused by a lack
of raw materials and defects in planning, and reparations to Russia
were still a burden. In its attitude to these problems the leadership of
the D.D.R. was divided. A 'liberal' wing, headed by Zaisser, Minister
for Security, and Herrnstadt, editor of the S.E.D. daily *Neues Deutschland*, advocated making concessions to the workers such as allocating
a higher proportion of resources to consumer goods. The hard or conservative line was represented by Ulbricht, the single most important
figure, but the 'liberals' had Russian backing, notably that of Semonov,
the Soviet High Commissioner.[55] Basically it was a wrangle between
those who wanted to get national unity in Germany before creating a
socialist society, and those who put socialism in one country (the
D.D.R.) before an all-German agreement.[56] While the party leaders
were arguing over these issues, unrest among the workers reached
breaking point. It was the classical situation for a revolution. A long
period of repression had been followed by a quasi-liberal policy of
unsure aims and duration. Then the government decided that the
workers' output must be increased and ordered a raising of work
norms. This meant more work for the same wages. In the highly
charged atmosphere this was the flashpoint which sparked off the rising.
It was led by the building workers, many of whom were employed in
the new Stalin-Allee, almost the only architectural showpiece of the
East German regime. In making a protest march the builders were
joined by thousands of other workers from the suburbs, who merged
with them in a huge demonstration which occupied the centre of East
Berlin. Word of the strike spread through the city, and the authorities
were patently not in control. Crowds, consisting mainly of young
people, came out in support of the strikers, surrounded the ministries and public buildings, tore down red flags, sickle and hammer
signs and other insignia of Communist rule, and set fire to them. The
red flag was hauled off the top of the Brandenburg Gate, while the
police were jeered and stoned. At least one minister was mobbed and
almost lynched. Most of the party bosses, including Ulbricht, were in
hiding. In the course of the afternoon Soviet tanks appeared on the
scene, and forced back the crowd. Shots were fired. By nightfall the
sector border had been sealed off and order was restored with martial
law. Reprisals followed with summary trials, executions and prison sentences. Similar risings occurred in the other main East German centres.
The total executed was 141; and 432 others, mostly demonstrators

but including police and a few Russians, also lost their lives.[57] Although the D.D.R. authorities predictably blamed the West for having used its spies and agents to incite the rising, it was in fact a spontaneous explosion of discontent and very much a working class affair. It is wholly explicable in terms of the economic situation and the general unpopularity of the government: one National Prize winner of the D.D.R. admitted a month later: 'We have not got ten per cent of the people with us.'[58] As Brecht wrote in one of his most ironic poems, the government had lost faith in the people.[59] Because the West was unaware of what was really happening in the D.D.R. and of the differences within the Communist camp, it was unable to take advantage of these difficulties. A more discerning and flexible policy in the West might have paid dividends in terms of German reunification. The fact that when the rising began, Reuter, the Governing Mayor of West Berlin, was away in Vienna was symptomatic of western unpreparedness.

All this was now changed. Ulbricht, who had been in great danger of being ousted, was unexpectedly saved, for the Russians could not dismiss him without loss of face. As for Zaisser and Herrnstadt, the events of 17 June made them close ranks with the hard-liners. Their fate depended on what happened in Moscow, where leading members of the party hierarchy were contending for mastery. Zaisser and Herrnstadt were backing Beria, who as Minister for Security was Zaisser's opposite number in the Soviet Union. They were unlucky: on 9 July Beria was arrested on charges of treason. His disgrace and execution followed. That was the end of Zaisser and Herrnstadt. Ulbricht remained the victor. He was forced to admit that mistakes had been made, especially in economic planning; and in future more notice was taken of the workers' wishes. Since East Berlin could not keep out of step with Moscow, Ulbricht had reluctantly to adopt a policy of 'creeping destalinisation', though this had little practical importance except in relation to the economy. If the June rising was the most serious challenge to his leadership, he continued to be embarrassed by other signs of discord within the Communist world. Khrushchev's criticisms of Stalin were indirectly a reflection on Ulbricht, and the revolts in Poland and Hungary in the same year (1956) were unsettling for East Germany. Further tensions within the S.E.D. over the acceptable degree of liberalisation led to a fresh purge, as a result of which three party veterans, Oelssner, Wollweber and Schirdewan, were expelled from the Politbüro. Perhaps, in retrospect, Ulbricht felt that the later disgrace of Khrushchev justified his own cautious orthodoxy.

In the 1960s Ulbricht ruled East Germany without a rival, a scarred but successful veteran of the Communist movement, the victorious sur-

vivor of many purges and intrigues. He was indeed the centre of a
remarkable personality cult, intended to present him as a genial kind-
hearted father of his people: this was no doubt necessary to neutralise
his notorious unpopularity. Pieck, the Republic's first and only President, died in 1960: his duties devolved on the chairman of a new
supreme body, the state council of the D.D.R., who was in fact
Ulbricht. Grotewohl, who had been little more than a figurehead, died
in 1964 after a long period of poor health. Ulbricht, younger than
Adenauer, was even longer in power; he resigned in 1970. Both
throve on the cold war, the intransigence of each sharpening the antagonism between them. Each blamed the other for dividing Germany.
For Adenauer Ulbricht was Germany's Stalin; for Ulbricht the Federal
Republic was a hotbed of militarism, 'revanchism' and American imperialism. It was often said that if the Russians really wanted a settlement over Germany they would have had to depose Ulbricht. He was
a liability in the early days when it might have suited the Russians to
liquidate the D.D.R. By the sixties he was too valuable to be discarded.
Ulbricht's name was held in particular detestation after his decision
in August 1961 – following an official denial – to build the Berlin Wall.
He did so only after consulting Moscow, and there is some reason to
believe that he may have acted only after Khrushchev rejected the
alternative, which Ulbricht himself might have preferred, of a separate
peace treaty between the D.D.R. and the Soviet Union.[60] Such a treaty
would have meant handing controls over traffic to and from West
Berlin to D.D.R. officials. This, if done without western agreement,
could have given rise to a more dangerous crisis than that provoked by
the Wall. The continuing loss of many of its most valuable citizens had
brought the D.D.R. near to collapse, and the gap in the state's economy
represented by West Berlin had caused a drain of resources. Before the
Wall western visitors were able to buy goods in East Berlin with cheap
East marks bought in the West. This was now made impossible.

The trading pattern of the East German economy was set in the
1950s. Dismantling stopped in 1948, reparations officially ended in
1953. Just as the Federal Republic was a member of the O.E.E.C. in
Paris, so the D.D.R. joined the equivalent organisation in Eastern
Europe, COMECON, in Warsaw. Since 1954 the policy of
COMECON has been to integrate the various national economies.
The resulting interdependence has made each member state less able
to practise economic autonomy. About four-fifths of East German
trade is with the Communist Eastern Europe, of which half is with the
Soviet Union itself. This meant a complete readjustment and adapta-
tion. Steel and hard coal no longer came as before from Western
Germany. A symbol of the new economic orientation is the new iron

and steel complex at Eisenhüttenstadt, where steel is made with the help of Polish coal and Russian ore. About 12 per cent of D.D.R. trade is with the Federal Republic. Interzonal commerce is highly political on both sides. In the East, distrust of capitalist states and fear of becoming too dependent on them are inhibiting factors. In the West, opinion is torn between people's desire to help their poor relations and unwillingness to relieve economic pressures which embarrass an unpopular government. Apart from this, for West Germans interzonal trade is significant in two ways. First it is one of the few ways in which ties between the two parts of their divided country can be maintained and still further estrangement avoided. Secondly, it is a lever which can be pulled, if necessary, to relieve pressure on West Berlin. For whenever the D.D.R. government makes a move against the city, almost the only retaliation open to the Bonn government is to threaten to cut off trade. In practice this threat is rarely acted on, and was not resorted to even when the Wall was built. For the rest, the D.D.R. economy followed the Russian example. A State Planning Commission was set up in 1950, and the first Five Year Plan began the following year. The 'Activist' movement to raise productivity through socialist competition in the fifties was the East German equivalent of the Stakhanov movement in Russia in the thirties, and Adolf Hennecke, the pioneer who raised his quota to 287 per cent above the norm and became a national hero, was also a miner. The collectivisation went on through the fifties and into the sixties: the 22 per cent of private industry in 1950 had sunk to 2.4 per cent in 1963; commerce, 42 per cent private in 1950, was only 11 per cent private in 1963; the percentage of agriculture in private hands fell from 88 to 10.[61] In two branches of the economy, agriculture and commerce, co-operatives outnumbered state enterprises, and there were mixed undertakings in which the state went into partnership with a private firm. Lessons were learned from the mistakes which preceded the 1953 rising. In the early sixties planning became less rigid and centralised. Following the Russian lead, especially those reforms advocated by the economist Yevsei Liberman, market forces were allowed more scope, and individual factories were expected to make a profit. Managers were given power of free decision and were even permitted to keep a share of their profits. To prevent inflation, wages were allowed to rise only after an increase in productivity. The man who successfully introduced these changes into the economy of the D.D.R. was Erich Apel, who, however, committed suicide in 1965 in protest against an unfavourable trade treaty with the Soviet Union. The Wall had stopped the outflow of labour and goods. As a result of a combination of these factors, East Germany produced its own 'economic miracle' in the sixties. Between 1950 and 1970 its national income was quadrupled.[62] A big contribution to the new prosperity was made by new or much expanded industries like shipbuilding. For the first time the East German consumer had a wide range of quality goods to choose from, and could obtain such things as tropical fruit and real coffee. More recently Western fashions and pop music have become acceptable. The D.D.R. is now the fifth industrial state in Europe and its living standards are the highest in the Communist world. Agricultural output has also risen since the setbacks caused by forced collectivisation were overcome, and productivity per acre again compares favourably with that of the other East European states. In January 1969 *Neues Deutschland* claimed that the D.D.R.'s industrial output was greater than that of the whole of Germany in 1936.[63]

The D.D.R. leaders are fond of boasting about the 'social achievements' of their state. By this they mean in the first place the claim that it is a workers' and farmers' regime. Power in fact is exercised by the Communist élite, of whom in 1963 only 33 per cent were classified as workers and 6·2 per cent as farmers.[64] The technical intelligentsia who run the country's increasingly sophisticated economy may be largely of working-class origin, but their academic and specialised training puts them in the middle class together with civil servants, teachers, clergymen, nurses and journalists. The D.D.R. is of course a welfare state. Its comprehensive insurance system is run within the national budget by the trade unions, who also look after the welfare side of industrial relations. The unions are not, as in a free enterprise society, pressure groups for raising wages, for in a workers' state there can, officially, be no conflict between wage-earners and society, and exploitation is absent by definition. As in the Soviet Union, the unions are really an instrument ('transmission belts') of the ruling party. The same could be said of another aspect of social policy, the schools and universities. The D.D.R. is proud of its educational progress. Universities have expanded and facilities for technological training have been greatly enlarged. In higher education preference was given to those with a working-class background, and in 1967 about two students out of five were in this category. At all levels there is indoctrination in Marxism-Leninism, and no university student can graduate without having taken such a course. Education is seen, not as a field within which an individual seeks truth or knowledge but as a discipline through which the state directs the citizens' minds and mobilises its human resources. Outside formal education the same aim is pursued. One of the most important agencies is the Free German Youth, the blue-shirted organisation to which the majority of boys and girls belong, entering the Young Pioneers at the age of six and proceeding at the age of fourteen to the main body. An innovation in the D.D.R. is the *Jugendweihe* or Youth Dedication ceremony for adolescents at which the candidate, having been prepared beforehand, solemnly promises to do his utmost for the 'great and noble cause of socialism'. This is a kind of secular equivalent to Confirmation and is not unnaturally regarded as an attempt to wean youth away from Christianity. The churches have not had an easy time. This is inevitable in a regime which makes totalitarian claims and which officially stands for atheism. Moreover, the churches' ties with their brethren in West Germany have been objected to: the West German Protestants are suspect because they allow their clergy to be chaplains in the NATO army. The measures to minimise West German influence in the D.D.R. have had a detrimental effect on the churches' efforts to maintain historic unity. Rather surprisingly, the 1968 constitution guarantees the right to profess a religious creed and to carry out religious activities, and of recent years more tolerance has been shown to the churches. This may be a measure of the regime's greater self-confidence. The worst sufferers are Jehovah's Witnesses, who were systematically persecuted during the Third Reich and were banned in the D.D.R. in 1950. Their offence, ironically enough, was 'incitement to war' because they refused military service on conscientious grounds: the East German army is described as a weapon of peace. Different as are its aims from those of Hitler, the methods used by the S.E.D. for indoctrinating its citizens and eliminating heretics are often strikingly similar. Like the Third Reich, the D.D.R. can generate enthusiasm and rouse devotion, especially among the young, and can stage spectacular demonstrations. One of the most impressive was the International Youth Rally in Berlin in 1951, a display which no one who saw it is likely to forget. With its ritual parades of athletes from many countries, its colourful national dances, choral competitions and appeals for peace and friendship in many languages, it carried an emotional appeal which made everyone forget the acres of grisly ruins, the drabness of daily life in the austerity republic. Perhaps the only comparable experience in Germany was the Nuremberg Rallies of the 1930s. Where the D.D.R. has lagged far behind the Federal Republic in its social policy is housing: between 1950 and 1964 it built only about 900,000 dwellings, compared with 8 million in the West.[65]

It is often suggested that as Communist regimes mature they become more mellow and more tolerant, that power passes from the party fanatics to the managerial class ('technical intelligentsia') whose outlook is pragmatic rather than ideological. The history of the D.D.R. so far hardly supports this thesis. In 1968 the regime adopted a new constitution. A comparison of this with the earlier constitution of 1949 is instructive.[66] All the changes point to a harder line. The D.D.R., described as a democratic republic in 1949, had become a socialist republic in 1968: the source of power, previously the people, was now the working people under the lead of the Socialist Unity Party (the party, the mainspring of the whole system, was at last given official recognition); the worker no longer was guaranteed the right to strike (because in a workers' state he would be striking against himself); another innovation was a pledge of co-operation with the Soviet Union for all time. There was little or nothing in the new constitution to indicate that the leaders of the D.D.R. were interested in a compromise with West Germany in order to end the country's division. It was significant that the East spoke about it (when at all) as German unification, whereas for the Federal Republic it was always *re*unification. The Russians seem to have decided – probably not later than the middle 1950s – that East Germany must not be given up on any terms because of its key position in the Soviet bloc. The treaty of friendship between the D.D.R. and the Soviet Union in 1964 was important mainly because of its assurance to the East Berlin government that it would not be sold out in a deal between Moscow and Bonn. While on the economic side the Stalinist-type controls which characterised the D.D.R. during its earlier years have been relaxed or abolished, there has been no similar liberalisation on the political side or in cultural policy. Nor has the evolution of the D.D.R. been such as to confirm the general assumption that economic decentralisation leads to political pluralisation.[67] The Ulbricht formula for government might be described as a combination of economic flexibility with rigidity in every other respect. Art and literature, the theatre and the cinema are subject to direction by the S.E.D. Even Brecht had to alter a play to suit the party line.[68] The press, broadcasting and television remain strictly controlled, and popular history books present the same oversimplified and distorted views, couched in the clichés of the cold war and in stale party jargon. The attitude towards the Soviet Union is still heavily sychophantic. Dissident intellectuals continue to be silenced and penalised. A well-known case was that of Wolfgang Harich, professor of philosophy at the Humboldt University in East Berlin, who in March 1957 was given a prison sentence of ten years for subversive activities. He was accused – inevitably – of trying to restore capitalism, whereas his real intention was to renew communism, as some of his fellow intellectuals tried to do in other East European countries with equal lack of success. In the D.D.R. there is no provision for legal opposition, other than the pseudo-opposition provided by the middle-class parties who are not allowed to offer any real alternative policy; and conspiratorial opposition is a crime. As far as Marxism is concerned the official attitude of the S.E.D. is highly conservative. The left-wing socialists such as Rudi Dutschke, who in 1967–8 created disturbances in West Berlin which led to bloodshed, were protesting against the fossilised and bureaucratic socialism of Ulbricht as well as against the complacent liberalism of the West. Another critic of the Ulbricht state was Robert Havemann, a scientist who had been in a Nazi prison; he too was expelled from the S.E.D. after losing his chair of chemistry at the Humboldt University. Other intellectuals who at various dates have fled from East to West Germany include two philosophers, Hans Mayer and Ernst Bloch, and a professor of literature, Alfred Kantorowicz. All three were Marxists. One of the effects of the Berlin Wall was to enable the D.D.R. government to pay less attention to public opinion and to take decisions which previously were too risky. For example, conscription was introduced in 1962, when recruits could no longer escape over the zonal border. When Willy Brandt became Chancellor, one of the hopes, or assumptions, which underlay his approach to relations with the East was that as the D.D.R. government felt more secure it could afford to be more liberal. Yet the meetings between Brandt and the East German Prime Minister Stoph at Erfurt in March 1970 and at Kassel in May showed that the D.D.R. had become, if anything, even more intransigent. The East Germans, prompted by Moscow, were willing to talk to the West Germans, but expected all the concessions to be made by the latter. This is understandable on the part of the S.E.D., but does not reflect the wishes of the East German population, who would like, if only for personal reasons, easier exchanges between both German states, and who suffer from the enforced isolation. The chilly response to West German initiatives is obviously due to the government's desire to shield the population from Western influences. This can never be wholly achieved, especially so long as East Germans continue to be able to hear broadcasts and see television from West Germany. It is safe to say that many East Germans compare this source of information with their own and realise the extent to which their own news is slanted; the amount of double-thinking and double-talk in the D.D.R. must be considerable.[69]

In its international relations the D.D.R. began modestly and uncertainly. More obviously than most East European countries it was a Soviet satellite. It was recognised only by its fellow members of the Communist bloc. Its first treaties were with its Polish and Czechoslovak neighbours, acknowledging the new frontiers (though in the early days of the Russian Zone there had been hope of getting back some of the territory ceded to Poland in 1945). The fact that in January 1953 the

Foreign Minister, Dertinger, was arrested on a charge of treason and removed from office hardly helped to give the new state credibility, nor was its prestige enhanced when later that year the popular rising was put down by Soviet tanks. In 1954 the D.D.R. became formally independent, with the Russian High Commissioner becoming ambassador. Although East Germany belonged to the East European economic organisation, COMECON, and to the Warsaw Pact, it remained rather isolated psychologically. It was the only German state in what was basically a Slav alliance, and to most Slavs all Germans were suspect, even when they were Communists. Nor was it easy for the East German population, brought up to believe in their superiority to the Slavs and especially the Russians, to accept the new relationship. The Russians themselves did not show much respect for the D.D.R. government, which before the 1964 treaty had reason to fear that it might be sacrificed if Russia's interests so required – despite the reliability and growing usefulness of Ulbricht. The prestige of the D.D.R. has however grown over the years, largely owing to its economic success, which has given it the leading place (apart from Russia) among the industrial countries of Eastern Europe. Its bargaining power is stronger, and it has been able to provide aid in the form of money and services to the developing countries. These tended to be countries with which the Soviet Union had friendly relations, such as Egypt and India, and some of the new African states. West Germany's special ties with Israel made the Arab world sympathetic to the D.D.R. Trade missions to uncommitted countries seemed to offer the best prospect of obtaining diplomatic recognition outside the Soviet orbit, for a trade mission could always be raised to the status of a consulate or even an embassy. In 1965 Ulbricht paid a much publicised visit to Cairo, but the Egyptians, while giving their visitor red carpet treatment, refused to establish full diplomatic relations at the time. (They have done so since.) East German trade missions exist in many countries, such as Algeria, Ghana and Tanzania, which have diplomatic representation with West Germany. The two German states are thus in open competition with one another, and more than one undeveloped nation has taken advantage of their rivalry. Another activity which could lead to greater recognition of the D.D.R. is sport. For East German teams and groups of athletes frequently take part in international sporting events, including the Olympic Games, and their list of successes is growing. When the question of visas arises (as in business relations) there is pressure for recognition. The problem has often been discussed in the West, and many, including members of parliament in search of détente and industrialists seeking contracts, have urged that the D.D.R. should be recognised.

The Western governments have so far adhered to the view of the Federal Republic that since the East German government is not freely elected, it has no mandate to speak for its citizens: to recognise it would be to deny recognition to the East German population. There is indeed something particularly artificial about the D.D.R. regime; its painful orthodoxy is less representative of local sentiment than that of the other regimes in Eastern Europe. It was characteristic that Ulbricht should have been foremost in urging Russian intervention in Czechoslovakia in 1968. Any deviation from the norm was a threat to his position, any *rapprochement* between a socialist Czechoslovakia and the West had to be presented as a sinister move by West German imperialists. Ulbricht showed that he was not interested in Brandt's policy of reconciliation between the two German states except on his terms, which meant prior recognition of the D.D.R. Such response as there was to western initiatives, for example the two meetings between Brandt and the East German Prime Minister Willy Stoph, seem to have been made under Russian pressure. Without the bogy of a vengeful and militarist West Germany it would be difficult for the East German regime to justify its continued repression, yet to abolish the repression would be to risk its existence. Ulbricht himself was so identified with the *status quo* that he was not expected to change. His resignation as general secretary of the S.E.D. in May 1971 may have been at Russian insistence in the interests of a settlement, though Honecker, his successor, a pre-1933 K.P.D. member who spent the Nazi years in gaol and concentration camp, has so far shown no more flexibility than Ulbricht. No doubt the D.D.R. has come to stay. Every effort is made to present it as a normal state, like any other in Eastern Europe. Yet the question remains whether the majority of its citizens will ever feel genuine loyalty towards it, whether an East German patriotism can develop. The citizens of the D.D.R. are rightly proud of what they have achieved, often against odds, especially in the economic field. Yet is this enough? Nationalism has been such a force in the present century that no nation willingly accepts its own division. Will the time come when ideology is thicker than blood, when the inhabitants of Dresden or Rostock have more in common with those of Prague and Warsaw than those of Frankfurt and Hamburg? Certainly so long as the Wall stands in Berlin the atmosphere of tension cannot disappear. The traveller to East Berlin from West Berlin has a choice of routes. If he goes by underground railway to Friedrichstrasse he will pass on the way two deserted and unused underground stations where in the sinister half-darkness the only animate object is a soldier with a machine gun, watching day and night. And if he takes the overhead railway to Friedrichstrasse he will pass above the Wall with its armed sentries, pill boxes and barbed wire and will see on one of the first buildings on the Eastern side a huge red caption boldly proclaiming: 'Our love for the D.D.R.'. This has the frightening quality of Orwell's *1984*, the point at which the utopian dream becomes a nightmare, and love, like power, flowers out of the barrel of a gun.

(v) THE POLITICS OF DÉTENTE: FROM ERHARD TO BRANDT

There were understandable signs of impatience in German politics in the early 1960s. The policy of reunification through strength was obviously producing negative rather than positive results (the Berlin Wall), and the new generation growing up in East Germany was increasingly alienated from its western compatriots. Urged on by the F.D.P., who since 1961 held the balance of power in the Bundestag, Erhard's Foreign Minister Gerhard Schröder decided to launch a policy of movement, a German counterpart to the search for peaceful co-operation between the super-powers which the American government had been pursuing, with limited success, for some years. The change of attitude was shown by the sending of West German trade missions to Poland (where Krupp's managing director, Berthold Beitz, who had saved Polish lives during the war, achieved remarkable personal success), Hungary, Roumania and Bulgaria. The assumption behind the policy was that economic agreements would lead to political ones, and would further the process of liberalisation within the Communist countries by helping them to develop into pluralist societies. Also they would become less dependent on the Soviet Union and therefore more receptive to western proposals. In March 1966 the Federal government issued a Note to the governments of Europe setting out its aims. Among them were readiness to assent to a reduction of nuclear force levels in Europe and to sign limited bi-lateral agreements with Eastern Europe. The significant feature of this document was its declaration that the Federal government was willing to limit the scope of its own activities in the interest of a *rapprochement* with Communist states. The time seemed propitious for a more ambitious initiative. 1966 was a year of flux. France left NATO, and the United States withdrew some troops from Germany. Roumania had already set out the course which was to give it a semi-independent status within the Warsaw Pact. In both foreign and economic policy the Roumanians were determined to pursue their own interests, which did not coincide with those of Moscow. Against the background of Russo-Chinese hostility, now fully in the open, there was talk of polycentric communism. In December 1966 the Grand Coalition came to power in Bonn, with Brandt as Foreign Minister. The new government affirmed its intention to develop its predecessor's policy favouring a relaxation of tension and the development of contacts in Eastern Europe, including, significantly, the D.D.R. (where the object was to moderate rather than eliminate the Communist regime). Full diplomatic relations were established with Roumania, and were resumed with Yugoslavia, despite Tito's earlier breach with Bonn and recognition of the D.D.R. In pursuing this policy, the Federal government drew upon itself even more than before the enmity of the D.D.R. government, which opposed any extension of West German influence in Eastern Europe and feared (with some reason, its own isolation. Ulbricht accused the Federal Republic of trying to get the East European states to support its claim to be the only legitimate German state. In political terms the distance between East and West Berlin was greater than between Berlin and Peking, but it became less as the political distance lengthened between Peking and Moscow. Moscow was also alarmed by the new relationship between West Germany and Roumania, and forced the other Warsaw Pact countries at a meeting at Karlovy Vary (Karlsbad) in Czechoslovakia to promise not to follow the Roumanian example. With the Dubček government in power in 1968 there was much speculation on how relations would develop between Czechs and West Germans. The latter were in a position to offer financial aid and trade on favourable terms. The Russian decision to invade Czechoslovakia in August (with the participation of the D.D.R. People's Army) put an end to any possible *rapprochement* between Bonn and Prague. It seemed for a moment that, faced with such a discouraging blow, West Germany would have to abandon its pursuit of a détente, but Kiesinger declared that the *Ostpolitik* must go on as there was no alternative. In the following year the situation changed again, this time in favour of the West. The Russians, having made their point and given an object lesson in what the West now called the Brezhnev doctrine (the Soviet right of intervention in any Socialist country) were anxious to show flexibility. They did not want to prejudice the talks in progress with the Americans on strategic arms limitation, and their deteriorating relations with China underlined the need for relaxation in Eastern Europe. The Soviet leaders appear also to have been afraid that the army generals were becoming too powerful, and the old fear of 'Bonapartism' was revived.[70] Finally, the Moscow government realised that with Brandt of the S.P.D. in power in Bonn they had a possibly unique opportunity to break the East-West deadlock, and that the old stereotype about West German imperialism could not be used to discredit him. Brandt's sincerity was patent, and his personal record, unlike that of Kiesinger, was irreproachable. Brandt himself defined his

Ostpolitik as designed to bring about the improvement of relations with the Soviet Union, the normalisation of relations with the other states of Eastern Europe, and a *modus vivendi* with the D.D.R.[71] These aims were pursued simultaneously. They had to be, if Brandt was not to be accused of trying to play off one section of the eastern bloc against another. Yet it was no easy matter to run the three policies together because under the common ideological cloak national jealousies persisted. Moscow held the key, and once Moscow, for the reasons just mentioned, decided to negotiate, it was difficult even for Ulbricht to hold out. As for Poland, in May 1969 Gomulka made a speech in which he announced that Poland would welcome the establishment of normal relations with the Federal Republic provided that the latter recognised the Oder-Neisse frontier. Shortly afterwards Klaus Schütz, Lord Mayor of West Berlin, met the Polish Foreign Minister at Poznan and had talks which eased German-Polish relations. Then in October 1969 the general election in West Germany resulted in the formation of yet another coalition, this time between the S.P.D. and the much smaller Free Democratic Party. It was a partnership in which the Socialists predominated and Brandt, as Chancellor, was able to continue his *Ostpolitik* with renewed confidence. At the same time he did not neglect relations with the western world. Instead of 'balancing' between East and West, he wanted to be trusted by both. He signed the treaty on the Non-Proliferation of Nuclear Weapons which previous German governments had left on the table. He emphasised his loyalty to the Common Market, which moved a step further on the road to an integrated Europe when the Coal and Steel Community and EURATOM, the atomic energy agency, were merged with it.

A turning point of some importance was the election of a new Federal President in March 1969. Since 1959, when Heuss retired, the President had been Heinrich Lübke, who in 1968 was nearing the end of his second term. A man of many private virtues with a strong sense of duty, he, like many other middle of the road politicians, had been caught up and compromised by events. An agrarian specialist who represented the Centre Party in the Prussian *Landtag* at the end of the Weimar Republic, Lübke was twice arrested and imprisoned by the Nazis, yet later, during the war, he became engaged in building workshops where prisoners from concentration camps were employed. As President he was criticised for disregard of constitutional propriety and for embarrassing *faux pas*, especially on foreign tours. A political innocent, he used his knowledge of agriculture to help many of the developing countries and to earn their goodwill. In October 1968, after the publication by East German propagandists of com-

promising documents concerning Lübke's political past, he decided
to retire the following spring, shortly before his final term was up,
and a few months before the Bundestag election was due. This time
the choice of President was more keenly contested than it had been
before. The two candidates were Gerhard Schröder, the former
Foreign Minister, who was the nominee of the C.D.U., and Gustav
Heinemann, the nominee of the S.P.D. After some hesitation the Free
Democrats decided to vote for Heinemann, while Schröder received the
support of the only other party in the Bundestag, the neo-Nazi N.P.D.
The voting was even enough to make three ballots necessary. In the end
Heinemann, who was leading marginally throughout, won by six votes
with five abstentions. It was a narrow victory, but significant because it
marked a further stage in the return to power of the German left, and
was a pointer to Brandt's chancellorship later that year. Heinemann
was in many ways the odd man out in German politics, a respected
but controversial figure. As a member of the Confessional Church he
had taken part in the famous Barmen synod of 1934. A lawyer with
deep Christian convictions, Heinemann was appointed President of
the Synod of the Evangelical Church in 1949, the same year in which
he became mayor of Essen, the much bombed town which suffered
also from extensive dismantling. A founder member of the C.D.U.,
Heinemann became Minister of the Interior in Adenauer's first cabinet.
In October 1950 he resigned over the plan to rearm the Federal
Republic. His stand, which received a good deal of publicity, was
made on moral and patriotic rather than pacifist grounds: Heinemann
rejected the official view that rearmament was compatible with German reunification. In 1952 Heinemann, who in the meantime had
left the C.D.U., founded the All-German People's Party with a policy
of neutrality. It had no electoral success and was discredited by using
funds believed to be of communist origin.[72] In 1957 he dissolved the
new party and joined the S.P.D., which was about to shed its earlier
anti-clericalism and to moderate its socialism. Heinemann was elected
to the Bundestag, and became Minister of Justice in the Grand Coalition. He introduced an unusually large number of legal reforms
and has been described as the most successful holder of the office in
the history of the Federal Republic. Though Heinemann had not
always been wise in his judgements he had never lacked courage, and
subsequent events vindicated his opposition to Adenauer in the eyes
of many who at the time disagreed with him. He was a man of
indisputable integrity, with an almost Puritan attitude to politics as
a public service, who struck an ascetic note in the new plutocratic
society. Whatever was thought of his changes of party they could not
be held against him as evidence of personal ambition. In many ways

he was the Nonconformist conscience which the Federal Republic needed. At the same time his directness and radicalism earned him the respect of rebellious students. His unconventionality, which some found endearing and others deplorable, was displayed in a controversial press interview given by the new President immediately after his election. With Heinemann's installation, the Social Democrats headed an establishment which hitherto had been dominated by men of other parties, and Brandt could be sure that his *Ostpolitik* would not be obstructed from that quarter. Heinemann had always shown more tolerance towards the Communists than most of his colleagues, and was the only cabinet minister who had actually visited the D.D.R. The dissolution of the Grand Coalition saw the end of the long reign of Christian Democrats, who had been continuously in office, alone or in coalition, since the start of the Federal Republic. Now they went into somewhat ineffectual opposition, though they still outnumbered the Social Democrats in the Bundestag. The Free Democrats, a much more left-wing party, at least in foreign policy, than they had been in the fifties, provided a new Foreign Minister in the person of Walter Scheel, who worked closely with Brandt.

The first results of the West German diplomatic offensive were seen in 1970, when a treaty renouncing the use of force was signed between the Federal Republic and the Soviet Union. Concurrently official talks were opened with the Poles. The great obstacle hitherto to relations with Poland had been the Polish insistence on recognition of the Oder-Neisse frontier. Brandt's acceptance of this was a turning point in the West German attitude. For years German political leaders had privately admitted that this recognition was inevitable, but had argued in public that it was a concession to be made during, not before, negotiations with Poland. In any case, public opinion in the Federal Republic would not have allowed any government to take this step. By 1970 a majority of West Germans appeared willing to accept the new frontier. The refugee organisations, a powerful lobby in the 1950s, had lost much of their importance, and the Refugees' party had ceased to be represented in the Bundestag. Every year saw a fall in the proportion of refugees and expellees, whose children, so far from longing for a homeland they had never seen, were integrated in the West. The Federal government actually closed down the Ministry for Refugees in October 1969. Brandt's view that in recognising the territories beyond the Oder and Neisse rivers as lost the Federal Republic was simply acknowledging reality and was giving up nothing that had not already been gambled away by Hitler. In East European eyes, and therefore for the Bonn government too, the frontier was just not negotiable. Polish opinion had in fact hardened since 1957, when Warsaw had been willing to open diplomatic relations with Bonn without any pre-conditions, saying that the frontier question could be left for subsequent discussion.[73] The change in the Polish attitude showed that time was not on the side of the West. Like Stresemann after the First World War, Brandt had to have the courage to pay the bills left by his predecessors. That he was able to pursue this policy and survive is a sign of the greater maturity of West German politics, the new freedom from illusions. The treaty between Poland and the Federal Republic was signed in December 1970. It confirmed the Oder-Neisse frontier and also pledged that differences between the two countries would not be settled by force. During his visit to Warsaw Brandt in a rare gesture knelt for half a minute in front of the monument commemorating the rising of the Jewish 'ghetto' in April 1942.

Brandt made it clear that his government would ratify the Russian and Polish treaties only if a solution was found for the problem of Berlin. This was the most difficult part of the deal to negotiate but at least it was a matter for the four former occupying powers and one in which the West was aided by the Russians' desire for agreement on strategic arms and a general détente on their western borders. For years the D.D.R. had used harassment of West Berlin as a means of extracting recognition. Recognition of the D.D.R. as a fully sovereign state was a price which even Brandt was unwilling to pay. The traditional objections, based on the East German government's credentials and policy, remained valid. Yet no settlement could be made over Berlin which did not include the D.D.R., since the supply routes passed through its territory. After months of long drawn-out negotiations agreement on Berlin was finally reached in August 1971. It was inevitably a compromise, in which both sides gave and took, and only time can show how it will work in practice. Its cardinal feature was that the Soviet Union acknowledged that access or transit to Berlin was still a four-power responsibility – in fact their own; in return certain concessions were made, such as the establishment of a Russian consulate in West Berlin. As the Russians had insisted since 1955 that their rights over civilian access had devolved on the D.D.R., the Berlin treaty represented a relative downgrading of the East German government. Ulbricht's resignation as general secretary of the S.E.D. in May 1971 may have been the result of his being overruled on this point by Moscow. The Russian calculation probably is that public opinion in West Germany will move sooner or later towards full recognition of the D.D.R., and it is significant that Brandt had already conceded that while there is only one German nation, there are two German states. At the moment the D.D.R. occupies a rather curious intermediate position between non-recognition and full sovereignty. West Berlin is pledged to reduce its formal ties with the Federal Republic, but in return for what is little more than a theoretical sacrifice it stands to gain in security and in much else. Apart from the hopes for increase in trade with the D.D.R. West Berliners will be able to visit their relations on the other side of the Wall. The Federal Republic's treaties with the Soviet Union and Poland were ratified by the Bundestag in May 1972 after a government crisis in which Willy Brandt and his coalition narrowly escaped defeat. Their objection, Christian Democrats declared, was not to the *Ostpolitik* as such but to unsatisfactory features, such as the failure of the Federal government to insist on the free movement of people and information between the two German states and the absence of a definite commitment by the Soviet Union to allow self-determination in the whole of Germany. More generally the C.D.U. feared a loosening of West Germany's ties with its allies and an upsurge of Communist influence. The Social Democrats claimed that they had obtained the best terms possible: it was wishful thinking to expect the Soviets not to support their East German satellite. In an attempt to meet his critics Brandt agreed to add certain documents to the treaties (accepted by the Russians) affirming the Germans' right to reunification. Nevertheless, when it came to the vote most Christian Democrats abstained, a gesture which gave Brandt and Scheel an unexpectedly large majority but revealed a certain ambiguity and indeed confusion in the C.D.U. ranks. Only time will show how far a general détente between East and West, symbolised by President Nixon's apparently successful visit to Moscow in May 1972, will bring about a change of attitude in East Berlin. Clearly Brandt's policy was one of long-term hope, undertaken despite many discouraging signs in the months preceding ratification of the treaties. In January 1972, for example, the D.D.R. opened its eastern frontier freely to the Poles but made its western border with the Federal Republic even more impassable by the use of booby-traps. Erich Honecker, the general secretary of the S.E.D., declared that there would never be unity between socialist East Germany and 'imperialist' West Germany, and that this was 'as certain and as clear as that rain falls to the ground and not up to the sky'.[74] There were other equally unmistakable manifestations of intransigence.[75] Nor is there any guarantee that even if Bonn pays the full price of recognition demanded by the D.D.R. government the latter will liberalise its policy, for it still fears western influence and contacts. No one can say when or even whether the ultimate objective of *Ostpolitik*, a united Germany, will be realised. To the Soviet Union East Germany remains strategically of the greatest importance, and economically its value has risen, not diminished. For Moscow to agree to the detachment of the D.D.R. from its bloc is something which it would do only under duress. No doubt the Russians and their East German allies also calculate that the time will come when not only the ruling élite but the majority of the East German population will be so indoctrinated and so wedded to their way of life that they will not wish to change it. Still, much depends on the course of Russia's relations with America and China, and the continuing feud between Moscow and Peking can only increase Russia's need for a more conciliatory policy towards West Germany. Meanwhile throughout Eastern Europe the Moscow and Warsaw treaties produced a great psychological change and were hailed as the beginning of a new chapter in Germany's relations with the Warsaw Pact countries.

Soon after the Second World War Friedrich Meinecke described Germany as the burnt-out volcano of world politics. The subsequent economic recovery of West Germany (and in its own way of East Germany too) has astonished the world. Even after the fearful bloodletting of two world wars German vitality remains, channelled now into activities that can cause admiration or envy but hardly fear among its neighbours. The Federal Republic's return to political importance has been slower and a good deal less certain; it is often described as an economic giant but a political pygmy. There are many reasons why the Germans have refrained from using their financial strength to assert their political will, and have allowed themselves to be overruled by the French in disputes within the Common Market.[76] The division of the country imposed a heavy mortgage on its foreign policy. Its dependence on America for defence, its exposed geographical position, its lack of nuclear power, above everything else the precariousness of Berlin, all imposed caution. The German nation bears, as Willy Brandt has reminded them, not only the burden of a second lost war and of the Nazi regime but the inherited distrust of foreigners who are doubtful of the sincerity of Germany's desire for reconciliation and of the permanence of its democracy.[77] National self-assertiveness in Bonn would revive too many latent fears and put the clock back. The need for French support over Berlin has also been a factor in determining Bonn's conciliatory policy towards Paris. The Federal Republic, Brandt has said, has no military ambition and does not aspire to a place in the sun that could easily turn to a place in the fire.[78] Nevertheless it is reasonable to suppose that the new freedom which the Federal Republic will gain through its new relationship with Eastern Europe and the security of Berlin will enable it to claim at least an equal voice with the French, and to exercise the political influence to which its economic strength entitles it. The decline of

American economic power is also bound to throw more responsibility onto the European states, including above all Germany.

(vi) CULTURE SINCE 1945: NEW ORIENTATIONS

'The German scene today', wrote a German exile in an English periodical soon after the end of the war. 'is an outward and visible sign of the collapse of the human spirit.'[79] It was the nadir of German culture as well as of the German state, and the gaping ruins seemed to imply a judgement on the country's intellectuals as well as on its political leaders. Yet the same opportunism which had prompted many artists and writers to offer their services to Hitler now led them to do so to the occupying Allies. A very well-known actor announced that he had a Jewish grandmother, while a radio commentator who had been one of Goebbels' closest collaborators applied for a post with the B.B.C. It was evident that one of Germany's needs was to create a society in which the individual would feel secure enough to behave with dignity and independence. The extent to which writers who had stayed in Germany were genuinely anti-Nazi was difficult to gauge because, of course, no work of this kind had been published during the Third Reich (Jünger's *On the Marble Cliffs* was an exception and its criticism too indirect to do much damage). Most of the younger writers had had their sensibilities blunted by the twelve years of Nazi rule, and by 1945 many of them were prisoners of war. Like most of the population, those who were still in or had returned to Germany were too preoccupied with the day to day problems of existence to have time for anything else. It was among the older generation that the first signs came of a revaluation and searching of conscience. The contributions of Meinecke and Jaspers have already been referred to: the former's *German Catastrophe* was an agonising reappraisal which also suggested positive remedies, while Jaspers became one of the Federal Republic's severest critics.[80] The first manifestation of a new trend among younger writers came with the formation of *Gruppe 47*, to which the novelist Heinrich Böll and the poet Günther Eich belonged: both had been prisoners of war with the Americans. These and other writers, including some who returned from exile, were broadly radical in their sympathies and prepared for engagement in politics. Their attitude was in sharp contrast to the traditional disdain for political involvement of many of their elders. The new men tended to side with the S.P.D. against the Bonn establishment and to be critical of the glossy materialism of the economic miracle. The best known post-war novelist, Günther Grass, is very much a committed writer, who has spoken at election meetings for the Social Democrats and helped Heinemann in his presidential campaign. The experience of the Third Reich went far to discredit the notion that the intellectual can or should confine himself to an ivory tower.

The cultural isolation which Hitler imposed on Germany brought its own reaction after the war in an inexhaustible demand for foreign literature.[81] The public wished to discover the new writers and artists who had appeared since 1933 and to re-discover those parts of their own cultural heritage which the Nazis had suppressed. The German intelligentsia was anxious to make contact with its opposite numbers abroad. Foreign plays dominated the theatre, then and for some years to come. There was particular interest in Thornton Wilder and Sartre. Other authors whose works were read or performed in translation included T. S. Eliot, Graham Greene and J. B. Priestley, Claudel, Giraudoux and Anouilh. Of the pre-war German writers, Thomas Mann added to his already great reputation: there was some regret that though he visited Germany (East as well as West) he did not return there to live, and his criticism of the writers who claimed to have belonged to 'inner emigration' led to a good deal of argument – he saw them as compromised, they accused Mann of giving patronising advice from the security of California. Kafka (new to the younger writers) became a literary influence, and the experience of totalitarian government gave his writing additional significance. Tucholsky, the most effective and best hated literary satirist of the Weimar Republic, was republished and eagerly read in both parts of Germany. Brecht was little performed in West Germany at first because of his identification with the East German regime; he had also fallen foul of the American authorities during his exile in California. In the more liberal sixties his plays returned to the stage, and his influence especially as an avant-garde producer was widely felt. As for Brecht's communism, there are many passages in his plays which can be read as an indictment of existing Communist regimes, a fact recognised by the suppression of such passages in Prague since 1968. In his play *The Plebeians rehearse the Uprising* Grass satirised Brecht as a revolutionary playwright who was too preoccupied with his theories to take part in the real workers' revolution when it broke out in 1953. Apart from Brecht, only two plays by German dramatists made much impact in the immediate post-war period. One was *Draussen vor der Türe* ('The Man Outside') by Wolfgang Borchert. This was an expressionist cry of despair by a young playwright who had been imprisoned for defeatism under the Nazi regime and died just before its first performance. Its theme was the familiar one of the soldier coming back from the war to find his wife unfaithful and his son killed in an air raid. His disillusion is complete: God is an old man who can give no help, and the 'hero' is not even allowed to commit suicide. Another war theme was the subject of the most successful play of the time, *The Devil's General* by Carl Zuckmayer, the well-known playwright who returned from exile. Its subject was a *Luftwaffe* general who, having supported Hitler to further his career, decides in the middle of the war to join the resistance, finally taking his own life. It was based on the actual life story of the air ace Ernst Udet, and its moral was that in the Third Reich there was only a choice of evils. As the play presented credible characters in a familiar situation and showed sympathetic insight into the tragic dilemma in which so many decent people had found themselves, it was widely acclaimed and performed on practically every stage. It crystalised the popular mood more than Zuckmayer's next play *Gesang im Feuerofen* ('The Song in the Fiery Furnace') whose theme was an episode in the occupation of France when a resistance group was burnt to death in the chapel of a château.

Two of the greatest influences on the German theatre in the fifties were the Swiss playwrights Max Frisch and Friedrich Dürrenmatt, whose subjects were often topical. Frisch's *Fireraisers* is a parable on middle-class complacency in face of a threat to society such as was presented by Hitler, and his *Andorra* is a psychological study of anti-semitism in a village community. Dürrenmatt's *The Visit* examines with equal subtlety the cowardice and corruptibility of a small town, while his *Physicists* deals with the moral dilemma of a scientist engaged in making an atomic bomb. The theatre of the absurd, led by Beckett and Ionesco, has had many followers in Germany, and Pinter's plays are popular. Osborne's *Look back in Anger*, which set a new trend in the British theatre, found few echoes in Germany whose post-war generation hardly knows the problems of a maladjusted class society. Plays of social protest in Germany were concerned with the graver questions of guilt and expiation. Dramatists like Peter Weiss, who had spent the war years in Sweden, were determined, as Borchert had been, not to let the newly affluent forget the crimes in which many of them had been in some sense involved. Weiss's *Marat/Sade* was an experimental drama which explored the relation between man's sexual nature and his revolutionary aspirations. His next play, called simply *The Investigation*, was documentary theatre, a form first used by Karl Kraus in his *Last Days of Mankind* about the First World War. It was a study, based on the evidence heard in court, of the trial at Frankfurt of a group of concentration camp guards charged with war crimes. In free verse, and using a dramatic structure modelled on Dante's *Inferno*, it uncomfortably recalled horrors which many of the audience would have liked to forget or ignore. Its main interest lay in the psychology

of the murderers and their victims. The most publicised of these
'expiatory' plays (in which there was no attempt to disguise the
characters) was *The Representative* by Rolf Hochhuth, which is a
critical examination of the attitude of Pius XII to the Nazi regime,
particularly in relation to the extermination of the Jews. It is a
powerful indictment of his failure to speak out on their behalf, which
is contrasted with the self-sacrifice of a young Jesuit priest who shares
the deportees' fate. Hochhuth's later play *Soldiers*, also on a Second
World War theme, was equally outspoken and even more controversial,
but was generally found less convincing. Hochhuth sees his task
as to rouse and enlighten the general public on the urgent moral issues
of the day; it is part of the process of exorcising the past in which
German writers, educators, churchmen and publicists have been engaged. Ever since Schiller in 1784 described it as a moral institution,
the German theatre has been expected to play a part in establishing
values and educating public opinion. This has never been truer than in
the 1960s.

The German cinema during the last quarter of a century has been
undistinguished by comparison with that of other countries, and by its
own earlier standards. There have been few outstanding films and
little originality. This is perhaps surprising since despite the exodus of
talent in 1933 a good deal remained behind. Some promising films
on topical themes were produced immediately after the war by the
East German film company, DEFA, which seemed to indicate a revival
of the Weimar tradition. Such were *Marriage in the Shadows*, the
story of an actor in the Third Reich and his Jewish wife (based on
the actual case of Joachim Gotthelf), who were driven to commit suicide; *The Murderers are among us*, about a respectable citizen in
post-war Germany who turns out to be a disguised war criminal; and
The Council of the Gods, the subject of which is a chemical works in
the Rhineland whose governing board ('the council of the gods') supports Hitler in 1933 in order to win armaments orders, and during
the war finds itself supplying poison gas for Auschwitz. Not only did
the factory receive American financial backing during the Nazi
regime but after the war under American military government it continued to manufacture its lethal products. Thus the viewer comes
away with the belief that American capitalists must share the blame
for Nazi atrocities. Even *The Underdog*, a film based on Heinrich
Mann's satirical novel about Wilhelmine Germany, was given an
anti-western slant in the DEFA studios. Wolfgang Staudte, the producer of *The Murderers are among us*, was sufficiently perturbed
by the pressures of the cold war to cross to West Germany where he
afterwards made films highly critical of the Bonn regime. The East

German studios continued to make powerful films about the Nazi past, but those dealing with contemporary problems, such as the refugees, were little more than exercises in propaganda. The German Democratic Republic gives great encouragement to artists provided they conform to its political and aesthetic standards; the ideal writer is a kind of court poet of the S.E.D. Peter Hacks, the most outstanding playwright in East Germany since Brecht, himself fell foul of the authorities for insufficient knowledge of Marxist ideology. 'The D.D.R.', Hacks has said, 'is the perfect greenhouse for forcing talents. But as soon as they are ripe they are forbidden.'

The theme of divided Germany was handled with realism and humour by Günther Neumann, a West Berliner, in his *Berlin Ballad*, the story of a prisoner of war who returns home to find his flat occupied by a black marketeer and his country the pawn of futile international conferences. The producer managed to avoid both despair and sentimentality. One of the most memorable films about Central Europe after the war was Carol Reed's *The Third Man*, based on Graham Greene's novel. Although this was set in Vienna, the ruins and black market milieu could have been in any German city, and the espionage was even more typical of Berlin. Pabst, now an elderly man, made two films on political subjects: one about Hitler's last days, the other about the 20 July plot. Neither added to his pre-1933 reputation. The West German cinema in the 1950s was characterised by an 'overproduction of easy entertainment'.[82] In the sixties a more interesting phase began, with technical experimentation and a more critical attitude to West German society. The film has also been much used to present the history of the Third Reich on television to a generation too young to have experienced it.

By comparison with its Weimar predecessor, the artistic achievements of the Federal Republic are unimpressive. Weimar was rich in talent ('creativity in the midst of suffering') but a political and economic failure: the Bonn regime has been just the opposite. If the first Republic was, in the words of a recent book, an idea seeking to become reality, the second could be described as reality in search of an idea.[83] The disruption brought by Hitler is still felt, and the absence of Jews has deprived the German dough of its yeast. It has even been suggested that Germany's growing prosperity has led to a kind of paralysis of the imagination.[84] Yet despite a lack of new plays by German authors, the theatre is flourishing, and continues to receive generous support from public authorities as it did in less prosperous times. The trade unions (D.G.B.) have also made a notable contribution to the arts with the annual Ruhr Festival at Recklinghausen, which was started in 1949 and brought plays, music and exhibitions to the heart of a great industrial concentration. In education too, especially for citizenship, the unions, like the schools and mass media have done much. Besides participating in adult education and vocational training the D.G.B. supports three academies: an Academy of Labour in Frankfurt, a Social Academy in Dortmund and an Academy for Economics and Politics in Hamburg. Over sixty years ago a German essayist wrote that the masses of the nation were more truly ambitious for education than for economic improvement or material advantage.[85] This continuing concern for the things of the mind – inevitably interrupted between 1933 and 1945 – on the part of ordinary people is an example of fruitful continuity which deserves to be recorded, one of many hopeful signs in a nation which like the phoenix has risen to new life from its own ashes.

Notes

CHAPTER I

1. W. N. Medlicott, *Bismarck and Modern Germany*, p. 171.
2. Hohenlohe described people's personalities as swelling like sponges in water after Bismarck's departure (Hohenlohe, *Memoirs*, ii, p. 416).
3. The historian Heinrich von Sybel told his younger colleague Meinecke in the 1890s of his fears for the future of Germany as a result of the accession of William II and the rise of Social Democracy, both of which he saw as portents of disaster. Bebel, the Socialist leader, described William as the future 'destroyer' of the Reich. (Letter from Bebel to V. Adler on 28 Feb. 1913). G. Kotowski, *Friedrich Ebert*, vol. 1, p. 1. Herbert Bismarck after his father's dismissal prophesied that the Reich would not last more than another twenty years, J. Ziekursch, *Politische Geschichte des neuen deutschen Kaiserreiches*, iii, p. 3.
4. By 1913 only 30 per cent of the officer corps was of noble birth, 70 per cent were of middle-class origin; even the guards regiments accepted commoners. K. Demeter, *The German Officer-Corps, 1650–1945*, pp. 25ff.
5. In the Prussian election of 1908 the Socialists needed 600,000 votes to obtain 7 seats in the *Landtag*, while the Conservatives with only 418,000 gained 212 seats. In 1913 the corresponding figures were: Socialists 775,000 votes and 10 seats, Conservatives 400,000 votes and 148 seats. W. H. Dawson, *The Evolution of Modern Germany*, p. 436, and O. E. Schüddekopf, *Die deutsche Innenpolitik und der konservative Gedanke im letzten Jahrhundert*, p. 106.
6. A contemporary described eighteenth-century Germany in the following words: 'without law and justice, without protection from arbitrary taxation, uncertain of the lives of our sons, and of our freedom and our rights, the impotent prey of despotic power, our existence lacking unity and a national spirit . . . this is the *status quo* of our nation'. Quoted in H. Marcuse, *Reason and Revolution*, p. 13.
7. For the influence of Hegel on German politics, see R. Dahrendorf, 'Conflict and Liberty: Some Remarks on the Social Structure of German Politics' in the *British Journal of Sociology*, *XIV* (1963), p. 197; also S. Avineri, 'Hegel revisited' in *J.C.H.*, vol. III, no. 2 (1968), p. 133.
8. The Austrian Emperor, too, failed to play the part assigned to him by *grossdeutsch* nationalists.
9. Quoted from F. Meinecke, *Die Staatsräson in der neueren Zeitgeschichte* (Munich, 1924) p. 493 in O. Pflanze, *Bismarck and the Development of Germany*, p. 42. The events of 1848 had shown that most liberals would sacrifice their liberalism if unity could be achieved by power politics. A. Ramm, *Germany, 1789–1919*, p. 211.

10. One of the few exceptions was Miquel, a National Liberal member of the Reichstag who became Minister of Finance in Prussia after resigning his seat as the constitution required.

11. For Ballin see A. Huldermann, *Albert Ballin* and L. J. C. Cecil, *Albert Ballin: Business and Politics in Imperial Germany, 1888–1918*. For Rathenau useful biographies are H. Kessler, *Walter Rathenau, his Life and Work* and Etta Federn-Kohlhaas, *Walther Rathenau, sein Leben und Wirken*.

12. W. Sombart, *Die deutsche Volkswirtschaft im neunzehnten Jahrhundert und am Anfang des zwanzigsten Jahrhunderts*, p. 470.

13. Kessler, p. 128. After the Russian Revolution of 1905 Rathenau wrote: 'The political climate of Europe is changing somewhat. In the East absolutism, in the West clericalism [a reference to the Dreyfus Affair] are running dry. How, we must ask, can we justify the fact that Germany is ruled in a more absolutist fashion than almost any other civilised country? . . . Germany is no longer the land of dreamers and professors. In the economic battle the Germans hold third place for achievement, and first place intellectually. It will be difficult to show . . . why by his constitution the German is allowed so much less influence in affairs of state than the Swiss, the Italian or the Roumanian. The continental barometer stands today at self-government, and we cannot very long continue to have a special climate of our own.'

14. J. P. Mayer, *Max Weber and German Politics*, p. 60.

15. F. Stampfer, *Die ersten Vierzehn Jahre der deutschen Republik*, p. 7.

16. F. Meinecke, *Die deutsche Katastrophe*, p. 26. Meinecke continued: 'But the shattering course of the First and still more of the Second World War makes it impossible to silence the question whether the seeds of the later evil were not essentially present from the beginning in Bismarck's Reich'.

17. In 1848 liberals believed that constitutional government, ministerial responsibility and protection against arbitrary police measures would be obtained in a united Germany. A. Dorpalen, *Heinrich von Treitschke*, p. 59.

18. Dawson, p. 8; for a similar view see also p. 5.

19. Kessler, p. 46.

20. When Bismarck was shown round the great port of Hamburg after his retirement he told his host, Ballin: 'Yes, this is a new age, a new world. I am stirred and moved.' B. von Bülow, *Imperial Germany*, p. 102.

21. Dawson, p. 87. It is possible that German industry might have expanded still faster without the tariffs that favoured the agrarians, but subsequent experience suggests that even a regime less representative of farming interests than that of Hohenzollern Germany would have continued to give German agriculture a good deal of protection. Dahrendorf speaks of the 'fruitful misalliance' between industrialisation and the dynastic state (*Gesellschaft und Demokratie in Deutschland*, p. 46).

22. The *Verein für Sozialpolitik*, founded in 1872, also favoured state action to improve the workers' lot; this had strong backing from academic economists ('socialists of the chair'). Bismarck's insurance legislation also brought considerable indirect benefits to the poorer classes. The Insurance Boards made available large sums for social and welfare purposes such as hospitals, convalescent homes, working-class housing, schools, baths and other amenities. Dawson, p. 160.

23. F. Fischer, *Griff nach der Weltmacht*, p. 20.

24. M. Balfour, *The Kaiser and his Times*, pp. 437ff. Agricultural production also rose. Between 1830 and 1900 output of wheat and oats nearly trebled, that of rye nearly doubled. Between 1879 and 1910 production per hectare

NOTES 571

(= 2.47 acres) of wheat, rye, barley, oats and potatoes went up by nearly
50 per cent (more in the case of rye). Sombart, p. 519.

25. Huldermann, *Albert Ballin*, p. 232.

26. C. Barnett, *The Swordbearers*, p. 193.

27. Balfour, p. 447; A. J. P. Taylor, *The Struggle for Mastery in Europe, 1848–1918*, p. xxviii.

28. Kessler, p. 174.

29. V. Chirol, *Fifty Years in a Changing World*, p. 274.

30. J. C. G. Röhl (ed.), *From Bismarck to Hitler*, p. 44.

31. In 1889 one of the anti-semitic groups, a German Social Reform party, met in conference at Hamburg and adopted a programme recommending drastic measures for dealing with the Jewish problem, including if necessary the destruction of the Jewish people, thus anticipating Hitler's 'final solution'. J. Bühler, *Vom Bismarckreich zum geteilten Deutschland*, p. 204. On the other hand, the Anti-Semitic party whinh had sixteen seats in the Reichstag in 1893, had only seven seats in 1912. The anti-semitic agitation failed to change the legal status of Jews, and a resolution moved at an International Congress of Anti-Semites at Dresden in 1882 in favour of expelling all Jews from Germany was defeated. P. W. Massing, *Rehearsal for Destruction*, pp. 107 and 113. For the numbers of the Anti-Semitic party in the Reichstag see Balfour, p. 447.

32. H. Kohn, *The Mind of Germany*, pp. 210–11.

33. Fischer, p. 26; Dawson, p. 353; E. L. Woodward, *Great Britain and the German Navy*, p. 26; G. Mann, *Deutsche Geschichte des 19ten und 20ten Jahrhunderts*, p. 504. Dawson describes the Navy League as having branches in every town and almost every village, and as supplying maps and charts to thousands of schools, libraries and offices. The country was deluged with the League's pamphlets and leaflets.

34. For the Pan-German League see A. Kruck, *Der Alldeutsche Verband, 1890–1939*; and M. S. Wertheimer, *The Pan-German League, 1890–1914*. Lagarde, a professor of oriental languages whose real name was Bötticher advocated *Lebensraum* at the expense of Russia in a book published in 1881.

35. W. L. Langer, *The Diplomacy of Imperialism* (2nd. edn., 1950), p. 528.

36. L. Dehio, *Germany and World Politics in the Twentieth Century*, p. 78.

37. J. H. Clapham, *Economic Development of France and Germany, 1815–1914*, p. 322.

38. Dawson, pp. 389 and 404.

39. A French professor, Leroy-Beaulieu, wrote in a book whose first edition was published in 1874: 'Colonisation is for France a matter of life and death: either France will become a great African power or in a century or two she will be no more than a secondary European power', quoted in C. J. H. Hayes, *A Generation of Materialism*, p. 222.

40. Röhl, p. 24.

41. Dawson, Chapter 3. The arrogance, often unconscious, of Germans towards Poles is illustrated by a remark attributed to the relatively liberal Max Weber: 'It is we [Germans] who made human beings of the Poles.' Dawson, p. 283. Weber belonged to the Pan-German League from 1891 to 1899. See also E. Wiskemann, *Germany's Eastern Neighbours*, pp. 10–14.

42. G. Masur, *Imperial Berlin*, p. 211.

43. J. Schoeps (ed.), *Zeitgeist im Wandel*, p. 127.

44. Schoeps, p. 105.

45. Dawson, p. 13.

46. N. Pevsner, *Pioneers of Modern Design* (rev. ed. 1970) p. 38.
47. W. Haftmann, *Painting in the Twentieth Century*, p. 119.
48. G. H. Hamilton, *Painting and Sculpture in Europe, 1880–1940*, p. 126.
49. An interesting biography of Harden is *Maximilian Harden, Censor Germaniae* by H. F. Young.
50. As a German officer observed later, militarism was the state of mind of the civilians. Demeter, p. 247.
51. For the Youth Movement see H. Becker, *German Youth, Bond or Free* and W. Z. Laqueur, *Young Germany*.
52. O. Baumgarten and others, *Geistige und sittliche Wirkungen des Krieges in Deutschland*, p. 253.
53. Schoeps, pp. 134 and 277.
54. Schoeps, pp. 181 and 196.
55. J. M. Roberts, Purnell's *History of the Twentieth Century*, vol. 1, p. 113.

CHAPTER II

1. Bismarck after his fall said that there was no constitutional objection to William being his own Chancellor. E. Eyck, *Das persönliche Regiment Wilhelms* II, pp. 15–16. It has been well said that William regarded the Chancellor as his chief civilian staff officer, M. Balfour, *The Kaiser and his Times*, p. 133. For the character of William II, see these two books, also Virginia Cowles, *The Kaiser*, and Kotowski, Pöls and Ritter, *Das Wilhelminische Deutschland*, pp. 9–26. For his 'personal rule' see J. C. G. Röhl, *Germany without Bismarck, passim*.
2. B. Bülow, *Memoirs*, 1, p. 76.
3. Balfour, p. 157.
4. Kotowski, Pöls and Ritter, p. 17; H. C. Meyer, *Mitteleuropa in German Thought and Action, 1815–1945*, p. 173.
5. H. Kessler, *Walther Rathenau, his Life and Work*, p. 173.
6. Kotowski, Pöls and Ritter, p. 15.
7. Meyer, p. 60.
8. Bülow wrote of Edward VII and William II: 'When the uncle talked politics with the nephew, I had the impression of a fat malicious tomcat playing with a shrewmouse.' Bülow, p. 339.
9. For Bismarck's resignation see Balfour, pp. 126ff; N. Rich, *Friedrich von Holstein*, I, pp. 243ff; Hohenlohe, *Memoirs*, II, p. 411; Röhl, pp. 45ff. The disintegration of the Conservative–National Liberal 'cartel' was brought about by Bismarck himself to make it harder for the Kaiser to do without him: by proving his indispensability he would postpone the hour of his dismissal.
10. Hohenlohe, p. 413.
11. The dramatic circumstances of Bismarck's dismissal make the change of policy which it signified appear more complete than it was in fact. Bismarck's elaborate structure of alliances, the main object of which was to keep France isolated and to remain on good terms with Russia without sacrificing the Austrian alliance, was showing signs of disruption while he was still in office. His refusal to allow German bankers to subscribe to a Russian loan, his use of the tariff to exclude Russian grain from the German market, his decision to strengthen the German army and his Mediterranean agreements with Britain all suggest that Bismarck at the end of his period

had few illusions about the durability of Russo–German friendship; while after 1887 the Russians refused to give Germany a free hand against France or to commit themselves to any further collaboration with Austria. For a recent brief assessment of Bismarckian diplomacy, see W. N. Medlicott, *Bismarck and Modern Germany*, pp. 171–2. On the other hand, according to Hohenlohe, Bismarck's successor but one as Chancellor, Bismarck, faced with an inescapable choice between Austria and Russia, was ready to abandon Austria, and William II's refusal to follow this course was one of the major points on which the two disagreed at the time of Bismarck's dismissal. Bismarck also spoke in this sense to Hatzfeldt, the German ambassador in London (E. Schiffer, *Ein Leben für der Liberalismus*, p. 151). It may be doubted whether Bismarck would really have taken a step so repugnant to nationalist feeling in Germany and so inconsistent with his desire to maintain the *status quo* in Europe; but whatever choice Bismarck might have made, the fact that he had to make it was an admission of failure. It is far from certain that, had he stayed in power after 1890, he could have prevented the Franco–Russian *rapprochement* which was foreshadowed during his last years of power and was quickly consummated under his successor. The comparatively rapid return by the German government after the failure of the New Course to the Bismarckian policy of wooing Russia and surpressing subversion at home is a further reason for not exaggerating the importance of Bismarck's departure as a turning-point.

12. J. Bühler, *Vom Bismarckreich zum geteilten Deutschland*, p. 178. Bülow once boasted: 'You've no idea how much I do prevent.' The Chancellor had to give way on small issues so as to get his way on bigger ones. For Caprivi and the New Course, see J. Alden Nichols, *Germany after Bismarck, The Caprivi Era, 1890–1894, passim*.

13. G. A. Craig, *From Bismarck to Adenauer*, p. 27; for Holstein see the *Holstein Papers* in 4 volumes edited by N. Rich and M. H. Fisher, and Rich's two-volume study, *Friedrich von Holstein*.

14. *History of the Times*, III, p. 839; Röhl p. 127.

15. *Grosse Politik*, VIII, p. 127; W. L. Langer, *Diplomacy of Imperialism*, p. 45.

16. Langer, p. 53; A. J. P. Taylor, *Struggle for Mastery in Europe, 1848–1918*, pp. 348ff.

17. What the Germans did not foresee was that the very difficulties which Britain experienced in the colonial field with France and Russia would provide material for an agreement between them (Morocco, Egypt and Persia).

18. *Grosse Politik*, IX, p. 155 (Salisbury to Hatzfeldt).

19. Nichols, p. 75.

20. Balfour, p. 171.

21. Bühler, p. 189.

22. W. H. Dawson, *Evolution of Modern Germany*, p. 265; J. H. Clapham, *Economic Development of France and Germany, 1815–1914*, p. 206.

23. Nichols, p. 191, quoting the *Times Literary Supplement* of 11 December 1948, p. 690.

24. J. Ziekursch, *Politische Geschichte des neuen deutschen Kaiserreiches*, vol. III, p. 79. Hohenlohe complained to his critics that if his government lacked drive, it was because it did not receive Reichstag backing.

25. N. F. Grant (ed.), *The Kaiser's Letters to the Tsar*, p. 8.

26. Waldersee, who had been chief of the General Staff from 1888 to 1891, and was an ambitious 'political' general, advised the Emperor to stage a *coup*

d'état against the Socialists and abolish manhood suffrage for the Reichstag. Had such a *coup* taken place, Waldersee would probably have been its leader. G. A. Craig, *The Politics of the Prussian Army, 1640–1945*, pp. 241–2; Ziekursch, pp. 81–2.

27. For the value to industrialists of military training see W. H. Dawson, *The Evolution of Modern Germany*, p. 151.

28. E. Eyck, *Das persönliche Regiment Wilhelms II*, p. 180.

29. Eyck, pp. 183–4.

30. For Naumann see Theodor Heuss, *Friedrich Naumann: der Mann, des Werk, die Zeit*. One of Naumann's *obiter dicta* was: 'The best armament for future wars is social reform', ibid., p. 137. Another aspect of Naumann was his interest in and appreciation of the new trends in architecture.

31. Balfour, p. 270. The writer was Count Monts.

32. F. Meinecke, *Cosmopolitanism and the National State*, p. 371.

33. In Prussia a member of the Social Democratic party could not become a professor, an army officer or a civil servant.

34. Craig, pp. 204–15.

35. Nichols, p. 316. The chief of each cabinet had the right to be present at all audiences of ministers with the Kaiser on a matter of concern to him and it was through the cabinets that the Kaiser sent directions to ministers.

36. G. Ritter, *Staatskunst und Kriegshandwerk*, II, p. 150.

37. Ibid., pp. 154–5.

38. Ibid., p. 155.

39. Ibid., pp. 163–5.

40. Craig, pp. 246–7.

41. In a telegram to his brother, Prince Henry, who was an admiral in the navy, Eyck, p. 161.

42. Craig, p. 295.

43. Ritter, p. 255.

44. Ritter, p. 255. See also N. Stone, 'Moltke–Conrad and relations between the Austro-Hungarian and German Chiefs of Staff', *H.J.*, vol. IX (1966) p. 201. Holland was originally included in the invasion plan but was later omitted. Bethmann Hollweg later explained that he considered it his duty not to interfere in any way with the generals' plans, for in the crisis of a war on two fronts any lack of success would have been blamed on such interference.

45. Craig, p. 288.

46. Craig, p. 296.

47. Yet Caprivi once said: 'The less [we have] of Africa, the better for us'. Ritter, p. 138.

48. In fact Germany's policy in the Far East followed a somewhat erratic course: after her exclusion from the first Chinese indemnity loan she inclined towards Britain, and the Deutsch–Asiatische Bank made an agreement with the Hongkong and Shanghai Bank for the joint financing of railway and government loans to China.

49. J. A. S. Grenville, *Lord Salisbury and Foreign Policy*, pp. 31ff.

50. Grenville, pp. 39–46.

51. Grenville, p. 52.

52. Langer, p. 52.

53. Langer, p. 646.

54. Ziekursch, pp. 140–1.

55. In 1900 a German diplomat summed up his country's policy in Turkey as follows: 'The point is to exploit Asiatic rivalry between England and Russia

in such a way that we shall slip our railway through to Kuwait on the Persian Gulf by making alternately a bow to the British lion and a curtsey to the Russian bear'. Ziekursch, p. 140. But the Russian bear remained suspicious, and German activity in Turkey did more than anything else to prevent a German–Russian *rapprochement*.

56. Ziekursch, p. 100.

57. E. L. Woodward, *Great Britain and the German Navy*, p. 27.

58. Langer, p. 243.

59. For Bülow see his *Memoirs* in four volumes (English translation, 1931–2). Marschall lost his job as Foreign Minister because he supported the bill to reform courts martial. Ritter, p. 166.

60. Rich, II, p. 547.

61. Balfour, p. 210.

62. For Tirpitz see his *Memoirs* (English translation, 1920), and Woodward, pp. 20ff. For Tirpitz and the first Navy Bill, see J. Steinberg, *Yesterday's Deterrent*.

63. A memorandum drawn up for the Kaiser by Tirpitz in June 1897 makes clear his intention to build a battle fleet that could be used against England. Steinberg, pp. 208–21.

64. See J. Steinberg, 'The Kaiser's Navy and German Society', *P. & P.*, vol. 28 (1964) p. 102.

65. Langer, p. 662.

66. Tirpitz's intention was eventually to exclude the Reichstag from any control over the navy, a development which would have added to the power of the Kaiser and dealt a heavy blow to the forces working in favour of parliamentary government. V. R. Berghahn, 'Zu den Zielen des deutschen Flottenbaus unter Wilhelm II', *H. Z.*, vol. 210 (1970), pp. 45ff.

67. Woodward, p. 28.

68. Woodward, pp. 32ff. Tirpitz believed that a strong German navy would not only deter England from attacking Germany but would also help to lever England in the direction Germany wanted. He also expected the smaller nations to support Germany's attempt to break Britain's monopoly of naval power, sometimes described as 'navalism'. Neither assumption proved valid. J. Steinberg, *Yesterday's Deterrent*, pp. 20–6.

69. Woodward, p. 53.

70. R. von Kühlmann, *Erinnerungen*, p. 292.

71. Bülow wired the Kaiser: 'Your Majesty is absolutely correct in the belief that the English must come to us . . . England's troubles will increase in the coming months, and with them will rise the price which we shall be able to demand.' Rich, p. 630. Another dictum of Holstein was: 'We can wait. Time is on our side.' German worries about Russia after 1909 suggested just the opposite conclusion.

72. When the Germans heard of the Anglo-Portuguese treaty they considered it an act of unexampled perfidy. 'With these people', Holstein exclaimed to one of his secretaries, 'it is impossible to enter into any engagement.' H. Nicolson, *Sir Arthur Nicolson, First Lord Carnock*, p. 128.

73. Langer, pp. 728–9.

74. *History of the Times*, III, p. 331. (Holstein's memorandum to Bülow of 1 November 1901.)

75. In a letter to Curzon of 8 April 1899 Salisbury referred to the 'impending disruption' of the Austrian Empire. F. L. Monger, *The End of Isolation*, p. 16.

76. *B.D.*, II, p. 64.
77. Langer, p. 773.
78. Bülow wanted the naval programme to go through, but 'only in an atmosphere of hostility to Britain could the great naval bills be passed in the Reichstag', Rich, p. 677.
79. Rich, p. 669. Relations between Germany and the United States, which had been strained since the appearance of German warships at Manila (Philippines) in 1898, further deteriorated as a result of German intervention in Venezuela.
80. *G.P.*, XVII, No. 4987 (letter to Bülow of 29 January 1901).
81. *B.D.*, II, p. 73.
82. Kipling both voiced and inflamed the popular indignation in some demagogic verses denouncing the 'shameless Hun'.
83. Woodward, p. 65.

CHAPTER III

1. The Germans believed, wrongly, that the Secret Convention signed at the same time as the treaty contained a clause regarding the Rhine frontier. This made them especially suspicious. Nicolson, *Sir Arthur Nicolson, Bart., First Lord Carnock*, p. 149.
2. N. Rich, *Friedrich von Holstein*, II, p. 675.
3. Rich, p. 683.
4. The Kaiser, alarmed by reports of a British naval concentration in home waters, wrote to Bülow on 5 December 1904: 'I now believe what I did not before – in the possibility of a war with England in which the attack would come from England', Rich, p. 689.
5. Rich., p. 694.
6. 'Holstein's Moroccan policy was intended as a means of forcing France into a friendly approach, and this by means of a double lever: political isolation at an international conference, accompanied by half-concealed military threats.' G. Ritter, *The Schlieffen Plan*, p. 114.
7. Rich, p. 718.
8. 'The Germans' strategical objective was to detach France from England and to incorporate her, together with Russia, in a continental alliance. Their tactical objective was to exploit the Morocco question as a means towards this end. Unfortunately however they were never clear in their own minds as to what was the strategy and what tactics. They ... confused the means with the ends.' Nicolson, pp. 158–9.
9. Whether Holstein himself really wanted war, as has been often supposed, is something on which the evidence is inconclusive. See Rich, pp. 696ff. From a military point of view this was the best opportunity Germany ever had of launching a preventive war.
10. *B.D.*, III, p. 263.
11. *B.D.*, III, pp. 397ff.
12. F. L. Monger, *The End of Isolation*, p. 82. Yet in January 1901 Selborne had written: 'I propose . . . . to consider our [naval] position abroad exclusively from its relative strength to that of France and Russia combined', p. 11.
13. Ibid., p. 70. Sir T. Sanderson, the Permanent Under-Secretary of the Foreign Office, wrote to Sir F. Lascelles, British ambassador in Berlin, that there was

in Britain a 'settled dislike' of the Germans, 'and an impression that they are ready and anxious to play us any shabby trick they can'. British public opinion, both official and otherwise, was also influenced by the reports of Saunders, who became *The Times* correspondent in Berlin in 1897. In an incisive memorandum drawn up by Saunders in June 1902 in reply to attempts by British germanophiles to influence *The Times* in favour of Germany, Saunders wrote: 'Any arrangement, any policy, any tendency which caused England to make a final choice for Germany against Russia and France, would be a *fatal, irrevocable* step. *The Times* ought to, and I trust can, prevent it . . . Germany is a *new*, crude, ambitious, radically unsound power . . .' *History of the Times*, III, p. 366. The use of *new* here in a pejorative sense is revealing.

14. J. Steinberg, 'The Copenhagen Complex', *J.C.H.*, Vol. I, No. 3 (1966) p. 38.
15. Steinberg, p. 31.
16. Steinberg, p. 38. 'Anglo-German relations never recovered from the shock of the war scare [of 1904–5].'
17. G. Ritter, *Staatskunst und Kriegshandwerk*, II, p. 186.
18. E. L. Woodward, *Great Britain and the German Navy*, p. 154.
19. *G.P.*, Vol. XXIV, No. 8217.
20. *G.P.*, Vol. XXIV, No. 8217.
21. *B.D.*, VI, No. 111.
22. *B.D.*, VI, No. 124. Hardinge's less colourful version of the interview agrees that the Emperor said he would go to war rather than accept 'dictation'. See also No. 116.
23. Woodward, p. 209.
24. Woodward, p. 220.
25. *B.D.*, VI, No. 174.
26. *B.D.*, VI, No. 169.
27. Bülow, *Memoirs*, II, pp. 415–16.
28. There were rumours in Germany that the next Habsburg emperor might pursue a pro-Slav policy and turn to Russia rather than Germany for support. B.D., VI, No. 96.
29. Nicolson, p. 261.
30. Bülow, p. 288.
31. E. Eyck, *Das persönliche Regiment Wilhelms II*, pp. 498–9.
32. In 1911 the Emperor denounced the attempt of a secretary of state to resign as a 'hair-raising' sign of 'disobedience'.
33. The only constitutional innovation in the years following the *Daily Telegraph* affair was that in 1912 the Reichstag was granted the right to question ministers. Such questions, called interpellations, could be followed by what amounted to a vote of no confidence in the government – but the government did not have to resign.
34. W. H. Dawson, *Imperial Germany*, II, p. 305.
35. Eyck, p. 349.
36. W. H. Dawson, *Evolution of Modern Germany*, p. 403.
37. J. Gebhardt, *Handbuch der deutschen Geschichte*, III, p. 289.
38. Behind the Junkers' opposition to the inheritance tax lay their fear of Prussian franchise reform, which would undermine their political predominance, and more generally their distrust of Bülow as a liberal. Eyck, pp. 530–1.
39. Bülow, p. 498; see also Eyck, p. 536.
40. Rich, p. 664.

41. A. von Tirpitz, *Memoirs*, II, p. 30.

42. Rich, p. 802.

43. Yet Tirpitz had moments of realism, as when he wrote to the Emperor on 24 October 1910: 'If the English fleet is permanently made and maintained so strong to make it safe to attack Germany, the German naval development, from a historical standpoint, was a mistake, and Your Majesty's fleet policy a historical fiasco.' Quoted from Tirpitz, *Politische Dokumente*, 184, in Brandenburg, *From Bismarck to the World War*, p. 299.

44. *B.D.*, VI, No. 208.

45. T. von Bethmann Hollweg, *Reflections on the World War*, I, p. 26. Now and during the First World War Bethmann Hollweg found himself unable to control public opinion. See W. J. Mommsen, 'Die Regierung Bethmann Hollweg und die öffentliche Meinung, 1914–17', *V.J.Z.G.* vol. 17 (1969), p. 117.

46. *B.D.*, VI, No. 195.

47. *B.D.*, VI, No. 204.

48. *B.D.*, VI, Nos. 207 and 208.

49. *G.P.*, XXVII (ii) No. 10167.

50. See J. S. Mortimer, 'Commercial Interests and German Diplomacy in the Agadir Crisis', *H.J.*, Vol. X (1967), p. 440. German policy was less sinister than it looked to the western powers, but they judged by the bellicose temper of the German press and in the light of their presuppositions about German intentions.

51. Eyck, op. cit., p. 584. Moltke wrote: 'The unfortunate Morocco business is beginning to get me down. If we slink out of this affair with our tails between our legs again (as in 1906), if we can't pull ourselves together for a vigorous demand which we are willing to enforce with the sword, then I despair of the future of the German Empire. Then I shall quit.' Quoted in F. Fischer, *Griff nach der Weltmacht*, pp. 32–3. Churchill wrote in his *World Crisis* of the 'deep and violent passions of humiliation and resentment' beneath the glittering uniforms which thronged the Kaiser's palaces.

52. The German Foreign Office tried to prevent the publication of Bernhardi's book, and he was reprimanded for it by the Imperial cabinet. G. Ritter, *Das deutsche Problem*, p. 149. According to Bethmann Hollweg (*Reflections*, I, p. 27) the public did not read Bernhardi's book, an assertion hardly borne out by its popularity.

53. Germany at the time was calling up only 52 per cent of men fit for military service, compared with 82 per cent in France. (W. Görlitz, *The German General Staff*, p. 148.)

54. Among the territories mentioned for possible cession to Germany were Pemba, Zanzibar, Portuguese Angola and Belgian Congo.

55. In his *Reflections on the World War* Bethmann Hollweg complained that Tirpitz had 'arrogated to himself a political authority far beyond his functions', vol. 1, p. 91.

56. *B.D.*, VI, No. 537. Grey never told the British people that the Germans were willing to discuss naval limitation in return for a suitable political agreement. But this was in line with Grey's general disinclination to reveal the details of his foreign policy even to parliament, which was unaware of the extent to which the military talks with the French involved Britain in a moral commitment in case of war with Germany. L. C. F. Turner, *Origins of the First World War*, p. 11, quoting A. J. Marder, *From the Dreadnought to Scapa Flow*, Vol. I, p. 232.

57. As late as October 1911 the German Admiralty was convinced that Britain

needed Germany's friendship in preference to France's. W. Hubatsch, *Die Ära Tirpitz*, p. 92.

58. Woodward, p. 378.

59. Since 1910 the three main radical groups had been united as the Progressive People's Party.

60. For the domestic policy of Bethmann Hollweg see H. G. Zmarzlik, *Bethmann Hollweg als Reichskanzler, 1909–1914, passim.*

61. Since 1906 there had been a federal tax on legacies to those not directly descended from the testators: to this extent the principle of no federal taxation of property had already been breached. (Zmarzlik, p. 45; and W. H. Dawson, *The German Empire*, II, p. 335.)

62. C. E. Schorske, *German Social Democracy*, p. 265.

63. P. Scheidemann, *Der Zusammenbruch*, p. 1.

64. For the S.P.D. generally in this period, see Schorske, *passim*. For the reformist socialists see also Dawson, *German Empire*, II, p. 353. Millerand was the French socialist who joined a coalition government to save the republic at the time of the Dreyfus crisis.

65. A. Kruck, *Geschichte des Alldeutschen Verbandes, 1890–1939*, pp. 59ff.

66. E. Federn-Kohlhaas, *Walther Rathenau*, p. 116.

67. B. Tuchman, *The Proud Tower*, p. 312.

68. Bethmann Hollweg, p. 86.

69. C. M. Bowra, *Poetry and Politics, 1900–1960*, p. 43. Marinetti in his first *Futurist Manifesto* (Paris, 1909), wrote of the new ideals as 'love of danger, fearlessness, rebelliousness, aggressiveness, patriotism and the glorification of war, the strong and healthy injustice of life'. W. Haftmann, *Painting in the Twentieth Century*, p. 106.

70. Sir Felix Cartwright, British ambassador at Vienna, wrote on 31 January 1913: 'Serbia will some day set Europe by the ears and bring about a universal war on the Continent.' Nicolson, p. 390. Fourteen years earlier a Serb had told the British Minister in Belgrade: 'We live in the hope of getting something for ourselves out of the general conflagration whenever it takes place.' *B.D.*, 1, No. 268. See also J. Remak, '1914 – The Third Balkan War' in *J.M.H.*, vol. 43 (1971) p. 353.

71. L. Albertini, *The Origins of the War of 1914*, 1, p. 371.

72. Ibid., p. 394.

73. This is sometimes called the Third Balkan war, the Second being the war of Montenegro against the powers in May 1913.

74. Albertini, op. cit., pp. 488ff. The Tsar of Russia visited Bucharest in June 1914. The visit was a great success.

75. Albertini, p. 396. Tschirschky, German ambassador at Vienna, quoted an Austrian officer at G.H.Q. as telling the German military attaché: 'We are ashamed of ourselves. And if we do not pull ourselves together we must draw the consequences and abdicate as a great power.'

76. Albertini, p. 402.

77. Albertini, p. 463. William's opinions varied according to whom he was talking to. On 16 October 1913 he assured the Austrian Chief of Staff that Germany would support Austria in a preventive war. A few days later he agreed with the leader of the Austrian 'peace group', the Archduke Franz Ferdinand, that Austria must seek the friendship of the Balkan people.

78. Eyck, p. 688.

79. Perhaps the high-water mark of the post-1911 Anglo-German *rapproche-*

ment was reached in an after-dinner conversation between Sir William Tyrrell, Grey's private secretary, and von Kühlmann, the German chargé d'affaires on 14 October 1912. Tyrrell said he was authorised to offer Germany 'heartfelt and durable conciliation', the 'olive branch of peace'. British wished to co-operate with Germany all over the world – in China, Persia, Turkey and Africa. This initiative, if it was one, was never followed up. Nicolson, p. 384. As early as 19 April 1911 Sir Arthur Nicolson had written, 'At the present moment there is in many circles here a move towards a friendly understanding with Germany.' *B.D.*, VI, No. 461. Lichnowsky, German ambassador in London from December 1912 to August 1914, reported to Bethmann Hollweg on 26 January 1913 that Anglo-German relations were friendlier than they had been for years. *G.P.*, XXXIV, No. 270.

80. *B.D.*, VI, No. 575. Nicolson wrote (p. 357): 'We had to accept the strangling of Persia ... to keep Russia friendly.' 'Over Persia the Anglo-Russian entente hung by a thread', *B.D.*, x (i), p. xi. As late as 16 June 1914 George V wrote to his cousin Nicholas II asking him to put an end to 'the unsatisfactory state of affairs in Persia'. *B.D.*, X (ii), No. 549.

81. *B.D.*, X (ii), p. xii. The Baghdad Railway had not been completed by the time war broke out in 1914.

82. Woodward, p. 430.

83. *B.D.*, X (ii), No. 454.

84. A. Huldermann, *Albert Ballin*, p. 272. The author of the book, which appeared anonymously, was a Dr Plehn who represented the *Kölnische Zeitung* in London, and was inspired or encouraged by Kühlmann.

85. Albertini, p. 414. 'Just as Germany, during the Bosnian annexation crisis had taken her stand at the side of Austria, ready to aid her against Russia if the latter made a *casus belli* of an Austrian attack on Serbia, reversing the practice of Bismarck in his alliances: so now, during the Balkan wars, France in a similar way promised armed assistance to Russia if Russia deemed it necessary to intervene against Austria in defence of Serbia, thus going beyond her obligations under the alliance as Poincaré himself had interpreted them in the spring of 1912.'

86. Albertini, p. 373.

87. *B.D.*, VI, No. 527. Crowe and Nicolson were convinced that friendship with Germany was not to be had on terms of equality.

88. *B.D.*, VI, No. 575. Nicolson wrote to Sir G. Buchanan, British ambassador in St Petersburg, on 21 April 1914: 'I am haunted by the same fear as you – lest Russia should become tired of us and strike a bargain with Germany.' Nicolson, p. 406. In the last years before the outbreak of war, Britain appeared to need Russia more than Russia needed Britain. See also Z. S. Steiner, *The Foreign Office and Foreign Policy, 1898–1914*, especially pp. 121ff.

89. 47 per cent of the population of the Habsburg Monarchy were Slavs.

90. Fischer, p. 40. William II told the Archduke Franz Ferdinand in October 1913: 'The Slavs are born not to rule but to obey.' Albertini, p. 488.

91. Woodward, p. 433. Albertini wrote in his Introduction that the leaders of the European nations were 'weak, undecided, short-sighted characters, not of a stature to deal with so grave a situation ... While fearing a European war, they deluded themselves that they could avert it by not showing fear of it ...' In fact they saw only the choice between defiance and surrender.

CHAPTER IV

1. L. Albertini, *Origins of the War of 1914*, I, p. 486.
2. Albertini, I, p. 484.
3. J. C. G. Röhl (ed.), *From Bismarck to Hitler*, p. 71.
4. Albertini, II, pp. 445–6; F. Fischer, *Griff nach der Weltmacht*, pp. 83–5.
5. Fischer, p. 59.
6. During the war Tirpitz was to admit that Germany's world policy had been premature and that his naval policy had been mistaken. W. Hubatsch, *Die Ära Tirpitz*, p. 116. After the war Groener confessed that Germany had unconsciously aimed at world domination before her continental position was secure.
7. Albertini, III, pp. 14 and 235.
8. Albertini, III, p. 53. See L. C. F. Turner, 'The Russian Mobilisation in 1914', *J.C.H.*, vol. 3 (i), (1968) p. 65.
9. J. C. G. Röhl, 'Admiral von Müller and the Approach of War, 1911–1914', *H.J.*, Vol. XII (1969) p. 651; A. Hillgruber, *Deutschlands Rolle in der Vorgeschichte der beiden Weltkriege*, p. 52.
10. L. F. C. Turner, *Origins of the First World War*, p. 109.
11. Albertini, III, pp. 171ff.
12. W. Groener, *Lebenserinnerungen*, p. 145.
13. J. Ziekursch, *Politische Geschichte des neuen deutschen Kaiserreiches*, III, pp. 292 and 306; A. von Tirpitz, *Memoirs*, p. 228.
14. Röhl, *H.J.*, XII, p. 652.
15. H. C. Meyer, *Mitteleuropa in German Thought and Action, 1815–1945*, p. 103.
16. Hillgruber, p. 35.
17. M. Erzberger, *Erlebnisse im Weltkrieg*, p. 20–1. The Italian view was that Austria had no right under the Triple Alliance to go to war without Italian consent and without some 'compensation' for Italy. Had Austria been willing to cede Trentino to Italy, the Italian government might even have been prepared to enter the war on the side of the Central Powers. See B. E. Schmitt, 'The Italian Documents for July 1914', *J.M.H.*, Vol. 37 (1965) p. 469.
18. Erzberger, p. 1.
19. Tirpitz, p. 265.
20. K. H. Janssen, *Der Kanzler und der General*, p. 19.
21. Röhl, *H.J.*, vol. XII, 1969, p. 670.
22. E. Bevan, *German Social Democracy during the War*, p. 9.
23. *Neue Zeit*, X, p. 586. Bebel had admitted that he would take part in a war against Russia, where tens of thousands were held as political prisoners.
24. K. Kautsky, *Sozialisten und Krieg*, pp. 461ff.
25. Fischer, p. 111.
26. Erzberger, p. 197. According to another account, Jagow refused to answer the question about Belgian neutrality. Fischer, pp. 44–5.
27. Erzberger, p. 198.
28. J. Braunthal, *In Search of the Millennium*, p. 148.
29. H. J. Varain, *Freie Gewerkschaften, Sozialdemokratie und Staat*, p. 81.
30. Groener, p. 150.
31. For the Schlieffen Plan, see G. Ritter, *The Schlieffen Plan*, and G. Ritter, *Staatskunst und Kriegshandwerk*, II, pp. 239–81.

32. For the battle of the Marne see Groener, pp. 150–77; C. Barnett, *The Swordbearers*, pp. 15–104. It was an irony that Moltke should have spoilt his reputation in carrying out a strategy in which, as he told the Kaiser in 1905, he had no faith. A country the size of France could not, he was sure, be conquered by a single stroke, and a long war would exhaust Germany too. Yet Moltke kept the Schlieffen Plan because he could not think of a better, just as he viewed with fatalism the coming of a war whose horrors he foresaw more clearly than most. Ziekursch, III, p. 312. Kluck afterwards blamed Bülow for expecting him to close the gap between their two armies, and claimed that he could have disposed of Maunoury's army on his flank had he not been ordered to retreat by Hentsch acting for Moltke. Lord d'Abernon, *Memoirs of an Ambassador of Peace*, I, p. 272.

33. Barnett, p. 76.

34. J. Buchan, *History of the Great War*, I, p. 204.

35. Janssen, p. 20; Groener, p. 211.

36. Falkenhayn wanted to tell the people the truth but was prevented from doing so by Bethmann Hollweg, who feared the effect on neutral opinion. Ziekursch, III, p. 328.

37. Fischer, p. 135.

38. Groener, pp. 179ff; E. von Falkenhayn, *General Headquarters, 1914–16, and its Crucial Decisions*, p. 13.

39. B. H. Liddell Hart, *History of the World War, 1914–18*, p. 90.

40. C. Falls, *The First World War*, p. 59.

41. Ritter, II, p. 59.

42. B. Tuchman, *August 1914*, p. 300.

43. Hhe choice of name irritated the Poles, whose help Germany needed against the Russians.

44. W. Görlitz, *The German General Staff*, p. 149. The War Ministry gave us its reason for refusing to create three extra army corps the impossibility of finding a suitable type of officer for them. K. Demeter, *The German Officer-Corps, 1650–1945*, pp. 14ff.

45. Groener, p. 166. Max Hoffmann, the able Chief of Staff to the Eastern Command, once wrote of Hindenburg: 'I don't believe he thinks at all.... No one ever became so famous with so little mental and physical exertion.' K. H. Janssen, 'Der Wechsel in der Obersten Heeresleitung 1916', *V.J.Z.G.*, vol. 7 (1959) p. 548.

46. Groener, p. 205.

47. G. A. Craig, *The Politics of the Prussian Army, 1640–1945*, p. 303.

48. Ritter, III, p. 68.

49. Janssen, p. 253.

50. Technically it was not a blockade in the proper sense of the term, but the word is sanctioned by general use.

51. Tirpitz, II, p. 377, also p. 358.

52. Tirpitz, p. 392.

53. Erzberger, p. 209.

54. Ritter, III, p. 151.

55. Ziekursch, III, p. 362.

56. Ziekursch, III, p. 364.

57. Ritter, III, p. 207.

58. Ritter, III, p. 212. The inhumanity of this method of warfare lay mainly in the small chance of survival of the crew and passengers of a torpedoed

vessel. The U-boats had no room for them, and in any case were unwilling to risk appearing on the surface where any submarine presented an easy target. Allied warships not infrequently sailed as unarmed neutrals. In practice, less than a third of all British ships torpedoed in 1915 and 1916 were sunk without warning. C. R. Cruttwell, *A History of the Great War*, p. 198.

59. Janssen, pp. 141ff.
60. W. Görlitz (ed.), *The Kaiser and his Court*, p. 145.
61. Janssen, pp. 173 and 248.
62. Ritter, III, p. 249.
63. Ritter, III, p. 248.
64. H. Herzfeld, *Der erste Weltkrieg*, p. 206. Contrast with this view that of Ludendorff in February 1918: 'A peace which only guarantees the territorial *status quo* would mean that we had lost the war', Fischer, p. 659. See also W. J. Mommsen, 'Die Regierung Bethmann Hollweg und die öffentliche Meinung, 1914–17', *V.J.Z.G.*, vol. 17 (1969) p. 117.
65. Ziekursch, III, p. 70. Annexationist fervour was found more among the civilian population than among the soldiers, according to Carl Zuckmayer whose Memoirs (*A Part of Myself*, London, 1971) describe the mood of the German army in August 1914 as one of enthusiasm but not of war fever or mass hysteria. (p. 137ff.)
66. Fischer, pp. 113ff.
67. H. W. Gatzke, *Germany's Drive to the West*, p. 120.
68. Gatzke, p. 27.
69. Gatzke, p. 66.
70. M. Hoffmann, War Diaries, published as *The War of Lost Opportunities*, I, p. 163 (entry for 21 December 1916).
71. Fischer, p. 214.
72. For nationalism in the S.P.D. see Bevan, *passim*.
73. Gatzke, p. 109.
74. In an unpublished pamphlet Kapp warned of the danger of a 'lukewarm peace' leading to a 'democratic dictatorship'. Gatzke, p. 129.
75. Erzberger, p. 198.
76. Fischer, p. 164.
77. Ritter, III, p. 279; Erzberger, p. 175.
78. Gatzke, p. 140.
79. Ritter, III, p. 325.
80. Ritter, III, pp. 359ff; Fischer, p. 392. For Bethman Hollweg and the Peace Note see W. J. Mommsen, 'Die Regierung Bethmann Hollweg und die öffentliche Meinung, 1914–17', *V.J.Z.G.*, vol. 17 (1969) p. 117.
81. E. Ludendorff, *Meine Kriegserinnerungen, 1914–1918*, p. 245.
82. Görlitz (ed.), p. 230; Ritter, III, p. 404.
83. Ritter, III, p. 403.
84. A. S. Link, *Wilson the Diplomatist*, pp. 84ff.
85. On 10 January 1917 Hindenburg asked the Kaiser to dismiss Bethmann Hollweg, Ritter, III, p. 417.
86. Ritter, III, p. 298.
87. R. Scheer, *Germany's High Seas Fleet in the World War*, pp. 260–1. The distribution of U-boats was as follows:– 57 in the North Sea, 8 in the Baltic, 38 on the Flanders coast, 31 in the Mediterranean.

CHAPTER V

1. J. Willett, *Expressionism*, pp. 102 and 104.
2. M. Mann (ed.), *Das Thomas Mann Buch*, p. 85. In a letter to his brother Heinrich on 7 August 1914 Thomas Mann, referring to Russia, wrote of his 'deepest sympathy for this execrated, indecipherable, fateful Germany which . . . is preparing to smash the most despicable police state in the world'. *Letters of Thomas Mann*, vol. 1, p. 70.
3. F. Meinecke, *Die deutsche Katastrophe*, p. 25.
4. W. Rathenau, *Tagebuch, 1907–22*, p. 36.
5. B. Bülow, *Memoirs*, III, p. 41.
6. Rathenau, p. 34.
7. H. W. Gatzke, *Germany's Drive to the West*, p. 136.
8. K. von Klemperer, *Germany's New Conservatism*, p. 50.
9. J. Joll, 'The 1914 Debate Continues', *P. & P.*, vol. 34 (1966) p. 109.
10. U. Trumpener, *Germany and the Ottoman Empire*, p. 109.
11. L. Albertini, *Origins of the War of 1914*, III, p. 35.
12. P. Lensch, *Drei Jahre Weltrevolution* is typical of many such writings.
13. H. Pross, 'Thomas Mann's Political Career', *J.C.H.*, vol. 2 (ii), (1967) pp. 65ff.
14. *Letters of Thomas Mann*, vol. 1, pp. 69–70. Contrast with this early impression the later judgement of a British Labour politician, Arthur Ponsonby: 'There must have been more deliberate lying in the world between 1914 and 1918 than in any other period of the world's history.' A. Ponsonby, *Falsehood in Wartime*, p. 19. Those who saw in war an exercise in chivalry were soon disillusioned by their experience of the trenches, or for that matter of the war at sea.
15. In a letter dated 3 August 1915 Thomas Mann suggested that, by comparison with Germany, France and England were old-fashioned: the future lay with Germany, whose mission was the social reorganisation of Europe. T. Mann, *Letters to Paul Amman*, pp. 44–5.
16. F. Fischer, *Griff nach der Weltmacht*, p. 317. See also H. C. Meyer, *Mitteleuropa in German Thought and Action, 1815–1945*.
17. H. Bechtel, *Wirtschaftsgeschichte Deutschlands im 19ten und 20ten Jahrhundert*, p. 369: A. C. Bell, *Blockade of the Central Empires, 1914–18*, especially pp. 671ff.
18. Average consumption of foodstuffs in the second half of 1918, expressed as a proportion of pre-war consumption, was as follows: Meat 12 per cent, fish 5 per cent, eggs 13 per cent, lard 7 per cent, butter 28 per cent, cheese 15 per cent, cereals 7 per cent, vegetable fats 17 per cent. J. Kuczynski, *A Short History of Labour Conditions under Industrial Capitalism*, vol. III, *Germany – 1800 to the Present Day*, p. 219.
19. Bell, p. 672.
20. G. Feldman, *Army, Industry and Labour in Germany, 1914–1918*, p. 174.
21. Feldman, p. 119.
22. W. F. Bruck, *Social and Economic History of Germany, 1888–1938*, pp. 134–43 and Bechtel, pp. 363–78.
23. M. Haussmann, *Schlaglichter*, p. 91.
24. Prince Max of Baden, *Memoirs*, 1, p. 112.
25. Gatzke, p. 178.
26. P. Scheidemann, *Memoirs of a Social Democrat*, II, p. 32.

27. K. Epstein, *Matthias Erzberger and the Dilemma of German Democracy*, pp. 153–213.
28. W. Görlitz (ed.), *The Kaiser and his Court*, p. 282. This book is the edited Diary of Admiral Georg Alexander von Müller, who was chief of the Kaiser's Naval Cabinet from 1908 to 1918. This Diary covers the war years. Eduard David in his subsequently published Diary records his bitter realisation after Bethmann's dismissal, that he (David) had been duped.
29. R. von Kühlmann, *Erinnerungen*, p. 47. Michaelis was afraid of Hindenburg and Ludendorff.
30. Epstein, p. 223.
31. 'Old Count Hertling cut a sorry figure as a politician', wrote von Müller in his Diary for 5 Nov. 1917 (Görlitz, p. 310).
32. M. Erzberger, *Erlebnisse im Weltkriege*, p. 299.
33. Quoted in Erzberger, p. 53.
34. Gatzke, p. 218.
35. Gatzke, p. 250. Ludendorff wrote on 1 Jan. 1918: 'I always hope that the Prussian franchise [reform] falls through. If I didn't have that hope, I would advise the conclusion of any peace.'
36. W. Groener, *Lebenserinnerungen*, p. 554.
37. A. J. Berlau, *German Social Democracy, 1914–21*, p. 75.
38. H. Heidegger, *Die deutsche Sozialdemokratie und der Nationalstaat, 1870–1921*, p. 159.
39. A. J. Ryder, *The German Revolution of 1918*, p. 104.
40. German strength on the western front increased by 30 per cent between Nov. 1917 and 21 March 1918. D. J. Goodspeed, *Ludendorff*, p. 192.
42. Epstein, p. 234.
43. Gatzke, p. 273.
44. A. Hillgruber, *Deutschlands Rolle in der Vorgeschichte der beiden Weltkriege*, p. 62ff.
45. E. Ludendorff, *Meine Kriegserinnerungen, 1914–1918*, II, p. 460.
46. Goodspeed, p. 195.
47. Fischer, pp. 828–9. Hindenburg told Brüning in 1931 that he knew the war was lost in February 1918. H. Brüning, *Memoiren, 1918–1934*, p. 455.
48. Max, II, p. 258.
49. G. A. Craig, *Politics of the Prussian Army, 1640–1945*, pp. 337ff.
50. Ludendorff, p. 472.
51. C. Tschuppik, *Ludendorff*, p. 209. During the offensive of March–April 1918 three German soldiers were killed or wounded for every two British.
52. R. A. Lutz (ed.), *Causes of the German Collapse*, p. 80. 'There can be no doubt that the Supreme Command wished to bring about the decision . . . by means of the offensive, and not to wear out our opponents by a series of partial offensives'. Kuhl, Chief of Staff to the Crown Prince of Bavaria, said: 'If the March offensive failed, the whole war would be lost'. Tschuppik, p. 199.
53. Ludendorff, p. 545.
54. Görlitz, p. 370; Fischer, pp. 845–6. Admiral von Müller's Diary of 14 July 1918 recorded: 'His Majesty went on to speak of the mission of McCormick, who had in the meantime sent news that the President was ready to open peace negotiations and wished to be informed of our terms. His Majesty had refused this through the Chancellor. The Americans must state their conditions.'
55. W. Förster, *Der Feldherr Ludendorff im Unglück*, pp. 22–3. Ludendorff

felt as if he was fighting a war on two fronts, against the external enemy and the internal revolution. Feldman, p. 513.

56. Görlitz, p. 377.

57. Ludendorff, p. 551.

58. *Ursachen des deutschen Zusammenbruches im Jahre 1918*, II, p. 224ff.

59. *Ursachen*, p. 236. 'There is no reason', said Hintze, 'to doubt our victory.'

60. Feldman, p. 511.

61. Feldman, p. 516. Speaking of the broad-based civilian government which was to conclude the armistice, Ludendorff said: 'They shall drink the soup they have cooked up for us.' Thus as early as 1 October, weeks before the first signs of revolution inside Germany, the home front was blamed for the defeat.

62. *Ursachen*, pp. 361ff. (Ludendorff's memorandum on the armistice offer, dated 31 October).

63. Förster, p. 118. When Ludendorff told von Payer, the Vice-Chancellor, that Wilson's Third Note was humiliating and should be rejected, Payer replied: 'I know nothing about soldier's honour. I am just an ordinary citizen, I see only starving people.'

64. Max, 11. pp. 323–4.

CHAPTER VI

1. For the November Revolution see A. J. Ryder, *The German Revolution of 1918*.

2. Ryder, p. 136.

3. Ryder, p. 181.

4. Quoted with slight changes from R. G. L. Waite, *Vanguard of Nazism*, p. 59.

5. Ryder, p. 219.

6. For Eisner see A. Mitchell, *Revolution in Bavaria*, especially pp. 34ff.

7. Mitchell, pp. 172 and 260.

8. T. Dorst and H. Neubauer (ed.), *Die Münchener Räte-Republik*, *passim*.

9. Thomas Mann, who was in Munich during the Bavarian soviet regime, wrote: 'The mixture of apathy, frivolity and bohemianism is disgusting and . . . capable of the bloodiest uncertainties'. *Letters of Thomas Mann*, 1, p. 95.

10. As economic or industrial units workers' councils were given a place in the Weimar constitution; this was supposed to be some compensation for their disappearance as political bodies.

11. E. Kolb, *Die Arbeiter-Räte in der deutschen Innenpolitik*, *1918–19*, p. 280. See also Kolb for a general discussion of the 'missed opportunity' presented by the workers' councils and for a criticism of Ebert's negative attitude to them.

12. Ryder, p. 229, also pp. 257ff for a discussion of the reasons for the reluctance of the S.P.D. to use the power it had been given.

13. Mitchell, p. 120.

14. F. L. Carsten, *Reichswehr and Politics*, *1918–33*, p. 61.

15. G. Feldman, *Army, Industry and Labor in Germany*, *1914–18*, pp. 519ff.

16. Quoted in H. Voigt, *The Burden of Guilt*, p. 37.

17. G. A. Craig and H. Holborn (ed.), *The Diplomats*, p. 145.

18. W. M. Jordan, *Great Britain, France and the German Problem, 1918–39*, p. 36.
19. Jordan, p. 12.
20. E. Bethge, *Dietrich Bonhoeffer*, p. 106.
21. Jordan, p. 49.
22. G. F. Kennan, *Russia and the West under Lenin and Stalin*, p. 221. See also the essay on Versailles in L. Dehio, *Germany and World Politics in the Twentieth Century*.
23. Jordan, p. 54.
24. E. Eyck, *History of the Weimar Republic*, vol. I, p. 71.
25. C. W. Guillebaud, *The Economic Recovery of Germany, 1933–1938*, p. 199.
26. R. N. Hunt, *German Social Democracy, 1918–33*, p. 252.
27. Eyck, p. 66.
28. Hugh Dalton in 1940, quoted in H. G. Atkins, *German Literature through Nazi Eyes*, p. 19.
29. H. Müller, *Die November-Revolution*, pp. 27ff.
30. Carsten, pp. 32–3.
31. Hunt, *German Social Democracy, 1918–33*, p. 182.
32. Ryder, p. 243.
33. Carsten, p. 92.
34. Lord d'Abernon, *An Ambassador of Peace*, Vol. I, p. 87.
35. W. Manchester, *The Arms of Krupp*, pp. 381ff.
36. J. W. Angell, *The Recovery of Germany*, pp. 379 and 282.
37. G. Stolper, *The German Economy, 1870 to the Present*, p. 82.
38. Stolper, p. 63.
39. This was equivalent to about 15 times the value of German exports in 1925.
40. Angell, pp. 33, 57, 379 and 382.
41. H. A. Turner, *Stresemann and the Politics of the Weimar Republic*, p. 82.
42. Kennan, p. 221.
43. Graf Kessler, *Tagebücher, 1918–37*, p. 606. For the diplomacy of Rapallo see H. Graml, 'Die Rapallo-Politik im Urteil der Westdeutschen Forschung', *V.J.Z.G.*, vol. 18 (1970) p. 366. Not everyone agrees with the interpretation of German policy at Rapallo given in the text. There is some evidence that the leaders of the German delegation, especially von Maltzan, the head of the East European department of the Foreign Ministry, were determined all along to come to terms with the Russians, and that the reasons given for the decision to sign the treaty were merely a pretext.
44. D. Felix, *Walther Rathenau and the Weimar Republic* (1971) is a useful study of Rathenau and the reparations problem.
45. G. Freund, *Unholy Alliance*, p. 83.
46. Freund, p. 72.
47. Carsten, p. 139.
48. Carsten, p. 140.
49. L. Kochan, *The Struggle for Germany, 1914–45*, p. 31. It does not appear that the Poles had any intention of attacking Germany.
50. The French, according to Lloyd George, greatly exaggerated the damage done to their country in order to swell the reparations bill (D. Lloyd George, *The Truth About Reparations and War Debts*, pp. 20ff.).
51. d'Abernon, I, p. 34.
52. W. Manchester, *The Arms of Krupp*, p. 373. Gustav Krupp's full name was Gustav Krupp von Bohlen und Halbach.
53. For a synoptic view of inflation by eye-witnesses and others, see F. K. Ringer (ed.), *The German Inflation of 1923*.

54. The social consequences of inflation are discussed in H. Ostwald, *Sitten-geschichte der Inflation*.
55. H. Speidel, 'Reichswehr und Rote Armee', *V.J.Z.G.* No. 1 (1953) p. 9.
56. Freund, pp. 152ff.
57. Freund, pp. 177–8.
58. I. Deak, *Weimar Germany's Left-wing Intellectuals*, p. 74.
59. Quoted in J. Willett, *Expressionism*, pp. 146 and 156.
60. G. Masur, *Imperial Berlin*, p. 228.
61. H. Lehmann-Haupt, *Art under a Dictatorship*, p. 18.
62. Willett, p. 189. But already some years before 1914 the virtues of *Sachlichkeit* had been proclaimed by an influential German architect, Hermann Muthesius.
63. P. Gay, *Weimar Culture*, p. 2. The phrase was first used, it seems, by Gustav Stolper, the author of *The German Economy, 1870 to the Present*.
64. Gay, p. 2.
65. For the Bauhaus, see L. Hirschfeld-Mack, *The Bauhaus*.
66. Gay, p. 101.
67. Deak, p. 206.
68. H. L. Poor, *Kurt Tucholsky and the Ordeal of Germany, 1918–1935*, p. 99.
69. For Georg Grosz see B. I. Lewis, *George Grosz: Art and Politics in the Weimar Republic*, especially pp. 162ff and 216, for the intellectuals generally also G. A. Craig, 'Engagement and Neutrality in Weimar Germany', *J.C.H.*, vol. 2 (ii) (1967) p. 49.
70. G. Rees, *A Bundle of Sensations*, p. 35.
71. For the pre-Nazi film, see S. Kracauer, *From Caligari to Hitler*, p. 272, and H. H. Wollenberg, *Fifty Years of German Films*. In his classic study Kracauer interprets many of the films made during the Republic as foreshadowing the Third Reich. In their recent study Manvell and Fraenkel find this thesis exaggerated, *The German Cinema*, p. 15.
72. T. Mann, *Betrachtungen eines Unpolitischen*, p. 74. 'I have long believed', wrote Mann on 25 November 1916, 'that it is impossible for internal more than external reasons to create an authentic political life in Germany.' *Letters*, 1, p. 82.
73. E. B. Wheaton, *Prelude to Calamity*, p. 386.
74. For Brecht see J. Willett, *The Theatre of Bertolt Brecht*; M. Esslin, *A Choice of Evils*.
75. B. Brecht, *Stücke*, IV, p. 265.
76. Brecht, *Stücke*, IV, p. 298.
77. On Brecht and Communism see Esslin, especially chapters 7 and 8.

CHAPTER VII

1. J. W. Angell, *The Recovery of Germany*, p. 400. In 1926 exports exceeded imports if reparations are included in the former.
2. G. Stolper, *The German Economy, 1870 to the Present*, p. 99; C. W. Guillebaud, *The Economic Recovery of Germany, 1933–38*, p. 13.
3. S. W. Halperin, *Germany tried Democracy*, p. 379.
4. Stolper, pp. 77 and 96.
5. Angell, pp. 316, 331 and 400.

6. Angell, p. 322.
7. Guillebaud, p. 13. There was always the possibility, ignored by critics of the Young Plan, that in the fairly rapidly changing climate of opinion, America might decide to cancel part of the war debt due to her, with the likely consequence of a reduction of reparations.
8. For Seeckt, see H. Meier-Welcker, *Seeckt*, the most recent biography, also B. H. Liddell Hart, *The Other Side of the Hill.*
9. Meier-Welcker, p. 114.
10. F. L. Carsten, *Reichswehr and Politics, 1918–33*, p. 117.
11. Meier-Welcker, p. 543. It was symptomatic that even in 1931 the phrase 'in peacetime' referred to the pre-1914 era. A. Dorpalen, *Hindenburg and the Weimar Republic*, pp. 164–5.
12. F. Neumann, *Behemoth*, pp. 478–9.
13. 'Can one be surprised that, in a state which never came to terms with itself, the army, burdened as it was with the very difficult task of forming a new tradition, did not find the right relationship to the state? . . . With the best will, the army could not integrate in something which was never integrated itself.' Golo Mann quoted in Meier-Welcker, p. 540.
14. H. von Seeckt, *Gedanken eines Soldaten*, p. 116.
15. Carsten, pp. 165ff. 'Seeckt himself believed that the only answer to Germany's difficulties was a dictatorship, but he disclaimed any wish to be the dictator.' Meier-Welcker, p. 411.
16. J. H. Morgan, *Assize of Arms*, Vol. I, pp. 266ff.
17. For Hindenburg, see A. Dorpalen, *Hindenburg and the Weimar Republic*, *passim*.
18. For Stresemann, see especially A. Thimme, *Gustav Stresemann*; H. A. Turner, *Stresemann and the Politics of the Weimar Republic*; and H. W. Gatzke, *Stresemann and the Rearmament of Germany*; also Gatzke, 'The Stresemann Papers' in *J.M.H.*, vol. 26 (1954) p. 49. It was ironical that when Gessler was suggested as presidential candidate, Stresemann objected on the ground that foreign opinion would not like a man so closely associated with the *Reichswehr*.
19. E. von Weizsäcker, *Erinnerungen*, p. 77.
20. *Akten zur deutschen auswärtigen Politik, 1918–1945*, Series B, 1, part 1 (Göttingen, 1966) pp. 727–53, quoted in *A.H.R.*, vol. 75 (1969) p. 77, footnote 13.
21. A. Cienciala, *Poland and the Western Powers, 1938–39*, Chapter 1. The Maginot Line, named after the then French Minister of War, was begun in 1929.
22. Shortly before his death Stresemann blamed the intransigence of the western powers for the continued opposition to his policy inside Germany. 'That', he is supposed to have said addressing them, 'is your crime and my tragedy.'
23. For the Nationalist Party (D.N.V.P.) see A. Chanady, 'The Disintegration of the German National People's Party, 1924–30', *J.M.H.*, vol. 39 (1967) p. 65.
24. For this subject see F. Stern, *The Politics of Cultural Despair* and G. L. Mosse, *The Crisis of German Ideology*, both *passim*.
25. Dorpaien, p. 164.
26. G. Jasper (ed.), *Von Weimar zu Hitler*, p. 137. For Zehrer and his associates see the chapter 'Der Tatkreis' by K. Sontheimer in Jasper, pp. 197–228. Sontheimer remarks that the *Tat* group with its intellectual sympathy for

Fascism bore the same relation to Nazism as the 'parlour pinks' (*Salonbolschewisten*) did to Communism. The *Tatkreis* also influenced the officers of the *Reichswehr*.

27. Möller van den Bruck, *Das Dritte Reich*, p. 138.

28. Quoted in E. Crankshaw, *The Gestapo*, p. 43.

29. K. D. Bracher, *Die Auflösung der Weimarer Republik*, p. 293.

30. In July 1930 Hindenburg arriving at Friedrichstrasse railway station in Berlin did not even recognise his own Chancellor. H. Brüning, *Memoiren, 1918–1934*, p. 183.

31. G. A. Craig, *Politics of the Prussian Army 1640–1945*, p. 438; Carsten, p. 274.

32. Carsten, p. 328.

33. E. Eyck, *History of the Weimar Republic*, ii, p. 394.

34. Dorpalen, p. 206.

35. E. W. Bennett, *Germany and the Diplomacy of the Financial Crisis, 1931*, p. 31.

36. A. Thimme, *Gustav Stresemann*, p. 69.

37. According to Curtius, German Foreign Minister at the time, it was French financial policy which led to the failure of the Austrian *Creditanstalt*. J. Curtius, *Sechs Jahre Minister der deutschen Republik*, p. 210.

38. Brüning told Hitler in October 1930 that he hoped to end reparations and make Germany able to defend itself, so that in the course of a year and a half or two years the whole treaty of Versailles would tacitly begin to crumble. Brüning, pp. 192–3.

39. For an assessment of Brüning, see Bennett, *passim*; Craig, *From Bismarck to Adenauer*, pp. 61ff; W. J. Helbich, *Die Reparationen in der Ära Brüning, 1930–32*, *passim*. According to Curtius his decision to resign was made independent of Brüning's undertaking to Hindenburg to reconstruct his cabinet. Curtius, p. 207.

40. With the wisdom of hindsight one can say that Brüning ought to have taken the kind of measures to relieve unemployment (while simultaneously protecting the mark) carried out shortly afterwards by the Hitler government with the help of Schacht. But Brüning did not have the authority to act as Hitler acted, nor did he have the necessary boldness and unorthodoxy.

41. Brüning speaks in his Memoirs (p. 492) of German indebtedness as a weapon against the treaty of Versailles and suggests that if the foreign powers proved recalcitrant Germany, like Samson among the Philistines, could pull down the pillars on which the world's prosperity rested.

42. Bracher, pp. 519 and 631.

43. W. Manchester, *The Arms of Krupp*, p. 399. One reason for the high unemployment was the rationalisation in the 1920s whereby new machinery had made many workpeople redundant.

44. Brüning, p. 612.

54. For Papen, see his *Memoirs*, *passim*. Papen accuses the British of driving a wedge between France and Germany. The basic Anglo-French clash over reparations arose because the French insisted on payments continuing when the British were more concerned to reactivate the German economy as a trading partner and also to get their short-term loans repaid. During the Reparations conference at Lausanne a characteristic incident occurred. Herriot and Macdonald, the French and British Prime Ministers, agreed to make a statement repudiating the guilt clause in the peace treaty provided Germany paid the final reparations sum they demanded. But they insisted

it must appear to be done spontaneously, not in response to pressure. As Papen, however, refused to pay the full amount on the ground that German public opinion would not stand for it, nothing was said on the other side about the guilt question. Agreement was reached in the end on the final sum, but Papen missed the boost to his government which Allied repudiation of German war guilt would have provided. Schwerin von Krosigk, *Es geschah in Deutschland*, p. 144.

46. *D.B.F.B.*, *1919–39*, Series 2, vol. iv, p. 460.
47. Carsten, pp. 368f.
48. R. N. Hunt, *German Social Democracy*, *1918–33*, p. 188; O. Braun, *Von Weimar zu Hitler*, p. 409.
49. S. Spender, *World Within World*, p. 129.
50. Guillebaud, pp. 32–8.
51. Carsten, pp. 368ff.
52. Hunt, p. 137.
53. *D.B.F.B.*, *1919–1939*, Second Series, vol. iii, p. 124.
54. For the testimony of Hammerstein, see Bracher, p. 733.
55. Eyck, ii, pp. 448ff; Carsten, p. 393; H. O. Meissner and H. Wilde, *Die Machtergreifung*, pp. 175ff; Brüning, pp. 645ff. The rumour was probably true, though the evidence is conflicting. According to Brüning, it was the news of Blomberg's appointment as Minister of Defence which provoked Schleicher to threaten a *coup d'etat* on 29 January, but other accounts make Blomberg arrive in Berlin from Geneva on 30 January, the day when the new cabinet was sworn in.
56. Dorpalen, p. 428.
57. L. J. Edinger, *German Exile Politics*, p. 16.
58. Braun, p. 5.
59. See Winston Churchill's essay on Hitler in *Great Contemporaries* (1937) for a characteristic British view in the mid 1930s.
60. W. Ulbricht, *Zur Geschichte der deutschen Arbeiterbewegung*, vol. i, p. 455. The admission was made by Wilhelm Pieck, later first President of the East German Republic. The K.P.D. 'Brussels' conference was actually held near Moscow in October 1935.
61. I. Deak, *Weimar Germany's Leftwing Intellectuals*, p. 226.
62. H. Schacht, *Account Settled*, p. 206.
63. For a general discussion of this problem, see article by Carl Schorske in the *New York Times Review of Books*, 21 May 1970, also an article by P. G. Pulzer, *H.J.*, vol. 13 (1970) p. 188.
64. A. Bullock, *Hitler*, p. 179. For middle-class attitudes during the Weimar Republic, see H. Lebovics, *Social Conservatism and the Middle Classes in Germany*, *1914–33*.
65. F. Thyssen, *I paid Hitler*, p. 134. Thyssen is vague on dates: he writes of contributions being given 'in the years before Hitler came to power'. For a critical discussion of Thyssen see H. A. Turner, 'Big Business and the Rise of Hitler', *A.H.R.*, vol. 75 (1969) pp. 56ff.
66. According to Brüning the *Vereinigte Stahlwerke* gave RM 5,000 for the candidature of Hindenburg but half a million marks for Hitler's in 1932. Brüning, p. 531.
67. Among those who thought that Hitler should be made Chancellor was Oskar Wassermann, a well-known banker and Zionist. *D.B.F.B.*, Series 2, vol. iii, p. 124.
68. Manchester, p. 407.

69. Hunt, pp. 38–9.
70. T. Wolff, *Through Two Decades*, p. 298.
71. Matthias and Morsey, p. 334.
72. Matthias and Morsey, p. 334.

CHAPTER VIII

1. F. L. Carsten, *The Rise of Fascism*, p. 78.
2. Carsten, p. 32 quoting A. J. May, *The Habsburg Monarchy, 1867–1914*, p. 177.
3. For Hitler's early life, see W. Maser, *Hitler's Mein Kampf*, especially pp. 85ff.
4. K. Heiden, *Hitler, a Man against Europe*, p. 50.
5. The Bavarian People's party (the Bavarian equivalent of the Centre) voted in the Reichstag against the adoption of the Weimar constitution.
6. Maser, p. 110.
7. N. H. Baynes, (ed.), *The Speeches of Adolf Hitler*, 1, p. 111.
8. Baynes, 1, p. 776.
9. H. Bennecke, *Hitler und die S.A.*, p. 24.
10. Carsten, p. 94.
11. Bennecke, p. 23.
12. J. Fest, *The Face of the Third Reich*, pp. 136ff.
13. Bennecke, p. 50.
14. Carsten, p. 177.
15. Bennecke, p. 9; K. Schwendt, *Bayern zwischen Monarchie und Diktatur*, p. 240.
16. A. Bullock, *Hitler*, p. 108.
17. Schwendt, p. 257.
18. Gregor Strasser, one of the strongest personalities among the Nazi leaders, represented the more constructive elements in the party, compared with nihilists like Goebbels, and belonged to the radical right-wing tradition of Sorel and the American Populists.
19. When Otto Strasser, brother of Gregor, accused Hitler of 'betraying' National Socialism, he was expelled by Goebbels from the party's Berlin organisation.
20. J. Noakes, 'Conflict and Development in the N.S.D.A.P. 1924–1927', *J.C.H.*, vol. 1 (iv) (1966) pp. 3ff.
21. For Goebbels, see biographies by L. Lochner and H. Heiber, also E. H. Bramsted, *Goebbels and National Socialist Propaganda, 1925–45*, and Z.A.B. Zeman, *Nazi Propaganda*.
22. Bramsted, p. 453.
23. G. Fergusson, 'A Blueprint for Dictatorship', *International Affairs*, Vol. 40 (1964) p. 247.
24. Zeman, p. 11.
25. Baynes, 1, p. 175.
26. S. Roberts, *The House that Hitler Built*, p. 76.
27. K. D. Bracher, *Die deutsche Diktatur*, p. 211.
28. G. Jasper (ed.), *Von Weimar zu Hitler*, p. 236.
29. F. Tobias, *The Reichstag Fire*, also H. Mommsen, 'Der Reichstagsbrand und seine politische Folgen', *V.J.Z.G.*, vol. 12 (1964) p. 351. A recent popular book on the Reichstag Fire is R. J. Pritchard, *Reichstag Fire: Ashes of*

Democracy (New York, 1972), which accepts the findings of Tobias and rejects the alternative explanation put forward by a special Commission of Inquiry into the Reichstag Fire set up by the European Committee for Scientific Research into the Origins and Consequences of the Second World War.

30. Fest, p. 145.
31. E. Matthias and R. Morsey (ed.), *Das Ende der Parteien*, chapter on the S.P.D., pp. 99ff.
32. Matthias and Morsey, chapter on the Centre party, pp. 281ff.
33. A. François-Poncet, *The Fateful Years*, p. 74.
34. A. Dorpalen, *Hindenburg and the Weimar Republic*, p. 445.
35. Bracher, p. 251.
36. Bracher, p. 380.
37. A. and V. Toynbee, *Hitler's Europe*, p. 21.
38. Jasper, p. 300.
39. L. J. Edinger, *German Exile Politics*, p. 22.
40. François-Poncet, p. 70.
41. Dorpalen, pp. 447ff.
42. M. Broszat, *Der Staat Hitlers*, pp. 407–8.
43. S. Kracauer, *From Caligari to Hitler*, p. 204.
44. B. Brecht, *Gedichte*, III, p. 25.
45. M. Broszat, 'Soziale Motivation und Führer-Binding des National Sozialismus', *V.J.Z.G.*, vol. 18 (1970) p. 393.
46. Broszat, p. 259.
47. Baynes, 1, p. 287.
48. R. J. O'Neill, *The German Army and the Nazi Party, 1933–39*, p. 38.
49. Blomberg hoped that the army would become the main pillar of Hitler's dictatorship, instead of the party, which would wither away. R. Koehl, 'The Character of the Nazi S.S.', *J.M.H.*, vol. 34 (1962) p. 275.
50. Broszat, p. 267.
51. O'Neill, p. 42.
52. E. Bethge, *Dietrich Bonhoeffer*, p. 299.
53. Dorpalen, pp. 482–3.
54. Bracher, p. 267.
55. The N.S.D.A.P. Nuremberg Rally of 1934 was the subject of one of the most remarkable propaganda films made during the regime, as mentioned in the next chapter.

CHAPTER IX

1. In his '*Second Book*', written in 1928 but discovered only in 1958, Hitler mentioned 500,000 square kilometres of space in Europe as his first goal. This alone shows that his ambitions went far beyond revision of Versailles. G. L. Weinberg, *The Foreign Policy of Hitler's Germany*, p. 6.
2. W. N. Medlicott, *Britain and Germany: the Search for Agreement, 1930–37*, p. 3. It was characteristic of the prevailing mood that the *Times* of 22 March 1933, the day after the Potsdam ceremony, spoke of modifying or cancelling harsh or unjust clauses in the peace treaty.
3. *D.B.F.P.*, Series 2, vol. VI, pp. 574ff (memorandum of 21 March 1934).
4. A. Cienciala, *Poland and the Western Powers, 1938–9*, p. 16.
5. D. C. Watt, 'German Plans for the Reoccupation of the Rhineland: a note'; *J.C.H.*, Vol 1 (iv) (1966) p. 193.

6. K. D. Bracher, *Die deutsche Diktatur*, pp. 389–92.
7. Medlicott, p. 12.
8. *D.G.F.P.*, Series D, 1, pp. 62–3.
9. *D.G.F.P.*, 1, p. 44.
10. *D.G.F.P.*, 1, pp. 29ff.
11. T. W. Mason, 'Some Origins of the Second World War', *P. & P.*, vol. 29 (1964) p. 76.
12. W. Warlimont, *Inside Hitler's Headquarters*, p. 6.
13. F. L. Carsten, *The Reichswehr and Politics, 1918–33*, p. 397; R. J. O'Neill, *The German Army and the Nazi Party*, p. 172.
14. O'Neill, pp. 40ff. This episode is important for the light it throws on Hitler's intentions, and helps to refute the thesis that Hitler in 1939 found himself at war by accident.
15. K. Demeter, *The German Officer-Corps, 1650–1945*, p. 210.
16. K. Robbins, 'Konrad Henlein, the Sudeten Question and British Foreign Policy', *H.J.*, vol. 12 (1969) p. 674.
17. O'Neill, p. 156.
18. H. Rothfels, *The German Opposition to Hitler*, p. 57.
19. E. von Manstein, *Lost Victories*, p. 80.
20. N. H. Baynes (ed.), *The Speeches of Adolf Hitler*, ii, p. 1746.
21. M. Beloff, *The Foreign Policy of Soviet Russia*, vol. ii, pp. 143ff; A. Ulam, *Expansion and Co-existence*, pp. 250ff.
22. Beloff, p. 158. Hodza resigned as Prime Minister on 22 September 1938.
23. Beloff, p. 166; G. F. Kennan, *Russia and the West under Lenin and Stalin*, pp. 322–4.
24. Ulam, p. 252.
25. Though appeasement, an emotive word in politics since the 1930s, was especially associated with Neville Chamberlain, it was also practised by Churchill (though for the most part unwillingly) and above all by Roosevelt in relation to the Soviet Union, especially in 1945. The case against Chamberlain is not that he sought an agreement with Germany but that he allowed this search to weaken the credibility of the Anglo-Polish treaty. Chamberlain seems to have viewed the guarantee to Poland (and probably also the guarantees to Roumania and Greece) as a 'diplomatic deterrent', a temporary and limited commitment. Cienciala, p. 224. The argument about appeasement has tended to exaggerate the difference between Chamberlain and the 'hard-liners' of the Foreign Office like Vansittart. The latter were not opposed to negotiating with Germany even if they were sceptical about an agreement with Hitler. Such negotiations were in their view necessary to gain time to prepare British defences, but Chamberlain too accepted the need to rearm and the impossibility of going to war before 1939. Medlicott, pp. 31–2. See also I. Colvin, *Vansittart in Office* (London, 1965), *passim*.
26. O'Neill, p. 159.
27. G. Ritter, *The German Resistance*, pp. 95ff; Rothfels, pp. 59ff.
28. Rothfels, p. 62.
29. O'Neill, pp. 67–8.
30. E. Zeller, *The Flame of Freedom*, p. 34.
31. W. Hofer, *Die Diktatur Hitlers*, p. 153.
32. L. Hill, 'Three Crises, 1938–39', *J.C.H.*, vol. 3 (i) (1968) pp. 113ff.
33. P. Schmidt, *Hitler's Interpreter*, p. 118. Hitler's optimism was based on a misunderstanding by Ribbentrop of remarks made to him by the French Foreign Minister, Bonnet, who was reckoned to be France's 'arch-appeaser'.

34. K. D. Bracher, *Die deutsche Diktatur*, p. 342.

35. *D.G.F.P.*, Series D., vol. VI, p. 168.

36. L. Gruchmann, *Geschichte des Zweiten Weltkrieges*, p. 13.

37. E. von Weizsacker, *Erinnerungen*, p. 237.

38. K. Feiling, *Life of Neville Chamberlain*, p. 407.

39. Cienciala, p. 243.

40. *D.G.F.P.*, Series D, VI, p. 1033; L. B. Namier, *Europe in Decay*, p. 223.

41. G. L. Weinberg, *Germany and the Soviet Union, 1939–41*, p. 170. The Russians were in no hurry to come to terms with Hitler, and Stalin did not finally make up his mind to sign until 19 August, or 21 August according to some accounts. Ulam, p. 275.

42. H. W. Koch, 'Hitler and the Origins of the Second World War', *H.J.*, vol. XI (1968) p. 125ff, J. Wheeler-Bennett, *The Nemesis of Power*, p. 452.

43. Lipski, Poland's ambassador to Germany, seems to have expected overt opposition to Hitler to show itself on the outbreak of war, and to have thought that the Polish army would get to Berlin. P. Kleist, *Zwischen Hitler and Stalin*, pp. 90–1.

44. *D.G.F.P.*, Series D., VI, pp. 566–7.

45. Weinberg, p. 18.

46. Cienciala, pp. 239–41.

47. 'If Hitler had had the decency to hand back a simulacrum of independence to the Czechs, he would have had the British government eating out of his hand', A. L. Rowse, *All Souls and Appeasement*, p. 99. This suggestion was actually made by Lord Lothian to Adam von Trott zu Solz when the latter visited Oxford in the summer of 1939.

48. *D.G.F.P.*, Series D., 1, p. 40.

49. M. Broszat, *Der Staat Hitlers*, p. 177.

50. D. Petzina, 'Hauptprobleme der deutschen Wirtschaft 1932–3', *V.J.Z.G.*, vol. XV (1967) pp. 18ff.

51. Another recent estimate puts the number of unemployed in 1938 at 300,000 out of a total labour force of 20·5 million. D. Petzina, 'Die Mobilisierung deutscher Arbeitskraefte vor und während des Zweiten Weltkrieges', *V.J.Z.G.*, vol. 18 (1970) p. 447.

52. A. E. Simpson, 'The Struggle for Control of the German Economy.' *J.M.H.*, vol. 31 (1959) pp. 37ff.

53. A. and V. Toynbee, *Hitler's Europe*, p. 209.

54. E. M. Carroll, *Design for Total War*, p. 176.

55. B. H. Klein, *Germany's Economic Preparations for War*, p. 61.

56. Carroll, pp. 93 and 122ff.

57. A. Hillgruber, *Hitler's Strategie*, p. 131.

58. M. Broszat, p. 212.

59. G. L. Mosse, *Nazi Culture*, p. 362.

60. Mosse, p. 363.

61. H. Schacht, *Account Settled*, p. 206.

62. T. W. Mason, 'Labour in the Third Reich, 1933–1939', *P. & P.*, vol. 33 (1966) pp. 82ff. For a general view of labour in the Third Reich see also D. Schoenbaum, *Hitler's Social Revolution*, especially chapter 3.

63. Broszat, p. 189.

64. Mosse, p. 342.

65. Klein, p. 66.

66. Bracher, p. 369.

67. Bracher, p. 362, A. J. Nicholls and E. Matthias, *German Democracy and the Triumph of Hitler*, p. 230.
68. Carroll, p. 142.
69. Carroll, p. 173.
70. Carroll, p. 73.
71. W. Speer, *Inside the Third Reich*, p. 540.
72. G. Stolper, *The German Economy, 1870 to the Present*, p. 142.
73. C. W. Guillebaud, *The Social Policy of Nazi Germany*, p. 115.
74. Klein, p. 13.
75. Mason, pp. 82ff.
76. Mosse, p. 360. From 1933 to the beginning of 1938 the average hourly earnings of workers in the most important industries rose by 10 per cent, and average earnings by 20 per cent, compared with a rise of 6 per cent in the official cost of living index.
77. Speer, p. 222.
78. Klein, p. 79.
79. Carroll, pp. 184 and 264. Resources had also to be found for the lavish building projects in Berlin and other cities for which Hitler ordered Speer to prepare plans.
80. Reluctance to employ women sprang from Hitler's well-known belief that woman's place is in the home, but here as elsewhere practical needs clashed with party doctrine. The shortage of men caused first by full employment then by the war caused the Nazis actually to encourage the use of women in public positions and even to give them professional training. By the end of 1942 Hitler's assumption that Germany's labour needs could be wholly met by importation of foreign labour including forced female labour from Eastern Europe was belied by events. Sauckel, the Reich Commissioner for Labour, ordered the conscription of three million women between the ages of seventeen and forty-five, but less than a third of these were actually used in industry. See also Speer, pp. 220–1 and 320, Nicholls and Matthias, pp. 211–12 and Kleist, p. 193.
81. A. S. Milward, *The German Economy at War*, pp. 63ff. In November 1939 General Thomas told leading German industrialists: 'We shall never defeat England with radio sets, vacuum cleaners and cooking utensils.' Nicholls and Matthias, p. 231.
82. Bracher, pp. 360–1. 'The rapid disintegration of the trade unions under the Nazi labour laws of 1933 remains one of the great surprises in the history of National Socialism in Germany.' J. P. Nettl, *The Eastern Zone and Soviet Policy in Germany*, p. 28.
83. Petzina, 'Die Mobilisierung deutscher Arbeitskraefte vor und während des Zweiten Weltkrieges', *V.J.Z.G.*, vol. 18 (1970) p. 449.
84. Bracher, p. 367.
85. D. Schoenbaum, *Hitler's Social Revolution*, chapters 8 and 9.
86. Broszat, p. 428.
87. Mosse, p. 345.
88. W. F. Bruck, *Social and Economic History of Germany, 1888–1938*, p. 263.
89. Bracher, p. 366.
90. Hofer, p. 115; D. Petzina, 'Hauptprobleme der deutschen Wirtschaftspolitik, 1932–3', *V.J.Z.G.*, vol. XV (1967) pp. 18ff.
91. Broszat, p. 238.
92. Toynbee, p. 216.
93. J. Fest, *The Face of the Third Reich*, p. 255.

94. Richard Strauss resigned this position two years later in protest against the regime's anti-semitism; the librettist for Strauss's opera *The Silent Woman* was Stefan Zweig, who was a Jew.

95. A. Chanady, 'The Disintegration of the German National People's Party, 1924–30', *J.M.H.*, vol. 39 (1967) p. 65.

96. S. D. Stirk, *The Prussian Spirit*, p. 83.

97. J. P. Stern, *Ernst Jünger, passim*, Fest, pp. 250 and 372.

98. No major National Socialist work of historical scholarship was produced.

99. G. H. Hamilton, *European Art and Architecture, 1880–1940*, p. 328; H. Lehmann-Haupt, *Art under a Dictatorship*, pp. 88ff; H. Brenner, *Die Kunstpolitik des Nationalsozialismus*, p. 112. A list of the artists and museums affected is in P. A. Rave, *Kunstdiktatur im Dritten Reich. sozialismus*, and P. A. Rave, *Kunstdiktatur im Dritten Reich*.

100. Speer, p. 59; Lehmann-Haupt, p. 117.

101. Speer, pp. 153 and 530.

102. Lehmann-Haupt, p. 124; B. N. Lane, *Architecture and Politics in Germany, 1918–1945*, pp. 185ff. See also H. Brenner, *Die Kunstpolitik des Nationalsozialismus*, and P. A. Rave, *Kunstdikatur im Dritten Reich*.

103. J. Wulff, *Theater und Film im Dritten Reich*, pp. 289ff.

104. R. Manvell and H. Fraenkel, *The German Cinema*, p. 78.

105. W. Zorn, 'Student Politics in the Weimar Republic', *J.C.H.*, vol. 5 (i) (1970) p. 136.

106. Fest, p. 252, Zorn, p. 136.

107. E. Y. Hartshorne, *German Universities and National Socialism*, p. 94.

108. R. H. Samuel and R. Hinton Thomas, *Education and Society in Modern Germany*, p. 133.

109. Bracher, p. 293.

110. Fest, p. 294.

111. Fest, p. 293.

112. Bracher, p. 287.

113. Fest, p. 233. Each of the four *Ordensburgen* could accommodate a thousand students.

114. Fest, p. 226.

115. Baynes, II, p. 1766. The psychologist was William Brown, Wilde Reader in Mental Philosophy at Oxford University. See also Broszat, 'Soziale Motivation und Führer-Binding des Nationalsozialismus', *V.J.Z.G.*, vol. 18 (1970), p. 392.

116. C. E. Schorske, 'Politics in a New Key: an Austrian Triptych', *J.M.H.*, vol. 39 (1967) p. 356.

117. 'One of the difficulties in the religious battles of the 1930s was the absence of clear-cut fronts', D. Schmidt, *Pastor Niemöller*, p. 95.

118. W. Dibelius, *In the Service of the Lord*, p. 139.

119. H. Rauschning, *Hitler speaks*, pp. 55ff.

120. *The Third Reich* (New York, 1955) p. 800.

121. J. S. Conway, *The Nazi Persecution of the Churches*, p. 21.

122. Conway, p. 26.

123. *Third Reich*, p. 806.

124. Dibelius, p. 111.

125. H. Graml and others, *The German Resistance to Hitler*, p. 204. (E. Wolf.)

126. K. W. Dahm, 'German Protestantism and Politics, 1918–39', *J.C.H.*, Vol. 3 (i) (1968) pp. 29ff.

127. Broszat, pp. 285–6.
128. Graml, p. 206. (Wolf.) For Nazi-Protestant relations generally in the pre-war period see also K. Scholder, 'Die Evangelische Kirche im Licht der Nationalsozialistischen Führung bis zum Kriegsausbruch', *V.J.Z.G.*, vol. 8 (1960) 1.
129. Graml, p. 214. (Wolf.)
130. Conway, p. 335. Conway speaks of the 'almost Manichaean conviction that the affairs of political and social life are irredeemable'.
131. Hofer, p. 182.
132. While Bonhoeffer was in Moabit Prison awaiting trial he was visited by the prison chaplain, who asked him: 'Brother, what are you doing here?' to which Niemöller replied: 'And, brother, why are *you* not here?' Schmidt, pp. 106–7.
133. Dibelius, p. 162.
134. Dibelius, p. 138; Conway, pp. 242ff.
135. Conway, p. 420.
136. Conway, p. 166.
137. Conway, p. 325.
138. S. Friedländer, *Pius XII and the Third Reich*, p. 34.
139. Conway, p. 398.
140. E. Bethge, *Dietrich Bonhoeffer*, p. 208.
141. Graml, p. 217. (Wolf.)
142. H. Brüning, *Memoiren, 1918–1934*, pp. 357ff.
143. Friedländer, p. 40, and *passim*; *Times Literary Supplement* of 1 December 1966, p. 1109; G. Bull, 'The Vatican, the Nazis and the Pursuit of Justice', *International Affairs*, Vol. 47 (1971) p. 353; H. Deutsch, *The Conspiracy against Hitler in the Twilight War*, pp. 107ff.
144. Conway, p. 326.
145. K. Bölling, *Republic in Suspense*, p. 26.
146. G. Lewy, *The Catholic Church and Nazi Germany*, pp. 292–3.

CHAPTER X

1. E. von Manstein, *Memoirs*, p. 46, S. Westphal, *Heer in Fesseln*, p. 7.
2. G. Reitlinger, *The S.S., Alibi of a Nation*, pp. 130–1; H. Höhne, *The Order of the Death's Head*, p. 308.
3. G. L. Weinberg, *Germany and the Soviet Union, 1939–41*, pp. 65ff.
4. Weinberg, p. 81.
5. Höhne, p. 296.
6. J. Fest, *The Face of the Third Reich*, p. 216.
7. Höhne, p. 294.
8. Höhne, p. 299.
9. A. Hillgruber, *Hitler's Strategie*, p. 250.
10. H. Deutsch, *The Conspiracy against Hitler in the Twilight War*, pp. 179 and 188–9.
11. Höhne, p. 368.
12. Manstein, pp. 83ff.
13. R. H. S. Stolfi, 'Equipment for Victory in France in 1940', *History*, Vol. 55 (1970) p. 1; A. Horne, *To lose a Battle, passim*.
14. S. Westphal, p. 38.

15. L. Hart, p. 812.
16. Weinberg, p. 109.
17. A. Bryant, *The Turn of the Tide, 1939–43*, pp. 188, 206.
18. Weinberg, p. 110.
19. Hillgruber, pp. 79ff; S. W. Roskill, *The War at Sea*, p. 88.
20. Hillgruber, p. 39.
21. Hillgruber, p. 176; Hinsley, *Hitler's Strategy*, p. 84.
22. Hillgruber, p. 177
23. B. Collier, *The Second World War*, p. 164. According to B. H. Liddell Hart (*The Second World War*, p. 108) German and British aircraft losses from July until the end of October were 1,733 and 915 respectively.
24. A. Bryant, p. 92.
25. S. W. Roskill, p. 92.
26. S. Friedländer, *Pius XII and the Third Reich*, p. 239.
27. A. and V. Toynbee, *Hitler's Europe*, p. 58.
28. Toynbee, p. 368.
29. Westphal, p. 85.
30. L. Gruchmann, *Der Zweite Weltkrieg*, p. 105.
31. L. Gruchmann, 'Die ,verpassten strategischen Chancen' der Achsenmaechte im Mittelmeerraum, 1940–1', *V.J.Z.G.*, vol. 18 (1970) p. 456.
32. Hart, p. 296.
33. Hart, p. 298.
34. Hart, p. 431.
35. D. Young, *Rommel*, p. 84.
36. H. A. Jacobsen (ed.), *Der Zweite Weltkrieg in Bildern und Dokumenten*, p. 32.
37. Hillgruber, p. 163.
38. Hillgruber, p. 161.
39. Hillgruber, p. 162.
40. Collier, p. 179.
41. K. Dönitz, *Memoirs*, p. 164.
42. A. Speer, *Inside the Third Reich*, p. 273.
43. Dönitz, p. 315.
44. H. Trevor-Roper, 'Hitler's Kriegsziele', *V.J.Z.G.*, vol. 8 (1960), p. 121.
45. Since for Japan the Tripartite Pact was a step towards her invasion of Russia's Far Eastern territory, for Soviet Russia to join the Pact was too much for even the optimistic Ribbentrop to expect.
46. Weinberg, p. 147.
47. Liddell Hart, p. 169.
48. W. Warlimont, *Inside Hitler's Headquarters*, p. 240.
49. A. Clark, *Barbarossa*, p. 107.
50. After Stalingrad Germany had little help from her Italian, Hungarian and Roumanian allies, and in the expectation of a second front she had nearly as many men under arms in the West (excluding Germany) as in Russia. A. Seaton, *The Russo-German War, 1941–5*, p. 352.
51. Gruchmann, p. 189.
52. When a German colonel was asked what would happen if a splendidly equipped army marched from the German frontier through Russia to Vladivostok without any hostile opposition, his reply was that it would arrive at its destination 'a mob'. P. Kleist, *Zwischen Hitler und Stalin*, p. 156.
53. A. V. Karasev, 'The People's War', Purnell's *History of the Twentieth*

Century, vol. 5, p. 1817. The first partisans in the Ukraine were dis-illusioned nationalists, not Nazi agents. Kleist, p. 190.

54. Höhne, p. 315.
55. According to Himmler, Russia would ultimately have been partitioned between Germany, Britain and the United States. R. Manvell and H. Fraen-kel, *Himmler*, p. 189.
56. G. Reitlinger, *The House built on Sand*, p. 62.
57. One of the difficulties about the use of Vlassov was that his ideas about Russia's future naturally differed from those of the non-Russian nationalities. Kleist, pp. 215ff.
58. H. Buchheim, *Anatomie des S.S. Staates*, p. 312.
59. Reitlinger, p. 446.
60. Reitlinger, pp. 216 and 353; A. Dallin, *German Rule in Russia*, p. 596. There were even Uzbek, Indian and Arab units in the *Waffen S.S.* by the end of the war.
61. Rosenberg had a reputation for indolence and indecisiveness, and his *Ostministerium* was nicknamed the Ministry of Chaos (a half-pun). Kleist, pp. 141ff.
62. Reitlinger, p. 182.
63. Reitlinger, p. 194.
64. Dallin, pp. 406–7 and 677–8.
65. A German official's account of Soviet peace feelers through the Soviet embassy in Stockholm is given in Kleist, pp. 230ff. The Russians spoke of restoring the Russo-German frontier of 1914.
66. L. B. Namier, *In the Nazi Era*, p. 100. For a contrary view, see H. Deutsch, *The Conspiracy against Hitler in the Twilight War*, p. 357. Beck refused to allow the archive of the German opposition to be destroyed because it contained proof that the conspiracy against Hitler began before Germany started to lose the war.
67. H. Rothfels, *The German Opposition to Hitler*, p. 83.
68. C. Stern, *Ulbricht*, pp. 86–7.
69. L. J. Edinger, *German Exile Politics*, especially pp. 83ff. Among those who took part in the underground activities of the S.P.D. was Willy Brandt, the later party leader and German Chancellor.
70. Stern, p. 106.
71. H. Graml and others, *The German Resistance to Hitler*, pp. 114ff (Mommsen). Popitz had been a member of the N.S.D.A.P. and had received the party's golden badge.
72. J. C. G. Röhl (ed.), *Germany from Bismarck to Hitler*, pp. 172ff.
73. For Adam Trott zu Solz see a recent and sympathetic biography by C. Sykes, *Troubled Loyalty*.
74. For Stauffenberg generally, see J. Kramarz, *Stauffenberg*.
75. Rothfels, p. 112.
76. Graml, p. 29. In October 1939 Trott wrote that the nationalism of the kind that found its extreme expression in Nazism had been on the decline for some time, Rothfels, p. 151.
77. A. W. Dulles, *Germany's Underground*, p. 171. As early as 4 October 1941 Hassell had written: 'If we wait until the impossibility of peace becomes clear to the whole world, we shall have lost the chance of a passable peace.' U. von Hassell, *Diaries*, p. 200.
78. F. von Schlabrendorff, *The Secret War against Hitler*, p. 277.
79. Schlabrendorff, p. 294.

80. Rothfels, p. 152.
81. Graml, p. 141 (H. Mommsen). One not uncommon criticism of the men of the 20 July plot is that they shared many of the assumptions of the Nazis and in some cases had a similar background. Certainly the majority had grown up as nationalists. This makes their revolt, late in the day as it was, all the more significant.
82. Dulles, p. 84.
83. Graml, p. 226 (E. Wolf).
84. Speer, p. 538.
85. B. H. Klein, *Germany's Economic Preparations for War*, p. 192.
86. E. M. Carroll, *Design for Total War*, p. 48.
87. Fest, p. 204.
88. Speer, pp. 536–7.
89. E. L. Homze, *Foreign Labour in Nazi Germany*, pp. 237–8. The treatment of prisoners of war, like that of imported labour, varied according to the country of origin – the further east the worse it became. Yet some of the displaced East Europeans worked with remarkable loyalty for the Reich, perhaps in the knowledge that they might not after all return to their homes after the war under a communist regime.
90. Homze, p. 130.
91. H. Rumpf, *Das war der Bombenkrieg*, p. 60. This figure is taken from an American post-war report on the strategic bombing of Germany.
92. Rumpf, pp. 90–1.
93. E. K. Bramsted, *Goebbels and National Socialist Propaganda, 1925–45*, p. 264.
94. A. S. Milward, *The German Economy at War*, pp. 192–3.
95. M. Steinert, *Capitulation, 1945*, p. 68.
96. N. Frankland, 'The Bombing of Germany', Purnell's *History of the Twentieth Century*, vol. 5, p. 1965. The question is more fully discussed in C. Webster and N. Frankland, *The Strategic Air Offensive against Germany, 1939–1945*, 4 vols. (London, 1961) (the official history).
97. For the bombing of Dresden, see D. Irving, *The Destruction of Dresden*. When the R.A.F. crews were being briefed for an attack on Chemnitz which was supposed to follow the raid on Dresden, they were told: 'Your reasons for going there are to finish off any refugees who may have escaped from Dresden' (p. 155). Also Webster and Frankland, vol. 3, pp. 95–119.
98. Irving, p. 229.
99. Höhne, chapter 3.
100. Höhne, p. 315.
101. H. Krausnick and others, *Anatomy of the S.S. State*, p. 248.
102. Höhne, p. 409.
103. Milward, p. 160; Homze, p. 308.
104. Bramsted, p. 351; for Bormann see J. McGovern, *Martin Bormann*.
105. D. Petzina, 'Die Mobilisierung deutscher Arbeitskraefte vor und während des Zweiten Weltkrieges', *V.J.Z.G.*, vol. 18 (1970) pp. 454–5. But according to another estimate the number of women called up for warwork in 1943–4 was just over 900,000. R. Grunberger, *A Social History of the Third Reich* (London, 1971) p. 256.
106. Bramsted, p. 354.
107. C. Wilmot, *The Struggle for Europe*, p. 538.
108. G. F. Kennan, *Russia and the West under Lenin and Stalin*, p. 365.
109. Steinert, p. 4.

110. Speer, p. 440.
111. Gruchmann, p. 438.
112. That the American generals were far from indifferent to the political implications of who captured what is shown by Eisenhower's reply to Montgomery when, in August 1944, the latter had suggested switching the main thrust of the advance into Germany from Patton's army to his. 'The American public would not stand for it' was Eisenhower's comment.
113. Manvell and Frankel, pp. 162ff.
114. C. Ryan, *The Last Battle*, p. 256. Those inhabitants of Berlin who remained in the city were without gas, electricity and sanitation, and the only water supply came from the hydrants.
115. Ryan, p. 452.
116. H. Trevor-Roper, *The Last Days of Hitler*, pp. xxxiii and 238.

CHAPTER XI

1. The documents of surrender signed by the German commanders made no mention of the surrender as having been authorised by the Dönitz government.
2. The supremacy of the Allied Control Council was in fact limited from the start because each Zone Commander had supreme authority in his own zone as well as a share of joint authority in matters affecting Germany as a whole through the A.C.C. In practice it was the former which counted, since decisions of the A.C.C. had to be unanimous and this became increasingly difficult to achieve. Each zone accordingly tended to go its own way.
3. H. Feis, *Churchill, Roosevelt, Stalin*, p. 269.
4. W. S. Churchill, *The Second World War*, vol. 6, p. 581; see also E. Wiskemann, *Germany's Eastern Neighbours*, pp. 109ff.
5. W. Bedell Smith, *My Moscow Mission*, p. 215. 'Foreigners who travelled by train from Berlin to Moscow reported that every railroad yard and siding was jammed with German machinery, much of it deteriorating in the rain and snow.'
6. M. Balfour and J. Mair, *Four Power Control in Germany and Austria, 1945–6*, p. 127.
7. Wiskemann, pp. 80–1 and 108.
8. Balfour and Mair, p. 121. Stalin was exaggerating: some two million Germans were still east of the Oder–Neisse line, and even many of those who had fled did so with the intention of returning when the outlook was more settled.
9. The Displaced Persons were at first the responsibility of U.N.R.R.A., a special international organisation set up during the war by the United Nations to look after refugees.
10. J. P. Nettl, *The Eastern Zone and Soviet Policy in Germany*, pp. 100–1.
11. North Rhine and Westphalia were at first separate *Länder* in the British zone: their merger in 1946 was said to be dictated by the wish to create a situation which would make it harder for France to detach the Ruhr from the rest of Germany as she at first intended.
12. For Prussia see S. D. Stirk, *The Prussian Spirit* and E. J. Feuchtwanger, *Prussia: Myth and Reality*.

13. Though in political and religious terms the main historic difference in Germany was between a largely Prussian North and a non-Prussian South, socially and economically the greater contrast lay between the industrialised West and the agrarian East, especially East Prussia, where living standards were much lower. Despite Hitler's professed admiration for Prussia, he did more than any other ruler of Germany to destroy its rights and independence as a state by merging it, with the other federal states, in his tightly unified and centralised Reich.

14. For the American attitude to Potsdam and German unity, see J. Gimbel, *The American Occupation of Germany, 1945–49,* especially pp. 82 and 202–3. This book is also informative about the French attitude, which up to 1948 was often in conflict with American policy. It has been argued that western historians have made Soviet policy in Germany look much more consistent than it was in fact: according to one West German writer the Russians had no clearly conceived German policy between 1945 and 1949. This view seems hardly tenable in the light of the changes brought about in the Russian Zone during that period. See also T. Vogelsang, 'Die Bemühungen um eine deutsche Zentralverwaltung 1945/46', *V.J.Z.G.,* vol. 18 (1970) p. 510.

15. B. Montgomery, *Memoirs,* p. 415.

16. K. Adenauer, *Memoirs, 1945–53,* p. 62; A. Grosser, *The Federal Republic,* p. 81.

17. Adenauer, p. 62.

18. Balfour and Mair, p. 139; Nettl, p. 276.

19. Balfour and Mair, p. 114. One farmer was quoted as saying: 'At last I have all I want except a carpet for the pigsty and a necklace for the pig.'

20. W. H. Chamberlin, *The German Phoenix,* p. 40. Other accounts put the price of butter at 400 marks a pound.

21. For a different aspect of the occupation see p. 475 below.

22. G. Stolper, *German Realities,* pp. 135–6. Stephen Spender in his 'Rhineland Journal' compared the inhabitants of Cologne with 'parasites sucking at a dead carcase . . . a tribe of wanderers who have discovered a ruined city in a desert and are living in the cellars and hunting among the ruins for the booty of a dead civilisation'. *Horizon,* vol. 15 (1947) pp. 394ff.

23. Balfour and Mair, p. 173.

24. C. Fitzgibbon, *Denazification,* pp. 133–4.

25. Balfour and Mair, p. 174.

26. The extent to which former Nazis hold positions of authority in East Germany is discussed in D. Childs, *East Germany,* pp. 72ff.

27. Fitzgibbon, p. 105.

28. L. D. Clay, *Decision in Germany,* p. 259.

29. Balfour and Mair, p. 174.

30. Clay, p. 259.

31. W. Stahl (ed.), *The Politics of Postwar Germany,* pp. 241–2.

32. Balfour and Mair, p. 223.

33. K. Bölling, *Republic in Suspense,* p. 194.

34. A film about the concentration camps and other crimes against humanity of the Nazi regime was shown at the Nuremberg trials and afterwards to a wider public. A film on the tragedy of the Polish Jews called *Long is the Road* made quite an impression on German audiences, wrote a contemporary critic, who added that the cinema seemed to have more power to evoke remorse than any other medium. R. Manvell and H. Fraenkel, *The German Cinema,* p. 109.

35. W. Brandt, *My Road to Berlin*, p. 122.

36. A remarkable contemporary tribute was paid to the British Chief Education Officer in Lower Saxony, Brigadier C. G. Maude, when he left, in a letter to his wife from a German official in the Ministry of Education: 'There was somewhat of an adoration of your husband in Hanover . . . he was one of those soldiers who always thought of peace, and helped us to build up a new education, by which men shall live in friendship with each other.' The sentiments expressed were not untypical of relations between many occupation officers and their German opposite numbers. For Anglo-German relations under the occupation see R. Ebsworth, *Restoring Democracy in Germany*, especially p. 138. The Control Commission for Germany was the name of the organisation set up by the three western governments to be in charge of the occupation in their respective zones. Its branches and offices in Germany were usually known as Military Government.

37. E. Deuerlin, *Deutschland nach dem Zweiten Weltkrieg, 1945–55*, p. 106.

38. See James Joll's Introduction to the English edition of F. Fischer's *Griff nach der Weltmacht*, published in 1967 as *Germany's Aims in the First World War*.

39. M. Djilas, *Conversations with Stalin*, p. 73.

40. W. Schlauch, 'American Policy towards Germany in 1945', *J.C.H.*, vol. 5 (iv) (1970) p. 124.

41. Balfour and Mair, p. 142. The Hoover Report concluded that the German standard of living as laid down at Potsdam would be roughly equivalent to that of 1932, the worst year of the depression. J. Gimbel, *The American Occupation of Germany, 1945–49*, p. 20.

42. L. J. Edinger, *Kurt Schumacher*, pp. 201–2.

43. Balfour and Mair, p. 11.

44. Bölling, pp. 84–5.

45. Clay, pp. 156ff.

46. Nettl, p. 264.

47. Clay, p. 26.

48. Nettl, p. 37.

49. P. Windsor, *Berlin: City on Leave*, p. 106.

50. Clay, p. 367.

51. Clay, p. 374.

52. Windsor, p. 126. The 8,000 tons brought to Berlin in a single day by air in the spring of 1949 was as much as had been brought in by rail, road and canal before the blockade.

54. Clay, p. 388.

55. E. B. Wheaton, *Prelude to Calamity*, p. 249.

56. Nettl, p. 109.

57. Brandt, p. 209.

58. The Berlin Wall effectively cut off Allied personnel from East Berlin, which they had hitherto entered without showing papers. A proviso of the Berlin Agreement of 1971 was that no more West German presidential elections should be held in the city.

59. *Der Spiegel*, 3 January 1972.

60. A. Grosser, *La Démocratie de Bonn*, p. 23.

61. U. Kitzinger, *German Electoral Politics*, pp. 17ff.

62. Grosser, pp. 76ff. R. Ebsworth's book, *Restoring Democracy in Germany* is an important testimony by a former British official who was closely concerned with administration and government in its various aspects, including denazi-

fication. For denazification in the American Zone see also Gimbel, Chapter 11.

63. Edinger, *passim*.
64. Bölling, pp. 96–8.
65. Bölling, p. 260.
66. H. Lebovics, *Social Conservatism and the Middle Classes in Germany, 1914–33*, p. 106.
67. Adenauer, p. 363.

CHAPTER XII

1. K. Adenauer, *Memoirs, 1945–53*, p. 365.
2. P. Weymar, *Adenauer*, p. 328.
3. Conscription has since been reduced to 15 months.
4. *Der Spiegel*, 10 January 1972.
5. An example of Adenauer's malice was his reference during the 1961 election campaign to the illegitimate birth of his opponent Willy Brandt, in a speech made only a day after the building of the Berlin Wall.
6. G. A. Craig, *From Bismarck to Adenauer*, p. 104.
7. Craig, p. 98.
8. T. Vogelsang, *Das geteilte Deutschland*, p. 264.
9. R. B. Tilford, 'German Coalition Politics', *The Political Quarterly*, Vol. 39 (1968) p. 169.
10. Pankow is the suburb of East Berlin where the Communist leaders have their official residences, hence it is used to describe the D.D.R. government.
11. *The Economist*, 15 January 1972. As the East German standard of living gradually approaches that of the Federal Republic, it has been argued that if the latter were to give up its intellectual freedom it would lose its distinctive character and even its *raison d'être*. See E. Nolte, 'Zeitgeschichtsforschung und Zeitgeschichte', *V.J.Z.G.*, vol. 18 (1970) p. 11.
12. For an assessment of the N.P.D. and more generally neo-Nazi and extreme right-wing groups in the Federal Republic see K. D. Bracher, *Die deutsche Diktatur*, chapter 9. An English translation has now appeared as *The German Dictatorship* (London, 1971).
13. A. Grosser, *Deutschland-Bilanz*, p. 324. This has been published in English as *Germany in our Time* (London, 1971).
14. Nolte, 'Zeitgeschichtsforschung und Zeitgeschichte', *V.J.Z.G.*, vol. 18 (1970) p. 8.
15. H. Schreiber & F. Sommer, *Gustav Heinemann, Bundespräsident*. The phrase is taken from the Introduction by Günther Grass.
16. R. B. Tilford and R. J. C. Preece, *Federal Germany*, p. 93.
17. H. Walton, *Germany*, p. 84.
18. K. S. Pinson, *Modern Germany: its History and Civilisation*, p. 581.
19. S. B. Clough, *An Economic History of Europe: Twentieth Century*, p. 21.
20. Walton, p. 88.
21. In the victorious countries people looked to peace to bring them the rewards of their efforts and sacrifices, but in Germany as defeat became certain the opposite was true. A joke circulating towards the end of the war was: 'Enjoy yourself while you can, the peace will be terrible'. H. C. Wallich, *Mainsprings of the German Revival*, p. 340.
22. M. Balfour, *West Germany*, pp. 177 and 311.

23. Wallich, p. 151.
24. Industrial relations in Germany are not, for example, handicapped by grievances dating back to the 1930s or even to the days before the First World War, as is not infrequently the case in Great Britain.
25. R. Hiscocks, *Germany's Recovery*, p. 134.
26. Hiscocks, p. 133.
27. G. Stolper, *The German Economy, 1870 to the Present*, p. 290.
28. N. J. G. Pounds, *The Economic Pattern of Modern Germany*, p. 50.
29. Pounds, p. 53.
30. Stolper, p. 266.
31. Balfour, p. 317.
32. Stolper, p. 277.
33. S. Holt, *Six European States*, p. 172. Space was also rationed according to the size of the family, with rent so much the square metre. Wallich, pp. 172–3.
34. *The Times*, 30 June 1971.
35. P. Windsor, *German Reunification*, pp. 57ff.
36. Vogelsang, p. 133.
37. Vogelsang, p. 138.
38. Vogelsang, pp. 135ff; Balfour, p. 213; Hiscocks, p. 224; Craig, pp. 114–15; Windsor, pp. 65ff.
39. W. Osten, *Die Aussenpolitik der D.D.R.*, p. 6.
40. Vogelsang, p. 213.
41. Windsor, p. 109.
42. W. F. Hanrieder, *West German Foreign Policy, 1949–63*, p. 197. The suggestion came from Walter Lippman, the American columnist.
43. American support for the M.N.F. was in fact designed not to satisfy but to forestall West Germany's alleged desire to become a nuclear power: it was a stratagem to prevent a possible nuclear pact between Paris and Bonn. W. F. Hanrieder, *The Stable Crisis*, pp. 18–22. It has been suggested that the Americans tacitly or explicitly 'compensated' the Russians for their relative restraint in Vietnam with an assurance that West Germany would not be allowed access to joint nuclear control. *Ibid.*, p. 26.
44. Hanrieder, *West German Foreign Policy*, p. 195.
45. H. Kroll, *Lebenserinnerungen eines Botschafters*, pp. 442ff.
46. G. Leptin, *Die deutsche Wirtschaft seit 1945*, p. 57. The trade figure was for the year 1968.
47. A. W. Dulles, *Germany's Underground*, p. 171.
48. W. Leonhardt, *Die Revolution entlässt ihre Kinder*, p. 317.
49. Leonhardt, p. 223.
50. J. P. Nettl, *The Eastern Zone and Soviet Policy in Germany*, p. 207.
51. Osten, p. 13.
52. Stolper, p. 305.
53. Vogelsang, p. 200.
54. Yet the congress also declared its aim to be to unite the whole German people under the banner of democratic and peace-loving Germany (itself). S. Dörnberg, *Kurze Geschichte der D.D.R.*, pp. 179ff; D. Childs, *East Germany*, especially chapter 1.
55. C. Stern, *Ulbricht*, pp. 168ff.
56. Osten, pp. 14–15.
57. E. Deuerlein, *Deutschland nach dem Zweiten Weltkrieg, 1945–55*, p. 230.
58. Childs, p. 34.
59. In a poem called 'The Solution'. M. Esslin, *Brecht: A Choice of Evils*,

p. 165.

60. Stern, pp. 230–1.

61. Stolper, pp. 310–11.

62. Dörnberg, p. 677.

63. Weber und Oldenburg, 25 *Jahre D.D.R.*, p. 34.

64. Childs, p. 47.

65. Stolper, p. 304. Owing to the decline in population the pressure on accommodation was not as heavy as in the Federal Republic.

66. Childs, pp. 96ff.

67. P. Windsor, *Germany and the Management of Détente*, p. 120. But on p. 151 it is suggested that the process of pluralisation is actually going on inside East Germany.

68. The play was 'The Trial of Lucullus', renamed 'The Sentencing of Lucullus'.

69. A small but not insignificant detail is that in a standard popular history of the D.D.R. containing a map showing arrows pointing to places abroad, only one place in West Germany is mentioned and nearly all the names included are those in Communist or Communist-orientated countries. Thus Peking is mentioned but not Tokyo, Hanoi but not Bombay, Tirana but not Athens, Pyöngyang but not Singapore. Dörnberg, p. 368.

70. Windsor, *Détente*, pp. 177ff.

71. For Willy Brandt see W. Brandt, *A Peace Policy for Europe* and K. Harpprecht, *Willy Brandt: Porträt und Selbstporträt.*

72. Schreiber and Sommer, p. 116.

73. Windsor, *Détente*, p. 79.

74. *The Economist*, 15 January 1972.

75. A recent East German film on Karl Liebknecht is at pains to show that for a Communist the S.P.D. under Brandt is no whit more worthy of co-operation or trust than the S.P.D. in 1919 under Ebert. *Der Spiegel*, 7 February 1972.

76. *The Economist*, 28 August 1971.

77. Brandt, p. 11.

78. Brandt, p. 29.

79. H. Fischer, 'German Writers of Today', *Horizon*, vol. 15 (1957) p. 3.

80. For example in his critical study, *Wohin treibt die Bundesrepublik?* (1966), in which Jaspers explains his fears for the future of German democracy.

81. One of the by-products of West Germany's post-war exposure to foreign cultural influences is a cult of English words and expressions, which are often used where their German equivalent appears quite adequate: anyone who reads one of the mass circulation magazines in the Federal Republic must have been struck by this phenomenon, which is no doubt an over-reaction against the linguistic nationalism of the Third Reich.

82. R. Manvell and H. Fraenkel, *The German Cinema*, p. 114.

83. P. Gay, *Weimar Culture*, p. 1.

84. Manvell and Fraenkel, p. 116.

85. W. H. Dawson, *The Evolution of Modern Germany*, p. 161. Dawson's own comment at the time was: 'The nation of which this may be said is sure of a future.'

Bibliography

The following list, which is not comprehensive, is intended simply as a guide to readers who may wish to go more deeply into the subject or an aspect of it. A useful general bibliography of German history during the period covered by this book can be found in: K. S. Pinson, *Modern Germany: its History and Civilisation.* There are specialised bibliographies in A. J. Nicholls, *Weimar and the Rise of Hitler* (for 1918–33); K. D. Bracher, *The German Dictatorship* (for 1933–45); A. Grosser, *Germany in our Time* (for the period since 1945).

Of documents, standard sources for pre-1914 foreign policy are: *Die grosse Politik der europäischen Kabinette, 1871–1914*, edited by J. Lepsius, A. Mendelssohn-Bartholdy and F. Thimme, Berlin, 1922–7; *British Documents on the Origins of the War, 1898–1914*, edited by G. P. Gooch and H. Temperley (London, 1926–38); and *Documents diplomatiques français, 1871–1914* (Paris, 1929–62). For the inter-war and second war years there are the *Documents on German Foreign Policy, 1918–45* (Series C and D), edited by American, British and French scholars (London, 1949 onwards), and *Documents on British Foreign Policy, 1919–39* (Series 1, 1a, 2 and 3) edited successively by E. L. Woodward, R. Butler, J. P. T. Bury, W. N. Medlicott, M. E. Lambert and D. Deakin (London, 1946 onwards), also *Soviet Documents on Foreign Policy, 1917–41*, edited by J. Degras, 3 vols (Oxford, 1951–3).

The collections of documents edited by R. A. Lutz, *The Fall of the German Empire, 1914–18*, 2 vols (Stanford, 1932) and *The Causes of the German Collapse in 1918* (Hoover War Library, Stanford, 1934) are informative for the First World War and the German Revolution; the latter volume is a much abridged summary in translation of the *Report of the Reichstag Committee of Inquiry into the German Collapse* (Die Ursachen des deutschen Zusammenbruches im Jahre 1918) 12 vols (Berlin, 1925–9). For the decade after the Second World War, Beate Ruhm von Oppen (ed.), *Documents on Germany under Occupation, 1945–54* (Oxford, 1955) is a work of reference.

General Books on Germany since 1890

G. A. Craig, *From Bismarck to Adenauer* rev. ed. (New York, 1965).

G. A. Craig, *The Politics of the Prussian Army, 1640–1945* (Oxford, 1955).

L. Dehio, *Germany and World Politics in the Twentieth Century* (London, 1959).

F. Ernst, *The Germans and their Modern History* (Columbia U.P., 1966).

H. Kohn (ed.), *German History – some new German Views* (London, 1954).

K. S. Pinson, *Modern Germany: Its History and Civilisation*, new edn (London, 1966).

J. C. G. Röhl (ed.), *From Bismarck to Hitler* (London, 1971).

G. Stolper, *The German Economy, 1870 to the Present* (rev. and expd. edn) (London, 1967).

Purnell's *History of the Twentieth Century* (8 vols), edited by A. J. P. Taylor and J. M. Roberts, contains many scholarly articles that serve as an introduction to German history in this period.

For those who read German the following volumes published by the Deutscher Taschenbuch Verlag are useful: H. Herzfeld, *Der erste Weltkrieg*; H. Heiber, *Die Republik von Weimar*; M. Broszat, *Der Staat Hitlers*; L. Gruchmann, *Der Zweite Weltkrieg*; T. Vogelsang, *Das geteilte Deutschland*. Each of these books has its own bibliography. A more general survey is J. Bühler, *Vom Bismarckreich zum geteilten Deutschland* (Berlin, 1960).

Wilhelmine Germany and its Background, 1890–1914

IN ENGLISH:

A. Albertini, *The Origins of the War of 1914*, 3 vols (London, 1952–1957).

P. R. Anderson, *The Background of Anti-English Feeling in Germany, 1890–1902* (Washington, D.C., 1939).

C. Andrew, *Théophile Delcassé and the Making of the Entente Cordiale* (London, 1968).

H. Becker, *German Youth, Bond or Free* (London, 1946).

E. Bernstein, *Evolutionary Socialism* (New York, 1961).

E. Brandenburg, *From Bismarck to the World War, 1890–1914* (London, 1927).

W. F. Bruck, *Economic and Social History of Germany, 1888–1938* (Cardiff, 1938).

B. von Bülow, *Imperial Germany* (London, 1914).

B. von Bülow, *Memoirs*, 4 vols (London, 1931–2).

E. M. Carroll, *Germany and the Great Powers, 1866–1914* (New York, 1938).

L. J. C. Cecil, *Albert Ballin: Business and Politics in Imperial Germany, 1888–1918* (Princeton, 1967).

V. Cowles, *The Kaiser* (New York, 1963).

R. Dahrendorf, *Society and Democracy in Germany* (London, 1968).

W. H. Dawson, *The Evolution of Modern Germany* (London, 1908).

W. H. Dawson, *The German Empire*, 2 vols (London, 1967) (reprinted).

K. Demeter, *The German Officer-Corps, 1650–1945* (London, 1965).

E. Eyck, *Bismarck and the German Empire* (London, 1950).

P. Frölich, *Rosa Luxemburg* (London, 1940).

P. Gay, *The Dilemma of Evolutionary Socialism: Eduard Bernstein's Challenge to Marx* (Columbia, 1952).

W. Görlitz, *The German General Staff* (London, 1953).

History of the Times, vol. 3, 1884–1912 (London, 1947).

Chlodwig Prince zu Hohenlohe-Schillingsfürst, *Memoirs*, 2 vols (London, 1906).

J. Joll, *The Second International* (London, 1955).

H. Graf Kessler, *Walther Rathenau: His Life and Work* (London, 1929).

H. Kohn, *The Mind of Germany* (London, 1961).

W. L. Langer, *The Diplomacy of Imperialism*, 2nd ed. (London, 1950).

W. Z. Laqueur, *Young Germany* (London, 1962).

G. Masur, *Imperial Berlin* (London, 1971).

J. P. Mayer, *Max Weber and German Politics*, 2nd ed. (London, 1956).

F. Meinecke, *Cosmopolitanism and the National State* (Princeton U.P., 1970).

J. P. Nettl, *Rosa Luxemburg*, 2 vols (Oxford, 1967).

J. A. Nichols, *Germany after Bismarck: the Caprivi Era* (Cambridge, Mass., 1958).

H. Nicolson, *Sir Arthur Nicolson, Bart., First Lord Carnock* (London, 1930).

N. Rich, *Friedrich von Holstein*, 2 vols (Cambridge, 1965).

Gerhard Ritter, *The Schlieffen Plan* (London, 1958).

J. C. G. Röhl, *Germany without Bismarck* (London, 1967).

C. E. Schorske, *German Social Democracy, 1905–17* (Harvard U.P., 1955).

J. Steinberg, *Yesterday's Deterrent* (London, 1965).

A. J. P. Taylor, *The Struggle for Mastery in Europe, 1848–1918* (Oxford, 1954).

A. von Tirpitz, *My Memoirs*, 2 vols (London, 1919).

L. C. F. Turner, *The Origins of the First World War* (London, 1970).

M. Wertheimer, *The Pan-German League, 1890–1914* (New York, 1924).

E. L. Woodward, *Great Britain and the German Navy* (London, 1964) (reprinted).

H. F. Young, *Maximilian Harden, Censor Germaniae* (The Hague, 1959).

IN GERMAN:

H. Booms, *Die Deutsche Konservative Partei* (Düsseldorf, 1954).

K. E. Born, *Staat und Sozialpolitik seit Bismarcks Sturz* (Wiesbaden, 1959).

E. Eyck, *Das persönliche Regiment Wilhelms II* (Zürich, 1948).

E. Federn-Kohlhaas, *Walther Rathenau, sein Leben und Wirken* (Dresden, 1928).

O. Hamann, *Bilder aus der letzten Kaiserzeit* (Berlin, 1922).

H. Heidegger, *Die deutsche Sozialdemokratie und der Nationale Staat, 1870–1920* (Göttingen, 1956).

T. Heuss, *Friedrich Neumann: der Mann, das Werk, die Zeit* (Stuttgart, 1937).

W. Hubatsch, *Die Ära Tirpitz* (Göttingen, 1955).

A. Huldermann, *Albert Ballin* (Oldenburg, 1922).

A. Kruck, *Der Alldeutsche Verband, 1890–1939* (Wiesbaden, 1954).

G. Kotowski, *Friedrich Ebert, eine politische Biographie*, vol. 1 (Wiesbaden, 1963).

T. Nipperdey, *Die Organisation der politischen Parteien vor 1918* (Düsseldorf, 1961).

G. Kotowski, W. Pöls and G. Ritter, *Das Wilhelminische Deutschland* (Frankfurt, 1965).

G. A. Ritter, *Die Arbeiterbewegung im Wilhelminischen Reich* (Berlin, 1959).

G. Ritter, *Staatskunst und Kriegshandwerk*, vol. 2 (Munich, 1965).

E. Schiffer, *Ein Leben für den Liberalismus* (Berlin, 1951).

H. J. Schoeps (ed.), *Zeitgeist im Wandel*, vol. 1, *Das Wilhelminische Zeitalter* (Stuttgart, 1967).

A. Thimme, *Hans Delbrück als Kritiker der Wilhelminischen Epoche* (Düsseldorf, 1955).

J. Ziekursch, *Politische Geschichte des neuen deutschen Kaiserreiches* 3 vols (Frankfurt, 1925).

H. G. Zmarzlik, *Bethmann Hollweg als Reichskanzler, 1909–14* (Düsseldorf, 1957).

THE FIRST WORLD WAR

IN ENGLISH:

C. Barnett, *The Swordbearers* (London, 1963).

M. Baumont, *The Fall of the Kaiser* (London, 1931).

A. J. Berlau, *German Social Democracy, 1914–21* (Columbia U.P., 1949).

E. Bevan, *German Social Democracy during the War* (London, 1918).

K. Epstein, *Matthias Erzberger and the Dilemma of German Democracy* (Princeton U.P., 1959).

M. Fainsod, *International Socialism and the World War* (Harvard U.P., 1935).

E. von Falkenhayn, *General Headquarters, 1914–16, and its crucial Decisions* (London, 1919).

G. Feldman, *Army, Industry and Labor in Germany, 1914–18* (London, 1967).

F. Fischer, *Germany's Aims in the First World War* (London, 1967).

P. Frölich, *Rosa Luxemburg* (London, 1940).

H. W. Gatzke, *Germany's Drive to the West* (Baltimore, 1950).

W. Görlitz (ed.), *The Kaiser and his Court* (the War Diary of Admiral von Müller) (London, 1961).

D. J. Goodspeed, *Ludendorff* (London, 1966).

M. Hoffmann, *The War of Lost Opportunities* (War Diary), 2 vols (London, 1927).

A. Horne, *The Price of Glory: Verdun, 1916* (London, 1964).

E. Ludendorff, *My War Memories of 1914–18*, 2 vols (London, 1920).

Prince Max of Baden, *Memoirs*, 2 vols (London, 1928).

A. J. Mayer, *Politics and Diplomacy of Peace-making, 1917–18* (London, 1968).

H. C. Meyer, *Mitteleuropa in German Thought and Action, 1815–1945* (The Hague, 1955).

A. Mendelssohn-Bartholdy, *The War and German Society* (Yale U.P., 1937).

A. Rosenberg, *The Birth of the German Republic* (London, 1931).

R. Scheer, *Germany's High Sea Fleet in the World War* (London, 1920).

P. Scheidemann, *Memoirs of a Social Democrat*, 2 vols (London, 1930).

C. Tschuppik, *Ludendorff* (London, 1932).

B. Tuchman, *August 1914* (London, 1962).

J. Wheeler-Bennett, *Brest-Litovsk: the forgotten Peace* (London, 1938).

Z. A. B. Zeman, *The Break-up of the Habsburg Empire, 1917–18* (London, 1961).

IN GERMAN:

T. von Bethmann Hollweg, *Betrachtungen zum Weltkrieg*, 2 vols (Berlin, 1919–21).

W. Conze, E. Matthias and R. Morsey (ed.), *Der Interfraktionelle Ausschuss, 1917–18* (Düsseldorf, 1959).

F. Ebert, *Schriften, Aufzeichunugen, Reden*, 2 vols (Dresden, 1926).

M. Erzberger, *Erlebnisse im Weltkrieg* (Stuttgart, 1920).

F. Fischer, *Griff nach der Weltmacht*, 3rd ed. (Düsseldorf, 1964).

W. Groener, *Lebenserinnerungen* (Göttingen, 1957).

D. Groener-Geyer, *General Groener – Soldat und Staatsmann* (Frankfurt, 1955).

M. Haussmann, *Schlaglichter* (Frankfurt, 1924).

W. Hubatsch, *Deutschland im Weltkrieg 1914–18* (Frankfurt, 1966).

F. H. Janssen, *Der Kanzler und der General: die Führungskrise um Bethmann Hollweg und Falkenhayn, 1914–16* (Göttingen, 1967).

R. von Kühlmann, *Erinnerungen* (Heidelberg, 1948).

T. Mann, *Betrachtungen eines Unpolitischen* (Frankfurt, 1919).

G. Ritter, *Staatskunst und Kriegshandwerk*, vols III & IV (Munich, 1964 and 1967). An English translation of this work has been published as *Sword and Scepter: The Problem of Militarism in Germany*, 2 vols (University of Miami Press, 1969).

H. J. Varain, *Freie Gewerkschaften, Sozial-Demokratie und Staat* (Düsseldorf, 1956).

THE PEACE SETTLEMENT, THE GERMAN REVOLUTION AND THE WEIMAR REPUBLIC

IN ENGLISH:

J. W. Angell, *The Recovery of Germany* (Yale U.P., 1929).

W. T. Angress, *Stillborn Revolution* (Princeton U.P., 1963).

E. W. Bennett, *Germany and the Diplomacy of the Financial Crisis, 1931* (Cambridge, Mass., 1962).

M. J. Bonn, *Wandering Scholar* (London, 1949).

E. H. Carr, *German-Soviet Relations between the two World Wars*, (Baltimore, 1951).

F. L. Carsten, *The Reichswehr and Politics, 1918 to 1933* (Oxford, 1966).

R. Coper, *Failure of a Revolution* (Cambridge, 1955).

G. A. Craig and F. Gilbert (eds.), *The Diplomats, 1919–1939* (Princeton U.P., 1953).

Lord d'Abernon, *An Ambassador of Peace*, 3 vols (London, 1929–30).

I. Deak, *Weimar Germany's Leftwing Intellectuals* (Univ. of California Press, 1968).

A. Dorpalen, *Hindenburg and the Weimar Republic* (Princeton U.P., 1964).

H. L. Dyck, *Weimar Germany and Soviet Russia, 1926–1933* (London, 1966).

E. Eyck, *A History of the Weimar Republic*, 2 vols (Oxford, 1962 and 1964).

Ruth Fischer, *Stalin and German Communism* (Cambridge, Mass., 1948).

G. Freund, *Unholy Alliance* (London, 1957).

H. W. Gatzke, *Stresemann and the Rearmament of Germany* (Baltimore, 1954).

P. Gay, *Weimar Culture* (London, 1969).

A. Grzesinski, *Inside Germany* (New York, 1939).

S. W. Halperin, *Germany tried Democracy* (New York, 1946).

L. Hertzman, *DNVP: Right-wing Opposition in the Weimar Republic* (Nebraska U.P., 1963).

G. Hilger and A. G. Meyer, *The Incompatible Allies* (New York, 1953).

R. N. Hunt, *German Social Democracy, 1918–33* (Yale U.P., 1953).

W. M. Jordan, *Great Britain, France and the German Problem, 1918–1939* (London, 1943).

J. M. Keynes, *The Economic Consequences of the Peace Treaty* (London, 1919).

K. von Klemperer, *Germany's New Conservatism* (Princeton U.P., 1957).

L. Kochan, *The Struggle for Germany, 1914–45* (Edinburgh U.P., 1963).

J. Kuczynski, *A Short History of Labour Conditions under Industrial Capitalism*, vol. III, *Germany – 1880 to the Present Day* (London, 1945).

H. Lebovics, *Social Conservatism and the Middle-Classes in Germany, 1914–1933* (Princeton U.P., 1969).

I. J. Lederer (ed.), *The Versailles Settlement* (Boston, Mass., 1960).

B. I. Lewis, *George Grosz: Art and Politics in the Weimar Republic* (Wisconsin U.P., 1971).

R. Manvell and H. Fraenkel, *The German Cinema* (London, 1971).

A. Mitchell, *Revolution in Bavaria* (Princeton U.P., 1965).

J. H. Morgan, *Assize of Arms* (London, 1945).

A. J. Nicholls and E. Matthias (ed.), *German Democracy and the Triumph of Hitler* (London, 1971).

H. Nicolson, *Peacemaking, 1919* (London, 1943).

F. K. Ringer (ed.), *The German Inflation of 1923* (Oxford, 1969).

A. Rosenberg, *Imperial Gèrmany: The Birth of the German Republic, 1871–1918* (Oxford, 1970) (reprinted).

A. Rosenberg, *The History of the Weimar Republic* (London, 1936).

H. Rudin, *Armistice, 1918* (Yale U.P., 1944).

A. J. Ryder, *The German Revolution of 1918* (Cambridge, 1967).

H. Stroebel, *The German Revolution and After* (London, 1923).

H. A. Turner, *Stresemann and the Politics of the Weimar Republic* (Princeton U.P., 1963).

R. G. L. Waite, *Vanguard of Nazism: The Free Corps Movement in Postwar Germany, 1918–1923* (Cambridge, Mass., 1952).

R. Watt, *The Kings Depart* (London, 1969).

T. Wolff, *Through Two Decades* (London, 1936).

J. W. Wheeler-Bennett, *The Nemesis of Power* (London, 1954).

J. W. Wheeler-Bennett, *Hindenburg, the Wooden Titan* (London, 1936).

IN GERMAN:

E. Barth, *Aus der Werkstaat der deutschen Revolution* (Berlin, n.d.).

E. Bernstein, *Die deutsche Revolution* (Berlin, 1921).

W. Besson, *Friedrich Ebert* (Göttingen, 1963).

K. Bracher, *Die Auflösung der Weimarer Republik*, 2nd ed. (Stuttgart, 1957).

H. Brüning, *Reden und Aufsaetze* (Münster, 1968).

H. Brüning, *Memoiren, 1918–1934* (Stuttgart, 1970).

O. Braun, *Von Weimar zu Hitler* (New York, 1940).

H. K. Buchheim, *Die Weimarer Republik* (Munich, 1960).

T. Dorst and H. Neubauer (ed.), *Die Münchener Räte-Republik* (Frankfurt, 1966).

O. K. Flechtheim, *Die K.P.D. in der Weimarer Republik* (Offenbach, 1948).

W. J. Helbich, *Die Reparationen in der Ära Brüning, 1930–32* (Berlin, 1962).

T. Heuss, *Erinnerungen, 1905–33* (Tübingen, 1963).

W. Hoegner, *Die Verratene Republik* (Munich, 1958).

G. Jasper (ed.), *Von Weimar zu Hitler, 1930–33* (Cologne, 1968).

H. Graf Kessler, *Tagebücher, 1918–1937* (Frankfurt, 1961).

E. Kolb, *Die Arbeiterräte in der deutschen Innenpolitik, 1918–19* (Düsseldorf, 1962).

G. Ledebour (ed.), *Der Ledebour-Prozess* (Berlin, 1969).

H. Meier-Welcker, *Seeckt* (Frankfurt, 1967).

E. Matthias and R. Morsey (ed.), *Das Ende der Parteien, 1933* (Düsseldorf, 1960).

H. Müller, *Die November-Revolution* (Berlin, 1928).

R. Müller, *Vom Kaiserreich zur Republik*, 2 vols (Vienna, 1925).

R. Müller, *Der Bürgerkrieg in Deutschland* (Berlin, 1925).

E. Niekisch, *Gewagtes Leben* (Cologne, 1958).

S. Neumann, *Die Parteien der Weimarer Republik* (Stuttgart, 1965).

G. Noske, *Von Kiel bis Kapp* (Berlin, 1920).

U. Ratz, *Georg Ledebour* (Berlin, 1969).

O. E. Schüddekopf (ed.), *Das Heer und die Republik: Quellen zur Politik der Reichswehrführung 1918 bis 1933* (Hanover and Frankfurt, 1955).

O. E. Schüddekopf, *Linke Leute von Rechts* (Stuttgart, 1960).

O. E. Schüddekopf, *Die deutsche Innenpolitik und der Konservative Gedanke im letzten Jahrhundert* (Brunswick, 1951).

A. Schwarz, *Die Weimarer Republik* (Konstanz, 1958).

C. Severing, *Mein Lebensweg*, 2 vols (Cologne, 1950).

F. Stampfer, *Die vierzehn Jahre der ersten deutschen Republik* (Karlsbad, 1936).

A. Thimme, *Gustav Stresemann* (Hanover, 1957).

W. Tormin, *Zwischen Rätediktatur und sozialer Demokratie* (Düsseldorf, 1954).

T. Vogelsang, *Reichswehr, Staat und N.S.D.A.P.* (Stuttgart, 1962).

O. E. Volkmann, *Revolution über Deutschland* (Oldenburg, 1930).

NATIONAL SOCIALISM AND THE SECOND WORLD WAR

IN ENGLISH:

N. H. Baynes (ed.), *The Speeches of Adolf Hitler*, 2 vols (London, 1942).

E. Bethge, *Dietrich Bonhoeffer* (London, 1970).

K. Bracher, *The German Dictatorship* (London, 1971).

E. K. Bramsted, *Goebbels and National Socialist Propaganda, 1925–1945* (London, 1965).

A. Bryant, *The Turn of the Tide, 1939–43* (London, 1957).

H. Buchheim, *The Third Reich: its Beginnings, its Developments, its End* (Munich, 1961).

A. Bullock, *Hitler* (rev. ed.) (London, 1964).

E. M. Carroll, *Design for Total War* (The Hague, 1968).

G. Ciano (ed. M. Muggeridge), *Diary, 1939–43* (London, 1946).

A. Clark, *Barbarossa* (London, 1965).

J. V. Compton, *The Swastika and the Eagle* (London, 1968).

J. S. Conway, *The Nazi Persecution of the Churches* (London, 1968).

A. Dallin, *German Rule in Russia, 1941–45* (London, 1957).

H. Deutsch, *The Conspiracy against Hitler in the Twilight War* (Minnesota U.P., 1968).

W. Dibelius, *In the service of the Lord* (London, 1965).

M. Dodd, *My Years in Germany* (London, 1939).

K. Dönitz, *Memoirs* (London, 1959).

A. W. Dulles, *Germany's Underground* (New York, 1947).

L. J. Edinger, *German Exile Politics* (Univ. of California Press, 1956).

D. D. Eisenhower, *Crusade in Europe* (London, 1948).

Th. Eschenburg and Others, *The Road to Dictatorship* (London, 1964).

H. Feis, *Churchill, Roosevelt, Stalin* (Princeton U.P., 1957).

J. Fest, *The Face of the Third Reich* (London, 1970).

A. François-Poncet, *The Fateful Years* (London, 1948).

S. Friedländer, *Pius XII and the Third Reich* (London, 1966).

H. B. Gisevius, *To the Bitter End* (London, 1947).

H. Graml, H. Mommsen, H. J. Reichardt and E. Wolf, *The German Resistance to Hitler* (London, 1970).

C. W. Guillebaud, *The Economic Recovery of Germany, 1933–38* (London, 1939).

C. W. Guillebaud, *The Social Policy of Nazi Germany* (Cambridge U.P., 1942).

U. von Hassell, *Diaries, 1938–44* (London, 1947).

N. Henderson, *Failure of a Mission* (London, 1940).

K. Heiden, *Hitler* (London, 1936).

F. H. Hinsley, *Hitler's Strategy* (Cambridge, 1951).

A. Hitler, *Mein Kampf* (tr. R. Manheim) (London, 1969).

H. Höhne, *The Order of the Death's Head* (London, 1969).

W. Hofer, *War premeditated* (London, 1955).

E. L. Homze, *Foreign Labour in Nazi Germany* (Princeton U.P., 1967).

D. Irving, *The Destruction of Dresden* (London, 1963).

W. Keitel, *Memoirs* (London, 1965).

B. H. Klein, *Germany's Economic Preparations for War* (Cambridge, Mass., 1959).

E. Kogon, *The Theory and Practice of Hell* (London, 1950).

J. Kramarz, *Stauffenberg* (London, 1970).

H. Krausnick, H. Buchheim, M. Broszat and H. A. Jacobsen, *Anatomy of the S.S. State* (London, 1968).

G. Lewy, *The Catholic Church and Nazi Germany* (London, 1964).

B. H. Liddell Hart, *The Other Side of the Hill* (London, 1948).

B. H. Liddell Hart, *The Second World War* (London, 1970).

E. von Manstein, *Lost Victories* (London, 1958).

R. Manvell and H. Fraenkel, *Dr. Goebbels* (London, 1960).

R. Manvell and H. Fraenkel, *Hermann Göring* (London, 1962).

R. Manvell and H. Fraenkel, *Himmler* (London, 1965).

W. Maser, *Hitler's Mein Kampf: An Analysis* (London, 1970).

W. N. Medlicott, *Britain and Germany: the Search for Agreement, 1930–37* (London, 1968).

F. Meinecke, *The German Catastrophe* (London, 1950).

A. Milward, *The German Economy at War* (London, 1965).

G. L. Mosse, *Nazi Culture* (London, 1966).

F. Neumann, *Behemoth* (London, 1944).

E. Nolte, *Three Faces of Fascism* (London, 1966).

R. J. O'Neill, *The German Army and the Nazi Party, 1933–39* (London, 1966).

D. Orlow, *The History of the Nazi Party*, vol. i, *1919–33* (Univ. of Pittsburgh Press, 1969).

F. von Papen, *Memoirs* (London, 1952).

R. J. Pritchard, *Reichstag Fire: Ashes of Democracy* (New York, 1972).

T. Prittie, *Germans against Hitler* (London, 1964).

H. Rauschning, *Germany's Revolution of Destruction* (London, 1939).

G. Reitlinger, *The Final Solution* (rev. ed., London, 1961).

G. Reitlinger, *The House built on Sand* (London, 1960).

G. Reitlinger, *The S.S., Alibi of a Nation, 1922–45* (London, 1956).

G. Ritter, *The German Resistance* (London, 1958).

K. Robbins, *Munich, 1938* (London, 1968).

E. M. Robertson, *Hitler's Pre-War Policy* (London, 1963).

E. M. Robertson (ed.), *The Origins of the Second World War* (London, 1971).

S. W. Roskill, *The War at Sea, 1939–45* (London, 1954).

H. Rothfels, *The German Opposition to Hitler* (London, 1961).

A. L. Rowse, *All Souls and Appeasement* (London, 1961).

H. Schacht, *Account Settled* (London, 1949).

H. Schacht, *My first Seventy Six Years* (London, 1955).

F. von Schlabrendorff, *The Secret War against Hitler* (London, 1966).

P. Schmidt, *Hitler's Interpreter* (London, 1951).

D. Schoenbaum, *Hitler's Social Revolution* (London, 1966).

A. Seaton, *The Russo-German War, 1941–45* (London, 1971).

W. M. Shirer, *The Rise and Fall of the Third Reich* (London, 1960).

J. L. Snell (ed.), *The Nazi Revolution, Germany's Guilt or Germany's Fate?* (Boston, Mass., 1959).

K. Sontheimer (ed.), *The Road to Dictatorship* (London, 1964).

W. Speer, *Inside the Third Reich* (London, 1969).

M. Steinert, *Capitulation, 1945* (London, 1969).

C. Sykes, *Troubled Loyalty* (London, 1969).

A. J. P. Taylor, *The Origins of the Second World War* (London, 1963).

F. Tobias, *The Reichstag Fire* (London, 1964).

A. and V. Toynbee (eds.), *Hitler's Europe* (London, 1954).

H. Trevor-Roper (ed.), *Hitler's War Directives, 1939–45* (London, 1966).

H. Trevor-Roper (ed.), *Hitler's Table Talk* (London, 1953).

R. G. L. Waite (ed.), *Hitler and Nazi Germany* (London, 1969).

W. Warlimont, *Inside Hitler's Headquarters, 1939–45* (London, 1964).

G. L. Weinberg, *Germany and the Soviet Union, 1939–41* (Leiden, 1964).

E. B. Wheaton, *Prelude to Calamity* (London, 1969).

J. Wheeler-Bennett, *The Nemesis of Power* (London, 1953).

C. Wighton, *Heydrich* (London, 1962).

C. Wilmot, *The Struggle for Europe* (London, 1952).

E. Wiskemann, *The Rome-Berlin Axis* (London, 1949).

E. Zeller, *The Flame of Freedom* (London, 1967).

Z. A. B. Zeman, *Nazi Propaganda* (London, 1964).

Various Authors, *The Third Reich* (A study published under the auspices of the International Council for Philosophy and Humanistic Studies with the assistance of UNESCO) (New York, 1955).

IN GERMAN:

H. Bennecke, *Hitler und die S.A.* (Munich, 1962).

K. D. Bracher, W. Sauer and G. Schulz, *Die Nationalsozialistische Machtergreifung* (Cologne, 1960).

R. Diels, *Lucifer ante portas* (Zürich, 1949).

A. Flitner, *Deutsches Geistesleben und Nationalsozialismus* (Tübingen, 1965).

P. J. Goebbels, *Vom Kaiserhof zur Reichskanzlei* (Berlin, 1934).

H. Heiber, *Joseph Goebbels* (Berlin, 1962).

A. Hillgruber, *Hitler's Strategie* (Frankfurt, 1965).

A. Hillgruber, *Deutschlands Rolle in der Vorgeschichte der beiden Weltkriege* (Göttingen, 1967).

W. Hofer, *Die Diktatur Hitlers bis zum beginn des Zweiten Weltkrieges* (Constance, 1960).

W. Hofer (ed.), *Der Nationalsozialismus: Dokumente, 1933–45* (Frankfurt, 1957).

A. Kubizek, *Adolf Hitler, mein Jugendfreund* (Graz, 1953).

H. A. Jacobsen (ed.), *Der Zweite Weltkrieg in Chronik und Dokumenten* (Weisbaden, 1961).

P. Kleist, *Zwischen Hitler und Stalin* (Bonn, 1950).

G. Meinck, *Hitler und die Deutsche Aufrüstung, 1933–37* (Wiesbaden, 1957).

H. O. Meissner and H. Wilde, *Die Machtergreifung* (Stuttgart, 1958).

J. von Ribbentrop, *Zwischen London und Moskau: Erinnerungen und letzte Aufzeichnungen* (Leoni, 1953).

P. A. Rave, *Kunstdiktatur im Dritten Reich* (Hamburg, 1949).

H. Rumpf, *Das war der Bombenkrieg* (Oldenburg, 1961).

K. Schwend, *Bayern zwischen Monarchie und Diktatur* (Munich, 1954).

L. Graf Schwerin von Krosigk, *Es geschah in Deutschland* (Tübingen, 1951).

T. Vogelsang, *Reichswehr, Staat und N.S.D.A.P.* (Stuttgart, 1962).

E. von Weizsäcker, *Erinnerungen* (Munich, 1952).

S. Westphal, *Heer in Fesseln* (Bonn, 1950).

J. Wulf (ed.), *Theater und Film im Dritten Reich* (Hamburg, 1966).

F. Zipfel, *Kirchenkampf in Deutschland, 1933–1945* (Berlin, 1965).

GERMANY SINCE 1945

IN ENGLISH:

K. Adenauer, *Memoirs, 1949–53* (London, 1966).

M. Balfour and J. Mair, *Four-Power Control in Germany and Austria, 1945-6* (London, 1956).

M. Balfour, *West Germany* (London, 1968).

K. Bölling, *Republic in Suspense* (London, 1964).

W. Brandt, *My Road to Berlin* (New York, 1963).

W. Brandt, *A Peace Policy for Europe* (London, 1969).

W. H. Chamberlin, *The German Phoenix* (London, 1963).

D. Childs, *East Germany* (London, 1969).

L. D. Clay, *Decision in Germany* (London, 1950).

R. Ebsworth, *Restoring Democracy in Germany* (London, 1961).

L. J. Edinger, *Kurt Schumacher* (Oxford, 1965).

J. Gimbel, *The American Occupation of Germany, 1945–49* (Stanford U.P., 1968).

A. Grosser, *Germany in our Time* (London, 1971).

W. F. Hanrieder, *West German Foreign Policy, 1949–1963* (Stanford U.P., 1967).

W. F. Hanrieder, *The Stable Crisis: Two Decades of German Foreign Policy* (New York, 1970).

R. Hiscocks, *Germany Revived* (London, 1966).

R. Hiscocks, *Democracy in Western Germany* (London, 1957).

W. Hubatsch and others, *The German Question* (New York, 1967).

E. McInnis, R. Hiscocks and R. Spencer, *The Shaping of Postwar Germany* (London, 1960).

P. H. Merkl, *The Origins of the West German Republic* (Oxford, 1963).

J. P. Nettl, *The Eastern Zone and Soviet Policy in Germany* (Oxford, 1951).

U. Kitzinger, *German Electoral Politics* (London, 1960).

J. Mander, *Berlin, Hostage for the West* (London, 1962).

T. Prittie, *Germany Divided* (London, 1960).

T. Prittie, *Konrad Adenauer* (London, 1972).

D. Schmidt, *Pastor Niemöller* (London, 1969).

W. Stahl (ed.), *The Politics of Post-War Germany* (New York, 1963).

G. Stolper, *German Realities* (London, 1947).

H. C. Wallich, *Mainsprings of the German Revival* (Yale U.P., 1955).

P. Weymar, *Adenauer* (London, 1947).

P. Windsor, *Berlin, City on Leave* (London, 1963).

P. Windsor, *German Reunification* (London, 1969).

P. Windsor, *Germany and the Politics of Détente* (London, 1970).

E. Wiskemann, *Germany's Eastern Neighbours* (Oxford, 1956).

IN GERMAN:

K. Adenauer, *Erinnerungen, 1945-1963*, 4 vols (Stuttgart, 1965-68).

W. Brandt and R. Löwenthal, *Ernst Reuter* (Munich, 1957).

E. Deuerlein, *Deutschland nach dem zweiten Weltkrieg, 1945-55* (Constance, 1965).

S. Dörnberg, *Kurze Geschichte der D.D.R.* (Berlin (East), 1969).

A. Grosser, *Deutschland-Bilanz* (Munich, 1970).

K. Harprecht, *Willy Brandt: Porträt und Selbstporträt* (Munich, 1970).

H. Kroll, *Lebenserinnerungen eines Botschafters* (Cologne, 1967).

W. Leonhardt, *Die Revolution entlässt ihre Kinder* (Cologne, 1955).

G. Leptin, *Die deutsche Wirtschaft seit 1945* (Opladen, 1971).

W. Osten, *Die Aussenpolitik der D.D.R.* (Opladen, 1969).

H. Schreiber and F. Sommer, *Gustav Heinemann, Bundespräsident* (Frankfurt, 1969).

C. Stern, *Ulbricht* (Cologne, 1963).

ARTICLES IN PERIODICALS

Articles on twentieth-century German history appear frequently in the standard historical periodicals, including the *American Historical Review, History*, the *Historical Journal, History Today*, the *Journal of*

Modern History and *Past and Present.* One very useful source is the *Journal of Contemporary History*, on which I have drawn heavily. The corresponding West German periodical, *Vierteljahrshefte für Zeitgeschichte*, published in Munich, is an even more prolific mine of information.

W. T. Angress and B. F. Smith, 'Diaries of Heinrich Himmler's Early Years', *J.M.H.* vol. 3 (1959) 206.

V. R. Berghahn, 'Zu den Zielen des deutschen Flottenbaus unter Wilhelm II, *H.Z.* vol. 210 (1970) 45.

M. D. Biddiss, 'Houston Stewart Chamberlain, Prophet of Teutonism', *History Today*, vol. 19 (1969) 10.

K. D. Bracher, 'Brünings unpolitische Politik und die Auflösung der Weimarer Republik', *V.J.Z.G.* vol. 19 (1971) 113.

M. Broszat, 'Betrachtungen zu Hitler's Zweites Buch', *V.J.Z.G.* vol. 9 (1961) 417.

M. Broszat, 'Soziale Motivation und Führerbindung des National-sozialismus', *V.J.Z.G.* vol. 18 (1970) 392.

G. Bull, 'The Vatican, the Nazis and the Pursuit of Justice', *International Affairs*, vol. 47 (1971) 353.

A. Chanady, 'The Disintegration of the German National People's Party', 1924-30, *J.M.H.* vol. 39 (1967) 30.

A. Chanady, 'The Dissolution of the German Democratic Party in 1930', *A.H.R.* vol. 73 (1968) 1433.

J. S. Conway, '*Machtergreifung* or Due Process of History? The Historiography of Hitler's Rise to Power', *H.J.* vol. 8 (1965) 399.

G. A. Craig, 'The World War Alliance of the Central Powers in Retrospect', *J.M.H.* vol. 37 (1965) 336.

G. A. Craig, 'Engagement and Neutrality in Weimar Germany', *J.C.H.* vol. 2 (ii) (1967) 49.

K. W. Dahm, 'German Protestantism and Politics, 1918-39', *J.C.H.* vol. 3 (i) (1968) 29.

W. Deist, 'Die Politik der Seekriegsleitung und die Rebellion der Flotte, Ende Oktober 1918', *V.J.Z.G.* vol. 14 (1966) 341.

E. Deuerlein, 'Hitlers Eintritt in die Politik und die Reichswehr', *V.J.Z.G.* vol. 7 (1959) 177.

A. Dorpalen, 'Wilhelmian Germany – a House divided against itself', *Journal of Central European Agairs*, vol. 15 (1955) 240.

A. Dorpalen, 'The Unification of Germany in East German Perspective', *A.H.R.* vol. 65 (1970) 1069.

K. Epstein, 'The Nazi Consolidation of Power', *J.M.H.* vol. 34 (1962) 74.

Th. Eschenburg, 'Die Rolle der Persönlichkeit in der Krise der

Weimarer Republik', *V.J.Z.G.* vol. 9 (1961) 1.

G. Fergusson, 'A Blueprint for Dictatorship', *International Affairs*, vol. 40 (1964) 247.

H. W. Gatzke, 'The Stresemann Papers', *J.M.H.* vol. 26 (1954) 49.

I. Geiss, 'The Outbreak of the First World War and German War Aims, *J.C.H.* vol. 1 (iii) (1966) 75.

H. Graml, 'Die Rapallo-Politik im Urteil der Westdeutschen Forschung', *V.J.Z.G.* vol. 18 (1970) 366.

H. Herzfeld, 'Die deutsche Kriegspolitik im ersten Weltkrieg', *V.J.Z.G.* vol. 11 (1963) 224.

L. Hill, 'Three Crises, 1938–9', *J.C.H.* vol. 3 (i) (1968) 113.

K. H. Janssen, 'Der Wechsel in der Obersten Heeresleitung 1916', *V.J.Z.G.* vol. 7 (1959) 537.

G. Jasper, 'Uber die Ursachen des Zweiten Weltkrieges', *V.J.Z.G.* vol. 10 (1962) 311.

J. Joll, 'The 1914 Debate continues', *P. & P.* vol. 34 (1966) 109.

C. Klessmann, 'Der Generalgouverneur Hans Frank', *V.J.Z.G.* vol. 19 (1971) 245.

H. W. Koch, 'Hitler and the Origins of the Second World War', *H.J.* vol. 11 (1968) 125.

R. Koehl, 'The Character of the Nazi S.S.', *J.M.H.* vol. 34 (1962) 275.

C. Kollman, 'Walther Rathenau and German Foreign Policy', *J.M.H.* vol. 24 (1952) 127.

W. H. Maehl, 'Recent Literature on the German Socialists, 1891–1952', *J.M.H.* vol. 33 (1961) 292.

T. W. Mason, 'Some Origins of the Second World War', *P. & P.* vol. 29 (1964) 76.

T. W. Mason, 'Labour in the Third Reich, 1933–39', *P. & P.* vol. 33 (1966) 82.

H. Metzmacher, 'Deutsch-Englische Ausgleichsbemühungen im Sommer 1939', *V.J.Z.G.* vol. 14 (1966) 369.

H. Mommsen, 'Der Reichstagsbrand und seine politische Folgen', *V.J.Z.G.* vol. 12 (1964) 351.

W. J. Mommsen, 'The Debate on German War Aims', *J.C.H.* vol. 1 (iii) (1966) 47.

W. J. Mommsen, 'Die Regierung Bethmann Hollweg und die öffentliche Meinung, 1914-17', *V.J.Z.G.* vol. 17 (1969) 237.

R. Morsey, 'Die Rolle Konrad Adenauers im Parlamentarischen Rat', *V.J.Z.G.* vol. 18 (1970) 62.

J. S. Mortimer, 'Commercial Interests and German Diplomacy in the Agadir Crisis', *H.J.* vol. 10 (1967) 440.

J. Noakes, 'Conflict and Development in the N.S.D.A.P., 1924-27', *J.C.H.* vol. 1 (iv) (1966) 3.

D. Orlow, 'Die Adolf Hitler-Schulen', *V.J.Z.G.* vol. 4 (1957) 272.

D. Petzina, 'Hauptprobleme der deutschen Wirtschaftpolitik, 1932-3', *V.J.Z.G.* vol. 15 (1967) 18.

D. Petzina, 'Die Mobilisierung deutscher Arbeitskraefte vor und während des Zweiten Weltkrieges', *V.J.Z.G.* vol. 18 (1970) 443.

D. Portner, 'The Writers' Revolution: Munich 1918-19', *J.C.H.* vol. 3 (iv) (1968) 137.

H. Pross, 'Thomas Mann's Political Career', *J.C.H.* vol. 2 (ii) (1967) 65.

J. Remak, '1914 – The Third Balkan War', *J.M.H.* vol. 43 (1971) 353.

J. C. G. Röhl, 'The Disintegration of the Kartell and Bismarck's Fall from Power, 1887-90', *H.J.* vol. 9 (1966) 60.

J. C. G. Röhl, 'Friedrich von Holstein', *H.J.* vol. 9 (1966) 379.

J. C. G. Röhl, 'Admiral von Müller and the Approach of War, 1911-1914', *H.J.* vol. 12 (1969) 651.

K. Robbins, 'Konrad Henlein, the Sudeten Question and British Foreign Policy', *H.J.* vol. 12 (1969) 674.

R. Rürup, 'Problems of the German Revolution 1918-19', *J.C.H.* vol. 3 (iv) (1968) 109.

Th. Schieder, 'Die Vertreibung der Deutschen aus dem Osten als Wissenschaftliches Problem', *V.J.Z.G.* vol. 8 (1960) 1.

W. Schlauch, 'American Policy towards Germany in 1945', *J.C.H.* vol. 5 (iv) (1970) 124.

B. E. Schmitt, 'The Italian Documents for July 1914', *J.M.H.* vol. 37, (1965) 469.

K. Scholder, 'Die Evangelische Kirche im Licht der Nationalsozialistischen Führung bis zum Kriegsausbruch', *V.J.Z.G.* vol. 16 (1968) 15.

A. E. Simpson, 'The Struggle for Control of the German Economy', *J.M.H.* vol. 31 (1969) 18.

J. L. Snell, 'Imperial Germany's Tragic Era, 1888-1918', *Journal of Central European Affairs*, vol. 18 (1959) 380.

H. Speidel, 'Reichswehr und Rote Armee', *V.J.Z.G.* vol. 1 (1953) 9.

J. Steinberg, 'The Kaiser's Navy and German Society', *P. & P.* vol. 28 (1964) 102.

J. Steinberg, 'The Copenhagen Complex', *J.C.H.* vol. 1 (iii) (1966) 38.

H. Stern, 'The Organisation Consul', *J.M.H.* vol. 35 (1963) 20.

R. H. S. Stolfi, 'Equipment for Victory in France in 1940', *History* vol. 55 (1970) 1.

N. Stone, 'Moltke-Conrad and Relations between the Austro-Hungarian and German Chiefs of Staff', *H.J.* vol. 9 (1966) 201.

R. B. Tilford, 'German Coalition Politics', *The Political Quarterly* vol. 39 (1968) 169.

H. Trevor-Roper, 'Hitler's Kriegsziele', *V.J.Z.G.* vol. 8 (1960) 121.

H. A. Turner, 'Big Business and the Rise of Hitler', *A.H.R.* vol. 75 (1969) 56.

L. C. F. Turner, 'The Russian Mobilisation in 1914', *J.C.H.* vol 3 (i) (1968) 63.

Th. Vogelsang, 'Die Bemühungen um eine Deutsche Zentralverwaltung 1945/46, *V.J.Z.G.* vol. 18 (1970) 510.

D. C. Watt, 'German Plans for the Re-occupation of the Rhineland', *J.C.H.* vol. 1 (iv) (1966) 13.

W. Zorn, 'Student Politics in the Weimar Republic', *J.C.H.* vol. 5 (i) (1970) 136.

Index